EXISTING HOLE

60.0

45.0

400.0

(70.0)

40.0

1500

(30.0)

EXISTING DIMPLE

SUPPORT ARM

D0023500

Graphics
for
Engineers

with AutoCAD® 2002
Sixth Edition

James H. Earle

Professor Emeritus
Texas A&M University

Pearson Education, Inc.
Upper Saddle River, New Jersey 07458

Library of Congress Cataloging-in-Publication Data

Earle, James H.
    Graphics for engineers with AutoCAD 2002 / James H. Earle.—6th ed.
      p. cm
    ISBN 0-13-008172-8
    1. Engineering graphics.   2. AutoCAD.   I. Title

  T353 .E3 2002
  620'.0042'02855369—dc21

                        2002070363

Vice President and Editorial Director, ECS: *Marcia J. Horton*
Executive Editor: *Eric Svendsen*
Associate Editor: *Dee Bernhard*
Vice President and Director of Production and Manufacturing, ESM: *David W. Riccardi*
Executive Managing Editor: *Vince O'Brien*
Managing Editor: *David A. George*
Production Editor: *Amy Rose*
Director of Creative Services: *Paul Belfanti*
Creative Director: *Carole Anson*
Art Director: *Wanda España*
Art Editor: *Xiaohong Zhu*
Manufacturing Manager: *Trudy Pisciotti*
Manufacturing Buyer: *Lisa McDowell*
Marketing Manager: *Holly Stark*

© 2003 by Pearson Education, Inc.
Pearson Education, Inc.
Upper Saddle River, NJ 07458

The author and publisher of this book have used their best efforts in preparing this book. These efforts include the development, research, and testing of the theories and programs to determine their effectiveness. The author and publisher make no warranty of any kind, expressed or implied, with regard to these programs or the documentation contained in this book. The author and publisher shall not be liable in any event for incidental or consequential damages in connection with, or arising out of, the furnishing, performance, or use of these programs.

AutoCAD and the AutoCAD logo are registered trademarks of Autodesk, Inc., 111 McInnis Parkway, San Rafael, CA 94903.

Printed in the United States of America

10 9 8 7 6 5 4 3 2 1

Pearson Education Ltd., *London*
Pearson Education Australia Pty. Ltd., *Sydney*
Pearson Education Singapore, Pte. Ltd.
Pearson Education North Asia Ltd., *Hong Kong*
Pearson Education Canada, Inc., *Toronto*
Pearson Educacíon de Mexico, S.A. de C.V.
Pearson Education—Japan, *Tokyo*
Pearson Education Malaysia, Pte. Ltd.
Pearson Education, Inc., *Upper Saddle River, New Jersey*

To Edna Bush Earle
1904–1998

Preface

New and Better

This sixth edition of *Graphics for Engineers* is the best edition since its introduction in 1985 in all categories: content, format, readability, clarity, and quality of illustrations. The challenge with each revision has always been, "How can the book be written and illustrated to make it easier for the student to learn and the teacher to teach?" Also asked is, "What should be the content for today's course that will fit tomorrow's needs?"

Meeting this goal is difficult for an author in any discipline, but it is especially awesome in the area of engineering design graphics, where 1500 illustrations, 620 problems, and a multitude of topics must be merged into a cohesive textbook as compactly as possible. Content must include fundamentals, design, computer graphics, industrial applications, and meaningful problems. We believe that we have met these goals.

Classic Content

Every paragraph and illustration has been revisited for evaluation, revision, improvement, or elimination so that all content makes a worthwhile contribution. No space has been squandered to make room for exotic illustrations of examples that are beyond the scope of a beginning freshman course. Instead, that valuable space has been used to better illustrate and present concepts in an understandable format so that the amount of classroom tutoring needed by the student is reduced.

Major content areas covered in this text are:

- design and creativity,
- computer graphics,

- engineering drawing, and

- problem solving.

Design and Creativity

The eight chapters devoted to the introduction of design and creativity have been revised and improved. New examples of case studies from industry, along with examples of worksheets applying the steps of design guide the student through the process of design.

Care has been taken to offer realistic design problems that are within the grasp of beginning students, rather than overwhelming them with problems beyond their capabilities. Since the primary objective of design instruction is to introduce the process of design, meaningful design assignments are given to make the process fun and to encourage the application of creativity and intuition. Most problems are adequately challenging to encourage creative and inspirational solutions that may lead to patentable products.

Chapter 9 has a variety of design problems that can be used as quickie problems, short assignments, or semester-long design projects. Additional design exercises are included at the ends of the chapters throughout the book.

Computer Graphics

AutoCAD® 2002 is presented in a step-by-step format to aid the student in learning how to use this popular software, not just read about it in the abstract. Steps of each illustration show the reader what will be seen on the screen as the example is followed. Chapter 26 gives an introduction to two-dimensional computer graphics and Chapter 27 covers three-dimensional computer graphics, solid modeling, and rendering.

The main purpose of *Graphics for Engineers* is to help students learn the principles of graphics, whether done on the drawing board or on the computer. This book can be used in courses where the entire course is done by computer, none is done by computer, or the course is partly done by computer.

Format: Make it Easy

Much effort has been devoted to the creation of illustrations separated into multiple steps to present the concepts as clearly and simply as possible. A second color is applied as a functional means of emphasizing sequential steps, key points, and explanations. Explanatory information and text is closely associated with the steps of each example.

Many three-dimensional pictorials that will aid the student in visualizing the example at hand have been drawn, modified, and refined. Photographs of actual industrial parts and products have been merged with explanatory examples of principles being covered.

The author has personally developed and drawn the illustrations in this book. Only after years of classroom experience and trial-and-error testing is it possible to present principles of graphics in a format that enables the student and teacher to cover more content with fewer learning obstacles.

The two-color, step-by-step format of presentation with conveniently located text has been classroom-tested to validate its effectiveness over a number of years.

We believe the results justify this added effort and expense.

Streamlined

The content in all chapters has been compressed, but no material essential to the adequate coverage of a topic has been eliminated. Chapters on descriptive geometry, civil engineering applications, and vector graphics have been eliminated to save over 100 pages.

Many new problems and illustrations have been added, and most of the existing figures have been edited and improved to make them more effective. No space in this book has been wasted.

A Book to Keep

Some material in this book may not be formally covered in the course for which it was adopted due to time limitations or variations in emphasis by different instructors. These briefly covered topics may be the ones that will be needed in later courses or in practice. Therefore, this book should be retained as a permanent reference by the engineer, technologist, or technician.

A Teaching System

Graphics for Engineers, used in combination with the supplements listed below, comprises a complete teaching system.

Textbook problems: Approximately 620 problems are offered to aid the student in mastering the principles of graphics and design.

Teachers' Solutions Manual: A manual containing the solutions to most of the problems in this book is available from Prentice Hall to assist the teacher with grading.

Problem Manuals: Nineteen problem books and teachers' guides (with outlines, problem solutions, tests, and test solutions) that are keyed to this book are available from Creative Publishing. Fifteen of the problem books are designed to allow problem solution by computer, by sketching, or on the drawing board. A listing of these manuals is given on the inside back cover of this book.

Acknowledgments

We are grateful for the assistance of many who have influenced the development of this edition. Many industries have furnished photographs, drawings, and applications, and have been acknowledged in the corresponding captions. The Engineering Design Graphics staff of Texas A&M University have been helpful in making suggestions for the revision of this book.

Professor Tom Pollock provided valuable information on metallurgy for Chapter 18. Professor Leendert Kersten of the University of Nebraska, Lincoln, kindly provided his descriptive geometry computer programs for inclusion; his cooperation is appreciated.

We are indebted to Jimm Meloy and Denis Cadu of Autodesk, Inc. for their assistance and cooperation. We are appreciative of the assistance of David Ratner of the Biomechanics Corporation Inc. for providing HUMANCAD® software. Also giving support were Melissa Campbell of Bresslergroup, and Henry Keck of Keck-Craig, Inc.

We are appreciative of the fine editorial and production team assembled by Eric Svendsen at Prentice Hall: Project Manager Amy Rose, Computer experts Mike and Sigrid Wile, and Proofreader Tara McCormick. Once more, Amy completed a complex project in a very skillful manner, handling virtually every paragraph and drawing to see that they were properly merged into the final book. Mike and Sigrid scanned and translated the illustrations into final form for printing. Tara sorted through every word, comma, semicolon, and character to make the text as error-free as possible. I am appreciative to all of you. *Thank You.*

Above all, we appreciate the many institutions who have thought enough of our publications to adopt them for classroom use. This is the highest honor that can be paid an author. We are hopeful that this textbook will fill the needs of engineering and technology programs. As always, comments and suggestions for improvement and revision will be appreciated.

Jim Earle
College Station, Texas

Contents

Contents • xiii

CHAPTER ONE

Engineering and Technology

1.1 Introduction

This book deals with the field of engineering design graphics and its application to the design process. Engineering graphics is the primary medium of design. Essentially all designs begin with graphics and end with graphical documents from which products and projects become realities. The solution of most engineering problems requires a combination of organization, analysis, problem-solving principles, graphics, skill, and communication (**Fig. 1.1**).

This book is intended to help you use your creativity and develop your imagination because innovation is essential to a successful career in engineering and technology. Albert Einstein said, "Imagination is more important than knowledge, for knowledge is limited, whereas imagination embraces the entire world . . . stimulating progress, or, giving birth to evolution."

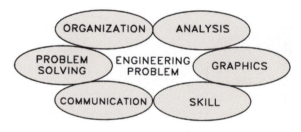

1.1 This text illustrates the total approach to engineering, with the engineering problem as the focal point.

1.2 Engineering Graphics

Engineering graphics covers the total field of graphical problem solving within two major areas of specialization: **descriptive geometry** and **documentation drawings**. Other areas of application are nomography, graphical mathematics, empirical equations, technical illustration, vector graphics, data analysis, and computer graphics. Graphics is one of the designer's most effective tools for developing design concepts and solving three-dimensional problems. It also is the designer's best means of communicating ideas to others.

MILESTONES OF THE 20TH CENTURY

1900	Vacuum cleaner	1950	A-bomb tests
	Airplane		Optical fibers
	Dial telephone		Soviet satellite
	Light bulb		Microchip
	Model T Ford	1960	Commun. satelite
1910	Washing machine		Indus. robot
	Refrigerator		Nuclear reactor
	Wireless phone		Heart transplant
1920	Radio broadcasts		Man on moon
	Telephone service	1970	Silicon chip
	35mm camera		Personal computer
	Cartoons & sound		Videocassette record.
1930	Tape recorder		Supersonic jet
	Atom split		Neutron bomb
	Jet engine	1980	Stealth bomber
	Television		Space shuttle
1940	Elect. computer		Artificial heart
	Missile		Soviet space station
	Transistor	1990	Compute voice
	Microwave		recoginition
	Polaroid camera		Artificial intelligence
			E-Mail and the
			internet

1.2 This chronology lists some of the significant technological advances of the twentieth century.

1.3 Technological and design team members, with their varying experiences and areas of expertise, must communicate and interact with each other. (*Courtesy of Toshiba America Information Systems, Inc.*)

Descriptive Geometry

Gaspard Monge (1746–1818), the "father of descriptive geometry," used graphical methods to solve design problems related to fortifications and battlements while he was a military student in France. His headmaster scolded him for not using the usual long, tedious mathematical process. Only after lengthy explanations and demonstrations of his technique was he able to convince his faculty that graphical methods (now called descriptive geometry) produced solutions in less time.

Descriptive geometry was such an improvement over mathematical methods that it was kept as a military secret for fifteen years before the authorities allowed it to be taught as part of the civilian curriculum.

Descriptive geometry is the projection of three-dimensional figures on the two-dimensional plane of paper in a manner that allows geometric manipulations to determine lengths, angles, shapes, and other geometric information about the figures.

1.3 Technological Milestones

Many of the technological advancements of the twentieth century are engineering achievements.

Since 1900, technology has taken us from the horse-drawn carriage to the moon and back and more advancements are certain in the future.

Figure 1.2 shows a few of the many technological mileposts since 1900. It identifies products and processes that have provided millions of jobs and a better way of life for all. Other significant achievements were building a railroad from Nebraska to California that met at Promontory Point, Utah, in 1869 in less than four years; constructing the Empire State Building with 102 floors in thirteen and a half months in 1931; and retooling industry in 1942 for World War II to produce 4.5 naval vessels, 3.7 cargo ships, 203 airplanes, and 6 tanks each day while supporting 15 million Americans in the armed forces.

One "miracle project" of the 1990s was the construction of the thirty-one-mile "Chunnel" that connects England and France under the English Channel for high-speed shuttle trains. It consists of three tunnels drilled 131 feet under the channel floor; two of the tunnels are 24 feet in diameter. The trip from London to Paris can be made in three and a half hours.

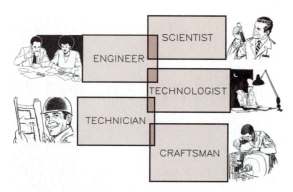

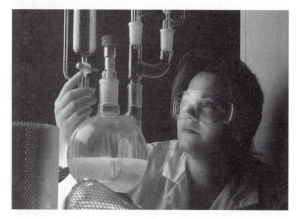

1.4 This ranking of the typical technological team is from the most theoretical level (scientists) to the least technical level (craftspeople).

1.6 Engineers and technologists combine their knowledge to work on an avionics modification. (*Courtesy of Cessna Aircraft Co.*)

1.5 This scientist is working to develop a new drug to protect the body from contracting AIDS. (*Courtesy of FMC Corporation.*)

1.4 The Technological Team

Technology and design have become so broad and complex that teams of specialists rather than individuals undertake most projects (**Fig. 1.3**). Such teams usually consist of one or more scientists, engineers, technologists, technicians, and craftspeople, and may include designers and stylists (**Fig. 1.4**).

Scientists

Scientists are researchers who seek to discover new laws and principles of nature through experimentation and scientific testing (**Fig. 1.5**).

They are more concerned with the discovery of scientific principles than with the application of those principles to products and systems. Their discoveries may not find applications until years later.

Engineers

Engineers receive training in science, mathematics, and industrial processes to prepare them to apply the findings of the scientists (**Fig. 1.6**). Thus engineers are concerned with converting raw materials and power sources into needed products and services. Creatively applying scientific principles to develop new products and systems is the design process, the engineer's primary function. In general, engineers use known principles and available resources to achieve a practical end at a reasonable cost.

Technologists

Technologists obtain backgrounds in science, mathematics, and industrial processes. Whereas engineers are responsible for analysis, overall design, and research, technologists are concerned with the application of engineering principles to planning, detail design, and production (**Fig. 1.6**). Technologists apply their knowledge

1.7 An engineering technician works on a phased-array radar antenna. (*Courtesy of Northrop Grumman Corporation.*)

of engineering principles, manufacturing, and testing to assist in the implementation of projects and production. They also provide support and act as liaisons between engineers and technicians.

Technicians

Technicians assist engineers and technologists at a less theoretical level than technologists and provide liaison between technologists and craftspeople (**Fig. 1.7**). They have backgrounds in mathematics, drafting, computer programming, and materials testing. Their work varies from conducting routine laboratory experiments to supervising craftspeople in manufacturing or construction.

Craftspeople

Craftspeople are responsible for implementing designs by fabricating them according to engineers' specifications. They may be machinists who make product parts or electricians who assemble electrical components. Their ability to produce a part according to design specifications is as necessary to the success of a project as engineers' ability to design it. Craftspeople include electricians, welders, machinists, fabricators, drafters, and members of many other occupational groups (**Fig. 1.8**).

1.8 A craftsman assembles a portion of an experimental aircraft. (*Courtesy of Cessna Aircraft Company.*)

Designers

Designers may be engineers, technologists, inventors, or industrial designers who have special talents for devising creative solutions. Designers do not necessarily have engineering backgrounds, especially in newer technologies where there is little design precedent. Thomas A. Edison, for example, had little formal education, but he created some of the world's most significant inventions.

Stylists

Stylists are concerned with the appearance and market appeal of a product rather than its fundamental design. They may design an automobile body or the exterior of an electric iron. Automobile stylists, for example, consider the car's appearance, driver's vision, passengers' enclosure, power unit's space requirement, and so on. However, they are not involved with the design of the car's internal mechanical functions, such as the engine, steering linkage, and brakes. Stylists must have a high degree of aesthetic awareness and an instinct for styling that appeals to the consumer.

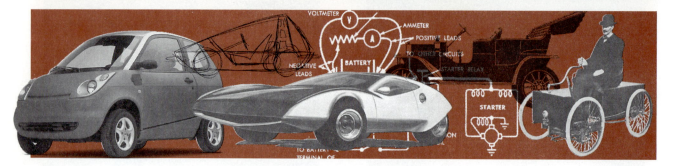

The Design Process

2.1 Introduction

The design process is the method of devising innovative solutions to problems that will result in new products or systems. Engineering graphics is the primary medium of design that is used for developing designs from initial concepts to final working drawings. Initially, a design consists of sketches that are refined, analyzed, and developed into precise, detailed drawings and specifications. They, in turn, become part of the contract documents for the parties involved in funding and implementing a project.

At first glance, the solution of a design problem may appear to involve merely the recognition of a need and the application of effort toward its solution, but most engineering designs are more complex than that. The engineering and design efforts may be the easiest parts of a project.

For example, engineers who develop roadway systems must deal with constraints such as ordinances, historical data, human factors,

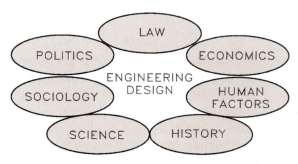

2.1 An engineering project may involve the interaction of people representing many professions and interests, with engineering design as the central function.

social considerations, scientific principles, budgeting, and politics (**Fig. 2.1**). Engineers can readily design driving surfaces, drainage systems, overpasses, and other components of the system. However, adherence to budgetary limitations is essential, and funding is closely related to politics on public projects.

Traffic laws, zoning ordinances, environmental impact statements, right-of-way acquisition, and liability clearances are legal aspects of roadway design that engineers must deal with. Past trends, historical data, human factors (including driver characteristics), and safety features affecting the function of the traffic system must be analyzed. Social problems may arise if proposed roadways will be heavily traveled and will attract commercial development such as shopping centers, fast-food outlets, and service stations. Finally, designers must apply engineering principles developed through research and experience to obtain durable roads, economical bridges, and fully functional systems.

2.2 Types of Design Problems

Most design problems fall into one of two categories: **product design** and **systems design**.

Product Design

Product design is the creation, testing, and manufacture of an item that usually will be mass produced, such as an appliance, a tool, a toy, or larger products such as automobiles (**Fig. 2.2**). In general, a product must have sufficiently broad appeal for meeting a specific need and performing an independent function to warrant its production in quantity. Designers of products, whether an automobile or a bicycle, must consider current market needs, production costs, function, sales, distribution methods, and profit predictions (**Fig. 2.3**).

Products can perform one or many functions. For instance, the primary function of an automobile is to provide transportation, but it also contains products that provide communication, illumination, comfort, entertainment, and safety. Because it is mass produced for a large consumer market and can be purchased as a unit, the automobile is regarded as a product. However, because it consists of many products that perform various functions, the automobile also is a system.

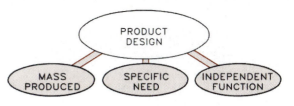

2.2 Product design seeks to develop a product that meets a specific need, that can function independently, and that can be mass produced.

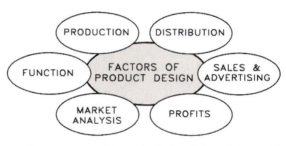

2.3 These are some of the major factors that must be considered when developing a product design.

Systems Design

Systems design combines products and their components into a unique arrangement and provides a method for their operation. A residential building is a system of products consisting of heating and cooling, plumbing, natural gas, electrical power, sewage, appliances, entertainment, and others that form the overall system, as shown in **Fig. 2.4**.

Systems Design Example

Suppose that you were carrying luggage to a faraway gate in an airport terminal. It would be easy for you to recognize the need for a luggage cart that you could use and then leave behind for others to use. If you have this need, then others do too. The identification of this need could

ENTERTAINMENT   ELECTRICITY   APPLIANCES

WATER   GAS

LIGHTING   COOLING

SEWAGE   FURNISHINGS   HEATING

2.4 The typical residence is a system composed of many components and products.

2.6 Luggage carts are dispensed from coin-operated centers at major entrances of airport terminals. (*Courtesy of Smarte Carte.*)

2.5 The luggage cart in an airport terminal is a product and part of a system. (*Courtesy of Smarte Carte.*)

2.7 The coin-operated gate (left) releases a cart from the cart dispenser. A vending machine (right) makes change for $5, $10, and $20 bills and issues baggage cards that can be used at any other airport terminal having the same cart system. (*Courtesy of Smarte Carte.*)

prompt you to design a cart like the one shown in **Fig. 2.5** to hold luggage, and even a child, and to make it available to travelers. The cart is a product.

How could you profit from providing such a cart? First you would need a method of holding the carts and dispensing them to customers, such as the one shown in **Fig. 2.6**. You would also need a method for users to pay for cart rental, so you could design a coin-operated gate for releasing them (**Fig. 2.7**).

For an added customer convenience, you could provide a vending machine that will take bills both to make change and to issue cards entitling customers to multiple use of carts at this and other terminals (**Fig. 2.7**). A mechanism to encourage customers to return carts to another, conveniently located dispensing unit would be helpful and efficient. A coin dispenser (**Fig. 2.6**) that gives a partial refund on the rental fee to customers returning carts to a dispensing unit at their destination might work.

The combination of these products and the method of using them is a system design. Such a system of products is more valuable than the sum of the products alone.

2.3 The Design Process

Design is the process of creating a product or system to satisfy a set of requirements that has mul-

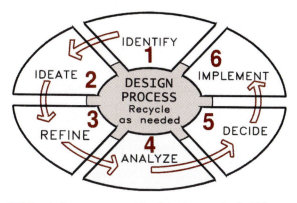

2.8 The design process consists of six steps, each of which can be repeated as necessary.

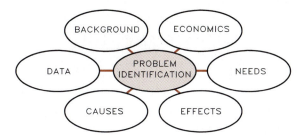

2.9 Problem identification requires that the designer accumulate as much information about a problem as possible before attempting a solution. The designer also should keep product marketing in mind at all times.

tiple solutions by using any available resources. In essentially all cases, the final design must be completed at a profit or within a budget.

The steps of the design process (**Fig. 2.8**) are:

1. problem identification,
2. preliminary ideas (ideation),
3. refinement,
4. analysis,
5. decision, and
6. implementation.

Designers should work sequentially from step to step but should review previous steps periodically and rework them if a new approach comes to mind during the process.

Problem Identification

Most engineering problems are not clearly defined at the outset and require identification before an attempt is made to solve them (**Fig. 2.9**). For example, air pollution is a concern, but we must identify its causes before we can solve the problem. Is it caused by automobiles, factories, atmospheric conditions that harbor impurities, or geographic features that trap impure atmospheres?

Another example is traffic congestion. When you enter a street where traffic is unusually con-gested, can you identify the reasons for the congestion? Are there too many cars? Are the signals poorly synchronized? Are there visual obstructions? Has an accident blocked traffic?

Problem identification involves much more than simply stating, "We need to eliminate air pollution." We need data of several types: opinion surveys, historical records, personal observations, experimental data, physical measurements from the field, and more. It is important that the designer resist the temptation to begin developing a solution before the identification step has been completed.

Preliminary Ideas

The second step of the design process is the development of as many ideas for problem solution as possible (**Fig. 2.10**). A brainstorming session is a good way to collect ideas at the outset that are highly creative, revolutionary, and even wild. Rough sketches, notes, and comments can capture and preserve preliminary ideas for further refinement. The more ideas, the better at this stage.

Refinement

Several of the better preliminary ideas are selected for refinement to determine their merits. The rough preliminary sketches are converted into scale drawings for spatial analysis, determination of critical measurements, and

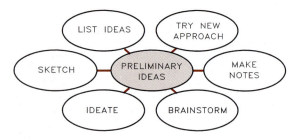

2.10 The designer gathers ideas from a brainstorming session and develops preliminary ideas for problem solution. Ideas should be listed, sketched, and noted in order to have a broad range of ideas to work with.

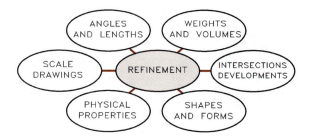

2.11 Refinement begins with the construction of scale drawings of the best preliminary ideas. Descriptive geometry and graphics are used to describe geometric characteristics.

the calculation of areas and volumes affecting the design (**Fig. 2.11**). Descriptive geometry aids in determining spatial relationships, angles between planes, lengths of structural members, intersections of surfaces and planes, and other geometric relationships.

Analysis

Analysis is the step during which engineering and scientific principles are used most intensively to evaluate the best designs and compare their merits with respect to function, strength, safety, cost, and optimization (**Fig. 2.12**). Graphical methods play an important role in analysis, also. Data can be analyzed graphically, forces analyzed as graphical vectors, and empirical data can be analyzed, integrated, and differentiated by other graphical methods. Analysis is less creative than the previous steps.

Decision

After analysis, a single design, which may be a compromise among several designs, is decided upon as the solution to the problem (**Fig. 2.13**). The designer alone, or a team, may make the decision. The outstanding aspects of each design usually lend themselves to graphical comparisons of manufacturing costs, weights, operational characteristics, and other data essential in decision making.

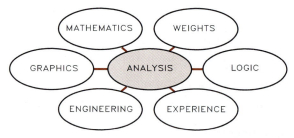

2.12 All available methods, from science to technology to graphics to experience, should be used to analyze a design.

Implementation

The final design must be described and detailed in working drawings and specifications from which the project will be built, whether it is a computer chip or a suspension bridge (**Fig. 2.14**). Workers must have precise instructions for the manufacture of each component, often measured within thousandths of an inch to ensure proper fabrication assembly. Working drawings must be sufficiently explicit to serve as part of the legal contract with the successful bidder on the job.

2.4 Graphics and Design

Whether by freehand sketching, with instruments, or on a computer, graphics is the

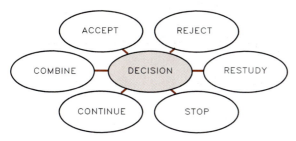

2.13 Decision involves the selection of the best design or design features to implement. This step may require an acceptance, a rejection, or a compromise of the proposed solution.

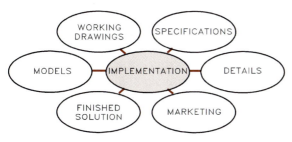

2.14 Implementation is the preparation of drawings, specifications, and documentation from which the product can be made. The product is produced and marketing is begun.

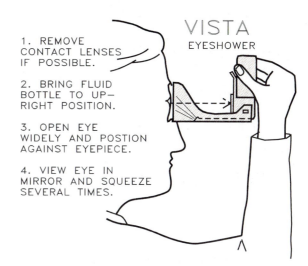

2.15 This freehand sketch with its accompanying notes describes the concept for an eye shower device. (*Courtesy Keck-Craig Inc.*)

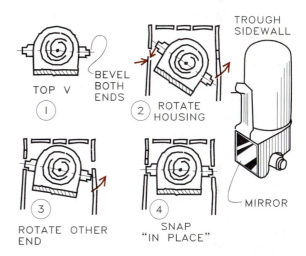

2.16 These freehand sketches show how the tank housing is snapped into position. (*Courtesy Keck-Craig Inc.*)

medium of design. Engineering, scientific, and analytical principles must be applied throughout the process, and graphics is the medium that is employed in each step from problem identification to implementation.

An example of how graphics is used by a design firm to develop a product is shown in **Fig. 2.15** through **Fig. 2.19**. A freehand sketch of the basic concept with notes explaining how the product is to be used to rinse out the eye of the user by spraying a solution is shown in **Fig. 2.15**.

The designer makes a series of four sketches in **Fig. 2.16** to study how the tank housing is snapped into position. These sketches represent his thinking process as well as a means of recording his ideas and for communicating with others.

A three-dimensional pictorial (**Fig. 2.17**) illustrates additional design features as the product evolves. The preliminary designs are studied and evaluated by several designers as a means of "troubleshooting" the design and applying all available experience and expertise to the eye shower.

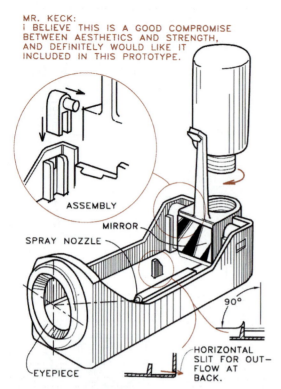

MR. KECK:
I BELIEVE THIS IS A GOOD COMPROMISE BETWEEN AESTHETICS AND STRENGTH, AND DEFINITELY WOULD LIKE IT INCLUDED IN THIS PROTOTYPE.

ASSEMBLY

MIRROR

SPRAY NOZZLE

90°

EYEPIECE

HORIZONTAL SLIT FOR OUT-FLOW AT BACK.

2.17 This three-dimensional pictorial clarifies additional production details that must be provided for the eye shower device. (*Courtesy Keck-Craig Inc.*)

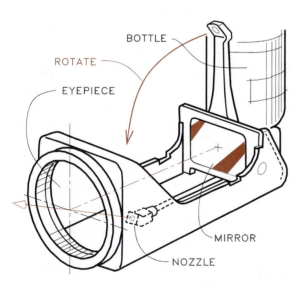

BOTTLE

ROTATE

EYEPIECE

MIRROR

NOZZLE

2.18 This pictorial shows the motion of the tank and the relationship of the mirror and nozzle to the eye shower. (*Courtesy Keck-Craig Inc.*)

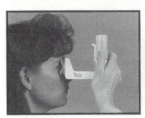

VISTA EYESHOWER

A. OPEN FOR USE   B. CLOSED FOR STORAGE

2.19 Photographs show how the eye shower is used and closed for carrying in a pocket or purse. (*Courtesy Keck-Craig Inc.*)

Additional design details are explained in the sketch in **Fig. 2.18**. The movements of the adjacent parts can be shown better in a three-dimensional drawing than in multiview drawings. These concepts must be refined and modified to attain the final design ready for production as a prototype, as shown in **Fig. 2.19**. A more detailed coverage of the steps of the design process will be given in the following chapters.

2.5 Application of the Design Process

The following example illustrates the application of the design process to a simple problem.

Hanger Bracket Problem

A bracket is needed to support a 2-inch diameter hot-water pipe from a beam or column 9 inches from the mounting surface. This design project is typical of an in-house assignment by an engineer of a company specializing in pipe hangers and supports.

Problem Identification

First, write a statement of the problem and a statement of need (**Fig. 2.20**). List limitations and desirable features and make descriptive sketches to better identify the requirements (**Fig. 2.21**). Even if much of this information may be obvious, writing statements and making

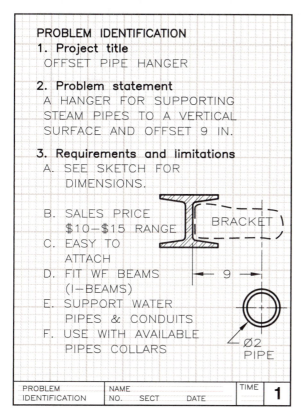

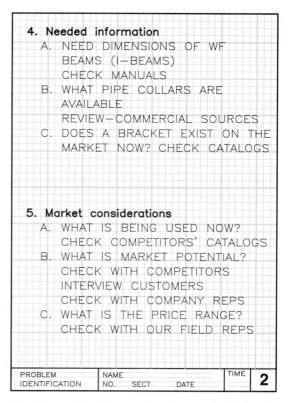

PROBLEM IDENTIFICATION
1. Project title
OFFSET PIPE HANGER

2. Problem statement
A HANGER FOR SUPPORTING STEAM PIPES TO A VERTICAL SURFACE AND OFFSET 9 IN.

3. Requirements and limitations
A. SEE SKETCH FOR DIMENSIONS.

B. SALES PRICE $10–$15 RANGE
C. EASY TO ATTACH
D. FIT WF BEAMS (I–BEAMS)
E. SUPPORT WATER PIPES & CONDUITS
F. USE WITH AVAILABLE PIPES COLLARS

BRACKET

9

Ø2 PIPE

| PROBLEM IDENTIFICATION | NAME | | TIME | 1 |
| | NO. SECT DATE | | | |

2.20 This worksheet shows aspects of problem identification, the first step of the design process.

4. Needed information
A. NEED DIMENSIONS OF WF BEAMS (I–BEAMS) CHECK MANUALS
B. WHAT PIPE COLLARS ARE AVAILABLE REVIEW—COMMERCIAL SOURCES
C. DOES A BRACKET EXIST ON THE MARKET NOW? CHECK CATALOGS

5. Market considerations
A. WHAT IS BEING USED NOW? CHECK COMPETITORS' CATALOGS
B. WHAT IS MARKET POTENTIAL? CHECK WITH COMPETITORS INTERVIEW CUSTOMERS CHECK WITH COMPANY REPS
C. WHAT IS THE PRICE RANGE? CHECK WITH OUR FIELD REPS

| PROBLEM IDENTIFICATION | NAME | | TIME | 2 |
| | NO. SECT DATE | | | |

2.21 This worksheet shows information needed before the designer can proceed, including sources from which it can be obtained.

sketches about the problem will help you "warm up" to the problem and begin the creative process. Also, you must begin thinking about sales outlets and marketing methods.

Preliminary Ideas

Brainstorm the problem for possible solutions with others, or alone if necessary. List the ideas obtained on a worksheet (**Fig. 2.22**), and summarize the best ideas and design features on a separate worksheet (**Fig. 2.23**). Then translate and expand these verbal ideas into rapidly drawn freehand sketches (**Fig. 2.24** and **Fig. 2.25**). You should develop as many ideas as possible during this step because a large number of ideas represents a high level of creativity. This is the most creative step of the design process.

Problem Refinement

Describe the design features of one or more preliminary ideas on a worksheet for comparison (**Fig. 2.26**). Draw the better designs to scale in preparation for analysis; you need to show only a few dimensions at this stage (**Fig. 2.27**).

Use instrument-drawn orthographic projections, computer drawings, and descriptive geometry to refine the designs and ensure precision. Let's say that you select ideas 3 and 5 for analysis. **Figure 2.27** depicts orthographic and auxiliary views of the two designs.

Analysis

Use an analysis worksheet to analyze the cast-iron bracket design as shown in **Figs. 2.28–2.31**.

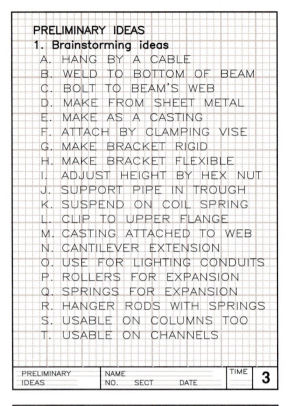

PRELIMINARY IDEAS
1. Brainstorming ideas
    A. HANG BY A CABLE
    B. WELD TO BOTTOM OF BEAM
    C. BOLT TO BEAM'S WEB
    D. MAKE FROM SHEET METAL
    E. MAKE AS A CASTING
    F. ATTACH BY CLAMPING VISE
    G. MAKE BRACKET RIGID
    H. MAKE BRACKET FLEXIBLE
    I. ADJUST HEIGHT BY HEX NUT
    J. SUPPORT PIPE IN TROUGH
    K. SUSPEND ON COIL SPRING
    L. CLIP TO UPPER FLANGE
    M. CASTING ATTACHED TO WEB
    N. CANTILEVER EXTENSION
    O. USE FOR LIGHTING CONDUITS
    P. ROLLERS FOR EXPANSION
    Q. SPRINGS FOR EXPANSION
    R. HANGER RODS WITH SPRINGS
    S. USABLE ON COLUMNS TOO
    T. USABLE ON CHANNELS

PRELIMINARY IDEAS	NAME			TIME	**3**
	NO.	SECT	DATE		

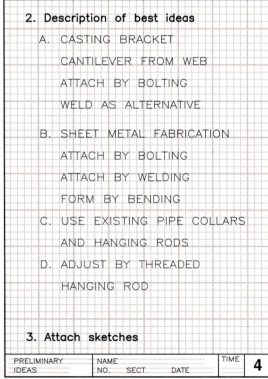

2. Description of best ideas

    A. CASTING BRACKET
        CANTILEVER FROM WEB
        ATTACH BY BOLTING
        WELD AS ALTERNATIVE

    B. SHEET METAL FABRICATION
        ATTACH BY BOLTING
        ATTACH BY WELDING
        FORM BY BENDING

    C. USE EXISTING PIPE COLLARS
        AND HANGING RODS

    D. ADJUST BY THREADED
        HANGING ROD

3. Attach sketches

PRELIMINARY IDEAS	NAME			TIME	**4**
	NO.	SECT	DATE		

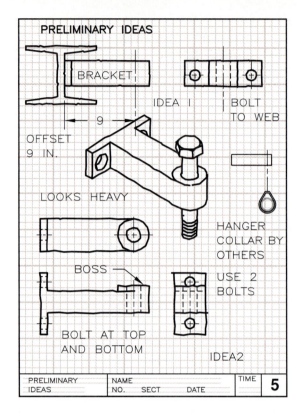

PRELIMINARY IDEAS

BRACKET
IDEA 1
BOLT TO WEB
OFFSET 9 IN.
LOOKS HEAVY
BOSS
BOLT AT TOP AND BOTTOM
HANGER COLLAR BY OTHERS
USE 2 BOLTS
IDEA2

PRELIMINARY IDEAS	NAME			TIME	**5**
	NO.	SECT	DATE		

2.22 (Sheet 3) A member of the brainstorming team records the ideas from the session.

2.23 (Sheet 4) The best ideas are selected from the brainstorming session to be developed as preliminary ideas.

2.24 (Sheet 5) Preliminary ideas are sketched and noted for further development. This is the most creative step of the design process.

2.25 (Sheet 6) Additional preliminary design solutions are sketched here.

2.26 (Sheet 7) Refinement of preliminary ideas begins with written descriptions of the better ideas.

2.27 (Sheet 8) Scale drawings of two designs are made to describe the designs. Almost no dimensions are needed.

2.28 (Sheet 9) A continuation of the analysis step.

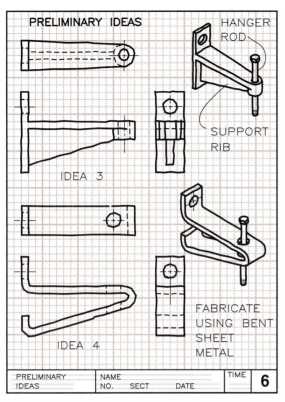

PRELIMINARY IDEAS

HANGER ROD

SUPPORT RIB

IDEA 3

IDEA 4

FABRICATE USING BENT SHEET METAL

PRELIMINARY IDEAS	NAME			TIME	**6**
	NO.	SECT	DATE		

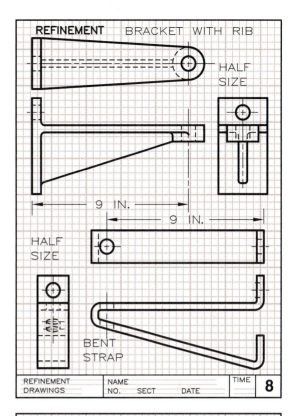

REFINEMENT BRACKET WITH RIB

HALF SIZE

9 IN.

9 IN.

HALF SIZE

BENT STRAP

REFINEMENT DRAWINGS	NAME			TIME	**8**
	NO.	SECT	DATE		

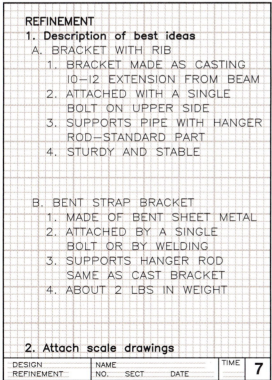

REFINEMENT

1. Description of best ideas

A. BRACKET WITH RIB
1. BRACKET MADE AS CASTING 10–12 EXTENSION FROM BEAM
2. ATTACHED WITH A SINGLE BOLT ON UPPER SIDE
3. SUPPORTS PIPE WITH HANGER ROD—STANDARD PART
4. STURDY AND STABLE

B. BENT STRAP BRACKET
1. MADE OF BENT SHEET METAL
2. ATTACHED BY A SINGLE BOLT OR BY WELDING
3. SUPPORTS HANGER ROD SAME AS CAST BRACKET
4. ABOUT 2 LBS IN WEIGHT

2. Attach scale drawings

DESIGN REFINEMENT	NAME			TIME	**7**
	NO.	SECT	DATE		

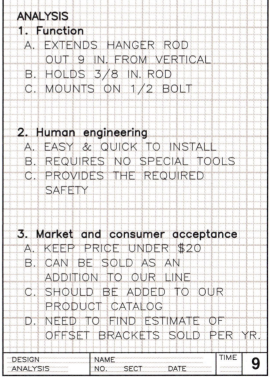

ANALYSIS

1. Function

A. EXTENDS HANGER ROD OUT 9 IN. FROM VERTICAL
B. HOLDS 3/8 IN. ROD
C. MOUNTS ON 1/2 BOLT

2. Human engineering

A. EASY & QUICK TO INSTALL
B. REQUIRES NO SPECIAL TOOLS
C. PROVIDES THE REQUIRED SAFETY

3. Market and consumer acceptance

A. KEEP PRICE UNDER $20
B. CAN BE SOLD AS AN ADDITION TO OUR LINE
C. SHOULD BE ADDED TO OUR PRODUCT CATALOG
D. NEED TO FIND ESTIMATE OF OFFSET BRACKETS SOLD PER YR.

DESIGN ANALYSIS	NAME			TIME	**9**
	NO.	SECT	DATE		

2.29 (Sheet 10) A continuation of the analysis step of the design process.

2.30 (Sheet 11) This portion of the analysis focuses on the production and economic considerations.

2.31 (Sheet 12) Graphics and descriptive geometry are used in analysis to determine the load carried by the support bolt.

2.32 (Sheet 13) A decision table is used to evaluate alternative designs in arriving at the final selection of the design that will be implemented.

2.33 (Sheet 14) The decision step is summarized to conclude this step of the design process.

```
4. Physical description
   A. BRACKET: 10–11 IN. LONG
      WITH RIB FOR STRENGTH
   B. ATTACHED WITH A SINGLE
      BOLT AT UPPER SIDE
   C. WEIGHT: ABOUT 3–4 LBS
   D. BOSS FOR EXTRA STRENGTH
      WHERE HANGER ROD ATTACHES
   E. FORMED AS A CASTING
      CAST IRON


5. Strength
   A. WILL SUPPORT ABOUT 200 LBS
      WITH A SAFETY FACTOR OF 5
   B. 1/2 BOLT SUFFICIENT FOR
      ATTACHMENT TO BEAM OR
      OR COLUMN
   C. 3/8 DIA HANGER ROD MORE
      THAN ADEQUATE TO SUPPORT
      200 LBS
```

| DESIGN ANALYSIS | NAME NO. SECT DATE | TIME | **10** |

```
6. Production procedures
   A. FABRICATE AS A CASTING
      USING CAST IRON
   B. DRILL .50 DIA HOLE FOR
      .375 DIA HANGER ROD
   C. DRILL .625 DIA HOLE FOR
      .50 DIA BOLT TO ATTACH
      BRACKET
   D. PAINT TO GIVE RUST–PROOF
      COATING

7. Economic analysis
   A. COSTS
      1. DEVELOPMENT  $0.20 ⎫
      2. CAST IRON       .50 ⎪
      3. CASTING COST   1.40 ⎬ 2.50
      4. DRILL 2 HOLES   .20 ⎪
      5. PAINTING        .20 ⎭
   B. LABOR                      .70
   C. PACKAGING                  .30
   D. PROFIT                    2.00
   E. WHOLESALE PRICE           6.50
   F. RETAIL PRICE           $12.00
```

| DESIGN ANALYSIS | NAME NO. SECT DATE | TIME | **11** |

If you are considering more than one solution, analyze each design separately.

By using the maximum load of 200 lbs. and the geometry of the bracket, it is possible to graphically determine the angle of the reaction that the bolt must support (456 lbs.) when the bracket carries its maximum design load of 200 lbs. (**Fig. 2.31**). Again, graphics is used as an important design tool.

Decision

The decision table (**Fig. 2.32**) compares two designs: the bracket with a rib and the bent strap. Apportion weighting factors of features to be analyzed by assigning points to them so that the sum of all factors is 10. You can then rank the designs on a 10-point scale from highest (10) to lowest (0).

Draw conclusions and summarize the features of the recommended design, along with a projection of its marketability (**Fig. 2.33**). In this case, we decide to implement the bracket with a rib.

Implementation

Detail the design of the bracket with a rib in a drawing which graphically describes and

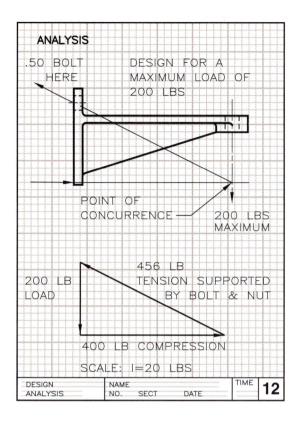

ANALYSIS

.50 BOLT HERE   DESIGN FOR A MAXIMUM LOAD OF 200 LBS

POINT OF CONCURRENCE — 200 LBS MAXIMUM

456 LB TENSION SUPPORTED BY BOLT & NUT

200 LB LOAD

400 LB COMPRESSION

SCALE: 1=20 LBS

| DESIGN ANALYSIS | NAME NO. SECT DATE | TIME | 12 |

DECISION

1. Decision table for evaluation

DESIGN 1: BRACKET WITH RIB
DESIGN 2: BENT STRAP
DESIGN 3:
DESIGN 4:
DESIGN 5:

MAX	FACTORS	1	2	3	4	5
2	FUNCTION	2	1.5			
2	HUMAN FACT.	1.5	1.5			
1	MARKET ANAL	.5	.2			
1	STRENGTH	1	.5			
1	PRODUCTION	.5	.5			
1	COST	.5	.2			
2	PROFITABILITY	1.0	1.0			
0	APPEARANCE	0	0			
10	TOTALS	7	5.4			

| DESIGN DECISION | NAME NO. SECT DATE | TIME | 13 |

dimensions each individual part (**Fig. 2.34**). A drawing of this type from which a design can be fabricated is called a working drawing.

Use notes to specify standard parts—the nuts, bolts, and hanger rod, but it will be unnecessary to draw them because they will be bought as standard parts. This working drawing shows the details and specifications for making the bracket. Now, you need to build a prototype or model of the product and test it for function.

Figure 2.35 shows the final product, the cast-iron bracket with a rib. After determining how it will be packaged and distributed, your next task will be to add it to your company's product line, list it in your catalog, and introduce it to the marketplace.

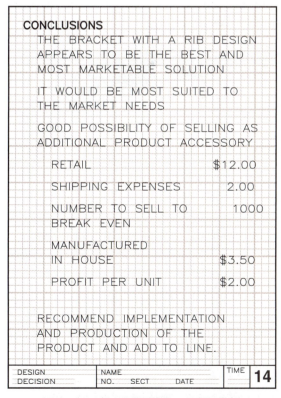

CONCLUSIONS

THE BRACKET WITH A RIB DESIGN APPEARS TO BE THE BEST AND MOST MARKETABLE SOLUTION

IT WOULD BE MOST SUITED TO THE MARKET NEEDS

GOOD POSSIBILITY OF SELLING AS ADDITIONAL PRODUCT ACCESSORY

RETAIL	$12.00
SHIPPING EXPENSES	2.00
NUMBER TO SELL TO BREAK EVEN	1000
MANUFACTURED IN HOUSE	$3.50
PROFIT PER UNIT	$2.00

RECOMMEND IMPLEMENTATION AND PRODUCTION OF THE PRODUCT AND ADD TO LINE.

| DESIGN DECISION | NAME NO. SECT DATE | TIME | 14 |

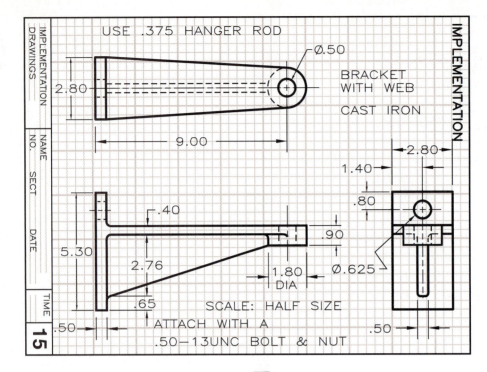

USE .375 HANGER ROD

Ø.50

BRACKET
WITH WEB

CAST IRON

2.80

9.00

2.80

1.40

.80

.40

.90

5.30

2.76

1.80
DIA

Ø.625

.65

SCALE: HALF SIZE

.50

ATTACH WITH A
.50-13UNC BOLT & NUT

2.34 The completed bracket design can be produced from this working drawing and brought to market.

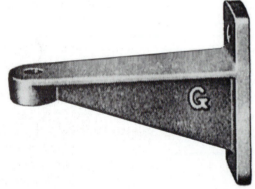

2.35 The completed bracket is shown here ready to be marketed. (*Courtesy of Grinnell Corporation.*)

Endorse each problem sheet with your name and file number, date, and problem number. Letter all points, lines, and planes with 1/8-inch letters, using guidelines. Letter the answers to essay problems with approved single-stroke Gothic lettering (see Chapter 11).

1. Outline your plan of activities for the weekend. Indicate aspects of your plans that you feel display creativity or imagination. Explain why.

2. Write a short report (not to exceed two pages) on the engineer or engineering achievement that you believe exhibits a high degree of creativity. Justify your selection by outlining the creative aspects of your choice.

Problems

Most of the following problems are to be solved on 8-1/2 × 11-inch paper, using instruments or by sketching freehand as assigned. Use a paper with a 0.20-inch printed grid or plain paper and an engineer's scale to lay out the problems.

3. Test your ability to recognize the need for new designs. List as many improvements as you can think of for the typical automobile. Make suggestions for implementing these improvements. Follow the same procedure for another product of your choice.

4. List as many systems as you can that affect your daily life. Separate several of these systems into their components (subsystems).

5. Subdivide the following items into their individual components: (a) a classroom, (b) a wristwatch, (c) a movie theater, (d) an electric motor, (e) a coffee percolator, (f) a golf course, (g) a service station, and (h) a bridge.

6. Indicate which of the items in Problem 5 are systems and which are products. Explain your answers.

7. Make a list of products and systems that you believe would be necessary for life on the moon.

8. You have been assigned the responsibility for organizing and designing a skateboard installation that will be a self-supporting. Write a paragraph on each of the six steps of the design process to explain how you would apply each step to the problem. For example, explain the action you would take to identify the problem.

9. Suppose that you are responsible for designing a motorized wheelbarrow to be marketed for home use. Write a paragraph on each of the six steps of the design process, explaining how you would apply each step to the problem. For example, what action would you take to identify the problem.

10. List and explain a sequence of steps that you believe would be adequate for, yet different from, the design process given in this chapter. Your version of the design process may contain any of the steps discussed.

11. Design a simple device for holding a fishing pole in a fishing position while the person fishing rows the boat. Make sketches and notes to describe your design.

12. Design a doorstop to keep a door from slamming into the wall behind it. Make rapid freehand sketches and notes using the six design steps. Do not spend more than thirty minutes on this problem. Indicate any information you would need at the decision and implementation steps that you may not have now.

13. List factors to consider during the problem identification step for designing (a) a skillet, (b) a bicycle lock, (c) a handle for a piece of luggage, (d) improving your grades, (e) a child's toy, (f) a stadium seat, (g) a desk lamp, (h) an umbrella, and (i) a hot dog stand.

14. Hanger Bracket identification: Make a worksheet that could follow Sheet 2 (Fig. 2.21) to provide additional identification information. For example, how much per linear foot will a 2″ XXS pipe weigh (9.03 lbs/ft) when it is full of water (refer to the Appendix for the weight of water). Show your calculations on the worksheet. How far apart should hangers be spaced if each is to carry no more than 200 lbs with a safety factor of 5 (the capacity to carry 5 times the design load)? Make sketches to clarify this information.

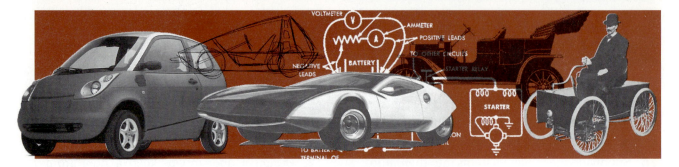

CHAPTER THREE

Problem Identification

3.1 Introduction

Problem identification is the initial step that a designer takes to solve a problem. It first involves recognizing a need and then proposing design criteria (**Fig. 3.1**).

Recognizing a need may begin with the observation of a problem or a defect in an existing product or system that needs to be corrected.

Or, you may have one of those rare moments where you think to yourself, "Why hasn't someone invented a gadget that . . ." The need may be for an improved automobile safety belt, a system allowing full wheelchair access to public buildings, or a new exercise apparatus. The solution may be a product or system improvement so that it will be more reliable and perhaps more profitable.

Proposing design criteria follows need recognition. Here the designer proposes the specifications a new product or system must meet.

3.2 Example: Ladder Attachment

When you use a ladder for house repairs, it works well enough when placed against the roof

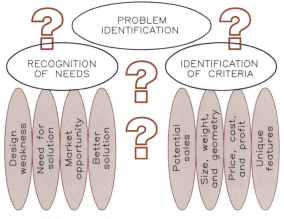

3.1 Problem identification has two aspects: Recognition of needs and identification of criteria.

or fascia at the eaves of the house (**Fig. 3.2**). However, if a gutter is attached to the fascia, the ladder damages the gutter when placed against it. The need is to prevent gutter damage by the ladder.

Now, you must propose design criteria before proceeding with a solution. You need to

20

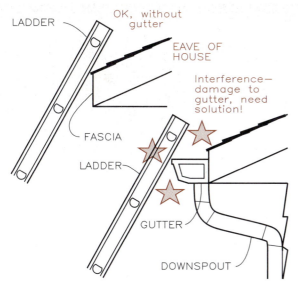

3.2 A ladder placed against the fascia or roof works fine, but when a gutter is attached to the fascia, the ladder damages the gutter. This problem needs a solution.

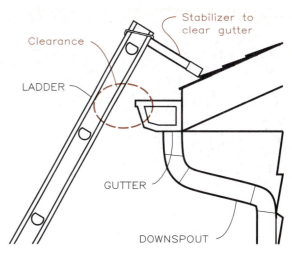

3.3 The problem recognized in Fig. 3.2 can be solved with a stabilizer attached to the ladder, which helps the ladder clear the gutter.

know the geometry and dimensions of typical gutters, pitches of roofs, angles of ladder placement, and the potential market for the solution.

Later in the design process, you might design a product that attaches to the ladder, allowing it to clear the gutter (**Fig. 3.3**). Other solutions are possible, but they all begin with recognizing the need.

3.3 The Identification Process

Problem identification requires the designer to determine requirements, limitations, and other background information before becoming involved in problem solution. The designer should take the following steps during problem identification (**Fig. 3.4**).

1. **Problem statement.** Describe the problem to begin the thinking process.

2. **Requirements.** List the conditions that the design must meet. Most will be questions to be answered after data are gathered.

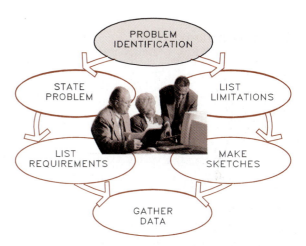

3.4 Problem identification requires a thorough investigation of background factors before attempting a design solution.

3. **Limitations.** List the factors affecting design specifications, such as maximum weight or size.

4. **Sketches.** Make sketches and add notes and dimensions to identify geometric and physical characteristics.

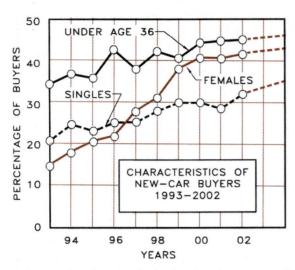

3.5 Data gathered to identify the changing characteristics of new-car buyers can be interpreted more easily when it has been graphed.

PROBLEM IDENTIFICATION

1. **Project title**
   AN EXERCISE BENCH FOR WEIGHT LIFTERS

2. **Problem statement**
   THERE ARE MANY PEOPLE WHO LIFT WEIGHTS IN ORDER TO KEEP PHYSICAL FITNESS. AN EXERCISE BENCH FOR HOME USE IS NEEDED THAT WILL HELP THEM WITH THEIR EXERCISE REGIMEN.

3. **Requirements and Limitations**

A. SHOULD BE AFFORDABLE $100−$200 PRICE RANGE
B. SIZE: SHOULD NOT TAKE MORE THAN 3 FT X 5 FT FLOOR SPACE
C. WEIGHT: LESS THAN 50 LBS FOR EASY MOVING
D. COLLAPSIBLE: WOULD BE GOOD IF IT WOULD FOLD UP FOR EASY STORAGE
E. MUST BE HELPFUL IN PERFORMING THE MOST COMMON WEIGHT EXERCISES —MUST DETERMINE FROM LIBRARY OR EXERCISE GYMS
F. MUST BE USABLE WITH THE TYPES OF WEIGHTS USED IN MOST EXERCISES —VISIT EXERCISE GYMS
G. MUST SUPPORT THE EXERCISER AND THE POUNDAGE OF THE WEIGHTS USED —OBSERVE AT EXERCISE GYMS
H. ATTRACTIVE AND COMFORTABLE TO APPEAL TO THE CUSTOMER
I. SUPPORT 275−LB PERSON

PROBLEM IDENTIFICATION	NAME			GRADE
	FILE	SEC	DATE	**1**

3.6 The problem identification step gives the project a title, describes what the product will be used for, and lists basic requirements and limitations for the design.

---

5. **Data collection.** Gather data on population trends, related designs, physical characteristics, sales records, and market studies. Graph the data, as in **Fig. 3.5**, for easier interpretation than the raw numbers or data tabulation permit.

3.4 Design Worksheets

Designers must make numerous notes and sketches on worksheets throughout the design process. They serve to document what has been done and allow periodic review of earlier ideas to avoid overlooking previously identified concepts. Moreover, a written and visual record of design work helps establish ownership of patentable ideas.

The following materials aid in maintaining permanent records of design activities.

1. **Worksheets** (8-1/2 by 11 inches). Sheets can be either grid-lined or plain and should be three-hole punched for a notebook or binder.

2. **Pencils.** A medium-grade pencil (F or HB) is adequate for most purposes.

3. **Binder or envelope.** Keep worksheets in a binder or envelope for reference.

3.5 Example: Exercise Bench

Design an exercise bench that can be used by those who lift weights for body fitness. This apparatus should be as versatile as possible and at the low end of the price range of exercise equipment. The contents of worksheets shown in **Figs. 3.6–3.9** identify the problem in a typical manner.

First, give the title of the project and a brief problem statement to describe the problem bet-

```
4. Needed information
   A. NUMBER OF PEOPLE WHO EXERCISE?
      —LIBRARY, INTERVIEW GYM OWNERS
   B. AGES OF EXERCISERS? OBSERVE GYM;
      HEALTH MAGAZINES
   C. WHAT IS THE POUNDAGE OF THE
      WEIGHTS USED BY MOST EXERCISERS
   D. WHERE DO MOST PEOPLE EXERCISE?
      HOME OR GYM? —LIBRARY AND INTER—
      VIEW GYM OPERATORS
   E. WHAT FEATURES WOULD BE DESIRABLE
      ON AN EXERCISE BENCH? —INTERVIEW
      USERS AT GYM
   F. IS HOME EXERCISING DONE INSIDE OR
      OUTSIDE? —INTERVIEW USERS AT GYM
   G. HOW OFTEN DO PEOPLE EXERCISE?
      —INTERVIEW USERS AT GYM

5. Market considerations
   A. SUITABLE MARKET PRICE? —CHECK
      RETAIL OUTLETS AND CATALOGS FOR
      COMPETING PRICES
   B. HOW MUCH IS SPENT ON EXERCISING
      AT GYMS? —CHECK YELLOW PAGES TO
      DETERMINE THE NUMBER OF GYMS
      AND RELATE POPULATION SIZE
   C. BRISKNESS OF SALES FOR EXERCISING
      BENCHES?  —INTERVIEW SALESMEN AT
      SPORTING GOODS STORES
   D. WHAT FEATURES DO BUYERS OF
      EQUIPMENT LIKE? —QUESTION SALESMEN
      AT SPORTING STORES
   E. IS THERE A VOID IN THE EXERCISE
      APPARATUS MARKET? —QUESTION SALES—
      PEOPLE AND INTERVIEW USERS AT GYMS
   F. HOW MANY PEOPLE HAVE MEMBERSHIPS
      AT GYMS? SPOT CHECK SEVERAL GYMS.
```

PROBLEM IDENTIFICATION	NAME FILE SEC DATE	GRADE 2

3.7 Continuation of problem identification for the exercise bench includes gathering information on market potential.

```
PROBLEM IDENTIFICATION
A. CHECK YELLOW PAGES FOR GYMS
   —8 GYMS FOR POPULATION OF 100,000
   —ONE GYM PER 12,500 PEOPLE
B. GYM MEMBERSHIP FOR STILLMAN'S GYM
```

YEAR	MEN	WOMEN
1992	75	20
1994	70	36
1996	110	70
1998	175	82
2000	180	120
2002	210	135

```
C. INTERVIEW RETAILERS OF EQUIPMENT
   —3 DEALERS POSITIVE ABOUT BENCH
   —2 DEALERS NEUTRAL
   —1 DEALER NEGATIVE ABOUT PROSPECTS

D. AGES OF EXERCISERS (BY OBSERVATION)
   —20% UNDER 20
   —40% BETWEEN 20 AND 30
   —30% BETWEEN 30 AND 50
   —10% OVER 50

E. PRICES AT STORES
   1. COMPLEX MULTI-USE          $1000
   2. MEDIUM-RANGE EQUIPMENT      700
   3. LIGHTWEIGHT BENCHES         130
   4. WEIGHTS                     100

F. TYPICAL BRANDS OF EQUIPMENT
   ON THE MARKET?
   1. WEIDER
   2. NAUTILUS
   3. BODY WONDERFUL
   4. HEALTH PLUS
```

PROBLEM IDENTIFICATION	NAME FILE SEC DATE	GRADE 3

3.8 This worksheet shows the data collected for use in designing the exercise bench.

ter. Then list requirements and limitations and add sketches as necessary. You will have to list some requirements as questions for the time being, but in all cases make estimates and give sources for the answers (**Fig. 3.6**). Make estimates as you go along; for example, it must cost between $100 and $200; it must weigh less than 50 pounds; and it must at least support a person weighing 250 pounds. Give estimates as ranges of prices or weights rather than exact numbers. Use catalogs offering similar products as sources for prices, weights, and sizes.

Next, make a list of the questions that need answers. Follow each question with a source for its answer and give a preliminary answer. How many people exercise? What are their ages? Do they buy exercise equipment? What are the most popular weight exercises? You may obtain this type of information from interviews, product catalogs, the library, and sporting-goods stores. Market considerations include the average income of a typical exerciser. How much does he or she spend on physical fitness per year? The opinions of sporting-goods dealers are helpful, and they should be able to direct you to other sources of information (**Fig. 3.7**).

Record the data that you gather by interviewing gym managers, looking at catalogs, and visiting sporting-goods stores to learn about the people who exercise and the equipment they

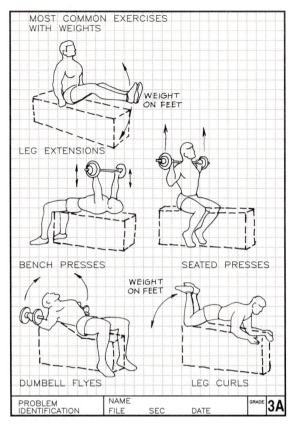

3.9 These sketches illustrate some of the typical exercises with weights.

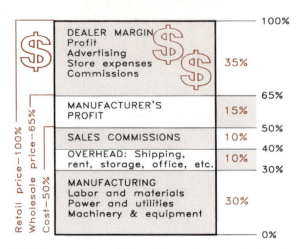

3.10 This chart shows the breakdown of costs involved in the retail price of a product.

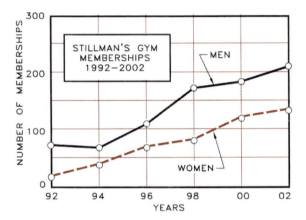

3.11 This graph describes visually the trends in potential customers for the exercise apparatus.

use (**Fig. 3.8**). Determine the most popular weight exercises of those for whom this bench is to be designed by surveying users, coaches, and sporting-goods outlets. Sketch those exercises on a worksheet (**Fig. 3.9**).

Think about costs and pricing the product even during problem identification. **Figure 3.10** shows how products may be priced from wholesale to retail, but these percentages vary by product. For instance, profit margins are smaller for food sales than for furniture sales. If an item retails for $50, the production and overhead cost cannot be more than about $20 to maintain the necessary margins.

Data are easier to interpret if they are presented graphically (**Fig. 3.11**). Thorough problem identification includes graphs, sketches, and schematics that improve the communication of your findings.

Problem identification is not complete at this point. However, this example should give you a basic understanding of the process.

3.6 Organization of Effort

The designer should prepare a schedule of required design activities after completing problem identification. The **project evaluation and review technique (PERT)**, developed by project managers for projects requiring coordination of many activities, aids in scheduling tasks. PERT is

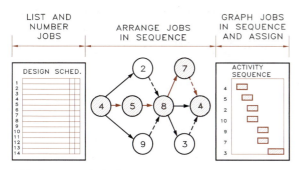

3.12 Planning and scheduling a project involves three steps.

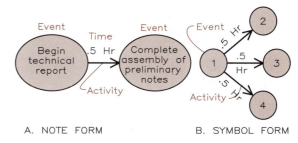

3.14 Two ways of preparing an Activities Network are (A) note form and (B) symbol form, both of which graphically arrange activities in sequence.

Design Schedule & Progress Record

TEAM __4__ PROJECT __PRODUCT DESIGN__

WORK PERIODS __11__ MAN HOURS __70__ FINISHING DATE __4-15__

JOB	ASSIGNMENT	Est. Hrs.	Act. Hrs.	PERCENT COMPLETE 0 20 40 60 80
7	WRITE REPORT—ALL	15		
6	BRAINSTORM—ALL	.5	1	
3	WRITE MFGRS—JHE	2		
10	GRAPH DATA—HLE	2		
5	MARKET ANALYSIS—DL	3	3	
12	COLLECT DATA—TT	2		

3.13 The Design Schedule and Progress Record (DS&PR) shows typical entries for a product design project.

a means of scheduling activities in sequence and reviewing progress made toward their completion.

The **critical path method (CPM)** of scheduling evolved from PERT and is used with it. The tasks that must be completed before others can begin are critical tasks and should be given priority. The critical path is the sequence of tasks requiring the longest time from start to finish and has the least flexibility. Activities not in the critical path receive less emphasis.

3.7 Planning Design Activities

The chart in **Fig. 3.12** illustrates the steps involved in planning a job (project): (1) list the tasks on a form called a Design Schedule and

Progress Record; (2) prepare an Activities Network Diagram, arranging the tasks in sequence; and (3) prepare an Activity Sequence Chart that graphs the tasks in the sequence shown in the network.

Design Schedule and Progress Record
The designer separates the job into tasks, numbers them, and lists them in the **Design Schedule and Progress Record (DS&PR)** without concern for their sequence (**Fig. 3.13**). Next, the designer estimates the amount of time required for each task and enters it in the third column. The designer adjusts the amount of time for each task so that the total matches the time allotted for the job.

Activities Network
The designer prepares an **Activities Network (AN)** by arranging the tasks from the DS&PR in their proper sequence in either note or symbol form. The note form identifies activities by task name (**Fig. 3.14**); the symbol form identifies activities by task number. Arrows connect activities, showing their sequence. Labels on the arrows indicate the amount of time needed to complete the activities. For example, the first activity in preparing the technical report is to assemble preliminary notes, which requires 0.5 hour (**Fig. 3.14A**).

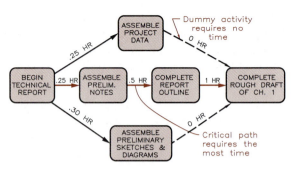

3.15 The critical path is the path from start to end of the project that requires the most time; shown here for a portion of the product design project.

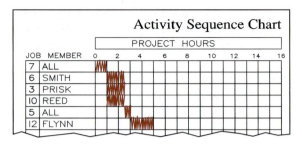

3.16 The Activity Sequence Chart (ASC) contains tasks, assignments, and initial time estimates from the DS&PR and activity sequence from the Activity Network.

Dummy activities simply indicate connections between activities that involve no work and no time, because activities must be connected in the network. The two dummy activities (dashed lines) in **Fig. 3.15** show sequential connections but no expenditure of time. In other words, the project data and the preliminary sketches and diagrams that were assembled were not needed to complete the draft of Chapter 1 but are available for later use in the project.

The critical path identified in the Activities Network (**Fig. 3.15**) is the longest time path from the project's beginning to its end. For the partial Activities Network shown, 1.75 hours are required to complete the draft of Chapter 1 of the technical report.

Activity Sequence Chart

Next, the designer lists the activities on the Activity Sequence Chart (ASC) (**Fig. 3.16**), which shows task numbers and team member assignments from the DS&PR. A bar graph shows the sequence of and the time allocated to each task. For example, 0.5 hour is scheduled for brainstorming, or task 2, from the DS&PR and is to be done first. The ASC also is the overall project schedule.

As work progresses, the designer graphs the status of each activity on the DS&PR (**Fig. 3.13**). The actual hours required to complete tasks

appear in column 4, for easy comparison with the original time estimates. When the extra time required becomes greater than that scheduled, the designer has to make adjustments in the ASC.

Problems

Problems should be presented on 8-1/2-by-11-inch paper, grid or plain. Notes, sketches, drawings, and graphs should be neatly executed. Written matter should be typed or lettered on paper with 1/8-in. guidelines.

General

1. Identify a need for a design solution that could be completed as a short class assignment in less than three hours. Submit a proposal outlining this need and your general plan for its solution. Limit the written proposal to two pages.

2. You are marooned on an uninhabited island with no tools or supplies. Identify the major problems that you would have to solve. List the factors that you would have to consider before attempting a solution for each problem. For example: There is the need for food. Determine (a) available sources of food on island, (b) methods of gathering/catching, (c) methods of storing a food supply, and (d) method of cooking.

3. While you were walking to class today, what irritants or discomforts did you recognize? Were the sidewalks too narrow? Were the entrances to the buildings inconvenient? Using worksheets, identify the cause of these problems, write a problem statement (including need recognition), and list the requirements for and limitations on solutions.

4. Repeat Problem 3, but use irritants or discomforts found in your (a) living quarters, (b) classroom, (c) recreation facilities, (d) dining facilities, or (e) another environment with which you are familiar.

Product Design Problems

5. Reconstruct the designer's approach to development of the tab-opening can. Even though the problem has been solved and its solution marketed, identify the need for the product and propose specifications for it. Is the existing solution the most appropriate one, or does your problem identification statement suggest others? Explain your answer.

6. Repeat Problem 5 for a travel iron for pressing clothes.

7. List the problems involved in designing a motorized wheelbarrow.

8. Suppose that you recognize the need for a device that could be attached to a bicycle to allow it to be ridden over street curbs to sidewalk level. Identify the problems involved in determining the marketability of such a device.

9. Identify the problems you might encounter in developing a portable engineering travel kit to give engineers the capability for making engineering calculations, notes, sketches, and drawings. The kit might include a carrying case, calculator, computer, drawing instruments, paper, reference material, and other accessories.

10. Use Section 3.7 as a guide and prepare a Design Schedule & Progress Record, an Activities Network, and an Activity Sequence Chart for the portion of your design project as assigned below:

- A. An overview of the entire project as you anticipate it at the present.
- B. The first three steps of the design process.
- C. The problem identification step only.

Use as many sheets as necessary.

11. Develop your ability to make educated guesses and estimates regarding your world. For example, can you guess how many McDonald's hamburger stores there are in a neighboring city? If you looked in the yellow pages of your town, counted the McDonald's there, and divided by the local population to find the population per store, would this factor help you with your estimate? Check a phone book from the neighboring city to see.

Using this approach, go to your library, look in the yellow pages, and determine the business outlets per 1000 of population for any of the following categories: Banks, gas stations, movie theaters, bookstores, fitness centers, restaurants, department stores, or other businesses that are of interest to you.

Learning to make intelligent guesses will help you be a better engineer and entrepreneur.

12. Pricing products is similar to making the estimates covered in Problem 11. Use your common sense and instincts (that you may not realize you have) to explain why mark-up and profit margins vary among various types of products. Give you explanation in a brief outline form that will make your key points easy to process by the reader.

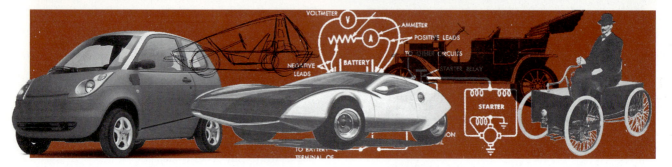

CHAPTER FOUR

Preliminary Ideas

4.1 Introduction

Creativity is highest during the preliminary idea step of the design process because there are no limitations on being innovative, experimental, and daring. During subsequent steps of the design process, freedom of creativity diminishes and the need for information and facts increases. **Figure 4.1** shows this relationship between creativity and information accumulation during the design process.

A unique design is the digital tire gauge used for checking air pressure with greater accuracy and convenience (**Fig. 4.2**). It is designed with a light in its nose to find the valve stem of a tire, even in the dark. Designs such as this will be limited in the future only by our imagination in applying technology.

Although the Instant Coffee spoon in **Fig. 4.3** is a less technical product, it is a unique design that prompts the question, "Why didn't I think of that?" Another example of a very simple but highly successful design is the Post-it®, the "sticky" removable note tab that was developed by the 3M Corporation.

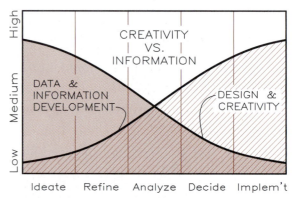

4.1 Creativity is highest during the early stages of the design process and information accumulation is highest at the end of the process.

A product that is expected to revolutionize pedestrian traffic is the Segway™ Human Transporter (**Fig. 4.4**), a battery-powered vehicle that will truly give the individual "wheels." It has a top speed of 12.5 miles per hour, a range of 17 miles, and a payload of 250 pounds.

4.2 This battery-operated digital tire gauge was designed to fit in the glove compartment of an automobile. It has a light in its nose to make it easy to find the valve stem in poor light. (*Courtesy Bresslergroup and Measurement Specialties, Inc.*)

4.3 A simple but unique design that solves several problems is the Coffee Spoon that preserves the instant coffee and is used as a spoon in the process. (*Courtesy of Aluminum Company of America.*)

4.4 The Segway (the human transporter) is expected to revolutionize pedestrian transportation. It is designed to move in response to leaning one's body forward or backward. (*Courtesy of Segway LLC.*)

A short time ago these products were considered futuristic fantasies. Progress in the future will be limited only by our imagination in applying technology.

4.2 Individual Versus Team

Designers work both as individuals and as members of design teams during the process of developing products. Both methods have their advantages and disadvantages.

Individual Approach

Designers working alone must make sketches and notes to communicate first with themselves and then with others. Their primary goal is to generate as many ideas as possible, because better ideas are more likely to come from long lists than from short lists. Rapidly-drawn sketches can capture fleeting thoughts that might otherwise be lost during ideation.

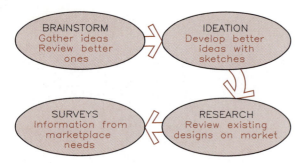

4.5 A plan of action is needed for the preliminary ideas step of the design process, which will probably involve most of the steps shown here.

4.6 The recorder should make a list of all brainstorming ideas during the session.

Team Approach

The team approach brings diversity and a broad range of ideas to the design process, but along with it comes problems of management and coordination. Groups perform better with a leader with the authority to guide their activities and make assignments.

Teams should alternate between individual and group work to take advantage of both approaches. For example, each team member could individually develop preliminary ideas, bring them to a team meeting, compare solutions, merge ideas, and return to individual work with a renewed outlook.

4.3 Plan of Action

The following steps are suggested for completing the preliminary ideas step of the design process: (1) hold brainstorming sessions, (2) prepare sketches and notes, (3) research background data, and (4) conduct surveys (**Fig. 4.5**). Periodically reviewing notes and worksheets made during problem identification ensures that efforts will stay focused on the design objectives.

4.4 Brainstorming

Brainstorming is a problem-solving technique in which members of a group spontaneously contribute ideas. The best session is one that adheres to the following rules.

Rules of Brainstorming

The guidelines for a brainstorming session are:[*]

1. **Criticism is ruled out.** Judgment of ideas must be withheld until later.

2. **Freewheeling is encouraged.** The wilder the idea, the better; it is easier to tame down than to think up. A good solution may emerge from a suggestion that was made as a joke.

3. **Quantity is wanted.** The larger the number of ideas, the greater will be the likelihood of useful ideas.

4. **Combination and improvement are sought.** Participants should seek ways of improving the ideas of others.

Brainstorming Session Organization

The organization of a brainstorming session involves selecting the panel, becoming familiar with the problem, selecting a moderator and recorder, holding the session, and following up.

Panel Selection The optimum number of participants in a brainstorming session is twelve people. For diversity, they should be people both with and without knowledge of the subject. Because supervisors may restrict the flow of ideas, panels should be composed of non-supervisory professionals of similar status.

[*]From Osborn, Alex, *Applied Imagination*. New York City: Scribner, 1963.

4.7 Designers use sketches and notes to develop preliminary ideas as a means of communicating with themselves and with others. (*Courtesy of Ford Motor Company.*)

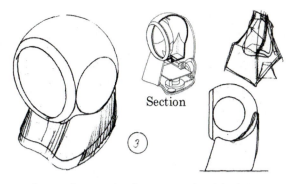

4.8 These preliminary sketches were made while designing a point-of-purchase pivoting sphere scanner. (*Courtesy of Besslergroup and Metrologic Instruments.*)

Preliminary Work An information sheet about the session should be given to panel members a couple of days before the session to allow ideas to incubate.

The Problem The problem to be brainstormed should be defined concisely. Instead of presenting the problem as "how to improve our campus," it should be presented by category, such as "how to improve student parking," or "how to improve food services."

The Moderator and Recorder The panel selects a moderator to be in charge of the session and a recorder to keep track of the ideas presented (**Fig. 4.6**).

The Session The moderator introduces the problem and recognizes the first member holding up a hand to respond. The person responding should state an idea as briefly as possible. The moderator then recognizes the next person holding up a hand, and the process continues. A suggestion made by one member often stimulates ideas in others, who snap their fingers to signify that they want to "hitchhike" on the pre-

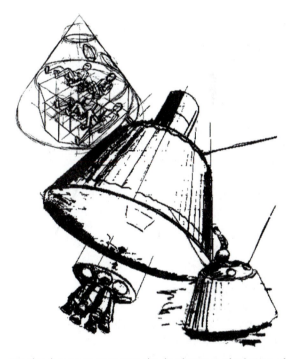

4.9 Sketches are important to the development of solutions of the most complex of engineering and scientific designs. These sketches illustrate preliminary ideas for the manned space capsule. (*Courtesy of the National Aeronautics and Space Administration.*)

vious idea. This interaction is central to a brainstorming session.

The moderator's most important job is to keep the ideas flowing and to prevent participants from giving long, drawn-out responses that dampen the spontaneous and "fun" aspects of the session.

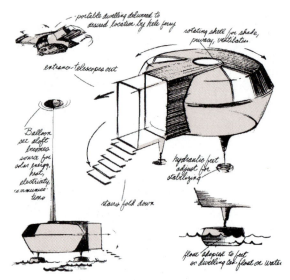

4.10 These preliminary sketches and notes depict a Transportable Uni-Lodge, a mobile dwelling of the future. (*Courtesy of Lippincott and Margulies, Inc., and Charles Bruning Company.*)

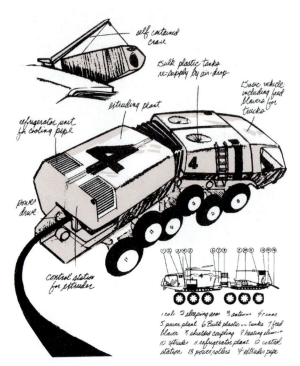

4.11 These sketches show a designer's ideas for a self-contained pipelayer for laying irrigation pipe in large tracts of desert areas. (*Courtesy of Donald Desky Associates, Inc. and Charles Bruning Company.*)

Length A session should move at a brisk pace and end when ideas slow to an unproductive rate. An effective session can last from a few minutes to an hour, but twenty minutes is considered about the best length.

Follow-up The recorder should reproduce the list of ideas gathered during the session and distribute them to the participants. As many as a hundred ideas may be gathered during a twenty-minute session. The designer should pare them down to those having the most merit.

4.5 Sketching and Notes

Sketching is an effective medium of design, its development, and its communication, whether it is a simple part or a complex product (**Fig. 4.7**). There are many instances where modification of designs and their descriptions are almost impossible without the ability to make simple and rapid freehand sketches. Sketching allows

the designer's ideas to take form as three-dimensional pictorials or as two-dimensional views that are visual extensions of the thinking process. The sketches shown in **Fig. 4.8** were several of many that were made in developing a design for a point-of-purchase pivoting-sphere scanner. **Figure 4.9** shows one of many sketches that were used in the design of the various components and systems of the space program, one of the most advanced design programs in history.

The preliminary ideas for the Transportable Uni-Lodge (**Fig. 4.10**) illustrate the importance of sketches in developing and communicating ideas. These ideas propose that the Uni-Lodge be transported by helicopter to previously

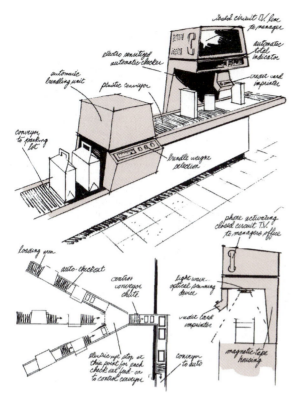

4.12 These sketches describe a concept for an automatic checkout/packaging unit for a supermarket. (*Courtesy of Lester Beall Inc. and Charles Bruning Company.*)

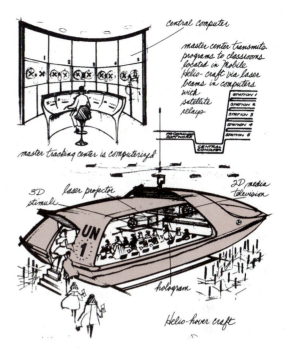

4.13 A flotilla of classrooms controlled from a master tracking center by lasers and computer relays is illustrated by sketches. (*Courtesy of Raymond Loewy/William Snaith, Inc. and Charles Bruning Company.*)

unreachable areas and lowered onto the site or the water. Its retractable legs can be equipped with pontoons, allowing it to float. Additional features are noted on the sketches.

Another concept is a self-contained pipelayer (**Fig. 4.11**) for laying irrigation pipe in desert areas. The tractor has a cab, sleeping accommodations, radio equipment, power plant, and bulk storage tanks for plastic. The van consists of an extrusion machine, a refrigeration unit, and a control station. The pipelayer transports bulk plastic and machinery that can extrude and lay approximately two miles of pipe from each pair of storage tanks. Empty tanks are discarded and replaced by full tanks that are air-dropped to the crew.

Figure 4.12 shows sketches of a proposed checkout system for a grocery store. The shopper sets the machine in operation by inserting a credit card in a slot. After the card is scanned, the customer receives an order number tag, and the conveyor moves the items under a scanner and totals the prices. If a question arises, the customer can stop the machine and talk to a store employee by lifting the phone. The conveyor moves the items to a unit where they are packaged in plastic containers and marked with the customer's number. A central conveyor transports large orders to an exterior pickup point near the area where the customer is parked.

Sketches in **Fig. 4.13** describe a teaching flotilla—mobile floating classrooms—that is connected to a master tracking center from which programs are transmitted by lasers and satellite relays. Each helio-hover craft is equipped with advanced technology, including two-dimensional and three-dimensional projectors and televisions. The computerized tracking center can transmit presentations to six different floating classrooms.

The concepts in these examples could not have been developed without the use of sketching as a medium of design and as a means of thinking. Rapid sketches capture a person's thought process, imagination, and creativity in a form that can be shared by others.

4.6 Design Sketching: Application

The previous sketches have ranged from simplistic to complicated, but they are typical of the drawings used in creating designs for automobiles, spacecraft, and all other products. Remember that sketching is the medium of developing concepts and details from idea to final design throughout the design process. The designer must develop numerous preliminary solutions to design problems, most of which will be rapidly-drawn freehand sketches (**Fig. 4.14**).

A series of sketches (**Fig. 4.15** through **Fig. 4.18**) illustrates how sketches are developed from rough sketches to more sophisticated drawings as the

4.14 The designer uses sketching as his primary means of developing preliminary design concepts. (*Courtesy I.N. Incorporated.*)

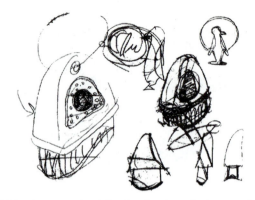

4.15 Design concepts of the shoe brush are brainstormed and sketched as two- and three-dimensional views. (*Courtesy Bresslergroup and Shoe Store Supplies.*)

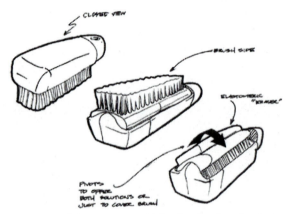

4.16 A second design concept of the shoe brush is sketched in three-dimensional views. (*Courtesy Bresslergroup and Shoe Store Supplies.*)

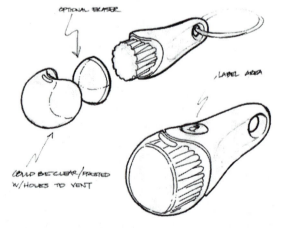

4.17 A third design concept of the shoe brush is sketched in three-dimensional views. (*Courtesy Bresslergroup and Shoe Store Supplies.*)

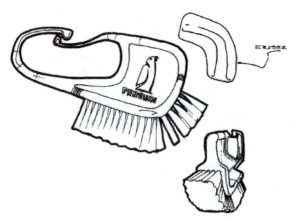

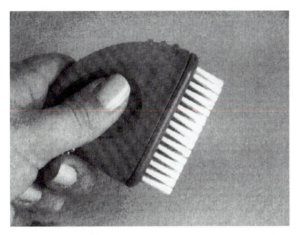

4.18 Another design concept of the shoe brush is sketched in three-dimensional views. (*Courtesy Bresslergroup and Shoe Store Supplies.*)

4.19 The final design for the shoe brush is shown here in product form. (*Courtesy Bresslergroup and Shoe Store Supplies.*)

preliminary idea process progresses. The product illustrated is a unique design for a shoe brush.

Figure 4.15 shows how rapidly-drawn sketches are used as an extension of the brainstorming process to develop initial concepts of the shoe brush. The designer uses sketches to communicate with himself.

Figure 4.16 illustrates another preliminary but better-developed concept for the shoe brush. Three-dimensional sketches are used by the designer to develop his design and communicate his ideas to others. Notes are used to clar-

ify significant features. A third and fourth design concept are sketched in **Fig. 4.17** and **Fig. 4.18**, respectively.

The final design for the shoe is shown as a prototype in **Fig. 4.19**. The concepts shown here are but a few of the many sketches that were made during the preliminary phase of the design process. The more concepts you have to choose from, the better your chances are of attaining the best design solution.

4.7 Quickie Design

Let's assume that we recognize the need for a product to protect walls and doorknobs where doors swing into walls. First, we make sketches on a worksheet to identify the problem and its geometry (**Fig. 4.20**). If we decide to develop a

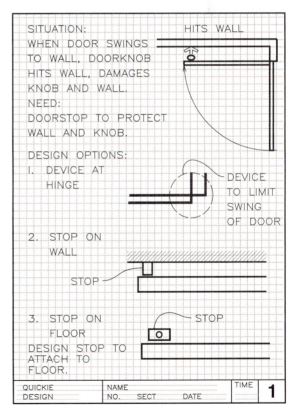

4.20 This worksheet shows sketches and notes to identify the need for a device to prevent damage caused by a door swinging in to a wall.

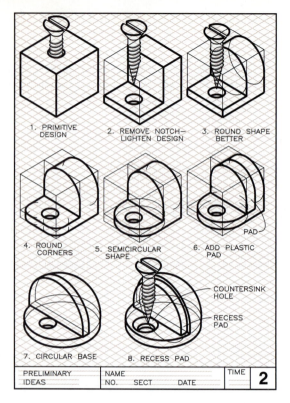

1. PRIMITIVE DESIGN
2. REMOVE NOTCH—LIGHTEN DESIGN
3. ROUND SHAPE BETTER
4. ROUND CORNERS
5. SEMICIRCULAR SHAPE
6. ADD PLASTIC PAD
PAD
7. CIRCULAR BASE
8. RECESS PAD
COUNTERSINK HOLE
RECESS PAD

PRELIMINARY IDEAS	NAME		TIME	2
	NO. SECT DATE			

FLOOR—MOUNTED STOPS

DOOR—MOUNTED STOPS

WALL—MOUNTED STOPS

QUICKIE DESIGN	NAME		TIME	4
	NO. SECT DATE			

4.21 (Sheet 2) A series of detailed sketches illustrates the evolution of the doorstop design.

4.22 (Sheet 3) Detailed sketches are used to refine the design and clarify it for others.

4.23 (Sheet 4) The doorstops shown here are examples of some that are available on today's market.

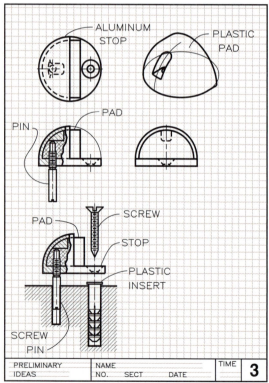

ALUMINUM STOP
PLASTIC PAD
PAD
PIN
PAD
SCREW
STOP
PLASTIC INSERT
SCREW
PIN

PRELIMINARY IDEAS	NAME		TIME	3
	NO. SECT DATE			

floor-mounted doorstop, we might begin with sketches (made by hand or by computer) of a design that begins as a basic block, which will do the job (**Fig. 4.21**). However, we can do better than that; we make additional sketches to refine and develop the design until we find a suitable and marketable solution.

We make more sketches (**Fig. 4.22, Sheet 3**) to develop the doorstop's details, which we show to others for consultation and evaluation. **Figure**

4.23 shows other solutions to this problem that are products already being marketed. These products were developed in a similar manner, by designers using graphics as the medium of design.

4.8 Background Information

One way of gathering preliminary ideas is to look for existing products and designs that are similar to the one being considered. Several sources of background information include magazines, patents, and consultants (**Fig. 4.24**).

Magazines

Articles in both general and technical magazines often present unique designs, complete with drawings and photographs. Advertisements in these magazines may give helpful information on materials and innovative devices. There are various magazines that specialize in most product areas that your librarian can help you find as a reference.

Patents

Patents from the U.S. Patent Office illustrate the details of all designs that were granted a patent. The designer can use them to understand competing products better and to ensure that there is no infringement on existing patents.

Consultants

Complex projects may require specialists in manufacturing, electronics, materials, and instrumentation. Manufacturers' representatives also provide valuable assistance with projects related to their companies' products. Having no knowledge of a project at the outset can be an advantage, since a fresh perspective is what is needed.

4.9 Opinion Surveys

Designers need to know the attitudes of consumers about a new product at the preliminary

4.24 The gathering of background information is helpful and necessary to the development preliminary ideas.

design stage. Is there a need for the product? Are consumers excited about the prospect of a particular product being designed? Would they buy the product? What features do they like or dislike? What price range would be acceptable to them? What price do retailers think it will sell for? Does size, weight, or color matter?

For a survey to be of value, the population for whom the product is being developed should be identified. Are they homeowners, high school males, or single women? A selected sample of the population can be surveyed by a personal interview, telephone survey, or mail questionnaire.

The Personal Interview

A personal interview survey should be organized to obtain and summarize reliable responses quickly and easily. For this reason, questions should be true-false or multiple choice for ease of tabulation.

Interviewers should introduce themselves, explain the purpose of the interview, and ask for

PRELIMINARY IDEAS

1. **Brainstorming Ideas**
   A. FEATURES
      1. HANG FROM CEILING
      2. CONVERT INTO A PIECE OF FURNITURE
      3. PADDED BENCH—INFLATED PAD—FOAM PAD, WATER—BED PAD
      4. USE SPRINGS, NOT WEIGHTS
      5. USE WATER FOR WEIGHTS
      6. FOLD OUT FROM WALL
      7. ADJUSTABLE HEIGHTS
      8. SAFETY DEVICE TO KEEP WEIGHTS FROM FALLING ON EXERCISER
      9. MOUNT ON WHEELS—MOUNT ON PADS
      10. MAKE WEIGHTS VARIABLE

   B. WHERE TO USE
      1. USE IN GARAGE
      2. USE IN BEDROOM, STORE IN CLOSET
      3. USE WHILE WATCHING TV
      4. MAKE FUN TO USE—ADD SOUND—USE WITH TV TAPE—RECORD ON TV TAPE
      5. USE IN DORM

   C. WHERE TO SELL
      1. DOOR TO DOOR
      2. SELL BY MAIL
      3. AT RETAIL OUTLES
      4. SELL AT EXERCISE GYMS
      5. SELL BY SCOUTS AS FUND RAISER
      6. SELL BY TV MARKETING
      7. SELL BY RADIO ADS
      8. ADVERTISE IN FITNESS MAGAZINES
      9. ADVERTISE IN GENERAL MAGAZINES
      10. RECOMMENDATIONS BY DOCTORS

| PRELIMINARY IDEAS | NAME | | | GRADE | 4 |
| | FILE | SEC | DATE | | |

PRELIMINARY IDEAS

2. Description of best ideas

   A. SUPPORT ON SOFT PAD TO PROTECT FLOORS

   B. PROVIDE A PADDED VINYL BENCH

   C. MAKE BENCH ADJUSTABLE TO DIFFERENT POSITIONS

   D. PROVIDE SUPPORT FOR WEIGHTS

   E. MAKE ADJUSTABLE TO FIT DIFFERENT SIZES OF USERS

   F. ADD FEATURES FOR POPULAR EXERCISES:

      1. BENCH PRESSES

      2. LEG CURLS

      3. ARM FLYES

      4. OVERHEAD PRESSES

   G. MAKE PORTABLE AND COLLAPSIBLE

   H. KEEP PRICE UNDER $150

   I. SHOULD BE ATTRACTIVE TO BE SUITABLE FOR HOME USE

| PRELIMINARY IDEAS | NAME | | | GRADE | 5 |
| | FILE | SEC | DATE | | |

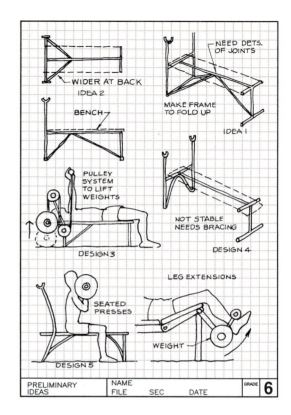

| PRELIMINARY IDEAS | NAME | | | GRADE | 6 |
| | FILE | SEC | DATE | | |

4.25 (Sheet 4) Ideas gathered during a brainstorming session are listed on a worksheet for future reference.

4.26 (Sheet 5) The best of the brainstorming ideas are selected and summarized for further development.

4.27 (Sheet 6) Preliminary concepts for the exercise bench are shown as sketches and notes.

permission to proceed. They should make the interview brief, record responses, and thank the interviewee for participating.

The Telephone Interview

If the opinions of the general public are desired, interviewers can talk to people selected from the telephone book. If opinions from a certain group—say, sporting-goods retailers—are needed, the Yellow Pages provide prospective interviewees.

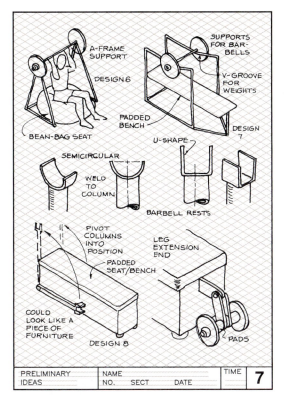

4.28 Sketches and notes describe additional ideas of the exercising bench.

The Mail Questionnaire

An economical method of contacting a large number of people in many locations is by mail questionnaire. To test the suitability of questions to be asked, the questionnaire can be mailed to a small group of people for their response as a test. The final questionnaire should be mailed to at least three times as many people as the number of responses desired. Inserting a self-addressed, stamped envelope will increase responses.

4.10 Preliminary Ideas: Exercise Bench

We introduced the design of an exercise bench in Chapter 3, where it was taken through the problem identification step. Recall that it is to be used by those who lift weights to maintain body fitness. This apparatus should be versatile and at the low end of the price range for exercise equipment.

Now, to apply the preliminary ideas step of the design process, begin holding a brainstorming session with team members to generate and record ideas on a worksheet (**Fig. 4.25**). Then select the better ideas, list their features, and summarize them on a worksheet (**Fig. 4.26**), even if they have more features than you could possibly use in a single design. The reason for this is to make sure that you do not forget or lose any concepts.

Using rapid freehand sketching techniques, such as orthographic views and three-dimensional pictorial sketches, sketch ideas on worksheets. Note on the drawings any ideas or questions that come to mind while you sketch. Do not erase and modify your sketches; instead make new sketches that incorporate revisions and modifications. By doing so, you will be able to review your thinking process from idea to idea. You should occasionally go back to previous steps to be sure that usable concepts have not been overlooked.

In **Fig. 4.27**, note the adaptation of ideas from various types of benches and exercise techniques. A number identifies each idea. Another worksheet (**Fig. 4.28**) shows other ideas and modifications of previous ideas. Additional sketches can be made of specific details of each design: connections, fabrication details, padding, and so forth.

Problems

Problems should be presented on 8–1/2-by-11-inch paper, grid or plain. All notes, sketches, drawings, and graphs should be neat and accurate. Written matter should be legibly lettered, using 1/8-in. guidelines.

1. Select one or more of the following items and list as many of their uses as possible: (a) empty vegetable cans (3-in. diameter by 5 in.), (b) 2000 sheets of 8–1/2-by-11-inch bond paper, (c) one cubic yard of dirt, (d) three empty oil drums (24-in. DIA by 36 in.), (e) a load of egg cartons, (f) twenty-five bamboo poles (10 ft. long), (g) ten old tires, or (h) old newspapers.

2. If you were going to select an ideal team to develop an engineering solution to a problem, what personal characteristics would you look for? Explain.

3. What are the advantages and disadvantages of working independently on a project? Of working as a member of a design team? Explain and give examples of instances in which each approach would have the advantage.

4. Gather background information on one of the following design problems or on one of your own selection: (a) a one-person canoe, (b) a built-in car jack, (c) an automatic blackboard eraser, (d) a built-in coffee maker for an automobile, (e) a self-opening door to permit a pet to leave or enter the house, (f) an emergency fire escape for a two-story building, (g) a rain protector for people attending outdoor spectator activities, (h) a new household appliance, or (i) a home exerciser. Consider costs, methods of construction, dimensions, existing products, estimates of need, and other information that will assist you in understanding the problem and its feasibility as a project. List your references and present your findings.

5. List and describe the type of consulting services required for the following design projects: (a) a zoning system for a city of 20,000 people, (b) a shopping center, (c) a go-cart operation, (d) a water-purification facility, (e) a hydroelectric system, (f) a nuclear fallout disaster plan, (g) a processing plant for refining petroleum products, and (h) a drainage system for residential areas.

6. The tensioner in **Fig. 4.29** keeps the chain taut that engages one side of the sprocket (the toothed wheel). Tension is applied to the chain by moving the position of the 6-in. DIA sprocket

4.29 (Problem 6) A chain tensioner with a 6-in. DIA sprocket mounted on a movable shaft. (*Courtesy of Brewer Machine and Gear Company.*)

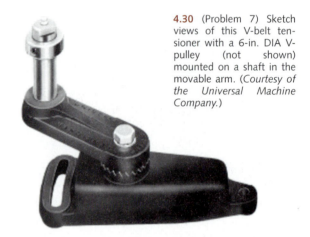

4.30 (Problem 7) Sketch views of this V-belt tensioner with a 6-in. DIA V-pulley (not shown) mounted on a shaft in the movable arm. (*Courtesy of the Universal Machine Company.*)

along its shaft by turning the nut on the threaded screw. The apparatus must be mounted with bolts at each end.

Although some of the parts are not clearly illustrated, make a series of freehand orthographic sketches to describe the parts as if you were the designer.

7. Another design for a belt tensioner is shown in **Fig. 4.30** that adjusts a pulley (not shown) instead of a sprocket. Notice that the base has a slot that is an arc of a circle for adjustment. An additional adjustment can be made by moving the arm to different positions. The V-pulley (6-in. DIA) for a flexible belt will be mounted on the shaft passing through the arm and held on by a collar with a setscrew.

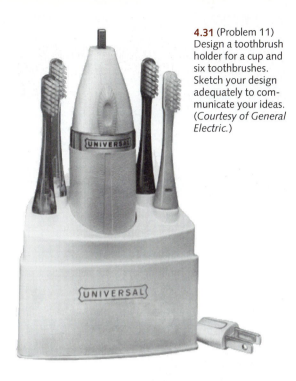

4.31 (Problem 11) Design a toothbrush holder for a cup and six toothbrushes. Sketch your design adequately to communicate your ideas. (*Courtesy of General Electric.*)

4.32 (Problem 12) Sketch views of the parts of the compressing coupling to better explain it to a classmate.

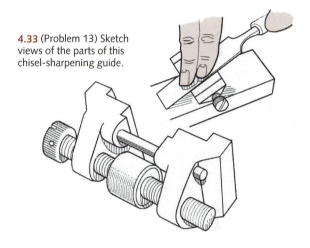

4.33 (Problem 13) Sketch views of the parts of this chisel-sharpening guide.

Make freehand orthographic sketches of the individual parts to better explain how they are made and their relationships to each other. Refer to Chapters 13 and 14 as needed.

8. Develop a questionnaire to determine the public's attitude toward a particular product of your selection. Explain how you would tabulate the responses to the questionnaire.

9. Organize a group of classmates and hold a brainstorming session to identify problems in need of solutions. Make a list of the ideas.

10. With a team of classmates, make a list of items that are in need of "invention." If you can't think of any, then make a list of problems and inconveniences that you are unhappy with. Their solution might lead to a new product or system.

11. Make sketches of a toothbrush holder that can sit on a table surface or be attached to the wall (**Fig. 4.31**). What options would make it most marketable?

12. The compression coupling (**Fig. 4.32**) is shown assembled and exploded. The coupling must fit snuggly with 1.50-diameter shafts. Make orthographic sketches of the parts to better understand their relationship.

13. Make orthographic sketches of the parts of the chisel-sharpening guide (**Fig. 4.33**). This device holds the chisel at a constant angle as it is moved back and forth on the whetstone for sharpening.

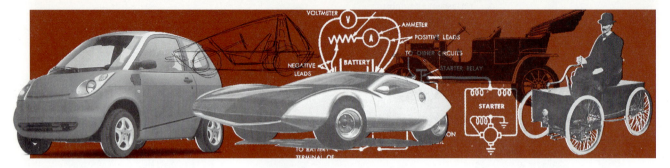

Refinement

5.1 Introduction

Refinement of preliminary ideas is the first departure from unrestricted creativity and imagination. The designer must now give primary consideration to function, cost, and practicality.

This step of the design process calls for the designer to make scale drawings with instruments to check dimensions and geometry that cannot be accurately measured in unscaled sketches. However, it is unnecessary to fully dimension these drawings. Descriptive geometry has its greatest application as a design tool in the idea refinement step of the design process.

5.2 Physical Properties

Important in refining an idea is determining the product's physical properties. An example of a refinement drawing is the profile of a Bell D326 Clipper helicopter that shows its overall dimensions (**Fig. 5.1**). The positions of the propeller

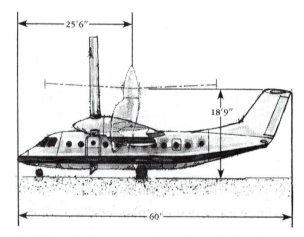

5.1 This scale drawing gives several overall dimensions to describe a helicopter body. It is important that refinement drawings be drawn to scale, but only major dimensions need be given at this stage. (*Courtesy of Bell Helicopter Textron.*)

blades are illustrated and dimensioned where they are rotated from vertical to horizontal.

Although most refinement drawings will be two-dimensional drawings where dimensions

5.2 The advanced steering technology of the BMW Street Carver is drawn to scale in this pictorial as a step in refining its design. The mechanism permits changes in directions when the weight of the rider is shifted. (*Courtesy of BMW Company.*)

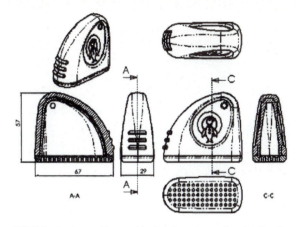

5.3 This six-view orthographic drawing shows the details of a shoe brush with major dimensions given. (*Courtesy Bresslergroup and Shoe Store Supplies.*)

can be accurately scaled and compared, three-dimensional drawings can also be used. **Figure 5.2** is an example of a three-dimensional view of the Street Carver that is drawn to scale so it can be measured on the drawing, even though no dimensions are given.

The configuration of a handle of a shoe brush is detailed in six orthographic views, along with an isometric view, that are all drawn to scale in **Fig. 5.3**. Only a few significant dimensions are given as shown.

The computer aids the designer in taking the refinement a step further. In **Fig. 5.4**, a model of the shoe brush is drawn as a computer model, permitting it to be viewed from any direction, or exploded apart for clarity. Mechanisms with moving parts can be made to operate on the computer's monitor to test their operation. An additional example is a machine part that is rendered as a three-dimensional model with AutoCAD® to permit viewing from any direction (**Fig. 5.5**).

5.3 Descriptive Geometry Application

Descriptive geometry is the study of points, lines, and surfaces in three-dimensional space,

5.4 Computer modeling affords an excellent means of refining a preliminary product design. (*Courtesy Bresslergroup and Shoe Store Supplies.*)

which are the geometric elements that comprise all forms. Before descriptive geometry can be applied, the designer must draw orthographic views to scale, from which auxiliary views can be projected. **Figure 5.6** shows how descriptive geometry is used to determine the clearance between a hydraulic cylinder and the fender of an automobile where the cylinder is attached with a clip. This construction can be performed either by pencil or by computer.

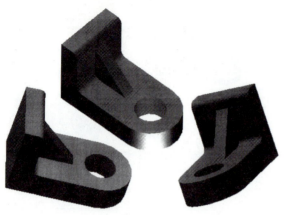

5.5 Designs can be constructed as three-dimensional models and revolved on the screen for visual inspection and refinement, much as if you were holding the part in your hand.

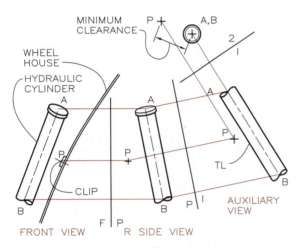

5.6 Descriptive geometry is an effective way to determine clearances between components, such as the clearance between a hydraulic cylinder and a fender.

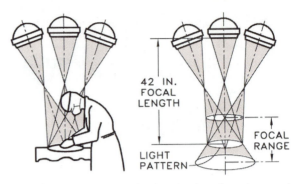

5.7 By using scale drawings developed in the refinement step of the design process, the designer can study the geometry of a surgical lamp. (*Courtesy of Sybron Corporation.*)

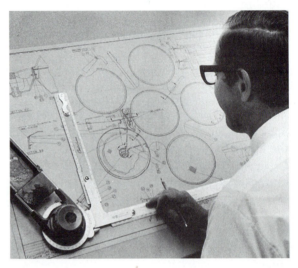

5.8 Refinement drawing shows the overall dimensions of the final design of the surgical lamp. (*Courtesy of Sybron Corporation.*)

The design of a surgical light requires the application of descriptive geometry. The light fixture must provide maximum light on the operating area with the least obstruction, as shown in **Fig. 5.7**. This scale drawing depicts the converging beams of light emitted from the reflectors, its position above the operating area, and approximate positions of the surgeons. The beams are positioned so their narrowest rays are at shoulder level to minimize shadows cast by the surgeon's shoulders, arms, and hands.

From these scale drawings, lengths, angles, areas, and other geometric relations can be determined by the designer at the drawing board or at the computer (**Fig. 5.8**). When the three-dimensional geometrical relationships have been determined, the engineering details can be developed for more analysis and testing. The major dimensions of the surgical lamp are shown in the refinement drawing in **Fig. 5.9**.

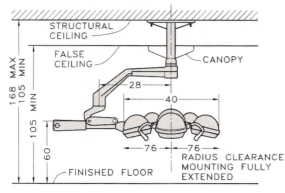

5.9 A well-designed surgical lamp emits light that passes around the surgeon's shoulders with the minimum of shadow. The focal range of this surgical lamp is between 30 and 60 inches. (*Courtesy of Sybron Corporation.*)

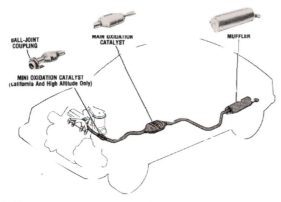

5.10 Descriptive geometry is useful in determining the lengths and angles of an automobile's exhaust system that are necessary to clear the structural members of the chassis. (Courtesy of Chrysler Corporation.)

5.4 Refinement Considerations

In advanced designs, such as that of a new model automobile, numerous features must be refined. The exhaust system shown in **Fig. 5.10** is the result of the many refinement drawings needed to determine its geometry. Descriptive geometry was used to determine the exhaust pipe's bend angles, its length, and clearances required for fitting it to the chassis without interference (**Fig. 5.11**).

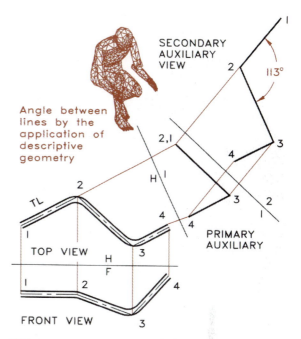

5.11 Descriptive geometry is applied to find the lengths and angles between exhaust pipe segments.

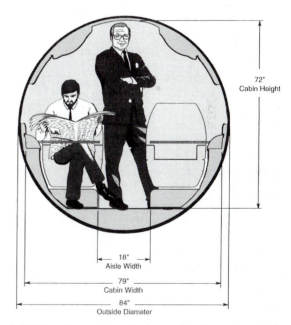

5.12 This refinement drawing is a section drawn through the fuselage of the Hawker Horizon, a business jet aircraft that shows the clearance, heights, and seat sizes of the interior. (*Courtesy of Raytheon Aircraft Corporation.*)

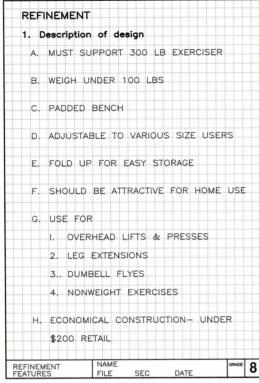

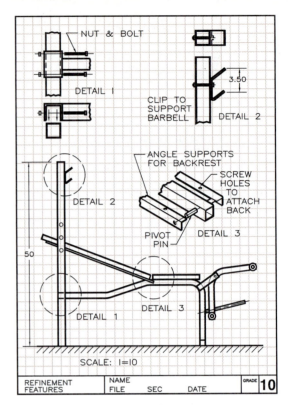

5.13 (Sheet 8) This list of desirable features is a refinement of the exercise bench.

5.14 (Sheet 9) This refinement drawing for the exercise bench is a scale drawing with only some of the major dimensions shown.

5.15 (Sheet 10) This refinement drawing is of another design concept for the exercise bench.

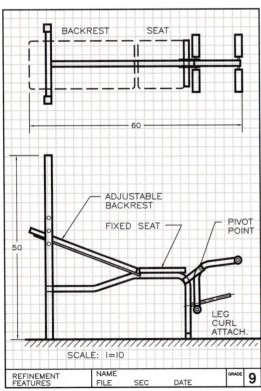

A designer's refinement drawing of the fuselage of business jet aircraft is shown as an orthographic section in **Fig. 5.12**. This drawing, although simple in concept, is effective in determining clearance, heights, and seat sizes for its passengers.

5.5 Refinement: Exercise Bench

In Chapter 3, the exercise bench design problem was identified and in Chapter 4 preliminary ideas for it were developed. Now, in this step, we

A. LEVELING   B. CASTERS FOR MOVABLE
    DEVICES   EQUIPMENT

5.16 A. The leveling devices are standard parts for leveling equipment on uneven floors.

B. Casters are attached to equipment that must be movable about a work area. They range from small sizes for TV sets to those that carry over 1000 pounds. (*Courtesy of Vlier Industries and Hamilton Casters.*)

refine the preliminary ideas for the exercise bench with instrument drawings.

First, list the features to be incorporated into the design on a worksheet (**Fig. 5.13**). Then refine a preliminary idea, say, idea 2 from **Fig. 4.27** in an orthographic scale drawing of the seat (**Fig. 5.14**). Block in extruded parts, such as the framework members, to expedite the drawing process and omit unneeded hidden lines.

Refinement drawings must be drawn to scale. The use of instruments is important to precisely portray the design from which angles, lengths, shapes, and other geometric elements will be obtained. The drawing shows only overall dimensions and several connecting joints are detailed to explain the design. **Figure 5.15** shows additional design features. These worksheets depict representative types of drawings required to refine a design; additional drawings would be required for a complete refinement of the design.

5.6 Standard Parts

When preparing refinement drawings, specify standard parts whenever possible because they are more economical and they are readily available. Merchandise catalogs, sales brochures, magazine advertisements, newspapers, and similar sources contain specifications for standard parts.

Make a practice of keeping files on stock items—such as leveling devices and casters (**Fig. 5.16**) that can be used in developing products and specified in refinement drawings by referring to literature from manufacturers and vendors. You can become a better designer by observing how standard parts and devices are made and how they function. When you see a device that you are unfamiliar with, ask yourself why it is made the way it is, how is it used, and what application can you think of for it in a design.

Problems

Problems should be presented on 8–1/2-by-11-inch paper, grid or plain. All notes, sketches, drawings, and graphical work should be neatly presented. Written matter should be lettered legibly using 1/8-inch guidelines.

1. When refining a design for a folding lawn chair, what physical properties would a designer need to determine? What physical properties would be needed for a (a) TV set base, (b) golf cart, (c) child's swing set, (d) portable typewriter, (e) shortwave radio, (f) portable camping tent, and (g) warehouse dolly used for moving heavy boxes?

2. Why should scale drawings, rather than freehand sketches, be used in the refinement of a design?

3. List five examples of problems involving spatial relationships that could be solved by the application of descriptive geometry. Explain your answers.

4. In the refinement step, how many preliminary designs should be refined? Why?

5. Make a list of refinement drawings that would be needed to develop the installation and design of a 100-foot radio antenna. Make rough

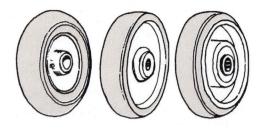

5.17 (Problem 8) Why are wheels not disks with holes through their centers? Why do they have raised hubs and bushings?

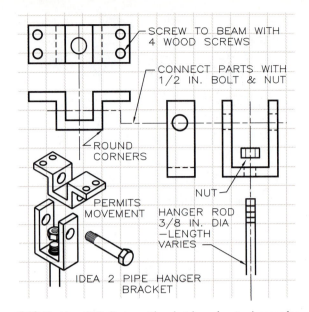

5.18 (Problem 9) Preliminary idea sketches of a pipe hanger for supporting steam pipes from an overhead beam on a hanger rod.

sketches of the types of drawings needed, with notes to explain their purposes.

6. If a design is eliminated as a possible solution after refinement drawings have been made, what should be the designer's next step? Explain.

7. For the exercise bench discussed in Section 5.5, what refinement drawings are necessary in addition to those presented? Make freehand sketches of the necessary drawings, with notes to explain what they should show.

Refinement Problems

8. Students often draw wheels as disks with holes at their centers, but even the simplest wheels have more sophistication in their design. Make a refinement drawing of one of the wheels shown in the sketches in **Fig. 5.17**. Why do wheels have raised hubs at their centers? Why do they have bushings in the holes through them?

9. Preliminary sketches for a pipe hanger bracket, used to support steam pipes from overhead beams, are given in **Fig. 5.18**. The sketches are sufficient for you to understand the concepts, but they need further refinement. Make refinement drawings of these sketches and, in the process, make whatever modifications in the design that you think would improve it.

10. The preliminary sketches in **Fig. 5.19** illustrate another concept for a pipe hanger bracket.

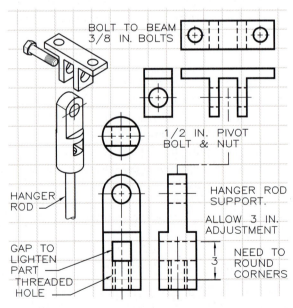

5.19 (Problem 10) Preliminary idea sketches of concepts for a hanger rod support for suspending steam pipes.

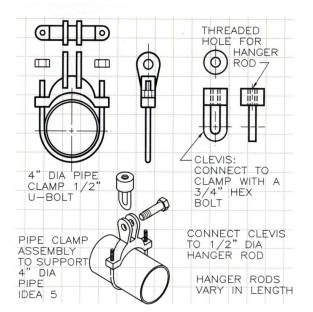

THREADED HOLE FOR HANGER ROD

CLEVIS: CONNECT TO CLAMP WITH A 3/4" HEX BOLT

4" DIA PIPE CLAMP 1/2" U-BOLT

CONNECT CLEVIS TO 1/2" DIA HANGER ROD

PIPE CLAMP ASSEMBLY TO SUPPORT 4" DIA PIPE IDEA 5

HANGER RODS VARY IN LENGTH

5.20 (Problem 11) Preliminary idea sketches of a pipe clamp assembly for holding steam pipes and connecting to an overhead hanger bracket.

Solve this problem by following the steps in Problem 9.

11. The preliminary sketches in **Fig. 5.20** illustrate a pipe clamp assembly that attaches to a hanger rod, which attaches to a hanger bracket of the type shown in the two previous figures. Solve this problem by following the same steps in Problem 9.

12. Gear puller (**Fig. 5.21**). Make orthographic refinement drawings of the parts of the gear puller. Make separate drawings of each part and make an assembly drawing showing how the parts fit together.

13. Metal-to-water discharge assembly (**Fig. 5.22**). Make orthographic refinement drawings of each part to better understand their relationship.

14. Make orthographic refinement drawings of the casters shown in **Fig. 5.16**.

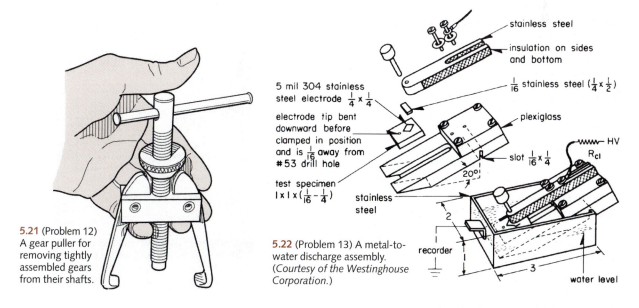

5.21 (Problem 12) A gear puller for removing tightly assembled gears from their shafts.

5 mil 304 stainless steel electrode $\frac{1}{4}$ x $\frac{1}{4}$

electrode tip bent downward before clamped in position and is $\frac{1}{16}$ away from #53 drill hole

test specimen 1 x 1 x ($\frac{1}{16}$ – $\frac{1}{4}$)

stainless steel

recorder

5.22 (Problem 13) A metal-to-water discharge assembly. (*Courtesy of the Westinghouse Corporation.*)

stainless steel

insulation on sides and bottom

$\frac{1}{16}$ stainless steel ($\frac{1}{4}$ x $\frac{1}{2}$)

plexiglass

HV

R_{cl}

slot $\frac{1}{16}$ x $\frac{1}{4}$

20°

water level

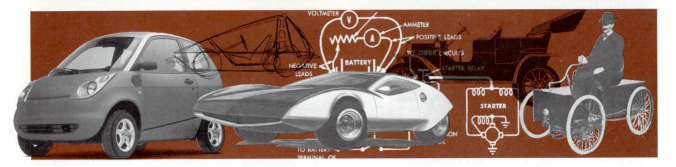

Design Analysis

6.1 Introduction

Analysis is the development and evaluation of a proposed design by objective thinking and the application of engineering and technology. For example, bridge designs are analyzed for loads, stresses, travel loads, dimensions, materials, sizes, function, economy, and much more. Less creativity is needed during analysis than during the previous steps of the design process. Analysis is the step in the design process most thoroughly covered in engineering courses.

6.2 Graphics and Analysis

Graphics and geometry are effective tools for analyzing a design in addition to the numerical methods normally used in engineering. Empirical data obtained from laboratory experiments and field observation can be transformed into formats suitable for graphical analysis and evaluation (**Fig. 6.1**).

Figure 6.2 shows an example of computer graphics applied to the analysis of a linkage sys-

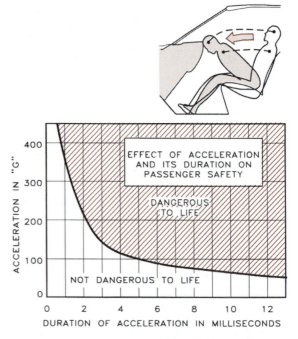

6.1 Designers analyze experimental data and human factors to determine comfortable and safe automobile designs. Graphics is a helpful tool in this step of the design process. (*Courtesy of General Motors Corporation.*)

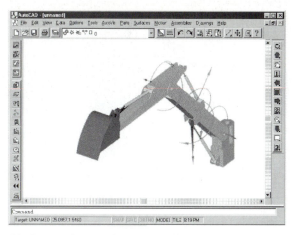

6.2 Clearance between functional parts and linkage systems can be analyzed efficiently with graphical methods by computer. (*Courtesy of Design Technologies International, Inc.*)

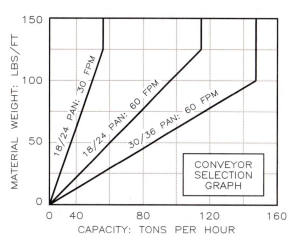

6.3 Graphics can be used to organize and present laboratory and field data to make it much easier to analyze for design applications.

tem to determine clearances, limits, and velocities of it members. Graphics also is an effective way to present and analyze technical information, background data, market surveys, population trends, and sales projections. The graph shown in **Fig. 6.3** enables the designer to quickly select the appropriate conveyor for transporting raw material at the desired rate.

6.3 Types of Analysis

Analysis includes evaluation of the following attributes:

1. function
2. human factors
3. product market
4. physical specifications
5. strength
6. economic factors
7. models

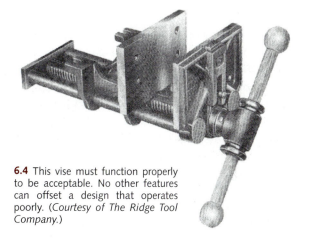

6.4 This vise must function properly to be acceptable. No other features can offset a design that operates poorly. (*Courtesy of The Ridge Tool Company.*)

Function

Function is the most important characteristic of a design because a product that does not function properly is a failure, regardless of its other desirable features (**Fig. 6.4**). Many products serve a narrow, utilitarian purpose, such as piston linkage of a gasoline engine (**Fig. 6.5**). In those cases, the designer is concerned with function to a much greater extent. Functional analysis usually involves the optimization of several aspects of the design, including safety,

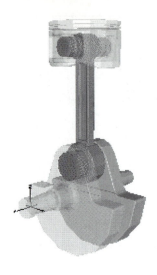

6.5 Graphical analysis is an efficient way to determine operating limits for the piston linkage of a gasoline engine. (*Courtesy Knowledge Revolution, Inc.*)

6.6 Human dimensions.

A Leonardo da Vinci analyzed body dimensions and proportions with graphics in 1473.

B Engineers used his techniques in the twentieth century to analyze motions by astronauts when restricted by radiation protection vests. (*Courtesy of General Dynamics Corporation.*)

economics, durability, appearance, and marketability. For example, despite high fuel costs, most consumers will not accept cars designed to get good mileage at the expense of comfort, safety, and styling. Buyers may be willing to give up some features, but few would give up air conditioning, tape decks, radios, comfortable seats, and safety features for improved gasoline mileage.

Human Factors

Human engineering (ergonomics) is the design of products and workplaces suited to the humans who use and occupy them. Safety and comfort are essential for efficiency, productivity, and profitability. Therefore the designer must consider the physical, mental, and emotional needs of the user and how to best satisfy them.

Leonardo da Vinci analyzed body dimensions in about 1473 (**Fig. 6.6A**). Nearly five hundred years later, NASA performed similar analyses to determine the range of mobility permitted by a radiation protection garment used by astronauts (**Fig. 6.6B**). Analysis of human factors is crucial in the space program because even the simplest, most familiar tasks require

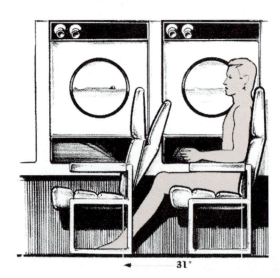

6.7 Analysis of human factors and living environments was part of designing the interior of this helicopter. (*Courtesy of Bell Helicopter Corporation.*)

training and adaptation when astronauts perform them while in a weightless state. The configuration of aircraft cabins shares many similarities with an automobile's interior (**Fig. 6.7**), because both must provide comfort and space in which to function, but the aircraft has the added restriction of less space to work within.

Dimensions and Ranges   A design must take into account the sizes, ranges of movement,

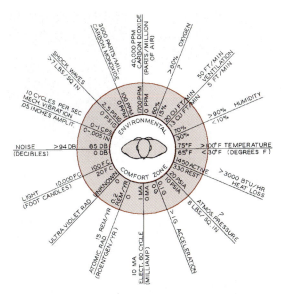

6.8 The inner circle represents the environmental comfort zone and the outer circle the bearable limit zone of the human environment. (*Courtesy of Henry Dreyfuss, The Measure of Man.*)

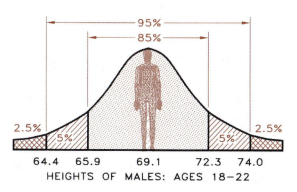

HEIGHTS OF MALES: AGES 18–22

6.9 This chart shows the distribution of average heights in inches of American men from 18 to 22 years of age. Fifty percent of American men in this age range are taller than 69.1 in., and fifty percent are shorter. (*Courtesy of HumanCAD.*)

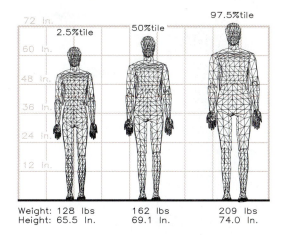

| Weight: 128 lbs | 162 lbs | 209 lbs |
| Height: 65.5 In. | 69.1 In. | 74.0 In. |

6.10 Men of average build have the body measurements shown. (*Courtesy of HumanCAD.*)

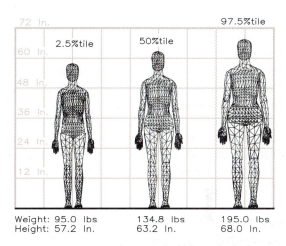

| Weight: 95.0 lbs | 134.8 lbs | 195.0 lbs |
| Height: 57.2 In. | 63.2 In. | 68.0 In. |

6.11 American women of average build have the body measurements shown. (*Courtesy of HumanCAD.*)

senses, and comfort zones of the people using the finished product (**Fig. 6.8**). Variations in people's physical characteristics conform to the normal distribution curve shown in **Fig. 6.9**. Designers must use the body dimensions of the average American man (**Fig. 6.10**) and the average American woman (**Fig. 6.11**) as the bases for industrial designs. It is challenging assignment to design accommodations that will be comfortable for the smallest as well as the largest subjects. **Figure 6.12** shows ranges of body movements of workers while performing maintenance on a spacecraft.

Motion The study of body motion begins with an understanding of the amount of space

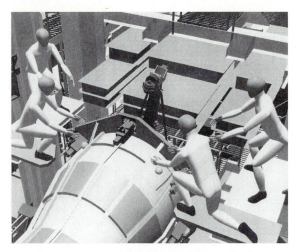

6.12 This computer model permits the analysis of body movements that are required to service a spacecraft. (*Courtesy of McDonal Douglas Space & Defense System.*)

6.13 A series of three-dimensional drawings are made from which to develop prototypes of a digital tire gauge for testing to ensure that the design is well-adapted to the hand. (*Courtesy Bresslergroup and Measurement Specialties, Inc.*)

required for a person to function comfortably, safely, and efficiently. **Figure 6.13** shows a three-dimensional drawing of a digital air gauge from which a prototype will be made and tested to ensure that it properly fits the hand.

Vision designs that include gauges and controls must provide the most visually effective means of aiding the operator. The welding helmet shown in **Fig. 6.14** is a futuristic shape for safety that is equipped with an auto-darkening lens to protect the welder's eyes. This design was developed to permit its user to function safely and efficiently with adequate vision and protection.

Sound   Sound must be within specified frequencies so as not to adversely affect a person's stress level and productivity. Many types of sound are both stressful and contribute to an unsafe work environment.

Environment   Working environments may include an entire industrial plant, a particular workstation, or a specialized location, such as the cockpit of a farm machine. Important environmental factors are temperature, lighting, color, sound, and comfort.

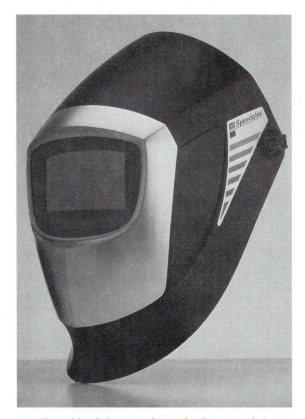

6.14 This welding helmet was designed with an auto-darkening lens and a stylish form that provides both safety and function to the welder. The designer must analyze human factors in order to develop a safe and efficient product. (*Courtesy of Momell International AB, Sweden.*)

Product Market

Designers study the market for a product during all stages of product development (Chapters 3–5) and review it more formally during the analysis step. Areas of product analysis are market prospects, retail outlets, sales features, and advertising.

Market Prospects Market information should be collected to learn about the age groups, income brackets, and geographical locations of prospective purchasers of the product. This information is helpful in planning advertising campaigns to reach potential customers.

Retail Outlets The product may be marketed through existing wholesale and retail channels, from newly established dealerships, or by the manufacturer directly. For example, mainframe computers are not suitable for distribution through retail outlets, so manufacturers' technical representatives work with clients individually. However, an exercise machine can be sold effectively through department stores, television commercials, direct mail, and sporting-goods outlets.

Sales Features The designer should itemize the unique features of a new design that would stimulate interest in the product and attract consumers. He must continually ask himself, "What features make this design better than my competitor's product?"

Advertising Manufacturers, wholesalers, and retailers use several media, including personal contact, direct mail, radio, TV, newspapers, and periodicals, to advertise their products to potential customers. Advertising costs vary widely and each medium should be analyzed for suitability before one or more is selected.

Physical Specifications

During the refinement step, the designer specified various measurements, such as lengths,

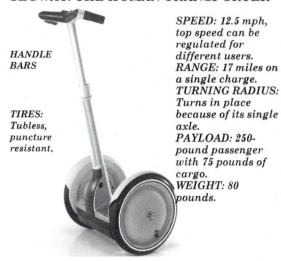

SEGWAY: THE HUMAN TRANSPORTER

HANDLE BARS

TIRES: Tubless, puncture resistant.

SPEED: 12.5 mph, top speed can be regulated for different users.
RANGE: 17 miles on a single charge.
TURNING RADIUS: Turns in place because of its single axle.
PAYLOAD: 250-pound passenger with 75 pounds of cargo.
WEIGHT: 80 pounds.

6.15 Designs must be analyzed to determine their physical properties, including weights, ranges, geometries, and capacities as shown for the Human Transporter (HT). (*Courtesy of Segway LCC.*)

areas, shapes, weight, and angles for the product. During the analysis step, the designer uses the product's geometry and measurements to calculate member sizes and dimensions, weights, volumes, capacities, velocities, operating ranges, packaging and shipping requirements, and similar information (**Fig. 6.15**).

Sizes and Dimensions The designer must evaluate product sizes and dimensions to ensure that they meet any standards specified, such as permissible widths, lengths, and weights in automobile design. For products that have moving parts, such as a construction crane, the designer must analyze the size of the product when extended, contracted, or positioned differently, as well as weight and balance requirements.

Ranges Many products have ranges of operation, capacities, and speeds that the designer

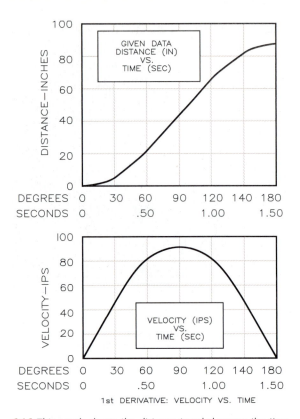

6.16 This graph shows the distance traveled versus the time required for a part on a conveyor. The designer graphically differentiates the plot of the data given to obtain a graph of velocity versus time as the first step in designing parts of sufficient strength for the conveyor.

6.17 An economic model that can be used as a guide in the economic analysis and pricing of a product.

must analyze before finalizing a design. For example, the designer must determine ranges and maximum limits such as seating capacity, miles per gallon, pounds of laundry per cycle, flows in gallons per minute, or power required.

Packaging and Shipping The designer must also be concerned with product packaging and shipping. Packaging relates both to product protection and consumer appeal: how the product is to be shipped—air, rail, mail, or truck—and whether it is to be shipped one at a time or in quantity are important considerations. Shipping and marketing a product assembled, partially assembled, or disassembled requires design

attention and analysis, as does the cost of each method.

Strength Much of engineering is devoted to analyzing a product's strength to support maximum design loads, withstand specified shocks, and endure necessary repetitive motions. **Figure 6.16** illustrates motion analysis for a moving part on a conveyor. The designer plots the data obtained and then uses graphical calculus to find the conveyor's velocity-versus-time profile as the first step in determining the strength needed by the part.

Economic Factors

Designs must be economically competitive to have a chance of being successful. Therefore, before releasing a product for production, the designer must analyze its cost and expected profit margin. Two methods of pricing a product are **itemizing** and **comparative pricing**.

Itemizing The process of totaling the costs of each part and its related overhead to determine its final cost is the first step in itemizing a product's price. From the working drawings, the designer (or an estimator) can estimate the costs of materials, manufacturing, labor, overhead,

39⁹⁹ Each

BLACK & DECKER TOOLS.
• 7¼" circular saw. No. CS1000.
• Mouse sander/polisher kit with 23 accessories. No. MS500K.
• VersaPak cordless drill with batteries and charger. No. VPD850K.

6.18 Each of these three products retails for approximately $40. They can be priced comparatively because they are similar in design and have essentially the same market size. (*Courtesy of Black & Decker Company.*)

6.19 This hunting seat and the exercise bench in Fig. 6.20 can be comparatively priced at between $90 and $100 because both have similar manufacturing requirements and market volume potential. (*Courtesy of Baker Manufacturing Company, Valdosta, Georgia.*)

and other items to arrive at the total production expense. The wholesale price is production cost plus profit. Dealer margin plus the wholesale cost gives the retail price. One example of an economic model is shown in **Fig. 6.17**; these percentages vary for different areas of manufacturing, marketing, and retailing.

Comparative Pricing The other method used to estimate the price of a proposed product is to compare it with the prices of similar products. For example, the power tools shown in **Fig. 6.18** are priced at $40 each. These tools are similar: All use the same type of power source, are made from the same materials, and have the same styling. **Most importantly, these products will have about the same market size.** Approximately the same number of drills, sanders, and saws are sold; consequently, production costs and retail prices are similar for each.

Another example of comparative pricing are the prices of the hunting seat (**Fig. 6.19**) and the

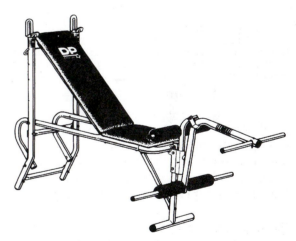

6.20 Priced at $100, this exercise apparatus is similar in manufacture and market appeal to the hunting seat shown in Fig. 6.19. (*Courtesy of Diversified Products Corporation.*)

exercise bench (**Fig. 6.20**), which have somewhat equal market sizes. Since both products' manufacturing requirements and market volumes are

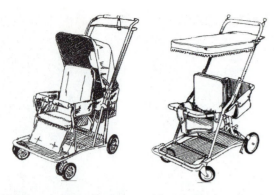

6.21 These baby strollers are priced from $55 to $75, considerably less than the hunting seat and exercise apparatus, because the stroller market is larger and competition for customers is greater. (*Courtesy of Strolee of California.*)

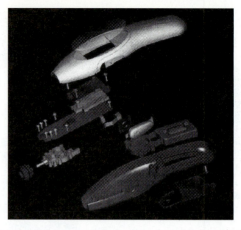

6.22 A computer-generated conceptual model of a digital tire gauge enables the designer to analyze the relationship of the device's components. (*Courtesy Bresslergroup and Measurement Specialties, Inc.*)

similar, both sell for about the same price of $90–$100. However, the baby stroller (**Fig. 6.21**) sells for about $50 because of its larger and more competitive market, even though it is very similar in configuration to the hunting seat and the exercise bench.

Manufacturers also use comparative pricing to estimate cost per square foot, per mile, per cubic foot, or per day. These factors yield rough cost estimates as a basis for doing more detailed studies.

Miscellaneous Expenses   Various expenses incurred in the development of new products can be easily overlooked and thereby affect a product's profitability projections. For example, warehousing and storage costs for finished products must be included in their price. Associated with warehousing are the costs of insurance, temperature control, shelving, forklifts, and employees.

Models

Models are effective aids for analyzing a design in the final stages of its development. Designers use three-dimensional models to study a product's proportion, operation, size, function, and efficiency. Types of models often used are **conceptual models**, **mock-ups**, **prototypes**, and **system layout models**.

Conceptual Models   Designers use preliminary models or computer models to analyze a preliminary design or feature concept (**Fig. 6.22**).

Mock-ups   Designers use full-size dummies of the finished design to demonstrate the product's size, appearance, and component relationships. Mock-ups give a visual impression rather than demonstrate its operation.

Prototypes   Designers use full-size working models to demonstrate the operation of a final product. Because prototypes are made mostly by hand, materials that are easy to fabricate are used instead of those to be used in final production.

System Layout Models   Designers use detailed scale models that show the relationships among components of large manufacturing systems, building complexes, and traffic layouts. Designers usually construct system layout models of refineries to supplement working drawings for contractors and construction supervisors during construction (**Fig. 6.23**).

Model Materials   Designers commonly use balsa wood, cardboard, and clay in model con-

6.23 This system layout model is used to analyze the details of construction of a refinery. (*Courtesy of E. I. du Pont de Nemours and Company.*)

6.24 A student's model demonstrates how a portable home caddy will fold flat for ease of storage.

struction because they are easy to shape and require few tools. Standard parts such as wheels, tubing, figures, dowels, and other structural shapes can be purchased, rather than made, to save time and effort. Plexiglas can be used to construct models that illustrate both inside and outside design features. Finished models should give a realistic impression of the design, especially when they are used for sales presentations and displays.

Model Scale   A model should be large enough to show the function of the smallest significant moving parts. For example, the student model of a portable home caddy shown in **Fig. 6.24** (made of balsa wood) demonstrates a linkage system that permits the wheels to be collapsed for storage. The model's scale is large enough to permit the linkage system to operate as it will in the final product. The transport cart shown in **Fig. 6.25**, which is currently on the market, has many of the features developed years earlier by the student design team.

Model Testing   Using models to test performance is helpful in determining how well a design meets requirements. Aerodynamic characteristics of the rear styling of an automobile can be evaluated by wind tunnel tests. Physical relationships and the functional workings of

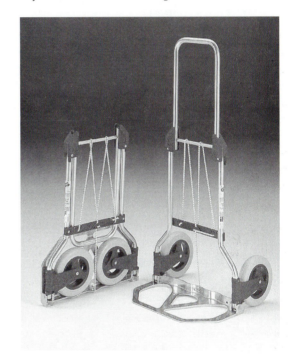

6.25 This folding transport cart folds to a thickness of 2.23 in., weighs 9.9 lb, and has a load capacity of 275 lb. (*Courtesy of Gebr. vom Braucke Cmb H & Co.*)

movable components, as for the hatch and storage area of a car, can be tested as a prototype. Products can be tested on the computer screen to economically obtain results of their operation. Designers also use models to test consumer reactions to new products before releasing the design for production.

```
ANALYSIS

1. Function

    A.  PROVIDES SUPPORT FOR BASIC
        EXERCISES

    B.  SUPPORTS BAR BELLS

    C.  ADJUSTABLE TO SUIT INDIVIDUAL

2. Human engineering

    A.  PADDED BENCH

    B.  ADJUSTABLE BACKREST

    C.  CONFORMS TO BODY MOTIONS

    D.  BARBELL BRACKETS FOR SAFETY

    E.  FOAM PADS FOR COMFORT

3. Market and consumer acceptance

    A.  POTENTIAL MARKET
        1.  STATE—56,000
        2.  NATION—7,000,000

    B.  MORE EFFECTIVE EXERCISING

    C.  AFFORDABLE AT $120—$150 RANGE

    D.  USABLE FOR NONWEIGHT EXERCISES
        ALSO
```

DESIGN ANALYSIS	NAME FILE SEC DATE	GRADE 11

```
6. Production procedures

    A.  STRUCTURAL MEMBERS HOLLOW REC-
        TANGULAR SECTIONS—STEEL, BENT TO
        SHAPE

    B.  PARTS WELDED OR BOLTED TOGETHER

    C.  VINYL SEAT COVERS STAPLED TO
        PLYWOOD SEAT AND BACKREST

    D.  PLASTIC CAPS AT ENDS OF OPEN
        SUPPORT MEMBERS

    E.  METAL PARTS NICKEL PLATED

7. Economic analysis

    MATERIALS            $15

    LABOR                 16

    SHIPPING               7

    WAREHOUSING            1
                    _____
            TOTAL          $39

    SALES COMMISSION    $ 4

    PROFIT              $20
                    _____
         WHOLESALE PRICE    $63

            RETAIL PRICE    $90
```

DESIGN ANALYSIS	NAME FILE SEC DATE	GRADE 13

```
4. Physical description

    A.  BENCH COMPOSED OF BACKREST & SEAT

    B.  BACKREST ADJUSTABLE FROM 0 DEG.
        TO +30 DEG. WITH HORIZONTAL

    C.  2 BAR HOLDER BRACKETS FOR BARBELLS

    D.  2 BUTTERFLY EXERCISE ATTACHMENTS

    E.  LEG CURL ATTACHMENT

    F.  WEIGHT: 45 LB

    G.  SIZE: 52" LONG X 31" WIDE X 50" TALL

5. Strength

    A.  RECOMMENDED WEIGHT SET: 160 LB

    B.  SUPPORT PERSON WEIGTHING UP TO
        300 LB

    C.  CROSS BRACED TO PROVIDE
        STABILITY

    D.  REPLACEABLE PLASTIC SLEEVES FOR
        BUTTERFLY ATTACHMENTS

    E.  MAX. LEG CURL WEIGHT: 100 LB.

    F.  MAX. RECOMMENDED BUTTERFLY
        WEIGHTS: 50 LB EACH
```

DESIGN ANALYSIS	NAME FILE SEC DATE	GRADE 12

6.26 (Sheet 11) A worksheet containing an analysis of function, human engineering, and market considerations for the exercise bench.

6.27 (Sheet 12) A worksheet giving the physical description and strength analysis for the exercise bench.

6.28 (Sheet 13) A worksheet that shows graphical analysis of the range of movements for the adjustable parts of the exercise bench.

6.4 Analysis: Exercise Bench

To illustrate a method of analyzing a product design, we return to our problem example, the exercise bench, which was carried through the first three steps of the design process in Chapters 3–5. The main areas of analysis listed on the worksheets in **Fig. 6.26** through **Fig. 6.29**

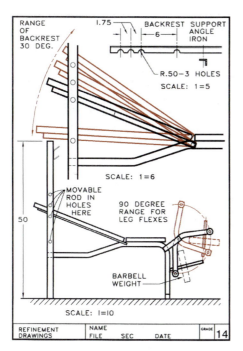

6.29 A worksheet containing an analysis of the production procedures for and economics of the exercise bench.

6.30 A full-size model of the exercise bench is tested for function and acceptability.

will assist you in analyzing the design. Additional worksheets and large sheet sizes for analysis drawings may be used if more space is needed.

Figure 6.29 shows how graphics are used to determine the range of positions of the backrest. Those positions affect the design of the angle-iron supports for the backrest and the locations of the semicircular holes in the angle irons for a range of settings of 30°.

The leg-exercising attachment at the end of the bench is designed to move through a 90° arc, which is sufficient for leg extensions. By determining the maximum loads on the backrest and the leg exerciser, you can select the member sizes and materials that provide the strength required. For further analysis, construct a model and test the design for suitability. A product that must support body weight plus weights that are being lifted should be rigorously tested to ensure that it is adequately sturdy.

Figure 6.30 illustrates a model of the exercise bench for testing its functional features. The cat-

alog description of the bench shown in **Fig. 6.31** lists the physical properties of the Weider® exercise bench to help the consumer understand its features. You should keep a list of descriptive characteristics of your design for its final catalog specifications. These points become very important to a consumer as he comes closer to being buying a product.

Problems

The following problems should be solved on 8–1/2-by-11-inch paper and the solution presented in drawing, note, and text forms. Answers to essay problems can be typed or lettered. All sheets should be placed in a binder or folder.

General

1. Make a list of human factors that must be considered in designing the following items: (a) canoe, (b) hairbrush, (c) water cooler, (d) automobile, (e) wheelbarrow, (f) drawing table,

6.31 This catalog description gives the key features of the exercise bench: Weider® bench with butterfly attachment. It features no-pinch supports, multiposition padded back and leg lift, and tubular steel frame. Total weight capacity is 1000 lb; butterfly capacity, 50 lb; leg lift capacity, 65 lb; overall size, 58″ × 45″ × 41″; weight, 48 lb; and price, $89.99. (*Courtesy of Sears, Roebuck and Company.*)

(g) study desk, (h) pair of binoculars, (i) baby stroller, (j) golf course, (k) seating in a stadium, (l) coffee table, (m) exercise apparatus, and (n) lunch box.

2. What physical quantities have to be determined for the designs in Problem 1?

3. Select one of the items in Problem 1 and outline the steps required to analyze: (a) function, (b) human factors, (c) product market, (d) physical specifications, (e) strength, (f) economic factors, and (g) a prototype model.

Human Engineering
4. Design a computer-graphics table for your body size to meet your own working and comfort needs. Make a drawing indicating the optimum working areas and tilt angle for the computer when you sit at the station. The drawing also should show the most efficient positioning of supplies, materials, and manuals.

5. Using the dimensions for the average man and woman (**Figs. 6.10** and **6.11**), design stadium benches to meet the optimum needs of spectators. Consider the slope of the stadium seating to allow for an adequate view of the playing field. Spectator comfort and provision for traffic along aisles in front of the benches also must be considered.

6. Compare the measurements of the male and female students in your class with the averages given in **Figs. 6.10** and **6.11**. Tabulate the results and compare them with the percentiles given in **Fig. 6.9**.

7. Design a backpack for use on a week-long camping trip. Determine the minimum number of articles a camper should carry; use their weights and volumes in establishing design criteria. Make sketches of the pack and the method of attaching it to the body to provide mobility, comfort, and capacity.

8. State the dimensions, facilities, and provisions needed for a one-person storm shelter to provide protection for forty-eight hours. Make sketches of the interior of the shelter in relationship to a person and the supplies.

9. Design a manhole access to an underground facility. Determine the diameter of the manhole required to permit a person to climb a ladder for a distance of ten feet with freedom of movement. Make a sketch of your design and explain your method of solving the problem.

10. Analyze the needs for an observation facility for temporary service in the Arctic. This facility is to be as compact as possible, but it must provide for the needs of one person during a seventy-two-hour duty watch. Make sketches of your design and explain the items considered essential to human survival in that harsh climate.

11. Design an automobile steering wheel that is different from current designs but that is just as functional. Base your design on human factors such as arm position, grip, and vision. Make sketches of your design and list the factors that you considered.

12. Assume that you prefer to alternate between sitting and standing when working at a study desk. Determine the ideal height of the table top for working in each position. Indicate how you would devise the table to permit instant conversion from the height for standing to the height for sitting.

13. Identify some human engineering problems that you believe need to be solved. Present several to your instructor for approval. Solve the approved problems. Make a series of sketches and notes to explain your approach.

Market Analysis

14. Conduct a market analysis for the drill shown in **Fig. 6.18**, covering the areas mentioned in the text. Assume that this power tool has never been introduced before. Outline the steps you would take in conducting a product market analysis.

15. Make a market analysis of the hunting seat shown in **Fig. 6.19**, following the steps suggested in the text. Determine a reasonable price, potential outlets, and other marketing information for the product.

16. Assume that the costs of producing hunting seats are estimated as: 100 seats, $35 each; 200 seats, $20 each; 400 seats, $10 each; 1000 seats, $8.50 each. Using these figures, determine the price at which you could introduce the seats to consumers on a trial basis and still make a profit. Explain your plan.

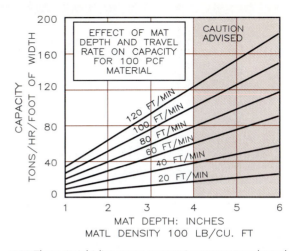

6.32 These straight-line curves represent conveyor speeds used for transporting materials of 100 lb per cubic foot. The capacity in tons per hour per foot of width of the conveyor is given on the y axis and mat depth is shown on the x axis. Mat depth is the thickness of the material applied to the conveyor.

Strength and Function Analysis

17. Refer to the integral curves plotted in **Fig. 6.16** and answer the following questions. At what point (in seconds) is velocity the greatest and what is this velocity? What is the velocity at 0.25 seconds? After how many seconds does deceleration begin? What would be the velocity at 360°?

18. The graph in **Fig. 6.32** can be used to estimate the capacities of material conveyors at various speeds and mat depths (thickness of the material on the conveyor). Answer the following questions: (a) For mat depth of 4 in. and a speed of 120 ft/min, how many tons per hour are transported? (b) To have 100 tons per hour transported, what is the slowest speed of the conveyor that would be safe (would avoid the "caution advised" area)? (c) For a mat depth of 5 in. and a speed of 20 ft per minute, what would be the capacity?

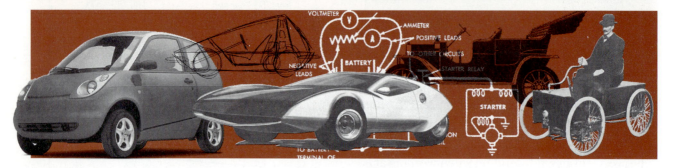

CHAPTER SEVEN

Decision

7.1 Introduction

After the designer has conceived, developed, refined, and analyzed several designs, one must be selected for implementation. The decision process begins with a presentation by the designer (or design team) of all significant findings, features, estimates, and recommendations. The presentation should be organized in an easy-to-follow form and it must communicate the designer's conclusions and recommendations because it is the means of gaining support for the project in order for it to become a reality. A committee usually makes the decision when funding must be obtained. Although decision-making is aided by facts, data, and analyses, it remains subjective at best.

7.2 Decision

The purpose of oral presentations and written reports is to present the findings of a project so that a decision can be made on whether to implement it. One of three types of decisions may be made:

Acceptance. A design may be accepted in its entirety, which indicates success by the designer.

Rejection. A design may be rejected in its entirety, which does not necessarily mean that the has designer failed. Changes in the economic climate, moves by competitors, or other factors beyond the designer's control may make the design obsolete, premature, or unprofitable.

Compromise. Parts of a design may have weaknesses and compromises may be suggested. For example, the initial production run might be increased or decreased, or various features might be eliminated, modified, merged, or added.

7.3 Decision: Exercise Bench

We have used the exercise bench problem introduced in Chapter 3 to illustrate the first four steps of the design process. We continue to use it here to help explain the decision step.

DECISION

1. Decision for evaluation

DESIGN 1 A–FRAME

DESIGN 2 U–FRAME

DESIGN 3 2–COLUMN FRAME

DESIGN 4

DESIGN 5

MAX	FACTORS	1	2	3	4
3.0	FUNCTION	2.0	2.3	2.5	
2.0	HUMAN FACTORS	1.6	1.4	1.7	
0.5	MARKET ANALYSIS	0.4	0.4	0.4	
1.0	STRENGTH	1.0	1.0	1.0	
0.5	PRODUCTION EASE	0.3	0.2	0.4	
1.0	COST	0.7	0.6	0.8	
1.5	PROFITABILITY	1.1	1.0	1.3	
0.5	APPEARANCE	0.3	0.4	0.4	
10	TOTALS	7.4	7.3	8.5	

DESIGN DECISION	NAME FILE SEC DATE	GRADE 16

7.1 This worksheet shows the decision table used to evaluate the design alternatives for the exercise bench.

CONCLUSIONS

THE 2–COLUMN FRAME IS THE BEST SOLUTION FOR IMPLEMENTATION BECAUSE

1. GOOD MARKET POTENTIAL
2. AIDS WELL IN EXERCISING
3. FULFILLS PRODUCT REQUIREMENTS
4. ATTRACTIVE PRICE
5. MANUFACTURED EASILY

RECOMMEND IMPLEMENTATION AND PRODUCTION OF THE DESIGN

ECONOMIC FORECAST

SALES PRICE	$ 90
SHIPPING EXPENSES	$ 12
CUSTOMER PRICE	$102
MANUFACTURER'S PROFIT	$ 20 EACH
BREAK–EVEN AT	500 UNITS

PRODUCTION: RECOMMEND THAT BENCHES BE MADE BY QUALIFIED MANUFACTURER ON A CONTRACT BASIS

PROFITABILITY: BENCH SHOULD YIELD AN ATTRACTIVE RETURN ON INVESTMENT

DESIGN CONCLUSION	NAME FILE SEC DATE	GRADE 17

7.2 This worksheet summarizes the designer's conclusions and recommendations of implementing that design.

Decision Table

Use a table like the one shown in **Fig. 7.1** to compare designs, where each idea is listed and given a number for identification. Assign maximum values for each factor of analysis, based on your best judgment, so they total to ten points. Rate each factor for the competing designs by entering points for each.

Sum the columns of numbers to determine the total for each design and compare the scores of each design. Your instincts may disagree with the outcome of this numerical analysis. If so, have enough faith in your judgment to go with your intuition. The scores from the decision table are meant to be a guide for you and not the absolute final word in your decision.

Conclusion

After making a decision, state it and the reasons for it clearly (**Fig. 7.2**). Record any additional information, such as number to be produced initially, selling price per unit, profit per unit, estimated sales during the first year, break-even number, and the product's most marketable features, that will help you prepare your presentation.

If you believe that none of your designs are satisfactory, you should recommend that they not be implemented. A negative recommendation is not a failure of the design process; it means only that the solutions you have developed so far are not feasible. Going forward with an inadequate solution could cause both monetary losses and wasted effort.

7.3 A decision may be the outcome of an informal presentation to an associate in which ideas and designs are discussed one-on-one. (*Courtesy of the Cessna Aircraft Company.*)

7.4 Planning cards are useful in preparing the sequence of a presentation by arranging the cards on a planning board (as shown here) or on a tabletop. (*Courtesy of Eastman Kodak.*)

Presentation

Until now your efforts have been self-directed and mostly free from supervision. The work is your own (or that of your team), you have solved the problem to the best of your ability, and you are ready to make recommendations regarding its implementation.

At this point the project usually involves the input of others besides the designers. These outsiders may be other engineers, managers, administrators, salespeople, company shareholders, investors, or bankers who will loan money for the project. You must prepare a presentation suitable for your audience in order to communicate the important features of your design, the data you gathered and analyzed, and the benefits to be gained by implementing your design.

Present your findings, conclusions, and recommendations as objectively as possible so that the group can make a valid decision. At no time should your enthusiasm for the project outweigh an impartial presentation of the facts.

7.4 Types of Presentations

Presentations may be made to groups ranging from a few knowledgeable design associates to a large number of laypeople unfamiliar with the project and its objectives. Presentations of the first type usually are informal; those of the second type are formal.

Informal Presentations

Informal presentations are made to several associates and perhaps a supervisor. Although formally prepared visual aids are unnecessary for presentations to a small group, the designer nevertheless needs to graph data, draw pictorials, sketch schematics, and build models to explain design concepts. Ideas and concepts may be sketched on a blackboard or informally discussed in a one-on-one situation (**Fig. 7.3**).

Formal Presentations

Formal presentations usually involve large groups that may include associates, administrators, and/or laypeople, or a combination of the three. They may be clients for whom the project is designed, potential investors, or politicians who will vote to approve or disapprove the design. Function and acceptability of a design are the primary concerns of engineering associates, and profitability is most important to investors.

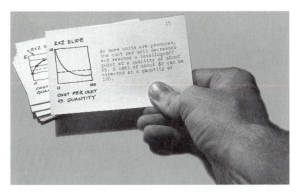

7.5 This layout on a 3-by-5-inch card, showing a sketch of the visual and its accompanying text, illustrates sound planning.

7.6 The flip chart is an effective method for presentation to small groups.

7.5 Organizing a Presentation

An effective method of planning oral and written reports is to use 3-by-5-inch index cards for the ideas to be presented. Placing the cards on a table or tacking them to a bulletin board (**Fig. 7.4**) allows an easy choice of sequence and rearrangement as needed. Each card (**Fig. 7.5**) should contain the following information:

1. **Number.** The card's position in the presentation sequence.
2. **Illustration.** A sketch of the illustration, if any.
3. **Text.** A brief outline of the points to be covered for that idea.

7.6 Visual Aids

Visual aids commonly used in presentations are flip charts, photographic slides, overhead visuals, models, computer images, and videotapes. The following suggestions apply to the preparation of visual aids:

1. Limit each visual to a single concept or point.
2. Reduce statements to key points to communicate thoughts clearly and concisely.
3. Make visuals containing text large enough to be readable.
4. Use illustrations, color, and attention-getting devices.

5. Prepare enough visuals so that notes are unnecessary.

Flip Charts

Flip charts consist of bold illustrations drawn on sheets (usually 30 × 36 inches) for presentation to groups no larger than about thirty people (**Fig. 7.6**).

Paper   Flip charts may be drawn on brown wrapping paper or white newsprint paper attached to a cardboard backing board. A stand or easel is needed to support the cardboard-backed set of sheets.

Lettering   Felt-tipped markers, ink, tempera, or sign paints are fine for lettering. When used correctly, felt-tipped markers can yield bold, visible lines in a variety of colors and with sophisticated effects. India ink is an effective medium for lettering and for adding emphasis to a chart.

Color   Construction paper cutouts mounted with rubber cement are especially effective for adding color to bar graphs. The use of felt-tipped markers and tempera colors also adds color and interest to a chart.

Assembly   Flip chart sheets should be arranged in order of presentation with a title page covered by a blank sheet of paper on top to prevent audience anticipation. The sheets are fastened at the top to the backing board.

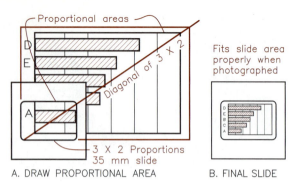

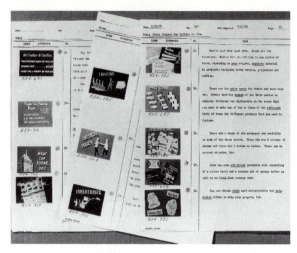

7.7 Use of this method of proportionally sizing artwork ensures that artwork will properly fill a photographic slide.

7.8 A slide script is useful for lengthy slide presentations and those that will be given repetitively. (*Courtesy of Eastman Kodak.*)

Presentation Each sheet is flipped in sequence after the presenter has covered the points on it. A pointer should be used to direct the audience's attention to specific items on the sheet. Well-prepared flip charts should require no additional notes.

Photographic Slides

Slides are effective for larger audiences and for showing actual scenes or examples of hardware.

Artwork The method for proportionally sizing artwork for a 35-mm slide is shown in **Fig. 7.7**. An 8-by-12-inch size is suitable for most slides. The artwork should contain color to make the slides more attractive and effective in maintaining audience interest. Colored construction paper, mat board, and other poster materials should be used in preparing slides.

Allow at least a one-inch margin on all artwork, so the edges will not show when photographed. Uppercase letters are best for slides, with the space between lines of text equal to the height of the letters. Do not use a white background for slide artwork, because it is tiring to the eyes.

Photographing Layouts To make slides, a camera, copy stand, and lights are required. A 35-mm reflex camera with through-the-lens viewfinder is best because the photographer sees exactly what is being photographed. The copy stand holds the camera steady. If all the artwork is uniform in size, the camera can be left in

the same position during photography. Small illustrations can be photographed with a close-up lens. The finished slides are reviewed, arranged in sequence, numbered, and loaded in a tray for showing.

Slide Scripts A slide script is useful when a presentation will be made repeatedly. Photographic copies of the slides attached to the left side of the script serve as prompts for the presenter (**Fig. 7.8**).

Overhead Projector Transparencies

Overhead projector transparencies are reproduced on 8–1/2 × 11-inch plastic sheets by the heat-transfer or diazo processes, or plotted by the computer. Tracing paper is the most commonly used drawing surface for preparing art from which transparencies are made. Tracing paper can be used in both the heat-transfer and diazo processes (opaque paper cannot be used in the diazo process). Computer plotting can be done directly onto plastic film with special pens. Diazo transparencies are reproduced on plastic film in the same manner in which blue-line prints are made.

Drawings should be made in black India ink. Stick-on shapes and graphing tapes can give the

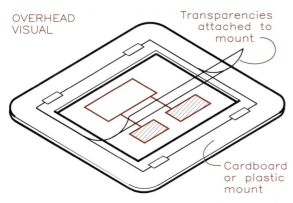

OVERHEAD VISUAL

Transparencies attached to mount

Cardboard or plastic mount

7.9 A transparency used on an overhead projector consists of an 8–1/2″ × 11″ transparency mounted on a 10″ × 12″ frame. The projection area within the frame is about 7–1/2″ × 9–1/2″. To show information sequentially, different-colored overlays can be flipped over, one at a time.

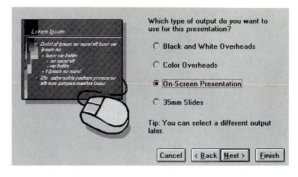

7.10 The dialogue screen illustrates a computer visual and the prompts for composing it. (*Courtesy of Microsoft*)

7.11 A model is an effective aid to a presentation to a small group (*Courtesy of Cessna Aircraft Company.*)

drawing a professional appearance. Lettering should be at least 0.20 in. high.

Color Overlays   Several color overlays can be hinged to the transparency mount for presentations with multiple steps (**Fig. 7.9**). Each color overlay requires a separate piece of artwork, which is drawn on tracing paper placed over the basic layout.

Computer Plotted-Transparencies   Computer-generated art and text can be plotted directly on plastic film with fiber-tipped pens, which come in many colors and match the film. The Romand font of AutoCAD is better suited for large lettering on transparencies than is the Romans font.

Presentation   The presenter stands or sits near the projector in a semilighted room and refers to the transparencies while facing the audience. The presenter can emphasize items on the stage of the projector with a pointer, which is projected onto the screen. In the same manner as multiple overlays are hinged to a mount, paper overlays can be attached to mounts in order to block out parts of the transparency to control audience attention.

Computer Visuals

Software programs such as Microsoft's *Power-Point* can be used for making slides that can be viewed on the computer monitor for small groups or projected onto a large screen connected to a computer for large groups. **Figure 7.10** shows a dialogue screen used in composing a computer visual with *PowerPoint.* Any drawing or photograph that can be seen on the computer monitor can be used as a visual.

When slides are made by the computer, there is no need for special art supplies, storage problems are eliminated, and the entire slide show can be shown on a laptop computer. Full-color artwork, special effects, and animation can be incorporated into these presentations.

7.12 A presentation should include graphical aids and models to help the speaker communicate with the audience. (*Courtesy of Hewlett Packard Corporation.*)

Models

A model is the most realistic visual aid for showing a final design (**Fig. 7.11**). Models should be large enough to be seen by all in the audience. A series of photographic close-ups of the model, taken from different angles, can be used to supplement the presentation. Obviously, a full-sized prototype of the completed design provides the most accurate description of the product and demonstrates its operation.

Videotapes

Videotaping presentations or visuals supplemented by a voice-over narration is an effective and sophisticated method. It may include various special effects such as music, sound effects, close-ups, motion, and precise realism. Formal presentations in the future will be multimedia shows using video and the computer in combination.

7.7 Making a Presentation

You should inspect the room in which the presentation is to be made in advance of the meeting. You also should view projected visuals from various audience locations. Projectors and visual-aid equipment must be positioned and focused before the audience arrives, and remote controls for slide projectors should be readied

for use. You should be aware of where to stand so as to not block anyone's view.

Delivery

You should move through the presentation at a moderate pace while emphasizing information on the visual aids with a pointer (**Fig. 7.12**). A positive approach in selling ideas should not become deceptive high-pressure salesmanship. The presenter should be frank in pointing out weaknesses in a design and show alternatives that compensate for them.

Conclusions and recommendations should be supported by data and analyses. A recommendation to reject or accept a design should be supported by reasons. A period for questions and answers should follow the presentation for clarification purposes. If available, a technical report should be given to the audience.

Critique

When your team gives a presentation to the class, both your design recommendations and the skill of your presentation will be evaluated and critiqued. The form shown in **Fig. 7.13** is typical of the evaluation form that may be used for your critique. It can also be used as a guide in preparing the presentation. The names of the team members are listed at the top of the sheet. As a group, your team must agree on the percent contribution of each member to the project prior to presentation. The sum of the percent contributions of all team members must equal 100 percent. The F-factor for each member is the number of members (N) times the contribution of each (C). The chart in Appendix 38 illustrates how an individual's contribution to the project is translated into his or her individual grade by using the F-factor.

The table below should be completed jointly by the team with only the grade column completed by the instructor who will use the chart on page 4 and the factor "F" that was computed for each member.

Oral Report

Team No. **5**   Project: **TOY MANUFACTURING**

Names	No. (N= **7**)	%Contri-bution (C)	F=NC	GRADE
1. Brown, George		17	119	91
2. Prisk, Helen		14.3	100	87
3. Smith, Roger		20	140	95
4. Reed, Ralph		5.7	40	63
5. Potter, Joyce		14.3	100	87
6. Flynn, Errol		14.3	100	87
7. Ross, Lawrence		14.4	100	87
8.				

Evaluation by instructor	Max.		Comments:
1. Introduction of team members	2	2.	Good introduction to project
2. Proper dress of team members	2	2.	
3. Statement of purpose of presentation	5	4.	
4. Use of visuals—point to important points, do not block screen, do not fumble, etc.	10	8.	Several visuals to complex to see very well
5. Adequate number of visual aids	9	9.	
6. Quality of visual aids	15	12.	
7. Clear presentation of recommended design	10	8.	Economic analysis could use a little more study
8. Presentation of alternate solutions considered	2	2.	
9. Consideration of human factors	5	5.	
10. Coverage of economics (manufacturing, shipping, packing, overhead, mark-up, etc.)	10	7.	Very good professional manner in giving the presentation
11. Presentation of an effective conclusion	5	4.	
12. Continuity of presentation	3	3.	
13. Poise and professionalism	2	2.	Good conclusion and proposed solution
14. Team participation (perfect score if all participate)	10	10.	
15. Use of allotted time	10	9.	

TOTAL 100   87

Instructor comments on back of this sheet.

7.13 An evaluation form for grading oral reports.

Problems

1. Prepare a checklist for evaluating an oral presentation by one of your classmates. List items to consider and develop a point scale for them. Devise a rating system to arrive at an overall evaluation.

2. Use 3-by-5-inch cards to plan a flip chart presentation that will last no more than five minutes. The subject of your presentation may be of your choosing or one assigned by your instructor. Some examples are (a) your career plans for the first two years after graduation, (b) the role of this course in your overall educational program, (c) the importance of effective communication, (d) the need for a design project that you are proposing, and (e) a comparison of engineering with another field.

3. Prepare graphical aids for an oral presentation using the methods and materials covered in this chapter.

4. Using the planning cards developed in Problem 2, prepare a five-minute briefing on a technique that you choose or is assigned by your instructor. Present this briefing to your class.

5. Assume that you are an engineer responsible for developing a proposal for a project that could result in a sizable contract. Make a list of instructions to give to your assistants for their help in preparing a presentation for a group of twenty people, ranging in background from bankers to engineers.

Your instructions should outline the materials needed, types and number of graphical aids required, method of projection or presentation, assistance needed during the presentation, room seating arrangements, length of time, and other factors. Select a topic or use one assigned by your instructor.

6. When giving a presentation, be sensitive to what the most important and significant points are. Important recommendations and findings must be stressed above all others. Do not get bogged down in ideas and approaches that were attempted but discarded at the expense of the points that are most helpful in attaining acceptance of your recommendations.

Make a list of the major points to emphasize if you were giving one of the following reports: (a) an application for a summer job; (b) a request for a loan from your parents; (c) a proposal to a banker for opening a hotdog stand or a business of your choice, (d) a resume of introduction to a prospective girl- or boyfriend; (e) a reason for talking your instructor into an excused absence; (f) a list of your qualifications as candidate for class president.

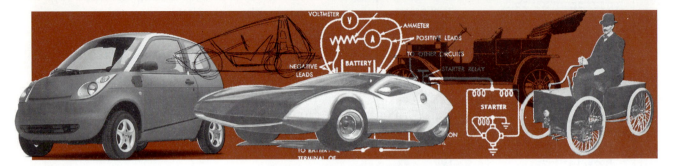

CHAPTER EIGHT

Implementation

8.1 Introduction

Implementation is the final step of the design process in which the design becomes a reality. The designer details the product in working drawings with specifications and notes for its fabrication. Graphical methods are particularly important during implementation, because all products are manufactured from working drawings and specifications. Implementation also involves the packaging, warehousing, distribution, and sales of the manufactured product.

8.2 Working Drawings

Working drawings, with orthographic views, dimensions, and notes, describe how to make the individual parts of a product. The wiper hanger in **Fig. 8.1** is drawn by computer as a working drawing for implementation in **Fig. 8.2.** Properly executed working drawings ensure that the resulting products will be identical when the

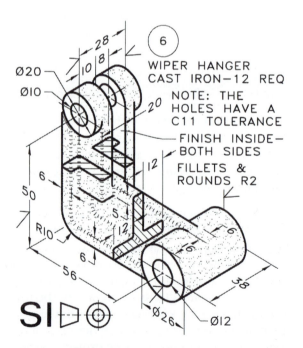

8.1 This wiper hanger is shown in a dimensioned working drawing in Figure 8.2 with three orthographic views.

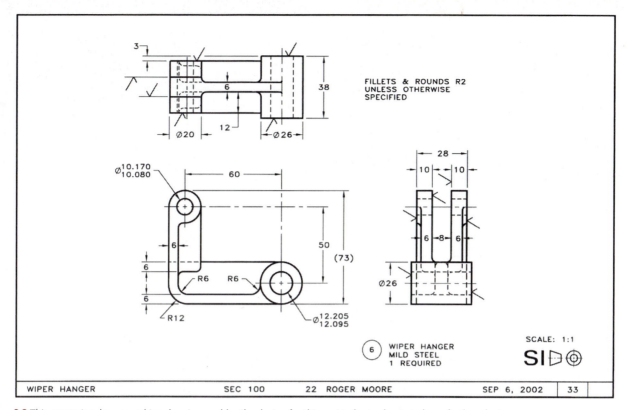

8.2 This computer-drawn working drawing enables the design for this part to be implemented as a final product.

instructions on the drawings are followed, regardless of the shop in which they are made.

When making working drawings, designers draw several parts on the same sheet without attempting to arrange them in relationship to each other or in order of their assembly. The names of the parts, their identifying numbers, the quantity required, and the materials to be used in making them are noted near the views.

8.3 Specifications

Specifications are written notes and instructions that supplement the information shown in drawings. Specifications may be prepared as separate typed documents that accompany drawings or that stand alone when graphical representation is unnecessary. Instructional notes such as the following are adequate as written specifications without drawings:

METALLURGICAL INSPECTION IS
REQUIRED BEFORE MACHINING,
or
PAINT WITH TWO COATS OF FLAT
BLACK PAINT (NO. 780)
AFTER FINISHING.

When space permits, specifications should be given on the working drawing rather than in a separate document.

8.4 Assembly Drawings

Assembly drawings illustrate how individual parts are to be put together to become the final product. They can be drawn as three-dimensional pictorials or orthographic views that are fully assembled, fully exploded, or partially exploded. **Figure 8.3** shows a partially exploded orthographic view of an assembly with part

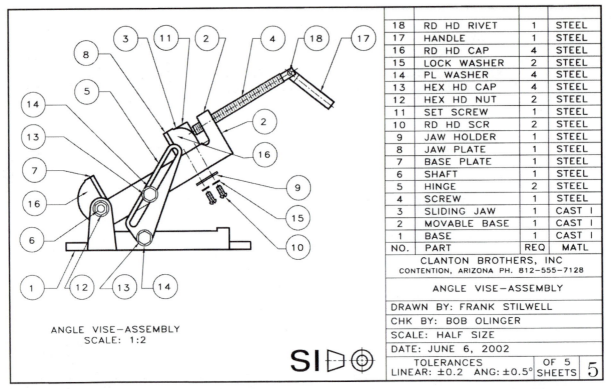

18	RD HD RIVET	1	STEEL
17	HANDLE	1	STEEL
16	RD HD CAP	4	STEEL
15	LOCK WASHER	2	STEEL
14	PL WASHER	4	STEEL
13	HEX HD CAP	4	STEEL
12	HEX HD NUT	2	STEEL
11	SET SCREW	1	STEEL
10	RD HD SCR	2	STEEL
9	JAW HOLDER	1	STEEL
8	JAW PLATE	1	STEEL
7	BASE PLATE	1	STEEL
6	SHAFT	1	STEEL
5	HINGE	2	STEEL
4	SCREW	1	STEEL
3	SLIDING JAW	1	CAST I
2	MOVABLE BASE	1	CAST I
1	BASE	1	CAST I
NO.	PART	REQ	MATL

CLANTON BROTHERS, INC
CONTENTION, ARIZONA PH. 812-555-7128

ANGLE VISE—ASSEMBLY

DRAWN BY: FRANK STILWELL
CHK BY: BOB OLINGER
SCALE: HALF SIZE
DATE: JUNE 6, 2002

| TOLERANCES | OF 5 | |
| LINEAR: ±0.2 ANG: ±0.5° | SHEETS | 5 |

ANGLE VISE—ASSEMBLY
SCALE: 1:2

SI▷◎

8.3 This partially exploded orthographic assembly drawing of a vise shows how individual parts fit together.

numbers in balloons. An assembly drawing usually contains a parts list for easy reference.

8.5 Miscellaneous Considerations

After preparing drawings and specifications, designers must consider other aspects of implementation: **product packaging**, **storage**, **shipping**, and **marketing**.

Packaging

In some industries such as the toy industry, packaging is elaborate and may be as expensive as the product. Designers must be aware of packaging problems as they develop a design because a product that is difficult to package will cost more. Many products are shipped partially disassembled to make packaging easier and cheaper.

Storage

Most manufacturers maintain an inventory of products for shipment. Therefore, warehousing costs must be figured into the product's final selling price.

Shipping

Industries that locate warehouse facilities in the middle of their market areas have lower shipping costs than those with warehouses at the edges of their market areas.

Marketing

Designers must be concerned with all aspects of a product after it enters the marketplace, including its marketability and consumer acceptance. Complaints about a product's reliability and function are important to designers, alerting them to design or manufacturing defects that must be overcome in future versions of the product.

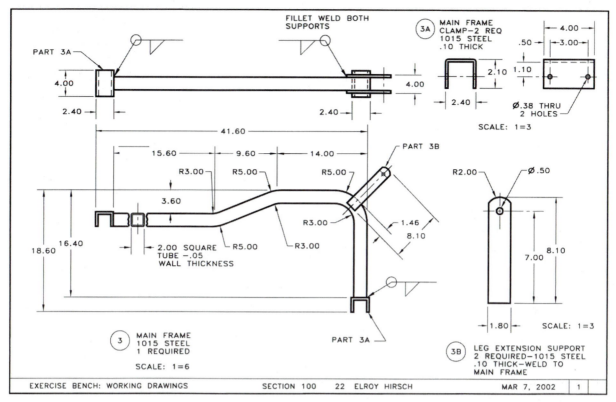

FILLET WELD BOTH SUPPORTS

PART 3A

4.00

2.40

41.60

15.60   9.60   14.00

R3.00   R5.00   R5.00

3.60

R3.00

R3.00

16.40

18.60

2.00 SQUARE
TUBE −.05
WALL THICKNESS

R5.00

R3.00

PART 3B

1.46

8.10

4.00

2.40

3A MAIN FRAME
CLAMP−2 REQ
1015 STEEL
.10 THICK

4.00

.50   3.00

2.10   1.10

2.40

Ø.38 THRU
2 HOLES

SCALE: 1=3

R2.00   Ø.50

8.10

7.00

1.80   SCALE: 1=3

3   MAIN FRAME
1015 STEEL
1 REQUIRED

SCALE: 1=6

PART 3A

3B LEG EXTENSION SUPPORT
2 REQUIRED−1015 STEEL
.10 THICK−WELD TO
MAIN FRAME

EXERCISE BENCH: WORKING DRAWINGS   SECTION 100   22 ELROY HIRSCH   MAR 7, 2002   1

8.4 A working drawing depicting exercise bench parts is shown here (sheet 1 of 5).

8.6 Implementation: Exercise Bench

To illustrate implementation of a product design, we return to the exercise bench, which was introduced in Chapter 3 and has been used to demonstrate the application of each step in the design process.

Working Drawings

The two working drawings shown in **Figs. 8.4** and **8.5** depict some details of the exercise bench design. Additional working drawings are required to show the other parts of the bench, which are dimensioned in decimal inches. Standard parts to be purchased from suppliers are not drawn but are itemized on the drawing,

given part numbers, and listed in the parts list on the assembly drawing.[*]

Assembly Drawing

Figure 8.6 shows an assembly drawing that illustrates how the parts are to be assembled after they have been made. The assembly is shown pictorially, with the different parts identified by numbered balloons attached to leaders. The parts list identifies each part by number and describes it generally.

Packaging

The Weider exercise bench is packaged in a corrugated cardboard box and weighs approximately

---

[*]This particular design was developed and patented and is marketed by Weider Health and Fitness, 2100 Erwin Street, Woodland Hills, CA 91367.

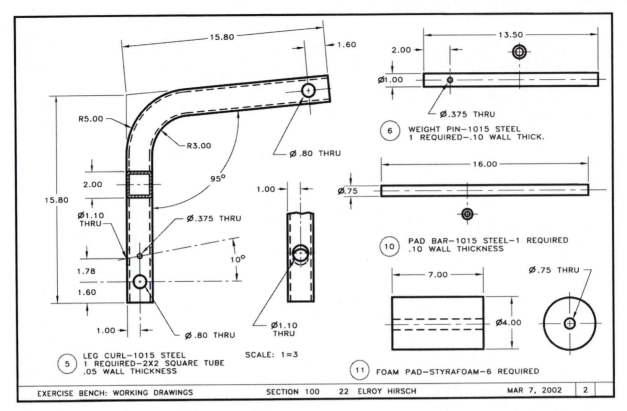

The drawing contains the following labeled text:

15.80 1.60 2.00 13.50
R5.00
R3.00
Ø.80 THRU
95°
2.00 1.00
15.80
Ø1.10 THRU
Ø.375 THRU
10°
1.78
1.60
1.00
Ø.80 THRU
Ø1.10 THRU
SCALE: 1=3

LEG CURL—1015 STEEL
5 1 REQUIRED—2X2 SQUARE TUBE
.05 WALL THICKNESS

Ø1.00
Ø.375 THRU
6 WEIGHT PIN—1015 STEEL
1 REQUIRED—.10 WALL THICK.

16.00
Ø.75
10 PAD BAR—1015 STEEL—1 REQUIRED
.10 WALL THICKNESS

7.00 Ø.75 THRU
Ø4.00
11 FOAM PAD—STYRAFOAM—6 REQUIRED

EXERCISE BENCH: WORKING DRAWINGS   SECTION 100   22 ELROY HIRSCH   MAR 7, 2002   2

8.5 Another working drawing describing exercise bench parts (sheet 2 of 5).

40 pounds. It is shipped unassembled so that it will fit into a smaller carton for ease of handling during shipment (**Fig. 8.7**).

Storage

An inventory of benches must be maintained to meet retailer demand. The need to hold inventory increases overhead costs for interest payments, warehouse rent, warehouse personnel, and loading equipment.

Shipping

Shipping costs for all types of carriers (rail, motor freight, air delivery, and mail services) must be evaluated. The shipping cost for a Weider bench with its accessories is $10–$15, depending on distance, when shipped one at a time by United Parcel Service. The cost per unit is about fifty percent less when units are shipped in bundles of ten to the same destination.

Accessories

Examples of accessories, or add-ons, are the butterfly attachments for arm exercises. Accessories enable buyers to upgrade the basic product in stages, which can increase product marketability and sales.

Prices

The retail price of the Weider bench is about $100. This type of product generally retails for about five or six times the cost of manufacturing it (including materials and labor). Retailers receive approximately a forty percent margin, distributors earn about ten percent, and the remainder of the price represents advertising costs and the other miscellaneous costs mentioned previously. The consumer pays all of these costs (prorated to each exercise bench) as part of the purchase price.

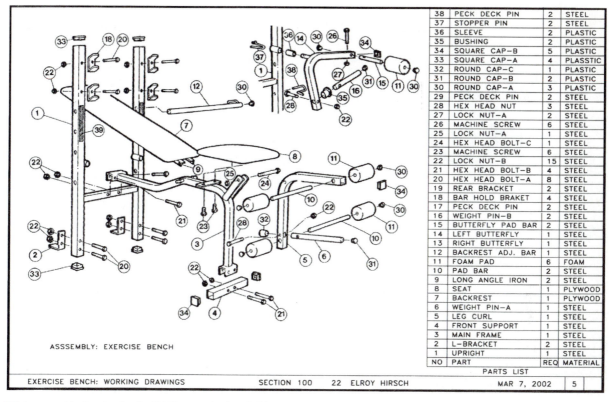

8.6 An assembly drawing for the Weider exercise bench (sheet 5 of 5). (Courtesy of Weider Health and Fitness.)

8.7 Patents

Inventors of processes or products should investigate the possibility of obtaining patents on them from the U.S. Patent and Trademark Office (PTO) before disclosing their inventions. The PTO issued its first patent in 1836, a patent for traction wheels. The patent procedure is outlined in *General Information Concerning Patents*, a publication available from the PTO from which the following material was extracted.

What May Be Patented?

Any person who "invents or discovers any new and useful process, machine, manufacture, or composition of matter, may obtain a patent," subject to the conditions and requirements of law. These categories include everything made

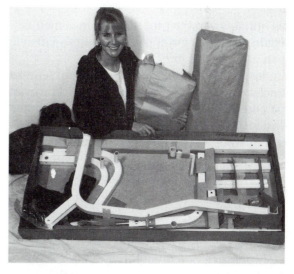

8.7 The exercise bench is packaged unassembled and flat for ease of packaging and handling during shipment.

T. A. EDISON.
Electric-Lamp.

No. 223,898.   Patented Jan. 27, 1880.

8.8 Thomas Edison received this patent for the electric lamp in 1880 that began the electrical/electronics revolution.

by humans and the processes for making them. **Figure 8.8** is the cover page of Thomas Edison's patent for the electric lamp.

Inventions used for the development of nuclear and atomic weapons for warfare are not patentable because they are not considered "useful." Also, a design for a mechanism that will not operate as described is not patentable. An idea or concept for a new invention is not patentable; it must be designed and described in detail before it can be considered for patent registration.

Who May Apply for a Patent?

Only the inventor may apply for a patent. A patent given to a person who was not the inven-tor would be void and the recipient subject to prosecution for perjury. However, the executor of a deceased inventor's estate may apply for a patent, and two or more people may apply for a patent as joint inventors.

Patent Rights

An inventor granted a patent has the right to exclude others from making, using, or selling the invention throughout the United States for twenty years from the time of application. At the end of that time, anyone may make, use, or sell the invention without authorization from the patent holder.

Application for a Patent

An inventor applying for a patent must provide: 1. a completed form that includes a petition, specification (description and claims), and oath or declaration; 2. a drawing, if a drawing is possi-ble; and 3. the filing fee.

Petition and Oath In the petition and oath (usually on one form) the inventor asks to be given a patent on the invention and declares that he or she is the original inventor of the device described in the application.

Specification The inventor must submit a written specification, describing the invention in detail so that a person skilled in the field to which the invention pertains can produce the item. Drawings should carry figure numbers and contain part numbers for text references (**Fig. 8.9**).

Claims The inventor's claims are brief descrip-tions of the invention's features that distinguish it from already patented items. The PTO studies claims to judge the novelty and patentability of an invention.

Fee As part of the application for a patent, the inventor must submit a $740 filing fee. Additional fees can be charged based on additional specifications and claims. An issue fee of $1320 is payable when the PTO grants the patent. As a general rule, patents cost the inventor about $4000–$6000, excluding attorney's fees.

8.8 Patent Drawings

A booklet, *Guide for Patent Draftsmen* (available from the U.S. Government Printing Office), outlines the required format for patent drawings. If the inventor cannot furnish drawings, the PTO will recommend a drafter who can prepare them at the inventor's expense.

Patent Drawing Standards

Patent drawings must meet the following standards.

Paper and Ink Drawings must be on pure white paper of the thickness of a two- or three-ply Bristol board with a surface that is calendared and smooth to permit erasure and correction. India ink is required for permanence and solid black lines. The use of white pigment to cover errors is not allowed.

Sheet Size and Margins Sheet size must be 8–1/2 by 14 inches (21.6 by 35.6 cm) or 21.0 by 29.7 cm. All sheets in a particular application must be the same size. One of the shorter sides is regarded as the top of the sheet. On 8–1/2-by-14-inch sheets, the top margin is 2 inches and the side and bottom margins are 1/4 inch. Margin border lines cannot be drawn on the sheets, but all work must be included within the margins. Sheets may be punched with two 1/4-inch holes, with their centerlines 11/16 inch below the top edge and 2–3/4 inches apart and centered from the sides of the sheet. The margins for 21.0 × 29.7cm sheets are 2.5 cm from the top, 2.5 cm from the left, 1.5 cm from the right, and 1 cm from the bottom.

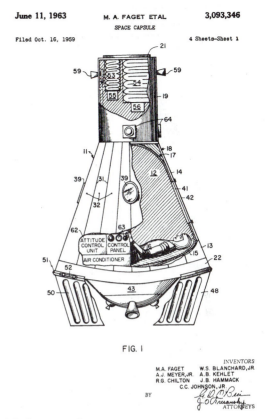

June 11, 1963   M. A. FAGET ETAL   3,093,346
SPACE CAPSULE
Filed Oct. 16, 1959   4 Sheets—Sheet 1

FIG. I

INVENTORS
M.A. FAGET   W.S. BLANCHARD, JR.
A.J. MEYER, JR.   A.B. KEHLET
R.G. CHILTON   J.B. HAMMACK
C.C. JOHNSON, JR.
BY
ATTORNEYS

8.9 This patent drawing of a space capsule was developed by the National Aeronautics and Space Administration (NASA).

Character of Lines All lines and lettering must be absolutely black regardless of line thickness. Freehand work is to be avoided.

Hatching and Shading Hatching lines used to shade the surface of an object should be parallel and at least 1/20 inch apart (**Fig. 8.10**). Heavy lines are used on the shade side of the views if they do not confuse the drawing. The light is assumed to come from the upper-left-hand corner at an angle of 45°. **Figure 8.11** depicts several types of surface delineation.

Scale The scale must be large enough to show the mechanism without crowding when the drawing is reduced for reproduction. Portions of

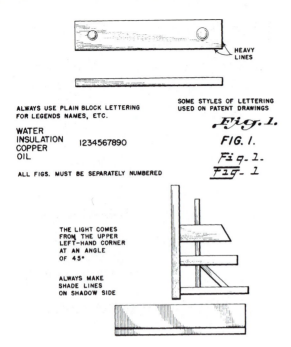

ALWAYS USE PLAIN BLOCK LETTERING
FOR LEGENDS NAMES, ETC.

SOME STYLES OF LETTERING
USED ON PATENT DRAWINGS

WATER
INSULATION   1234567890
COPPER
OIL

ALL FIGS. MUST BE SEPARATELY NUMBERED

Fig. 1.

FIG. 1.

Fig. 1.

FIG. 1

HEAVY
LINES

THE LIGHT COMES
FROM THE UPPER
LEFT—HAND CORNER
AT AN ANGLE
OF 45°

ALWAYS MAKE
SHADE LINES
ON SHADOW SIDE

8.10 These are typical examples of lines and lettering recommended for patent drawings.

the mechanism may be drawn at a larger scale to show details.

Reference Characters The drafter should identify different views of a mechanism by consecutive plain, legible numerals of at least 1/8-inch high figure numbers, not encircled, and placed close to their parts. A blank space should be provided on hatched surfaces if numbers are to be placed on them. The same part appearing in more than one view on the drawing should be labeled with the same numeral.

Symbols Symbols used to represent various materials in sections, electrical components, and mechanical devices are recommended by the PTO and conform to engineering drawing standards.

Signature and Names The signature or name of the applicant and the signature of the attor-

ney or agent are placed in the lower right-hand corner of each sheet within the marginal lines or below the lower marginal line.

Views Figures should be numbered consecutively in order of their appearance. Figures may be plan, elevation, section, perspective, or detail views. Exploded views may be used to describe an assembly of multiple parts. Large parts may be broken into sections and drawn on several sheets if this approach is not confusing. Removed sections may be used if the cutting plane is labeled to indicate the section by number. All sheet headings and signatures are to be placed in the same position on the sheet, whether the drawing is read from the bottom or the right of the sheet. Completed drawings should be sent flat, protected by heavy board, or rolled in a suitable mailing tube.

8.9 Patent Searches

A patent can be granted only after PTO examiners have searched existing patents to verify that the invention has not been patented previously. With more than 6,000,000 patents on record, a search is the most time-consuming part of obtaining a patent. Most inventors employ patent attorneys or agents to do preliminary searches for possible infringement on other patents.

8.10 Questions and Answers

We used the PTO's pamphlet, *Questions and Answers About Patents*, to answer the following questions. Additional information can be found on the Web at **www.uspto.gov**.

Nature and Duration of Patents

1. **Q.** *What is a patent?*

   A. A patent is a grant issued by the U.S. Government, giving an inventor the right to exclude all others from making, using, or selling his or her invention within the United States, its territories, and possessions.

2. Q. *For how long is a patent granted?*

A. Twenty years from the date on which and application is filed; except for patents on ornamental designs, which are granted for terms of 3-1/2, 7, or 14 years.

3. Q. *May the term of a patent be extended?*

A. Only by a special act of Congress, which occurs rarely and only under exceptional circumstances.

4. Q. *Does the person granted the patent have any control over the patent after it expires?*

A. No. Anyone has the right to use an invention covered in an expired patent so long as they do not use features covered in other unexpired patents.

5. Q. *On what subject matter may a patent be granted?*

A. A patent may be granted to the inventor or discoverer of any new and useful process, machine, manufacture, or composition of matter, or any new and useful improvement thereof, or on any distinct and new variety of plant, or on any new, original, and ornamental design for an article of manufacture.

6. Q. *What may not be patented?*

A. A patent may not be granted on a useless device, on printed matter, on a method of doing business, on an improvement in a device that would be obvious to a person skilled in the art, or on a machine that will not operate, particularly on alleged perpetual motion machines.

7. Q. *What do "patent pending" and "patent applied for" mean?*

A. They are used by a manufacturer or seller of an article to indicate that a patent application for that article is on file with the U.S.

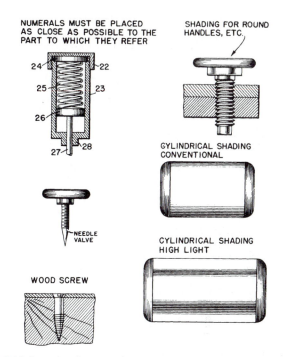

8.11 Several techniques of representing surfaces and beveled planes may be used on patent drawings.

Patent and Trademark Office. Those using these terms falsely to deceive the public can be fined.

8. Q. *I have made some changes and improvements in my invention after my patent application was filed with the PTO. May I amend my patent application by adding a description or illustration of these features?*

A. No. The law provides that new matter shall not be introduced into a patent application. You should call to the attention of your patent agent any such changes you may make, or plan to make, so steps may be taken for your protection.

9. Q. *How does someone apply for a patent?*

A. By making application to the Commissioner of Patents, Patent and Trademark Office, Washington, DC, 20231.

10. Q. *What are the PTO's fees in connection with filing of an application for patent and issuance of the patent?*

A. A filing fee of $790 plus certain additional charges for claims, depending on their number and the manner of their presentation, are required when the application is filed. An issue fee of $1320 plus certain printing charges are required if the patent is to be granted.

11. Q. *Are models required as a part of the application?*

A. Only in the exceptional cases. The PTO has the authority to require that a model be submitted, but rarely exercises it.

12. Q. *Is it necessary for me to go to the PTO in Washington, DC to transact business concerning patent matters?*

A. No. Most business is conducted by correspondence. Interviews regarding pending applications can be arranged with examiners if necessary and often are helpful.

13. Q. *Can the PTO give me advice about whether to apply for a patent?*

A. No. It can only consider the patentability of an invention when an application comes before it.

14. Q. *Is there any danger that the PTO will give others information contained in my application while it is pending?*

A. No. All patent applications are kept secret until the patent is issued. After the patent is issued, the PTO file containing the application and all correspondence leading to its issuance is made available in the Patent Office Search Room to anyone, and copies may be purchased from the PTO.

15. Q. *May I write to the PTO about my application after it is filed?*

A. The PTO will answer your inquiries about the status of the application and indicate whether the application has been rejected, allowed, or is awaiting action. However, you should forward correspondence through your patent attorney or agent.

16. Q. *What happens when two inventors apply separately for a patent on the same invention?*

A. The PTO declares an "interference" and requires that testimony be submitted to determine which inventor is entitled to the patent.

17. Q. *May applications be examined out of their regular order?*

A. No. All applications are examined in the order in which they are filed, except under special conditions.

When to Apply for a Patent

18. Q. *I have been making and selling my invention for the past thirteen months and have not filed any patent application. Is it too late for me to apply?*

A. Yes. A patent may not be obtained if the invention has been in public use or for sale in this country for more than a year prior to application. Your own use and sale of it for more than a year before filing will bar your right to a patent as though someone else had done so.

19. Q. *I published an article describing my invention in a magazine thirteen months ago. Is it too late to apply for a patent?*

A. Yes. The inventor is not entitled to a patent if the invention has been described in a printed publication anywhere in the world more than a year before filing an application.

20. **Q.** *If two or more people work together on an invention, to whom will the patent be granted?*

    A. If each had a share in the ideas forming the invention, they are joint inventors and a patent will be issued to them jointly if an application is filed by them jointly. If one person provided all the ideas and the other has only followed instructions in making the device, the person contributing the ideas is the sole inventor and the patent application and patent should be in his or her name only.

21. **Q.** *If one person furnishes all the ideas for an invention and someone else employs that person or furnishes the money for building and testing the invention, should the patent application be filed by them jointly?*

    A. No. The application must be signed, executed, sworn to, and filed in the name of the inventor, who is the person furnishing the ideas, not the employer or the person furnishing the money.

22. **Q.** *May a patent be granted if an inventor dies before filing an application?*

    A. Yes. The application may be filed by the executor or administrator of the inventor's estate.

23. **Q.** *While in England this summer, I found an ingenious article that has not been introduced into the United States or patented. May I obtain a U.S. patent on it?*

    A. No. A U.S. patent may be obtained only by the inventor, not by someone learning of someone else's invention.

24. **Q.** *May the inventor sell or otherwise transfer the right to the patent or patent application to someone else?*

    A. Yes. The inventor may sell all or part of the interest in the patent application or patent to anyone by a properly worded legal assignment. However, the application for a patent must be filed in the name of the inventor, not in the name of the purchaser.

25. **Q.** *Is it advisable to conduct a search of patents and other records before applying for a patent?*

    A. Yes. If the device has been patented previously, making application is useless. A patent search avoids the expense of filing a needless application.

Technical Knowledge Available from Patents

26. **Q.** *May I obtain information through patents of what has been done by others to solve a particular problem?*

    A. The patents in the Patent Office Search Room in Washington, DC contain a wealth of technical information. It is organized so that you can easily find and review previous work related to your problem or general field of interest. You may review these patents personally, or hire a patent practitioner to do so and send you copies of patents related to your problem.

27. **Q.** *Can I obtain information about patents and the patent process on the World Wide Web?*

    A. Yes. You may contact the Patent Office at **www.uspto.gov** to obtain information about patents and trademarks, plus most answers to questions that you will have about patents. Although the patents are accessible by computer, the patent drawings are not available by computer.

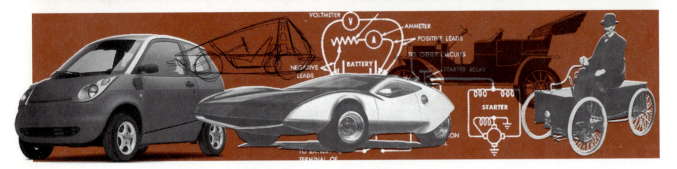

CHAPTER NINE

Design Problems

9.1 Introduction

This chapter offers problems that are suitable for both individual assignments and team projects to provide experience in applying the methods of creative problem-solving presented in this textbook. Graphics has many applications during the design process. All new products begin with sketches at the preliminary idea step and end with documentation drawings at the implementation step.

9.2 The Individual Approach

The solution of short problems (one to two hours) is best suited to students working alone. Although simple design problems may involve fewer details and less depth than comprehensive problems do, the same design steps are involved.

9.3 The Team Approach

An effectively organized team working on a problem has more talent than the typical individual possesses. However, management of talent becomes as much of the process as solving the problem. It is essential that the team process be learned since most of the engineering activities in industry are done by teams.

Team Size

Student design teams should have from three to eight members. Three is the minimum number needed for a valid team experience, and four is the number needed to minimize the possibility of domination by one or two members.

Team Composition

In practice, an engineering team often consists of representatives of different departments, or even of different firms, who may be unacquainted. This situation can be advantageous because it reduces the impact of preconceived notions about individuals.

Team Leader

A leader is necessary for teams to function effectively. The leader is responsible for making assignments, ensuring that deadlines are met, and mediating disagreements.

9.4 Selection of a Problem

The best problem for a student design project is one that involves familiar and accessible conditions that can be observed, measured, and inspected. A design for a water-ski rack for an automobile is more feasible than is a design for a support bracket for an airplane. When a student design team selects a design problem, the team should prepare a written proposal identifying the problem and outlining its limits. Assignment of problems by the instructor in the classroom is analogous to assignments by a supervisor in the workplace.

9.5 Problem Specifications

An individual or team may be expected to complete any or all of the following tasks.

Short Problems (One or Two Hours)

1. Worksheets that record development of a design procedure (Chapter 2).

2. Freehand sketches of the design for implementation (Chapters 4 and 13).

3. Instrument drawings of the solution (Chapters 8 and 22).

4. Pictorial sketches (or drawings made with instruments or a computer) illustrating the design (Chapters 4, 13, and 24).

5. Visual aids, flip charts, or other media for presentation to a group (Chapter 7).

Comprehensive Problems (40 to 100 Hours)

1. A proposal identifying the problem and outlining an approach for solving it (Chapters 2, 3, and 7).

2. Worksheets documenting the preliminary ideas for a solution (Chapter 4).

3. Schematic diagrams, flowcharts, or other graphics to illustrate refinements of the design (Chapter 5).

4. A market survey evaluating the product's possible acceptance and estimated profit (Chapters 3 and 6).

5. A model or prototype for analysis and/or presentation (Chapter 6).

6. Pictorials to illustrate features of the final design solution (Chapters 7 and 24).

7. Dimensioned working drawings and assembly drawings to give details and specifications (Chapters 8 and 22).

8. An oral report, illustrated with graphs and diagrams, to explain the method of solution and present conclusions and recommendations (Chapter 7).

9.6 Scheduling Team Activities

The semester schedule shown in **Fig. 9.1** is suggested for a comprehensive design project. Spreading design projects over the semester allows time for thinking about the problem, gathering information, and working on the solution. Refer to the exercise bench example in Chapters 3 through 8 as a guide for carrying out your project.

9.7 Short Design Problems

The following short design problems can be completed in less than two hours.

1. Lamp bracket. Design a bracket to attach a desk lamp to a vertical wall for reading in bed. It should be removable for use as a conventional desk lamp.

	MONDAY	WEDNESDAY	FRIDAY
1			
2			
3		Assign teams	
4		Identify problem	
5		Identify problem	
6		Brainstorm	
7		Preliminary ideas	
8		Refinement	
9		Refinement	
10		Analysis	
11		Decision	
12		Implementation	
13		Prepare	
14		Present	
15			
16			

9.1 The semester schedule for the integration of a design project is shown here.

9.2 (Problem 6) Base redesign.

2. Towel bar. Design a towel bar for a kitchen or bathroom. Determine optimum size and consider styling, ease of use, and method of attachment.

3. Bicycle rack. Design a rack (or basket) for a bicycle for carrying books and class materials.

4. Boot puller. Design a device for helping you remove cowboy boots from your feet.

5. Side-mounted mirror. Design an improved side-mounted rearview mirror for an automobile. Consider aerodynamics, protection from inclement weather, visibility, and other factors.

6. Part modification. Modify the base that supports the 2″ diameter shaft by changing the square base to a circular base with six holes instead of four (**Fig. 9.2**). Modify the ribs accordingly.

7. Pipe column support. Design a base that can be attached to a concrete slab with bolts that would provide a base for 3 inch diameter pipe columns.

8. Motor bracket (Fig. 9.3). Design a bracket to support a motor. The plate should be the upper part of the finished bracket.

9. Pipe bracket clamp (Fig. 9.4). Design a clamp that can be attached to an overhead I-beam to support a pipe without welding or drilling holes in the beam.

10. Pipe roll stand (Fig. 9.5). Design an alternative design to this roll stand that supports pipes up to 10 inches in diameter with a roller that allows expansion and contraction.

11. Foot scraper. Design a device that can be attached to the sidewalk for scraping mud from your shoes.

12. Audio cassette storage unit. Design a storage unit for an automobile that will hold several audio cassettes, making them accessible to the driver but not to a thief.

13. Slide projector elevator. Design a device for raising a slide projector to the proper angle for projection on a screen. It may be part of the

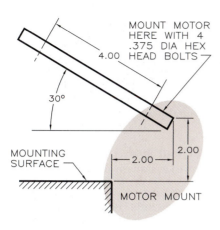

9.3 (Problem 8) Base redesign.

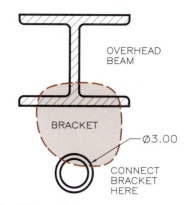

9.4 (Problem 9) Base redesign.

9.5 (Problem 10) Pipe roll stand. (*Courtesy of Grinnell Company, Inc.*)

original projector or an accessory to be attached to existing projectors.

14. Book holder. Design a holder to support a textbook or reference book at a workstation for ease of reading and accessibility.

15. Table leg design. Do-it-yourselfers build a variety of tables using hollow doors or plywood for the tops and commercially available legs. Determine standard heights for various types of tables and design a family of legs that can be attached to table tops with screws.

16. Pipe clamp (Fig. 9.6). A pipe with a 4-in. diameter must be supported by angles that are spaced 8 ft. apart. Design a clamp that will support the pipe without drilling holes in the angles.

17. Toothbrush holder. Design a toothbrush holder for a cup and two toothbrushes that can be attached to a bathroom wall.

18. Framing fixture. Design a device to hold the rails of a picture frame in position to aid in assembly and insure that the corners will be square.

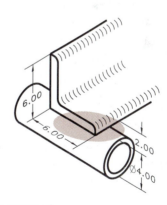

9.6 (Problem 16) Pipe clamp.

19. Clothes hook. Design a clothes hook that can be attached to a closet door for hanging clothes on.

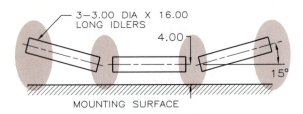

3—3.00 DIA × 16.00 LONG IDLERS

4.00

15°

MOUNTING SURFACE

9.7 (Problem 23) Roller brackets.

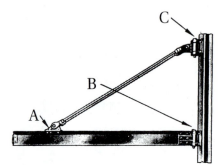

9.8 (Problem 24) Jib crane bracket.

9.9 (Problem 28) Sit-up bench.

9.10 (Problem 29) Trash can cover.

20. Hammock support. Design a hammock support that will fold up and that will require minimal storage space.

21. Door stop. Design a door stop that can be attached to a wall or floor to prevent a door knob from hitting the wall.

22. Basketball goal. Design a basketball goal that is easy to install for the 8-10 age range.

23. Roller brackets (Fig. 9.7). The rollers are to be positioned as shown to support a conveyor belt that carries bulk material. Design brackets to support the rollers.

24. Jib crane brackets. Design the brackets at the joints indicated (**Fig. 9.8 A**, **B**, and **C**) to form a jib crane made of an 8″ × 4″ × 8 ft.-long I-beam and a steel connecting rod. The crane should have at least a 180° swing.

25. Drawer handle. Design a handle for a standard file cabinet drawer.

26. Handrail bracket. Design a bracket that will support a tubular handrail to be used on a staircase.

27. Flagpole socket. Design a flagpole socket that is to be attached to a vertical wall.

28. Sit-up bench (Fig. 9.9). Design a sit-up bench for exercising. Can you make it serve multiple purposes?

29. Trash can cover. Design a functional lid with an appropriate opening through which to put garbage (**Fig. 9.10**).

30. Conduit connector hanger (Fig. 9.11). Design an attachment for a 3/4-in. conduit to support a channel used as a raceway for electrical wiring.

31. Hose spool. Design a spool/rack on which a garden hose can be wound and left neatly near the outside faucet.

32. Gate hinge. Design a hinge that can be attached to a 3-in.-diameter tubular post to support a 3-ft-wide wooden gate.

33. Cup holder. Design a holder that will support a soft-drink can or bottle in an automobile.

34. Channel bracket (Fig. 9.12). The bracket shown is designed to fit on the flat side of the channel. Design a method of attaching the bracket to the slotted side so the inside nut will not drop down inside the channel.

9.8 Systems Design Problems

Systems problems require analysis of the inter-relationship of various components and products.

35. Archery range. Determine the feasibility of providing an archery range that can be operated profitably. Investigate the potential market for such a facility and factors such as location, equipment needed, method of operation, utilities, concessions, parking, costs, and fees.

36. Bicycle rental system. Investigate the feasibility of a student-operated bicycle rental system. Determine student interest, cost factors, number of bikes needed, prices, personnel needs, storage, maintenance, and so on. Summarize your location, operating cost, and profitability conclusions.

37. Model-airplane field. Investigate the need for a model-airplane field, including space requirements, types of surface needed, sound control, safety factors, and method of operation. Select a site on or near your campus that is adequate for this facility, and evaluate the equipment, utilities, and site preparation required.

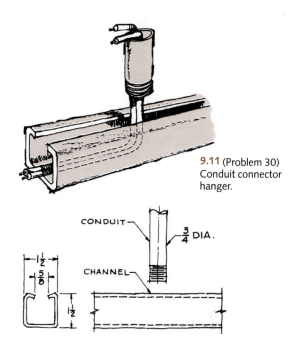

9.11 (Problem 30) Conduit connector hanger.

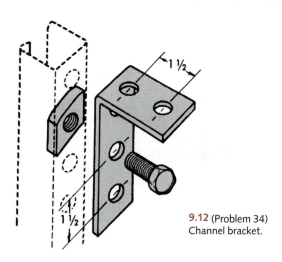

9.12 (Problem 34) Channel bracket.

38. Overnight campsite. Analyze the feasibility of converting a vacant tract of land near a major highway into sites for overnight campers. Determine the facilities required by the campers and the venture's profitability.

39. Skateboard facility study. Determine the cost of building and operating a skateboard facility on your campus. Consider where it could be located, how many students would use it, and the amounts of equipment and labor necessary to operate it. Would it be financially feasible?

40. Hot-water supply. Your weekend cottage does not have a hot-water supply, but cold water is available from a private well. Design a system that uses the sun's energy in the summer to heat water for bathing and kitchen use. Devise a system for heating the water in the winter by some other source. Determine whether one or both of these systems could be made portable for showers on camping trips and, if so, how.

41. Information center. Design a drive-by information center to help campus visitors find their way around. Determine the best location for it and the informational material needed, such as slides, photographs, maps, sound, and other audiovisual aids.

42. Golf driving range ball-return system. Balls at golf driving ranges are usually retrieved by hand or with a specially designed vehicle. Design a system capable of automatically returning balls to the tee area.

43. Car wash. Design a car wash facility for your campus that would be self-supporting and would provide the basics needs for washing cars. Think simple and economical.

44. Instant motel. Many communities need temporary housing for celebrations and sporting events. Investigate methods of providing an "instant motel" involving the use of tents, vans, trailers, train cars, or other temporary accommodations. Estimate profitability.

45. Drive-in garbage system. Design a system for leaving wrappers, boxes, and napkins left over after eating in your car at a hamburger drive-in. It would be preferred if this could be done without getting out of your car.

46. Computer wiring system (**Fig. 9.14**). Computer installations become cluttered with wiring as accessories are attached and access to connections becomes difficult. Design a system whereby the electrical wiring can be more organized, convenient, and accessible.

47. Injury-proof playground. Design a playground that permits the greatest degree of participation by children with the least risk of injury.

48. Modification of an existing facility. Select a facility on your campus or in your community that is inadequate, such as a street intersection, parking lot, recreational area, or classroom. Identify its deficiencies and propose improvements to it.

49. Patio table production. Determine the procedures for production of a plywood patio table: materials, equipment, methods, storage, and sales. Determine the number to be manufactured per month to break even and the selling price. Establish quantity breaks for quantities that exceed the break-even level.

9.9 Product Design Problems

Product design involves developing a device that will perform a specific function, be mass-produced, and be sold to a large number of consumers.

50. Hunting blind. Design a portable hunting blind adequate for hunting geese or ducks that can be easily taken to its site. Consider making the blind of degradable materials so it can be left at the site.

51. Self-adjusting assembly jig. A concept for an assembly jig for holding together parts for bonding thin pieces to thick pieces by furnace brazing is shown in **Fig. 9.13**.

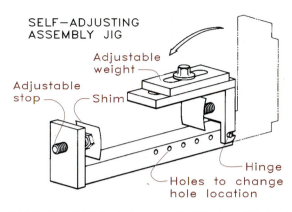

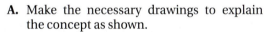

9.13 (Problem 51) Self-adjusting assembly. (*Courtesy of National Aeronautics and Space Administration.*)

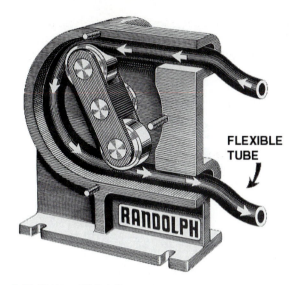

FLEXIBLE TUBE

9.14 (Problem 53) Rotating pump.

A. Make the necessary drawings to explain the concept as shown.

B. Design an alternative jig of your own.

52. Mailbox. Design a residential mailbox that either attaches to the house or is supported on a pole near the street.

53. Rotating pump. A portion of the Randolph pump is shown in **Figure 9.14.** Make the necessary drawings to complete the total design. The flexible tube is 0.50 in. in diameter.

54. Utility rack. Design a rack that can be attached to a pickup truck to aid in hauling equipment and tools (**Fig. 9.14**).

55. Rescue litter (Fig. 9.15). Design a rescue litter than can be folded in a number of positions in order to care for the injured. It should be lightweight and collapsible for convenient storage.

56. Yard helper (Fig. 9.16). Design a movable container that can be used for gardening and yard work.

57. Computer mount. Design a device that can be clamped to a desktop for holding a computer,

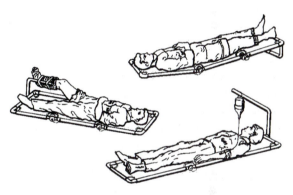

9.15 (Problem 55) Rescue litter. (*Courtesy of National Aeronautics and Space Administration.*)

9.16 (Problem 56) Yard helper.

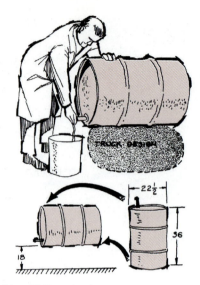

9.17 (Problem 59) Drum truck.

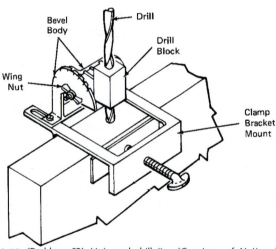

9.18 (Problem 62) Universal drill jig. (*Courtesy of National Aeronautics and Space Administration.*)

permitting it to be adjusted to various positions while leaving the desktop free to work on.

58. Workers' stilts. Design stilts to give workers access to an 8-ft-high ceiling, permitting them to nail 4 × 8-ft ceiling panels into position.

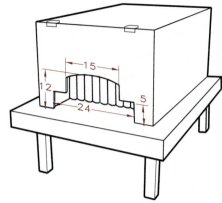

9.19 (Problem 63) Carry-on template.

59. Drum truck (Fig. 9.17). Design a truck that can be used for handling 55-gal drums of turpentine (7.28 lb per gallon), one at a time. Drums are stored in a vertical position and used in a horizontal position. The truck should be useful in tipping a drum into a horizontal position (as shown), as well as for moving the drum.

60. Pole-vault uprights. Pole-vault uprights must be adjusted for each vaulter by moving them forward or backward 18 in. The crossbar must be replaced at heights of over 18 ft by using poles and ladders. Develop a more efficient set of uprights that can be readily adjusted and that allow the crossbar to be replaced easily.

61. Sportsman's chair. Design a sportsman's chair that can be used for camping, for fishing from a bank or boat, at sporting events, and for other purposes.

62. Universal drill jig. A concept for a drill jig that can be used to guide a drill bit at a variety of angles is shown in **Fig. 9.18**.

    A. Make the necessary drawings to depict the design as it is given.

    B. Design your own version of a drill jig of this type. Consider how drills of various diameters could be accommodated.

9.20 (Problem 64) Can crusher.

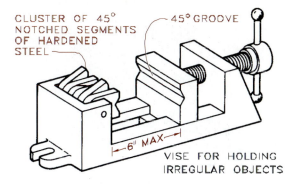

9.21 (Problem 65) Specialty vise. (*Courtesy of National Aeronautics and Space Administration.*)

63. Carry-on template. In an attempt to limit the size of carry-on luggage, airlines are testing designs for an effective template that can be used to screen luggage at check-in time. Design a template that would solve this problem using the specifications shown in **Fig. 9.19**.

64. Can crusher (Fig. 9.20). Design a device for flattening aluminum cans.

65. Self-adjusting assembly jig. A concept for an assembly jig that holds together parts for bonding thin pieces to thick pieces by furnace brazing is shown in **Fig. 9.21**.

    A. Make the necessary drawings to explain the concept that is given.

    B. Design an alternative jig of your own.

66. Monitor support. Design a computer monitor arm to support and position the screen for ease of use.

67. Projector cabinet. Design a cabinet to serve as an end table or some other function while housing a slide projector and slide trays ready for use.

68. Heavy appliance mover. Design a device for moving large appliances—stoves, refrigerators, and washers—about the house for the purposes of rearranging, cleaning, and servicing them.

69. Map holder. Design a map holder to give the driver a view of the map in a convenient

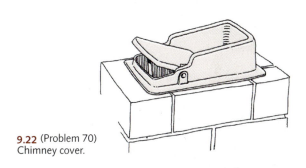

9.22 (Problem 70) Chimney cover.

location in the car while driving. Provide a method of lighting the map that will not distract the driver.

70. Chimney cover (Fig. 9.22). Design a chimney cover that can be closed from inside the house for repelling rain and reducing temperature loss.

71. Gate opener. An annoyance to farmers and ranchers is the necessity of opening and closing gates. Design a manually operated gate that could be opened and closed by the driver from his vehicle.

72. Automobile coffee maker. Design a device that will provide hot coffee from the dashboard of an automobile. Consider the method of changing and adding water, the spigot system, and similar details.

Drawing Instruments

10.1 Introduction

The preparation of technical drawings requires the ability to use a variety of drawing instruments and the computer. Even people with little artistic ability can produce professional technical drawings when they learn to use drawing instruments properly.

The drawing instruments covered in this chapter are traditional ones that are used by hand, as opposed to computer instruments. Traditional instruments will always have an application in the development of drawings, but to a lesser degree than in the past.

Computer Instruments

Electronic drawing instruments—computers, plotters, scanners, and similar equipment—are covered in Chapter 26. The ability to use computer graphics and its associated hardware is a necessary skill for members of the engineering team because of its efficiency and uniformity in producing graphics for industrial applications.

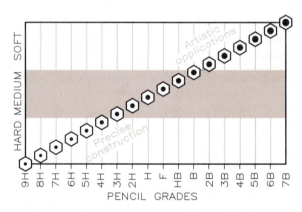

10.1 The hardest pencil lead is 9H and the softest is 7B. The diameters of hard leads are progressively smaller than those of the softer leads.

10.2 Drawing Media

Pencils

A good drawing begins with the correct pencil grade and its proper use. Pencil grades range from the hardest of 9H to the softest, 7B (**Fig. 10.1**). The pencils in the medium-grade range of

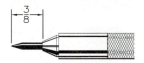

A. LEAD HOLDER

Holds any size lead; point must be sharpened.

B. FINE—LINE HOLDER

Must use different size holder for different lead sizes; does not need to be sharpened.

C. WOOD PENCIL

Wood must be trimmed and lead must be pointed.

D. THE PENCIL POINT

Sharpen point to a conical point with a lead pointer or a sandpaper pad.

10.2 Sharpen the drafting pencil to a tapered conical point (not a needle point) with a sandpaper pad or other type of sharpener.

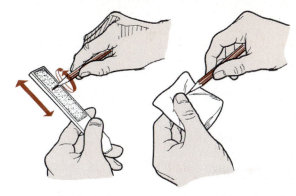

10.3 Revolve the drafting pencil about its axis while stroking the sandpaper pad to form a conical point. Wipe away the graphite from the point with a tissue.

4H to B are used most often for drafting work of the type covered in this textbook.

Figure 10.2 shows three standard pencils used for most drawings. The leads used in the lead holder shown in **Fig. 10.2A** (the best all-around pencil of the three) are marked in white at the ends to indicate their grade.

The fine-line leads used in the lead holder in **Fig. 10.2B** are more difficult to identify because their sizes are smaller and they are unmarked. A different fine-line holder must be used for each size of lead. The common sizes are 0.3 mm, 0.5 mm, and .007 mm, which are the diameters of the leads. A disadvantage of the fine-line pencil is the tendency of the lead to snap off when you apply pressure to it.

Although you have to sharpen it and point its lead, the wood pencil shown in **Fig. 10.2C** is a very satisfactory pencil. The grade of the lead is marked on one end of the pencil; therefore, the opposite end should be sharpened so the identity of the grade of lead will be retained. The wood can be sharpened with a knife or a drafter's pencil sharpener to leave about 3/8 inch of lead exposed.

You must sharpen a pencil's lead properly to obtain a point, as shown in **Fig. 10.2D.** To obtain a conical point, stroke the pencil lead against a sandpaper board and revolve the pencil about its axis in the process (**Fig. 10.3**). Wipe excess graphite from the point with a cloth or tissue.

Although sharpening a pencil point with a sandpaper board may seem outdated, it is a very practical way to sharpen pencil points and about the only way to sharpen compass points. However, there are a multitude of pencil pointers available, some of which work well and others that do not.

Papers and Films

Sizes Sheet sizes are specified by the letters A through E. These sizes are multiples of either the standard 8-1/2 × 11-inch sheet (used by engineers) or the 9 × 12-inch sheet (used by architects), as shown in **Fig. 10.4**. The metric sizes (A4 through A0) are equivalent to the 8-1/2 × 11-inch modular sizes.

Detail Paper When drawings are not to be reproduced by the diazo (blue-line process), an opaque paper, called **detail paper**, can be used as the drawing surface. The higher the rag content (cotton additive) of the paper, the better is its quality and durability. You may draw preliminary layouts on detail paper and then trace them onto the final surface.

	ENGINEERS'	ARCHITECTS'		METRIC		
A	11" X 8.5"	12" X 9"	A4	297	X	210
B	17" X 11"	18" X 12"	A3	420	X	297
C	22" X 17"	24" X 18"	A2	594	X	420
D	34" X 22"	36" X 24"	A1	841	X	594
E	44" X 34"	48" X 36"	A0	1189	X	841

10.4 Standard sheet sizes vary by purpose.

10.5 The drafting machine is used for drawings made by hand. (*Courtesy of Keuffel & Esser Company.*)

Tracing Paper Tracing paper, or tracing vellum, is a thin, translucent paper which permits light to pass through it, allowing reproduction by the blue-line process. Tracing papers that yield the best reproductions are the most translucent ones. Vellum is a tracing paper that has been chemically treated to improve its translucency, but vellum does not retain its original quality as long as do high-quality, untreated tracing papers.

Tracing Cloth Tracing cloth is a permanent drafting medium used for both ink and pencil drawings. It is made of cotton fabric and is coated with a starch compound to provide a tough, erasable drafting surface that yields excellent blue-line reproductions. Tracing cloth does not change shape as much as tracing paper with variations in temperature and humidity. It can withstand erasures to a higher degree than tracing papers.

Polyester Film An excellent drafting surface is polyester film, which is available under several trade names such as *Mylar*®. It is more transparent, stable, and tougher than paper or cloth and is waterproof. Mylar film is used for both pencil and ink drawings. A plastic-lead pencil must be used with some films, whereas standard lead pencils may be used with others.

10.3 Drawing Equipment

Drafting Machine
Most professional drafters prefer the mechanical drafting machine (**Fig. 10.5**), which is attached to the drawing table top and has fin-

10.6 The professional drafter or engineer may work in this type of environment. (*Courtesy of Martin Instrument Company.*)

gertip controls for drawing lines at any angle. A modern, fully equipped drafting station is shown in **Figure 10.6**. Today, most offices are equipped with computer graphics stations, which have replaced much of the manual equipment (**Fig. 10.7**).

Triangles
The two types of triangles used most often are the 45° triangle and the 30°–60° triangle. The size

10.7 A typical engineering workstation used in industry. (*Courtesy of Jervis B. Webb Co.*)

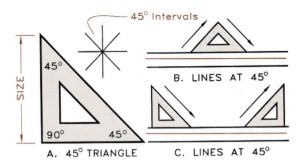

10.9 Use the 45° triangle to draw lines at 45° angles throughout 360°.

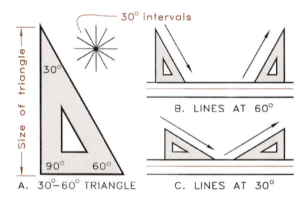

10.8 The 30°–60° triangle is used to draw lines at 30° intervals throughout 360°.

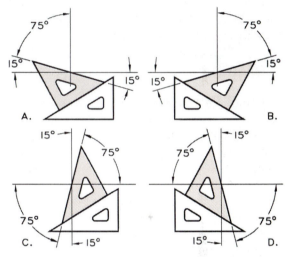

10.10 By using a 30°–60° triangle in combination with a 45° triangle, angles can be drawn at 15° intervals.

of a 30°–60° triangle is specified by the longer of the two sides adjacent to the 90° angle (**Fig. 10.8**). Standard sizes of 30°–60° triangles range in 2-inch intervals from 4 to 24 inches.

The size of a 45° triangle is specified by the length of the sides adjacent to the 90° angle. These range in 2-inch intervals from 4 to 24 inches, but the 6-inch and 10-inch sizes are adequate for most classroom applications. **Figure 10.9** shows the various angles that you may draw with this triangle. By using the 45° and 30°–60°

triangles in combination, you may draw angles at 15° intervals throughout 360° (**Fig. 10.10**).

Protractor

When drawing or measuring lines at angles other than multiples of 15°, a protractor is used (**Fig. 10.11**). Protractors are available as semicircles (180°) or circles (360°). Adjustable triangles with movable edges that can be set at different angles with thumbscrews also are available.

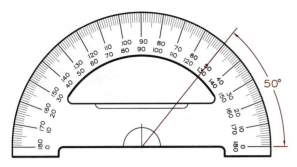

10.11 This semicircular protractor is used to measure angles.

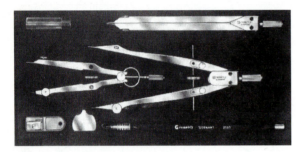

10.12 This is a typical cased set of drawing instruments. (*Courtesy of Gramercy Guild.*)

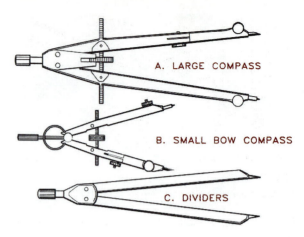

10.13 Drawing instruments can be purchased individually or as a set.

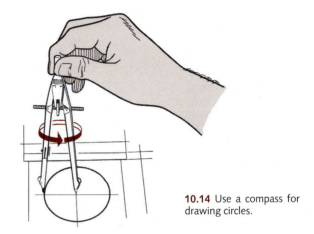

10.14 Use a compass for drawing circles.

Instrument Set

Figure 10.12 shows a cased set of some of the basic drawing instruments that are available individually as well. The three most important instruments for hand drawing are the large compass, small compass, and divider shown in **Fig. 10.13.**

Compass Use the compass to draw circles and arcs in pencil or ink (**Fig. 10.14**). To draw circles well with a pencil compass, sharpen the lead on its outside with a sandpaper board to bevel cut as shown in **Fig. 10.15.** You cannot draw a thick arc in pencil with a single sweep. You must draw a series of thin concentric circles by adjusting the radius of the compass slightly.

When setting the compass pivot point in the drawing surface, insert it just enough for a firm set, not to the shoulder of the point. If your table-top has a hard surface, you must place several sheets of paper under the drawing to provide a seat for the compass point.

Use a small bow compass (**Fig. 10.16**) to draw circles of up to 2 inches in radius. For larger circles, use an extension bar included in most sets to extend the range of the large bow compass. You may draw small circles conveniently with a circle template aligned with the centerlines of the circles (**Fig. 10.17**).

Divider The divider looks like a compass without a drawing point. It is used for laying off and transferring dimensions onto a drawing. For example, you can step off equal divisions rapidly

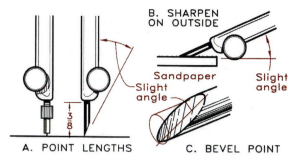

10.17 Circle templates are convenient for drawing small circles without a compass.

10.15 Compass lead

A. Adjust the pencil point to be the same length as the compass point.

B. & C. Sharpen the lead from the outside with a sandpaper pad.

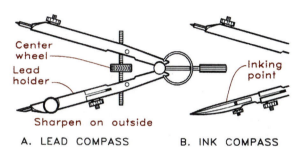

A. LEAD COMPASS　　**B. INK COMPASS**

10.16 Use a small bow compass for drawing circles of up to a 2-in. radius in pencil or in ink.

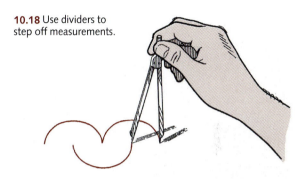

10.18 Use dividers to step off measurements.

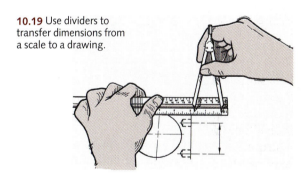

10.19 Use dividers to transfer dimensions from a scale to a drawing.

and accurately along a line (**Fig. 10.18**). As you make each measurement, the divider's points make a slight impression mark in the drawing surface.

Also, use dividers to transfer dimensions from a scale to a drawing (**Fig. 10.19**) or to divide a line into a number of equal parts. Bow dividers (**Fig. 10.20**) are useful for transferring smaller dimensions, such as the spacing between lettering guidelines.

10.4 Lines

The type of line produced by a pencil depends on the hardness of its lead, drawing surface, and your drawing technique. You must experiment in order to achieve the ideal combination.

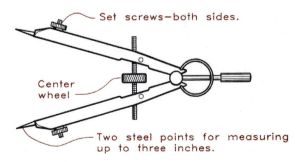

10.20 Bow dividers are used to transfer small dimensions, such as spacing for guidelines for lettering.

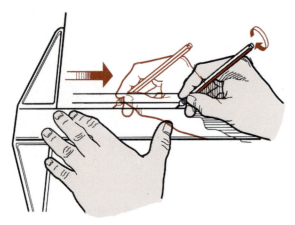

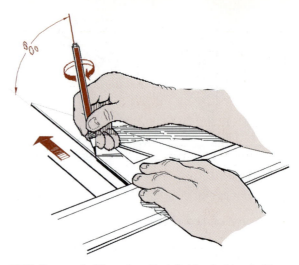

10.21 Draw horizontal lines along the upper edge of a straightedge while holding the pencil in a plane perpendicular to the paper and at 60° to the surface and rotate the pencil about its axis.

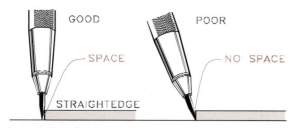

10.22 While drawing, hold the pencil or pen point in a plane perpendicular to the paper, leaving a space between the point and the straightedge.

10.23 Draw vertical lines along the left side of a triangle (if you are right-handed) in an upward direction, holding the pencil or pen in a plane perpendicular to the paper and at 60° to the surface.

Horizontal Lines

To draw a horizontal line, use the upper edge of your horizontal straightedge and make strokes from left to right, if you are right-handed (**Fig. 10.21**), and from right to left if you are left-handed. Rotate the pencil about its axis so that its point will wear evenly. Darken pencil lines by drawing over them with multiple strokes. For drawing the best line, leave a small space between the straightedge and the pencil or pen point (**Fig. 10.22**).

Vertical Lines

Use a triangle and a straightedge to draw vertical lines. Hold the straightedge firmly with one hand and position the triangle where needed and draw the vertical lines with the other hand (**Fig. 10.23**). Draw vertical lines upward along the left side of the triangle if you are right-handed and upward along the right side of the triangle if you are left-handed.

Irregular Curves

Curves that are not arcs must be drawn with an irregular curve (sometimes called French curves). These plastic curves come in a variety of sizes and shapes, but the one shown in **Fig. 10.24** is typical. Here, we use the irregular curve to connect a series of points to form a smooth curve.

Erasing Lines

Always use the softest eraser that will do a particular job. For example, do not use ink erasers to erase pencil lines because ink erasers are coarse and may damage the surface of the paper. When working in small areas, you should use an erasing shield to avoid accidentally erasing adjacent lines (**Fig. 10.25**). Follow erasing by brushing away the "crumbs" with a dusting brush. Wiping the

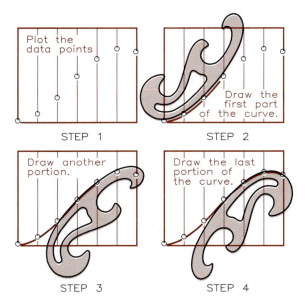

| Plot the data points | STEP 1 | Draw the first part of the curve. | STEP 2 |
| Draw another portion. | STEP 3 | Draw the last portion of the curve. | STEP 4 |

10.24 Using the irregular curve

Step 1 Plot data points with a circle template.

Step 2 Position the curve to pass through as many points as possible and draw that portion of the curve.

Step 3 Reposition the irregular curve and draw another portion of the curve.

Step 4 Draw the last portion to complete the curve.

10.25 Use an erasing shield for erasing in tight spots. Use a brush, not your hand, to brush away the erasure crumbs.

crumbs away with your hands will smudge the drawing. A typical cordless electric eraser that can be used with several grades of erasers to meet your needs is shown in **Fig 10.26**.

10.5 Measurements

Scales

All engineering drawings require the use of scales for measuring lengths and sizes. Scales may be flat or triangular in cross section and are made of wood, plastic, or metal. **Figure 10.27**

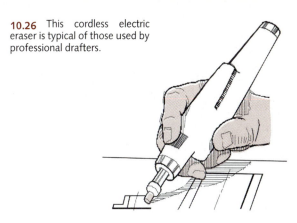

10.26 This cordless electric eraser is typical of those used by professional drafters.

A. ARCHITECTS' SCALE

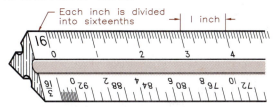

B. ENGINEERS' SCALE

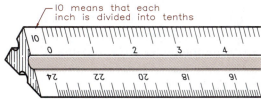

C. METRIC SCALE

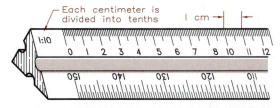

10.27 The architects' scale (A) measures in feet and inches. The engineers' scale (B) and the metric scale (C) are calibrated in decimal units.

shows triangular architects', engineers', and metric scales. Most scales are either 6 or 12 inches long.

Architects' Scale

Drafters use architects' scales to dimension and scale features such as room size, cabinets,

BASIC FORM SCALE: $\frac{X}{X}=1'-0$ *From end of scale*

TYPICAL SCALES

SCALE: FULL SIZE (USE 16-SCALE)

SCALE: HALF SIZE (USE 16-SCALE)

SCALE: $3=1'-0$ SCALE: $\frac{1}{4}=1'-0$

SCALE: $1\frac{1}{2}=1'-0$ SCALE: $\frac{3}{4}=1'-0$

SCALE: $\frac{1}{2}=1'-0$ SCALE: $\frac{3}{8}=1'-0$

SCALE: $\frac{3}{16}=1'-0$ SCALE: $\frac{1}{8}=1'-0$

SCALE: $\frac{3}{32}=1'-0$ SCALE: $1=1'-0$

10.28 Use this basic form to indicate the scale on a drawing made with an architects' scale.

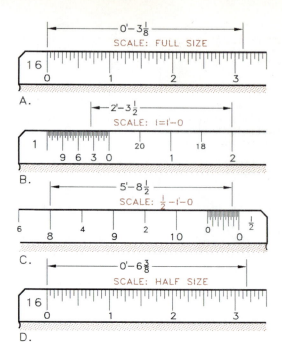

10.29 Lines measured with an architects' scale in feet and inches.

plumbing, and electrical layouts. Most indoor measurements are made in feet and inches with the architects' scale. **Figure 10.28** shows how to indicate the scale you are using on a drawing. Place this scale designation in the title block or in a prominent location on the drawing. Because dimensions measured with the architects' scale are in feet and inches, you must convert all dimensions to decimal equivalents (all feet or all inches) before making calculations.

Use the 16 scale for measuring full-size lines (**Fig. 10.29A**). An inch on the 16 scale is divided into sixteenths to match the ruler used by carpenters. The measurement shown is 3-1/8″. When the measurement is less than 1 ft, a zero may precede the inch measurements, with inch marks omitted, or 0′–3-1/2. (Inch marks are omitted since inches are understood to be the units of measurement in the English system.)

Figure 10.29B shows the use of the 1 = 1′–0 scale to measure a line. Read the nearest whole foot (2 ft in this case) and the remainder in inches from the end of the scale (3-1/2 in.) for a total of 2′–3-1/2. Note that at the end of each scale, a foot is divided into inches for measuring fractional parts of feet in inches. The scale 1″ =

1′–0 is the same as saying that 1 in. is equal to 12 in. or that the drawing is 1/12 the actual size of the object.

When you use the 1/2 = 1′–0 scale, 1/2 in. represents 12 in. on a drawing (1/24th size). The line in **Fig. 10.29C** measures 5′–8-1/2.

To obtain a half-size measurement, divide the full-size dimension by 2 and measure it with the 16 scale. Half size is sometimes specified as SCALE: 6 = 12 (inch marks omitted). The line in **Fig. 10.29D** measures to be 0′–6-3/8.

Letter dimensions in feet and inches as shown in **Fig. 10.30,** with fractions twice as tall as whole numerals.

Engineers' Scale

On the engineers' scale, each inch is divided into multiples of 10. Because it is used for making drawings of outdoor projects—streets, structures, tracts of land, and other topographical features—it is sometimes called the civil engineers' scale.

Omit inch marks   Zero here   Zero optional

10.30 Omit inch marks but show foot marks (according to current standards). When the inch measurement is less than a whole inch, use a leading zero.

FROM END OF SCALE

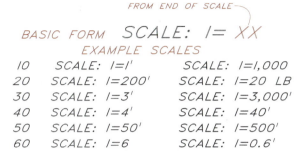

BASIC FORM   SCALE: 1= XX

EXAMPLE SCALES

10	SCALE: 1=1'	SCALE: 1=1,000	
20	SCALE: 1=200'	SCALE: 1=20 LB	
30	SCALE: 1=3'	SCALE: 1=3,000'	
40	SCALE: 1=4'	SCALE: 1=40'	
50	SCALE: 1=50'	SCALE: 1=500'	
60	SCALE: 1=6	SCALE: 1=0.6'	

10.31 Use this basic form to indicate the scale on a drawing made with an engineers' scale.

Figure **10.31** shows the form for specifying scales when using the engineers' scale. For example, scale: 1 = 10'. With measurements already in decimal form, calculations are easier because there is no need to convert common fractions, as there is when using the architects' scale.

Each end of the scale is labeled 10, 20, 30, and so on, which indicates the number of units per inch on the scale (**Fig. 10.32**). You may obtain many combinations simply by mentally moving the decimal places of a scale.

Figure **10.32A** shows the use of the 10 scale to measure a line 32.0 ft long drawn at the scale of 1 = 10'. Figure **10.32B** shows use of the 20 scale to measure a line 540.0 ft long drawn at a scale of 1 = 200'. Figure **10.32C** shows use of the 30 scale to measure a line of 9.6 in. long at a scale of 1 = 3. Figure **10.33** shows the proper format for indicating measurements in feet and inches.

English System of Units

The English (Imperial) system of units has been used in the United States, Great Britain (until

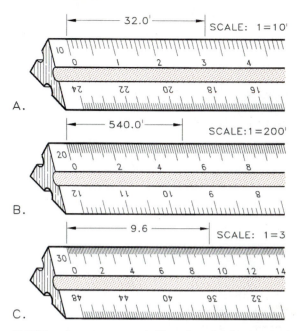

A.

B.

C.

10.32 These lines are measured with engineers' scales.

Omit zeros and inch marks

.13   2.13   0.15   0.13"

GOOD   GOOD   GOOD   POOR

No zero in front of decimal   Space for decimal   Zero for fractional feet   Decimal point crowded

10.33 For decimal fractions in inches, omit leading zeros and inch marks. For feet, leave adequate space for decimal points between numbers and show foot marks.

recently), and Canada since it was established. This system is based on arbitrary units (of length) of the inch, foot, cubit, yard, and mile. Because there is no common relationship among these units, calculations are cumbersome. For example, finding the area of a rectangle that measures 25 in. × 6-3/4 yd. first requires conversion into common units.

Metric System (SI) of Units

France proposed the metric system in the fifteenth century. In 1793 the French National Assembly agreed that the meter (m) would be

Value			Prefix	Symbol	Pronunciation
1 000 000	=	10^6	= Mega	M	"Megah"
1 000	=	10^3	= Kilo	k	"Keylow"
100	=	10^2	= Hecto	h	"Heck tow"
10	=	10^1	= Deka	da	"Dekah"
1	=				
0.1	=	10^{-1}	= Deci	d	"Des sigh"
0.01	=	10^{-2}	= Centi	c	"Cen'—ti"
0.001	=	10^{-3}	= Milli	m	"Mill lee"
0.000 001	=	10^{-6}	= Micro	μ	"Microw"

10.34 These prefixes and abbreviations indicate decimal place-ment for SI measurements.

one ten-millionth of the meridian quadrant of the earth and fractions of the meter would be expressed as decimal fractions. An international commission officially adopted the metric system in 1875.

The worldwide organization responsible for promoting the metric system is the **International Standards Organization (ISO).** It has endorsed the Syst'me International d'Unites (International System of Units), abbreviated **SI**. Prefixes to SI units indicate placement of the decimal, as **Fig. 10.34** shows.

Metric Scales

The meter is 39.37 inches. The basic metric unit of measurement for an engineering drawing is the millimeter (mm), which is one-thousandth of a meter, or one-tenth of a centimeter. Dimensions on a metric drawing are understood to be in millimeters unless otherwise specified.

The width of the fingernail of your index finger is a convenient way to approximate the dimension of one centimeter, or ten millimeters (**Fig. 10.35**). Depicted in **Fig. 10.36** is the format for specifying metric scales on a drawing.

Decimal fractions are unnecessary on most drawings dimensioned in millimeters. Thus dimensions are rounded off to whole numbers except for dimensions with specified tolerances. For measurements of less than 1, a zero goes in front of the decimal. In the English system, the

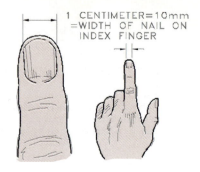

10.35 The nail width of your index finger is approximately equal to 1 centimeter, or 10 millimeters.

1 CENTIMETER=10mm =WIDTH OF NAIL ON INDEX FINGER

From end of scale

BASIC FORM   SCALE: 1= $\overline{XX}$

EXAMPLE SCALES

SCALE: 1:1   (1mm=1mm; 1cm=1cm)
SCALE: 1:2   (1mm=2mm; 1mm=20mm)
SCALE: 1:3   (1mm=30mm; 1mm=0.3mm)
SCALE: 1:4   (1mm=4mm; 1mm=40mm)
SCALE: 1:5   (1mm=5mm; 1mm=500mm)
SCALE: 1:6   (1mm=6mm; 1mm=60mm)

10.36 Use this basic form to indicate the scale of a drawing made with a metric scale.

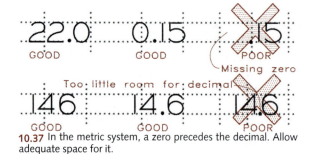

10.37 In the metric system, a zero precedes the decimal. Allow adequate space for it.

zero is omitted from measurements of less than an inch (**Fig. 10.37**).

Metric scales are expressed as ratios: 1:20, 1:40, 1:100, 1:500, and so on. These ratios mean that one unit represents the number of units to the right of the colon. For example, 1:10 means that 1 mm equals 10 mm, or 1 cm equals 10 cm, or 1 m equals 10 m. The full-size metric scale (**Fig. 10.38**) shows the relationship between the metric units of the decimeter, centimeter, millimeter, and micrometer. The line shown in **Fig. 10.39A** measures 59 mm. Use the 1:2 scale when

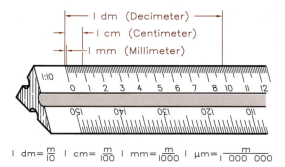

$1\ dm=\frac{m}{10}\quad 1\ cm=\frac{m}{100}\quad 1\ mm=\frac{m}{1000}\quad 1\ \mu m=\frac{m}{1\ 000\ 000}$

10.38 A decimeter is one tenth of the meter, a centimeter is one hundredth of a meter, a millimeter is one thousandth of a meter, and a micrometer is one millionth of a meter.

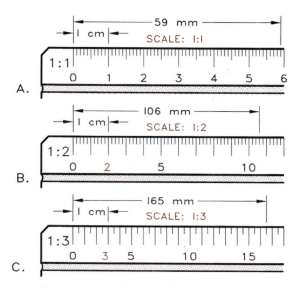

10.39 Measurements with metric scales.

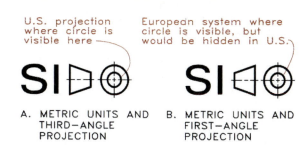

A. METRIC UNITS AND THIRD–ANGLE PROJECTION

B. METRIC UNITS AND FIRST–ANGLE PROJECTION

10.40 The large SI indicates that measurements are in metric units. The partial cones indicate whether the views are drawn in (A) the third-angle of projection (U.S. system), or (B) the first-angle of projection (European system).

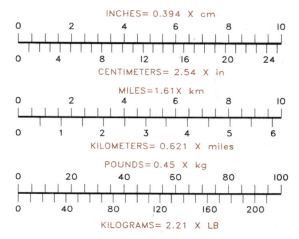

10.41 These scales show a comparison of the English system units with the metric system units.

1 mm represents 2 mm, 20 mm, 200 mm, and so on. The line shown in **Fig. 10.39B** measures 106 mm. **Figure 10.39C** shows a line measuring 165 mm, where 1 mm represents 3 mm.

Metric Symbols   To indicate that drawings are in metric units, insert SI in or near the title block (**Fig. 10.40**). The two views of the partial cone denote whether the orthographic views were drawn in accordance with the U.S. system (third-angle projection) or the European system

(first-angle projection). **Figure 10.41** shows several comparisons of English and SI units.

Expression of Metric Units   The general rules for expressing SI units are given in **Fig. 10.42.** Do not use commas to separate digits in large numbers; instead, leave a space between them, as shown.

Scale Conversion

The Appendix gives factors for converting English to metric lengths and vice versa. For example, multiply decimal inches by 25.4 to

Omit commas and group into threes	1 000 000 GOOD	1,000,000 POOR
Use a raised dot for multiplication	N•M GOOD	NM POOR
Precede decimals with zeros	0.72 mm GOOD	.72 mm POOR
Methods of division	kg/m or GOOD	kg•m⁻¹ GOOD

10.42 Follow these general gules for showing SI units.

obtain millimeters, and divide millimeters by 0.394 to obtain inches.

Multiply an architects' scale by 12 to convert it to an approximate metric scale. For example, Scale: 1/8 = 1'–0 is the same as 1/8 in. = 12 in. or 1 in. = 96 in., which closely approximates the metric scale of 1:100. You cannot convert most metric scales exactly to English scales, but the metric scale of 1:60 does convert exactly to 1 = 5', which is the same as 1 in. = 60 in.

10.6 Presentation of Drawings

The following formats are suggested for the presentation of drawings. Most problems can be drawn and solved on size A (8-1/2 × 11-inch) sheets in a vertical format with a title strip, as **Fig. 10.43** shows. Size A sheets can also be laid out in a horizontal format as **Fig. 10.44** shows.

Figure 10.44 shows the standard sizes of sheets, from size A through size E, and an alternative title strip for sizes A through E. Always use guidelines for lettering title strips.

Problems

Problems 1–9 (Figs. 10.45 -10.47): Draw these problems on size A sheets, with or without a printed grid, using the format shown in **Fig. 10.45.** You may be assigned to solve two half-size drawings per sheet on size A sheets. Each grid represents 0.25 in. or 6 mm.

Problems 10–20 (Figs. 10.48-10.58): Draw full-

size views on size A sheets (horizontal format) and omit the dimensions.

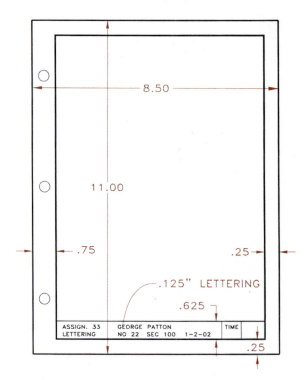

10.43 Use the format and title strip shown for a size A (vertical format) to present the solutions to problems at the end of each chapter.

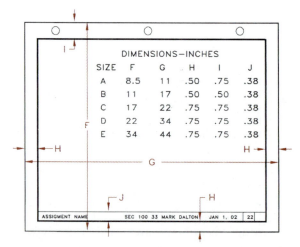

DIMENSIONS—INCHES					
SIZE	F	G	H	I	J
A	8.5	11	.50	.75	.38
B	11	17	.50	.50	.38
C	17	22	.75	.75	.38
D	22	34	.75	.75	.38
E	34	44	.75	.75	.38

10.44 Format sizes for A through E sheets are shown here in columns F through J.

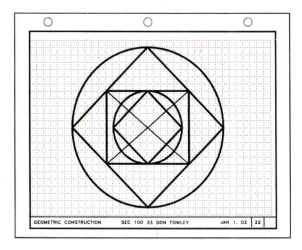

10.45 Problem 1 and sheet format.

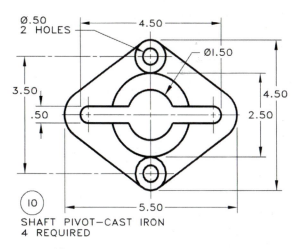

10.48 Problem 10.

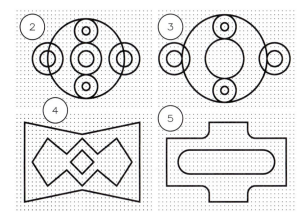

10.46 Problems 2–5.

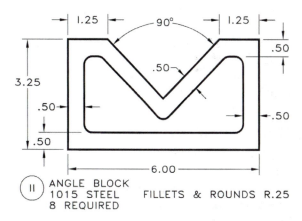

10.49 Problem 11.

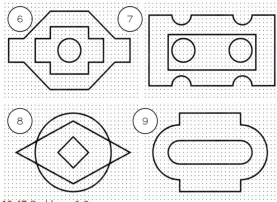

10.47 Problems 6-9.

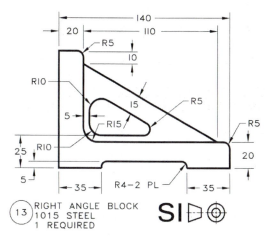

10.50 Problem 12.

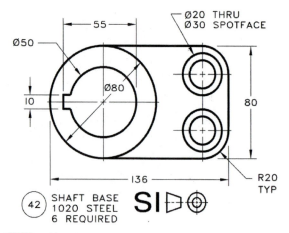

10.51 Problem 13.

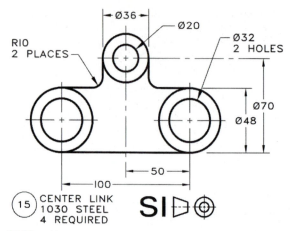

10.54 Problem 16.

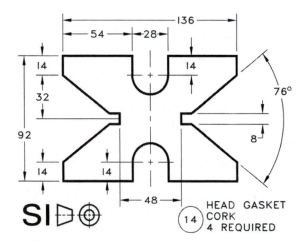

10.52 Problem 14.

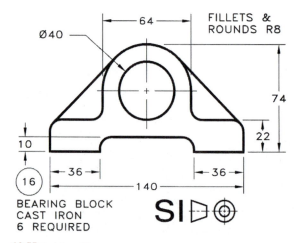

10.55 Problem 17.

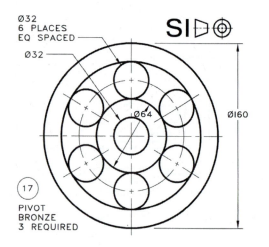

10.53 Problem 15.

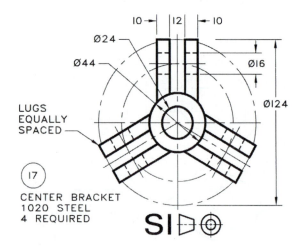

10.56 Problem 18.

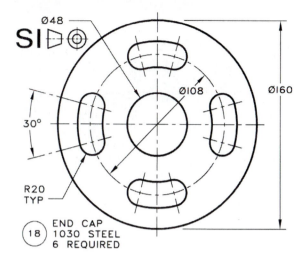

10.57 Problem 19.

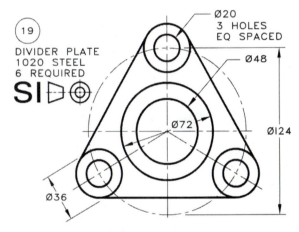

10.58 Problem 20.

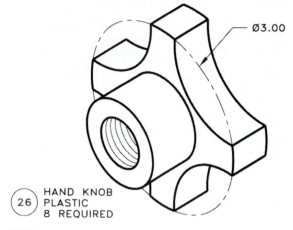

10.59 Problem 21.

Design Application

Design 1.

The knob in **Fig. 10.59** has a diameter of 3 in. (flat-to-flat). Make an instrument drawing of the descriptive end of this part; estimate the dimensions as if you were its designer.

Design 2.

Make an instrument drawing of the film reel in **Fig. 10.60** as it is shown, or design your own configuration of it using your own geometry while adhering to the overall dimensions.

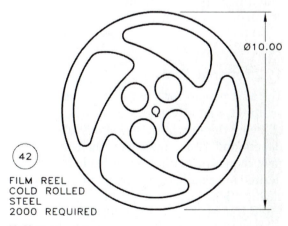

10.60 Problem 22.

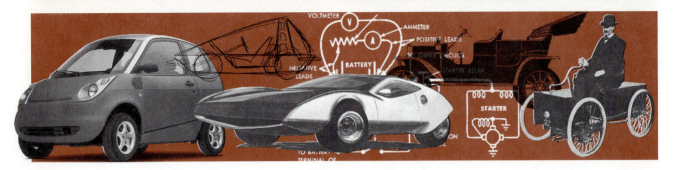

CHAPTER ELEVEN

Lettering

11.1 Introduction

Notes, dimensions, and specifications, which must be lettered, supplement all drawings. The ability to letter freehand is an important skill to develop because it affects the use and interpretation of drawings. It also displays an engineer's skill with graphics, and may be taken as an indication of professional competence.

11.2 Lettering Tools

The best pencils for lettering on most surfaces are the H, F, and HB grades, with an F grade pencil being the one most commonly used. Some papers and films are coarser than others and may require a harder pencil lead. To give the desired line width, round the point of the pencil slightly (**Fig. 11.1**), because a needle point is likely to snap off when you apply pressure to it.

Revolve the pencil about its axis with each stroke so that the lead will wear evenly. For good reproduction, bear down firmly to make letters

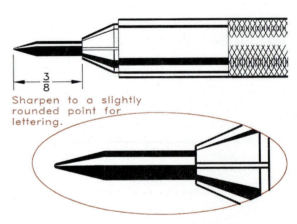

Sharpen to a slightly rounded point for lettering.

11.1 Good lettering begins with a properly sharpened pencil point. The F grade pencil is good for lettering.

black and bright with a single stroke. Prevent smudging while lettering by placing a sheet of paper under your hand to protect the drawing (**Fig. 11.2**). And, by all means, keep your hands clean to avoid smudges.

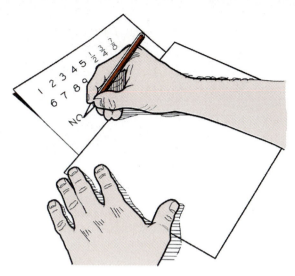

11.2 Place a protective sheet under your hand to prevent smudges and work from a comfortable position for natural strokes.

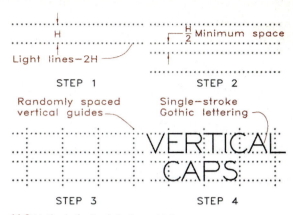

11.3 Method of using lettering guidelines

Step 1 Lay off letter heights, H, and draw light guidelines with a 2H pencil.

Step 2 Space lines no closer than H/2 apart.

Step 3 Draw vertical guidelines as light, thin, randomly spaced lines.

Step 4 Draw letters with single strokes using a medium-grade pencil: H, F, or HB. Leave the guidelines.

11.3 Guidelines

The most important rule of lettering is to **use guidelines at all times**, whether you are lettering a paragraph or a single letter. **Figure 11.3** shows how to draw and use guidelines. Use a sharp pencil in the 2H, 3H, or 4H grade range and draw light guidelines, just dark enough to be seen.

Most lettering on an engineering drawing is done with capital letters that are 1/8 inch (3 mm) high. The spacing between lines of lettering should be no closer than half the height of the capital letters, or 1/16 inch in this case.

Lettering Guides

Two instruments for drawing guidelines are the **Braddock-Rowe** lettering triangle and the **Ames** lettering instrument.

The Braddock-Rowe triangle contains sets of holes for spacing guidelines (**Fig. 11.4**). The numbers under each set of holes represent thirty-seconds of an inch. For example, the numeral 4 represents 4/32 inch or 1/8 inch for making uppercase (capital) letters. Some triangles have millimeter markings. Intermediate

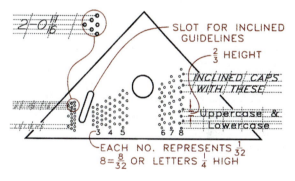

11.4 The Braddock-Rowe triangle is used for drawing guidelines for lettering. The numbers near the guideline holes represent thirty-seconds of an inch.

holes provide guidelines for lowercase letters, which are not as tall as capital letters.

While holding a horizontal straightedge firmly in position, place the Braddock-Rowe triangle against its upper edge. Insert a sharpened 2H pencil point in the desired guideline hole to contact the drawing surface and guide the pencil point across the paper, drawing the guideline

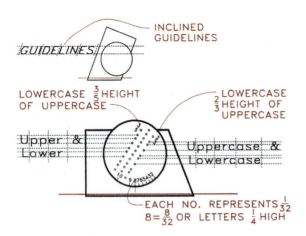

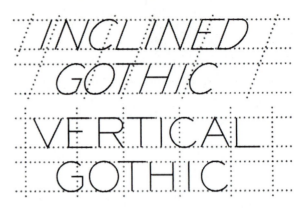

11.6 Use either vertical or inclined single-stroke Gothic lettering on engineering drawings.

11.5 The Ames guide is used for drawing guidelines for lettering. Set the dial to the desired number of thirty-seconds of an inch for the height of uppercase letters.

while the triangle slides along the straightedge. Repeat this procedure by moving the pencil point to each successive hole to draw other guidelines. Use the slanted slot in the triangle to draw guidelines, spaced randomly, for inclined lettering.

The **Ames lettering guide (Fig. 11.5)** is a similar device but has a circular dial for selecting guideline spacing. The numbers around the dial represent thirty-seconds of an inch. For example, the number 8 represents 8/32 inch, or guidelines for drawing capital letters that are 1/4 inch tall.

11.4 Gothic Lettering

The lettering recommended for engineering drawings is single-stroke Gothic lettering, so called because the letters are a variation of the Gothic style made with a series of single strokes. Gothic lettering may be vertical or inclined (**Fig. 11.6**), but only one style or the other should be used on a single drawing.

Vertical Letters
Uppercase Figure 11.7 shows the alphabet in the single-stroke Gothic uppercase (capital) let-

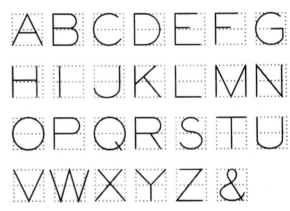

11.7 This alphabet shows the form of single-stroke Gothic vertical uppercase letters. Letters are drawn inside squares to show their proportions.

ters. Each letter is drawn inside a square box of guidelines to show their correct proportions. Draw straight lines with a single stroke; for example, draw the letter A with three single strokes. Letters composed of curves can best be drawn in segments; for example, draw the letter O by joining two semicircles.

The shape (form) of each letter is important. Small wiggles in strokes will not detract from your lettering if the letter forms are correct. **Figure 11.8** shows common errors in lettering that you should avoid.

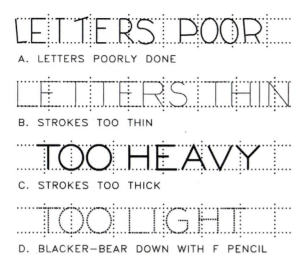

A. LETTERS POORLY DONE

B. STROKES TOO THIN

C. STROKES TOO THICK

D. BLACKER—BEAR DOWN WITH F PENCIL

11.8 Avoid these common errors when lettering.

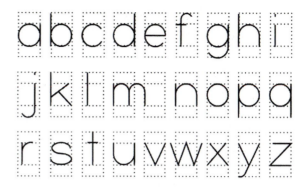

11.9 The alphabet is drawn here in single-stroke Gothic vertical lowercase letters.

A. Lowercase $\frac{2}{3}$ height of caps

B. Lowercase $\frac{3}{5}$ height of caps

From Ames guide

11.10 The ratio of lowercase letters to uppercase letters should be either two-thirds (A) or three-fifths (B). The Ames guide has both ratios, but the Braddock-Rowe triangle has only the two-thirds ratio.

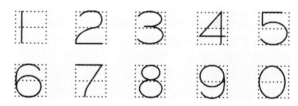

11.11 These numerals are used with single-stroke Gothic, vertical letters.

Lowercase   The alphabet of lowercase letters is shown in **Figure 11.9**, which should be either two-thirds or three-fifths as tall as uppercase letters. Both lowercase ratios are labeled on the Ames guide, but only the two-thirds ratio is available on the Braddock-Rowe triangle.

Some lowercase letters, such as the letter b, have ascenders that extend above the body of the letter; some, such as the letter p, have descenders that extend below the body. Ascenders and descenders are equal in length.

The guidelines in **Fig. 11.9** that form squares about the body of each letter are used to illustrate their proportions. Letters that have circular bodies may extend slightly beyond the sides of the guideline squares. **Figure 11.10** shows examples of capital and lowercase letters used together.

Numerals   Vertical numerals for use with single-stroke Gothic lettering are shown in **Fig. 11.11**; each numeral is enclosed in a square of guidelines. Numbers should be the same height as the capital letters being used, usually 1/8 inch. The numeral 0 (zero) is an oval, whereas the letter O is a circle in vertical lettering.

Inclined Letters

Uppercase   Inclined uppercase (capital) letters have the same heights and proportions as vertical letters; the only difference is their 68° inclination (**Fig. 11.12**). Guidelines for inclined lettering can be drawn with both the Braddock-Rowe triangle and the Ames guide.

11.12 This is an alphabet of single-stroke Gothic, inclined upper-case letters.

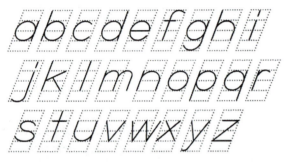

11.13 This is an alphabet of single-stroke Gothic, inclined lowercase letters.

Lowercase Inclined lowercase letters are drawn in the same manner as vertical lowercase letters (**Fig. 11.13**), but circular features are drawn as ovals (ellipses). Their angle of inclination is 68°, the same as for uppercase letters.

Numerals Examples of inclined numerals and letters used in combination are shown in **Fig. 11.14** and **Fig. 11.15**. The ratio of lowercase to uppercase letters should be either two-thirds (A) or three-fifths (B). The Ames guide has both ratios, but the Braddock-Rowe triangle has only the two-thirds ratio. Inclined letters and numbers are used in combination in **Fig. 11.15**. Guidelines are drawn using the Braddock-Rowe triangle or the Ames lettering guide, as shown in **Fig. 11.16**.

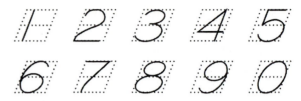

11.14 Single-stroke Gothic, inclined numerals.

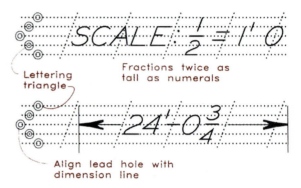

11.15 Inclined common fractions are twice as tall as single numerals. Omit inch marks in dimensions.

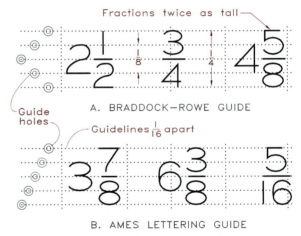

11.16 Guidelines are drawn for fractions so they can be twice as tall as single numerals.

Spacing Numerals and Letters

Allow adequate space between numerals for the decimal point in fractions (**Fig. 11.17**). Common fractions are twice as tall as single numerals (**Fig. 11.17**). Both the Braddock-Rowe triangle and the Ames guide have separate sets of holes

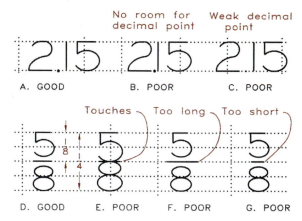

A. GOOD   B. POOR   C. POOR

No room for decimal point   Weak decimal point

Touches   Too long   Too short

D. GOOD   E. POOR   F. POOR   G. POOR

11.17 Avoid making these errors in lettering fractions.

A. GOOD—EQUAL AREAS BETWEEN LETTERS

B. POOR—EQUAL LINEAR SPACING

11.18 Letters should be spaced so that the areas between them are about equal.

Leave at least one-half letter height between lines!

DON'T EVEN THINK ABOUT LETTERING LIKE THIS

Drawing guidelines is not enough. You must USE them!

USE THE GUIDELINES

11.19 Always use guidelines (vertical and horizontal), whether you are lettering a paragraph or a single letter.

ABCDEFGHIJKLMNO
PQRSTUVWXYZ&%
01234567890abcd
efghijklmnopqrstu
vwxyz

11.20 *Romans* is the text (font) that is most like Gothic lettering and is recommended for engineering drawings. *Romand* is the same letter form drawn with a double stroke, which is often better when plotted with a laser printer.

spaced 1/16 inch apart for common fractions. The center guideline locates the fraction's cross-bar (**Fig. 11.15**).

When grouping letters to spell words, make the areas between the letters approximately equal for the most visually pleasing result (**Fig. 11.18**). **Figure 11.19** shows the incorrect use of guidelines and other violations of good lettering practice that you should avoid.

11.5 Computer Lettering

Although AutoCAD offers a wide range of lettering (text) fonts, the *Romans* font shown in **Fig. 11.20** is the Gothic single-stroke text recommended for engineering drawings. *Dtext* (dynamic text found under *Draw> Text> Single Line Text,* or by typing *Dtext)* is the command that applies text to a drawing on the screen as it is typed at the keyboard:

Command: DTEXT (Enter)
Specify start point of text or [Justify/Style]: I (Enter)
[Align/Fit/Center/Middle/Right/TL/TC/ TR/ML/MC/MR/BL/BC/BR]:

Some of the abbreviations in the last line above are insertion points for lines of text defined in **Fig. 11.21**.

By typing *Style* at the command line (or selecting *Text Style* under *Format,* a dialogue box appears on the screen that enables you to name a *New* text file, RS, for example (**Fig. 11.22**). You can select and assign a font to RS, specify the text height (zero is preferred because it lets you specify any desired height on the screen), assign a width factor, and specify an obliquing angle.

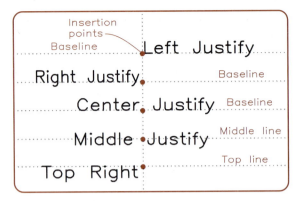

11.21 The options of *Dtext/Justify* are available for variations in text (lettering) placement.

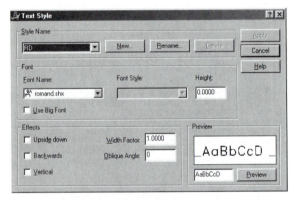

11.22 The *Text Style* menu *(Format> Text Style)* can be used to assign various characteristics to the letter form (text) being used. (See Chapter 27 for more details.)

Once these settings have been made, type *Dtext* at the command line and respond to the options shown in **Fig. 11.23**, and at the prompt *Enter text*, type the text and it will appear on the screen as it is typed.

RS is now the current style with the font of *Romans;* it has a height of zero, and each letter has a width that is 120 percent (1.2 times) the default width. The width of 1.2 matches the recommended letter proportions of Gothic engineering lettering. Assigning zero permits you to change heights by responding when prompted by the *Dtext* command. Had a height been specified, it would remain constant until you modified using the *Style* command. Additional

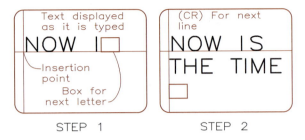

11.23 The *Dtext* command
Step 1 *Command:* DTEXT (Enter)
Specify start point of text or [Justify/Style]: (Cursor-select)
Specify height <.18>: .125 (Enter)
Specify rotation angle of text <0>: 0 (Enter)
Enter text: NOW IS (Enter)
Step 2 (Box moves to start of next line.)
Enter text: THE TIME (Enter) (Box moves to start of next line. Press (Enter) to save text.)

information on AutoCAD lettering is covered in Section 38 of Chapter 26.

Problems

Complete these lettering exercises on size A (11 × 8-1/2-in., horizontal format) sheets, with or without printed grids, using the format shown in **Fig. 11.24**.

1. Draw the alphabet in vertical, uppercase letters as shown in **Fig. 11.24**. Draw each letter three times: three As, three Bs, and so on. Use a medium-weight pencil: H, F, or HB.

2. Draw vertical numerals and the alphabet in lowercase letters, as shown in **Fig. 11.25**. Construct each letter and numeral two times: two 1s, two 2s, two a's, two b's, and so on. Use a medium-weight pencil: H, F, or HB.

3. Draw the alphabet as inclined uppercase letters, as shown in **Fig. 11.12**. Construct each letter three times with a medium-weight pencil (H, F, or HB), as shown in **Fig. 11.24**.

4. Draw the vertical numerals and the alphabet in lowercase letters, as shown in **Figs. 11.13** and

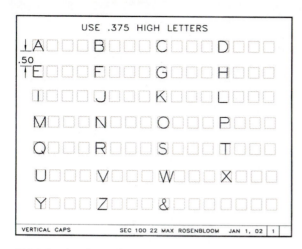

11.24 The sheet layout for lettering assignments.

11.25 A typical sheet layout for lettering assignments.

11.14. Draw each letter two times (**Fig. 11.25**). Use a medium-weight pencil: H, F, or HB.

5. Construct guidelines for 1/8-in. capital letters starting 1/4 in. from the top border of a sheet similar to the one shown in **Fig. 11.25**. Each guideline should end 1/2 in. from the left and right borders. Letter the first paragraph of the text of this chapter using all vertical capitals. Spacing between the lines should be 1/8 in.

6. Repeat Problem 5, but use inclined capital (uppercase) letters. Use inclined guidelines to help you slant letters uniformly.

7. Repeat Problem 5, but use vertical capital and lowercase letters in combination. Capitalize only those words capitalized in the text.

8. Repeat Problem 5, but use inclined capital and lowercase letters in combination. Capitalize only those letters that are capitalized in the text. Use single-stroke Gothic vertical lowercase letters.

> We, the people of the United States, in order to form a more perfect Union, establish justice, insure domestic tranquility, provide for the common defense, promote the general welfare, and secure the blessings of liberty to ourselves and our posterity, do ordain and establish this Constitution for the United States of America.
>
> PREAMBLE: CONSTITUTION   SEC 100 22 TOM JEFFERSON   JAN 1, 03   3

11.26 The Preamble of the Constitution of the United States.

9. As a fun project, experiment with the available fonts of AutoCAD and select an appropriate one to make a copy of the Preamble of the Constitution of the United States (Fig. 11.26), a very significant document for all Americans. Try to make your version look as much like the original as possible, maybe do a little research.

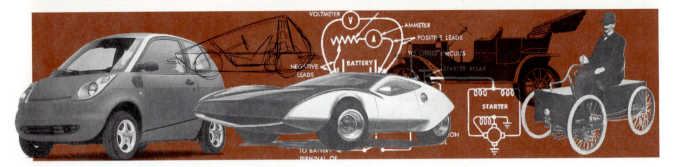

Geometric Construction

12.1 Introduction

Many graphical problems are solved by geometry and geometric construction. Because mathematics was an outgrowth of graphical construction, the two areas are closely related. The proofs of many principles of plane geometry and trigonometry can be developed by using graphics. Graphical methods can be applied to solve some types of problems in algebra and arithmetic, and virtually all types of problems in analytical geometry.

12.2 Constructing Polygons

A **regular polygon**, a polygon that has sides of equal lengths, can be inscribed in or circumscribed about a circle. When it is inscribed, all corner points of the polygon will lie on the circle For example, a 10-sided polygon (called a **decagon**) is constructed by dividing a circle into ten sectors to locate points on the circle and

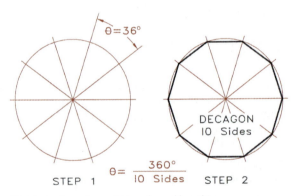

12.1 A regular polygon (sides of equal length)

Step 1 Divide the circle into the correct number of sectors, 10 in this example.

Step 2 Connect the division points with straight lines where they intersect the circle. A ten-sided polygon is a decagon.

connecting them to form the polygon, as shown in **Fig. 12.1**.

Triangles

The polygon with the fewest number of sides is the triangle. When you know the lengths of all

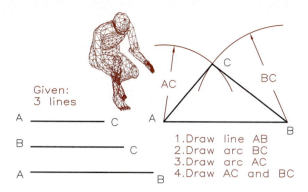

Given:
3 lines

A _____ C

B _____ C

A _____ B

1. Draw line AB
2. Draw arc BC
3. Draw arc AC
4. Draw AC and BC

12.2 A triangle, the polygon with the fewest sides, can be constructed by triangulation with a compass when three sides are given.

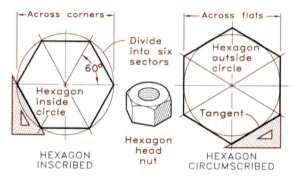

12.3 A hexagon can be inscribed in or circumscribed about a circle with a 30°–60° triangle.

three sides of a triangle, you may construct it with a compass by triangulation, as shown in **Fig. 12.2**.

Hexagons

The **hexagon**, a six-sided regular polygon, can be inscribed in or circumscribed about a circle (**Fig. 12.3**). Use a 30°–60° triangle to divide the circle into six sectors and draw the hexagon. The circle represents the distance from corner to corner for an inscribed hexagon, and from flat to flat when the hexagon is circumscribed about a circle.

Octagons

The **octagon**, an eight-sided regular polygon, can be inscribed in or circumscribed about a cir-

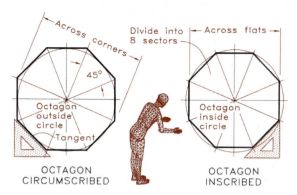

12.4 An octagon can be inscribed in or circumscribed about a circle with a 45° triangle.

cle, as shown in **Fig. 12.4**. Use a 45° triangle to divide the circle into eight sectors. When the octagon is circumscribed, the sides are drawn tangent to the circle. When the octagon is inscribed, the corner points found on the circle are connected.

Pentagons

The **pentagon**, a five-sided regular polygon, can be inscribed in or circumscribed about a circle with the same techniques as used in drawing other regular polygons. The steps of constructing a pentagon in the classic manner with a compass and straightedge are shown in **Fig. 12.5**, where the five corners lie on the circle.

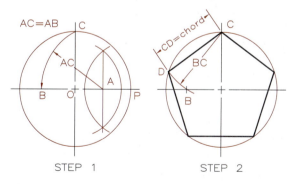

12.5 Constructing an inscribed pentagon:

Step 1 Bisect radius OP to locate point A. With center A and radius AC, locate point B on the diameter.

Step 2 With point C as the center and BC as the radius, locate point D. Use line CD as the chord to locate the other corners of the pentagon.

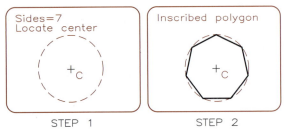

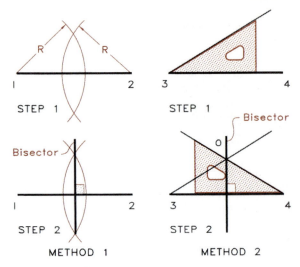

STEP 1 · STEP 1

STEP 2 — METHOD 1 · STEP 2 — METHOD 2

12.6 A polygon by computer: (Draw Menu)

Step 1 *Command:* Polygon (Enter)

Enter number of sides: 7 (Enter)

Specify center of polygon or [Edge]: (Locate with cursor.)

Enter and option [Inscribed in circle/Circumscribed about circle] I: I (Enter)

Step 2 *Specify radius of circle:* (Drag cursor to select R. Polygon is inscribed inside the imaginary circle.)

12.7 Bisecting a line:

Method 1 Use a compass and any radius.

Method 2 Use a triangle and a straightedge.

Computer Method You may use one of two *Polygon* options from under the *Draw* command to draw polygons (**Fig. 12.6**). The *Center* option asks you to give the number of sides, select the center, specify the radius, and indicate whether the polygon is to be inscribed in or circumscribed about an imaginary circle. The *Edge* option allows you to specify the number of sides and specify the length and direction of one edge of the polygon before drawing it.

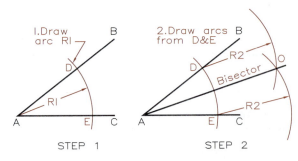

STEP 1 · STEP 2

12.8 Bisecting an angle:

Step 1 Swing arc R1 to locate points D and E.

Step 2 Draw equal arcs from D and E to locate point O. Line AO is the bisector of the angle.

12.3 Bisecting Lines and Angles

Bisecting Lines

Two methods of finding the midpoint of a line with a perpendicular bisector are shown in **Fig. 12.7**. In the first method, a compass is used to construct the perpendicular bisector of the line. In the second method, a standard triangle and a straightedge are used in combination.

Bisecting Angles

You may bisect angles by using a compass and drawing three arcs, as shown in **Fig. 12.8**.

Computer Method Use the *Arc* command (with *Osnap* set to *Midpoint*) and draw an arc of

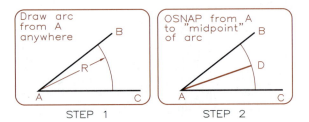

STEP 1 · STEP 2

12.9 Bisecting an angle by computer: (*Draw* menu)

Step 1 Use the *Arc* command, any radius, and center A, to draw an arc that *Osnaps*, *Nearest* to AC and AB.

Step 2 *Command:* Line (Enter)

Specify first point or [Undo]: Mid (Enter)

(Midpoint option) and select the arc to snap to D. Draw line AD as the bisector of the angle.

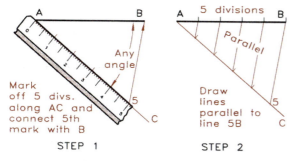

STEP 1

STEP 2

12.10 Dividing a line

Step 1 To divide line AB into five equal lengths, lay off five equal divisions along line AC, and connect point 5 to end B with a construction line.

Step 2 Draw a series of five construction lines parallel to 5B to divide line AB into five equal parts.

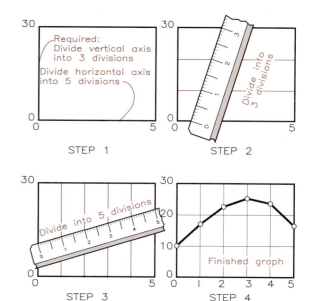

STEP 1

STEP 2

STEP 3

STEP 4

12.11 Dividing axes on a graph

Step 1 Draw the outline of the graph.

Step 2 Divide the y axis into equal segments with a scale of three units that span the graph with 0 and 3 located on the top and bottom lines. Mark points 1 and 2 and draw horizontal lines through them.

Step 3 Divide the x axis into equal segments with a scale of five units that span the graph with 0 and 5 on the left- and right-hand vertical lines. Mark points 1, 2, 3, and 4 and draw vertical lines through them.

Step 4 Plot the data points and draw the curve to complete the graph.

a convenient radius between the two lines with its center at vertex A (**Fig. 12.9**). Use the *Line* command (with *Osnap* set to *Midpoint)* to draw a line from vertex A to the arc's midpoint at D. Line AD is the bisector.

12.4 Division of Lines

Dividing a line into several equal parts is often necessary. **Figure 12.10** shows the method used to solve this type of problem where the line AB is divided into five equal lengths by using a convenient scale to lay off the five divisions.

The same principle applies to locating equally spaced lines on a graph (**Fig. 12.11**). Lay scales with the desired number of units (0 to 3 and 0 to 5, respectively) across the graph up and down and then left to right. Make marks at each whole unit and draw vertical and horizontal index lines through these points. These index lines are used to show data in a graph.

12.5 An Arc Through Three Points

An arc can be drawn through three points (**Fig. 12.12**) by connecting the points with two lines and drawing perpendicular bisectors through each line to locate the center of the circle at C.

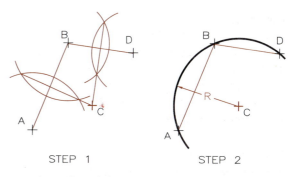

STEP 1

STEP 2

12.12 An arc through three points

Step 1 Connect points A, B, and D with two lines and construct their perpendicular bisectors, which intersect at center C.

Step 2 Use center C and the distance to the points as the radius, R, to draw the arc through the points.

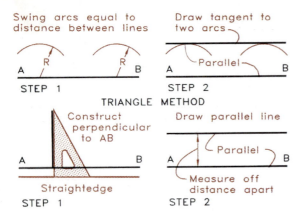

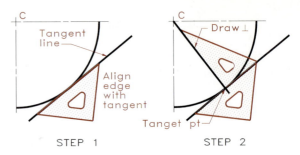

STEP 1   STEP 2

TRIANGLE METHOD

12.13 Drawing parallel lines

Compass Method

Step 1 Swing two equal arcs from line AB.

Step 2 Draw the parallel line tangent to the arcs.

Triangle Method

Step 1 Draw a line perpendicular to AB.

Step 2 Measure the desired distance, R, along the perpendicular and draw the parallel line through it.

12.14 Locating a tangent point

Step 1 Align a triangle with the tangent line and hold it firmly in position.

Step 2 With a second triangle, draw a line from center C perpendicular to the first triangle to locate the tangent point.

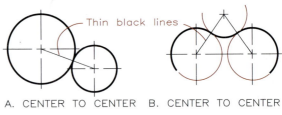

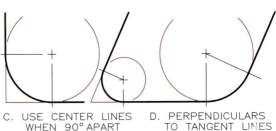

A. CENTER TO CENTER   B. CENTER TO CENTER

C. USE CENTER LINES   D. PERPENDICULARS
   WHEN 90° APART   TO TANGENT LINES

12.15 Use thin, black lines that extend from the centers slightly beyond the arcs to mark tangency points.

Draw the arc, and lines AB and BD become chords of the arc.

To find the center of a circle or an arc, reverse this process by drawing two chords that intersect at a point on the circumference and bisecting them. The perpendicular bisectors intersect at the center of the circle.

12.6 Parallel Lines

You may draw one line parallel to another by using either method shown in **Fig. 12.13**. In the first method, use a compass and draw two arcs having radius R to locate a parallel line at the desired distance (R) from the first line. In the second method, measure the desired perpendicular distance R from the first line, mark it, and draw the parallel line through it with your drafting machine.

12.7 Tangents

Marking Points of Tangency

A point of tangency is the theoretical point at which a line joins an arc or two arcs join without crossing. **Figure 12.14** shows how to find the

point of tangency with triangles by constructing a perpendicular line to the tangent line from the arc's center. **Figure 12.15** shows the conventional methods of marking points of tangency.

Line Tangent to an Arc

The classical compass method of finding the point of tangency between a line and a point is shown in **Fig. 12.16**. Connect point A to the arc's center and bisect line AC (step 1); swing an arc from point M through point C locating tangent point T (step 2); draw the tangent to T (step 3); and mark the tangent point (step 4).

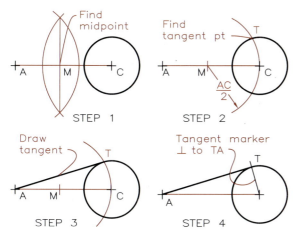

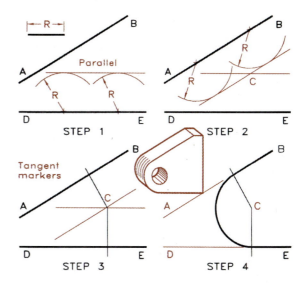

12.16 A line tangent to an arc from a point

Step 1 Draw a line from point A to center C; bisect AC to find point M.

Step 2 Use center M and radius MC to locate point T on the arc.

Step 3 Draw a line from A to T on the circle.

Step 4 Draw the tangent line from the center perpendicular to TA and past the arc as a thin, dark line.

12.18 An arc tangent to lines making an acute angle

Step 1 Draw a light line parallel to DE with radius R.

Step 2 Draw a second light line parallel to and R distant from line AB to locate center C.

Step 3 Draw thin, dark lines from center C perpendicular to AB and DE to locate the tangency points.

Step 4 Draw the arc and darken lines.

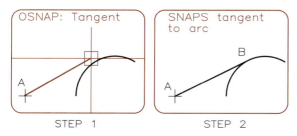

12.17 A line tangent to an arc by computer

Step 1 *Command:* Line (Enter)

Specify first point or [Undo]: A (Select point A)

Specify next point or [Undo]: Tan (Enter)

Step 2 *to:* (Select point on arc near tangent point.)

Line AB is drawn tangent to the arc.

Computer Method   A line can be drawn from a point tangent to an arc by using the *Osnap Tangent* option (**Fig. 12.17**). When prompted for the second point, select a point on the arc near the tangent point and the line will be drawn to the true tangent point.

Arc Tangent to Two Lines

Figure 12.18 shows how to construct an arc of a given radius tangent to two nonparallel lines

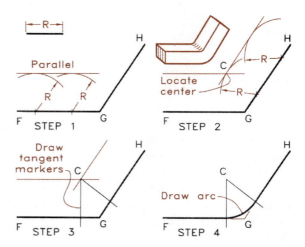

12.19 An arc tangent to lines making an obtuse angle

Step 1 Use radius R to draw a line parallel to FG.

Step 2 Construct another light line parallel to GH that is R distant from it to locate center C.

Step 3 Draw thin, dark lines from center C perpendicular to FG and GH to locate the tangency points.

Step 4 Draw the tangent arc and darken your lines.

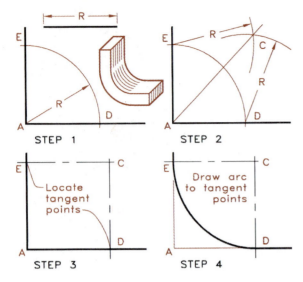

STEP 1   STEP 2

STEP 3   STEP 4

12.20 An arc tangent to perpendicular lines

Step 1 Using radius R and center A, locate D and E.

Step 2 Find C by swinging two arcs with radius R.

Step 3 Perpendiculars CE and CD locate tangent pts.

Step 4 Draw the tangent arc and darken your lines.

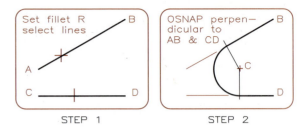

STEP 1   STEP 2

12.21 An arc tangent to two lines by computer

Step 1 *Command: Fillet* (Enter)

Select first object or [Polyline/Radius/Trim]: <u>R</u> (Enter)

Specify fillet radius [0.0000]: <u>.75</u> (Enter)

Command: (Enter)

Select first object or [Polyline/Radius/Trim]: (Select points on AB and CD.)

Step 2 *Command:* <u>Line</u> (Enter)

Line from first point: <u>Center</u> (Enter) *of* (Select point on the arc.)

Specify next point or [Undo]: <u>Perpen</u> (Enter) *to* (Select line AB; a perpendicular is drawn to the point of tangency. Locate the tangent point on CD in the same manner.)

that form an acute angle. The same steps apply to constructing an arc tangent to two lines that form an obtuse angle (**Fig. 12.19**). In both cases, the points of tangency are located with thin, dark lines drawn from their centers perpendicular to and past the original lines. **Figure 12.20** shows the steps for finding an arc tangent to lines that are perpendicular.

Computer Method   Draw an arc tangent to two nonparallel lines with the *Fillet* command from the *Modify* menu (**Fig. 12.21**). When the radius length has been set and a point selected on each line, the arc is drawn and the lines trimmed. To mark the tangent points, *Snap* to the center of the arc with the *Center* option of *Osnap* and draw two lines perpendicular (use *Osnap's Perpend* option) to lines AB and CD from center C.

Arc Tangent to an Arc and a Line

Figure 12.22 shows the steps for constructing an arc tangent to an arc and a line. **Figure 12.23**

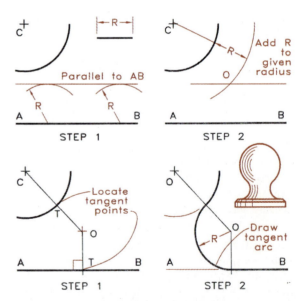

STEP 1   STEP 2

STEP 1   STEP 2

12.22 An arc tangent to an arc and a line

Step 1 Draw a line parallel to AB that is R distant from it.

Step 2 Add radius R to the radius from center C. Swing the extended radius to find the center O.

Step 3 Lines OC and OT locate the tangency pts.

Step 4 Draw the tangent arc between the points of tangency with radius R and center O.

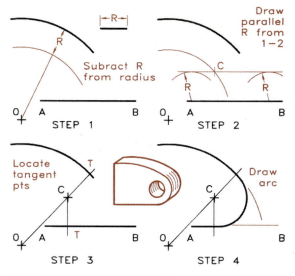

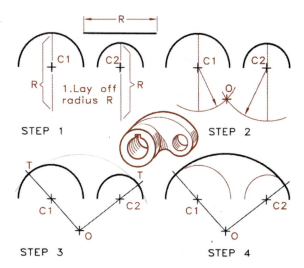

12.23 An arc tangent to an arc and a line

Step 1 Subtract radius R from the radius through center O. Draw a concentric arc.

Step 2 Draw a line parallel to line AB and R distant from it to locate center C.

Step 3 Locate the tangency points with lines OC and from C perpendicular to AB.

Step 4 Draw the arc between the tangent points with radius R and center C.

12.25 A convex arc tangent to two arcs

Step 1 Extend each radius from the arc past its center by a distance of radius R along these radii.

Step 2 Use the distances from C1 and C2 to the ends of the radii and swing arcs to locate center O.

Step 3 Draw thin, dark lines from center O through centers C1 and C2 to locate the points of tangency.

Step 4 Draw the arc between the tangent points using radius R and center O.

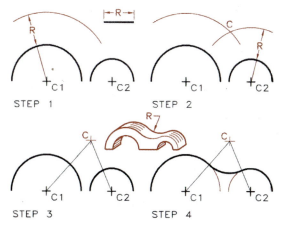

12.24 A concave arc tangent to two arcs

Step 1 Add radius R to the radius from center C1. Draw a concentric arc with the extended radius.

Step 2 Add radius R to the radius from center C2 of the other circle. Draw a concentric arc with this extended radius to locate center C.

Step 3 Draw thin, dark lines from center C to centers C1 and C2 to locate the tangency points.

Step 4 Draw the arc between the points of tangency using radius R and center C.

shows a variation of this technique for an arc drawn tangent to a given arc and line where the arc is reversed.

Arc Tangent to Two Arcs

Figure 12.24 shows how to draw a concave arc tangent to two arcs. Lines drawn from center C to centers C1 and C2 locate the points of tangency. The resulting tangent arc is concave from the upper side of the arcs. Drawing a convex arc tangent to the given arcs requires that its radius be greater than the radius of either of the given arcs, as shown in **Fig. 12.25**.

One variation of this problem (**Fig. 12.26**) is to draw an arc of a given radius tangent to the top of one arc and the bottom of the other. Another variation (**Fig. 12.27**) is to draw an arc tangent to a circle and a larger arc. You will notice that the same basic principles apply in each of these examples.

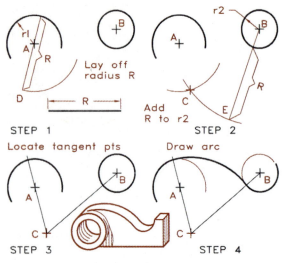

12.26 An arc tangent to two circles

Step 1 Lay off radius R from the arc along the extended radius to locate point D. Swing arc AD.

Step 2 Extend the radius from center B and add radius R to it. Use radius BE to locate center C.

Step 3 Draw thin, dark lines from center C through centers A and B to locate the points of tangency.

Step 4 Draw the tangent arc between the tangent points using radius R and center C.

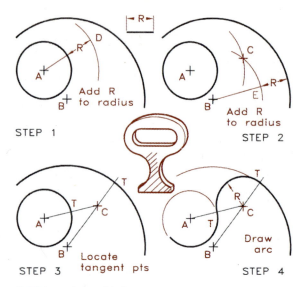

12.27 An arc tangent to two arcs

Step 1 Add radius R to the radius from A. Use radius AD to draw a concentric arc from center A.

Step 2 Subtract radius R from the radius through B. Use radius BE to draw an arc to locate center C.

Step 3 Draw thin, dark lines to connect the centers and mark the points of tangency.

Step 4 Draw the tangent arc between the tangency points using radius R and center C.

Computer Method Use the *Fillet* command (**Fig. 12.28**) to draw an arc tangent to two arcs. After entering the command, specify the radius when prompted. Press (Enter) twice to return to the *Command* mode, and the *Fillet* command is ready for use.

Select the two arcs with your cursor; the tangent arc is drawn and the arcs are trimmed at the points of tangency. Mark the tangency points by drawing lines from centers C1 and C2 a little past the arc.

12.8 Conic Sections

Conic sections are plane figures that can be described both graphically and mathematically. They are formed by passing imaginary cutting planes through a right cone, as shown in **Fig. 12.29**.

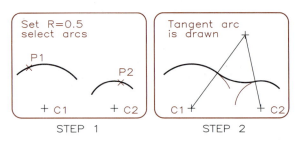

12.28 An arc tangent to two arcs by computer
Step 1 *Command:* FILLET (Enter)
Select first object for [Polyline/Radius/Trim]: R (Enter)
Specify fillet radius [0.0000]: .5 (Enter)
Step 2 *Command:* (Enter)
Select first object or [Polyline/Radius/Trim]: P1
Select second object or [Polyline/Radius/Trim]: P2
(Tangent arc is drawn. Locate tangent points with lines between the center.)

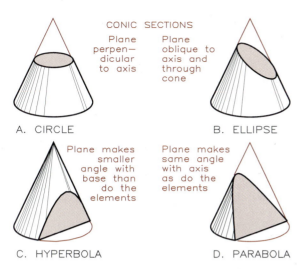

CONIC SECTIONS

Plane perpendicular to axis

A. CIRCLE

Plane oblique to axis and through cone

B. ELLIPSE

Plane makes smaller angle with base than do the elements

C. HYPERBOLA

Plane makes same angle with axis as do the elements

D. PARABOLA

12.29 The conic sections are the (A) circle, (B) ellipse, (C) hyperbola, and (D) parabola. They are formed by passing imaginary cutting planes through a right cone.

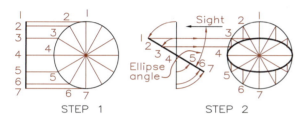

STEP 1

Sight

Ellipse angle

STEP 2

12.30 An ellipse by revolution

Step 1 When the edge of a circle is perpendicular to the projectors from its adjacent view, it appears as a circle. Mark equally spaced points around the circle's circumference and project them to the edge.

Step 2 Revolve the edge of the circle and project the points to the circular view. Project each point vertically downward from their points on the circle to obtain the elliptical view.

Ellipses

The ellipse is a conic section formed by passing a plane through a right cone at an angle as shown in (**Fig. 12.29B**). Mathematically, the ellipse is the path of a point that moves in such a way that the sum of the distances from two focal points is a constant. The largest diameter of an ellipse—the major diameter—is always the true length. The shortest diameter—the minor diam-

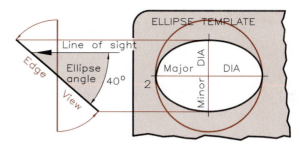

ELLIPSE TEMPLATE

Line of sight

Edge View

Ellipse angle / 40°

Major DIA / DIA

Minor DIA

2

12.31 When the line of sight is not perpendicular to a circle's edge, it appears as an ellipse. The angle between the line of sight and the edge of the circle is the ellipse template angle.

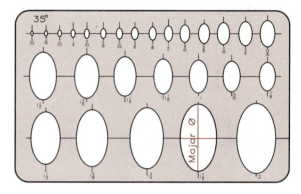

35°

Major Ø

12.32 Ellipse templates are calibrated at 5° intervals from 15° to 60°.

eter—is perpendicular to the major diameter at its midpoint.

Revolving the edge view of a circle yields an ellipse (**Fig. 12.30**). The ellipse template shown in **Fig. 12.31** is used to draw the same ellipse. The angle between the line of sight and the edge of the circle is the angle of the ellipse template (or the one closest to this size) that should be used to draw the ellipse. Ellipse templates are available in 5° intervals and in major diameter sizes that vary in increments of about 1/8 inch (**Fig. 12.32**).

Instead of using the ellipse template, you may construct an ellipse inside a rectangle or parallelogram by plotting a series of points to form the ellipse as shown in **Fig. 12.33**. The

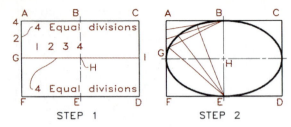

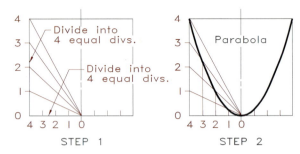

12.33 An ellipse by the parallelogram method

Step 1 Divide the horizontal distance GI and the vertical distance AF into the same number of equal divisions. (Construction for only one quadrant is shown.)

Step 2 Use the construction shown with rays from B and E to locate points on the ellipse in the other quadrants.

12.35 A parabola by the parallelogram method

Step 1 Draw a parallelogram or rectangle to contain the parabola; draw its axis parallel to the sides through 0. Divide the sides into equal segments and draw rays from 0.

Step 2 Draw lines parallel to the sides (vertical in this case) to locate points along the rays from 0 and draw a smooth curve through them.

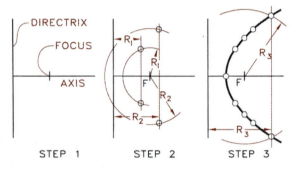

12.34 A parabola by the mathematical method

Step 1 Draw an axis perpendicular to the directrix (a perpendicular line). Choose a point for the focus, F.

Step 2 Use a series of selected radii to find points on the curve. For example, draw a line parallel to the directrix and R2 from it. Swing R2 from F to intersect the line and plot the point.

Step 3 Continue this process with a series of arcs of varying radii until you find an adequate number of points to complete the curve.

(called a directrix) and a focal point. The parabola is the conic section formed by a cutting plane that makes the same angle with the cone's base as the elements on the cone's surface as shown in **Fig. 12.29D**.

Figure 12.34 shows the construction of a parabola by using its mathematical definition as is done in analytical geometry. The mathematical equation of the parabola is:

$$y = ax^2 + bx + c, \text{ where a is not 0}$$

A second method of drawing a parabola, which involves the use of a rectangle or parallelogram, is shown in **Fig. 12.35**. An irregular curve must be used to connect the plotted points on the ellipse to represent the curve of the ellipse.

plotted points must then be connected with an irregular curve.

An ellipse can be drawn on the x and y axes by plotting its x and y coordinates that have been calculated from its mathematical equation. The equation of an ellipse is

$$\frac{x^2 + y^2}{a^2 + b^2} = 1, \text{ where a, b are not 0.}$$

Parabolas

The **parabola** is defined as a plane curve, each point of which is equidistant from a straight line

Hyperbolas

The hyperbola is a two-part conic section defined as the path of a point that moves in such a way that the difference of its distances from two focal points is a constant, as illustrated in **Fig. 12.29C**. **Figure 12.36** shows construction for drawing a hyperbola by applying this definition. By selecting a series of radii until enough points

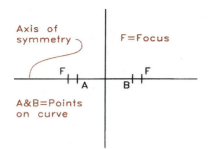

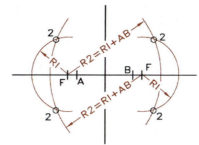

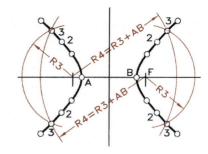

12.36 A hyperbola:

Step 1 Draw a perpendicular through the axis of symmetry. Locate focal points F equidistant from it on both sides. Locate points A and B equidistant from the perpendicular at a distance of your choice but between the focal points.

Step 2 Use radius R1 to draw arcs using focal points F as the centers. Add R1 to AB (the nearest distance between the hyperbolas) to find R2. Draw arcs using radius R2 and the focal points as centers. R1 and R2 locate points S2.

Step 3 Select other radii and add them to AB to locate additional points as shown in Step 2. Draw a smooth curve through the points with an irregular curve.

have been located, the hyperbolic curve can be accurately drawn by using an irregular curve.

Problems

Present your solutions to these problems on size A (8-1/2 × 11 inch), vertical format sheets. The printed grid represents 0.20-in. intervals, so you can use your engineers' 10 scale to lay out the problems. By equating each grid interval to 5 mm, you also can use your full-sized metric scale to lay out and solve the problems. Show your construction and mark all points of tangency, as recommended in the chapter.

1. Basic constructions (**Sheet 1**):

   (A) Draw triangle ABC using the given sides.

   (B) Inscribe a three-sided regular polygon inside the circle.

   (C) Circumscribe a four-sided regular polygon about the circle.

   (D) Inscribe a five-sided regular polygon inside the circle. Refer to **Fig. 12.5**.

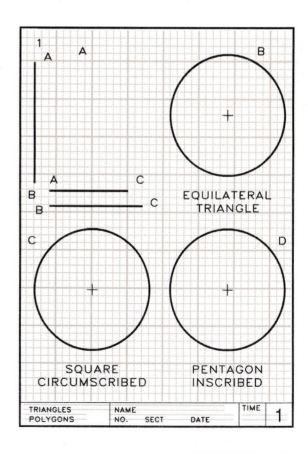

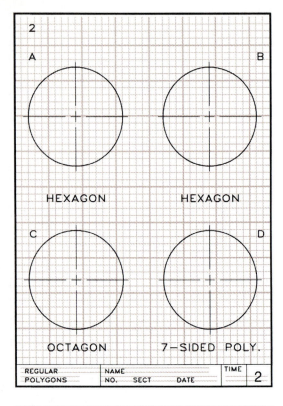

HEXAGON   HEXAGON

OCTAGON   7—SIDED POLY.

REGULAR POLYGONS | NAME | | TIME | 2
| NO. SECT DATE | |

2. Construction of regular polygons (Sheet 2):

(A) Circumscribe a hexagon about the circle.

(B) Inscribe a hexagon in the circle.

(C) Circumscribe an octagon about the circle.

(D) Construct a 7-sided regular polygon inside the circle using the compass method.

3. Basic constructions (Sheet 3):

(A) Bisect the lines.

(B) Bisect the angles.

(C) Bisect the sides of the triangle.

4. Line division and tangencies (Sheet 4):

(A) Divide AB into seven equal parts using a construction line through point A.

(B) Divide the space between the two vertical lines into four equal segments. Draw three vertical lines that are equal in length to the given lines at the division points.

(C) Draw an arc with radius R that is tangent to the line at J and that passes through P.

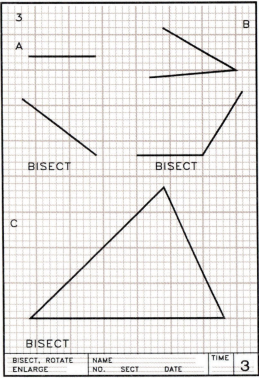

BISECT   BISECT

BISECT

BISECT, ROTATE ENLARGE | NAME | | TIME | 3
| NO. SECT DATE | |

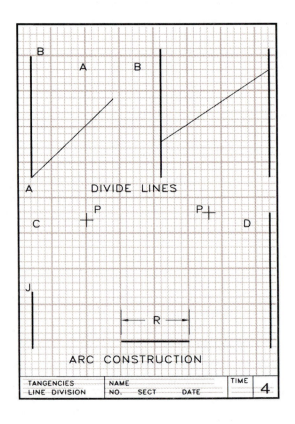

DIVIDE LINES

ARC CONSTRUCTION

TANGENCIES LINE DIVISION | NAME | | TIME | 4
| NO. SECT DATE | |

(D) Construct an arc with radius R that is tangent to the line and passes through P.

5. Tangency construction (Sheet 5):

(A) Using the compass method, draw a line from P tangent to the arc. Mark the points of tangency.

(B–D) Construct arcs with the given radii tangent to the lines. Mark the points of tangency.

6. Tangency construction (Sheet 6):

(A–D) Construct arcs that are tangent to the arcs or lines shown. The radii are given for each problem. Mark the points of tangency.

7. Tangency construction (Sheet 7):

(A–B) Using the given radius, connect the circles with the tangent arcs as indicated in the sketches.

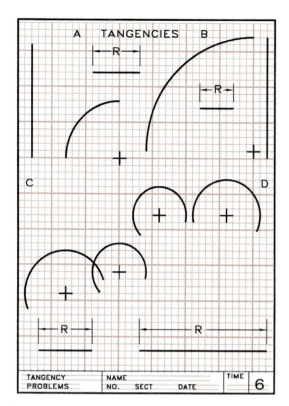

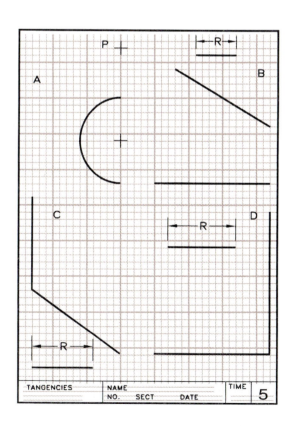

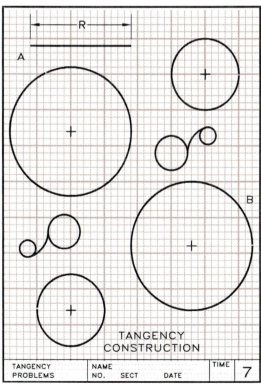

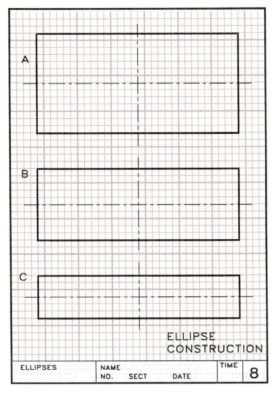

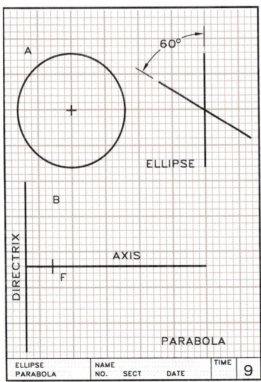

8. Ellipse construction (Sheet 8):

(A–C) Construct ellipses inside the rectangles given. Use enough divisions to make it possible to draw accurate ellipses with your irregular curve.

9. Ellipse and parabola (Sheet 9):

(A) Construct an ellipse inside the circle when the edge view has been rotated as shown.

(B) Using the focal point F and the directrix, plot and draw the parabola formed by these elements.

10. Hyperbola and spiral (Sheet 10):

(A) Using the focal point F, points A and B on the curve, and the axis of symmetry, construct the hyperbola.

(B) Construct a parabola by using the parallelogram method and five divisions along each axis for each half of the parabola.

Practical applications **(Figures 12.37–12.48)**. Construct the given shapes on size A sheets, one problem per sheet. Select the scale that will best fit the problem to the sheet. Mark all points of points of tangency and strive for good line quality.

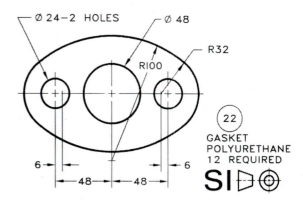

12.39 Problem 13.

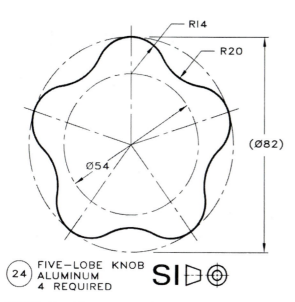

12.37 Problem 11.

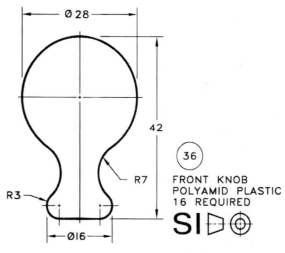

12.40 Problem 14.

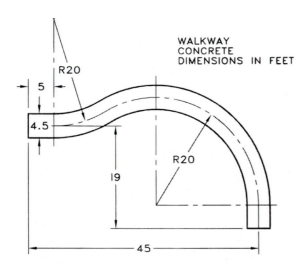

12.38 Problem 12.

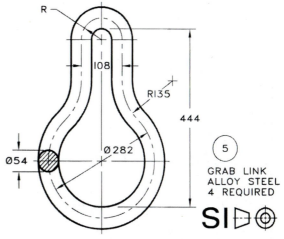

12.41 Problem 15.

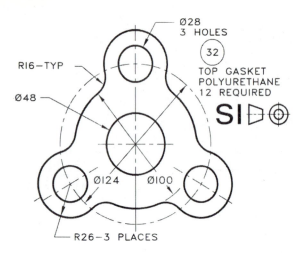

12.42 Problem 16.

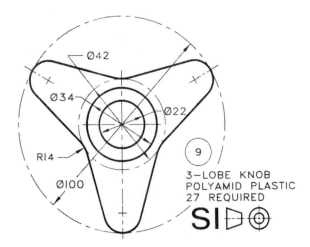

12.45 Problem 19.

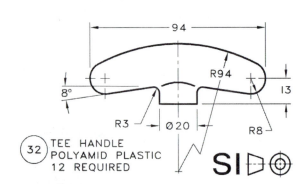

12.43 Problem 17.

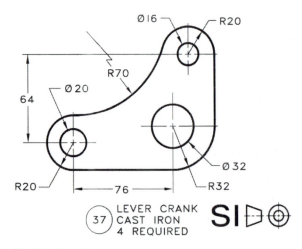

12.46 Problem 20.

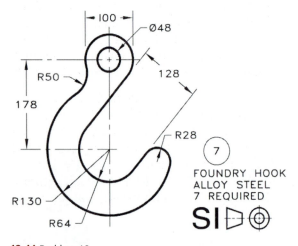

12.44 Problem 18.

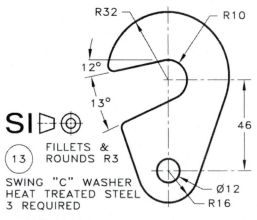

12.47 Problem 21.

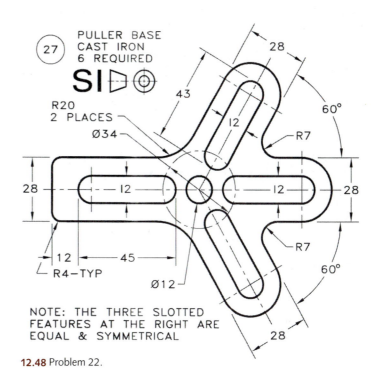

27 PULLER BASE
CAST IRON
6 REQUIRED

SI ⊳ ⊙

R20
2 PLACES

Ø34

28

12

43

28

60°

12

R7

12

28

12

45

R4–TYP

Ø12

R7

60°

28

NOTE: THE THREE SLOTTED
FEATURES AT THE RIGHT ARE
EQUAL & SYMMETRICAL

12.48 Problem 22.

Word Problems

1. For an arc between two points with a radius of 10 ft., calculate its length for the following radial angles: (a) 10°, (b) 20°, (c) 30°, (d) 90°, (e) 135°, (f) 210°, (g) 310°, and (h) 340°.

2. By referring to Fig. 12.10, draw a horizontal line that is 8 in. long to represent 5 in. with 0.2 in. calibrations marked on the upper side. Use a metric scale to construct the equivalent distance in millimeters calibrated along the lower side of the line in 5 mm divisions. This is a nomograph for converting measurements from one system to the other.

3. Construct by computer an arc tangent to two lines, as shown in Fig. 12.18. Using AutoCAD's *List* command (type *List*), select each line and the arc to determine the lengths of the final lines and the arc.

4. Use the *List* command described in Problem 3 to find the areas and perimeters of the follow-ing figures that you have drawn by computer: (a) triangle, (b) square, (c) hexagon, (d) octagon, and (e) decagon.

5. Draw the single views of one of the following objects using instruments and geometric con-struction. If these objects are not available to work from, draw them from memory as if you were designing them: (a) the blade of a buzz fan, (b) the side view of a hand-held telephone, (c) the side view of a desk lamp shade, (d) a baseball diamond, (e) a cross-sectional view of light bulb.

6. Observe the products and objects in the envi-ronment where you are presently sitting. List examples of geometric construction that were applied to their design. For example, list what types of tangencies, curves, and conic sections were used to design a door knob, a light fixture, a bathroom lavatory, a toothbrush, and so forth.

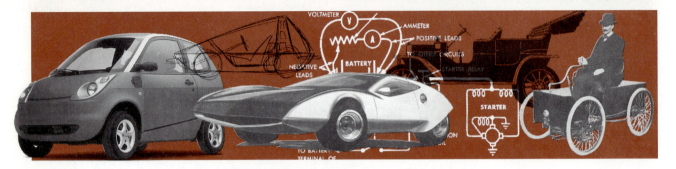

Freehand Sketching

13.1 Introduction

Sketching is a rapid, freehand method of drawing without the use of drawing instruments. Sketching is also a thinking process as much as it is a method of communication. Designers and engineers make many sketches as a method of developing ideas before arriving at the final solution. Many new products and projects have begun as sketches made on the back of an envelope or on a napkin at a restaurant (**Fig. 13.1**).

Sketching is used by the engineer throughout the engineering process, including the making of free-body diagrams during the analysis step of the design process (**Fig. 13.2**).

The ability to communicate by any means is a great asset, and sketching is one of the best ways to transmit ideas. Engineers must use their sketching skills to explain their ideas before they can delegate assignments and obtain the assistance of their team members.

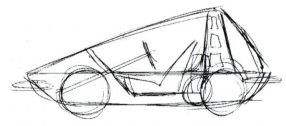

13.1 Designs begin with rough, freehand sketches as a means of developing concepts. (*Courtesy of Chrysler Corporation.*)

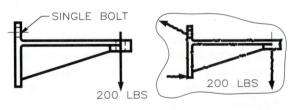

13.2 Sketching is a necessary skill used in all aspects of design, from free-body diagrams to design documentation.

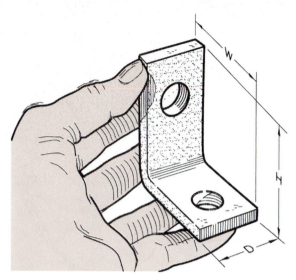

13.3 How can you sketch this angle bracket to convey its shape effectively?

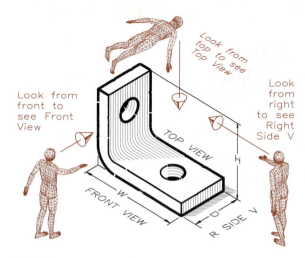

13.4 These positions give the viewpoints for three orthographic views of the angle bracket: top, front, and right side.

13.2 Shape Description

Although the angle bracket in **Fig. 13.3** is a simple three-dimensional object, describing it with words is difficult. Most untrained people would think that drawing it as a three-dimensional pictorial would be a challenge. To make drawing such objects easier, engineers devised a standard system called **orthographic projection** for showing objects in multiple views.

In orthographic projection, separate views represent the object at 90° intervals as the viewer moves about it (**Fig. 13.4**). **Figure 13.5** shows two-dimensional views of the bracket from the front, top, and right side. The top view is drawn above the front view and both share the dimension of width. The right-side view is drawn to the right of the front view and both share the dimension of height.

The views of the bracket are drawn with three types of lines: **visible lines**, **hidden lines**, and **centerlines**. Visible lines are the thickest. Thinner hidden lines (dashed lines) represent features that are invisible or hidden in a view. The thinnest lines are centerlines, which are imaginary lines composed of long and short

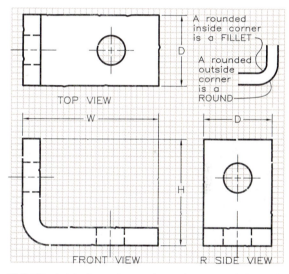

13.5 This sketch shows three orthographic views of the angle bracket.

dashes to show the centers of arcs and the axes of cylinders.

The space between views may vary, but the views must be positioned as shown here. This arrangement is logical, the views are easiest to interpret in this order, and the drawing process is most efficient because the views project from each other. **Figure 13.6** illustrates the lack of

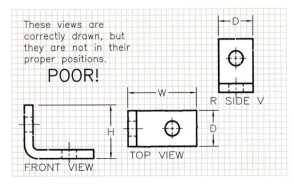

These views are correctly drawn, but they are not in their proper positions.

POOR!

W

R SIDE V

D

H

D

TOP VIEW

FRONT VIEW

13.6 Views must be sketched in their standard orthographic positions. If they are incorrectly positioned, the object cannot be readily understood.

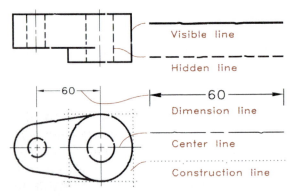

Visible line

Hidden line

60

60

Dimension line

Center line

Construction line

13.7 The alphabet of lines for sketching are shown here. The lines at the right are full size.

clarity when views are incorrectly positioned, even though each view is properly drawn.

13.3 Sketching Techniques

You need to understand the application of line types used in sketching (freehand) orthographic views before continuing with the principles of projection. The "alphabet of lines" for sketching is illustrated in **Fig. 13.7**. All lines, except construction lines, should be black and dense. Construction lines, which serve as guides, are drawn lightly so that they need not be erased. The other lines are distinguished by their line widths (line thicknesses), but they are equal in darkness.

Medium-weight pencils, such as H, F, or HB grades, are best for sketching the lines shown in

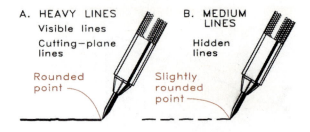

A. HEAVY LINES
Visible lines
Cutting-plane lines
Rounded point

B. MEDIUM LINES
Hidden lines
Slightly rounded point

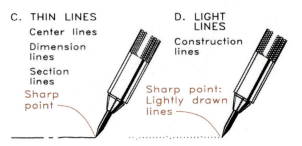

C. THIN LINES
Center lines
Dimension lines
Section lines
Sharp point

D. LIGHT LINES
Construction lines
Sharp point: Lightly drawn lines

13.8 An F pencil is a good choice for sketching all lines if you sharpen it for varying line widths.

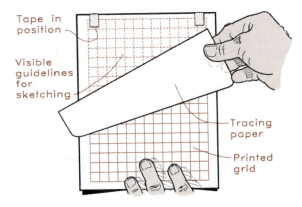

Tape in position

Visible guidelines for sketching

Tracing paper

Printed grid

13.9 A grid placed under a sheet of tracing paper will provide guidelines as an aid in freehand sketching.

Fig. 13.8. By sharpening the pencil point to match the desired line width, you may use the same grade of pencil for all these lines. Lines sketched freehand should have a freehand appearance; do not attempt to make them appear mechanical. Using a printed grid or laying translucent paper over a printed grid can aid your sketching technique (**Fig. 13.9**).

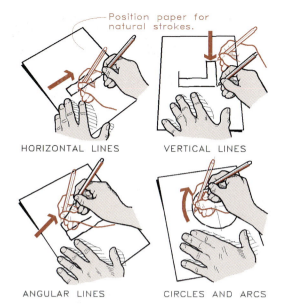

HORIZONTAL LINES   VERTICAL LINES

ANGULAR LINES   CIRCLES AND ARCS

Position paper for natural strokes.

13.10 Sketch lines as shown here for the best results; rotate your drawing sheet for comfortable sketching positions.

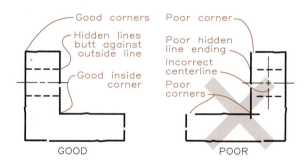

Good corners
Hidden lines butt against outside line
Good inside corner
GOOD

Poor corner
Poor hidden line ending
Incorrect centerline
Poor corners
POOR

13.11 For good sketches, follow the examples of good technique and avoid the common errors of poor technique shown here.

When you make a freehand sketch, lines will be vertical, horizontal, angular, and/or circular. By not taping your drawing to the table top, you can easily position the sheet that is most comfortable for each drawing stroke, usually from left to right (**Fig. 13.10**). Examples of correctly sketched lines are contrasted with incorrectly sketched ones in **Fig. 13.11**. Notice that gaps should not be left at the corners of a view.

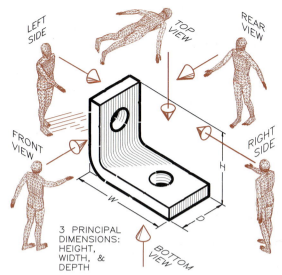

LEFT SIDE   TOP VIEW   REAR VIEW

FRONT VIEW   RIGHT SIDE

BOTTOM VIEW

3 PRINCIPAL DIMENSIONS: HEIGHT, WIDTH, & DEPTH

13.12 Six principal views of the angle bracket can be sketched from the viewpoints shown.

13.4 Six-View Sketching

The maximum number of principal views that can be drawn in orthographic projection is six, as the viewer changes position at 90° intervals (**Fig. 13.12**). In each view, two of the three dimensions of **height**, **width**, and **depth** are seen.

These views must be sketched in their standard positions (**Fig. 13.13**). The width dimension is shared by the top, front, and bottom views. The height dimension is shared with the right-side, front, left-side, and rear views. Note the simple and effective dimensioning of each view with two dimensions. Seldom is an object so complex that it requires six orthographic views.

13.5 Three-View Sketching

You can adequately describe most objects with three orthographic views; usually the top, front, and right-side views. **Figure 13.14** shows a typical three-view sketch of a T-block with height, width, and depth dimensions and the front, top, and right-side views labeled.

The object shown in **Fig. 13.15** is represented by three orthographic views on a grid in **Fig.**

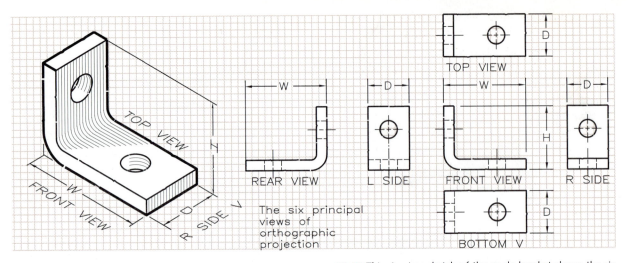

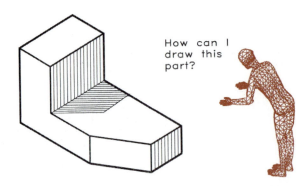

13.13 This six-view sketch of the angle bracket shows the six principal views of orthographic projection. Note the placement of dimensions on the views.

13.14 This sketch shows the standard orthographic arrangement for three views of a T nut, with dimensions and labels.

13.15 Sketches of three orthographic views describe this fixture block in Fig. 13.16.

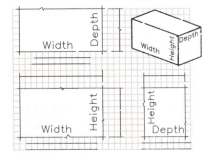

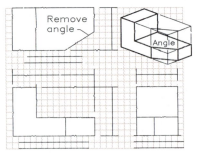

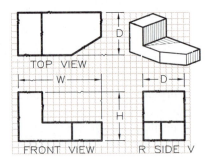

13.16 Three-view sketching

Step 1 Block in the views with light construction lines. Allow proper spacing for labeling and dimensioning the views.

Step 2 Remove the notches and project the resulting lines of intersection to the adjacent views.

Step 3 Check for correctness, darken the lines, add the dimensions, and letter the labels for each view.

13.16. To obtain those views, block in the views of the object with its overall dimensions, then sketch the slanted surface in the top view and project it to the other two views. Finally, darken the lines, label the views, and letter the overall dimensions of height, width, and depth.

Slanted surfaces will appear as **edges** or **foreshortened** (not-true-size) **planes** in the principal views of orthographic projection (**Fig. 13.17**). In **Fig. 13.17C,** two intersecting planes of the object slope in two directions; thus both appear foreshortened in the front, top, and right-side views.

A good way to learn orthographic projection is to construct a missing third view (the front view in **Fig. 13.18**) when two views are given. In **Fig. 13.19**, we construct the missing right-side view from the given top and front views. To obtain the depth dimension for the right-side view, transfer it from the top view with dividers;

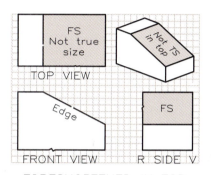

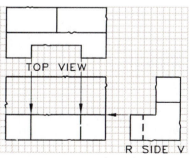

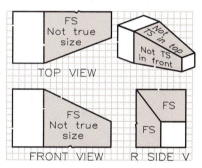

FORESHORTENED IN TOP

FORESHORTENED IN FRONT

FORESHORTENED IN ALL

13.17 Views of planes

A The plane appearing as an angular edge in the front view is foreshortened in the top and side views.

B The plane appearing as an angular edge in the top view is foreshortened in the front and side views.

C Two sloping planes appear foreshortened in the top, front, and right-side views.

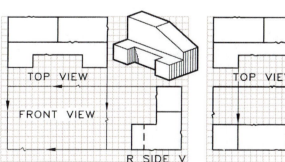

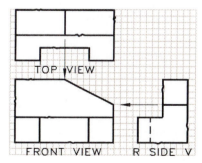

13.18 Sketching a missing view

Step 1 Begin by blocking in the front view with light construction lines that will not need to be erased.

Step 2 Project the notch from the top view to the front view and darken these lines as final lines.

Step 3 Project the ends of the angular notch from the top and right-side views, check the views, and darken the lines.

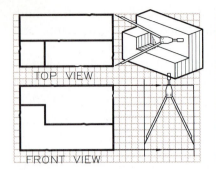
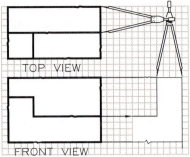
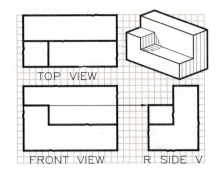

13.19 Sketching a missing side view

Step 1 Transfer the depth with dividers and project the height from the front. Block in the side view with construction lines.

Step 2 Locate the notch in the side view with your dividers and project its base from the front view. Use light construction lines.

Step 3 Project the top of the notch from the front view, check for correctness, darken the lines, and label the view.

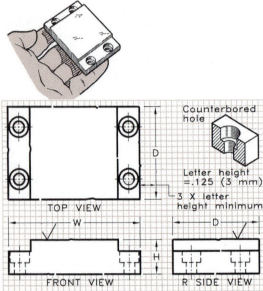

13.20 Three orthographic views adequately describe the rest pad. Space dimension lines at least three letter heights from the views. Finish marks (V marks) indicate that the top surface has been machined to a smooth finish. Counterbored holes allow bolt heads to be recessed.

to obtain the height dimension, project it from the front view.

Figure 13.20 shows a fixture pad sketched in three views. The pad has a **finished surface**, indicated by V marks in the two views where the surface appears as an edge, and four **counter-**

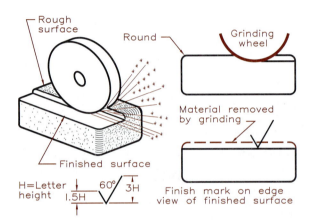

13.21 Place a finish mark on all edge views of a surface (visible or hidden) that is to be smoothed by machining. Grinding is one of the methods used to finish a surface.

bored holes. Dimension lines for the height, width, and depth labels should be spaced at least three letter heights from the views. For example, when you use 1/8-inch letters, position them at least 3/8 of an inch from the views.

Apply the finish mark symbol to the edge views of any finished surfaces, visible or hidden, to specify that the surface is to be machined to make it smoother. The surface in **Fig. 13.21** is being finished by grinding, which is one of many methods of smoothing a surface.

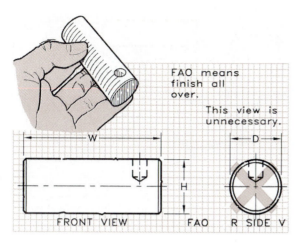

FAO means
finish all
over.

This view is
unnecessary.

FRONT VIEW   FAO   R SIDE V

13.22 This pulley shaft is a typical cylindrical part that can be represented adequately by two views.

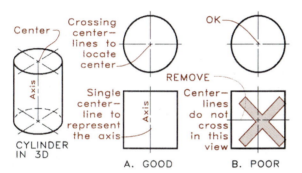

Center

Crossing
center-
lines to
locate
center

OK

Axis

REMOVE

Single
center-
line to
represent
the axis

Axis

Center-
lines
do not
cross
in this
view

CYLINDER
IN 3D

A. GOOD   B. POOR

13.23 Centerlines identify the centers of circles and axes of cylinders. Centerlines cross only in the circular view and extend about 1/8 inch beyond the outside lines.

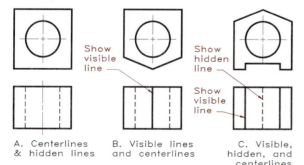

First priority: Visible lines
Second priority: Hidden lines
Third priority: Centerlines

Show
visible
line

Show
hidden
line

Show
visible
line

A. Centerlines
& hidden lines

B. Visible lines
and centerlines

C. Visible,
hidden, and
centerlines

13.24 When visible lines coincide with hidden lines, show the visible lines. When hidden lines coincide with centerlines, show the hidden lines.

13.6 Circular Features

The pulley shaft depicted in **Fig. 13.22** in two views is composed of circular features. **Centerlines** are added to better identify these cylindrical features. **Figure 13.23** shows how to apply centerlines to indicate the center of the circular ends of a cylinder and its vertical axis. Perpendicular centerlines cross in circular views to locate the center of the circle and extend beyond the arc by about 1/8 inch. Centerlines consist of alternating long and short dashes, about 1 inch and 1/8 inch in length, respectively.

When centerlines coincide with visible or hidden lines, the centerline should be omitted because object lines are more important and centerlines are imaginary lines. **Figure 13.24** shows the precedence of lines.

The centerlines shown in **Fig. 13.25** clarify whether the circles and arcs are concentric (share the same centers). **Figure 13.26** shows the

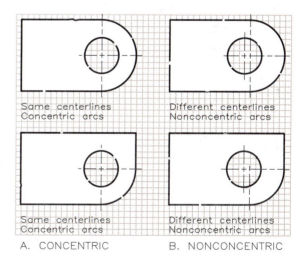

Same centerlines
Concentric arcs

Different centerlines
Nonconcentric arcs

Same centerlines
Concentric arcs

Different centerlines
Nonconcentric arcs

A. CONCENTRIC   B. NONCONCENTRIC

13.25 Centerlines

A Extend centerlines beyond the last arc that shares the same center.

B Sketch separate centerlines when the arcs are not concentric.

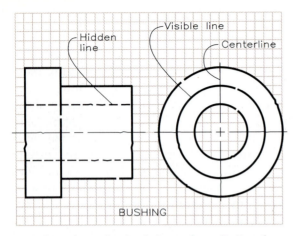

13.26 This orthographic sketch depicts the application of centerlines to concentric cylinders and the relative weights of various lines.

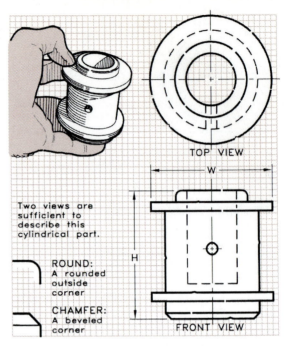

13.28 Two views adequately describe this cylindrical pivot base.

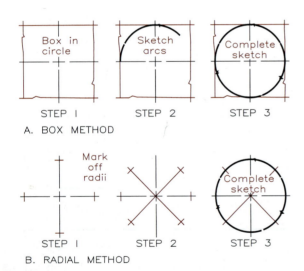

13.27 Sketching circles

Method 1

Step 1 Block in the diameter of the circle about its centerlines.

Step 2 Sketch an arc tangent to two tangent points.

Step 3 Complete the circle with other arcs.

Method 2

Step 1 Mark off radii on the centerlines.

Step 2 Mark off radii on two construction lines drawn at 45°.

Step 3 Sketch the circles with arcs passing through the marks.

correct manner of applying centerlines to orthographic views of an object composed of concentric cylinders.

Sketching Circles

Circles can be sketched by either of the methods shown in **Fig. 13.27**. Use light guidelines and dark centerlines to block in the circle. Drawing a freehand circle in one continuous arc is difficult, so draw arcs in segments with the help of the guidelines.

A typical part having circular features is represented by two sketched views in **Fig. 13.28**. Note the definitions of a **round** and a **chamfer**. The steps for constructing three orthographic views of a part having circular features are shown in **Fig. 13.29**.

13.7 Pictorial Sketching: Obliques

An oblique pictorial is a three-dimensional representation of an object's height, width, and depth. It approximates a photograph of an

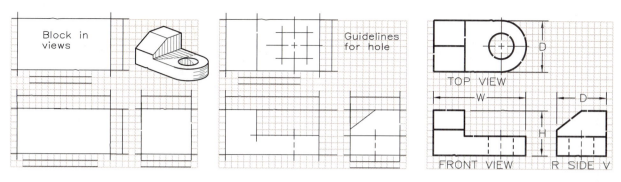

13.29 Sketching circular features

Step 1 Block in the overall dimensions with construction lines. Leave room for labels and dimensions.

Step 2 Draw the centerlines and the squares that block in the diameter of the circle. Find the slanted surface in the side view.

Step 3 Sketch the arcs, darken the lines, label the views, and show the dimensions of W, D, and H between the views.

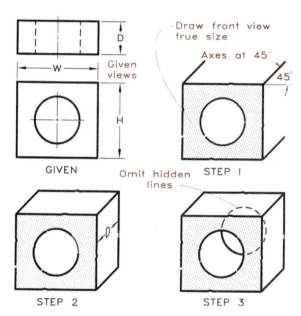

13.30 Sketching oblique pictorials

Step 1 Sketch the front of the part as an orthographic front view and the receding lines at 45° to show the depth dimension.

Step 2 Measure the depth along the receding axes and sketch the back of the part.

Step 3 Locate the circle on the rear plane, show the visible portion of it, and omit the hidden lines.

object, making the sketch easier to understand at a glance than do orthographic views. Sketch the front of the object as a true-shape orthographic view (**Fig. 13.30**). Sketch the receding

axes at an angle of between 20° and 60° oblique with the horizontal in the front view. Lay off the depth dimension at its true length along the receding axes. **Figure 13.31** shows an oblique sketch of a saddle. When the depth is true length, the oblique is a **cavalier** oblique.

The major advantage of an oblique pictorial is the ease of sketching circular features with

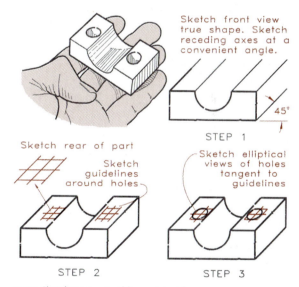

13.31 Sketching arcs in oblique pictorials

Step 1 Sketch the front view of the saddle as a true front view. Sketch the receding axes from each corner.

Step 2 Sketch the rear of the part by measuring its depth along the receding axes. Sketch guidelines that will enclose the holes.

Step 3 Sketch the circular features as ellipses on the upper planes tangent to the guidelines.

true circular arcs on the true-size front plane rather than as ellipses. Circular features on the receding planes appear as ellipses, requiring slanted guidelines as shown.

13.8 Pictorial Sketching: Isometrics

Another type of three-dimensional representation is the isometric pictorial, in which the axes make 120° angles with each other (**Fig. 13.32**). Specially printed isometric grids with lines intersecting at 60° angles make isometric sketching easier, as shown in **Fig. 13.33**, by transferring dimensions from the square grid in the orthographic views to the isometric grid.

You cannot measure angles in isometric pictorials with a protractor; you must find them by

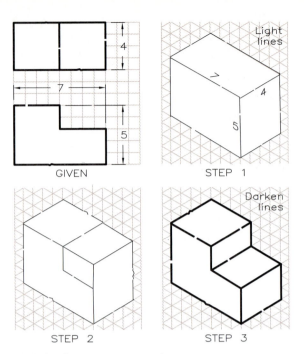

GIVEN   STEP 1

STEP 2   STEP 3

13.33 Sketching isometric pictorials

Step 1 Use an isometric grid, transfer the overall dimensions from the given views, and sketch a box having those dimensions.

Step 2 Locate the notch by measuring over four squares and down two squares, as shown in the given views.

Step 3 Finish the notch and darken the lines.

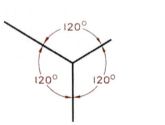

A. ISOMETRIC AXES   B. ISOMETRIC DRAWING

13.32 An isometric sketch

A Begin an isometric pictorial by sketching three axes spaced 120° apart. One axis usually is vertical.

B Sketch the isometric shapes parallel to the three axes by transferring their true measurements as the dimensions.

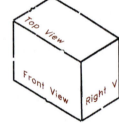

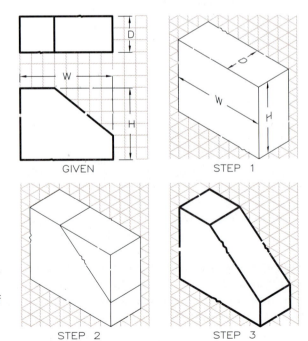

GIVEN   STEP 1

STEP 2   STEP 3

13.34 Sketching angles in isometric pictorials

Step 1 Sketch a box using the overall dimensions given in the orthographic views.

Step 2 Angles cannot be measured with a protractor. Find each end of the angle with coordinates measured along the axes.

Step 3 Connect the ends of the angle and darken the lines.

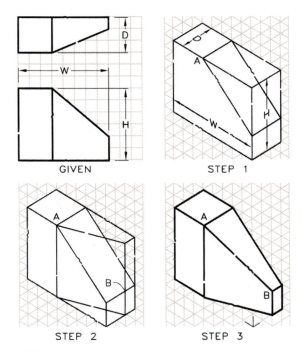

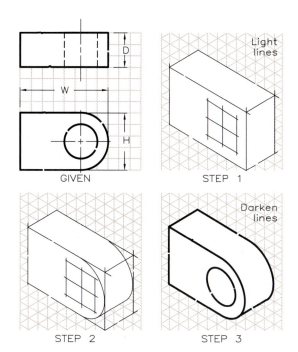

13.35 Sketching double angles in isometric

Step 1 This object has two sloping angles that intersect. Begin by sketching the overall box and draw one of the angles.

Step 2 Find the second angle, which locates point B, the intersection line between the planes.

Step 3 Connect points A and B and darken the lines. Line AB is the line of intersection between the two sloping planes.

13.36 Sketching circles in isometric pictorials

Step 1 Sketch a box using the overall dimensions given. Sketch the centerlines and a rhombus blocking in the circular hole.

Step 2 Sketch the isometric arcs tangent to the box. These arcs are elliptical, rather than circular.

Step 3 Sketch the hole and darken the lines. Hidden lines usually are omitted in isometric pictorial sketches.

connecting coordinates of the angle laid off along the isometric axes. In **Fig. 13.34**, locate the ends of the angular plane by using the coordinates for width and height. When a part has two sloping planes that intersect (**Fig. 13.35**), you must sketch them one at a time to find point B. Line AB is found as the line of intersection between the planes. A more thorough coverage of isometric drawing is given in Chapter 24.

Circles in Isometric

Circles appear as ellipses in isometric pictorials. When you sketch them, begin with their centerlines and construction lines, enclosing their diameters as shown in **Fig. 13.36**. The end of the

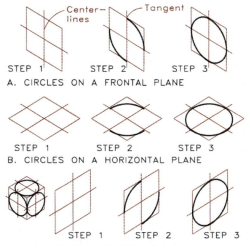

13.37 Sketching circular features in isometric

Step 1 Sketch the centerlines and guidelines.

Step 2 Sketch the two large arcs on opposite sides.

Step 3 Sketch the two small arcs at the ends of the ellipse.

block is semicircular in the front view, so its center must be equidistant from the top, bottom, and end of the front view. Circles and ellipses are easier to sketch when you use construction lines.

Figure 13.37 shows how to use centerlines and construction lines to draw ellipses in the three isometric planes: frontal, horizontal (top), and profile (side) views. This technique is used to sketch a cylinder in **Fig. 13.38** and an object having semicircular ends in **Fig. 13.39.** Hidden lines are usually omitted in isometric drawings.

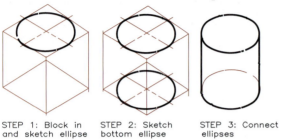

STEP 1: Block in and sketch ellipse

STEP 2: Sketch bottom ellipse

STEP 3: Connect ellipses

13.38 Sketching a cylinder in isometric

Step 1 Block in the cylinder with guidelines and sketch the upper ellipse.

Step 2 Sketch the lower ellipse.

Step 3 Connect the ellipses with lines tangent to the elliptical ends and darken the lines.

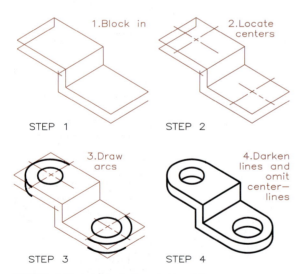

1.Block in

2.Locate centers

STEP 1

STEP 2

3.Draw arcs

4.Darken lines and omit center-lines

STEP 3

STEP 4

13.39 Sketching circular features in isometric

Step 1 Block in the isometric shape of the object with light lines.

Step 2 Locate the centerlines of the holes and the rounded ends.

Step 3 Sketch the semicircular ends of the part and the holes.

Step 4 Draw the bottoms of the holes and darken the lines.

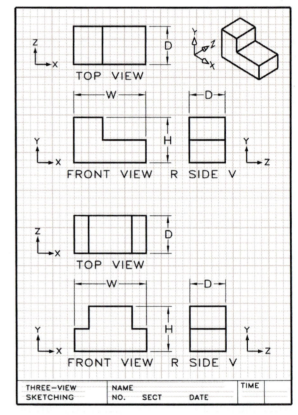

13.40 Use this layout of a size A sheet for sketching problems. You may sketch two problems on each sheet.

Problems

Sketch the problems in Figs. 13.41–13.43 on size A sheets, with or without a printed grid, as shown in Figure 13.40. Each grid is equal to 0.20 in. or 5 mm.

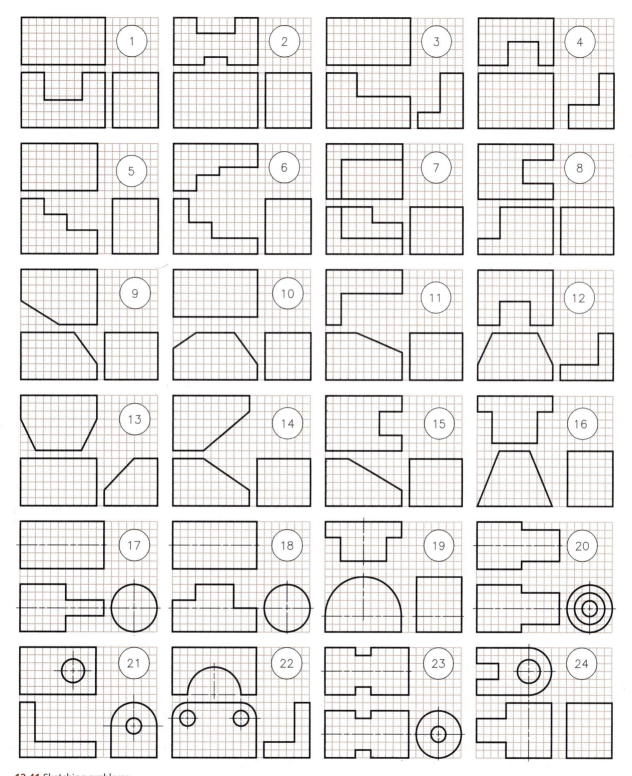

13.41 Sketching problems.

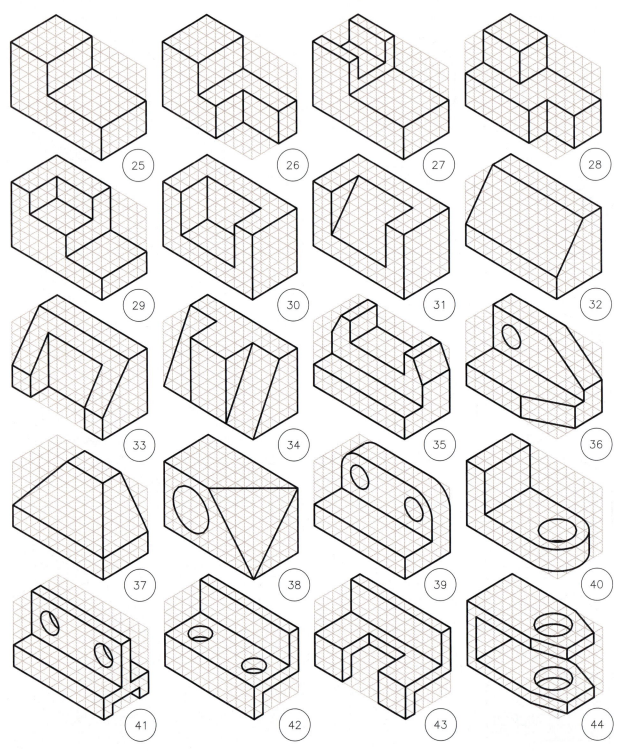

13.42 Sketching problems.

13.43 Sketching problems.

Design Sketching

General dimensions are given on the following problems. You must determine all missing information as if you were the original designer of the parts. Sketch your solutions on size A sheets (8-1/2 × 11), with either a vertical or a horizontal format.

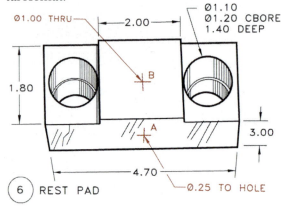

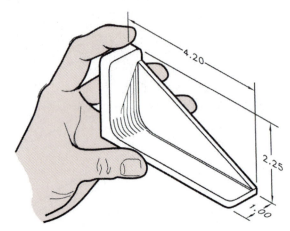

Design 1: Sketch the necessary views of the rest pad and add the two new holes as specified.

Design 3: Modify the aircraft bracket to have the triangular rib moved to the center of the part. Show fillets and rounds. Sketch the necessary orthographic views.

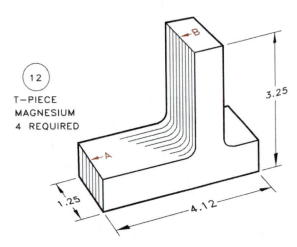

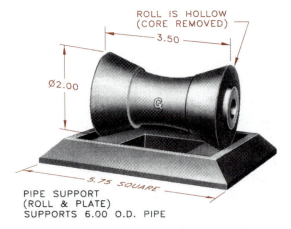

Design 2: Modify the T-piece to have a 0.25 in.-thick rib from point A to point B. Sketch the necessary orthographic views to describe the part.

Design 4: Sketch orthographic views of both parts of the pipe support. The inside of the roll is hollow.

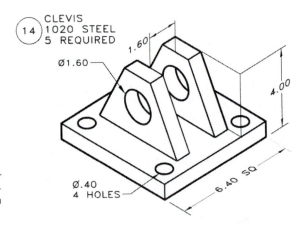

Design 5: Modify the clevis to have semicircular ends about the 1.60 DIA holes and make concentric rounded corners at each 0.40 DIA hole. Sketch the necessary views.

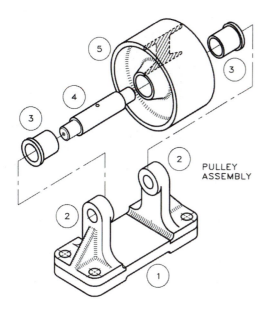

Design 6: There are five parts in the pulley assembly, which has a 1 in. DIA shaft (Part 4). Sketch one part per A size sheet, following the instructions below.

Option 1: Make a two-view sketch of the shaft (Part 4). Do you know why there are holes in the shaft?

Option 2: Make a two-view drawing of the bushing (Part 3). What are bushings and why are they used? What type of material is best for a bushing?

Option 3: Make a two-view drawing of the base (Part 1). How are the brackets (Part 2) connected to the base?

Option 4: make a three-view drawing of the shaft bracket (Part 2). How do the brackets support the shaft?

Option 5: Make a two-view drawing of the pulley (Part 5). Why does it have a boss (hub) protruding from it through which the shaft (Part 4), passes?

Option 6: Redesign the bracket (Part 2) and show your proposed modification in a three-view sketch.

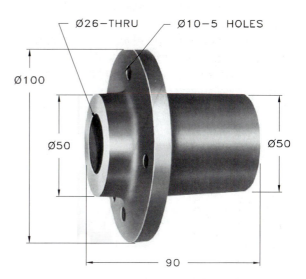

Design 7: Modify the socket by moving the flange to the center of the part's length. Sketch the necessary views to describe the part on a size A sheet.

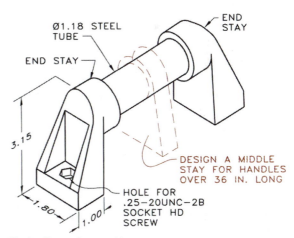

Design 8: Handle assembly

Option 1 Draw the necessary freehand orthographic views to describe the parts of the assembly.

Option 2 Draw orthographic sketches of your own design of the middle stay that can be used to provide additional strength for longer handles.

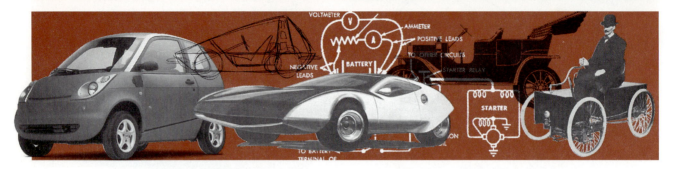

Orthographic Projection With Instruments

14.1 Introduction

In Chapter 13, you were introduced to orthographic projection by freehand sketching, which is an excellent way to develop design concepts. Now, you must convert these sketches into orthographic views drawn to scale with instruments, or by computer, to precisely define your design. Afterwards, you will add dimensions and notes to convert these drawings into working drawings from which the design will become a reality.

Orthographic drawings are three-dimensional objects represented by separate views arranged in a standard manner that are readily understood by the technological team. Because multiview drawings usually are executed with instruments and drafting aids, they are often called **mechanical drawings**. They are called **working drawings**, or **detail drawings**, when sufficient dimensions, notes, and specifications are added to enable the product to be manufactured or built from the drawings.

14.2 Orthographic Projection

An artist has the option of representing objects impressionistically, but the engineer must represent them precisely. Orthographic projection is used to prepare accurate, scaled, and clearly presented drawings from which the project depicted can be produced.

Orthographic projection is the system of drawing views of an object by projecting them perpendicularly onto projection planes with parallel projectors. Figure 14.1 illustrates this concept by imagining that the object is inside a glass box and three of its views are projected onto planes of the orthographic box.

Figure 14.2 illustrates the principle of orthographic projection where the front view is projected perpendicularly onto a vertical projection plane, the **frontal plane**, with parallel projectors. The projected front view is two-dimensional because it has only width and height and lies in a single plane. Similarly, the top view is projected onto a horizontal projection plane, and the side

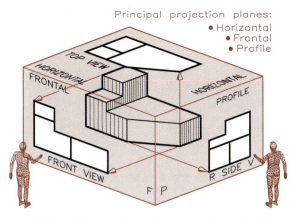

Principal projection planes:
• Horizontal
• Frontal
• Profile

14.1 Orthographic projection is the system of projecting views onto an imaginary glass box with parallel projectors that are perpendicular to the three mutually perpendicular projection planes.

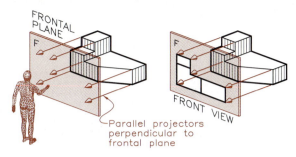

Parallel projectors perpendicular to frontal plane

14.2 An orthographic view is found by projecting from the object to a projection plane with parallel projectors that are perpendicular to the projection plane.

view is projected onto a second vertical projection plane.

Imagine that the box is opened into the plane of the drawing surface, as shown in **Fig. 14.3A**, to yield the three-view arrangement of views shown in **Fig 14.3B.** This layout of views gives the standard positions for three orthographic views that describe the object. These views are the **front**, **top**, and **right-side views.**

The principal projection planes of orthographic projection are the **horizontal (H)**, **frontal (F)**, and **profile (P)** planes. Views projected onto these principal planes are principal views. The dimensions used to give the sizes of principal views are **height (H)**, **width (W)**, and **depth (D)**.

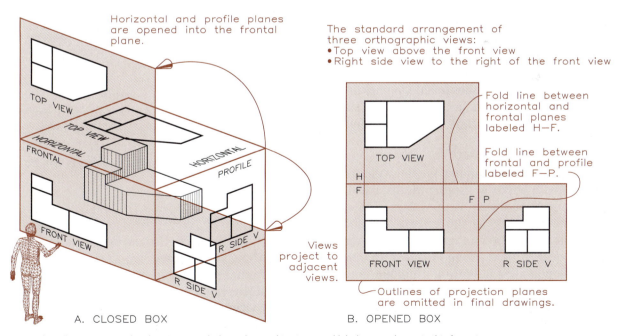

Horizontal and profile planes are opened into the frontal plane.

Views project to adjacent views.

A. CLOSED BOX

The standard arrangement of three orthographic views:
• Top view above the front view
• Right side view to the right of the front view

Fold line between horizontal and frontal planes labeled H–F.

Fold line between frontal and profile labeled F–P.

Outlines of projection planes are omitted in final drawings.

B. OPENED BOX

14.3 When the imaginary glass box is opened, the orthographic views and labeling are drawn in this format.

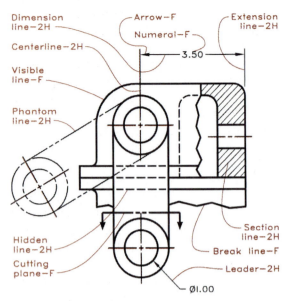

14.4 The alphabet of lines and recommended pencil grades for drawing orthographic views are shown here.

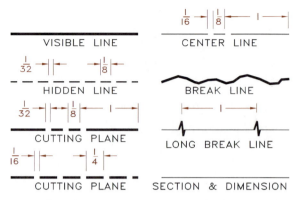

14.5 Full-size line weights recommended for drawing orthographic views are shown above.

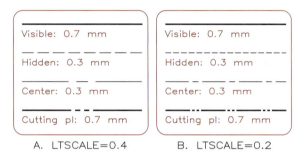

A. LTSCALE=0.4   B. LTSCALE=0.2

14.6 These lines were drawn using AutoCAD's standard *Linetypes* and two pens (P.3 and P.7 points). A. The *Ltscale* factor of 0.4 gives relatively long dashes and spaces between dashes. B. By contrast, the *Ltscale* factor of 0.2 produces dashes and spaces that are half as long as the *Ltscale* factor of 0.4.

14.3 Alphabet of Lines

Draw all orthographic views with dark and dense lines, as if they were drawn with ink. Only the line widths should vary except for guidelines and construction lines, which are drawn very lightly for layout and lettering. **Figure 14.4** gives examples of lines used in orthographic projection and the recommended pencil grades for them. The lengths of dashes in hidden lines and centerlines are drawn longer as a drawing's size increases. **Figure 14.5** further describes these lines.

Computer Lines Computer graphics plotters use pens with points of varying widths, usually 0.7 mm and 0.3 mm wide, to draw lines of different thicknesses. To vary the lengths of dashes and the spaces between them in dashed lines, use *Ltscale* (**Fig. 14.6**). When *Ltscale* is used, **all** noncontinuous (centerlines and hidden lines) on the drawing are changed at the same time.

The laser and dot-matrix printers are also widely used for producing A- and B-size drawings. The ability to print with a high degree of

sharpness and in many colors is the major advantage of laser printers over the pen plotter. However, drawings in the 36 in. size range are plotted mostly on the pen plotter. Line widths can be specified in similar methods on both types of plotters.

14.4 Six-View Drawings

When you imagine that an object is inside a glass box, you will see two horizontal planes, two frontal planes, and two profile planes (**Fig. 14.7**). Therefore, the maximum number of principal views that can be used to represent an object is six. The top and bottom views are projected onto horizontal planes, the front and rear

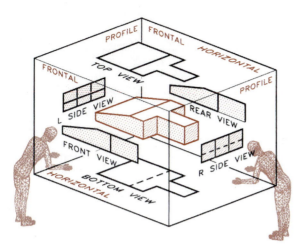

14.7 Six principal views of an object can be drawn in orthographic projection. Imagine that the object is in a glass box with the views projected onto its six planes.

views onto frontal planes, and the right- and left-side views onto profile planes.

To draw the six views on a sheet of paper, imagine that the glass box is opened up into the plane of the drawing paper, as shown in **Fig. 14.8**. Place the top view over and the bottom view under the front view; place the right-side view to the right and the left-side view to the left of the front view; and place the rear view to the left of the left-side view.

Projectors align the views both horizontally and vertically about the front view. Each side of the fold lines of the glass box is labeled **H**, **F**, or **P** (horizontal, frontal, or profile) to identify the projection planes on each side of the imaginary fold lines (**Fig. 14.8**).

Height (H), width (W), and depth (D), the three dimensions necessary to dimension an object, are shown in their recommended positions in **Fig. 14.8**. The standard arrangement of

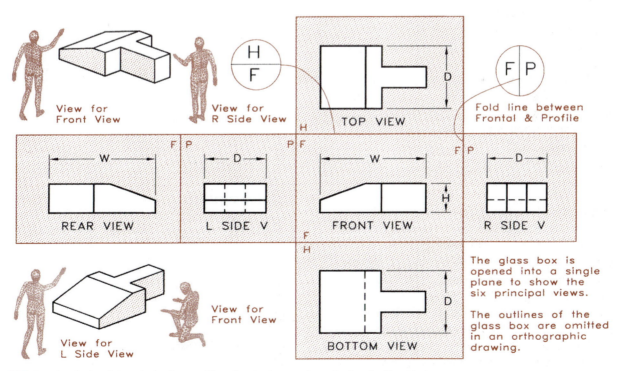

14.8 Opening the box into a single plane positions the six views as shown to describe the object.

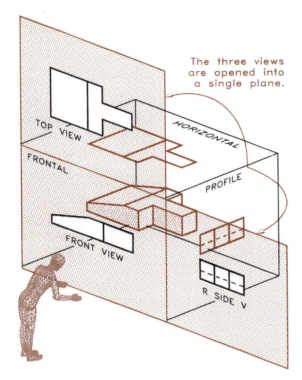

The three views are opened into a single plane.

14.9 Three-view drawings are usually adequate for describing most small objects, such as machine parts.

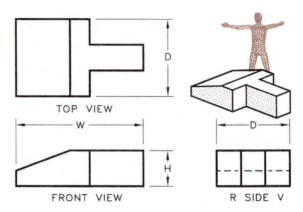

14.10 This three-view drawing depicts the object shown in Fig. 14.9.

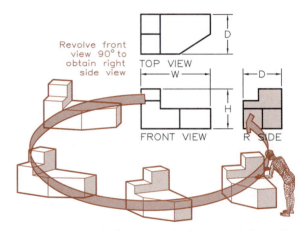

Revolve front view 90° to obtain right side view

14.11 By rotating the front view 90° about a vertical axis, the side view is found.

the six views allows the views to share dimensions by projection. For example, the height dimension, which is shown only once between the front and right-side views, applies to the four horizontally aligned views. The width dimension is placed between the top and front views, but applies to the bottom view also.

14.5 Three-View Drawings

The most commonly used orthographic arrangement of views is the three-view drawing, consisting of front, top, and right-side views. Imagine that the views of the object are projected onto the planes of the glass box (**Fig. 14.9**) and the three planes are opened into a single plane, the frontal plane. **Figure 14.10** shows the resulting three-view drawing, where the views are labeled and dimensioned with H, W, and D.

In addition to using the glass-box approach for visualizing orthographic projection, imagine

that the object is revolved until the desired view is obtained. For example, if the front view of the part in **Fig. 14.11** is revolved 90°, you will see its side view true shape (TS). Placed in its proper position, the side view aligns with the projectors from the front view at its right.

14.6 Arrangement of Views

Figure 14.12 shows the standard positions for a three-view drawing: The top and side views are projected from and aligned with the front view.

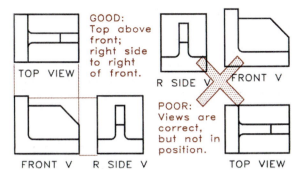

14.12 Orthographic views must be arranged in their proper positions in order for them to be interpreted correctly.

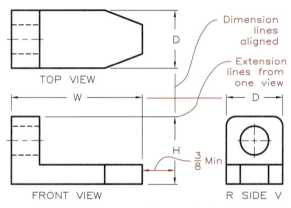

14.13 Dimension and extension lines used in three-view orthographic projection should be aligned. Draw extension lines from only one view when dimensions are placed between views.

Improperly arranged views that do not project from view to view are also shown. **Figure 14.13** illustrates the rules of projection and shows the proper alignment of dimension lines. Orthographic projection shortens layout time, improves readability, and reduces the number of dimensions required because they are placed between and are shared by the views to which they apply.

14.7 Selection of Views

Select the sequence of orthographic views with the fewest hidden lines. **Figure 14.14A** shows that the right-side view is preferable to the left-side view because it has fewer hidden lines.

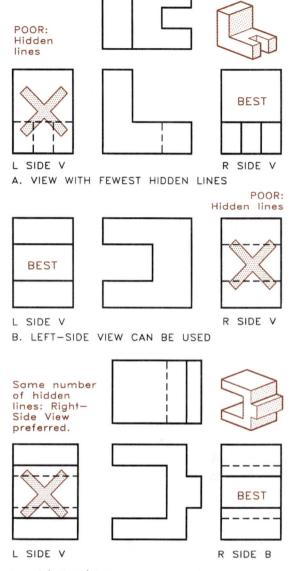

14.14 Selection of views

A Select the set of views with the fewest hidden lines.

B Select the left-side view because it has fewer hidden lines than the right-side view.

C When both views have an equal number of hidden lines, select the right-side view.

Although the three-view arrangement of top, front, and right-side views is more commonly used, the top, front, and left-side view arrangement is acceptable (**Fig. 14.14B**) if the left-side view has fewer hidden lines than the right-side view.

The most descriptive view usually is selected as the front view. If an object, such as a chair, has predefined views that are generally recognized as the front or top views, you should use the accepted front view as the orthographic front view.

Although the right-side view usually is placed to the right of the front view, the side view can be projected from the top view (**Fig. 14.15**). This alternative position is advisable when the object has a much larger depth than height.

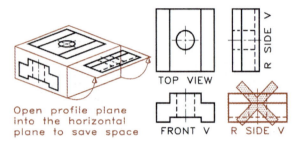

4.15 The side view can be projected from the top view instead of the front view. This alternate position saves space when the depth of an object is considerably greater than its height.

14.8 Line Techniques

Figure 14.16 illustrates techniques for handling most types of intersecting lines, hidden lines, and arcs in combination. Proper application of these principles improves the readability of orthographic drawings.

Become familiar with the order of importance (precedence) of lines (**Fig. 14.17**). The most important line, the visible object line, is shown regardless of any other line lying behind it. Of next importance is the hidden line, which is more important than the imaginary centerline.

14.9 Point Numbering

Some orthographic views are difficult to draw due to their complexity. By numbering the endpoints of the lines of the parts in each view as

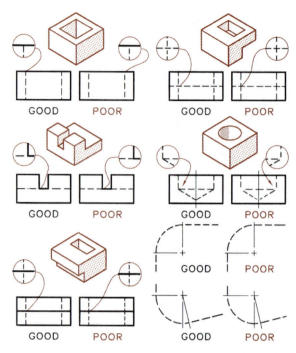

14.16 These drawings show proper intersections and other line techniques in orthographic views.

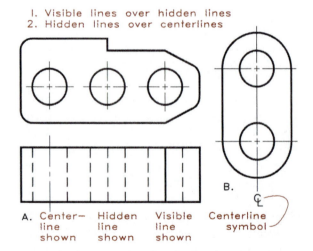

14.17 When lines coincide with each other, the more important lines take precedence over (cover up) the other lines. The order of importance is: visible lines, hidden lines, and center lines.

you construct it (**Fig. 14.18**), the location of the object's features will be easier to see. For example, using numbers on the top and side views of

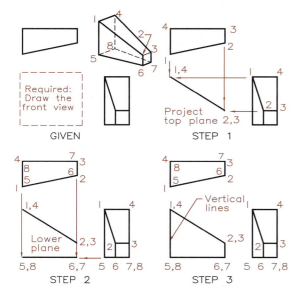

14.18 Point numbering

Required: Find the front view.

Step 1 Number the corners of plane 1–2–3–4 in the top and side views and project them to the front view.

Step 2 Number the corners of plane 5–6–7–8 in the top and side views and project them to the front view.

Step 3 Connect the numbered lines to complete the front view.

this object aids in the construction of the missing front view. Projecting points from the top and side views to the intersections of the projectors locates the object's front view.

14.10 Drawing with Triangles

Two triangles can be effectively used to make instrument drawings on 8-1/2 × 11 sheets without taping the sheet to the drawing surface. It is better that the sheet can be moved about to comfortably position the triangles.

Parallel lines The 45° triangle or the 30°–60° triangle can be used to draw parallel lines as shown in **Fig. 14.19**. One triangle or a straightedge is held in position while the other triangle is moved to where the parallel line is drawn.

Perpendiculars To draw a line perpendicular to AB in **Fig. 14.20**, align the 30°–60° triangle's hypotenuse side with AB and against the lower triangle or straightedge. Hold the lower triangle

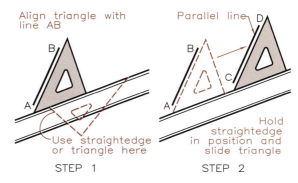

14.19 Drawing parallel lines

Step 1 Align the upper triangle with AB and in contact with the lower triangle (or straightedge).

Step 2 Hold the lower triangle in position and slide the upper triangle to where CD is drawn parallel to AB.

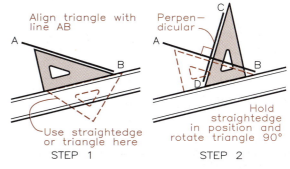

14.20 Drawing perpendiculars

Step 1 Align your triangle with line AB and in contact with the lower triangle (or straightedge).

Step 2 Hold the lower triangle in position, rotate your triangle, and draw CD perpendicular to AB.

in position and rotate it so that its hypotenuse is perpendicular to AB and line CD can be drawn.

Angles To draw a line making 30° with AB, use the steps shown in **Fig. 14.21**. Two triangles can be used in other combinations as a means of making instrument drawings in this informal manner, and yet with a sufficient degree of accuracy.

14.11 Views by Subtraction

Figure 14.22 illustrates how three views of a part are drawn by beginning with a blocked-in outline having the overall dimensions of height,

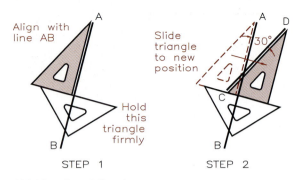

14.21 Drawing a 30° angle

Step 1 Hold the 30°–60° triangle aligned with AB and in contact with the lower triangle (or straightedge).

Step 2 Hold the straightedge in position and slide the triangle and draw CD at 30° to AB.

width, and depth of the finished part and removing volumes from it. This drawing procedure is similar to the steps of making the part in the shop.

14.12 Three-View Drawing Layout

The depth dimension applies to both the top and side views, but these views usually are positioned where depth does not project between them. The depth dimension must be transferred between the top and side views with dividers or by using a 45° miter line, as illustrated in **Fig. 14.23**.

Layout Rules The basic rules of making orthographic drawings are summarized below. Refer to the examples in **Fig. 14.24** thru **Fig. 14.28** and observe how these rules have been used. Notice how the dimensions have been applied and how the views have been labeled.

1. Draw orthographic views in their proper positions.
2. Select the most descriptive view as the front view, if the object does not have a predefined front view.
3. Select the sequence of views with the fewest hidden lines.
4. Label the views; for example, top view, front view, and right-side view.
5. Place dimensions between the views to which they apply.

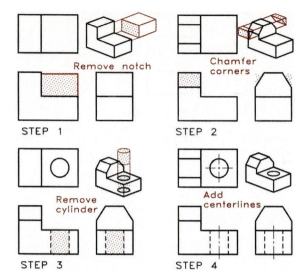

14.22 Views by subtraction

Step 1 Block in the views of the object using overall dimensions of H, W, and D. Remove the notch.

Step 2 Remove the triangular solids at the corners.

Step 3 Remove the cylindrical volume of the hole.

Step 4 Add centerlines to complete the views.

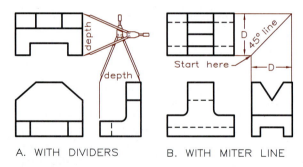

A. WITH DIVIDERS   B. WITH MITER LINE

14.23 Transferring depth

A Transfer the depth dimension from the top view to the side view with your dividers.

B Use a 45° miter line to transfer the depth dimension between the top and side views by projection.

6. Use the proper alphabet of lines.
7. Leave adequate room between the views for labels and dimensions.
8. Draw the views necessary to describe a part. Sometimes fewer or more views are required.

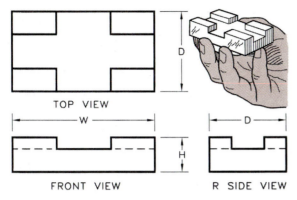

TOP VIEW

FRONT VIEW   R SIDE VIEW

14.24 A three-view drawing depicts an object with only horizontal and vertical planes.

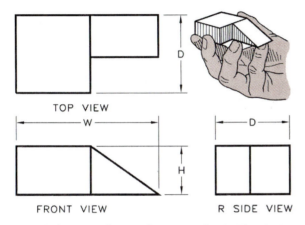

TOP VIEW

FRONT VIEW   R SIDE VIEW

14.25 A three-view drawing showing an object with a sloping plane.

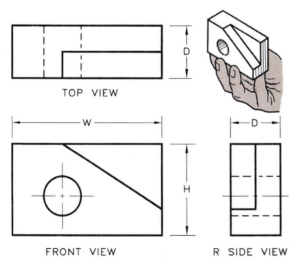

TOP VIEW

FRONT VIEW   R SIDE VIEW

14.26 A three-view drawing showing an object with a sloping plane and a cylindrical hole through it.

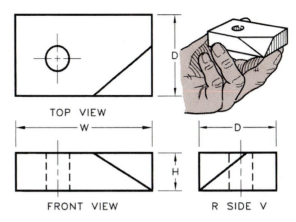

TOP VIEW

FRONT VIEW   R SIDE V

14.27 This three-view drawing depicts an object that has a corner plane with a compound slope.

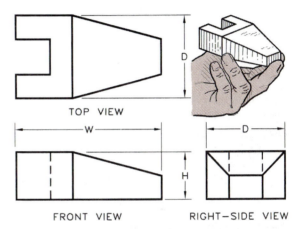

TOP VIEW

FRONT VIEW   RIGHT–SIDE VIEW

14.28 This three-view drawing shows an object that has multiple planes with compound slopes.

14.13 Views by Computer

The steps of drawing three orthographic views of an object by computer are shown in **Fig. 14.29**, where the *Line* command is used to block in three views using their overall dimensions. Other visible and hidden lines are added in by projecting from view to view. The *Dtext* command is used to label the views if this is desired. Additional details of using the *Line* command can be found in Chapter 26.

Three-dimensional (3D) Solids The object in **Fig. 14.30A** was used as the example in **Fig. 14.31** to show how a 3D solid can be constructed

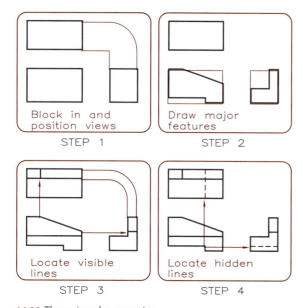

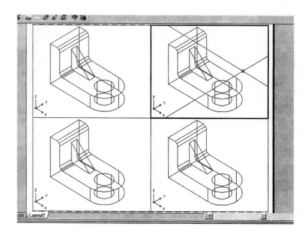

14.31 Create floating viewports

Step 1 *Command:* Tilemode> 0. (The screen is set to *Paper Space (PS)* with a triangle icon in the lower left corner.)

Step 2 *Command:* Mview> (Select 4 to specify 4 viewports)> Fit (The screen is filled with four viewports with the part shown in each one.) An *X–Y–Z Model-Space* icon appears in each viewport. Type MS (model space) and select a viewport with your cursor to make it the active one.

14.29 Three views by computer

Step 1 Use the *Line* command block in the views.

Step 2 Draw the major external features.

Step 3 Draw the visible lines in each view.

Step 4 Draw the hidden lines in each view.

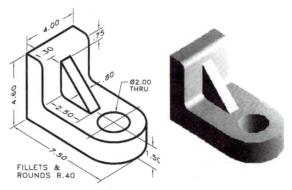

14.30 The given problem (left) was constructed as a 3D solid and rendered as shown at the right by using AutoCAD.

and *rendered,* as in **Fig. 14.30B**. Once the part is drawn as a 3D solid, it can be viewed from different directions to obtain the standard orthographic views.

In order to make a three-view orthographic layout, open the drawing of the part in *Model Space* and set *Tilemode* to 0, which changes the screen to *Paper Space (PS)* and blanks the screen. Before the 3D solid can be seen, you

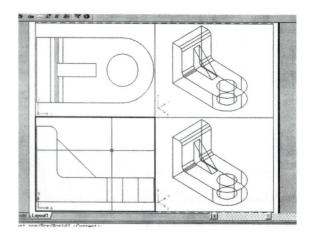

14.32 Creating top and front views

Step 1 Select the upper right viewport, pick *UCS> Save> Desired UCS name:* ISO (Enter)

Step 2 Select the upper left viewport and type Plan to obtain a view parallel to the X–Y axes, the top view. Pick *UCS> Save> Desired UCS name:* TOP (Enter). This saves the top view *UCS*.

Step 3 Select the lower left viewport; pick *UCS> X> Rotation>* 90 to make the X–Y axes parallel to the front of the object. Type Plan to get a front view; pick *UCS> Save> Name>* Front (Enter) to save the UCS.

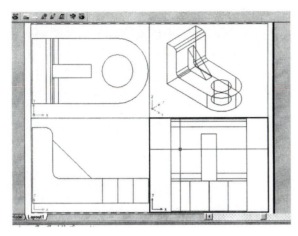

14.33 Create a side view

Step 1 Select the lower right viewport and pick *UCS> X> 90* to make the X–Y icon line in vertical plane. Type *UCS> Y> 90* to make the X–Y axes parallel to the side of the part. Type Plan to obtain the side view.

Step 2 Pick *UCS> Save> Name > SIDE*, to save the *UCS* named SIDE for the side view. Now the three orthographic views are obtained.

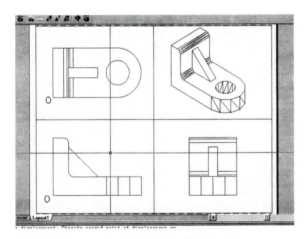

14.34 Scaling and aligning the views

Step 1 Select the top view by cursor; pick *UCS> Restore> Name?> TOP*, to restore the X–Y icon parallel to the top view. Type *Zoom> 1.2* and the top view is sized to properly fill the viewport. Repeat this step for the front and side views to size the views equally.

Step 2 Align the views by typing *Mvsetup* (Multi View Set Up), which changes the screen to *Paper space (PS)*. Select *Align> Vertical> Specify basepoint>* (select a point in the top view)> *Specify point in viewport to be panned:>* (select the same corner in the front view to align the top and front views). Repeat but use the horizontal option to align the front and side views.

must create *Floating Viewports* with the *Mview* command (make view) and select *4* and the *Fit* option to create 4 viewports on the screen (**Fig. 14.31**). Type *MS* to enter *Model Space* and select the upper right port to make it active. Type *UCS* (*User Coordinate System*) and select the option of *Save* and after *Desired UCS name*, type ISO to keep this isometric view (**Fig. 14.32**).

Select the upper left port with the cursor to make it active where the X–Y axes of the icon are parallel to the top of the object. Type *UCS*, select *Save*, and name the view TOP. The X–Y axes of the icon must be rotated 90° to be parallel with the front of the part; pick *UCS> X> 90*. Then type *Plan* to display the front view. Type *UCS> Save> Name> FRONT*.

Select the lower right port to make it active and make the X–Y icon parallel to the side view (**Fig. 14.33**). Type *UCS> X> 90*. Then type *UCS> Y> 90* to align the X–Y axes with the side view; type *UCS> Save> Name> SIDE*.

The three views that have been found may appear at different sizes and aligned incorrectly as orthographic views should. Select each view one at a time and restore the saved views. For example, select the top viewport, type *UCS> Restore> Name> TOP* and the X–Y icon returns parallel to the top view. Type *Zoom> 1.2* to size the top view to appropriately fill the viewport. Select the front- and side-view ports, restore the views by name, and use *Zoom> 1.2* to make them equal in size to each other.

Type *MVsetup* (Model View Setup), which changes the screen to *Paper Space (PS)*, to align the views as shown in **Fig. 14.34**. *MVsetup> Align> Vertical> Specify base point>* (Select a corner point of the top view)> *Other point>* (Pick the same point in the front viewport) and the views are automatically aligned. Now, you have three orthographic views drawn from a single 3D solid. Refer to Chapter 27 for more coverage of solid modeling.

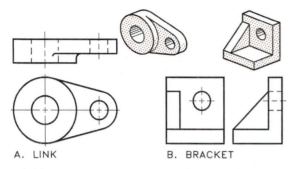

A. LINK   B. BRACKET

14.35 These objects can be adequately described with two orthographic views.

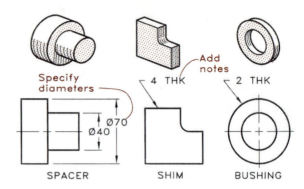

SPACER   SHIM   BUSHING

14.37 Objects that are cylindrical or of a uniform thickness can be described with only one orthographic view and supplementary notes.

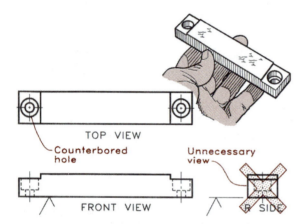

14.36 Two views are adequate for describing this part.

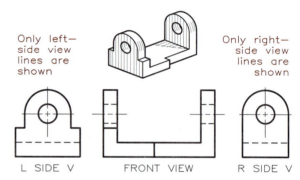

L SIDE V   FRONT VIEW   R SIDE V

14.38 Use simplified views with unnecessary and confusing hidden lines omitted to improve clarity.

14.14 Two-View Drawings

Time and effort can be saved by drawing only the views and features that are necessary to describe a part. **Figure 14.35** shows typical objects that require only two views in order to be described. The fixture block in **Fig. 14.36** is another example of a part needing only two views to be adequately described. You can see that the top and front views are the best for this part. The front and side views would not be as good.

14.15 One-View Drawings

Simple cylindrical parts and parts of a uniform thickness can be described by only one view, as shown in **Fig. 14.37**. Supplementary notes clarify features that would have been shown in the omitted views. Diameters are labeled with diameter signs and thicknesses are given in notes.

14.16 Simplified and Removed Views

The right- and left-side views of the part in **Fig. 14.38** would be harder to interpret if all hidden lines were drawn by rigorously following the rules of orthographic projection. Simplified views, in which confusing and unnecessary lines have been omitted, are better and more readable.

When it is difficult to show a feature with a standard orthographic view because of its location, a **removed view** can be drawn (**Fig. 14.39**). The removed view, indicated by the directional arrows, is clearer and less confusing when moved to an isolated position.

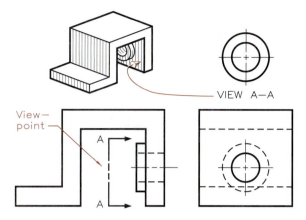

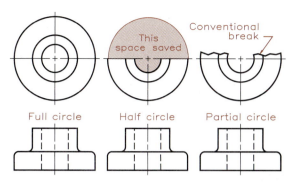

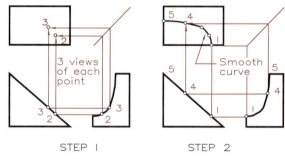

14.39 Use a removed view, indicated by the directional arrows, to show hard-to-see views in removed locations.

14.40 Save space and time by drawing the circular view of a cylindrical part as a partial view.

14.17 Partial Views

Partial views of symmetrical or cylindrical parts may be used to save time and space. Omitting the rear of the circular top view in **Fig. 14.40** saves space without sacrificing clarity. To clarify that a part of the view has been omitted, a conventional break is used in the top view as an option.

14.18 Curve Plotting

An irregular curve can be plotted by following the rules of orthographic projection, as shown in **Fig. 14.41**. Begin by numbering the points in the given front and side views along the curve. Next, project from the points having the same numbers in the front and side views to the top, where the projectors intersect. Continue projecting in this manner and connect the points in the top view with a smooth curve drawn with an irregular curve. **Figure 14.42** shows an ellipse plotted in the top view by projecting points from front and side views. It is best to number the points as they are transferred one at a time to avoid getting lost in your construction.

14.41 Curve plotting

Step 1 Locate points 2 and 3 in the front and side views by projection. Project points 2 and 3 to the top view.

Step 2 Locate the remaining points in the three views and connect them in the top view with a smooth curve.

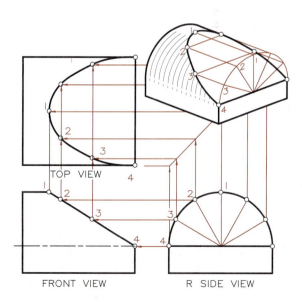

14.42 The ellipse in the top view was found by numbering points in the front and side views and projecting them to the top view.

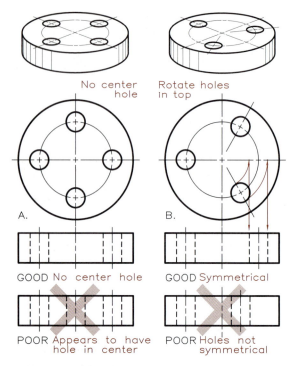

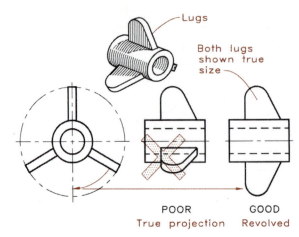

14.43 Placement of holes

A Omit the center hole found by true projection that gives an impression that a hole passes through the center of the plate.

B Use a conventional view to show the holes located at their true radial distances from the center. They are imagined to be rotated to the centerline in the top view.

14.44 Symmetrically positioned external features, such as webs, ribs, and these lugs, are imagined to be revolved to their true-size positions for the best views.

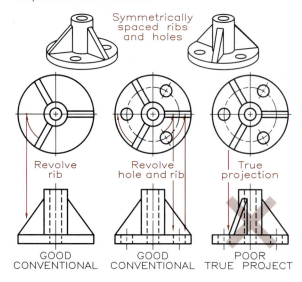

14.45 Conventional methods of revolving holes and ribs in combination improve clarity.

14.19 Conventional Practices

The readability of an orthographic view may be improved if the rules of projection are violated. Violations of rules customarily made for the sake of clarity are called **conventional practices**.

Symmetrically spaced holes in a circular plate (**Fig. 14.43**) are drawn at their true radial distance from the center of the plate in the front view as a conventional practice. Imagine that the holes are revolved to the centerline in the top view before projecting them to the front view.

This principle of revolution also applies to symmetrically positioned features such as ribs, webs, and the three lugs on the outside of the part shown in **Fig. 14.44**. **Figure 14.45** shows the applications of conventional practices to holes and ribs in combination.

Another conventional revolution is illustrated in **Fig. 14.46**, where the front view of an inclined arm is imagined to be revolved to a horizontal position so that it can be drawn true size in the top view. The arm in its revolved position in the front view is not drawn because the revolution is imaginary.

Figure 14.47 shows how to clarify views of parts by conventional revolution. By revolving

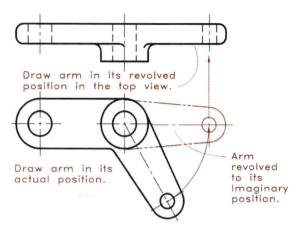

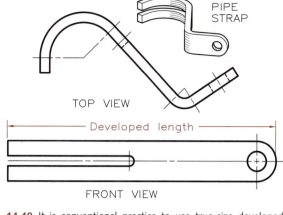

14.46 Imagine that the front view of the arm is revolved so its true length can be drawn in the top view as a conventional practice.

14.48 It is conventional practice to use true-size developed (flattened-out) views of parts made of bent sheet metal.

the top views of these parts 45°, slots and holes no longer coincide with the centerlines and can be seen more clearly. Draw the front views of the slots and holes true size by imagining that they have been revolved 45°.

Another type of conventional view is the true-size development of a curved sheet-metal part drawn as a flattened-out view (**Fig. 14.48**). The top view shows the part's curvature.

14.20 Conventional Intersections

In orthographic projection, lines are drawn to represent the intersections (fold lines) between planes of object. Wherever planes intersect, forming an edge, this line of intersection is projected to its adjacent view. Examples showing where lines are required are given in **Fig. 14.49**.

Figure 14.50 shows how to draw intersections between cylinders, rather than plotting

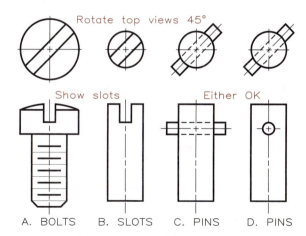

14.47 It is conventional practice to draw the slots and holes at 45° in the top view and at true size in the front view.

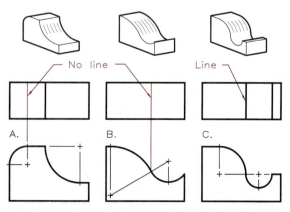

14.49 Object lines are drawn only where there are sharp intersections or where arcs are tangent at their centerlines, as at C.

14.20 CONVENTIONAL INTERSECTIONS • 169

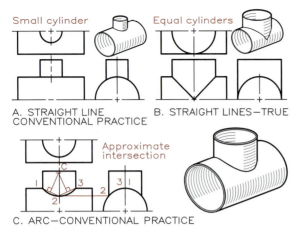

A. STRAIGHT LINE
CONVENTIONAL PRACTICE

B. STRAIGHT LINES—TRUE

Approximate
intersection

C. ARC—CONVENTIONAL PRACTICE

14.50 Intersections between cylinders

A and **C** Use these methods of representation.

B Equal-size cylinders have straight-line intersections.

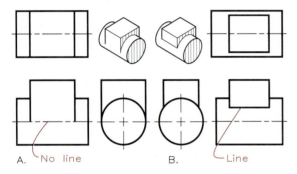

A. No line

B.

Line

14.51 These are true intersections between cylinders and prisms.

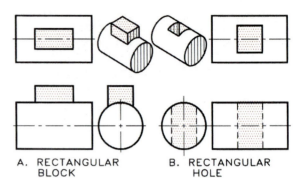

A. RECTANGULAR
BLOCK

B. RECTANGULAR
HOLE

14.52 These are conventional intersections between cylinders and prisms.

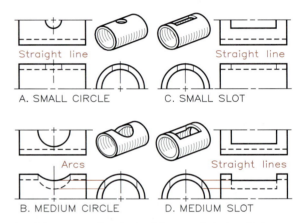

Straight line

Straight line

A. SMALL CIRCLE

C. SMALL SLOT

Arcs

Straight lines

B. MEDIUM CIRCLE

D. MEDIUM SLOT

14.53 Conventional methods of depicting holes in cylinders are easier to draw and to understand than true projections.

more complex, orthographically correct lines of intersection. **Figures 14.50A** and **C** show conventional intersections, which means they are approximations drawn for ease of construction while being sufficiently representative of the object. **Figure 14.50B** shows an easy-to-draw intersection between cylinders of equal diameters, and this is a true intersection as well. **Figures 14.51** and **14.52** show other cylindrical intersections, and **Fig. 14.53** shows conventional practices for depicting intersections formed by holes in cylinders.

14.21 Fillets and Rounds

Fillets and rounds are rounded intersections between the planes of a part that are used on castings, such as the body of the pillow block in **Fig. 14.54**. A fillet is an inside rounding and a round is an external rounding on a part. The radii of fillets and rounds usually are small, about 1/4 inch. Fillets give added strength at inside corners, rounds improve appearance, and both remove sharp edges (**Fig. 14.55**).

A casting will have square corners after its surface has been finished, which is the process of machining away part of the surface to a smooth finish (**Fig. 14.56**). Finished surfaces are indicated by placing a finish mark (V) on all edge views of finished surfaces, whether the edges are visible or hidden. **Figure 14.57** shows

14.54 The edges of this pillow block are rounded with fillets and rounds. The surface of the casting is rough except where it a has been machined. (*Courtesy of Dodge Mfgr. Company.*)

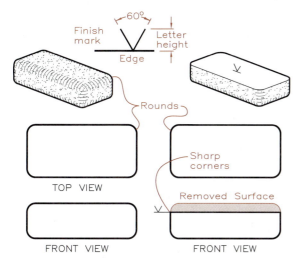

14.55 When a surface is finished (machined), the cut removes the rounded corners and leaves sharp corners. The finish mark placed on the edge of the surface indicates that it is to be finished.

four types of finish marks. A more detailed surface texture symbol is presented in Chapter 20. **Figure 14.58** illustrates several techniques for showing fillets and rounds on orthographic views with a circle template.

Computer Method Fillets and rounds are drawn by computer as shown in **Fig. 14.59**. The object is first drawn with angular intersections, and the *Fillet* command is used to round the corners for both fillets and rounds.

14.58 These examples show both poorly drawn and conventionally drawn fillets and rounds.

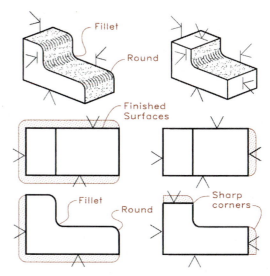

14.56 Fillets and rounds are rounded inside and outside corners, respectively, that are standard features on castings. When surfaces are finished, fillets and rounds are removed, as shown here.

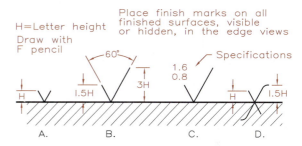

14.57 Any of these finish marks are placed on all edge views of finished surfaces, whether visible or hidden.

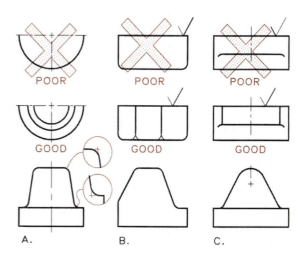

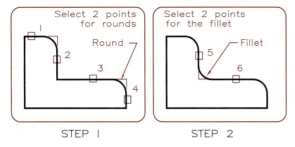

STEP 1 | STEP 2

14.59 Fillets and rounds by computer

Step 1 *Command: Fillet* (Enter)

Select first object or [Polyline/Radius/Trim]: R (Enter)

Specify fillet radius [0.000]: .50 (Enter)

Command: (Enter)

Select first object or [Polyline/Radius/Trim]:(Select 1 and 2; a round is drawn.) (Enter) (Select 3 and 4 to draw another round.)

Step 2 *Command:* (Enter) (Select 5 and 6 when prompted and the fillet is drawn. The lines are trimmed at the fillets and rounds.)

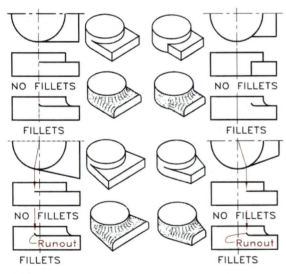

14.60 These examples show conventional intersections and runouts on cylindrical features. Runouts result from fillets and rounds intersecting cylinders.

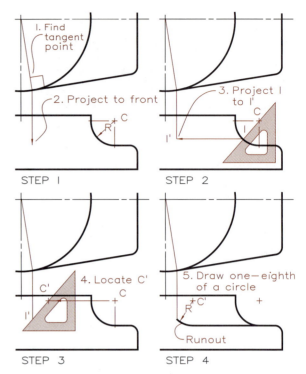

STEP 1 | STEP 2

STEP 3 | STEP 4

14.61 Plotting runouts

Step 1 Find the tangency point in the top view and project it to the front view.

Step 2 Find point 1 with a 45° triangle; project it to 1′.

Step 3 Move the 45° triangle to locate point C′ on the horizontal projector from center C.

Step 4 Use the radius of the fillet to draw the runout with C′ as its center. The runout arc is drawn as one-eighth of a circle.

Figure 14.60 gives a comparison of intersections and **runouts** of parts with and without fillets and rounds. Large runouts are constructed as an eighth of a circle with a compass, as shown in **Fig. 14.61**. Small runouts are drawn with a circle template. Runouts on orthographic views

reveal much about the details of an object. For example, the runout in the top view of Fig. **14.62A** tells us that the rib has rounded edges, whereas the top view of **Fig. 14.62B** tells us the rib is completely round. **Figures 14.63** and **14.64** illustrate other types of filleted and rounded intersections.

Computer Method A drawing of a part with runouts at its tangent points is shown in **Fig. 14.65**. The runouts are plotted by using the *Line* command, then using the *Arc* command, and finally pressing (Enter) to obtain the first point of an arc tangent to and connected to the end of

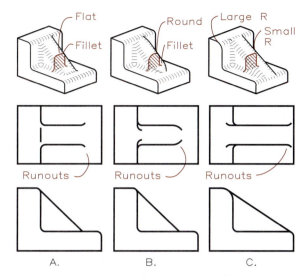

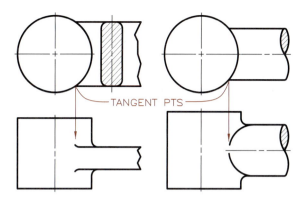

14.62 These are conventional representations of runouts.

14.64 These are conventional runouts for cylinders of different cross sections.

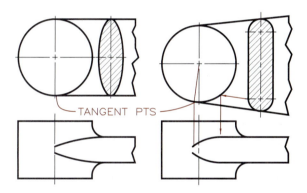

14.63 Conventional representation of runouts.

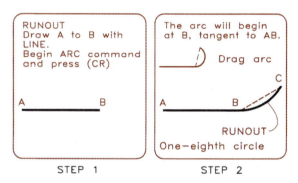

the line. Locate the other end of the arc to complete the runout.

14.22 First-Angle Projection

The examples in this chapter are third-angle projections in which the top view is placed over the front view and the right-side view is placed to the right of the front view, as shown in **Fig. 14.66**. This method is used in the United States,

RUNOUT Draw A to B with LINE. Begin ARC command and press (CR) A ————————— B	The arc will begin at B, tangent to AB. Drag arc A ———————— B RUNOUT One-eighth circle
STEP 1	STEP 2

14.65 Runouts by computer
Step 1 *Command:* Line (Enter)
Specify first point: A (Enter)
Specify next point or [Undo]: B (Enter)
Step 2 *Command:* Arc (Enter)
Specify start point or arc or [CEnter]: (Enter)
Specify end point of arc: C (Drag to point C.)

14.66 Third-angle projection is used for drawing orthographic views in the U.S., Great Britain, and Canada. The top view is placed over the front view and the right-side view is placed to the right of the front view. The truncated cone is the symbol used to designate third-angle projection.

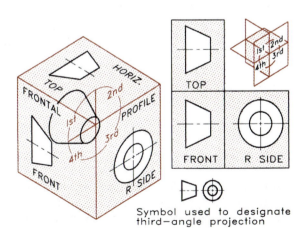

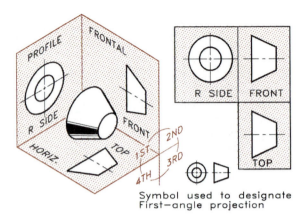

14.67 First-angle projection is used in most of the world. It shows the right-side view to the left of the front view and the top view under the front view. The truncated cone designates first-angle projection.

14.68 These symbols are placed on drawings to specify first-angle or third-angle projection and metric units of measurement.

Great Britain, and Canada. However, most of the world uses first-angle projection.

The first-angle system is illustrated in **Fig. 14.67**, in which an object is placed above the horizontal plane and in front of the frontal plane. When these projection planes are opened onto the surface of the drawing paper, the front view projects over the top view, and the right-side view to the left of the front view.

The angle of projection used in making a drawing is indicated by placing the truncated cone in or near the title block (**Fig. 14.68**). When metric units of measurement are used, the SI symbol is given in combination with the cone on the drawing.

14.23 Summary

The techniques of orthographic projection introduced in this chapter can be used to design and communicate designs from the simple to the complex. Orthographic projection is an important medium of design and the language of engineering, without which the marvels of the twentieth century could not have come into being.

With the advent of computer graphics, many designs are depicted as three-dimensional pictorials in order to show objects in views as if they had been photographed by a camera. Despite these powerful computer capabilities, a precisely drawn and dimensioned orthographic view may give the fabrication details with greater clarity.

You will use orthographic projection throughout your career as a valuable means of developing design concepts.

Problems

1–7. (Figs. 14.69–14.75) Draw the given views on size A sheets, two per sheet, using the dimensions given and draw the missing top, front, or right-side views. Lines may be missing in the given views.

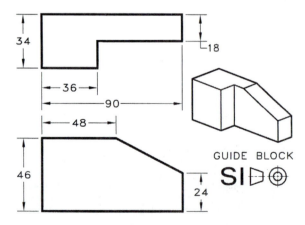

14.69 Problem 1.

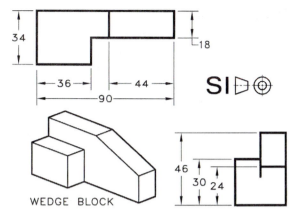

14.70 Problem 2.

WEDGE BLOCK

SI

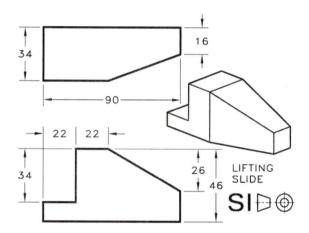

14.71 Problem 3.

LIFTING SLIDE

SI

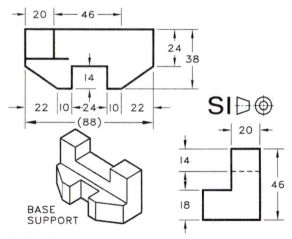

14.72 Problem 4.

BASE SUPPORT

SI

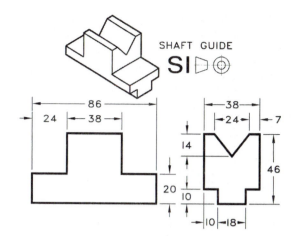

SHAFT GUIDE

SI

14.73 Problem 5.

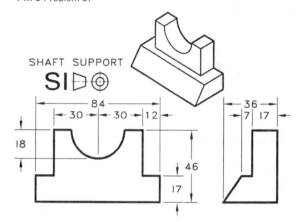

SHAFT SUPPORT

SI

14.74 Problem 6.

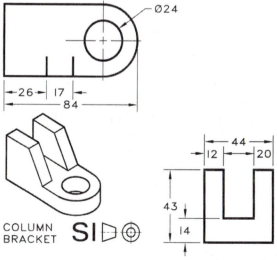

COLUMN BRACKET

SI

Ø24

14.75 Problem 7.

8–29. (Fig. 14.76- Fig. 14.97) Construct the necessary orthographic views to describe the objects on B-size sheets at an appropriate scale. Label the views and show the overall dimensions of W, D, and H.

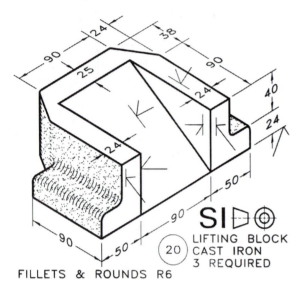

14.76 Problem 8.

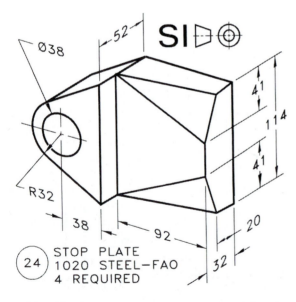

14.77 Problem 9.

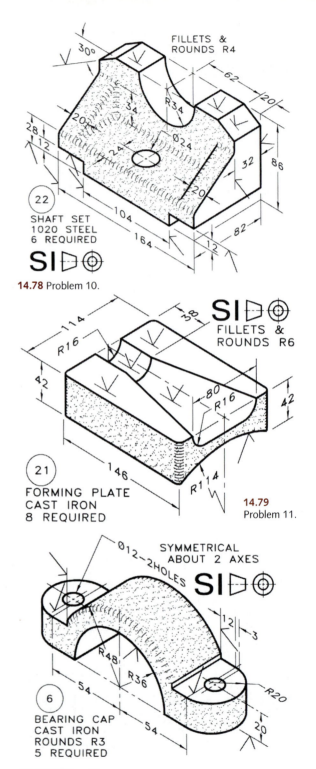

14.78 Problem 10.

14.79 Problem 11.

14.80 Problem 12.

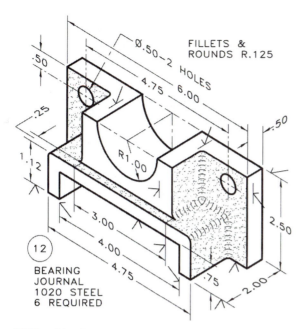

14.81 Problem 13.

FILLETS &
ROUNDS R.125

Ø.50-2 HOLES

4.75
6.00

.50
.25
1.12
3.00
4.00
4.75
.50
2.50
.75
2.00

12

BEARING
JOURNAL
1020 STEEL
6 REQUIRED

R1.00

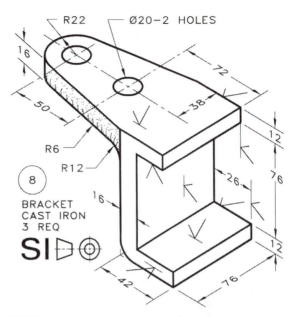

14.83 Problem 15.

R22
Ø20-2 HOLES
16
50
72
38
12
76
26
16
42
76
12

R6
R12

8

BRACKET
CAST IRON
3 REQ

SI

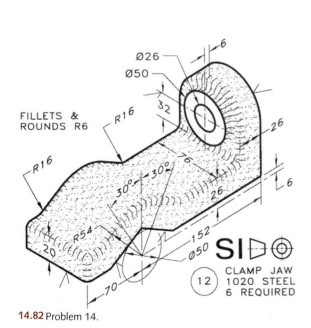

14.82 Problem 14.

Ø26
Ø50
6

FILLETS &
ROUNDS R6

R16
R16
32
26
6

30°
30°
76
26
152
Ø50

R54
20
70

SI

12

CLAMP JAW
1020 STEEL
6 REQUIRED

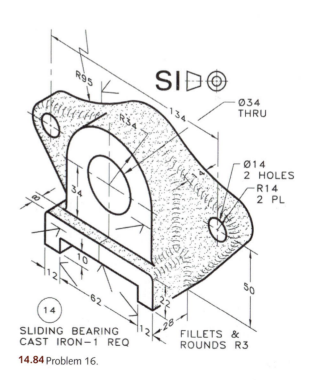

14.84 Problem 16.

R95
134
SI
Ø34
THRU
R34
Ø14
2 HOLES
R14
2 PL
34
8
10
12
62
12
28
22
50

14

SLIDING BEARING
CAST IRON-1 REQ

FILLETS &
ROUNDS R3

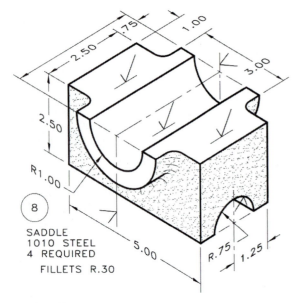

8

SADDLE
1010 STEEL
4 REQUIRED
FILLETS R.30

14.85 Problem 17.

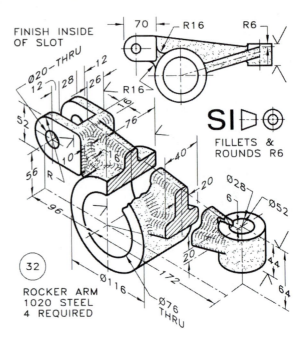

FINISH INSIDE
OF SLOT

SI ▷⊙

FILLETS &
ROUNDS R6

32

ROCKER ARM
1020 STEEL
4 REQUIRED

14.87 Problem 19.

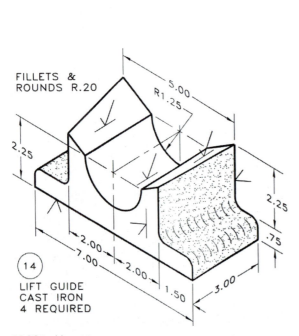

FILLETS &
ROUNDS R.20

14

LIFT GUIDE
CAST IRON
4 REQUIRED

14.86 Problem 18.

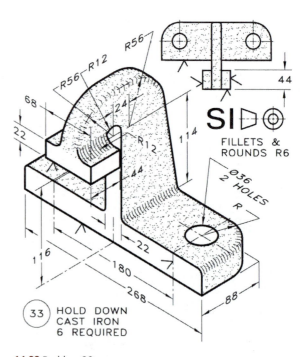

SI ▷⊙

FILLETS &
ROUNDS R6

33

HOLD DOWN
CAST IRON
6 REQUIRED

14.88 Problem 20.

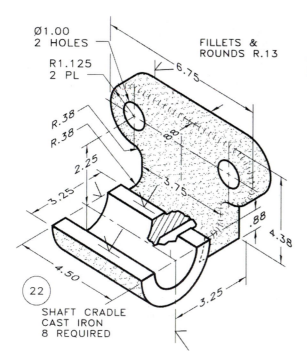

Ø1.00
2 HOLES

FILLETS &
ROUNDS R.13

6.75

R1.125
2 PL

R.38
R.38

2.25

3.25

.88

3.75

.88

4.38

4.50

(22)

3.25

SHAFT CRADLE
CAST IRON
8 REQUIRED

14.89 Problem 21.

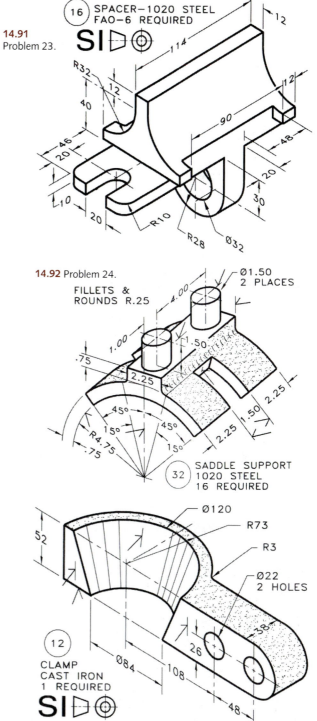

14.91
Problem 23.

(16) SPACER-1020 STEEL
FAO-6 REQUIRED

SI▷◉

12

114

R32

12

40

90

12

46

20

48

10

20

R10

R28

Ø32

20

30

14.92 Problem 24.

Ø1.50
2 PLACES

FILLETS &
ROUNDS R.25

4.00

1.00

.75

1.50

2.25

45°

45°

15°

15°

R4.75

.75

2.25

1.50

2.25

1.50

SADDLE SUPPORT
1020 STEEL
16 REQUIRED

(32)

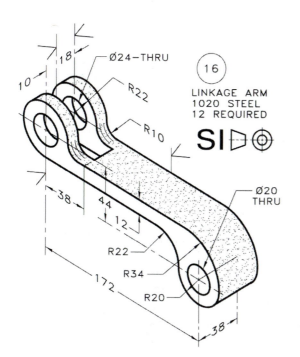

18

10

Ø24-THRU

R22

(16)

LINKAGE ARM
1020 STEEL
12 REQUIRED

SI▷◉

R10

Ø20
THRU

38

44

12

R22

R34

172

R20

38

14.90 Problem 22.

Ø120

R73

52

R3

Ø22
2 HOLES

(12)

CLAMP
CAST IRON
1 REQUIRED

SI▷◉

Ø84

26

108

38

48

14.93 Problem 25.

PROBLEMS • 179

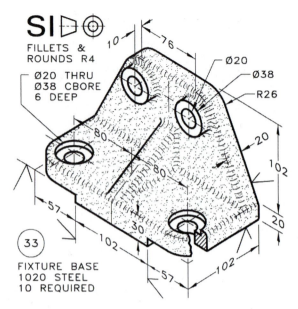

SI⬠⊕

FILLETS & ROUNDS R4

Ø20 THRU
Ø38 CBORE
6 DEEP

10
76
Ø20
Ø38
R26
80
80
20
102
20
57
102
30
102
57

33

FIXTURE BASE
1020 STEEL
10 REQUIRED

14.94 Problem 26.

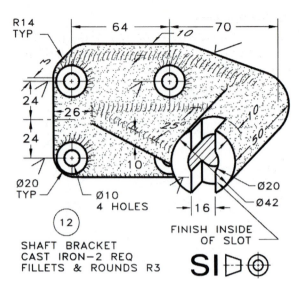

R14 TYP
64
70
10
3
24
26
25°
10
24
50
10
Ø20 TYP
Ø10
4 HOLES
10
Ø20
Ø42
16

12

FINISH INSIDE
OF SLOT

SI⬠⊕

SHAFT BRACKET
CAST IRON—2 REQ
FILLETS & ROUNDS R3

14.96 Problem 28.

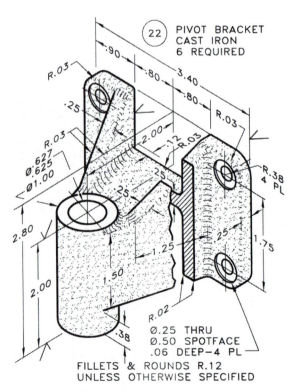

22 PIVOT BRACKET
CAST IRON
6 REQUIRED

R.03
.90
.80
3.40
.80
R.03
.25
2.00
.12
R.03
R.03
.627
Ø.625
Ø1.00
.25
.25
R.38
4 PL
2.80
.25
2.00
1.25
1.75
1.50
R.02
.38
Ø.25 THRU
Ø.50 SPOTFACE
.06 DEEP—4 PL

FILLETS & ROUNDS R.12
UNLESS OTHERWISE SPECIFIED

14.95 Problem 27.

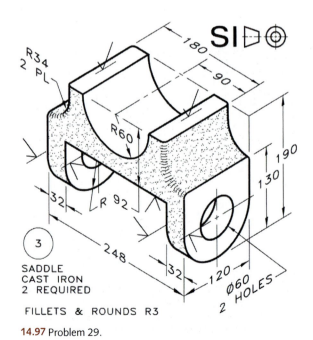

SI⬠⊕

R34
2 PL
180
90
R60
R 92
190
130
32
32
248
120
Ø60
2 HOLES

3

SADDLE
CAST IRON
2 REQUIRED

FILLETS & ROUNDS R3

14.97 Problem 29.

Design Problems:

Follow the instructions for each of the partially-dimensioned problems given below as if you were the original designer.

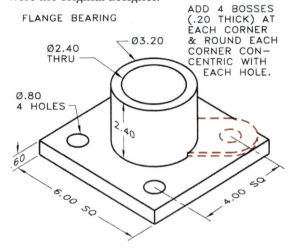

FLANGE BEARING

Ø2.40 THRU

Ø3.20

ADD 4 BOSSES (.20 THICK) AT EACH CORNER & ROUND EACH CORNER CONCENTRIC WITH EACH HOLE.

Ø.80 4 HOLES

2.40

.60

6.00 SQ

4.00 SQ

Design 1 Redesign the flange bearing to have four bosses and round each corner as noted. Draw the necessary views to describe the part.

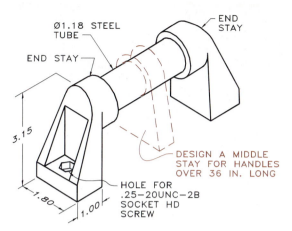

Ø1.18 STEEL TUBE

END STAY

END STAY

3.15

1.80

1.00

DESIGN A MIDDLE STAY FOR HANDLES OVER 36 IN. LONG

HOLE FOR .25-20UNC-2B SOCKET HD SCREW

Design 3 Handle assembly

Option 1: Draw the views of the end stays of the door handle to adequately describe them.

Option 2: Design a middle stay that can be used for handles over 36 in. and draw the necessary orthographic views to describe your design.

Option 3: Design a completely different handle and make the necessary instrument drawings (orthographic views) to describe it adequately.

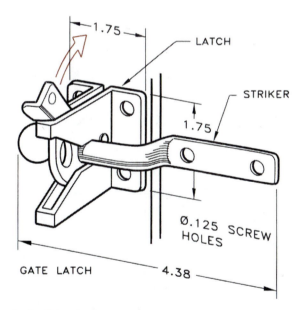

1.75

LATCH

STRIKER

1.75

Ø.125 SCREW HOLES

GATE LATCH

4.38

Design 2 Gate latch

Option 1: Make instrument drawings of the parts of the partially dimensioned gate latch on size A sheet or sheets.

Option 2: Design a different gate latch and make the necessary instrument drawings to describe your design.

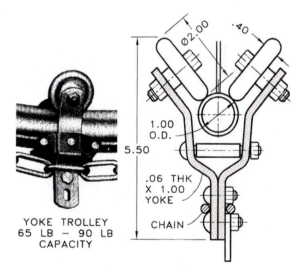

Ø2.00

.40

1.00 O.D.

5.50

.06 THK X 1.00 YOKE

CHAIN

YOKE TROLLEY 65 LB – 90 LB CAPACITY

Design 4 Yoke trolley

Option 1: Make the necessary orthographic freehand sketches of the parts of the trolley.

Option 2: Make the necessary orthographic views of the parts of the trolley using instruments.

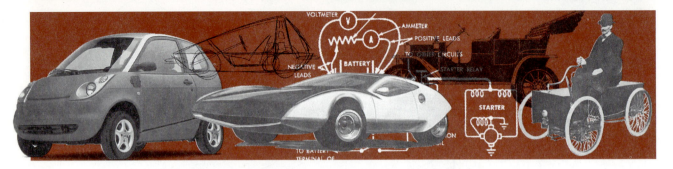

Primary Auxiliary Views

15.1 Introduction

Objects often are designed to have sloping or inclined surfaces that do not appear true size in principal orthographic views. A plane of this type is not parallel to a principal projection plane (horizontal, frontal, or profile) and is, therefore, a **nonprincipal plane**. Its true shape must be projected onto a plane that is parallel to it. This view is called an **auxiliary view**.

An auxiliary view projected from a primary view (principal view) is called a **primary auxiliary view**. An auxiliary view projected from a primary auxiliary view is a **secondary auxiliary view**. By the way, get out your dividers; you must use them all the time in drawing auxiliary views.

The inclined surface of the part shown in **Fig. 15.1A** does not appear true size in the top view because it is not parallel to the horizontal projection plane. However, the inclined surface will appear true size in an auxiliary view projected perpendicularly from its edge view in the front view **(Fig. 15.1B).**

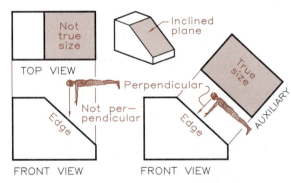

15.1 A surface that appears as an inclined edge in a principal view can be seen true size in an auxiliary view. (A) The top view is foreshortened, but the inclined plane is true size in the auxiliary view at (B).

The relationship between an auxiliary view and the view it was projected from is the same as that between any two adjacent orthographic views. **Figure 15.2A** shows an auxiliary view pro-

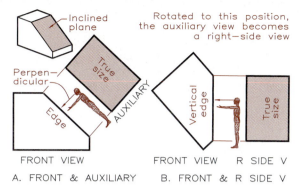

A. FRONT & AUXILIARY   B. FRONT & R SIDE V

15.2 An auxiliary view has the same relationship with the view it is projected from as that of any two adjacent principal views.

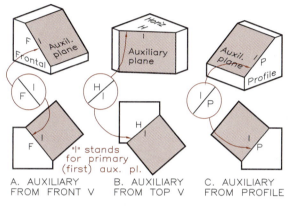

A. AUXILIARY FROM FRONT V   B. AUXILIARY FROM TOP V   C. AUXILIARY FROM PROFILE

15.3 A primary auxiliary plane can be folded from the frontal, horizontal, or profile planes. The fold lines are labeled F–1, H–1, and P–1, with 1 on the auxiliary plane side and P on the principal plane side.

jected perpendicularly from the edge view of the sloping surface. By rotating these views (the front and auxiliary views) so that the projectors are horizontal, the views have the same relationship as regular front and right-side views (**Fig. 15.2B**).

15.2 Folding-Line Principles

The three principal orthographic planes are the **frontal** (F), **horizontal** (H), and **profile** (P) planes. An auxiliary view is projected from a principal orthographic view (a top, front, or side view), and a primary auxiliary plane is perpendicular to one of the principal planes and oblique to the other two.

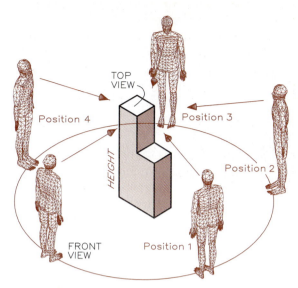

15.4 By moving your viewpoint around the top view of an object, you will see a series of auxiliary views in which the height dimension (H) is true length in all of them.

Think of auxiliary planes as planes that fold into principal planes along a folding line (**Fig. 15.3**). The plane in **Fig. 15.3A** folds at a 90° angle with the frontal plane and is labeled F–1, where F is an abbreviation for frontal and 1 represents the first, or primary, auxiliary plane. **Figures 15.3B** and **15.3C** illustrate the positions for auxiliary planes that fold from the horizontal and profile planes, labeled H–1 and P–1, respectively.

It is important that reference lines be labeled as shown in **Fig. 15.3**, with the numeral 1 placed on the auxiliary side and the letter H, F, or P on the principal-plane side.

15.3 Auxiliaries from the Top View

By moving your position about the top view of a part as shown in **Fig. 15.4**, each line of sight is perpendicular to the height dimension. One of the views, the front view, is a principal view while the other positions see nonprincipal views called **auxiliary views**.

Figure 15.5 illustrates how these five views (one of which is a front view) are projected from the top view. The line of sight for each auxiliary view is parallel to the horizontal projection plane; therefore the height dimension is true length in each view projected from a top view. The height (H) dimensions are transferred from the front to each of the auxiliary views by using your dividers.

Folding-Line Method

The inclined plane shown in **Fig. 15.6** is an edge in the top view and is perpendicular to the horizontal plane. If an auxiliary plane is drawn parallel to the inclined surface, the view projected onto it will be a true-size view of the inclined surface. **A surface must appear as an edge in a principal view in order for it to be found true size in a primary auxiliary view**. When the auxiliary

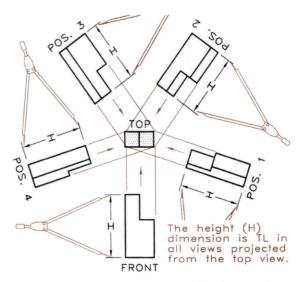

15.5 The views shown in Fig. 15.4 would be drawn as shown here with the same height dimension common to each view.

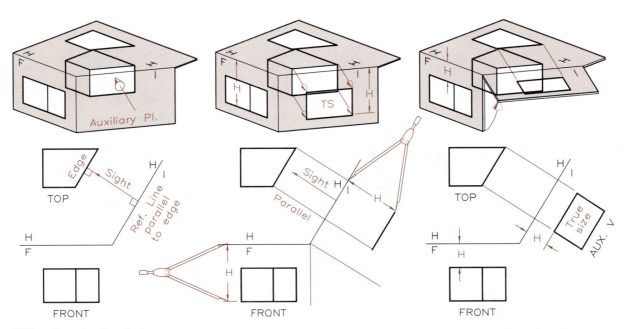

15.6 Auxiliary view from the top

Step 1 Draw the line of sight perpendicular to the edge view of the inclined surface. Draw the H–1 line parallel to its edge and draw the H–F reference line between the top and front views.

Step 2 Project from the edge view of the inclined surface parallel to the line of sight. Transfer the H dimensions from the front to locate a line in the auxiliary view.

Step 3 Locate the other corners of the inclined surface by projecting to the auxiliary view and locating the points by transferring the height (H) from the front view.

view is projected from the top view, the height dimensions in the front view must be transferred to the auxiliary view with your dividers.

15.4 Auxiliaries from the Top: Application

Figure 15.7 illustrates how the folding-line method is used to find an auxiliary view of a part that is imagined to be in a glass box. The semicircular end of the part does not appear true size in front or side views, making these views difficult to draw and to interpret if they were drawn. However, because the inclined surface appears as an edge in the top view, it can be found true size in a primary auxiliary view projected from the top view. The height dimension (H) in the frontal view will be the same as in the auxiliary plane because both planes are perpendicular to the horizontal projection plane. Height is transferred from the front to the auxiliary view with your dividers. In **Fig. 15.8**, the auxiliary plane is rotated about the H–1 fold line into the plane of the top view, the horizontal projection plane. This rotation illustrates how the placement of the views is determined when drawing the views.

When drawn on a sheet of paper, the views of this object appear as shown in **Fig. 15.9**. The top view is a complete view, but the front view is drawn as a partial view because the omitted portion would have been hard to draw and would not have been true size. The auxiliary view also is drawn as a partial view because the front view shows the omitted features better, which saves drawing time and space on a drawing.

Reference-Plane Method

A second method of locating an auxiliary view uses reference planes instead of the folding-line method. **Figure 15.10A** shows a horizontal reference plane (HRP) drawn through the center of the front view. Because this view is symmetrical, equal height dimensions on both sides of the HRP can be conveniently transferred from the

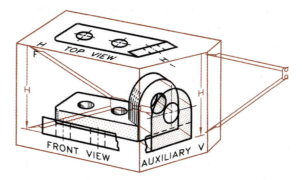

15.7 By imagining that the object is inside a glass box, you can see the relationship of the auxiliary plane, on which the true-size view is projected, and the horizontal projection plane.

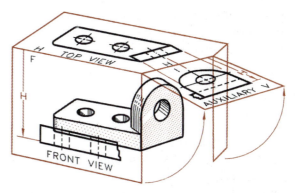

15.8 Fold the auxiliary plane into the horizontal projection plane by revolving it about the H–1 fold line.

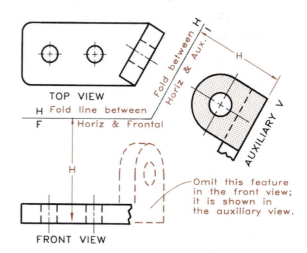

15.9 The front and auxiliary views are shown as partial views. The omitted portions of these views are unnecessary because their details are explained by the adjacent views.

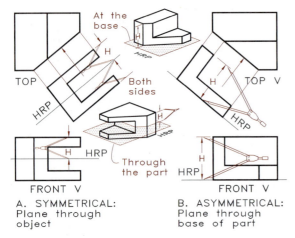

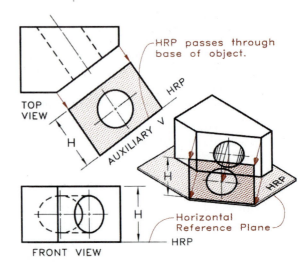

15.10 A horizontal reference plane (HRP) can be positioned through the part or in contact with it. The dimension of height (H) is measured from the HRP and transferred to the auxiliary view with your dividers.

15.11 An auxiliary view projected from the top view is used to draw a true-size view of the inclined surface using a horizontal reference plane. The HRP is drawn through the bottom of the front view.

front view to the auxiliary view and laid off on both sides of the HRP.

The reference plane can be placed at the base of the front view, as shown in **Fig. 15.10B**. In this case, the height dimensions are measured upward from the HRP in both the front and auxiliary views. You may draw a reference plane (the HRP in this example) in any convenient position in the front view: through the part, above it, or below it.

A similar example of an auxiliary view drawn with a horizontal reference plane is shown in **Fig. 15.11**. In this example, the hole appears as a true circle in the auxiliary view instead of as an ellipse.

15.5 Rules of Auxiliary Construction

Now that several examples of auxiliary views have been discussed, it would be helpful to summarize the general rules of construction, which are outlined in **Fig. 15.12**.

1. An auxiliary view that shows a surface true size must be projected perpendicularly from

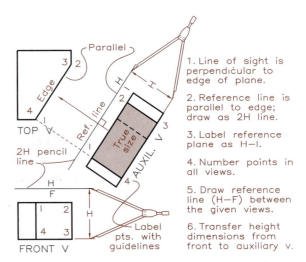

15.12 Rules of Auxiliary view construction

Step 1 Draw a line of sight perpendicular to the edge of the inclined surface. Draw the H–1 fold line parallel to the edge of the inclined surface and draw an H–F fold line between the given views.

Step 2 Find points 1 and 2 by transferring the height (H) dimensions with your dividers from the front view to the auxiliary view.

Step 3 Find points 3 and 4 in the same manner by transferring the H dimensions.

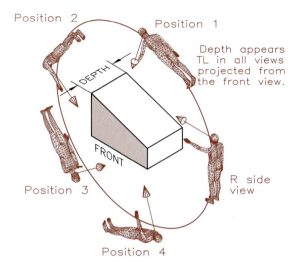

15.13 By moving your viewpoint around the frontal view of an object, you will see a series of auxiliary views in which the depth dimension (D) is true length in all views.

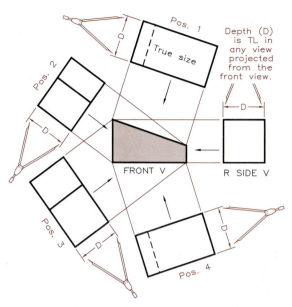

15.14 The auxiliary views shown in Fig. 15.13 would be seen in this arrangement when viewing the front view.

the edge view of the surface. Usually, the inclined surface, or a partial view, is all that is needed in the auxiliary view, but the entire object can be drawn in the auxiliary view if desired, as shown here.

2. Draw the sight line perpendicular to the inclined edge of the plane you wish to find true size (TS).

3. Draw the reference line, H–1 for example, parallel to the edge view of the inclined plane, which will be perpendicular to the line of sight.

4. Draw and label a reference line between the given views (front and top in this example). Draw reference lines (fold lines) as thin, dark lines with a 2H or 3H pencil.

5. If an auxiliary is projected from the front view, it will have an F-1 reference line; if it is projected from the horizontal view (top view), it will have an H–1 reference line; and if projected from the side view (profile view), it will have a P–1 reference plane.

6. Transfer measurements from the other given view with your dividers (not the view you are projecting from)—height in the front view in this example.

7. It would be helpful to number the points one at a time in the primary views and the auxiliary views as they are plotted.

8. Do your lettering in a professional manner with guidelines.

9. Connect the points with light construction lines and use light gray projectors that do not have to be erased with a pencil in the 2H–4H range.

10. Draw the outlines of the auxiliary view as thick, visible lines, the same weight as visible lines in principal views, with an F or HB pencil.

15.6 Auxiliaries from the Front View

By moving about the front view of the part as shown in **Fig. 15.13**, you will be looking parallel to the edge view of the frontal plane. Therefore, the depth dimension (D) will appear true size in each auxiliary view projected from the front view. One of the positions gives a principal view, the right-side view, and position 1 gives a true-size view of the inclined plane. **Figure 15.14**

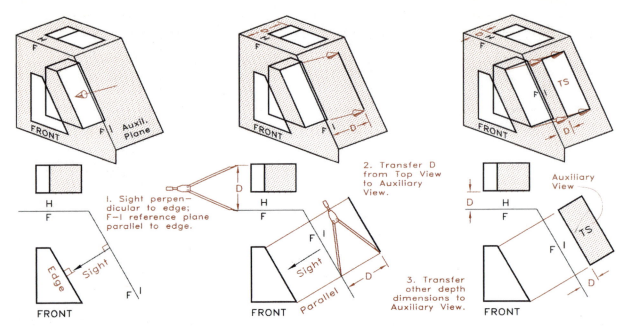

15.15 Auxiliary from the front: Folding-line method

Step 1 Draw the line of sight perpendicular to the edge of the plane and draw the F–1 line parallel to it. Draw the H–F fold line between the top and front views.

Step 2 Project perpendicularly from the edge view of the inclined surface and parallel to the line of sight. Transfer the depth dimensions (D) from the top to the auxiliary view with dividers.

Step 3 Locate the other corners of the inclined surface by projecting to the auxiliary view. Locate the points by transferring the depth dimensions (D) from the top to the auxiliary view.

illustrates the relationship between the auxiliary views projected from the front view.

Folding-Line Method

A plane of an object that appears as an edge in the front view (**Fig. 15.15**) is true size in an auxiliary view projected perpendicularly from it. Draw fold line F–1 parallel to the edge view of the inclined plane in the front view at a convenient location.

Draw the line of sight perpendicular to the edge view of the inclined plane in the front view. When observed from this direction, the frontal plane appears as an edge; therefore measurements perpendicular to the frontal plane depth dimensions (D) will be seen true length. Transfer depth dimensions from the top view to the auxiliary view with your dividers.

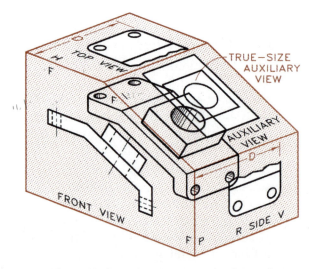

15.16 This part is shown in an imaginary glass box to illustrate the relationship of the auxiliary plane, on which the true-size view of the inclined surface is projected, to the principal planes.

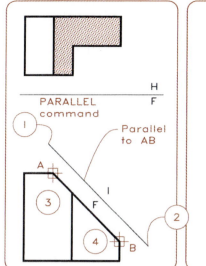
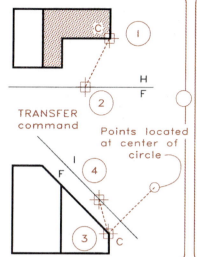
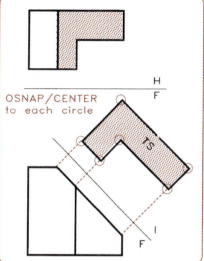

15.18 Auxiliary view by AutoCAD

Step 1 Type *Parallel* to receive the prompts for the first end of the reference line (1) and its approximate second endpoint (2). You are then prompted for the ends of line AB, to which the reference line is parallel.

Step 2 Type *Transfer*; you are prompted for a point in the top view (1) and its distance from the H-F line (2) to transfer. You are prompted for the front view of the point to project (3) and the reference line (4). Point C is projected to the auxiliary view.

Step 3 Continue using *Transfer* to locate the other corner points of the inclined plane. Connect the points using the *Center* option of *Osnap* to snap to the centers of the circles. *Erase* the circles after connecting their centers.

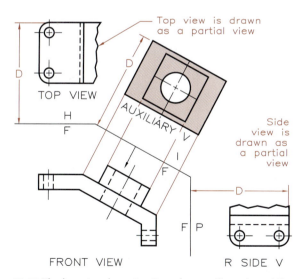

15.17 The layout and construction of an auxiliary view of the object shown in Fig. 15.16 is shown here.

The object in **Fig. 15.16** is imagined to be enclosed in a glass box and an auxiliary plane is folded from the frontal plane to be parallel to the inclined surface. When drawn on a sheet of paper, the views appear as shown in **Fig. 15.17**. The top and side views are drawn as partial views because the auxiliary view eliminates the need for drawing complete views. The auxiliary view, located by transferring the depth dimension measured perpendicularly from the edge view of the frontal plane in the top view and transferred to the auxiliary view, shows the surface's true size.

Computer Method Find the true-size view of the inclined surface that appears as an edge in the front view (**Fig. 15.18**) by using the *Lisp* commands, *Parallel* and *Transfer* (see Section 26.2).

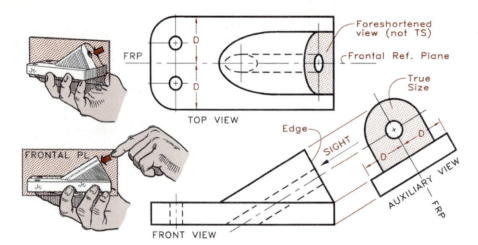

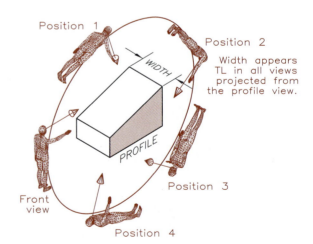

15.19 Because the inclined surface is symmetrical, a frontal reference plane (FRP) that passes through the object is used. Project the auxiliary view perpendicularly from the edge view of the plane. The FRP appears as an edge in the auxiliary view, and depth dimensions (D) are transferred from both sides of it in the top view to find its true-size view of the inclined surface.

(This program is not a regular part of AutoCAD, but it is an excellent addition to have available for solving auxiliary problems. It was developed by Professor Leendert Kersten of the University of Nebraska. Once copied as a *Lisp* file, it is accessed by typing (Load "*ACAD*") at the command line, and be sure to use the parentheses.)

While in AutoCAD's drafting mode, type *Parallel* to draw the reference line parallel to edge AB. Type *Transfer* to obtain prompts for transferring measurements from the top view, as if you were using your dividers. Connect the circular points to complete the auxiliary view.

Reference-Plane Method

The object shown in **Fig. 15.19** has an inclined surface that appears as an edge in the front view; therefore this plane can be found true size in a primary auxiliary view. It is helpful to draw a reference plane through the center of the symmetrical top view because all depth dimensions can be located on each side of the frontal reference plane. Because the reference plane is a frontal plane, it is labeled FRP in the top and auxiliary views. In the auxiliary view, the FRP is drawn parallel to the edge view of the inclined plane at a convenient distance from it. By transferring depth dimensions from the FRP in the top view

to the FRP in the auxiliary view, the symmetrical view of the part is drawn.

15.7 Auxiliaries from the Profile View

By moving your position about the profile view (side view) of the part as shown in **Fig. 15.20**, you will be looking parallel to the edge view of the profile plane. Therefore, the width dimen-

15.20 By moving your viewpoint around a profile (side) view of an object, you will obtain a series of auxiliary views in which the width dimension (W) is true length.

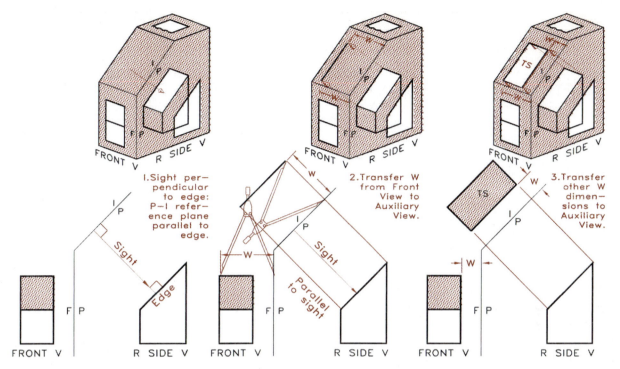

15.22 Auxiliary from the side: Folding-line method

Step 1 Draw a line of sight perpendicular to the edge of the inclined surface. Draw the P–1 fold line parallel to the edge view, and draw the F–P fold line between the given views.

Step 2 Project the corners of the edge view parallel to the line of sight. Transfer the width dimensions (W) from the front view to locate a line in the auxiliary view.

Step 3 Find the other corners of the inclined surface by projecting to the auxiliary view. Locate the points by transferring the width dimensions (W) from the front view to the auxiliary view.

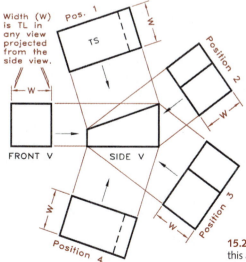

15.21 The auxiliary views shown in Fig. 15.20 would be seen in this arrangement when projected from the side view.

sion will appear true size in each auxiliary view projected from the side view. One of the positions gives a principal view, the front view, and position 1 gives a true-size view of the inclined plane. **Figure 15.21** illustrates the arrangement of the auxiliary views projected from the side view as if they were drawn on a sheet of paper.

Folding-Line Method

Because the inclined surface in **Fig. 15.22** appears as an edge in the profile plane, it can be found true size in a primary auxiliary view pro-

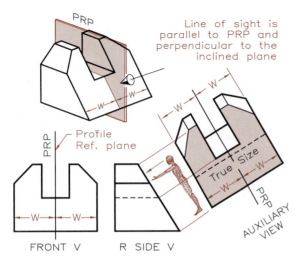

15.23 An auxiliary view is projected from the right-side view by using a profile reference plane (PRP) to show the true-size view of the inclined surface.

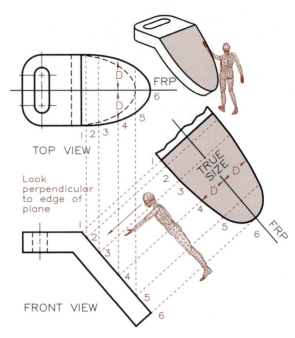

15.25 The auxiliary view of this curved surface required that a series of points located in the top view be projected to the front view, and then projected to the auxiliary view. The FRP was passed through the center of the top view.

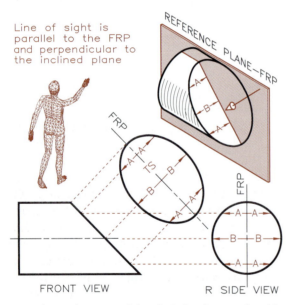

15.24 The auxiliary view of this elliptical surface was found by projecting a series of points found about its perimeter. The frontal reference plane (FRP) is drawn through its center in the side view since the object is symmetrical.

jected from the side view. The auxiliary fold line, P–1, is drawn parallel to the edge view of the inclined surface. A line of sight perpendicular to the auxiliary plane shows the profile plane as an edge. Therefore, width dimensions (W) transferred from the front view to the auxiliary view appear true length in the auxiliary view.

Reference-Plane Method

The object shown in **Fig. 15.23** has an inclined surface that appears as an edge in the right-side view, the profile view. This inclined surface may be drawn true size in an auxiliary view by using a profile reference plane (PRP) that is a vertical edge in the front view. Draw the PRP through the center of the front view, because this view is symmetrical. Then find the true-size view of the inclined plane by transferring equal width dimensions (W) with your dividers from the edge view of the PRP in the front view to both sides of the PRP in the auxiliary view.

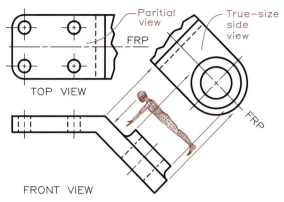

15.26 Partial views with foreshortened portions omitted can be used to represent objects. The FRP reference line is drawn through the center of the object in the top view because the object is symmetrical. This makes point location easier.

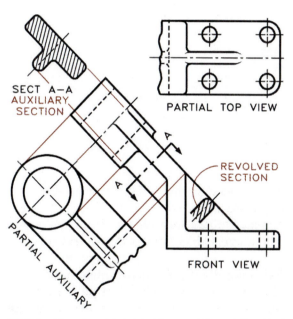

15.27 A cutting plane labeled A–A is passed through the object and the auxiliary section, section A–A, is drawn as a supplementary view to describe the part. The top and front views are drawn as partial views.

15.8 Curved Shapes

The cylinder shown in **Fig. 15.24** has an inclined surface that appears as an edge in the front view. The true-size view of this plane can be seen in an auxiliary view projected from the front view.

Because the cylinder is symmetrical, a frontal reference plane (FRP) is drawn through the center of the side view so that equal dimensions can be laid off on both sides of it. Points located about the circular side view are projected to its edge view in the front view.

In the auxiliary view, the FRP is drawn parallel to the edge view of the plane in the front view, and the points are projected perpendicularly from the edge view of the plane. Dimensions A and B are shown as examples of depth dimensions used for locating points in the auxiliary view. To construct a smooth elliptical curve, more points than shown in this example are needed.

A true-size auxiliary view of a surface bounded by an irregular curve is shown in **Fig. 15.25**. Project points from the curve in the top view to the front view. Locate these points in the auxiliary view by transferring depth dimensions (D) from the FRP in the top view to the auxiliary view.

15.9 Partial Views

Auxiliary views are used as supplementary views to clarify features that are difficult to depict with principal views alone. Consequently, portions of principal views and auxiliary views may be omitted, provided that the partial views adequately describe the part. The object shown in **Fig. 15.26** is composed of a complete front view, a partial auxiliary view, and a partial top view. These partial views are easier to draw and are more descriptive without sacrificing clarity.

15.10 Auxiliary Sections

In **Fig. 15.27**, a cutting plane labeled A–A is passed through the part to obtain the auxiliary section labeled section A–A. The auxiliary section provides a good and efficient way to describe features of the part that could not be as easily described by additional principal views.

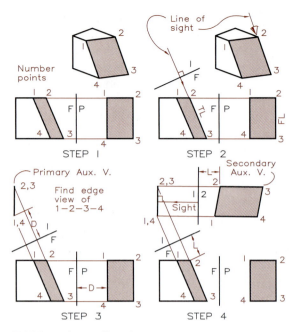

15.28 Secondary auxiliary views

Step 1 Draw a fold line F–P between the front and side views. Label the corner points in both views.

Step 2 Line 2–3 is a true-length frontal line in the front view. Draw reference line F–1 perpendicular to line 2–3 with a line of sight parallel to line 2–3.

Step 3 Find the edge view of plane 1–2–3–4 by transferring depth dimensions (D) from the side view.

Step 4 Draw a line of sight perpendicular to the edge view of 1–2–3–4 and draw the 1–2 fold line parallel to the edge view. Find the true-size auxiliary view by transferring the dimensions (L) from the front view to the auxiliary view.

15.11 Secondary Auxiliary Views

Figure 15.28 shows how to project an auxiliary, called a **secondary auxiliary view**, from a primary auxiliary view. An edge view of the oblique plane is found in the primary auxiliary view by finding the point view of a true-length line (2–3) that lies on the oblique surface. A line of sight perpendicular to the edge view of the plane gives a secondary auxiliary view that shows the oblique plane as true size.

Note that the reference line between the primary auxiliary view and the secondary auxiliary

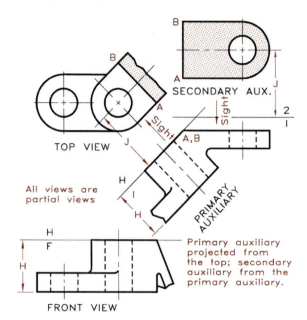

15.29 A secondary auxiliary view projected from a primary auxiliary view that was projected the top view is shown here. All views are drawn as partial views.

view is labeled 1–2 to represent the fold line between the primary plane (1) and the secondary plane (2). The 1 label is placed on the primary side and the 2 label is placed on the secondary side.

Figure 15.29 illustrates the construction of a secondary auxiliary view that gives the true-size view of a surface on a part using these same principles and a combination of partial views. A secondary auxiliary view must be used in this case because the oblique plane does not appear as an edge in a principal view.

Find the point view of a line (AB) on the oblique plane to find the edge view of the plane in the primary auxiliary view. The secondary auxiliary view is projected perpendicularly from the edge view of the plane found in the primary auxiliary view to find the true-size view of the plane. In this example, all of the views are drawn as partial views, which are adequate to describe the part.

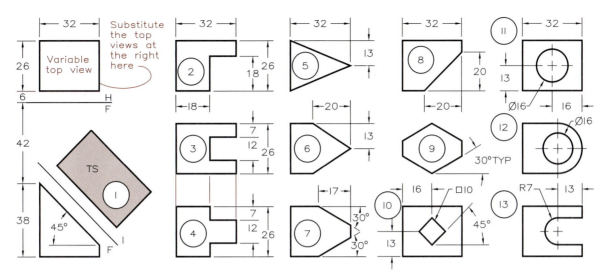

15.31 (Problems 1-13) Primary auxiliary views.

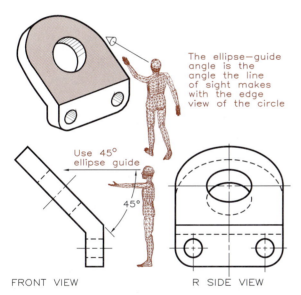

15.30 The ellipse guide angle is the angle that the line of sight makes with the edge view of the circular feature. The ellipse angle for the right-side view is 45°.

15.12 Elliptical Features

Occasionally, circular shapes will project as ellipses, which must be drawn with an irregular curve or an ellipse template. The ellipse tem-plate (guide) is by far the most convenient method of drawing ellipses. The angle of the ellipse template is the angle the line of sight makes with the edge view of the circular feature. In **Fig. 15.30** the angle is found to be 45° where the curve is an edge in the front view, so the right-side view of the curve is drawn as a 45° ellipse.

Problems

1–13. (Fig. 15.31) Using the example layout, change the top and front views by substituting the top views given at the right for the one given in the example. The angle of inclination in the front view is 45° for all problems, and the height is 38 mm (1.5 inches) in the front view. Construct auxiliary views that show the inclined surface true size. Draw two problems per size A sheet.

14–32. (Figs. 15.32–15.50) Draw the necessary primary and auxiliary views to describe the objects assigned. Draw one per size A or size B sheet. Adjust the scale of each to utilize the space on the sheet.

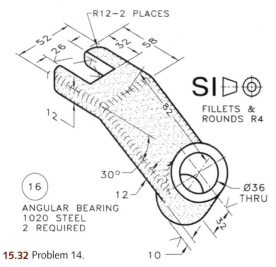

15.32 Problem 14.

R12–2 PLACES
52
26
32
58
12
82
SI
FILLETS &
ROUNDS R4
30°
12
16
ANGULAR BEARING
1020 STEEL
2 REQUIRED
Ø36
THRU
32
10

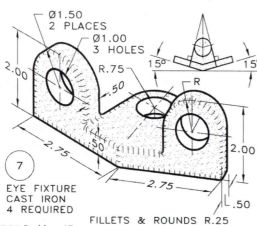

15.33 Problem 15.

Ø1.50
2 PLACES
Ø1.00
3 HOLES
2.00
R.75
.50
R
15°   15°
2.75
.50
7
EYE FIXTURE
CAST IRON
4 REQUIRED
2.00
2.75
.50
FILLETS & ROUNDS R.25

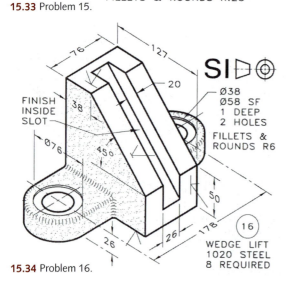

15.34 Problem 16.

76
127
20
FINISH
INSIDE
SLOT
38
Ø76
45°
50
26
178
26
SI
Ø38
Ø58 SF
1 DEEP
2 HOLES
FILLETS &
ROUNDS R6
16
WEDGE LIFT
1020 STEEL
8 REQUIRED

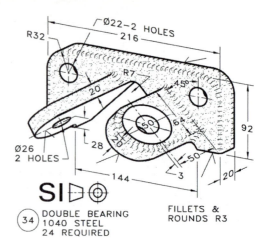

15.35 Problem 17.

R32
Ø22–2 HOLES
216
R7
20
45°
.50
64
92
Ø26
2 HOLES
28
20
50
3
144
20
SI
34
DOUBLE BEARING
1040 STEEL
24 REQUIRED
FILLETS &
ROUNDS R3

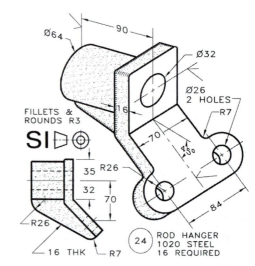

15.36 Problem 18.

Ø64
90
Ø32
Ø26
2 HOLES
16
R7
FILLETS &
ROUNDS R3
SI
70
45°
35   R26
32
70
R26
84
16 THK   R7
24
ROD HANGER
1020 STEEL
16 REQUIRED

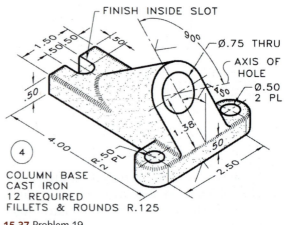

15.37 Problem 19.

FINISH INSIDE SLOT
1.50
.50 .50
.50
900
Ø.75 THRU
AXIS OF
HOLE
.50
45°
Ø.50
2 PL
1.38
4.00
R.50
2 PL
.50
2.50
4
COLUMN BASE
CAST IRON
12 REQUIRED
FILLETS & ROUNDS R.125

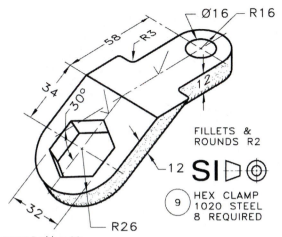

Ø16 — R16
58
R3
34
30°
12
FILLETS &
ROUNDS R2
12 SI▷◉
⑨ HEX CLAMP
1020 STEEL
8 REQUIRED
32
R26

15.38 Problem 20.

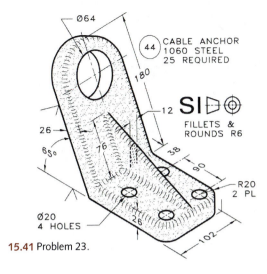

Ø64
④④ CABLE ANCHOR
1060 STEEL
25 REQUIRED
180
26
12 SI▷◉
FILLETS &
ROUNDS R6
65°
76
38
R20
2 PL
Ø20
4 HOLES
26
102

15.41 Problem 23.

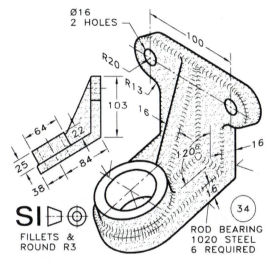

Ø16
2 HOLES
100
R20
R13
103
16
64
22
16
38
84
120°
16
16
SI▷◉
FILLETS &
ROUND R3
③④ ROD BEARING
1020 STEEL
6 REQUIRED

15.39 Problem 21.

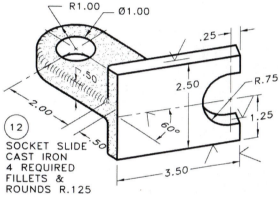

R1.00 Ø1.00
.25
.50
2.50
R.75
2.00
60°
1.25
.50
⑫ SOCKET SLIDE
CAST IRON
4 REQUIRED
FILLETS &
ROUNDS R.125
3.50

15.42 Problem 24.

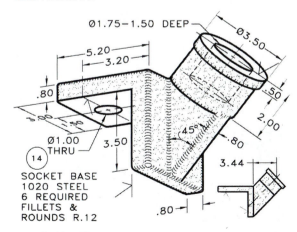

Ø1.75–1.50 DEEP
Ø3.50
5.20
3.20
.80
.50
2.00
Ø1.00
THRU
3.50
45°
.80
⑭
SOCKET BASE
1020 STEEL
6 REQUIRED
FILLETS &
ROUNDS R.12
3.44
.80

15.40 Problem 22.

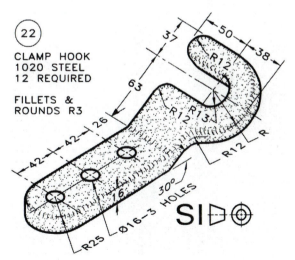

②②
CLAMP HOOK
1020 STEEL
12 REQUIRED

FILLETS &
ROUNDS R3
37
50
38
R12
63
R12
R13
26
42
42
R12 R
16
30°
Ø16–3 HOLES
SI▷◉
R25

15.43 Problem 25.

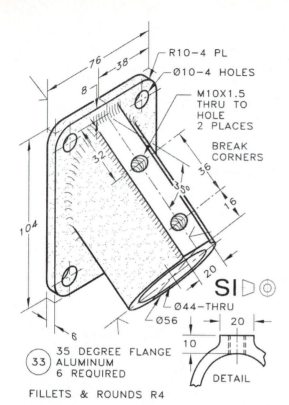

R10-4 PL
Ø10-4 HOLES
M10X1.5
THRU TO
HOLE
2 PLACES

BREAK
CORNERS

76
38
8
32
36
350
16
104
20
SI▷◎
Ø44-THRU
Ø56
6

20
10
DETAIL

(33) 35 DEGREE FLANGE
ALUMINUM
6 REQUIRED

FILLETS & ROUNDS R4

15.44 Problem 26.

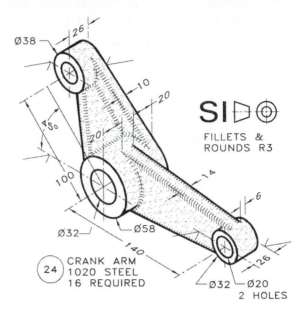

Ø38
26
10
20
450
20
100
14
6
Ø32
Ø58
140
126
Ø32 Ø20
2 HOLES

SI▷◎
FILLETS &
ROUNDS R3

(24) CRANK ARM
1020 STEEL
16 REQUIRED

15.46 Problem 28.

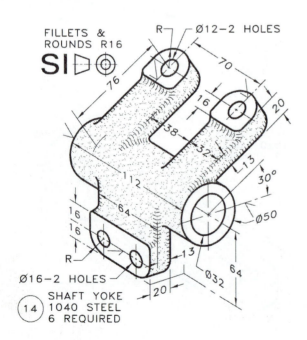

FILLETS &
ROUNDS R16
SI▷◎

R Ø12-2 HOLES
76
70
16
20
38
32
13
30°
112
Ø50
16
64
16
R
13
Ø32
64
20
Ø16-2 HOLES

(14) SHAFT YOKE
1040 STEEL
6 REQUIRED

15.45 Problem 27.

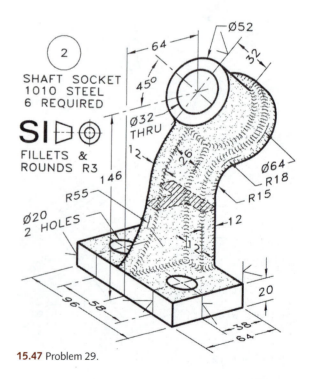

(2) SHAFT SOCKET
1010 STEEL
6 REQUIRED

SI▷◎
FILLETS &
ROUNDS R3

Ø52
64
32
450
Ø32
THRU
12
146
26
Ø64
R18
R15
R55
Ø20
2 HOLES
12
12
96
58
20
38
64

15.47 Problem 29.

198 • **CHAPTER 15   PRIMARY AUXILIARY VIEWS**

15.48 (Problem 30) Lay out the necessary orthographic views of the oblique bracket on a size B sheet. Construct the true-size auxiliary view that shows the inclined surface true size. Select the appropriate scale.

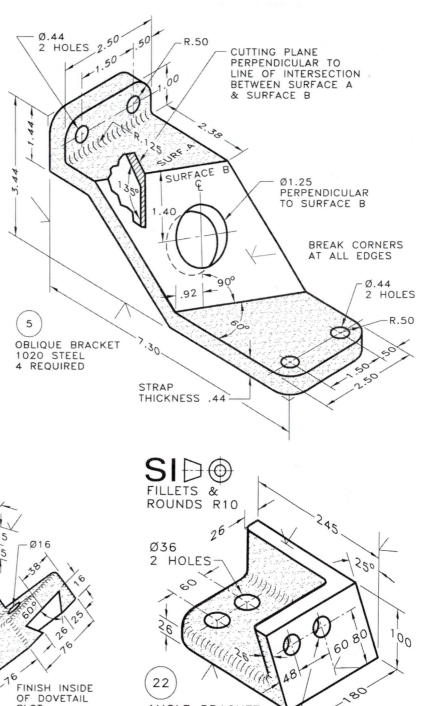

Ø.44
2 HOLES

CUTTING PLANE
PERPENDICULAR TO
LINE OF INTERSECTION
BETWEEN SURFACE A
& SURFACE B

R.50

SURF. A

SURFACE B

Ø1.25
PERPENDICULAR
TO SURFACE B

BREAK CORNERS
AT ALL EDGES

Ø.44
2 HOLES

R.50

⑤

OBLIQUE BRACKET
1020 STEEL
4 REQUIRED

90°

60°

STRAP
THICKNESS .44

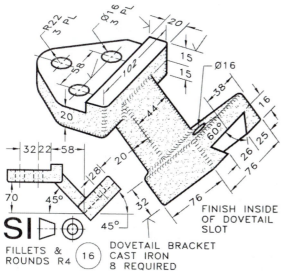

SI⊅⊙
FILLETS &
ROUNDS R4 ⑯

DOVETAIL BRACKET
CAST IRON
8 REQUIRED

FINISH INSIDE
OF DOVETAIL
SLOT

15.49 Problem 31.

SI⊅⊙
FILLETS &
ROUNDS R10

Ø36
2 HOLES

㉒

ANGLE BRACKET
CAST IRON
2 REQUIRED

Ø32–2 HOLES
2 HOLES

15.50 Problem 32.

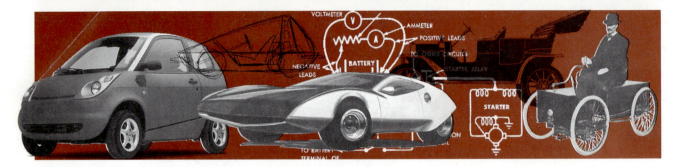

Sections

16.1 Introduction

Correctly drawn orthographic views that show all hidden lines may not clearly describe an object's internal details. The gear housing shown in **Fig. 16.1** is such an example, which is better understood when a section has been cut from it. The technique of constructing imaginary cross-sectional cuts through a drawing of a part results in an orthographic view called a **section.**

16.2 Basics of Sectioning

In **Fig. 16.2A**, standard views of a cylinder are shown as top and front views where its interior features are drawn as hidden lines. If you imagined a knife edge cutting through the top view, the front view would become a **section**. This section is a **full section** since the cutting plane passes fully through the part (**Fig. 16.2B**). The portion of the part that was cut by the imaginary plane is crosshatched, and hidden lines usually

16.1 This gear housing has many internal features that cannot be described clearly in a standard orthographic view. Sections are used to clarify interior parts.

are omitted in sectional views because they are not needed.

Figure 16.3 shows two types of cutting planes. Either is acceptable, although the one with pairs of short dashes is most often used.

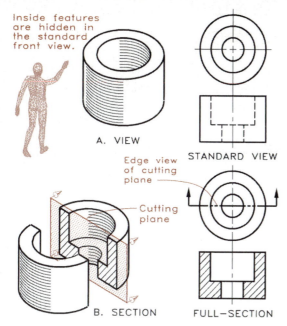

16.2 A part with internal features can be better shown with sectional views than in standard views with hidden lines.

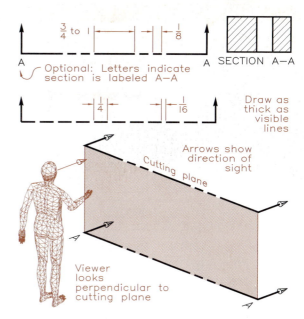

16.3 Cutting planes can be thought of as knife edges that pass through views to reveal interior features in sections. The cutting plane marked A–A results in a section labeled SECTION A–A.

The spacing and proportions of the dashes depend on the size of the drawing. The line thickness of the cutting plane is the same as the visible object line. Letters placed at each end of the cutting plane are used to label the sectional view, such as **SECTION A–A.**

The sight arrows at the ends of the cutting plane are always perpendicular to the cutting plane. In the sectional view, the observer is looking in the direction of the sight arrows, perpendicular to the surface of the cutting plane.

Figure 16.4 shows the three basic positions of sections and their respective cutting planes. In each case perpendicular arrows point in the direction of the line of sight. For example, the cutting plane in **Fig. 16.4A** passes through and removes the front of the top view, and the line of sight is perpendicular to the remainder of the top view.

The top view appears as a section when the cutting plane passes through the front view and

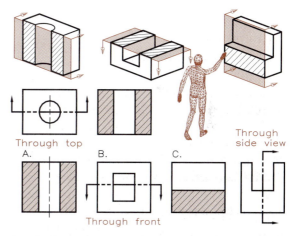

16.4 The three examples of cutting planes that pass through the principal views, (A) top, (B) front, and (C) side views, are shown here. The arrows point in the direction of your line of sight for each section.

the line of sight is downward (**Fig. 16.4B**). When the cutting plane passes vertically through the side view (**Fig. 16.4C**), the front view becomes a section.

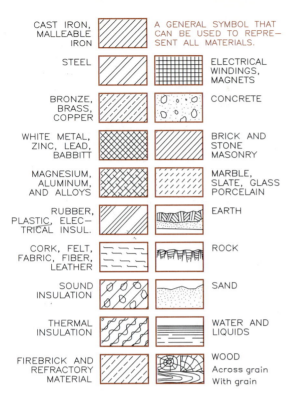

16.5 Use these symbols for hatching parts in section. The cast-iron symbol may be used for any material.

16.3 Sectioning Symbols

The hatching symbols used to distinguish between different materials in sections are shown in **Fig. 16.5**. Although these symbols may be used to indicate the materials in a section, you should provide supplementary notes specifying the materials to ensure clarity.

The cast-iron symbol (evenly spaced section lines) may be used to represent any material and is the symbol used most often. Draw cast-iron symbols with a 2H pencil, slant the lines upward and to the right at 30°, 45°, or 60° angles, and space the lines about 1/16 inch apart (close together in small areas and farther apart in larger areas).

Computer Method A few of the many cross-sectional symbols available with AutoCAD are shown in **Fig. 16.6**. The spacing between the lines and the dash lengths can be changed by setting the pattern scale factor, *Ltscale*.

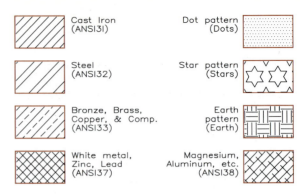

16.6 These are a few of the hatching symbols available in AutoCAD. The spacing and size of the symbols can be varied by setting the pattern scale factor, *Ltscale*.

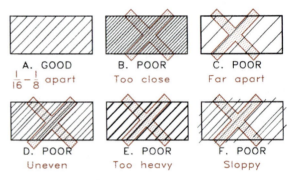

16.7 Hatching techniques

A Section lines are thin, dense lines drawn from 1/16 to 1/8 in. apart.

B–F Avoid these common errors of section lining.

Properly drawn section lines—ones that are thin and evenly spaced—are shown in **Fig. 16.7**. **Figure 16.7B–F** show common errors of section lining.

Thin parts such as sheet metal, washers, and gaskets are sectioned by completely blacking in their areas (**Fig. 16.8**) because space does not permit the drawing of section lines. On the other hand, large parts are sectioned with an **outline section** to save time and effort.

Sectioned areas should be hatched with symbols that are neither parallel nor perpendicular to the outlines of the parts, lest they be confused with serrations or other machining treatments of the surface (**Fig. 16.9**).

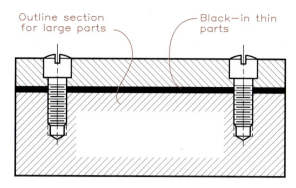

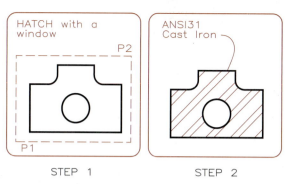

16.8 Large sectional areas are hatched with outline sectioning (around their edges) and thin parts are blacked in solid.

16.10 Hatching by computer

Step 1 *Command:* <u>Hatch</u> (Enter)

Enter pattern name or (? /Solid/User defined) [ANSI31]: <u>ANSI32</u> (Enter)

Specify a scale for the pattern [1.00]: <u>.50</u> (Enter)

Specify an angle for pattern [0]: <u>0</u> (Enter)

Step 2 *Select objects:* <u>W</u> (window option)

Specify first corner: <u>P1</u>

Specify opposite corner: <u>P2</u> (Enter) (The hatching is applied.)

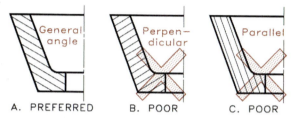

16.9 Draw section lines that are neither parallel nor perpendicular to the outlines of the part, so that they are not misunderstood as features of the part.

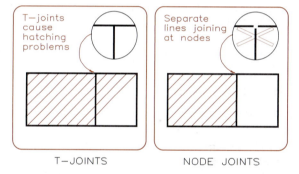

16.11 For the *Hatch* command to work properly, the outlines of areas to be hatched must be drawn with perfect closing outlines. T-joints, overlaps, or gaps at intersections can give irregular results.

Computer Method The most basic principal of applying section symbols to an area with AutoCAD is shown in **Fig. 16.10**. After assigning the proper hatch symbol with the *Hatch* command, select the area to be sectioned with a window and the hatch lines are drawn. To vary the spacing of the section lines, change the patterns scale of the *Hatch* command. *Bhatch* and other hatching commands are covered in Chapters 26 and 27.

The lines that outline areas to be hatched must intersect perfectly at each corner point; no T-joints are permitted (**Fig. 16.11**). Poor intersections can cause hatching symbols to fill the desired area improperly.

16.4 Sectioning Assemblies of Parts

When sectioning an assembly of several parts, draw section lines at varying angles to distinguish the parts from each other (**Fig. 16.12A**).

Using different material symbols in an assembly also helps distinguish between the parts and their materials. Crosshatch the same part at the same angle and with the same symbol, even though portions of the part may be separated (**Fig. 16.12B**).

16.5 Full Sections

A cutting plane passed fully through an object and removing half of it forms a **full section** view. **Figure 16.13** shows two orthographic views of

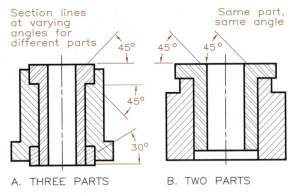

Section lines at varying angles for different parts

45°
45°
45°
45°
30°

A. THREE PARTS   B. TWO PARTS

16.12 Hatching parts in assembly

A Draw section lines of different parts in an assembly at varying angles to distinguish between them.

B Draw section lines on separated portions of the same part (both sides of a hole here) in the same direction.

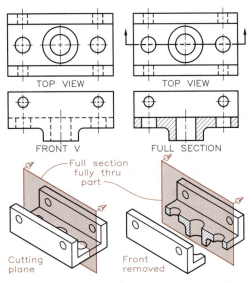

TOP VIEW   TOP VIEW

FRONT V   FULL SECTION

Full section fully thru part

Cutting plane   Front removed

16.13 A full section is found by passing a cutting plane fully through the top view of this part, removing half of it. The arrows on the cutting plane give the direction of your sight. The front sectional view shows the internal features clearly.

an object with all its hidden lines. We can describe the part better by passing a cutting plane through the top view to remove half of it. The arrows on the cutting plane indicate the direction of sight. The front view becomes a full

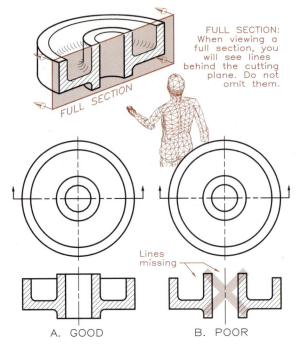

FULL SECTION: When viewing a full section, you will see lines behind the cutting plane. Do not omit them.

FULL SECTION

Lines missing

A. GOOD   B. POOR

16.14 Full section: Cylindrical part

A When a front view of a cylinder is shown as a full section, as shown here, visible lines will be seen behind the cut surface.

B If only the lines of the cut surface (the section) are shown, the view will be incomplete.

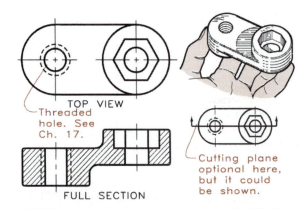

TOP VIEW

Threaded hole. See Ch. 17.

FULL SECTION

Cutting plane optional here, but it could be shown.

16.15 The cutting plane of a section can be omitted if its location is obvious.

section, showing the surfaces cut by the cutting plane. **Figure 16.14** shows a full section through a cylindrical part, with half the object removed. **Figure 16.14A** shows the correctly drawn sectional view. A common mistake in constructing

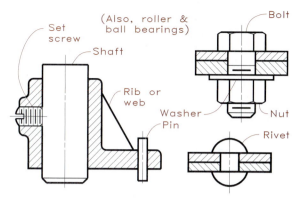

16.16 By conventional practice, these parts are not section-lined even though cutting planes pass through them.

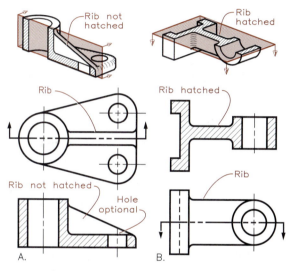

16.17 Ribs in section

A Do not hatch a rib cut in a flatwise direction.

B Ribs are hatched when cutting planes pass through them, showing their true thicknesses.

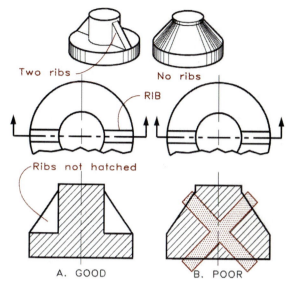

16.18 Ribs in section

A Ribs are not hatched in section to better describe the part.

B If ribs were hatched in section, a misleading impression of the part would be given.

sections is the omission of the visible lines behind the cutting plane (**Fig. 16.14B**).

Omit hidden lines in sectional views unless you consider them necessary for a clear understanding of the view. Also, cutting planes may be omitted if you consider them unnecessary. **Figure 16.15** shows a full section of a part from which the cutting plane was omitted because its path is obvious.

Parts Not Requiring Section Lining

Many standard parts, such as nuts and bolts, rivets, shafts, and set screws, do not require section lining even though the cutting plane passes through them (**Fig. 16.16**). These parts have no internal features; therefore sections through them would be unnecessary. Other parts not requiring section lining are roller bearings, ball bearings, gear teeth, dowels, pins, and washers.

Ribs

Ribs are not section-lined when the cutting plane passes flatwise through them (**Fig. 16.17A**), because to do so would give a misleading impression of the rib. But ribs do require section lining when the cutting plane passes perpendicularly through them and shows their true thickness (**Fig. 16.17B**).

By not section-lining the ribs in **Fig. 16.18A**, we provided a descriptive section view of the part. Had we hatched the ribs, the section would

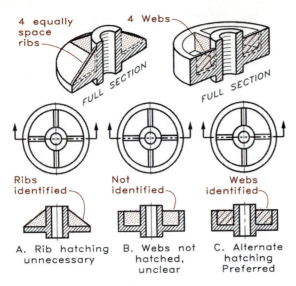

16.19 Ribs and webs in section

A These ribs are well-defined in this section and are not hatched.

B These webs are poorly defined when not hatched in the sectional view.

C Alternate hatch lines are drawn to call attention to poorly-defined webs.

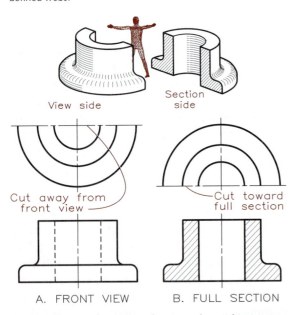

16.20 Half views of symmetrical parts can be used to conserve space and drawing time as an approved conventional practice. (A) The external portion of the half view is toward the front view. (B) The internal portion of the half view is toward the front view when it is a section. In half sections, the omitted half view can be either toward or away from the section.

give the impression that the part was solid and conical (**Fig. 16.18B**).

Figure 16.19 shows an alternate method of section-lining webs and ribs. The outside ribs in **Fig. 16.19A** do not require section-lining because the cutting plane passes flatwise through them and they are well-identified. As a rule, webs do not require crosshatching, but the webs shown in **Fig. 16.19B** are not well-identified in the front section and could go unnoticed. Therefore, using alternate section lines, as shown in **Fig. 16.19C**, is better. Here, extending every other section line through the webs ensures that they can be identified easily.

16.6 Partial Views

A conventional method of representing symmetrical views is the half view that requires less space and less time to draw than full views (**Fig. 16.20**). A half top view is sufficient when drawn adjacent to the section view or front view. For half views (not sections), the removed half is away from the adjacent view (**Fig. 16.20A**). For full sections, the removed half is the half nearest the section (**Fig. 16.20B**). When drawing partial views with half sections, you may omit either the front or rear halves of the partial views.

16.7 Half Sections

A **half section** is a view obtained by passing a cutting plane halfway through an object and removing a quarter of it to show both external and internal features. Half sections are used with symmetrical parts, and with cylinders in particular, as shown in **Fig. 16.21**. By comparing the half section with the standard front view, you can see that both internal and external features show more clearly in a half section than in a view. Hidden lines are unnecessary, and we've omitted them to simplify the section. **Figure 16.22** shows a half section of a pulley.

Note omission of the cutting plane from the half section shown in **Fig. 16.23** because the cut-

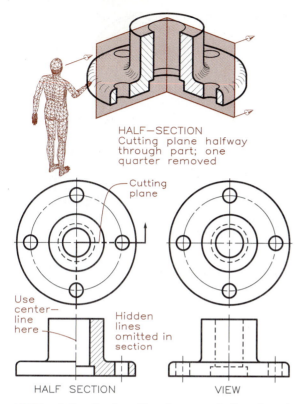

HALF—SECTION
Cutting plane halfway through part; one quarter removed

16.21 In a half section the cutting plane passes halfway through the object, removing a quarter of it, to show half the outside and half the inside of it. Omit hidden lines in sectional views unless they are needed for clarity.

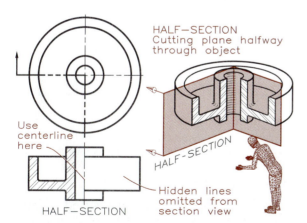

HALF—SECTION
Cutting plane halfway through object

16.22 This half section describes the part that is shown orthographically and pictorially. The parting line for cylinders is a centerline.

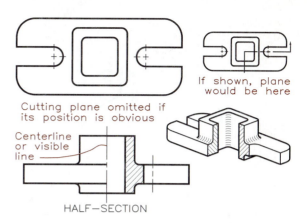

If shown, plane would be here

Cutting plane omitted if its position is obvious

Centerline or visible line

HALF—SECTION

16.23 The cutting plane can be omitted when its location is obvious. The parting line between the section and the view may be a visible line or a centerline if the part is not cylindrical.

ting plane's location is obvious. Because the parting line of the half section is not at a centerline, you may use a solid line or a centerline to separate the sectional half from the half that appears as an external view.

16.8 Offset Sections

An **offset section** is a full section in which the cutting plane is offset to pass through important features that do not lie in a single plane. **Figure 16.24** shows an offset section in which the plane is offset to pass through the large hole and one of the small holes. The cut formed by the offset is not shown in the section because it is imaginary.

16.9 Broken-Out Sections

A **broken-out section** shows a partial view of a part's interior features. The broken-out section of the part shown in **Fig. 16.25** reveals details of the wall thickness to describe the part better. The irregular lines representing the break are conventional breaks (discussed later in this chapter).

The broken-out section of the pulley in **Fig. 16.26** clearly depicts the keyway and threaded hole for a setscrew. This method shows the part efficiently, with the minimum of views.

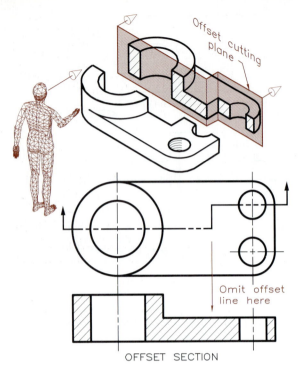

OFFSET SECTION

16.24 An offset section is formed by a cutting plane that must be offset to pass through features not in a single plane.

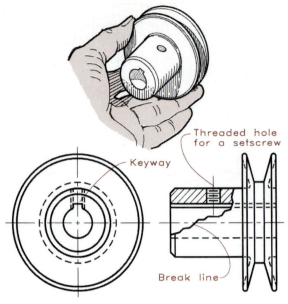

16.26 This broken-out section shows the keyway and the threaded hole for the setscrew in the pulley.

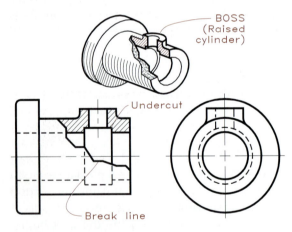

16.25 A broken-out section is one in which a part of the object has been broken away to show internal features.

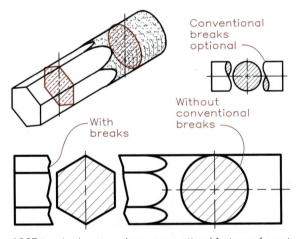

16.27 Revolved sections show cross-sectional features of a part and eliminate the need for additional orthographic views. Revolved sections may be superimposed on the given views or conventional breaks can be used to separate them from the given view.

16.10 Revolved Sections

A **revolved section** describes a part when you revolve its cross section about an axis of revolution and place it on the view where the revolu-

tion occurred. Note the use of revolved sections to explain two cross sections of the shaft shown in **Fig. 16.27** (with and without conventional breaks). Conventional breaks are optional; how-

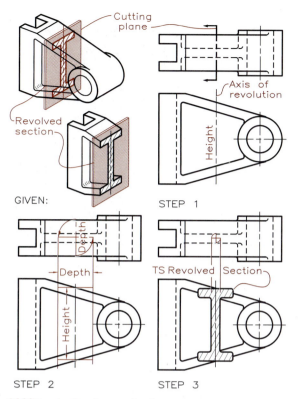

GIVEN:

STEP 1

STEP 2

STEP 3

16.28 Revolved section construction

Given: The part is shown pictorially with a cutting plane showing the cross section that will be revolved.

Step 1 An imaginary cutting plane is located in the top view and the axis of rotation is drawn the front view.

Step 2 The depth in the top view is rotated and is projected to the front view. The height and depth in the front view give the overall dimensions of the revolved view.

Step 3 The revolved section is drawn, fillets and rounds are added, and the section lines are applied to finish the view.

ever, you may draw a revolved section on the view without them.

A revolved section helps to describe the part shown in **Fig. 16.28**. Imagine passing a cutting plane through the top view of the part (step 1). Then imagine revolving the cutting plane in the top view and projecting it to the front (step 2). The true-size revolved section is completed in step 3. Conventional breaks could be used on each side of the revolved section.

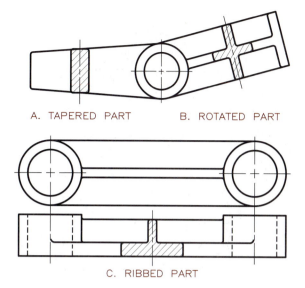

A. TAPERED PART   B. ROTATED PART

C. RIBBED PART

16.29 These revolved sections describe the cross sections of the two parts that would be difficult to depict in supplementary orthographic views, such as a side view.

Figure 16.29 demonstrates how to use typical revolved sections to show cross sections through parts, eliminating the need to draw additional orthographic views.

16.11 Removed Sections

A **removed section** is a revolved section that is shown outside the view in which it was revolved (**Fig. 16.30**). Centerlines are used as axes of rotation to show the locations from which the sections are taken. Where space does not permit revolution on the given view (**Fig. 16.31A**), removed sections must be used instead of revolved sections (**Fig. 16.31B**).

Removed sections do not have to be positioned directly along an axis of revolution adjacent to the view from which they were revolved. Instead, removed sections can be located elsewhere on a drawing if they are properly labeled (**Fig. 16.32**). For example, the plane labeled with an A at each end identifies the location of section A–A, and the same applies to section B–B.

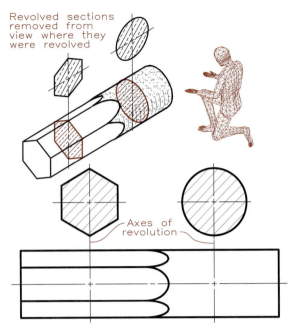

16.30 Removed sections are revolved sections that are drawn outside the object and along their axes of revolution.

When a set of drawings consists of multiple sheets, removed sections and the views from which they are taken may appear on different sheets. When this method of layout is necessary, label the cutting plane in the view from which the section was taken and the sheet on which the section appears (**Fig. 16.33**).

16.12 Conventional Practices

In **Fig. 16.34A**, the middle hole is omitted because it does not pass through the center of the circular plate. However, in **Fig. 16.34B**, the hole does pass through the plate's center and is shown in the section. Although the cutting plane does not pass through one of the symmetrically spaced holes in the top view (**Fig. 16.34C**), the hole is revolved to the cutting plane to show the full section.

When ribs are symmetrically spaced about a hub (**Fig. 16.35**), it is conventional practice to

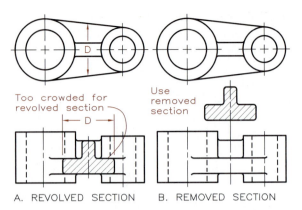

16.31 Removed sections are necessary when space does not permit the revolved section to be superimposed on the part.

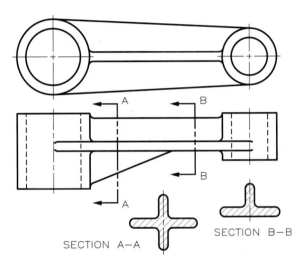

16.32 Letters at each end of a cutting plane (such as A–A) identify the removed section labeled SECTION A–A drawn elsewhere on the drawing.

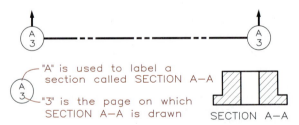

16.33 When a removed section is placed on another page of a set of drawings, label each end of the cutting plane with a letter and a number. The letters identify the section and the numerals indicate the page on which the removed section it is drawn.

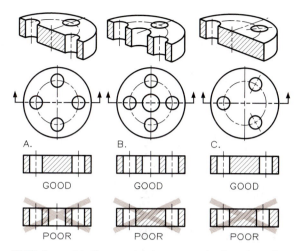

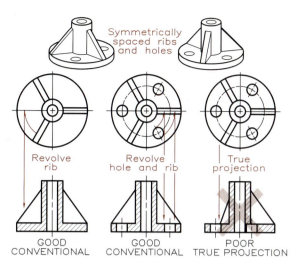

16.34 Symmetrically spaced holes are revolved to show their true radial distance from the center of a circular part in sectional views. (A) Omit the middle holes; they are not at the center of the plate. (B) Show the middle hole; it is at the center of the plate. (C) Rotate the holes to the centerline and project to make the section symmetrical.

16.36 Symmetrically spaced ribs and holes should be shown in sections with the ribs rotated to show them true size and the holes rotated to show them at their true radial distance from the center.

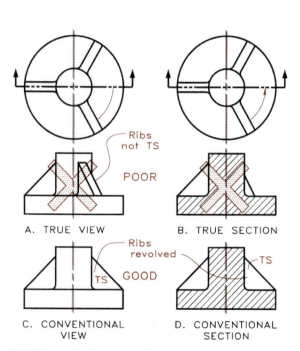

16.35 Symmetrically spaced ribs are revolved and drawn true size in their orthographic and sectional views as a conventional practice.

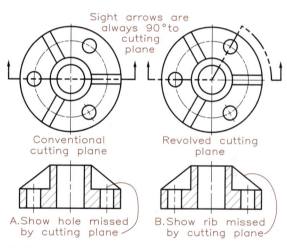

16.37 Rotate symmetrically spaced ribs to show them true size, whether or not the cutting plane passes through them. As an alternative, the cutting plane can be drawn to pass through the ribs for clarity.

revolve them so that they appear true size in both views and sections. **Figure 16.36** illustrates the conventional practice of revolving both holes and ribs (or webs) of symmetrical parts. Revolution gives a better description of the parts in a manner that is easier to draw.

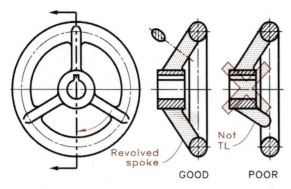

16.38 Revolve spokes to show them true size in section. Do not section line (hatch) spokes.

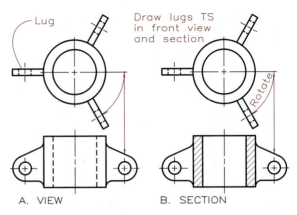

16.40 Lugs are revolved to show their true size in (A) the front view, and also in (B) the sectional view.

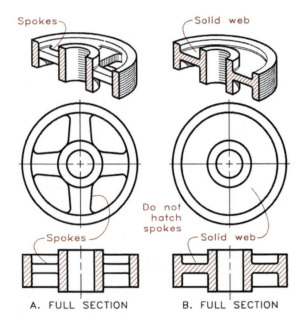

16.39 Spokes and webs in section

A. Spokes are not hatched even though the cutting plane of the section passes through them.

B. Webs are hatched when cut by the cutting plane.

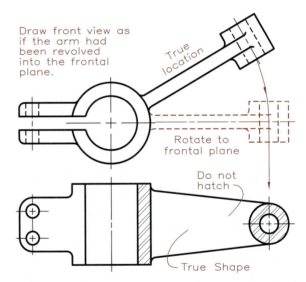

16.41 It is conventional practice to revolve parts with inclined features in order to show them true size in both sections and regular orthographic views.

A cutting plane may be positioned in either of the two ways shown in **Fig. 16.37**. Even though the cutting plane does not pass through the ribs and holes in **Fig. 16.37A**, they may appear in section as if the cutting plane passed through them. The path of the cutting plane also may be revolved, as shown in **Fig. 16.37B**. In this case the ribs are revolved to their true-size position in the section view, although the plane does not cut through them.

The same principles apply to symmetrically spaced spokes (**Fig. 16.38**). Draw only the revolved, true-size spokes and do not section-line them. If the spokes shown in **Fig. 16.39A**

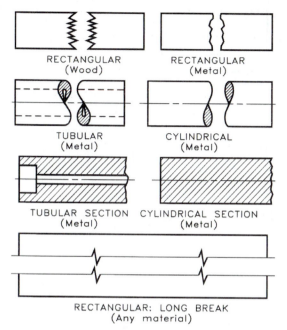

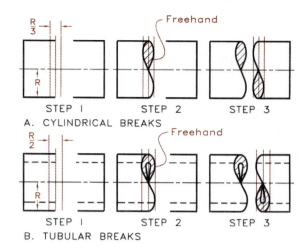

16.42 These conventional breaks indicate that a portion of an object has been omitted.

16.43 It is essential that you use guidelines in drawing conventional breaks freehand for both (A) solid cylinders and (B) tubular cylinders. The radius R is used to determine the widths.

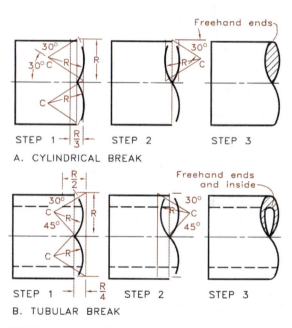

16.44 These steps can be followed to draw conventional breaks with a compass.

were hatched, they could be misunderstood as a solid web, as shown in **Fig. 16.39B**.

Revolving the symmetrically positioned lugs shown in **Fig. 16.40** gives their true size in both the front view and the sectional view. The same principles of rotation apply to the part shown in **Fig. 16.41**, where the inclined arm appears in the section as if it had been revolved to the centerline in the top view and then projected to the sectional view. These conventional practices save time and space on a drawing and also make the views more understandable by the reader.

16.13 Conventional Breaks

Figure 16.42 shows types of conventional breaks to use when you remove portions of an object. You may draw the "figure-eight" breaks used for cylindrical and tubular parts freehand (**Fig. 16.43**) or with a compass when they are larger, as shown in **Fig. 16.44**.

Conventional breaks can be used to shorten a long piece by removing the portion between

the breaks so that it may be drawn at a larger scale (**Fig. 16.45**). The dimension specifies the true length of the part, and the breaks indicate that a portion of the length has been removed.

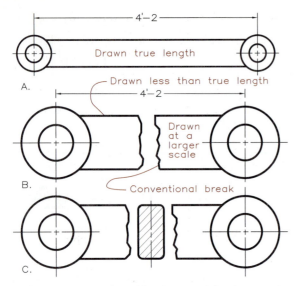

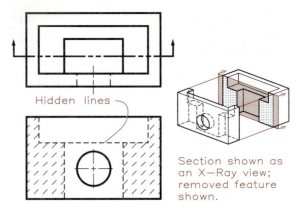

16.46 Phantom sections give an "X-ray" view of a part to show features on both sides of the cutting plane. Section lines are drawn as dashed lines.

16.45 By using conventional breaks, part of the object can be removed so it can be drawn at a larger scale and space can be saved. A revolved section can also be inserted between the breaks to further describe the part.

16.14 Phantom (Ghost) Sections

A **phantom or ghost section** depicts parts as if they were being X-rayed. In **Fig. 16.46**, the cutting plane is used in the normal manner, but the section lines are drawn as dashed lines. If the object were shown as a regular full section, the circular hole through the front surface could not be shown in the same view. A phantom section lets you show features on both sides of the cutting plane.

16.15 Auxiliary Sections

You may use **auxiliary sections** to supplement the principal views of orthographic projections (**Fig. 16.47**). Pass auxiliary cutting plane A–A through the front view and project the auxiliary view from the cutting plane as indicated by the sight arrows. Section A–A gives a cross-sectional description of the part that would be difficult to depict by other principal orthographic views.

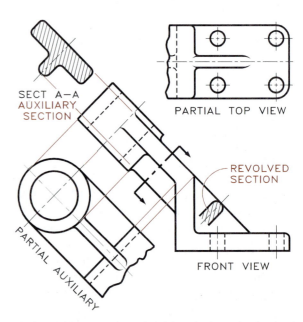

16.47 Auxiliary sections are helpful in clarifying the details of inclined features of a part.

Problems

1–24. Solve the problems shown in **Fig. 16.48** on size A sheets by drawing two solutions per sheet. Each grid space equals 0.20 in., or 5 mm.

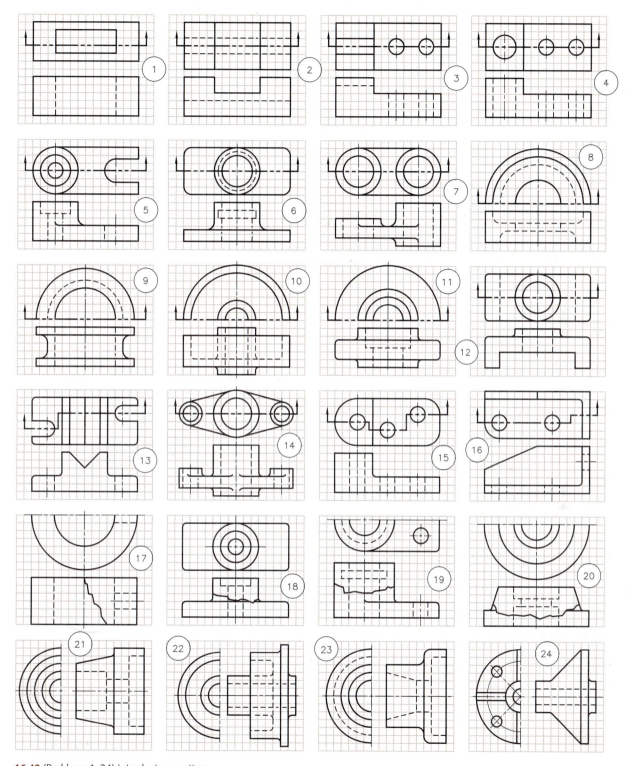

16.48 (Problems 1–24) Introductory sections.

25–36. (Figs. 16.49–16.60) Complete these drawings as full sections. Draw one problem per size A sheet (horizontal format). Each grid space equals 0.20 in., or 5 mm. Show the cutting planes in each problem.

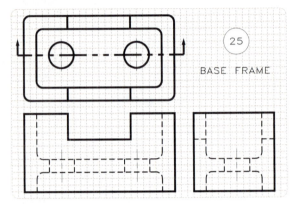

16.49 (Problem 25) Full section.

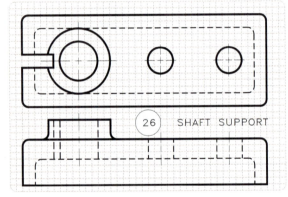

16.50 (Problem 26) Full section.

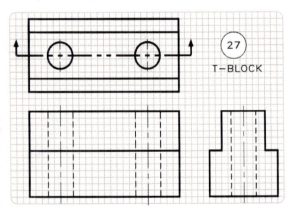

16.51 (Problem 27) Full section.

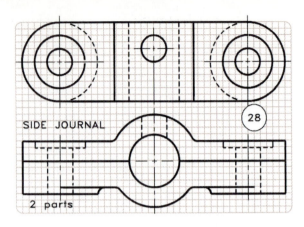

16.52 (Problem 28) Offset section.

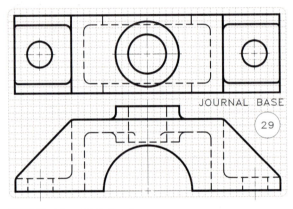

16.53 (Problem 29) Full section.

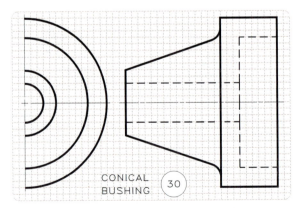

16.54 (Problem 30) Half section.

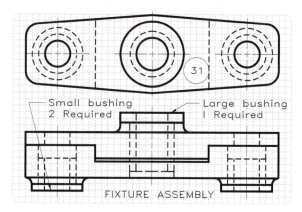

16.55 (Problem 31) Half section.

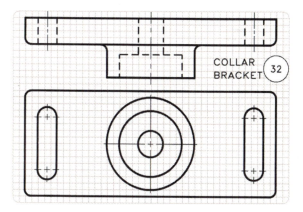

16.56 (Problem 32) Half section.

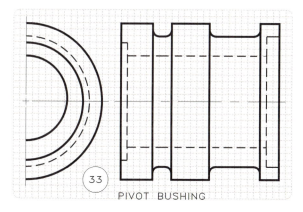

16.57 (Problem 33) Half section.

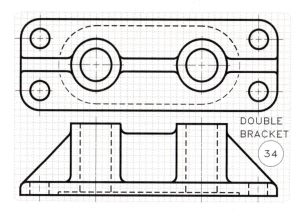

16.58 (Problem 34) Half section.

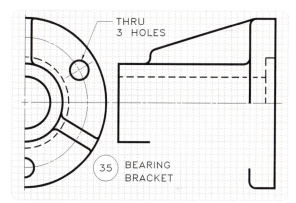

16.59 (Problem 35) Half section.

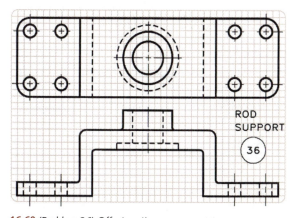

16.60 (Problem 36) Offset section.

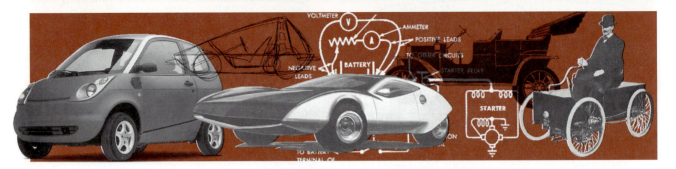

CHAPTER SEVENTEEN

Screws, Fasteners, and Springs

17.1 Introduction

Screws provide a fast and easy method of fastening parts together, adjusting the positions of parts, and transmitting power. **Screws, sometimes called threaded fasteners, should be purchased rather than made as newly designed parts for each product.** Screws are available through commercial catalogs in countless forms and shapes for various specialized and general applications. Such screws are cheap, interchangeable, and easy to replace.

The types of threaded parts most often used in industry are covered by current ANSI Standards and include both Unified National (UN) and International Organization for Standardization (ISO) threads. Adoption in 1948 of the UN thread, a modification of the American Standard and the Whitworth thread, by the United States, Great Britain, and Canada (sometimes called the ABC Standards) was a major step in standardizing threads. The ISO developed metric thread standards for even broader worldwide applications. Other types of fasteners include **keys**, **pins**, and **rivets**.

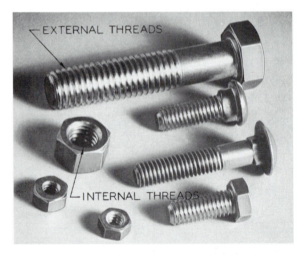

17.1 This photograph shows examples of internal and external threads and three head types. (*Courtesy of Russell, Burdsall & Ward Bolt and Nut Company.*)

Also introduced are **springs** that resist and react to forces and have applications varying from pogo sticks to automobiles. Springs also are available in many forms and styles from specialty manufacturers who supply most of them to industry.

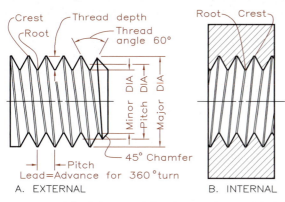

17.2 Most of the definitions of thread terminology are labeled for (A) external and (B) internal threads.

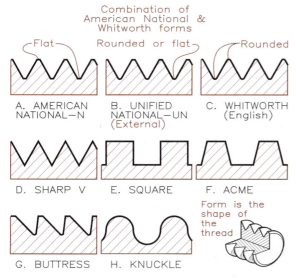

17.3 The various types of thread forms for external threads are shown here.

17.2 Thread terminology

Understanding threaded parts begins with learning their definitions and terminology, which is used throughout this chapter.

External thread: a thread on the outside of a cylinder, such as a bolt (**Fig. 17.1**).

Internal thread: a thread cut on the inside of a part, such as a nut (**Fig. 17.1**).

Major diameter: the largest diameter on an internal or external thread (**Fig. 17.2**).

Minor diameter: the smallest diameter on an internal or external thread (**Fig. 17.2**).

Crest: the peak edge of a screw thread (**Fig. 17.2**).

Root: the bottom of the thread cut into a cylinder to form the minor diameter (**Fig. 17.2**).

Depth: the depth of the thread from the major diameter to the minor diameter; also measured as the root diameter (**Fig. 17.2**).

Thread angle: the angle between threads cut by the cutting tool, usually 60° (**Fig. 17.2**).

Pitch (thread width): the distance between crests of threads, found by dividing 1 inch by the number of threads per inch of a particular thread (**Fig. 17.2**).

Pitch diameter: the diameter of an imaginary cylinder passing through the threads at the points where the thread width is equal to the space between the threads (**Fig. 17.2** and **Fig. 17.4**).

Lead (pronounced leed): the distance a screw will advance when turned 360°.

Form: the shape of the thread cut into a threaded part (**Fig. 17.3**).

Series: the number of threads per inch for a particular diameter, grouped into coarse, fine, extra fine, and eight constant-pitch thread series.

Class of fit: the closeness of fit between two mating parts. Class 1 represents a loose fit and Class 3 a tight fit.

Right-hand thread: one that will assemble when turned clockwise. A right-hand external thread slopes downward and to the right when its axis is horizontal and in the opposite direction on internal threads.

Left-hand thread: one that will assemble when turned counterclockwise. A left-hand external thread slopes downward and to the left when its axis is horizontal and in the opposite direction on internal threads.

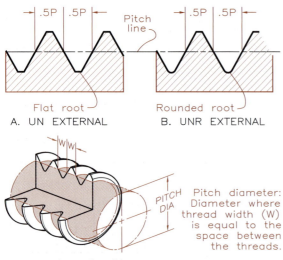

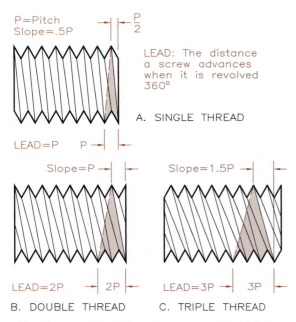

17.4 UN and UNR thread forms

A The UN external thread has a flat root (a round root is optional) and a flat crest.

B The UNR thread has a rounded root, formed by rolling rather than by cutting. The UNR form does not apply to internal threads.

17.5 Threads can be (A) single, (B) double, or (C) triple, which represents the ratio that each advances when turned 360°.

17.3 English System Specifications

Form　Thread form is the shape of the thread cut into a part (**Fig. 17.3**). The Unified National form, denoted by UN in thread notes, is the most widely used form in the United States. The American National form, denoted by N, appears occasionally on older drawings. The sharp V thread is used for set screws and in applications where friction in assembly is desired. Acme, square, and buttress threads are used in gearing and other machinery applications (**Fig. 17.3**).

The Unified National Rolled form, denoted UNR, is used for external threads only, because internal threads cannot be formed by rolling. The standard UN form has a flat root (a rounded root is optional) (**Fig. 17.4A**), and the UNR form (**Fig. 17.4B**) has a rounded root formed by rolling a cylinder across a die. The UNR form can be used instead of the UN form where precision of assembly is less critical.

Series　The thread series designates the spacing of threads that vary with diameter. The American National (N) and the Unified National (UN/UNR) forms include three graded series: **coarse (C), fine (F),** and **extra fine (EF).** Eight **constant-pitch** series (4, 6, 8, 12, 16, 20, 28, and 32 threads per inch) are also available.

Coarse　Unified National threads are denoted UNC or UNRC, which is a combination of form and series designation. The coarse thread (UNC/UNRC or NC) has the largest pitch of any series and is suitable for bolts, screws, nuts, and general use with cast iron, soft metals, and plastics when rapid assembly is desired. An American National (N) form for a coarse thread is written NC.

Fine threads　(NF or UNF/UNRF) are used for bolts, nuts, and screws when a high degree of tightening is required. Fine threads are closer together than coarse threads, and their pitch is graduated to be smaller on smaller diameters.

Extra-fine threads　(UNEF/UNREF or NEF) are suitable for sheet metal screws and bolts, thin nuts, ferrules, and couplings when the length of engagement is limited and high stresses must be withstood.

Constant-pitch threads (4 UN, 6 UN, 8 UN, 12 UN, 16 UN, 20 UN, 28 UN, and 32 UN) are used on larger diameter threads (beginning near the 1/2-inch size) and have the same pitch size regardless of the diameter size. The most commonly used constant-pitch threads are the 8 UN, 12 UN, and 16 UN members of the series, which are used on threads of about 1 inch in diameter and larger. Constant-pitch threads may be specified as UNR or N thread forms. The ANSI table in the Appendix 3 shows constant-pitch threads for larger thread diameters instead of graded pitches of coarse, fine, and extra fine.

Class of Fit The class of fit is the tightness between two mating threads, as between a nut and bolt, and is indicated in the thread note by the numbers 1, 2, or 3 followed by the letters A or B. For UN forms, the letter A represents an external thread and the letter B represents an internal thread. The letters A and B do not appear in notes for the American National form (N).

Class 1A and 1B threads are used on parts that assemble with a minimum of binding and precision. **Class 2A** and **2B** threads are general-purpose threads for bolts, nuts, and screws used in general and mass-production applications. **Class 3A** and **3B** threads are used in precision assemblies where a close fit is required to withstand stresses and vibration.

Single and Multiple Threads A single thread (**Fig. 17.5A**) is a thread that advances the distance of its pitch in a revolution of 360°; that is, its pitch is equal to its lead. The crest lines have a slope of 1/2 P since only 180° of the revolution is visible in the view.

Multiple threads are used where quick assembly is required. A double thread is composed of two threads that advance a distance of 2P when turned 360° (**Fig. 17.5B**); that is, its lead is equal to 2P. The crest lines have a slope of P because only 180° of the revolution is visible in

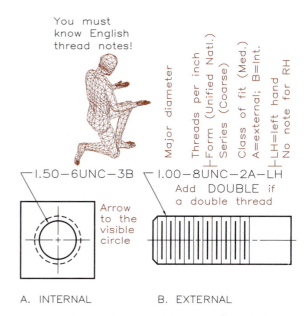

A. INTERNAL   B. EXTERNAL

17.6 Thread notes of the English form that are applied to (A) internal and (B) external threads are defined here.

the view. A triple thread advances 3P in 360° with a crest line slope of 1-1/2 P in the view where 180° of the revolution is visible (**Fig. 17.5C**).

17.4 English Thread Notes

Drawings of threads are only symbolic depictions and are inadequate representations of threads unless accompanied by notes (**Fig. 17.6**). In a thread note, the major diameter is given first, followed by the number of threads per inch, the form, the series, the class of fit, and the letter A or B to denote external or internal threads, respectively. For a double or triple thread, include the word double or triple in the note, and for left-hand threads add the letters LH.

Figure 17.7 shows a UNR thread note for the external thread. (UNR does not apply to internal threads.) When inches are the unit of measurement, fractions can be written as decimals or as

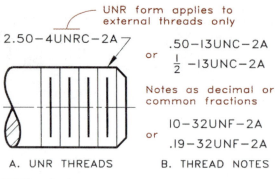

A. UNR THREADS   B. THREAD NOTES

17.7 Thread notes

A The UNR thread note is applied to only external threads.

B Diameters in thread notes can be given as decimal fractions or common fractions.

AMERICAN NATIONAL STANDARDS INSTITUTE
UNIFIED INCH SCREW THREADS (UN AND UNR)

Nominal Diameter	Basic Diameter	Coarse NC & UNC		Fine NF & UNF		Extra Fine NEF/UNEF	
		Thds per In.	Tap Drill DIA	Thds per In.	Tap Drill DIA	Thds per In.	Tap Drill DIA
1	1.000	8	.875	12	.922	20	.953
1-1/16	1.063	...	...	...	...	18	1.000
1-1/8	1.125	7	.904	12	1.046	18	1.070
1-3/16	1.188	...	...	...	...	18	1.141
1-1/4	1.250	7	1.109	12	1.172	18	1.188
1-5/16	1.313	...	...	...	...	18	1.266
1-3/8	1.375	6	1.219	12	1.297	18	1.313
1-7/16	1.438	...	...	...	...	18	1.375
1-1/2	1.500	6	1.344	12	1.422	18	1.438

17.8 This is a portion of the ANSI tables for UN and UNR threads in Appendix 2.

common fractions. The information for thread notes comes from ANSI tables in Appendices 2 and 3.

Using Thread Tables

A portion of Appendix 2 is shown in **Fig. 17.8**, which gives the UN/UNR thread table from which specifications for standardized interchangeable threads can be selected. Note that a 1.50-inch-diameter bolt with fine thread (UNF) has 12 threads per inch, and its thread note is written as

1.500-12 UNF-2A or 1-1/2-12 UNF-2A.

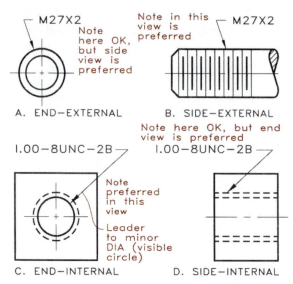

17.9 Notes for external threads are best if they are placed on the rectangular view of the threads. Notes for internal threads are best applied in the circular view if space permits. Metric notes are given at A and B, and English notes are given at C and D.

If the thread were internal (nut), the thread note would be the same but the letter B would be used instead of the letter A. For constant-pitch thread series, selected for larger diameters, write the thread note as

1.750-12 UN-2A or 1-3/4-12 UN-2A.

For the UNR thread form (for external threads only), substitute UNR for UN in the last three columns; for example, UNREF for UNEF (extra fine). **Figure 17.9** shows the preferred placement of thread notes (with leaders) for external and internal threads.

17.5 Metric Thread Notes

Metric thread notes are simpler than English notes since only the major diameter and the pitch are given, as shown in A and B of **Fig. 17.9**. The letter M (for metric) precedes diameter and pitch: M27 × 2, for example, where 27 is the major diameter and 2 is the pitch in millimeters. A portion of the ISO thread table in Appendix 4 is shown in **Fig. 17.10**, from which thread notes

COARSE			FINE		
MAJ. DIA & THD PITCH		TAP DRILL	MAJ. DIA & THD PITCH		TAP DRILL
M20 X 2.5		17.5	M20 X 1.5		18.5
M22 X 2.5		19.5	M22 X 1.5		20.5
M24 X 3		21.0	M24 X 2		22.0
M27 X 3		24.0	M27 X 2		25.0
M30 X 3.5		26.5	M30 X 2		28.0
M33 X 3.5		29.5	M33 X 2		31.0
M36 X 4		32.0	M36 X 2		33.0
M39 X 4		35.0	M39 X 2		36.0
M42 X 4.5		37.5	M42 X 2		39.0

17.10 This portion of the metric (ISO) thread tables in Appendix 4 shows specifications for metric thread notes.

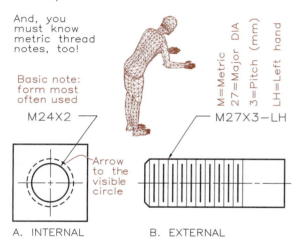

17.11 This is the basic thread note that will be used for (A) internal and (B) external threads.

can be selected. Notice that metric threads come in two series: **coarse** and **fine**. The tap drill, the approximate diameter of the minor diameter, is also given.

Basic Designation Examples of metric thread notes that were taken directly from the tables are shown in **Fig. 17.11**. These are basic designation notes that are sufficient for general applications. Metric notes do not distinguish between internal and external threads, as in the English system where the letters A and B are given. But like the English system, left-hand threads are labeled LH at the end of the note.

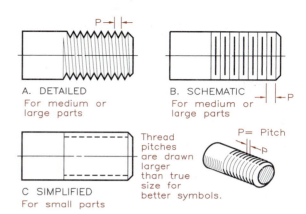

17.12 The three types of thread symbols used for drawing threads are (A) simplified, (B) schematic, and (C) detailed.

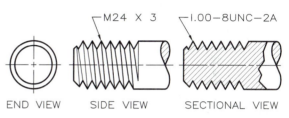

17.13 These detailed symbols represent external threads in view and in section.

17.6 Drawing Threads

Threads may be represented by **detailed**, **schematic**, and **simplified** symbols (**Fig. 17.12**). Detailed symbols represent a thread most realistically, simplified symbols represent a thread least realistically, and schematic symbols are a compromise between the two. Detailed and schematic symbols can be used for drawing larger threads on a drawing (1/2″ diameter and larger) and simplified symbols are best for smaller threads.

17.7 Detailed Symbols

UN/UNR Threads

Detailed thread symbols for external threads in view and in section are shown in **Fig. 17.13**. Instead of drawing helical curves, straight lines are used to depict crest and root lines. Variations of detailed thread symbols for internal threads

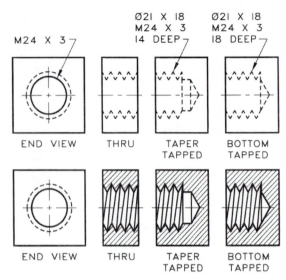

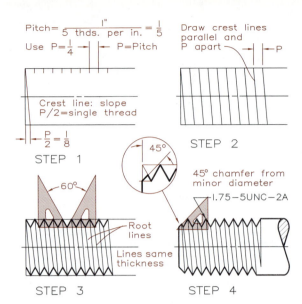

17.14 These detailed symbols represent internal threads. Approximate the minor diameter as 75% of the major diameter. Tap drill diameters are found in Appendix 4.

17.15 Detailed representation of threads

Step 1 For a 1.75-5 UNC-2A thread, find the pitch by dividing 1 inch by the number of threads per inch, 5 in this case. Use a pitch of 1/4 instead of 1/5 to space the threads farther apart. Lay off the pitch along the thread's length and draw a crest line at a slope of P/2.

Step 2 Draw the other crest lines as dark, visible lines parallel to the first crest line.

Step 3 Draw 60° vees between the crest lines and draw root lines from the bottom of the vees. Root lines are parallel to each other but not to crest lines.

Step 4 Draw a 45° chamfer from the minor diameter at the thread's end. Darken lines and add a thread note.

drawn in views and sections are shown in **Fig. 17.14**.

The steps of drawing a detailed thread representation, whether in English or metric threads, are shown in **Fig. 17.15**. When using the English tables, calculate the pitch by dividing 1 inch by the number of threads per inch. In the metric system, pitch is given in the tables. **Draw the spacing between crest lines larger than the actual pitch size to avoid "clogged-up" lines.**

Computer Method You can draw detailed thread symbols by computer (**Fig. 17.16**) and duplicate them with the *Copy* command's *Multiple* option. The program produces a typical set of threads in step 1 and then copies it repetitively in step 2.

Square Threads **Figure 17.17** shows how to draw and note a detailed drawing of a square thread. Follow the same basic steps to draw views and sections of square internal threads (**Fig. 17.18**). In section, draw both the internal crest and root lines, but in a view draw only the

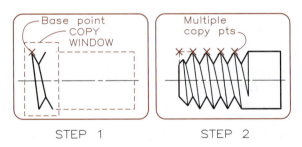

17.16 Detailed thread symbols by computer

Step 1 Draw a typical detailed thread symbol at the end of the screw with the *Line* command.

Step 2 Duplicate the typical set of threads with the *Copy* command and the *Multiple* option along the predetermined snap points of the screw.

outline of the threads. Place thread notes for internal threads in the circular view, whenever

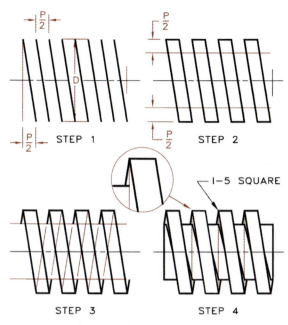

17.17 Drawing the square thread

Step 1 Lay out the major diameter. Space the crest lines 1/2P apart and slope them downward and to the right for right-hand threads.

Step 2 Connect every other pair of crest lines. Find the minor diameter by measuring 1/2P inward from the major diameter.

Step 3 Connect the opposite crest lines with light construction lines to establish the profile of the thread form.

Step 4 Connect the inside crest lines with light construction lines to locate the points on the minor diameter where the thread wraps around the minor diameter. Darken the final lines.

possible, with the leader pointing toward the center and stopping at the visible circle.

When a square thread is long, it can be represented by using phantom lines, without drawing all the threads (**Fig. 17.19**). This conventional practice saves time and effort without reducing the drawing's effectiveness.

Acme Threads A modified version of the square thread is the Acme thread, which has tapered (15°) sides for easier engagement than square threads. The steps involved in drawing detailed Acme threads are shown in **Fig. 17.20**.

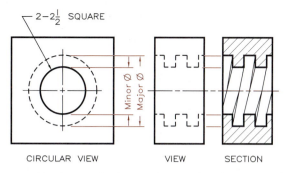

17.18 This drawing shows internal square threads in view and section.

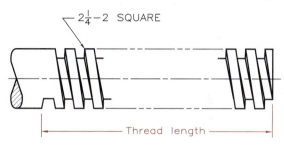

17.19 The conventional method of showing square threads is to draw sample threads at each end and to connect them with phantom lines.

Acme threads are heavy threads that are used to transmit force and power in mechanisms such as screw jacks, leveling devices, and lathes. Appendix 5 contains the table for Acme thread specifications and dimensions.

Internal Acme threads are shown in view and section in **Fig. 17.21**. Left-hand internal threads in section appear the same as right-hand external threads.

17.8 Schematic Symbols

Figure 17.22 shows schematic representations of external threads with metric notes. Because schematic symbols are easy to draw and adequately represent threads, it is the thread symbol used most often for medium-size threads. Draw schematic thread symbols by using thin, parallel crest lines and thick root lines. Schematic drawings of left-hand and right-hand threads are identical; only the LH in the thread

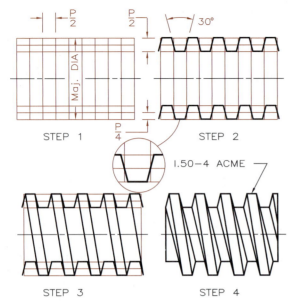

STEP 1   STEP 2

1.50−4 ACME

STEP 3   STEP 4

17.20 Drawing the Acme thread

Step 1 Lay out the major diameter and thread length and divide the shaft into equal divisions 1/2P apart. Locate the minor and pitch diameters by using distances 1/2P and 1/4 P.

Step 2 Draw lines at 15° angles with the vertical along the pitch diameter to make a total angle of 30°.

Step 3 Draw the crest lines across the screw.

Step 4 Darken the lines, draw the root lines, and add the thread note to complete the drawing.

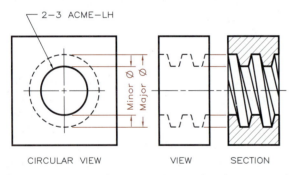

2−3 ACME−LH

CIRCULAR VIEW   VIEW   SECTION

17.21 This drawing shows internal Acme threads in view and section.

note indicates that a thread is left-handed. Right-hand threads are not marked RH, but are understood to be right-hand threads.

Figure 17.23 shows threaded holes in view and in section drawn with schematic symbols.

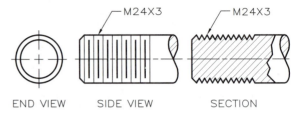

END VIEW   SIDE VIEW   SECTION

17.22 These schematic symbols represent external threads in view and section.

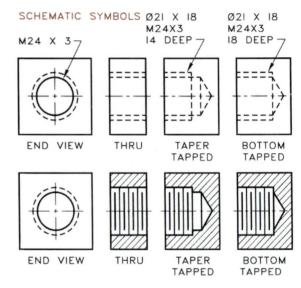

SCHEMATIC SYMBOLS   Ø21 X 18   Ø21 X 18
                    M24X3   M24X3
M24 X 3   14 DEEP   18 DEEP

END VIEW   THRU   TAPER   BOTTOM
                  TAPPED   TAPPED

END VIEW   THRU   TAPER   BOTTOM
                  TAPPED   TAPPED

17.23 These schematic symbols represent internal threads in view and section. Tap drill diameters for their minor diameters are given in Appendix 2.

The size of the tap drill diameter is approximately equal to the major diameter minus the pitch. However, the minor diameter usually is drawn a bit smaller to provide better separation between the lines representing the major and minor diameters.

Figure 17.24 shows how to draw schematic threads using English specifications. Draw the minor diameter at approximately three-quarters of the major diameter and the chamfer (bevel) 45° from the minor diameter. Draw crest lines as thin lines and root lines as thick visible lines.

Computer Method You may draw schematic thread symbols by computer (**Fig. 17.25**) and

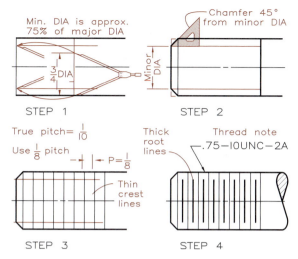

Min. DIA is approx. 75% of major DIA

$\frac{3}{4}$ DIA

STEP 1

Chamfer 45° from minor DIA

Minor DIA

STEP 2

True pitch = $\frac{1}{10}$

Use $\frac{1}{8}$ pitch

$P = \frac{1}{8}$

Thin crest lines

STEP 3

Thick root lines

Thread note
.75–10UNC–2A

STEP 4

17.24 Schematic representation of threads

Step 1 Lay out the major diameter and locate the minor diameter (about 75% of the major diameter). Draw the minor diameter with light construction lines.

Step 2 Chamfer the end of the threads with a 45° angle from the minor diameter.

Step 3 Find the pitch of a .75-10UNC-2A thread (.01) by dividing 1 inch by the number of threads per inch (10). Use a larger pitch, 1/8 inch in this case, for spacing the thin crest lines.

Step 4 Draw root lines as thick as the visible lines between the crest lines to the construction lines representing the minor diameter. Add a thread note.

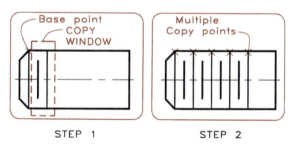

Base point
COPY
WINDOW

STEP 1

Multiple Copy points

STEP 2

17.25 Schematic threads by computer

Step 1 With the *Line* command, draw the outline of the shaft with a chamfer. Draw typical minor and major diameters and window them for a *Multiple Copy*.

Step 2 Repetitively *Copy* the threads along the screw by *Snapping* to the ends of the crest lines.

duplicate them with the *Copy* command's *Multiple* option. The program lets you draw a typical set of threads in step 1 and copies it repetitively in step 2.

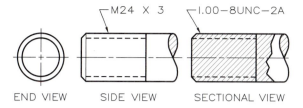

M24 X 3

1.00–8UNC–2A

END VIEW   SIDE VIEW   SECTIONAL VIEW

17.26 These simplified thread symbols represent external threads in view and section.

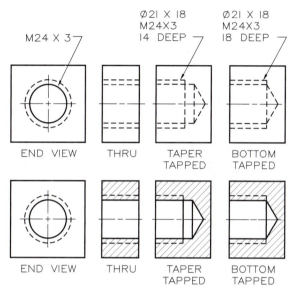

M24 X 3

Ø21 X 18
M24X3
14 DEEP

Ø21 X 18
M24X3
18 DEEP

END VIEW   THRU   TAPER TAPPED   BOTTOM TAPPED

END VIEW   THRU   TAPER TAPPED   BOTTOM TAPPED

17.27 These simplified thread symbols represent internal threads in view and section. Draw minor diameters at about 75% of the major diameter.

17.9 Simplified Symbols

Examples of external threads drawn with simplified symbols and noted with both metric and English formats are shown in **Fig. 17.26**. Simplified symbols are the easiest to draw and are the best suited for drawing small threads where drawing using schematic and detailed symbols would be too crowded. Various techniques of applying simplified symbols to threads are shown in **Fig. 17.27**. The minor diameter is drawn as hidden lines spaced at about three-quarters of the major diameter. **Figure 17.28** shows the steps of drawing simplified threads. With experience, you will be able to approximate the location of the minor diameter of simplified threads by eye.

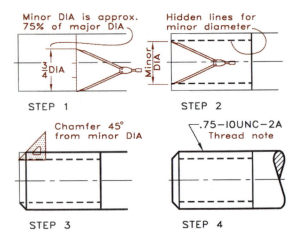

STEP 1

STEP 2

Chamfer 45° from minor DIA

STEP 3

.75–10UNC–2A Thread note

STEP 4

17.28 Simplified representation of threads:

Step 1 Lay out the major diameter. Locate the minor diameter (about 75% of the major diameter).

Step 2 Draw hidden lines to represent the minor diameter.

Step 3 Draw a 45° chamfer from the minor diameter to the major diameter.

Step 4 Darken the lines and add a thread note.

Drawing Small Threads

Remember, a drawing of a thread is a pictorial symbol; therefore, do not try to draw the true spacing of the threads. True spacing will be too close and hard to read. Instead, select a wider spacing between root and crest lines for a drawing that is easier to read and draw (**Fig. 17.29**). This conventional practice of enlarging the thread's pitch to separate thread symbols is applied in drawing all three types of symbols (simplified, schematic, and detailed). Add a thread note to the drawing to give the necessary detailed specifications.

17.10 Nuts and Bolts

Nuts and bolts (**Fig. 17.30**) come in a variety of forms and sizes for many different applications. Some common types of threaded fasteners are shown in **Fig. 17.31**. A **bolt** is a threaded cylinder with a head that is used with a nut to hold parts together. A **stud** is a headless bolt, threaded at

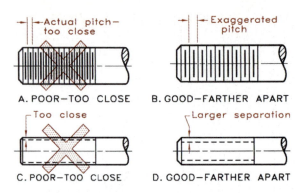

A. POOR–TOO CLOSE   B. GOOD–FARTHER APART

C. POOR–TOO CLOSE   D. GOOD–FARTHER APART

17.29 Most threads must be drawn using exaggerated dimensions instead of actual measurements to prevent the drawing from having lines drawn too closely together.

17.30 This photo shows a nut, bolt, and washers in combination. (Courtesy of Lamson & Sessions.)

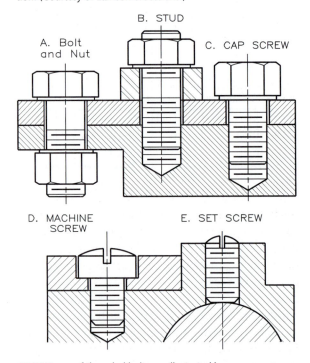

17.31 Types of threaded bolts are illustrated here.

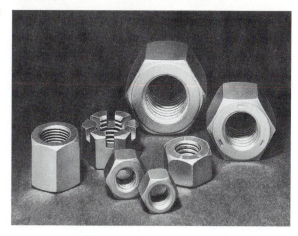

17.32 Examples of types of nuts. (*Courtesy of Russell, Burdsall & Ward Bolt and Nut Company.*)

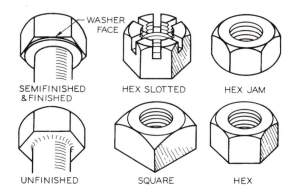

17.33 Finished and semifinished bolts and nuts have raised washer faces. Several types of nuts are shown here also.

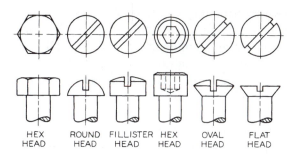

17.34 These are standard types of bolt and screw heads.

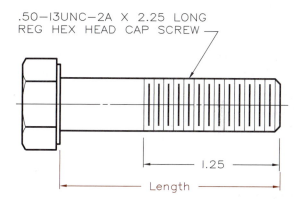

17.35 A properly dimensioned and noted hexagon-head bolt.

both ends, that is screwed into one part with a nut attached to the other end.

A **cap screw** usually does not have a nut, but passes through a hole in one part and screws into a threaded hole in another part. A hexagon-head **machine screw** is similar to but smaller than a cap screw. Machine screws also come with other types of heads. A **set screw** is used to hold one part fixed in place with another, usually to prevent rotation, as with a pulley on a shaft.

Types of heads used on **regular** and **heavy** bolts and nuts are shown in **Fig. 17.32** and **Fig. 17.33**. Heavy bolts have thicker heads than regular bolts for heavier usage. A **finished head** (or

nut) has a 1/64-inch-thick washer face (a circular boss) to provide a bearing surface for smooth contact. **Semifinished bolt heads** and **nuts** are the same as finished bolt heads and nuts. Unfinished bolt heads and nuts have no bosses and no machined surfaces.

A **hexagon jam nut** does not have a washer face, but it is chamfered (beveled at its corners) on both sides. **Figure 17.34** shows other standard bolt and screw heads for cap screws and machine screws.

Dimensions
Figure 17.35 shows a properly dimensioned bolt. The ANSI tables in Appendices 7–10 give nut and bolt dimensions, but you may use the following guides for hexagon-head and square-head bolts.

Overall Lengths   Hexagon-head bolts are available in 1/4-inch increments up to 8 inches long, in 1/2-inch increments from 8 to 20 inches long, and in 1-inch increments from 20 to 30 inches long. Square-head bolts are available in 1/8-inch increments from 1/2 to 3/4 inch long, in 1/4-inch increments from 3/4 inch to 5 inches long, in 1/2-inch increments from 5 to 12 inches long, and in 1-inch increments from 12 to 30 inches long.

Thread Lengths   For both hexagon-head and square-head bolts up to 6 inches long,

$$\text{Thread length} = 2D + 1/4 \text{ in.}$$

where D is the diameter of the bolt. For bolts more than 6 inches long,

$$\text{Thread length} = 2D + 1/2 \text{ in.}$$

Threads for bolts can be coarse, fine, or 8-pitch threads. The class of fit for bolts and nuts is understood to be 2A and 2B if no class is specified in the note.

Dimension Notes

Designate standard square-head and hexagon-head bolts by notes in one of three forms:

3/8–16 × 1–1/2 SQUARE HEAD BOLT- STEEL;

1/2–13 × 3 HEX CAP SCREW—SAE
GRADE 8-STEEL;

.75 × 10 UNC–2A HEX HD LAG SCREW.

The numbers (left to right) represent bolt diameter, threads per inch, bolt length, screw name, and material (material designation is optional). When not specified in a note, each bolt is assumed to have a class 2 fit. Three types of notes for designating nuts are:

1/2–13 SQUARE NUT-STEEL;

3/4–16 HEAVY HEX NUT;

1.00–8UNC–2B HEX HD THICK SLOTTED NUT
CORROSION-RESISTANT STEEL.

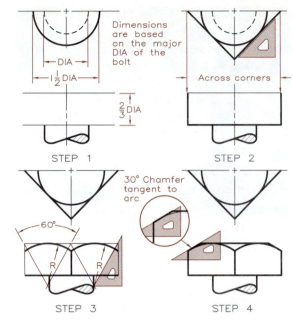

17.36 Drawing the square head

Step 1 Draw the major diameter, DIA, of the bolt. Use 1.5 DIA to draw the hexagon-head's diameter and 2/3 DIA to establish its thickness.

Step 2 Draw the top view of the square head at a 45° angle to give an across-corners view.

Step 3 Show the chamfer in the front view by using a 30°–60° triangle to find the centers for the radii.

Step 4 Show a 30° chamfer tangent to the arcs in the front view. Darken the lines.

When nuts are not specified as heavy, they are assumed to be regular. When the class of fit is not specified in a note, it is assumed to be 2B for nuts.

17.11 Drawing Square Heads

Appendix 7 gives dimensions for square bolt heads and nuts. However, it is conventional practice to draw nuts and bolts by using the general proportions shown in **Fig. 17.36**. Your first step in drawing a bolt head or nut is to determine whether the view is to be across corners or across flats—that is, whether the lines at either side of the view represent the square's corners or flats. Drawing across corners shows nuts and bolts best, but occasionally you must draw one across flats when the head or nut is truly in this orientation.

17.12 Drawing Hexagon Heads

Figure 17.37 shows the steps for drawing the head of a hexagon bolt across corners by using the bolt's major diameter, D, as the basis for all other proportions. Begin by drawing the top view of the head as a circle of diameter of 1-1/2 D. For a regular head, the thickness is 2/3 D and for a heavy head it is 7/8 D. Circumscribe a hexagon about the circle. Then draw outside arcs in the rectangular view and tangent chamfers (bevels) to complete the drawing.

Computer Method You may draw a hexagon head for a bolt by computer, as shown in step 1 of **Fig. 17.38**. Use a bolt diameter of 1 inch for easy scaling. You may then scale and rotate the block as desired when you use the *Insert* command. Step 2 shows the drawing *Blocked* and *inserted* at scales of 50% and 75%. To insert a thread with a diameter of 0.50 inch, assign a size factor of 0.50 when prompted by the *Insert* and *Block* commands.

Drawing Nuts

Use the same steps you used to draw bolt heads to draw a square nut and a hexagon nut (shown across corners in **Fig. 17.39**). The difference is that nuts are thicker than bolt heads: The thickness of a regular nut is 7/8 D, and the thickness of a heavy nut is 1 D, where D is the bolt diameter. Hidden lines may be inserted in the front view to indicate threads, or they may be omitted. Exaggerate the thickness of the 1/64-inch washer face on the finished and semifinished hexagon nuts to about

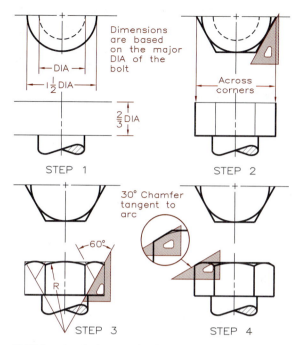

17.37 Drawing the hexagon head

Step 1 Draw the major DIA of the bolt, find the diameter of the head as 1.5 DIA, and thickness as 2/3 DIA.

Step 2 Construct a hexagon head with a 30°–60° triangle to give an across-corners view.

Step 3 Find arcs in the front view to draw the chamfer of the head.

Step 4 Draw a 30° chamfer tangent to the arcs in the front view. Darken the lines.

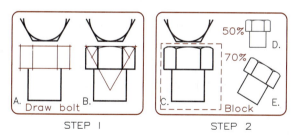

17.38 A bolt head representation drawn by computer

Step 1 Draw a hexagon head using the steps of geometric construction in Fig. 17.37. Base the size of the head on a bolt diameter of 1 inch to form a *Unit Block* for easy scaling.

Step 2 Convert the drawing into a *Block* by using a window. *Insert* the block at any size and position and scale with the desired factor as shown at D and E.

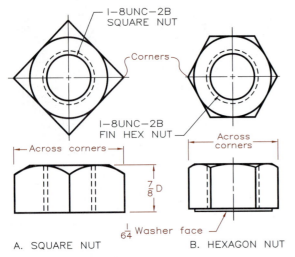

A. SQUARE NUT   B. HEXAGON NUT

17.39 Drawing square and hexagon nuts across corners involves the same steps used for drawing bolt heads. Add notes to give nut specifications.

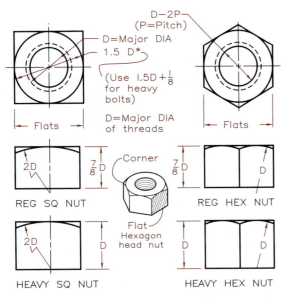

17.40 These square and hexagon nuts are drawn across flats with notes added to give their specifications. Square nuts are unfinished.

1/32 inch to make it more noticeable. Place thread notes on circular views with leaders when space permits. Square nuts that are not labeled as heavy are assumed to be regular nuts.

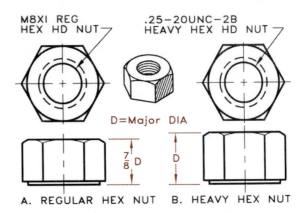

A. REGULAR HEX NUT   B. HEAVY HEX NUT

17.41 These regular and heavy hexagon nuts are drawn across corners, with notes added to give their specifications.

Figure 17.40 shows how to construct square and hexagon nuts across flats. For regular nuts, the distance across flats is 1-1/2 × D (D = major diameter of the thread), and 1-5/8 D for heavy nuts. Draw the top views in the same way you drew across-corner top views, but rotate them to give across-flat front views. **Figure 17.41** depicts dimensioned and noted hexagon regular and heavy nuts drawn across corners.

Drawing Nut and Bolt Combinations

Nuts and bolts in assembly are drawn in the same manner as they are drawn individually (**Fig. 17.42**). Use the major diameter, D, of the bolt as the basis for other dimensions. Here, the views of the bolt heads are across corners, and the views of the nuts are across flats, although both views could have been drawn across corners. The half end views are used to find the front views by projection. Add a note to give the specifications of the nut and bolt.

17.13 Types of Screws

Cap Screws

The cap screw passes through a hole in one part and screws into a threaded hole in the other part so the two parts can be held together without a

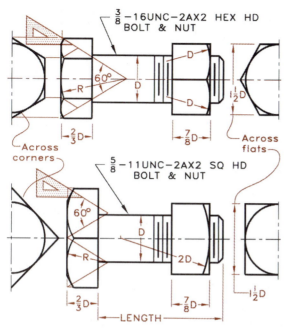

17.42 The proportions and the geometry for drawing square nuts and bolts and hexagon nuts and bolts are shown here.

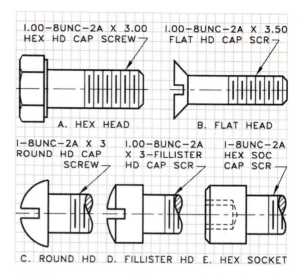

17.43 These cap screws are drawn on a grid to give the proportions for drawing them at different sizes. Notes give thread specifications, length, head type, and bolt name (cap screw).

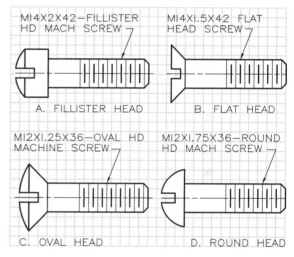

17.44 These are standard types of machine screws. The same proportions may be used to draw machine screws of all sizes.

nut. Cap screws are usually larger than machine screws and they may also be used with nuts. **Figure 17.43** shows the standard types of cap screw heads drawn on a grid that can be used as a guide for drawing cap screws of other sizes. Appendices 11–15 gives cap screw dimensions, which can aid in drawing them.

Machine Screws

Smaller than most cap screws, **machine screws** usually are less than 1 inch in diameter. They screw into a threaded hole in a part or into a nut. Machine screws are fully threaded when their length is 2 inches or less. Longer screws have thread lengths of 2D + 1/4 inch (D = major diameter of the thread). **Figure 17.44** shows four types of machine screws, along with notes, drawn on a grid that may be used as an aid in drawing them without dimensions from a table. Machine screws range in diameter from No. 0 (0.060 inch) to 3/4 inch, as shown in Appendix

16, which gives the dimensions of round-head machine screws.

Set Screws

Set screws are used to hold parts together, such as pulleys and handles on a shaft, and prevent rotation. **Figure 17.45** shows various types of set screws with dimensions denoted by letters that

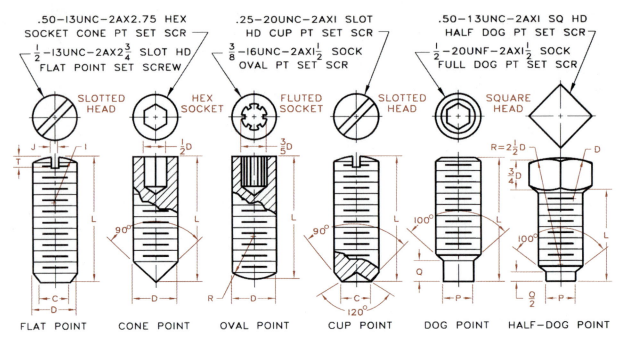

.50–13UNC–2AX2.75 HEX
SOCKET CONE PT SET SCR

½–13UNC–2AX2¾ SLOT HD
FLAT POINT SET SCREW

.25–20UNC–2AXI SLOT
HD CUP PT SET SCR

⅜–16UNC–2AXI½ SOCK
OVAL PT SET SCR

.50–13UNC–2AXI SQ HD
HALF DOG PT SET SCR

½–20UNF–2AXI½ SOCK
FULL DOG PT SET SCR

SLOTTED HEAD   HEX SOCKET   FLUTED SOCKET   SLOTTED HEAD   SQUARE HEAD

FLAT POINT   CONE POINT   OVAL POINT   CUP POINT   DOG POINT   HALF–DOG POINT

17.45 Set screws are available with various combinations of heads and points. Notes give their measurements. (See Appendix 17.)

correspond to the tables of dimensions in Appendix 17.

Set screws are available in combinations of points and heads. The shaft against which the set screw is tightened may have a machined flat surface to provide a good bearing surface for a dog or flat-point set screw end to press against. The **cup point** gives good gripping when pressed against round shafts. The **cone point** works best when inserted into holes drilled in the part being held. The **headless set screw** has no head to protrude above a rotating part. An **exterior square head** is good for applications in which greater force must be applied with a wrench to hold larger set screws in position.

Wood Screws

A wood screw is a pointed screw having sharp coarse threads that will screw into wood, making its own internal threads in the process. **Figure 17.46** shows the three most common

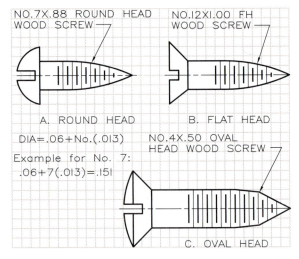

NO.7X.88 ROUND HEAD WOOD SCREW

NO.12X1.00 FH WOOD SCREW

A. ROUND HEAD

DIA=.06+No.(.013)

Example for No. 7:
.06+7(.013)=.151

B. FLAT HEAD

NO.4X.50 OVAL HEAD WOOD SCREW

C. OVAL HEAD

17.46 Standard types of wood screws are drawn on a grid to give their proportions for drawing them at other sizes.

types of wood screws drawn on a grid to show their relative proportions.

Sizes of wood screws are specified by single numbers, such as 0, 6, or 16. From 0 to 10, each digit represents a different size. Beginning at 10,

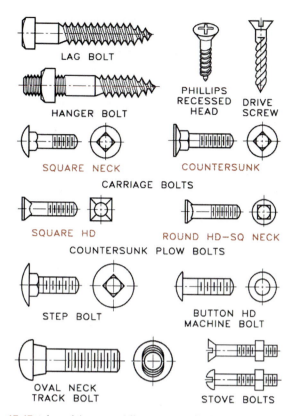

17.47 A few of the many different types of bolts and screws are illustrated here.

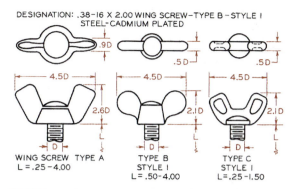

17.48 These wing screw proportions are for screw diameters of about 5/16 inch. The same proportions may be used to draw wing screws of any diameter. Type A screws are available in diameters of 4, 6, 8, 10, 12, 0.25", 0.313", 0.375", 0.438", 0.50", and 0.625". Type B screws are available in diameters of 10 to 0.625". Type C screws are available in diameters of 6 to 0.375".

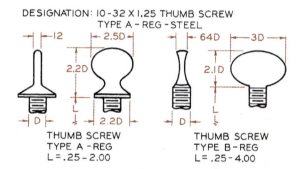

17.49 These thumb screw proportions are for screw diameters of about 1/4 inch. The same proportions may be used to draw thumb screws of any diameter. Type A screws are available in diameters of 6, 8, 10, 12, 0.25", 0.313", and 0.375". Type B thumb screws are available in diameters of 6 to 0.50".

only even-numbered sizes are standard, that is, 10, 12, 14, 16, 18, 20, 22, and 24. Use the following formula to translate these numbers into the actual diameter sizes:

Actual DIA = 0.06 + (screw number × 0.013).

For example, the diameter for the No. 7 wood screw shown in **Fig. 17.46** is calculated as follows:

DIA = 0.06 + 7(0.013) = 0.151.

17.14 Other Threaded Fasteners

Only the more standard types of nuts and bolts are covered in this chapter. **Figure 17.47** illustrates a few of the many other types of threaded fasteners that have their own special applications. Three types of wing screws that are turned by hand are available in incremental lengths of 1/8 inch (**Fig. 17.48**). **Figure 17.49** shows two types of thumb screws, which serve the same purpose as wing screws, and **Fig. 17.50** shows wing nuts that can be screwed together by fingertip without wrenches or screwdrivers.

17.15 Tapping a Hole

An internal thread is made by drilling a hole with a tap drill that has a 120° point (**Fig. 17.51**). The

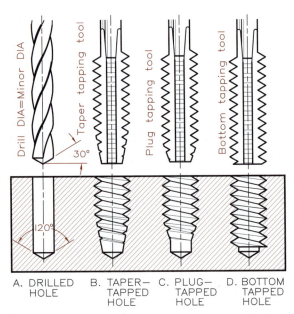

.7D .5D .7D

4D 4.6D 4.3D

2.5D 2D 2D

WING NUT-TYPE A   TYPE B   TYPE C
                      STYLE I   STYLE I

17.50 These wing nut proportions are for screw diameters of 3/8 inch. The same proportions may be used to draw thumb screws of any size. Type A wing nuts are available in screw diameters of 3, 4, 5, 6, 8, 10, 12, 0.25″, 0.313″, 0.375″, 0.438″, 0.50″, 0.583″, 0.625″, and 0.75″. Type B nuts are available in sizes from 5 to 0.75″. Type C nuts are available in sizes from 4 to 0.50″.

Drill DIA=Minor DIA   Taper tapping tool   Plug tapping tool   Bottom tapping tool

30°

120°

A. DRILLED   B. TAPER—   C. PLUG—   D. BOTTOM
   HOLE   TAPPED   TAPPED   TAPPED
                 HOLE   HOLE   HOLE

17.51 Three types of tapping tools are used to thread internal drilled holes: taper tap, plug tap, and bottom tap.

depth of the drilled hole is measured to the shoulder of the conical point, not to the point. The diameter of the drilled hole is approximately equal to the root diameter, calculated as the major diameter of the screw thread minus its pitch (Appendices 2 and 3). The hole is **tapped**,

or threaded, with a tool called a **tap** of one of the types shown.

The **taper**, **plug**, and **bottoming** hand taps have identical measurements except for the chamfered portion of their ends. The taper tap has a long chamfer (8 to 10 threads), the plug tap has a shorter chamfer (3 to 5 threads), and the bottoming tap has the shortest chamfer (1 to 1-1/2 threads).

When tapping is to be done by hand in open or "through" holes, the taper tap should be used for coarse threads and in harder metals because it ensures straighter alignment and starting. The plug tap may be used in soft metals and for fine-pitch threads. When a hole is tapped to its bottom, all three taps—taper, plug, and bottoming—are used in that sequence on the same internal threads.

Notes are added to specify the depth of a drilled hole and the depth of the threads within it. For example, a note reading 7/8 DIA-3 DEEP × 1/8 UNC-2A × 2 DEEP means that the hole is to be drilled deeper than it is threaded and that the last usable thread will be 2 inches deep in the hole.

17.16 Washers and Pins

Various types of washers are used with nuts and bolts to improve their assembly and increase their fastening strength.

Plain washers are noted on a drawing as

.938 × 1.750 × 0.134 TYPE A
PLAIN WASHER,

where the numbers (left to right) represent the washer's inside diameter, outside diameter, and thickness (Appendices 22 and 23).

Lock washers reduce the likelihood that threaded parts will loosen because of vibration and movement. **Figure 17.52** shows several common types of lock washers. Appendix 28 contains a table of dimensions for regular and extra-heavy-duty, helical-spring lock washers. Designate them with a note in the form:

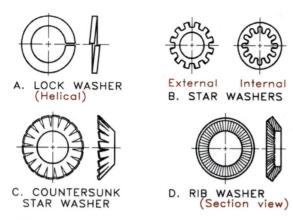

A. LOCK WASHER
(Helical)

External   Internal
B. STAR WASHERS

C. COUNTERSUNK
STAR WASHER

D. RIB WASHER
(Section view)

17.52 Lock washers are used to keep threaded parts from vibrating apart.

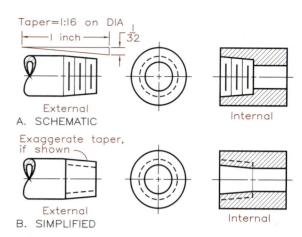

Taper=1:16 on DIA

External
A. SCHEMATIC

Internal

Exaggerate taper, if shown

External
B. SIMPLIFIED

Internal

17.54 Pipe threads are shown with schematic and simplified symbols here.

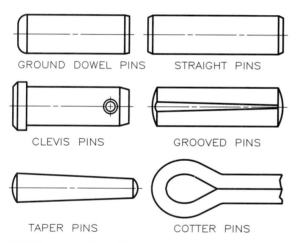

GROUND DOWEL PINS   STRAIGHT PINS

CLEVIS PINS   GROOVED PINS

TAPER PINS   COTTER PINS

17.53 Pins are used to hold parts together in assembly.

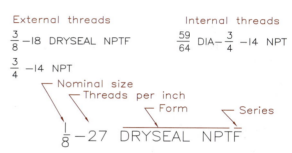

External threads

$\frac{3}{8}$ –18 DRYSEAL NPTF

$\frac{3}{4}$ –14 NPT

Internal threads

$\frac{59}{64}$ DIA– $\frac{3}{4}$ –14 NPT

Nominal size

Threads per inch

Form

Series

$\frac{1}{8}$ –27 DRYSEAL NPTF

17.55 These are typical pipe thread notes.

HELICAL-SPRING LOCK WASHER
1/4 REGULAR—PHOSPHOR BRONZE,

where the 1/4 is the washer's inside diameter. You can designate tooth lock washers with a note in one of two forms:

INTERNAL-TOOTH LOCK WASHER
1/4-TYPE A—STEEL;

EXTERNAL-TOOTH LOCK WASHER
.562-TYPE B—STEEL.

Pins (**Fig. 17.53**) are used to hold parts together in a fixed position. Appendix 19 gives dimensions for taper pins. The **cotter pin** is another locking device that you will remember held the wheels on your toy wagon. Appendix 18 contains a table of dimensions for cotter pins.

17.17 Pipe Threads and Fittings

Pipe threads are used for connecting pipes, tubing, and various fittings, including lubrication fittings. The most commonly used pipe thread is tapered at a ratio of 1 to 16 on its diameter, but straight pipe threads also are available (**Fig. 17.54**). Tapered pipe threads will engage only for an effective length of

$$L = (0.80 D + 6.8) P,$$

where D is the outside diameter of the threaded pipe and P is the pitch of the thread.

The pipe threads shown in **Fig. 17.54** have a taper exaggerated to 1:16 on radius (instead of on diameter) to emphasize it. Drawing them with no taper obviously is easier. You may use either schematic or simplified symbols to show the threaded features.

Use the following ANSI abbreviations in pipe thread notes. All begin with NP (for National Pipe thread).

NPT: national pipe taper

NPTF: national pipe thread (dryseal, for pressure-tight joints)

NPS: straight pipe thread

NPSC: straight pipe thread in couplings

NPSI: national pipe straight internal thread

NPSF: straight pipe thread (dryseal)

NPSM: straight pipe thread for mechanical joints

NPSL: straight pipe thread for locknuts and lock nut pipe threads

NPSH: straight pipe thread for hose couplings and nipples

NPTR: taper pipe thread for railing fittings

To specify a pipe thread in note form, give the nominal pipe diameter (the common-fraction size of its internal diameter), the number of threads per inch, and the thread-type symbol:

3-8 NPT or 5-8 NPTR

Appendix 6 gives a table of dimensions for pipe threads. **Figure 17.55** shows how to present specifications for external and internal threads in note form. Dryseal threads, either straight or tapered, provide a pressure-tight joint without the use of a lubricant or sealer.

Grease Fittings
Grease fittings (**Fig. 17.56**) allow the application of lubrication to moving parts. Threads of grease

Thread size	$\frac{1}{8}$ 3mm		$\frac{1}{4}$ 6mm		$\frac{3}{8}$ 10mm	
Overall length	L=in.	mm	L=in.	mm	L=in.	mm
Straight	.625	16	1.000	25	1.200	30
90° Elbow	.800	20	1.250	32	1.400	36
45° Angle	1.000	25	1.500	38	1.600	41

GREASE FITTINGS
Threads may be NPT or UN form

A. STRAIGHT   B. 90° ANGLE   C. 45° ANGLE

17.56 Three standard types of grease fittings used to lubricate moving parts with a grease gun are shown here.

fittings are available as tapered and straight pipe threads. The ends, where grease is inserted with a grease gun, are available straight or at 90° and 45° angles. A one-way valve, formed by a ball and spring, permits grease to enter the fitting (forced through by a grease gun) but prevents it from escaping.

17.18 Keys

Keys are used to attach pulleys, gears, or crank handles to shafts to hold them securely in place while moving and transmitting power. The four types of keys shown in **Fig. 17.57** are the most commonly used ones. Appendices 20 and 21 contain tables of dimensions for keyways, keys, and keyseats.

17.19 Rivets

Rivets are fasteners that permanently join thin overlapping materials (**Fig. 17.58**). The rivet is inserted in a hole slightly larger than the diameter of the rivet, and the application of pressure to the projecting end forms the headless end into shape. Forming may be done with either hot or cold rivets, depending on the application.

Figure 17.59 shows typical shapes and proportions of small rivets that vary in diameter

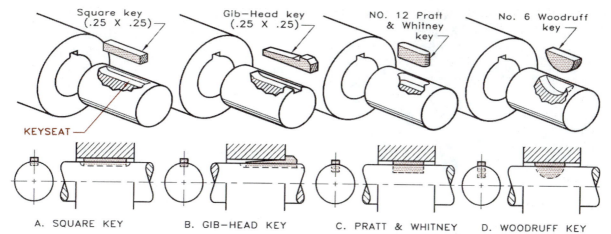

Square key
(.25 X .25)

Gib-Head key
(.25 X .25)

NO. 12 Pratt
& Whitney
key

No. 6 Woodruff
key

KEYSEAT

A. SQUARE KEY   B. GIB-HEAD KEY   C. PRATT & WHITNEY   D. WOODRUFF KEY

17.57 Standard types of keys used to hold parts on a shaft.

17.58 Rivets are used to permanently fasten structural elements together. (*Courtesy of Russell, Burdsall & Ward Bolt and Nut Company.*)

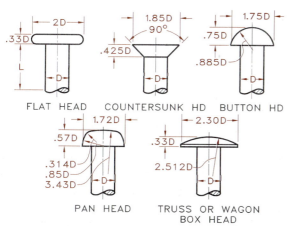

2D
.33D
L
D

FLAT HEAD

1.85D
90°
.425D
D

COUNTERSUNK HD

1.75D
.75D
.885D
D

BUTTON HD

1.72D
.57D
.314D
.85D
3.43D
D

PAN HEAD

2.30D
.33D
2.512D
D

TRUSS OR WAGON
BOX HEAD

17.59 The proportions of small rivets with shanks up to 1/2 inch diameter are shown here.

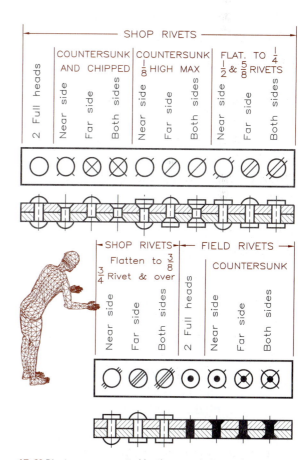

SHOP RIVETS

2 Full heads	COUNTERSUNK AND CHIPPED			COUNTERSUNK $\frac{1}{8}$ HIGH MAX			FLAT. TO $\frac{1}{4}$ $\frac{1}{2}$ & $\frac{5}{8}$ RIVETS		
	Near side	Far side	Both sides	Near side	Far side	Both sides	Near side	Far side	Both sides

	SHOP RIVETS			FIELD RIVETS		
	Flatten to $\frac{3}{8}$ $\frac{3}{4}$ Rivet & over			COUNTERSUNK		
2 Full heads	Near side	Far side	Both sides	Near side	Far side	Both sides

17.60 Rivets are represented by these symbols in a drawing.

17.19 RIVETS • 239

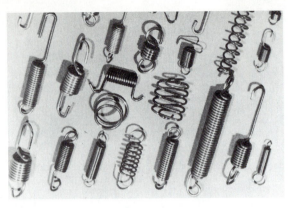

17.61 Springs are available for numerous special applications.

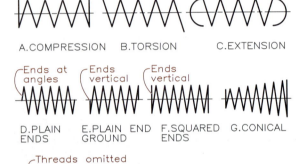

A.COMPRESSION   B.TORSION   C.EXTENSION

Ends at angles | Ends vertical | Ends vertical

D.PLAIN ENDS   E.PLAIN END GROUND   F.SQUARED ENDS   G.CONICAL

Threads omitted

H.SINGLE—LINE REPRESENTATIONS: SIMPLIFIED

17.62 Single-line spring drawings

A–C These are single-line representations of various types of springs.

D–G These single-line representations of springs show various types of ends.

H These are simplified single-line representations of the springs depicted in D–G.

from 1/16 to 1-3/4 inches. Rivets are used extensively in pressure-vessel fabrication, heavy construction (such as bridges and buildings), and sheet-metal construction.

Figure 17.60 shows some of the standard ANSI symbols for representing rivets. Rivets that are driven in the shop are called **shop rivets**, and those assembled at the job site are called **field rivets**.

17.20 Springs

Springs are devices that absorb energy and react with an equal force (**Fig. 17.61**). Most springs are **helical**, as are bed springs, but they can also be **flat** (leaf), as in an automobile chassis. Some of the more common types of springs are **compression**, **torsion**, **extension**, **flat**, and **constant force** springs. **Figures 17.62A-C** show single-line conventional representations of the first three types. **Figures 17.62D-F** represent the types of ends used on compression springs.

Plain ends of springs simply end with no special modification of the coil. **Ground plain ends** are coils that have been machined by grinding to flatten the ends perpendicular to their axes. **Squared ends** are inactive coils that have been closed to form a circular flat coil at the spring's end, which may also be ground.

In **Fig. 17.62G** a conical helical spring is shown in its simplified form. **Figure 17.62H** shows schematic single-line representations of the same types of springs depicted in **Fig. 17.62D-G** with phantom outlines instead of all the coils. This is the conventional method of drawing springs that saves time and effort.

Working drawing specifications of a compression spring drawn as a double-line representation are shown in **Fig. 17.63**. Two coils are drawn at each end of the spring and phantom lines are drawn between them in order to save drawing time. A dimension is given with the diameter and free length of the spring on the drawing. The remaining specifications are given in a table placed near the drawing.

A working drawing of an extension spring (**Fig. 17.64**) is similar to that of a compression spring. An extending spring is designed to resist stretching, whereas a **compression spring** is designed to resist squeezing. In a drawing of a helical torsion spring, which resists and reacts to a twisting motion (**Fig. 17.65**), angular dimensions specify the initial and final positions of the spring as torsion is applied. Again, dimension

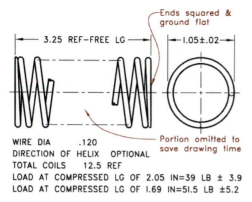

WIRE DIA   .120
DIRECTION OF HELIX   OPTIONAL
TOTAL COILS   12.5 REF
LOAD AT COMPRESSED LG OF 2.05 IN=39 LB ± 3.9
LOAD AT COMPRESSED LG OF 1.69 IN=51.5 LB ±5.2

17.63 This conventional double-line drawing is of a compression spring and includes its specifications.

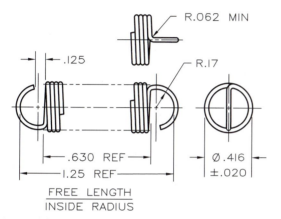

FREE LENGTH
INSIDE RADIUS

WIRE DIA   0.42
DIRECTION OF HELIX   OPTIONAL
TOTAL COILS   14 REF
RELATIVE POSITION OF ENDS   180° ±20°
EXTENDED LENGTH INSIDE ENDS
WITHOUT PERMANENT SET   2.45 IN (MAX)
INITIAL TENSION   1.00 LB ±.10 LB
LOAD   4.0 LB ±.4 LB AT 1.56 IN
EXTENDED LG INSIDE ENDS
LOAD   6.30 LB ±.63 LB AT 1.95

17.64 This conventional double-line drawing shows an extension spring and its specifications.

the drawing and add specifications to describe their details.

17.21 Drawing Springs

Springs may be represented with single-line drawings (**Fig. 17.62**) or as more realistic double-line drawings (**Fig. 17.66**). Draw each type

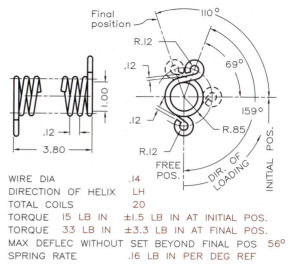

WIRE DIA   .14
DIRECTION OF HELIX   LH
TOTAL COILS   20
TORQUE   15 LB IN   ±1.5 LB IN AT INITIAL POS.
TORQUE   33 LB IN   ±3.3 LB IN AT FINAL POS.
MAX DEFLEC WITHOUT SET BEYOND FINAL POS 56°
SPRING RATE   .16 LB IN PER DEG REF

17.65 This conventional double-line drawing is of a helical torsion spring and includes its specifications.

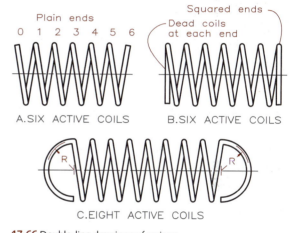

17.66 Double-line drawings of springs

A This double-line drawing shows a spring with six active coils.

B This double-line drawing shows a spring with six active coils and a "dead" coil (inactive coil) at each end.

C This double-line drawing shows an extension spring with eight active coils.

shown by first laying out the diameters of the coils and lengths of the springs and then dividing the lengths into the number of active coils (**Fig. 17.66A**). In **Fig. 17.66B**, both end coils are "dead" (inactive) coils, and only six coils are active. **Figure 17.66C** depicts an extension spring with eight active coils.

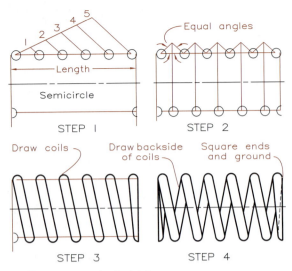

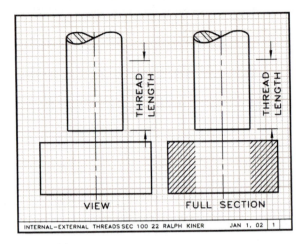

17.68 Problems 1–3.

17.67 Drawing a spring in detail

Step 1 Lay out the diameter and length of the spring and locate the five coils by the diagonal-line technique.

Step 2 Locate the coils on the lower side along the bisectors of the spaces between the coils on the upper side.

Step 3 Connect the coils on each side. This is a right-hand coil; a left-hand spring would slope in the opposite direction.

Step 4 Construct the back side of the spring and the end coils to complete the drawing. The spring has a square end that is to be ground.

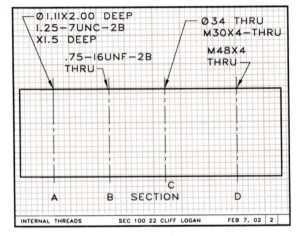

17.69 Problems 4–6.

The steps of drawing a double-line detailed representation of a compression spring are shown in **Fig. 17.67**. Springs can be drawn right-hand or left-hand, but like threads, most are drawn as right-hand coils. The ends of the spring in this case are to be squared by grinding the ends to make them flat and perpendicular to the axis of the spring.

Problems

Solve and draw these problems on size A sheets. Each grid space equals 0.20 inch, or 5 mm.

1. (Fig. 17.68) Draw detailed representations of Acme threads with 2-in. major diameters. Show both external and internal threads as views and sections. Give a thread note by referring to Appendix 8.

2. Repeat Problem 1, but draw detailed representations of square threads.

3. Repeat Problem 1, but draw detailed representations of UN threads with a class 2 fit.

4. (Fig. 17.69) Using the notes, draw detailed representations of the internally threaded holes in section.

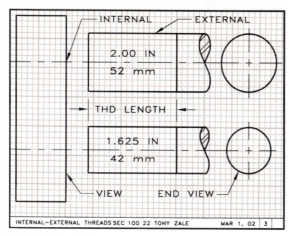

17.70 Problems 7–9.

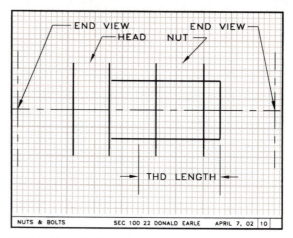

17.71 Problems 10–12.

5. Repeat Problem 4, but use schematic symbols.

6. Repeat Problem 4, but use simplified symbols.

7. **(Fig. 17.70)** Complete the partial views using detailed thread symbols, and draw external, internal, and end views of the full-size threaded parts. Provide thread notes for UNC threads with a class 2 fit.

8. Repeat Problem 7, but use schematic symbols.

9. Repeat Problem 7, but use simplified symbols.

10. **(Fig. 17.71)** Complete the drawing of the finished hexagon-head bolt and a heavy hexagon nut. Draw the bolt head and nut across corners using schematic thread symbols. Provide metric or English thread notes.

11. Repeat Problem 10, but draw the nut and bolt with unfinished square heads. Use schematic thread symbols.

12. Repeat Problem 10, but draw the bolt with a regular finished hexagon head across flats, using

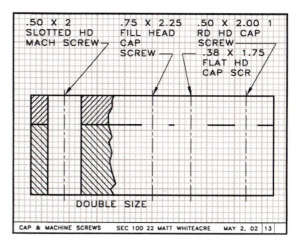

17.72 Problems 13–15.

simplified thread symbols. Draw the nut across flats and provide thread notes for both.

13. **(Fig. 17.72)** Draw the screws with detailed symbols in accordance with the notes and complete the broken-out section; show all cross-hatching. Provide thread notes to the parts.

14. Repeat Problem 13, but with schematic thread symbols.

15. Repeat Problem 13, but with simplified thread symbols.

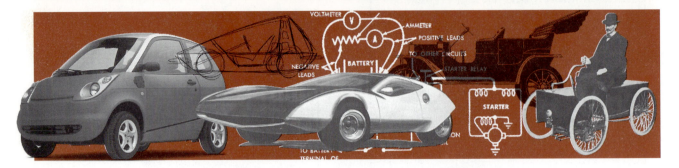

Materials and Processes

18.1 Introduction

Various materials and manufacturing processes are commonly used to make parts similar to those discussed in this textbook. A large proportion of parts designed by engineers are made of metal, but other materials such as plastics, fibers, and ceramics are available to the designer in increasingly useful applications.

Metallurgy, the study of metals, is a field that is constantly changing as new processes and alloys are developed (**Fig. 18.1**). These developments affect the designer's specification of metals and their proper application for various purposes and applications. Three associations have standardized and continually update their guidelines for designating various types of metals: the American Iron and Steel Institute (AISI), the Society of Automotive Engineers (SAE), and the American Society for Testing Materials (ASTM).

18.1 These workmen are assembling a sand casting mold to produce a transmission housing weighing 186 pounds of aluminum alloy. The shape in the foreground is part of the mold assembly. (*Courtesy of the Aluminum Company of America.*)

18.2 Commonly Used Metals

Iron*

Metals that contain iron, even in small quantities, are called **ferrous** metals. Three common types of iron are **gray iron**, **white iron**, and **ductile iron**.

Gray iron contains flakes of graphite, which results in the low strength and low ductility that make it easy to machine. Gray iron resists vibration better than other types of iron. **Figure 18.2** shows designations of and typical applications for gray iron.

White iron contains carbide particles that are extremely hard and brittle, enabling it to withstand wear and abrasion. Because the composition of white iron differs from one supplier to another, there are no designated grades of white iron. It is used for parts on grinding and crushing machines, digging teeth on earthmovers and mining equipment, and wear plates on reciprocating machinery used in textile mills.

Ductile iron (also called nodular or spheroidized iron) contains tiny spheres of graphite, making it stronger and tougher than most types of gray iron and more expensive to produce. Three

---

*This section on iron was developed by Dr. Tom Pollock, a metallurgist at Texas A&M University.

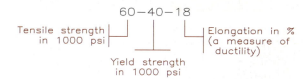

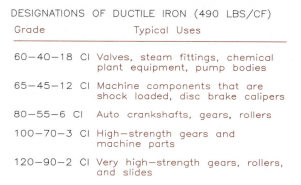

18.3 Ductile iron is specified with numerical notes in this format.

DESIGNATIONS OF DUCTILE IRON (490 LBS/CF)

Grade	Typical Uses
60−40−18 CI	Valves, steam fittings, chemical plant equipment, pump bodies
65−45−12 CI	Machine components that are shock loaded, disc brake calipers
80−55−6 CI	Auto crankshafts, gears, rollers
100−70−3 CI	High−strength gears and machine parts
120−90−2 CI	Very high−strength gears, rollers, and slides

18.4 These are the numbering designations of ductile iron and its typical uses.

sets of numbers (**Fig. 18.3**) describe the most important features of ductile iron. **Figure 18.4** shows the designations of and typical applications for the commonly used alloys of ductile iron.

Malleable iron is made from white iron by a heat-treatment process that converts carbides into carbon nodules (similar to ductile iron). The numbering system for designating grades of malleable iron is shown in **Fig. 18.5**. Some of the commonly used grades of malleable iron and their typical applications are shown in **Fig. 18.6**.

Cast iron is iron that is melted and poured into a mold to form it by casting, a commonly used process for producing machine parts. Although cheaper and easier to machine than steel, iron does not have steel's ability to withstand shock and force.

DESIGNATION OF GRAY IRON (450 LBS/CF)

ATSM Grade (1000 psi)	SAE Grade	Typical Uses
ASTM 25 CI	G 2500 CI	Small engine blocks, pump bodies, clutch plates, transmission cases
ASTM 30 CI	G 3000 CI	Auto engine blocks, heavy castings, flywheels
ASTM 35 CI	G 3500 CI	Diesel engine blocks, tractor transmission cases, heavy and high−strength parts
ASTM 40 CI	G 4000 CI	Diesel cylinders, pistons, camshafts

18.2 These are the numbering designations of gray iron and its typical uses.

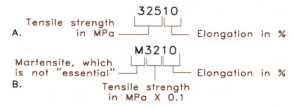

18.5 These notes illustrate the numbering designations for malleable iron.

DESIGNATIONS OF MALLEABLE IRON (490 LBS/CF)

ASTM Grade	Typical Uses
35018 CI	Marine and railroad valves and fittings, "black—iron" pipe fittings (similar to 60—40—18 ductile CI)
45006 CI	Machine parts (similar to 80—55—6 ductile CI)
M3210 CI	Low—stress components, brackets
M4504 CI	Crankshafts, hubs
M7002 CI	High—strength parts, connecting rods, universal joints
M8501 CI	Wear—resistant gears and sliding parts

18.6 These are the numbering designations of malleable iron and its typical uses.

DESIGNATIONS OF STEEL (490 LBS/CF)

Type of steel	Number	Applications
Carbon steels		
Plain carbon	10XX	Tubing, wire, nails
Resulphurized	11XX	Nuts, bolts, screws
Manganese steel	13XX	Gears, shafts
Nickel steel	23XX	Keys, levers, bolts
	25XX	Carburized parts
	31XX	Axles, gears, pins
	32XX	Forgings
	33XX	Axles, gears
Molybdenum	40XX	Gears, springs
Chromium—moly.	41XX	Shafts, tubing
Nickel—chromium	43XX	Gears, pinions
Nickel—moly.	46XX	Cams, shafts
	48XX	Roller bearings, pins
Chromium steel	51XX	Springs, gears
	52XX	Ball bearings
Chrom. vanadium	61XX	Springs, forgings
Silicon manganese	92XX	Leaf springs

18.7 These are the numbering designations of steel and its applications.

Steel

Steel is an alloy of iron and carbon, which often contains other constituents such as manganese, chromium, or nickel. Carbon (usually between 0.20% and 1.50%) is the ingredient having the greatest effect on the grade of steel. The three major types of steel are **plain carbon steels**, **free-cutting carbon steels**, and **alloy steels**.

ALUMINUM DESIGNATIONS (169 LBS/CF)

Composition	Alloy Number	Application
Aluminum (99% pure)	1XXX	Tubing, tank cars
Aluminum alloys		
Copper	2XXX	Aircraft parts, screws, rivets
Manganese	3XXX	Tanks, siding, gutters
Silicon	4XXX	Forging, wire
Magnesium	5XXX	Tubes, welded vessels
Magnesium and silicon	6XXX	Auto body, pipes
Zinc	7XXX	Aircraft structures
Other elements	8XXX	

18.8 These are the numbering designations of aluminum and aluminum alloys and their applications.

Figure 18.7 gives the types of steels and their SAE designations by four-digit numbers. The first digit indicates the type of steel: 1 is carbon steel, 2 is nickel steel, and so on. The second digit gives content (as a percentage) of the material represented by the first digit. The last two or three digits give the percentage of carbon in the alloy: 100 equals 1%, and 50 equals 0.50%.

Steel weighs about 490 pounds per cubic foot. Some frequently used SAE steels are 1010, 1015, 1020, 1030, 1040, 1070, 1080, 1111, 1118, 1145, 1320, 2330, 2345, 2515, 3130, 3135, 3240, 3310, 4023, 4042, 4063, 4140, and 4320.

Copper

One of the first metals discovered, copper is easily formed and bent without breaking. Because it is highly resistant to corrosion and is highly conductive, it is used for pipes, tubing, and electrical wiring. It is an excellent roofing and screening material because it withstands the weather well. Copper weighs about 555 pounds per cubic foot.

Copper has several alloys, including brasses, tin bronzes, nickel silvers, and copper nickels.

ALUMINUM CASTINGS AND INGOT DESIGNATIONS

Composition	Alloy Number
Aluminum (99% pure)	1XX.X
Aluminum alloys	
Copper	2XX.X
Silicon with copper and/or magnesium	3XX.X
Silicon	4XX.X
Magnesium	5XX.X
Magnesium and silicon	6XX.X
Zinc	7XX.X
Tin	8XX.X
Other elements	9XX.X

18.9 These are the numbering designations of cast aluminum, ingots, and aluminum alloys.

Brass (about 530 pounds per cubic foot) is an alloy of copper and zinc, and bronze (about 548 pounds per cubic foot) is an alloy of copper and tin. Copper and copper alloys are easily finished by buffing or plating; joined by soldering, brazing, or welding; and machining.

Wrought copper has properties that permit it to be formed by hammering. A few of the numbered designations of wrought copper are C11000, C11100, C11300, C11400, C11500, C11600, C10200, C12000, and C12200.

Aluminum

Aluminum is a corrosion-resistant, lightweight metal (approximately 169 pounds per cubic foot) that has numerous applications. Most materials called aluminum actually are aluminum alloys, which are stronger than pure aluminum.

The types of wrought aluminum alloys are designated by four digits (**Fig. 18.8**). The first digit (2 through 9) indicates the alloying element that is combined with aluminum. The second digit indicates modifications of the original alloy or impurity limits. The last two digits identify other alloying materials or indicate the aluminum's purity.

Figure 18.9 shows a four-digit numbering system used to designate types of cast aluminum and alloys. The first digit indicates the alloy group, and the next two digits identify the aluminum alloy or aluminum purity. The number to the right of the decimal point represents the aluminum form: XX.0 indicates castings, XX.1 indicates ingots with a specified chemical composition, and XX.2 indicates ingots with a specified chemical composition other than the XX.1 ingot. Ingots are blocks of cast metal to be remelted, and billets are castings of aluminum to be formed by forging. A few of the often-used aluminum are 1100, 2001, 3003, 5005, 6061, and 7075.

Magnesium

Magnesium is a light metal (109 pounds per cubic foot) available in an inexhaustible supply because it is extracted from seawater and natural brines. Magnesium is an excellent material for aircraft parts, clutch housings, crankcases for air-cooled engines, and applications where lightness is desirable.

Magnesium is used for die and sand castings, extruded tubing, sheet metal, and forging. Magnesium and its alloys may be joined by bolting, riveting, or welding. Some numbered designations of magnesium alloys are M10100, M11630, M11810, M11910, M11912, M12390, M13320, M16410, and M16620.

18.3 Properties of Metals

All materials have properties that designers must utilize to the best advantage. The following terms describe these properties.

Ductility: a softness in some materials, such as copper and aluminum, which permits them to be formed by stretching (drawing) or hammering without breaking.

Brittleness: a characteristic that will not allow metals such as cast irons and hardened steels to stretch without breaking.

Malleability: the ability of a metal to be rolled or hammered without breaking.

Hardness: the ability of a metal to resist being dented when it receives a blow.

Toughness: the property of being resistant to cracking and breaking while remaining malleable.

Elasticity: the ability of a metal to return to its original shape after being bent or stretched.

Modifying Properties by Heat Treatment

The properties of metals can be changed by various types of heat treating. Although heat affects all metals, steels are affected to a greater extent than others.

Hardening: heating steel to a prescribed temperature and quenching it in oil or water.

Quenching: rapidly cooling heated metal by immersing it in liquids, gases, or solids (such as sand, limestone, or asbestos).

Tempering: reheating previously hardened steel and cooling it, usually by air, to increase its toughness.

Annealing: heating and cooling metals to soften them, release their internal stresses, and make them easier to machine.

Normalizing: heating metals and letting them cool in air to relieve their internal stresses.

Case hardening: hardening a thin outside layer of a metal by placing the metal in contact with carbon or nitrogen compounds that it absorbs as it is heated; afterward, the metal is quenched.

Flame hardening: hardening by heating a metal to within a prescribed temperature range with a flame and then quenching the metal.

18.4 Forming Metal Shapes

Casting

One of the two major methods of forming shapes is casting, which involves preparing a mold in the shape of the part desired, pouring molten metal into it, and cooling the metal to form the part. The types of casting, which differ in the way the molds are made, are **sand casting**,

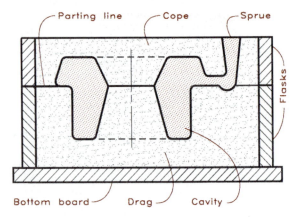

18.10 A two-section sand mold is used for casting a metal part.

18.11 This pattern is held in the bottom half (the drag) of a sand mold to form a mold for a casting.

permanent-mold casting, **die casting**, and **investment casting**.

Sand-Casting In the first step of sand casting, a wood or metal form or pattern is made in the shape of the part to be cast. The pattern is placed in a metal box called a flask and molding sand is packed around the pattern. When the pattern is withdrawn from the sand, it leaves a void forming the mold. Molten metal is poured into the mold through sprues or gates. After cooling, the casting is removed and cleaned (**Fig. 18.10**).

Cores formed from sand may be placed in a mold to create holes or hollows within a casting.

18.12 The tailstock casting for a lathe has raised bosses and contact surfaces that were finished to improve the effectiveness of nuts and bolts. Fillets and rounds were added to the inside and outside corners. (*Courtesy L. W. Chuck Company.*)

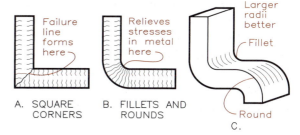

A. SQUARE CORNERS   B. FILLETS AND ROUNDS   C.

18.13 Fillets and Rounds

A Square corners cause a failure line to form, causing a weakness at this point.

B Fillets and rounds make the corners of a casting stronger and more attractive.

C The larger the radii of fillets and rounds, the stronger the casting will be.

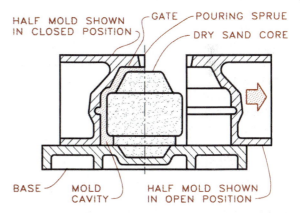

18.14 Permanent molds are made of metal for repetitive usage. Here, a sand core made from another mold is placed in the permanent mold to create a void within the casting.

After the casting has been formed, the cores are broken apart and removed, leaving behind the desired void within the casting.

Because the patterns are placed in and removed from the sand before the metal is poured, the sides of the patterns must be tapered, called **draft**, for ease of withdrawal from the sand. The angle of draft depends on the depth of the pattern in the sand and varies from 2° to 8° in most applications. **Figure 18.11** shows a pattern held in the sand by a lower flask. Patterns are made oversize to compensate for shrinkage that occurs when the casting cools.

Because sand castings have rough surfaces, features that come into contact with other parts must be machined by drilling, grinding, finishing, or shaping. The tailstock base of the lathe shown in **Fig. 18.12** illustrates raised bosses that have been finished. The casting must be made larger than finished size where metal is to be removed by machining.

Fillets and **rounds** are used at the inside and outside corners of castings to increase their strength by relieving the stresses in the cast metal (**Fig. 18.13**). Fillets and rounds also are used because forming square corners by the sand-casting process is difficult and because rounded edges make the finished product more attractive (**Fig. 18.12**).

Permanent-Mold Casting Permanent molds are made for the mass production of parts. They are generally made of cast iron and coated to prevent fusing with the molten metal poured into them (**Fig. 18.14**).

Die Casting Die castings are used for the mass production of parts made of aluminum, magnesium, zinc alloys, copper, and other materials. Die castings are made by forcing molten metal into dies (or molds) under pres-

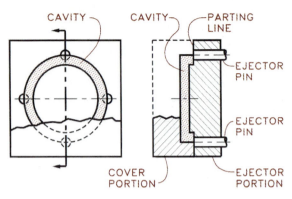

18.15 This die is used for casting a simple part. The metal is forced into the die to form the casting.

18.16 An investment casting (lost-wax process) is used to produce complex metal objects and art pieces.

18.17 This aircraft landing gear-component was formed by forging. (*Courtesy of Cameron Iron Works.*)

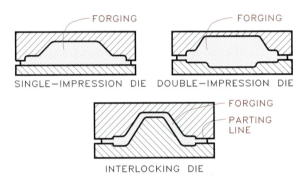

18.18 This drawing shows three types of forging dies.

sure. They are inexpensive, meet close tolerances, and have good surface qualities. The same general principles of sand castings—using fillets and rounds, allowing for shrinkage, and specifying draft angles—apply to die castings (**Fig. 18.15**).

Investment Casting Investment casting is used to produce complicated parts or artistic sculptures that would be difficult to form by other methods (**Fig. 18.16**). A new pattern must be used for each investment casting, so a mold or die is made for casting a wax master pattern. The wax pattern, identical to the casting, is placed inside a container and plaster or sand is poured (invested) around it. Once the investment has cured, the wax pattern is melted, leaving a hollow cavity to serve as the mold for the molten metal. After the casting has set, the plaster or sand is broken away from it.

Forgings

The second major method of forming shapes is forging, which is the process of shaping or forming heated metal by hammering or forcing it into a die. Drop forges and press forges are used to hammer metal billets into forging dies. Forgings have the high strength and resistance to loads and impacts required for applications such as aircraft landing gears (**Fig. 18.17**).

Figure 18.18 shows three types of dies. A single-impression die gives an impression on one side of the parting line between the mating dies; a double-impression die gives an impression on both sides of the parting line; and the interlocking dies give an impression that may cross the parting line on either side. **Figure 18.19** shows how an object is forged with horizontal dies and a vertical ram to hollow the object.

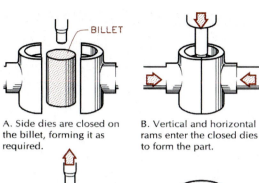

A. Side dies are closed on the billet, forming it as required.

B. Vertical and horizontal rams enter the closed dies to form the part.

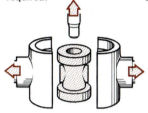

C. Rams are withdrawn, the dies open, and the forging extracted.

D. Result: A forging having multiple planes, no flash, and no draft.

18.19 These are the steps involved in forging a part with external dies and an internal ram.

18.20 Steps A through G are required to forge a billet into a finished connecting rod. (*Courtesy of the Drop Forging Association.*)

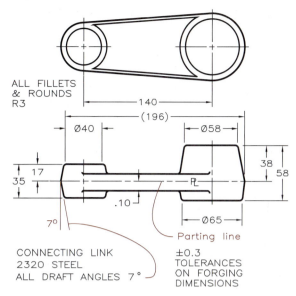

ALL FILLETS & ROUNDS R3

140

(196)

Ø40

Ø58

17

35

38

58

.10

7°

Ø65

CONNECTING LINK 2320 STEEL ALL DRAFT ANGLES 7°

Parting line

±0.3 TOLERANCES ON FORGING DIMENSIONS

18.21 This working drawing for a forging shows draft angles and the parting line (PL) where the dies come together.

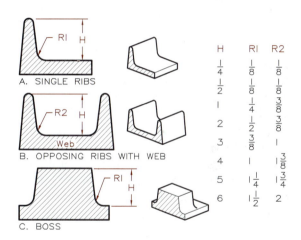

A. SINGLE RIBS

B. OPPOSING RIBS WITH WEB

C. BOSS

H	RI	R2
$\frac{1}{4}$	$\frac{1}{8}$	$\frac{1}{8}$
$\frac{1}{2}$	$\frac{1}{8}$	$\frac{1}{8}$
1	$\frac{1}{4}$	$\frac{3}{8}$
2	$\frac{1}{2}$	$\frac{3}{8}$
3	$\frac{3}{8}$	1
4	1	$1\frac{3}{8}$
5	$1\frac{1}{4}$	$1\frac{3}{4}$
6	$1\frac{1}{2}$	2

18.22 These guidelines are for determining the minimum radii for fillets (inside corners) on forged parts.

Figure 18.20 illustrates the sequence of forging a part from a billet by hammering it into different dies. It is then machined to its proper size within specified tolerances.

Figure 18.21 shows a working drawing for making a forged part. When preparing forging drawings, you must consider (1) draft angles and parting lines, (2) fillets and rounds, (3) forging

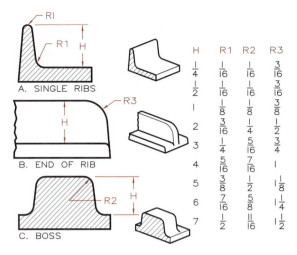

A. SINGLE RIBS

B. END OF RIB

C. BOSS

H	R1	R2	R3
$\frac{1}{4}$	$\frac{1}{16}$	$\frac{1}{16}$	$\frac{3}{16}$
$\frac{1}{2}$	$\frac{1}{16}$	$\frac{1}{16}$	$\frac{3}{16}$
1	$\frac{1}{8}$	$\frac{1}{8}$	$\frac{3}{8}$
2	$\frac{3}{16}$	$\frac{1}{4}$	$\frac{1}{2}$
3	$\frac{1}{4}$	$\frac{5}{16}$	$\frac{3}{4}$
4	$\frac{5}{16}$	$\frac{7}{16}$	1
5	$\frac{3}{8}$	$\frac{1}{2}$	$1\frac{1}{8}$
6	$\frac{7}{16}$	$\frac{5}{8}$	$1\frac{1}{4}$
7	$\frac{1}{2}$	$\frac{11}{16}$	$1\frac{1}{2}$

18.23 These guidelines are for determining the minimum radii of rounds (outside corners) on forged parts.

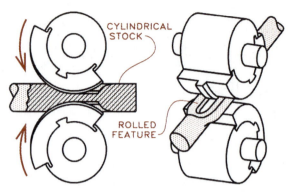

18.24 Features on parts may be formed by rolling. Here, a part is being rolled parallel to its axes. (*Courtesy of General Motors Corporation.*)

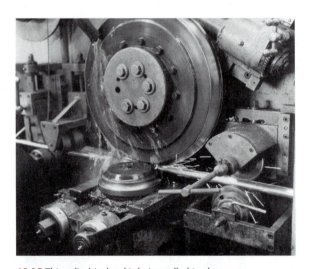

18.25 This cylindrical rod is being rolled to shape.

tolerances, (4) extra material for machining, and (5) heat treatment of the finished forging.

Draft, the angle of taper, is crucial to the forging process. The minimum radii for inside corners (fillets) are determined by the height of the feature (**Fig. 18.22**). Similarly, the minimum radii for the outside corners (rounds) are related to a feature's height (**Fig. 18.23**). The larger the radius of a fillet or round, the better it is for the forging process.

Some of the standard steels used for forging are designated by the SAE numbers 1015, 1020, 1025, 1045, 1137, 1151, 1335, 1340, 4620, 5120, and 5140. Iron, copper, and aluminum also can be forged.

Rolling Rolling is a type of forging in which the stock is rolled between two or more rollers to shape it. Rolling can be done at right angles or parallel to the axis of the part (**Fig. 18.24**). If a high degree of shaping is required, the stock usually is heated before rolling. If the forming requires only a slight change in shape, rolling can be done without heating the metal, which is called cold rolling (CR); CRS means cold-rolled steel. **Figure 18.25** shows a cylindrical rod being rolled.

Stamping

Stamping is a method of forming flat metal stock into three-dimensional shapes. The first step of stamping is to cut out the shapes, called blanks, which are formed by bending and pressing them against forms. **Figure 18.26** shows three types of box-shaped parts formed by stamping, and **Fig. 18.27** shows a design for a flange to be formed by stamping. Holes in stampings are made by punching, extruding, or piercing (**Fig. 18.28**).

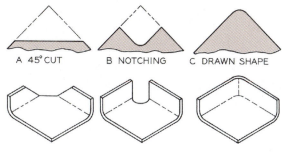

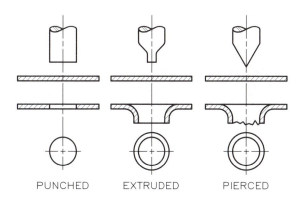

18.26 Box-shaped parts formed by stamping

A A corner cut of 45° permits flanges to be folded with no further trimming.

B Notching has the same effect as the 45° cut and is often more attractive.

C A continuous corner flange requires that the blank be developed so that it can be drawn into shape.

18.28 These three methods are used to form holes in sheet metal by punching.

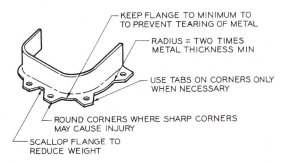

18.27 This drawing shows a sheet metal flange design with notes that explain design details.

18.5 Machining Operations

After metal parts have been formed, machining operations must be performed to complete them. The machines used most often are **lathe**, **drill press**, **milling machine**, **shaper**, and **planer**. Some of these machines require manual operation; others are computer-programmed to run at high speeds automatically and they require minimal or no operator attention.

Lathe

The **lathe** shapes cylindrical parts while rotating the work piece between its centers (**Fig. 18.29**).

18.29 This typical metal lathe holds and rotates the work piece between its centers for machining. (*Courtesy of the Clausing Corporation.*)

The fundamental operations performed on the lathe are **turning**, **facing**, **drilling**, **boring**, **reaming**, **threading**, and **undercutting** (**Fig. 18.30**).

Turning forms a cylinder with a tool that advances against and moves parallel to the cylinder being turned between the centers of the lathe (**Fig. 18.31**). Facing forms flat surfaces

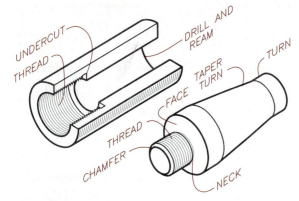

18.30 The basic operations that are performed on a lathe are shown here.

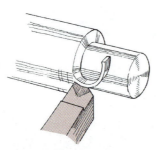

18.31 The most basic operation performed on the lathe is turning, whereby a continuous chip is removed by a cutting tool as the part rotates.

A. Start drilling

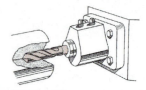

B. Twist drilling

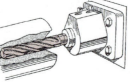

C. Core drilling

18.32 The three steps in drilling a holes in the end of a cylinder are: **A** start drilling, **B** twist drilling, and **C** core drilling.

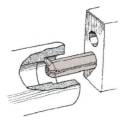

A. Boring

B. Undercutting

18.33 A. This hole is being bored with a cutting tool attached to a boring bar of a lathe. **B.** An undercut is being cut by the tool and boring bar.

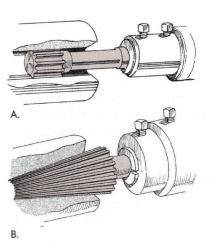

A.

B.

18.34 Fluted reamers can be used to finish the inside of **A** cylindrical and **B** conical holes within a few thousandths of an inch.

perpendicular to the axis of rotation of the part being rotated.

Drilling is performed by mounting a drill in the tail stock of the lathe and rotating the work while the bit is advanced into the part (**Fig. 18.32A–C**). **Boring** makes large holes by enlarging smaller drilled holes with a tool mounted on a boring bar (**Fig. 18.33A**). **Undercutting** is a groove cut inside a cylindrical hole with a tool mounted on a boring bar. The groove is cut as the tool advances from the center of the axis of revolution into the part (**Fig. 18.33B**). **Reaming** removes only thousandths of an inch of material inside cylindrical and conical holes to enlarge them to their required tolerances (**Fig. 18.34**). **Figure 18.35** shows a close-up view of reaming by honing.

Threading of external shafts and internal holes can be done on the lathe. The die used for cutting internal holes is called a **tap** (**Fig. 18.36**).

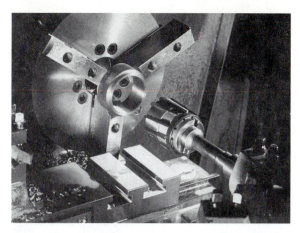

18.35 This hole is being reamed by honing. (*Courtesy of Barber-Coleman Company.*)

18.37 A die is being used on a lathe to cut internal threads in this part. (*Courtesy of the Landis Machine Company.*)

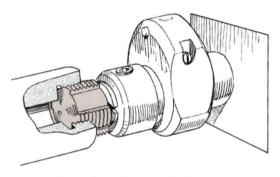

18.36 Internal threads can be cut on a lathe with a die called a **tap**. A recess, called a **thread relief**, was formed at the end of the threaded hole.

A tapping die being used to thread a hole held in the chuck of a lathe is illustrated in **Fig. 18.37**.

The **turret lathe** is a programmable lathe that can perform sequential operations, such as drilling a series of holes, boring them, and then reaming them. The turret is a multi-sided tool holder that sequentially rotates each tool into position for its particular operation (**Fig. 18.38**).

Drill Press

The **drill press** is used to drill small- and medium-sized holes (**Fig. 18.39**). The stock being drilled is held securely by fixtures or clamps. The drill press can be used for counter-drilling, countersinking, counter-boring, spotfacing, and threading (**Fig. 18.40**). Multiple-head

18.38 A turret lathe performs a sequence of operations by revolving the turret on which are mounted various tools.

drill presses can be programmed to perform a series of drilling operations for mass production applications (**Fig. 18.41**).

Measuring Cylinders The diameters of cylindrical features of parts made on a drill press

18.39 This small drill press is used to make holes in parts. (*Courtesy of Clausing Corporation.*)

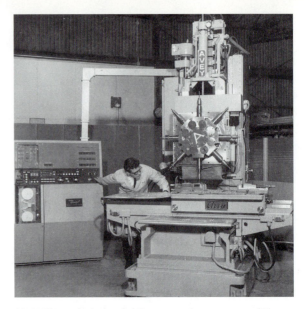

18.41 This multiple-head drill press can be programmed to perform a series of operations sequentially.

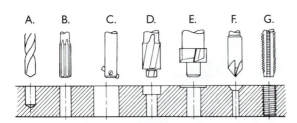

18.40 The basic operations performed on the drill press are (A) drilling, (B) reaming, (C) boring, (D) counterboring, (E) spotfacing, (F) countersinking, and (G) tapping (threading).

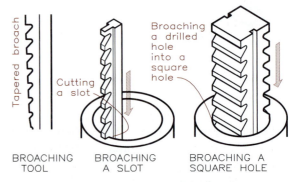

18.42 A broaching tool can be used to cut slots and holes with square corners on the interior and exterior of parts. Other shapes may be broached also.

or a lathe are measured (not their radii), to determine their sizes. Internal and external micrometer calipers are used for this purpose to measure to within one ten-thousandth of an inch.

Broaching Machine

Cylindrical holes can be converted into square, rectangular, or hexagonal holes with a **broach** mounted on a special machine (**Fig. 18.42**). A broach has a series of teeth graduated in size along its axis, beginning with teeth that are nearly the size of the hole to be broached and tapering to the final size of the hole. The broach is forced through the hole by pushing or pulling in a single pass, with each tooth cutting more from the hole as it passes through. Broaches can be used to cut external grooves, such as keyways or slots, in a part.

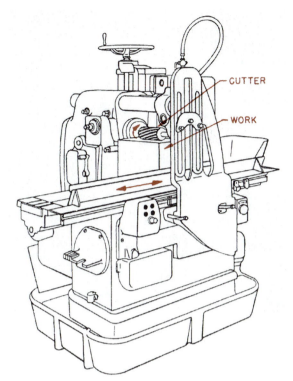

18.43 The milling machine operates by mounting the work on a bed that moves beneath revolving cutters. (*Courtesy of the General Motors Corporation.*)

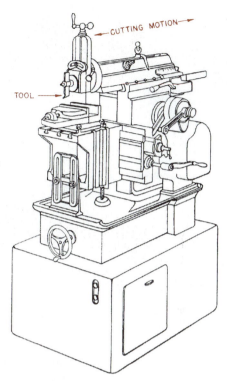

18.44 The shaper holds the work stationary while the machine's cutting tool makes strokes back and forth across the part to cut the desired shape in the work piece. (*Courtesy of the General Motors Corporation.*)

Milling Machine

The **milling machine** uses a variety of cutting tools, rotated about a shaft (**Fig. 18.43**), to form different grooved slots, threads, and gear teeth. The milling machine can cut irregular grooves in cams and finish surfaces on a part within a high degree of tolerance. The cutters revolve about a stationary axis while the work is passed beneath them.

Shaper

The shaper is a machine that holds a work piece stationary while the cutter passes back and forth across it to shape the surface or to cut a groove one stroke at a time (**Fig. 18.44**). With each stroke of the cutting tool, the material is shifted slightly to align the part for the next overlapping stroke (**Fig. 18.45**).

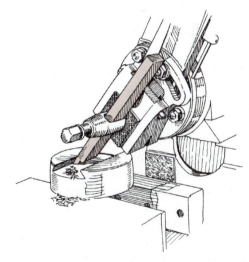

18.45 The shaper moves back and forth across the part, removing metal as it advances, to shape surfaces, cut slots, and perform other operations.

18.46 This planer has stationary cutters and a 30-foot bed. Work is fed past the cutters to finish large surfaces. (*Courtesy of Gray Corporation.*)

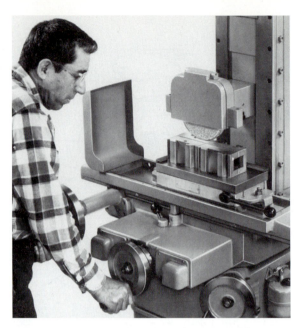

18.47 The operator is grinding the upper surface of this part to a smooth finish with a grinding wheel. (*Courtesy of the Clausing Corporation.*)

Planer

Unlike the shaper, which holds the work piece stationary, the **planer** passes the piece under the cutters to machine large flat surfaces (**Fig. 18.46**). Like the shaper, the planer can cut grooves or slots and finish surfaces that must meet close tolerances.

18.6 Surface Finishing

Surface finishing produces a smooth, uniform surface. It may be accomplished by **grinding**, **polishing**, **lapping**, **buffing**, and **honing**.

Grinding involves holding a flat surface against a rotating abrasive wheel (**Fig. 18.47**). Grinding is used to smooth surfaces, both cylindrical and flat, and to sharpen edges used for cutting, such as drill bits (**Fig. 18.48**). Polishing is done in the same way as grinding, except that the polishing wheel is flexible because it is made of felt, leather, canvas, or fabric.

Lapping produces very smooth surfaces. The surface to be finished is held against a lap, which is a large, flat surface coated with a fine abrasive powder that finishes a surface as the lap rotates. Lapping is done only after the surface has been previously finished by a less accurate technique,

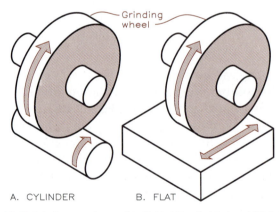

A. CYLINDER   B. FLAT

18.48 Grinding may be used to finish (**A**) cylindrical and (**B**) flat surfaces.

such as grinding or polishing. Cylindrical parts can be lapped by using a lathe with the lap.

Buffing removes scratches from a surface with a belt or rotating buffer wheel made of wool, cotton, felt, or other fabric. To enhance the buffing, an abrasive mixture is applied to the buffed surface during the process.

Honing finishes the outside or inside of holes within a high degree of tolerance (see **Fig.**

18.49 These are the characteristics of and typical applications for commonly used plastics and other materials.

	MACHINABILITY	FORMABILITY	CASTABILITY	WELDABILITY	CORROSION RES.	ABRASION RES.	LB/CU FT	YIELD: 1000 PSI	Typical Applications
THERMOPLASTICS									
ACRYLIC	G	G	E	A	E	F	74	9	Aircraft windows, TV parts, Lenses, skylights
ABS	G	G	G	A	E	G	66	66	Luggage, boat hulls, tool handles, pipe fittings
POLYMIDES (NYLON)	E	G	G	—	G	E	73	15	Helmets, gears, drawer slides, hinges, bearings
POLYETHYLENE	G	F	G	A	F	F	58	2	Chemical tubing, containers, ice trays, bottles
POLYPROPYLENE	G	G	G	A	E	G	56	5.3	Card files, cosmetic cases, auto pedals, luggage
POLYSTYRENE	G	E	G	A	P	G	67	7	Jugs, containers, furniture, lighted signs
POLYVINYL CHLORIDE	E	E	G	A	G	G	78	4.8	Rigid pipe and tubing, house siding, packaging
THERMOSETS									
EPOXY	F	G	G	—	E	G	69	17	Circuit boards, boat bodies, coatings for tanks
SILICONE	F	G	G	—	G	G	109	28	Flexible hoses, heart valves, gaskets
ELASTOMERS									
POLYURETHANE	G	G	G	A	G	E	74	6	Rigid: Solid tires, bumpers; Flexible: Foam, sponges
SBR RUBBER	—	—	E	—	F	E	39	3	Belts, handles, hoses, cable coverings
GLASSES									
GLASS	F	G	—	—	F	F	160	10+	Bottles, windows, tumblers, containers
FIBERGLASS	G	—	E	A	G	G	109	20+	Boats, shower stalls, auto bodies, chairs, signs

18.35). The honing tool is rotated as it is passed through the holes to produce the types of finishes found in gun barrels, engine cylinders, and other products requiring a high degree of smoothness.

18.7 Plastics and Other Materials

Plastics (polymers) are widely used in numerous applications ranging from clothing, containers, and electronics to automobile bodies and components. Plastics are easily formed into irregular shapes, have a high resistance to weather and chemicals, and are available in limitless colors. The three basic types of plastics are **thermoplastics**, **thermosetting plastics**, and **elastomers**.

Thermoplastics may be softened by heating and then formed to the desired shape. If a polymer returns to its original hardness and strength after being heated, it is classified as a **thermoplastic**. In contrast, thermosetting plastics cannot be changed in shape by reheating after they have permanently set. **Elastomers** are rubber-like polymers that are soft, expandable, and elastic, which permits them to be deformed greatly and then return to their original size.

Figure 18.49 shows commonly used plastics and other materials, including **glass** and **fiber-**

18.50 The use of Dow plastic in this motorized wheelchair (made by Amigo, Inc.) reduced the number of parts by 97% and the weight by 10%. It is also safe and easy to clean. (*Courtesy of Dow Chemical Corporation.*)

glass. The weights and yields of the materials are given, along with examples of their applications.

The motorized wheelchair shown in **Fig. 18.50** is made of plastic. It has fewer parts and weighs less than motorized wheelchairs made of metal. Its rounded corners make it safe, eliminate joints, and make it easy to fabricate and clean.

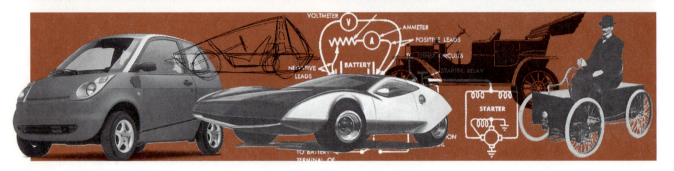

CHAPTER NINETEEN

Dimensioning

19.1 Introduction

Working drawings have dimensions and notes that convey sizes, specifications, and other information necessary to build a project. Drawings with their details, dimensions, and specifications serve as construction documents, which become legal contracts.

The techniques of dimensioning presented here are based primarily on the standards of the American National Standards Institute (ANSI), especially Y14.5M, *Dimensioning and Tolerancing for Engineering Drawings*. Standards of companies such as the General Motors Corporation also are referenced.

19.2 Terminology

The strap shown in **Fig. 19.1** is described in **Fig. 19.2** with orthographic views to which dimensions were added. This example introduces the basic terminology of dimensioning.

Dimension lines: thin lines (2H-4H pencil) with arrows at each end and numbers placed near their midpoints to specify size.

Extension lines: thin lines (2H-4H pencil) extending from the part and between which dimension lines are placed.

Centerlines: thin lines (2H-4H pencil) used to locate the centers of cylindrical parts such as holes.

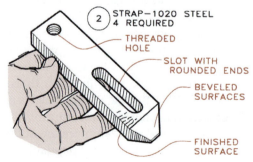

19.1 This tapered strap is a part of a clamping device that is dimensioned in Fig. 19.2.

Leaders: thin lines (2H-4H pencil) drawn from a note to the feature to which it applies.

Arrowheads: drawn at the ends of dimension lines and leaders (F-HB pencil) and the same length as the height of the letters or numerals, usually 1/8 inch, as shown in **Fig. 19.3**.

Dimension numbers: placed near the middle of the dimension line (F-HB pencil) and usually 1/8-inch high, with no units of measurement shown (″, in., or mm).

19.3 Units of Measurement

The two commonly used units of measurement are the **decimal inch** in the English (imperial) system, and the **millimeter** in the metric system (SI) (**Fig. 19.4**). Giving fractional inches as decimals rather than as common fractions makes arithmetic easier.

Figure 19.5 demonstrates the proper and improper dimensioning techniques with millimeters, decimal inches, and fractional inches. In general, round off dimensions in millimeters to whole numbers without fractions. However, when you must show a metric dimension of less than a millimeter, use a zero before the decimal point. Do not use a zero before the decimal point when inches are the units.

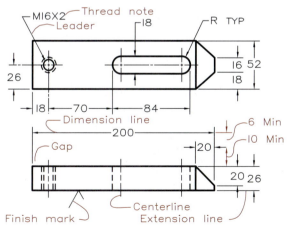

19.2 This dimensioned drawing of the tapered strap shown in Fig. 19.1 introduces the terminology of dimensioning.

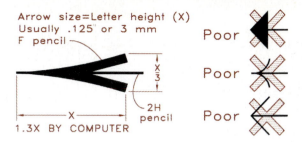

19.3 Draw arrowheads as long as the height of the letters used on the drawing and one third as wide as they are long. When drawn by computer, they can be drawn about 30% longer.

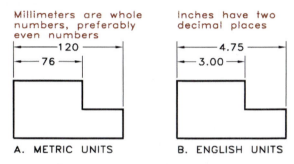

19.4 For the metric system, round millimeters to the nearest whole number. For the English system, show inches with two decimal places even for whole numbers such as 3.00.

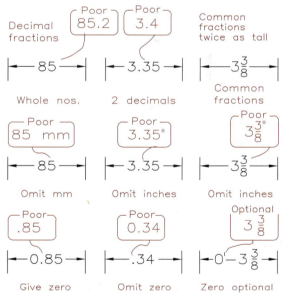

19.5 Basic principles of specifying measurements in SI and English units on a drawing.

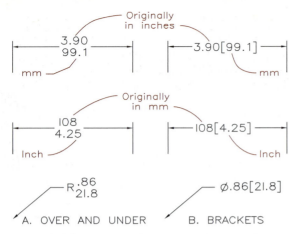

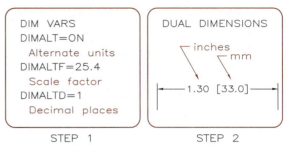

A. OVER AND UNDER   B. BRACKETS

19.6 In dual dimensioning, place size equivalents in millimeters under or to the right of the inches (in brackets). Place the equivalent measurement in inches under or to the right of millimeters (in brackets). Show millimeters converted from inches as decimal fractions.

19.7 Alternate (dual) dimensions by computer

Step 1 Type *Dimalt* and select *On* to activate dual dimensioning, type *Dimaltf* to assign the scale factor, type *Dimaltd*, and specify the number of decimal places.

Step 2 Find the linear dimensions by using the same steps, as shown in **Fig. 19.33**. The dimension in brackets is the metric equivalent of the inch dimensions.

Show decimal inch dimensions with two-place decimal fractions, even if the last numbers are zeros. Omit units of measurement from the dimension, because they are understood to be in millimeters or inches. For example, use 112 (not 112 mm) and 67 (not 67″ or 5′-7″).

Architects use combinations of feet and inches in dimensioning and show foot marks, but usually omit inch marks; for example, 7′-2. Engineers use feet and decimal fractions of feet to dimension large-scale projects such as road designs; for example, 252.7′.

19.4 English/Metric Conversions

To convert dimensions in inches to millimeters, multiply by 25.4. To convert dimensions in millimeters to inches, divide by 25.4.

When millimeter fractions are required as a result of conversion from inches, one-place fractions usually are sufficient, but two-place fractions are used in some cases. Rules of rounding of dimensions are given here:

- Retain the last digit if it is followed by a number less than 5; for example, round 34.43 to 34.4.

- Increase the last digit retained by 1 if it is followed by a number greater than 5; for example, round 34.46 to 34.5.

- Leave the last digit unchanged if it is an even number and is followed by the digit 5; for example, round 34.45 to 34.4.

- Increase the last digit retained by 1 if it is an odd number and is followed by the digit 5; for example, round 34.75 to 34.8.

19.5 Dual Dimensioning

On some drawings you may have to give both metric and English units, called **dual dimensioning** (**Fig. 19.6**). Place the millimeter equivalent either under or over the inch units, or place the converted dimension in brackets to the right of the original dimension. Be consistent in the arrangement you use on any set of drawings.

(Note: Brief examples of dimensioning by computer are shown throughout this chapter. Refer to Chapter 26 for a more thorough coverage of this topic.)

Computer Method As shown in **Fig. 19.7**, the dimensioning property *Dimalt* must be set to *On* to obtain alternative (dual) dimensions in brackets following the units originally used. Set the property *Dimaltf* (scale factor) to the value

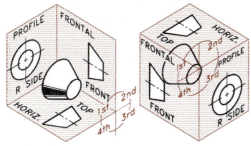

A. 1ST ANGLE   **B. 3RD ANGLE**

19.8 Projection systems

A The SI system uses the first angle of orthographic projection, in which the top view is placed under the front view.

B The American system uses the third angle of projection, which places the top view over the front view.

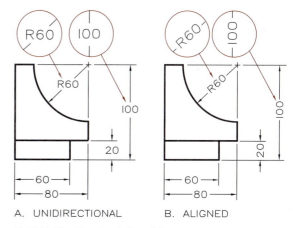

A. METRIC UNITS & THIRD ANGLE OF PROJECTION

B. METRIC UNITS & FIRST ANGLE OF PROJECTION

19.9 The SI symbol

A The SI symbol indicates that the millimeter is the unit of measurement and this truncated cone specifies that third-angle projection was used to position the orthographic views.

B Again, the SI symbol denotes use of the millimeter, but this truncated cone designates that first-angle projection was used.

of the multiplier to be used to change the first dimension. Use *Dimaltd* to assign the desired number of decimal places for the second dimension. Then select dimensions by using the *Dimlinear* command, the same way you do to find single-value dimensions (**Fig. 19.34**). Dimensioning variables can be set also from *Dimension Style* dialogue boxes.

19.6 Metric Units

Recall that in the metric system (SI), the first-angle of projection positions the front view over the top view and the right-side view to the left of the front view (**Fig. 19.8**). You should label metric drawings with one of the symbols shown in **Fig. 19.9** to designate the angle of projection. Display either the letters SI or the word METRIC prominently in or near the title block to indicate that the measurements are metric.

19.7 Numerals and Symbols

Vertical Dimensions

Numerals on vertical dimension lines may be **aligned** or **unidirectional**. When the unidirectional method is used, all dimensions are given in the standard horizontal position (**Fig. 19.10A**). When the aligned method is used, numerals are given parallel with vertical and

A. UNIDIRECTIONAL   **B. ALIGNED**

19.10 Unidirectional and aligned dimensions

A Dimensions are unidirectional when they are horizontal in both vertical and horizontal dimension lines.

B Dimensions are aligned when they are lettered parallel to angular and vertical dimension lines to read from the right side of the drawing (not from the left).

angular dimension lines and read from the right-hand side of the drawing, never from the left-hand side (**Fig. 19.10B**). Aligned dimensions are used almost entirely in architectural drawings where dimensions composed of feet, inches, and fractions are too long to fit unidirectionally (for example, 22'-10-1/2).

Computer Method   The variable *Dimtih* (Text inside dimension lines is horizontal), a *Dim Vars*

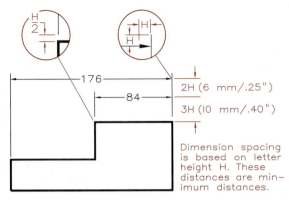

19.11 Place dimensions on a view as shown here, where all dimensioning geometry is based on the letter height (H) used.

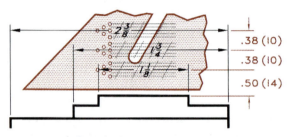

19.12 Draw guidelines for common fractions in dimensions by aligning the center holes in the Braddock-Rowe triangle with the dimension line.

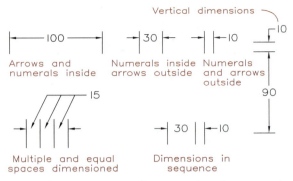

19.13 When space permits, place numerals and arrows inside extension lines. For smaller spaces use other placements, as shown.

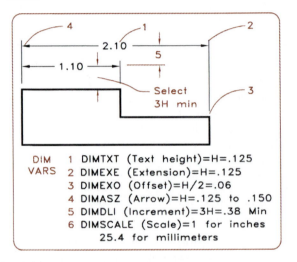

DIM VARS		
	1	DIMTXT (Text height)=H=.125
	2	DIMEXE (Extension)=H=.125
	3	DIMEXO (Offset)=H/2=.06
	4	DIMASZ (Arrow)=H=.125 to .150
	5	DIMDLI (Increment)=3H=.38 Min
	6	DIMSCALE (Scale)=1 for inches
		25.4 for millimeters

19.14 The dimensioning properties (*Dim>Status*) to be applied by AutoCAD are shown here. They remain active with the file in use. *Dimscale* can be used to enlarge or reduce all of these variables. Arrowheads in computer drawing are better if drawn larger than the letter height.

of the *Dim* command of AutoCAD, must be set to *Off* for aligned dimensions and to *On* for unidirectional dimensions. The *Dimtoh* mode controls the position of text lying outside dimension lines where the numerals do not fit within a short dimension line. When *Dimtoh* is *On*, numerals will be horizontal; when it is *Off*, numerals will align with the dimension line.

Placement

Dimensions should be placed on the most descriptive views of the part being dimensioned. The first row of dimensions should be at least three times the letter height (3H) from the object (**Fig. 19.11**). Successive rows of dimensions should be spaced equally at least two times the letter height apart (0.25 inch or 6 mm, when 1/8-inch letters are used). Use the Braddock-Rowe

lettering guide triangle to space the dimension lines (**Fig. 19.12**).

Figure 19.13 illustrates how to place dimensions in limited spaces. Regardless of space limitations, do not make numerals smaller than they appear elsewhere on the drawing.

Computer Method Dimensioning variables and their minimum settings are shown in **Figure 19.14**. You may change variables set at these proportions at the same time by using *Dimscale*. For example, *Dimscale* = 25.4 would convert all

Dim Vars	Default	Description
DIMADEC	-1	Decimal places for ang. dims.
DIMALT	OFF	Alternate units selected
DIMALTD	2	Alternate unit decimal places
DIMALTF	25.4	Alternate unit scale factor
DIMALTTD	2	Alternate tolerance dec. places
DIMALTTZ	0	Alternate tolerance zero suppress.
DIMALTU	2	Alternate units
DIMALTZ	0	Alternate unit zero suppression
DIMAPOST	-	Default suffix for alternate text
DIMASO	ON	Create associative dimensions
DIMASZ	.125	Arrow length
DIMAUNIT	0	Angular unit format
DIMBLK	-	Arrow block name
DIMBLK1	-	First arrow block name
DIMBLK2	-	Second arrow block name
DIMCEN	.09	Center mark size
DIMCLRD	BYLAYER	Dimension line color
DIMCLRE	BYLAYER	Extension line & leader color
DIMCLRT	BYLAYER	Dimension & extension color
DIMDEC	4	Decimal places for dimensions
DIMDLE	0	Dimension line extension
DIMDLI	.38	Dim. increment for continuation
DIMEXE	.125	Extension beyond dimension line
DIMEXO	.06	Extension line offset
DIMFIT	3	Fit text
DIMGAP	.06	Justification of text on dim. line
DIMJUST	0	Gap from dimension line to text
DIMLFAC	1	Length factor
DIMLIM	OFF	Gives tolerances in limit form
DIMPOST	-	Character suffix after dimensions
DIMRND	0	Rounding value for distances
DIMSAH	OFF	Separate arrowheads at each end
DIMSCALE	1	Scale factor for all dim. vars.
DIMSD1	OFF	Suppress first dimension line
DIMSD2	OFF	Suppress second dimension line
DIMSE1	OFF	Suppress first extension line
DIMSE2	OFF	Suppress second extension line
DIMSHO	ON	Changes dimens. while dragging
DIMSOXD	OFF	Suppress outside dimension lines
DIMSTYLE	STANDARD	Current dimensioning style
DIMTAD	0	Text placed above dimension line
DIMTDEC	4	Tolerance decimal places
DIMTFAC	1	Tolerance text scale factor
DIMTIH	ON	Text inside extension lines horiz.
DIMTIX	OFF	Text forced inside extension lines
DIMTM	0	Minus tolerance value
DIMTOFL	OFF	Forces dim. line inside, text out
DIMTOH	ON	Text outside ext. lines is horiz
DIMTOL	OFF	Applies tolerances to dimensions
DIMTOLJ	1	Tolerance vertical justification
DIMTP	0	Plus tolerance value
DIMTSZ	0	Tick size
DIMTVP	0	Text over or under dimen. line
DIMTXSTY	STANDARD	Text style
DIMTXT	.125	Text height
DIMTZIN	0	Tolerance zero suppression
DIMUNIT	2	Unit format
DIMUPT	OFF	User positioned text
DIMZIN	0	Zero suppression

19.15 Most of AutoCAD's dimensioning variables (Dim> Status) are shown here. Chapter 30 covers more details of their application.

dimensioning variables from inch to millimeter proportions. **Figure 19.15** shows other AutoCAD dimensioning variables. The full list of variables and their definitions can be obtained on the screen by typing *Dim* and then *Status* (see Chapter 26 also).

Dimensioning Symbols

Figure 19.16 shows standard dimensioning symbols and their sizes based on the letter

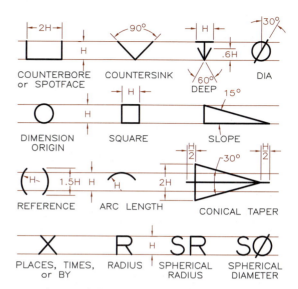

19.16 These symbols can be used instead of words to dimension parts. Their proportions are based on the letter height, H, which usually is 1/8 inch.

height, usually 1/8 inch. By using these symbols, lengthy notes can be replaced and drawing time saved.

19.8 Dimensioning by Computer

Figure 19.17 shows several combinations of dimensioning variables that are available with the *Dim* command (type *Dim*).

You can place text inside the dimension line *(Dimtad: Off)* or above it *(Dimtad: On)*. You may place arrowheads at the ends of dimension lines *Dimasz>0* or use tick marks (slashes) instead when *Dimtsz* is set to a value greater than 0, usually about half the letter height. You may select *Units* as architectural (feet and inches), metric (no decimal fractions), decimal inches (two or more decimal fractions), or engineering units (feet and decimal inches).

The text font (letter form) used in dimensioning numerals is the same as the currently-used text font or the font assigned by the *Dimstyle* procedure and a *Style* is selected for dimensioning. In both cases, the text height should be set to 0 (zero) in order for *Dimscale* (an option with the *DIM* command) to change the text height when invoked (**Fig. 19.18**).

Had you set text to a specified height under the *Dimstyle* command, the text would not change with different *Dimscale* values, but would remain at its constant specified height. Text size is the most critical aspect of dimensioning since it must be sufficiently large to be readable (**Fig. 19.19**). Using *Dimscale* enables text height, arrows, and extension line offsets to be changed at the same time.

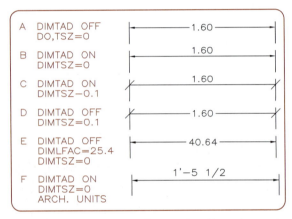

19.17 These dimension lines illustrate the effects of using the different dimensioning variables in AutoCAD.

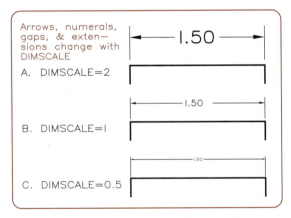

19.18 *Dimscale*, a subcommand under *Dim*, permits changing the sizes of all dimensioning variables by typing a single scale factor. It changes the text size, arrows, offsets, and extensions at the same time.

19.9 Dimensioning Rules

There are many rules of dimensioning that you should become familiar with in order to place dimensions and notes on drawings in the conventional approved manner. Each geometrical shape has its own set of rules: prisms, angular surfaces, cylindrical features, pyramids, cones, spheres, and arcs.

Dimensioning rules should be considered more as guidelines rather than as rigid rules. Quite often, rules of dimensioning must be violated or applied in a different manner because of the complexity of the part or the lack of space that is available.

Prisms

The fundamental rules of dimensioning prisms are illustrated in **Figs. 19.20** through **19.32**. All rules are presented in the simplest of examples in the most fundamental manner in order to focus on the specific rules one point at a time. These generally accepted dimensioning rules were not arrived at arbitrarily, but they are based on a logical approach to aid in their application and interpretation, as you will recognize as you become more familiar with dimensioning.

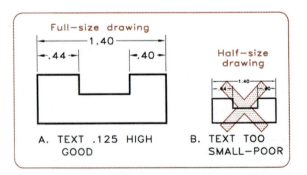

19.19 When dimensioning a drawing, be aware of its final plotted size so that you can properly size the dimensioning variables for reduction or enlargement. *Dimscale* is the most efficient command for assigning the proper scale to dimensioning variables.

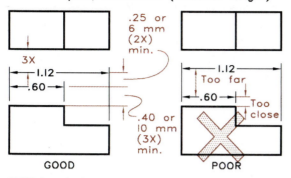

RULE 1: First row 3 times letter height from part, minimum. (X=Letter height)

.25 or 6 mm (2X) min.

3X

1.12

.60

Too far

Too close

.40 or 10 mm (3X) min.

GOOD   POOR

19.20 Place the first row of dimensions at least three times the letter height from the object. Successive rows should be at least two times the letter height apart.

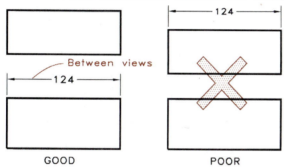

RULE 2: Place dimensions between the views

124

Between views

124

GOOD   POOR

19.21 Place dimensions between the views sharing these dimensions.

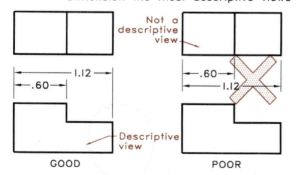

RULE 3: Dimension the most descriptive views

Not a descriptive view

1.12

.60

.60

1.12

Descriptive view

GOOD   POOR

19.22 Place dimensions on the most descriptive views of an object.

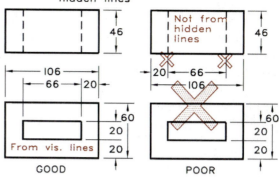

RULE 4: Dimension from visible lines, not hidden lines

46

Not from hidden lines

46

106

66   20

20   66

106

60

20

20

From vis. lines

60

20

20

GOOD   POOR

19.23 Dimension visible features, not hidden features.

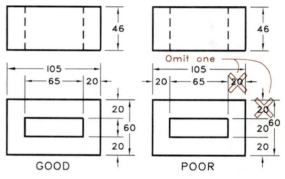

RULE 5: Give an overall dimension and omit one of the chain dimensions

46

46

105

65   20

Omit one

105

20   65   20

20

60

20

20

60

20

GOOD   POOR

19.24 Leave the last dimension blank in a chain of dimensions and give an overall dimension.

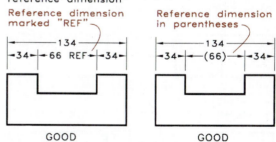

RULE 5 (DEVIATION): When one chain dimension is not omitted, mark one dimension as a reference dimension

Reference dimension marked "REF"

134

34   66 REF   34

Reference dimension in parentheses

134

34   (66)   34

GOOD   GOOD

19.25 If you give all dimensions in a chain, mark the reference dimension (the one that would be omitted) with REF or place it in parentheses. Giving a reference dimension is a way of eliminating mathematical calculations in the shop.

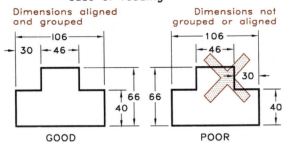

RULE 6: Organize and align dimensions for ease of reading

19.26 Place dimensions in well-organized lines for uncluttered drawings.

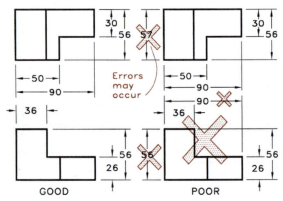

RULE 7: Do not repeat dimensions

19.27 Do not duplicate dimensions on a drawing in order to avoid errors or confusion.

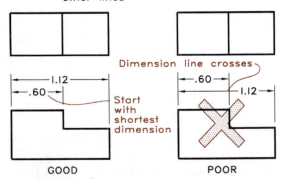

RULE 8: Dimension lines should not cross other lines

19.28 Dimension lines should not cross any other lines unless absolutely necessary.

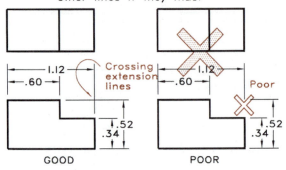

RULE 9: Extension lines may cross other lines if they must

19.29 Extension lines may cross other extension lines or object lines if necessary.

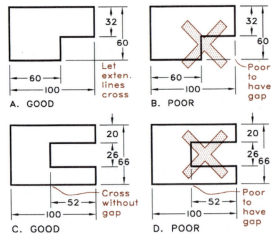

RULE 9 (Cont.): Crossing extension lines

19.30 Leave a small gap from the edges of an object to extension lines that extend from them. Do not leave gaps where extension lines cross object lines or other extension lines.

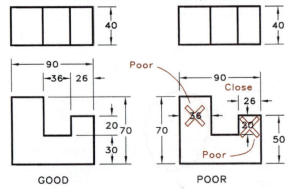

RULE 10: Do not place dimensions within the views unless necessary

19.31 Whenever possible, place dimensions outside objects rather than inside their outlines.

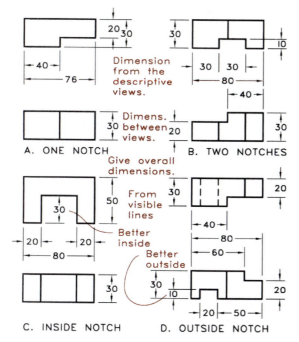

19.32 Dimensioning Prisms

A–B Dimension prisms from descriptive views and between views.

C You may dimension a notch inside the object if doing so improves clarity.

D Dimension visible lines, not hidden lines.

Computer Method Dimension the part shown in **Fig. 19.33** by typing *Dimlinear,* selecting the *First extension line origin* and the *Second extension line origin* when prompted, and picking *Horizontal* and a point on the dimension line. Alternatively, extension lines can be found automatically by responding to the prompt, *Select object to dimension,* selecting the line to be measured, specifying the direction of the dimension line, and locating the dimension line.

By setting the dimensioning variable *Dimaso* to *On,* dimensions will be associative dimensions. That is, the measurements in the dimension lines will change as the size of the objects are changed. For example, the *Stretch* command updates the dimensioning measurements as part's size is modified (**Fig. 19.34**). Associative dimensions can be erased as a unit (extension

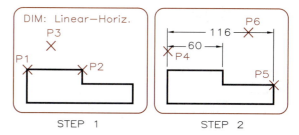

19.33 Linear dimensioning by computer

Step 1 Command: <u>Dimlinear</u> (Enter)

Specify extension line origin or <select object>: <u>P1</u>

Specify second extension line origin: <u>P2</u>

Specify dimension line location or [Mtext/Text/Angle/ Horizontal/Vertical/Rotated]: <u>P3</u> (*Mtext* and *Text* can be used as options for overriding the measured distance.)

Step 2 Command: (Enter) (*Dimlinear* is repeated.)

Specify extension line origin or <select object>: <u>P4</u>

Specify second extension line origin: <u>P5</u>

Specify dimension line location or [Mtext/Text/Angle/ Horizontal/Vertical/Rotated]: <u>P6</u>

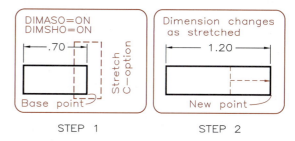

19.34 Associative dimensions

Step 1 Set dimensioning variables *Dimaso* and *Dimsho* to *On* to associate the dimensions with the size of the part to which they apply. Use the C option of the *Stretch* command to window the ends of an extension line and dimension lines.

Step 2 Select a base point and a new point. Dragging the size of the part recalculates the dimensions dynamically.

lines, dimension lines, arrows, and number). When *Dimsho* is *On,* you will be able to see the dimensioning numerals changing dynamically on the screen as you *Stretch* the part to a new size.

Angles

You may dimension angles either by coordinates locating the ends of sloping surfaces or by angular measurements in degrees (**Fig. 19.35**).

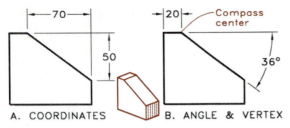

19.35 Dimensioning angles

A Dimension angular planes by using coordinates.

B Measure angles by locating the vertex and measuring the angle in degrees. When accuracy is essential, specify angles in degrees, minutes, and seconds.

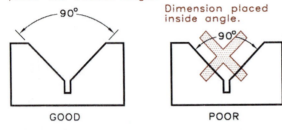

19.36 Place angular dimensions outside the object by using extension lines.

Fractional angles can be specified in decimal units or in degrees, minutes and seconds. Recall that there are 60 minutes in a degree and 60 seconds in a minute. It is seldom that you will need to measure angles to the nearest second. **Figures 19.36** and **19.37** illustrate basic rules for dimensioning angles.

Computer Method Type *Dimangular* at the command line to dimension angles (**Fig. 19.38**). If room is not available for the arrows between the extension lines, AutoCAD will generate them outside the extension lines.

Cylindrical Parts and Holes

The diameters of cylinders are measured with a micrometer (**Figs. 19.39** and **19.40**). Therefore,

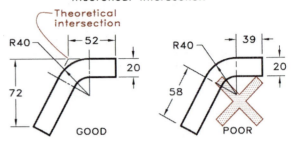

19.37 Dimension a bent surface rounded corner by locating its theoretical point of intersection with extension lines.

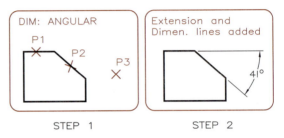

19.38 Angular dimensions by computer

Step 1 Command: *Dimangular* (Enter)

Select arc, circle, line: P1

Select second line: P2

Step 2 *Specify dimension arc line location or (Mtext/Text/Angle):* P3 (To accept measured angle.)

Dimension text <41>: (Enter)

Command: (Continue angular dimensioning or enter a new command.)

dimension cylinders in their rectangular views with a diameter as a graphical simulation of how the dimension is measured (**Figs. 19.41** and **19.42**). Place diameter symbols in front of the diametral dimensions to indicate that the dimension is a diameter. You will recall that the diametric symbol is a circle with a slash through it. In the English system the abbreviation DIA placed after the diametral dimension is still sometimes used, but the metric diameter symbol is preferred.

Space is almost always a problem in dimensioning, and all means of conserving space must be used. Stagger dimensions for concentric

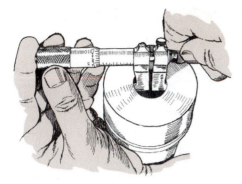

19.39 This internal micrometer caliper measures internal cylindrical diameters (radii cannot be measured).

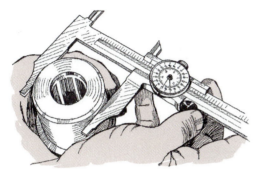

19.40 This external micrometer caliper measures the diameter of a cylinder.

RULE 13: Dimension cylinders in their rectangular views with diameters

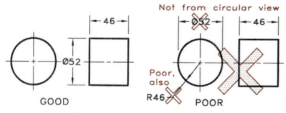

19.41 Dimension the diameter (not the radius) of a cylinder in the rectangular view.

cylinders to avoid crowding, as shown in **Fig. 19.43**. Dimension cylindrical holes in their circular view with leaders (**Fig. 19.44**). The circular view is the view that would be used when the hole is located and drilled. Draw leaders specify-

RULE 13 (Cont.): Dimensioning cylinders

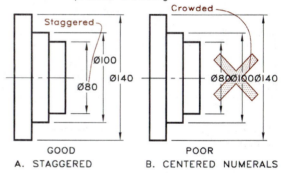

19.42 Dimension holes in their circular views with leaders. Dimension concentric cylinders with a series of diameters.

RULE 14: Stagger dimension numerals to prevent crowding

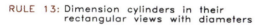

19.43 Numerals on concentric cylinders are easier to read if they are staggered within their dimension lines.

RULE 15: Give hole sizes as diameters with leaders in the circular views.

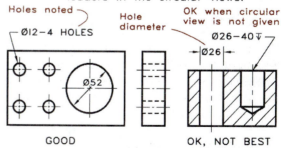

19.44 Dimension holes in their circular view with leaders whenever possible, but dimension them in their rectangular views if necessary.

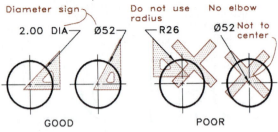

RULE 16: Leaders have horizontal elbows and point toward the hole centers.

GOOD   POOR

19.45 Draw leaders pointing toward the centers of holes.

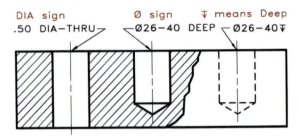

DIA sign   Ø sign   ⊽ means Deep
.50 DIA–THRU   Ø26–40 DEEP   Ø26–40⊽

19.46 These are examples of holes noted in their rectangular views when they cannot be dimensioned in their circular views.

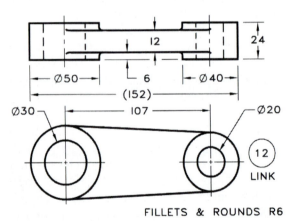

FILLETS & ROUNDS R6

19.47 This drawing illustrates the application of dimensions to cylindrical features. Fillets and rounds have a 6 mm radius.

ing hole sizes, as shown in (**Fig. 19.45**). When you must place diameter notes for holes in the rectangular view instead of the circular view, draw them as shown in **Fig. 19.46**. Examples of

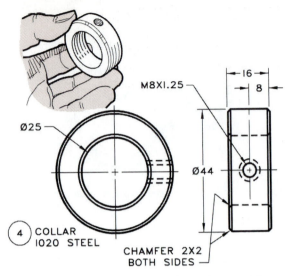

Ø25   M8X1.25   16   8
Ø44   4 COLLAR 1020 STEEL
CHAMFER 2X2 BOTH SIDES

19.48 This cylindrical part, a collar, is shown drawn and dimensioned with properly applied dimensions and notes.

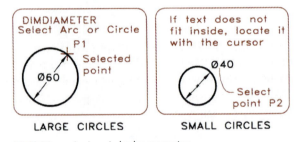

DIMDIAMETER
Select Arc or Circle
P1
Selected point
Ø60
LARGE CIRCLES

If text does not fit inside, locate it with the cursor
Ø40
Select point P2
SMALL CIRCLES

19.49 Dimensioning circles by computer

Step 1 Type *Dimdiameter* to dimension a circle. Select P1 on the arc (an endpoint of the dimension) to produce the dimension. You have the option of replacing the dimension measured by the computer with a different value.

Step 2 When text does not fit you can position it with the cursor. Select a point, P2, and the leader and dimension are drawn.

correctly dimensioned parts with cylindrical features are shown in **Figs. 19.47** and **19.48**.

Computer Method Dimension circles in the circular view, as shown in **Fig. 19.49**. Dimension lines begin with the point selected on the circle and pass through the circle's center. The diameter symbol appears in front of the dimension

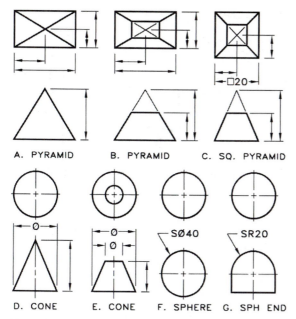

19.50 This drawing shows the proper way to dimension pyramids, cones, and spheres.

19.51 Extend leaders from the first or the last word of a note with a horizontal elbow.

numerals. Small circles are dimensioned with the arrows inside the circle and the dimension numerals outside, connected by a leader. Circles that are smaller have both the arrows and dimension outside the circle.

Pyramids, Cones, and Spheres

Figures 19.50A-C show three methods of dimensioning pyramids. **Figures 19.50D-E** show two acceptable methods of dimensioning cones. Spheres are dimensioned by giving their diameter, as shown in **Fig. 19.50F**. If the spherical shape is less than a hemisphere (**Fig. 19.50G**), use a spherical radius (SR). Only one view is needed to describe a sphere.

Leaders

Leaders are used to reference notes and dimensions to features and are most often drawn at standard angles of triangles (**Fig. 19.47**). Leaders should begin at either the first or the last word of a note with a short horizontal line (elbow) from

the note and extend to the feature being described, as shown in **Fig. 19.51**.

Computer Method To produce a leader that begins with an arrow, type *Qleader* or (*Dimension> Leader*) (**Fig. 19.52**). To ensure that the arrow touches the circle, use *Osnap* and *Nearest* to snap the point of the arrow to the circumference. The program will prompt you to *Specify next point* twice, allowing a leader with an angular bend prior to locating the horizontal elbow at the end of the leader. When prompted with *Enter first line of annotation text*, type a note. Additional prompts will allow you to add more notes in a vertical "stack." The leader command does not measure circles or lines; therefore, you must type in the desired values because it applies the last number it used.

If the previous option was *Dimdiametr*, the diameter symbol will precede the dimension. If the previous option was *Dimradius*, the radius symbol R will precede the dimension.

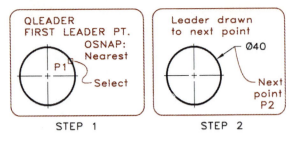

STEP 1 STEP 2

19.52 Leaders by computer:

Step 1 *Command:* <u>Qleader</u> (Enter)

Specify first leader point or [Settings]: <u>P1</u>

Step 2 *Select next point:* <u>P2 </u>(Enter)

Specify text width <0.00>: (Enter)

Enter first line of annotation text <Mtext>: <u>% %C40</u> (Enter)

Enter next line of annotation text: (Enter)

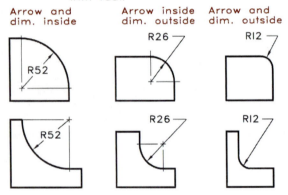

19.53 When space permits, place dimensions and arrows between the center and the arc. When the number will not fit, place it outside and the arrow inside. If the arrow will not fit inside, place both the dimension and arrow outside the arc with a leader.

Arcs and Radii

Full circles are dimensioned with diameters while arcs are dimensioned with radii (**Fig. 19.53**). Current standards specify that radii be dimensioned with an R preceding the dimension (for example, R10). The previous standard specified that the R follow the dimension (10R, for example). Thus both methods are seen on drawings.

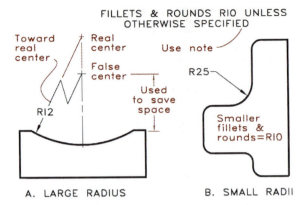

A. LARGE RADIUS B. SMALL RADII

19.54 Dimensioning radii

A Show a long radius with a false radius (a line with a zigzag) to indicate that it is not true length. Show its false center on the centerline of the true center.

B Specify fillets and rounds with a note to reduce repetitive dimensions of small arcs.

You may dimension large arcs with a false radius (**Fig. 19.54**) by drawing a zigzag to indicate that the line does is not the true radius. Where space is not available for radii, dimension small arcs with leaders.

Computer Method Type *Dimradius* and select a point on the arc as the starting point to dimension an arc (**Fig. 19.55**). If space permits, the dimension will appear between the center and the arrow. For smaller arcs, the arrows will appear inside and the dimensions outside the arc.

When space is not available for arrows inside, both the arrow and the dimension will appear outside the arc. Decimal values are preceded with a zero unless you override them by typing in R and the value without a preceding zero. Leading zeros will be omitted if the variable *Dimzin* = 4.

Fillets and Rounds

When all fillets and rounds are equal in size, you may place a note on the drawing stating that condition or use separate notes (**Fig. 19.56**). If

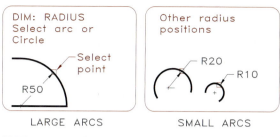

LARGE ARCS   SMALL ARCS

19.55 Type *Dimradius* to select a point on the arc. The program generates the dimension with its arrow at this point and precedes the dimension with an R. The program dimensions smaller arcs by positioning the dimension outside the arc or, because of even more limited space, by placing both the arrows and the dimension outside the arc.

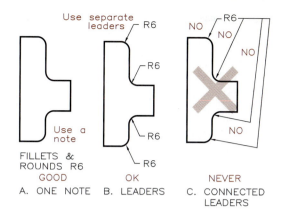

A. ONE NOTE   B. LEADERS   C. CONNECTED LEADERS

19.56 Indicate fillets and rounds by (A) notes, or (B) separate leaders and dimensions. Never use confusing leaders (C).

most, but not all, of the fillets and rounds have equal radii, the note may read

ALL FILLETS AND ROUNDS R6
UNLESS OTHERWISE SPECIFIED

(or abbreviated as F&R R6), with the fillets and rounds of different radii dimensioned separately.

You may note repetitive features as shown in **Fig. 19.57** by using the notes TYPICAL or TYP, which means that the dimensioned feature is typical of those not dimensioned. You may use the note PLACES or PL to specify the number of places that identical features appear although only one is dimensioned.

Figure 19.58 shows how the views of a pulley are dimensioned. This example demonstrates proper application of many of the rules discussed in this section.

19.10 Curved and Symmetrical Parts

Curved Parts

An irregular shape comprised of tangent arcs of varying sizes can be dimensioned by using a series of radii, as shown in **Fig. 19.59**. Irregular curves are dimensioned by using coordinates to locate a series of points along the curve (**Fig.**

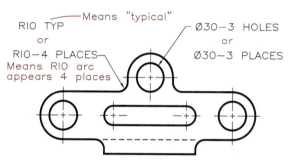

19.57 Use notes to indicate that identical features and dimensions are repeated to simplify dimensioning.

19.60). You must use your judgement in determining how many located points are necessary to define the curve. Placing extension lines at an angle provides additional space for showing dimensions.

Symmetrical Parts

Dimension an irregular symmetrical curve with coordinates as shown in **Fig. 19.61**. Note the use of dimension lines as extension lines, a permissible violation of dimensioning rules in this case.

Dimension symmetrical objects by using coordinates to imply that the dimensions are

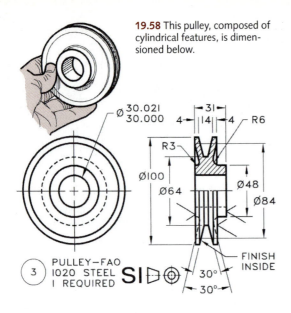

19.58 This pulley, composed of cylindrical features, is dimensioned below.

Ø 30.021
30.000

PULLEY—FAO
1020 STEEL
I REQUIRED

FINISH INSIDE

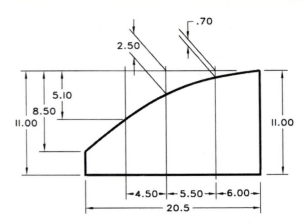

19.60 Use coordinates to dimension points along an irregular curve on a part.

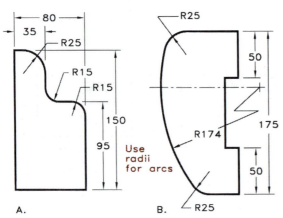

A.

B.

Use radii for arcs

19.59 Use radii to dimension parts composed of arcs of partial circles.

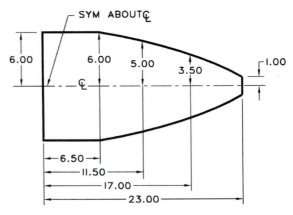

SYM ABOUT ℄

19.61 Use coordinates to dimension points along curves of a symmetrical part.

symmetrical about the centerline (abbreviated CL), as shown in **Fig. 19.62A**. **Figure 19.62B** shows a better method of dimensioning this type of object, where symmetry is dimensioned with no interpretation required on the part of the reader.

19.11 Finished Surfaces

Parts formed in molds, called **castings**, have rough exterior surfaces. If these parts are to

assemble with and move against other parts, they will not function well unless their contact surfaces are machined to a smooth finish by grinding, shaping, lapping, or similar processes.

To indicate that a surface is to be finished, finish marks are drawn on edge views of surfaces to be finished (**Fig. 19.63**). Finish marks should be shown in every view where finished surfaces appear as edges, even if they are hidden lines.

The preferred finish mark for the general cases is the uneven mark shown in **Fig. 19.63B**.

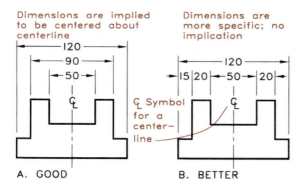

19.62 Symmetrical parts

A You may dimension symmetrical parts implicitly about their centerlines.

B The better way is to dimension symmetrical parts explicitly about their centerlines.

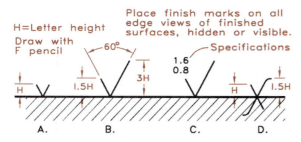

19.63 Finish marks indicate that a surface is to be machined to a smooth surface.

A The traditional V can be used for general applications.

B The unequal finish mark is the best for general applications.

C Where surface texture must be specified, this finish mark is used with texture values.

D The f-mark is the oldest and least-used symbol.

When an object is finished on all surfaces, the note FINISHED ALL OVER (abbreviated as FAO) can be placed on the drawing.

19.12 Location Dimensions

Location dimensions give the positions, not the sizes, of geometric shapes (**Fig. 19.64**). Locate rectangular shapes by using coordinates of their

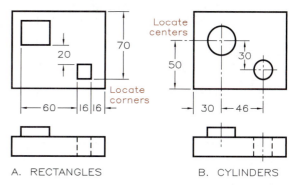

19.64 Location dimensions give the positions of geometric features with respect to other geometric features, but not their sizes.

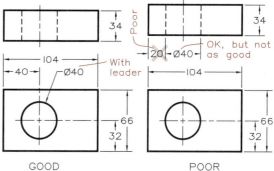

RULE 19: Locate holes in circular views and dimension diameters with a leader.

19.65 Locate cylindrical holes in their circular views by coordinates to their centers.

corners and cylindrical shapes by using coordinates of their centerlines. In each case, dimension the view that shows both measurements. Always extend coordinates from any finished surfaces (even if a finished surface is a hidden line), because smooth machined surfaces allow the most accurate measurements. Locate and dimension single holes as shown in **Fig. 19.65** and multiple holes as shown in **Fig. 19.66**. **Figure 19.67** shows the application of location dimensions to a typical part with size dimensions omitted.

Baseline dimensions extend from two baselines in a single view (**Fig. 19.68**). The use of

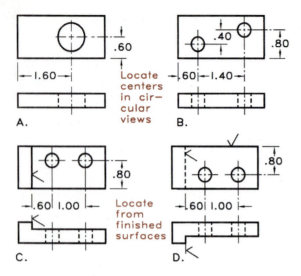

19.66 Location rules in summary

A Locate cylindrical holes in their circular views from two surfaces of the object.

B Locate multiple holes from center to center.

C Locate holes from finished surfaces, even if the finished surfaces are hidden as in (D).

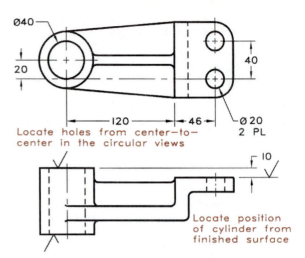

19.67 This example of a dimensioned shaft arm shows the application of location dimensions, with feature sizes omitted.

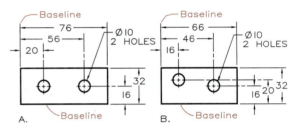

19.68 Measuring holes from two datum planes is a more accurate way to locate them, since the accumulation of errors that occur in chain dimensioning is reduced.

baselines eliminates the possible accumulation of errors in size that can occur from chain dimensioning.

Holes through circular plates can be located by using coordinates or a note, as shown in **Fig. 19.69**. Dimension the diameter of the imaginary circle passing through the centers of the holes in the circular view as a reference dimension and locate the holes by using coordinates (**Fig. 19.69A**) or a note (**Fig. 19.69B**). This imaginary circle is called the **bolt circle** or **circle of centers**.

You may also locate holes with radial dimensions and their angular positions in degrees (**Fig. 19.70**). Holes may be located on their bolt circle even if the shape of the object is not circular.

Objects with Rounded Ends

Dimension objects with rounded ends from one rounded end to the other (**Fig. 19.71A**) and show their radii as R without dimensions to specify that the ends are arcs. Obviously, the end radius

is half the height of the part. If you dimension the object from center to center (**Fig. 19.71B**), you must give the radius size. You may specify the overall width as a reference dimension (116) to eliminate the need for calculations.

Dimension parts with partially rounded ends as shown in **Fig. 19.72A**. Dimension objects with rounded ends that are smaller than a semicircle with a radius and locate the arc's center (**Fig. 19.72B**).

Dimension a single slot with its overall width and height (**Fig. 19.73A**). When there are two or more slots, dimension one slot and use a note to

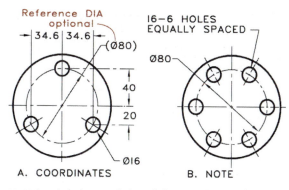

19.69 Locate holes on a bolt circle by using (A) coordinates or (B) notes.

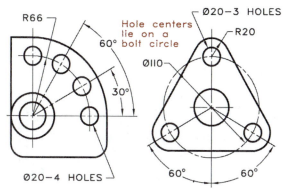

19.70 Locate centers of holes by using (A) a combination of radii and degrees, or (B) a circle of centers.

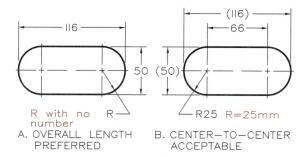

19.71 Rounded ends

A Dimension objects having rounded ends from end to end and give the diameter.

B A less desirable choice is to dimension the rounded ends from center to center and give the radius.

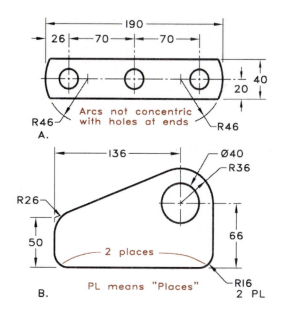

19.72 These examples show dimensioned parts having (A) rounded ends that are not concentric with the holes and (B) rounds and cylinders.

indicate that there are other identical slots (**Fig. 19.73B**).

The tool holder table shown in **Fig. 19.74** illustrates dimensioning of arcs and slots. To prevent dimension lines from crossing, several dimensions are placed on a less descriptive view. Notice that the diameters of the semicircular features are given; therefore, notes of R are given to indicate radii but the radius sizes are unnecessary since that can be easily calculated as half of the diameters.

19.13 Outline Dimensioning

Now that you are familiar with most of the rules of dimensioning, you can better understand outline dimensioning, which is a way of applying dimensions to a part's outline (silhouette). By taking this approach, you have little choice but to place dimensions in the most descriptive views of the part. For example, imagine that the T-block shown in **Fig. 19.75** has no lines inside its outlines. It is dimensioned beginning with its location dimensions. When the inside lines are

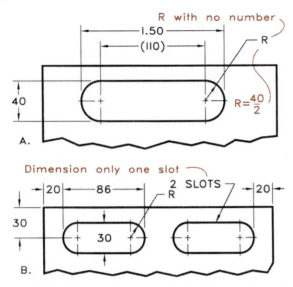

19.73 These drawings illustrate methods of dimensioning parts that have (A) one slot and (B) more than one slot.

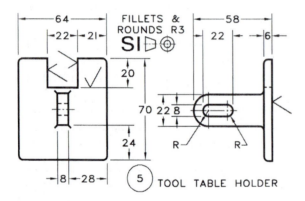

19.74 This dimensioned part has both slots and arcs.

19.75 Outline dimensioning is the placement of dimensions on views as if they had no internal lines. Applying this concept will aid you in placing dimensions on their most descriptive views.

A. DIMENSION OUTLINES   B. ADD INSIDE LINES

19.76 This drawing illustrates the use of the outline method to dimension the cap in its most descriptive views.

considered, additional dimensions are seldom needed.

Figure 19.76 shows an example of outline dimensioning. Note the extension of all dimensions from the outlines of well-defined features.

19.14 Machined Holes

Machined holes are formed by machine operations, such as drilling, boring, or reaming (**Fig. 19.77**). Occasionally a machining operation is specified in the note, such as 32 DRILL, but it is

preferred to omit the specific machining operation. Give the diameter of the hole with its diameter symbol (a circle with a slash through it) in front of its dimension with a leader extending from the circular view. You may also note hole diameters with DIA after their size (for example, 2.00 DIA).

Drilling is the basic method of making holes. Dimension the size of a drilled hole with a leader pointing to the circumference and extending from its circular view. The hole's depth can be given in the note from the circular view or specified in the rectangular view with a conventional

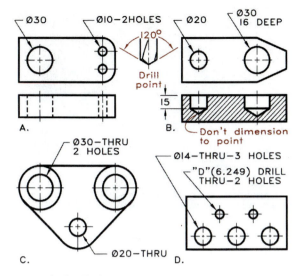

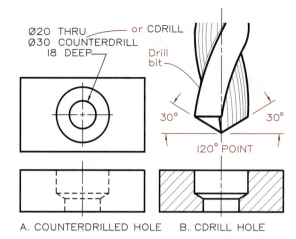

19.77 Cylindrical holes

A–B Dimension cylindrical holes by either of these methods.

C–D When only one view is used, notes must be used to specify THRU holes or to specify their depths.

A. COUNTERDRILLED HOLE   B. CDRILL HOLE

19.78 Counterdrilling notes give the specifications for drilling a larger hole inside a smaller hole. Do not dimension the 120° angle, because it is a byproduct of the drill point. Noting the counterdrill with a leader from the circular view is preferable.

dimension (**Fig. 19.77B**). Dimension the depth of a drilled hole to the usable part of the hole, not to its conical point.

Counterdrilling involves drilling a large hole inside a smaller hole to enlarge it (**Fig. 19.78**). The drill point leaves a 120° conical shoulder as a byproduct of counterdrilling.

Countersinking is the process of forming conical holes for receiving screw heads (**Fig. 19.79**). Give the diameter of a countersunk hole (the maximum diameter on the surface) and the angle of the countersink in a note. Countersunk holes also are used as guides in shafts, spindles, and other cylindrical parts held between the centers of a lathe.

Spotfacing is the process of finishing the surface around holes to provide bearing surfaces for washers or bolt heads (**Fig. 19.80A**). **Figure 19.80B** shows the method of spotfacing a boss (a raised cylindrical element).

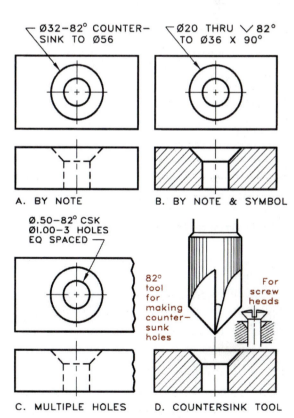

A. BY NOTE   B. BY NOTE & SYMBOL

C. MULTIPLE HOLES   D. COUNTERSINK TOOL

19.79 These illustrations show methods of noting and specifying countersunk holes for receiving screw heads.

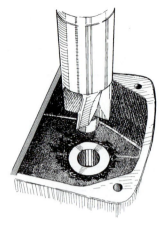

19.80 This spotfacing tool is used to finish the cylindrical boss to provide a smooth seat for a bolt head. Spotfacing is the process of smoothing the surface where it will contact a washer, nut, or bolt, and is noted as shown below.

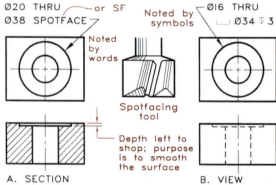

Ø20 THRU — or SF
Ø38 SPOTFACE

Noted by words

Noted by symbols

Ø16 THRU
⌴ Ø34 ▽3

Spotfacing tool

Depth left to shop; purpose is to smooth the surface

A. SECTION   B. VIEW

19.81 This photo shows the use of a lathe to bore a large hole with a boring bar. (*Courtesy of Clausing Corporation.*)

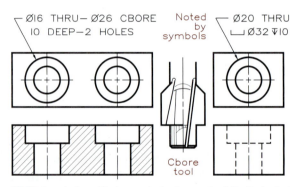

Ø16 THRU — Ø26 CBORE
10 DEEP — 2 HOLES

Noted by symbols

Ø20 THRU
⌴ Ø32 ▽10

Cbore tool

19.82 Counterbored holes are similar to counterdrilled holes but have flat bottoms instead of tapered sides. Dimension them as shown.

Boring is used to make large holes and it is usually done on a lathe with a bore or a boring bar (**Fig. 19.81**).

Counterboring is the process of enlarging the diameter of a drilled hole (**Fig. 19.82**) to give a flat bottom to the hole without the tapers in counterdrilled holes.

Reaming is the operation of finishing or slightly enlarging drilled or bored holes within their prescribed tolerances. A ream is similar to a drill bit.

19.15 Chamfers

Chamfers are beveled edges cut on cylindrical parts, such as shafts and threaded fasteners, to eliminate sharp edges and to make them easier to assemble. When the chamfer angle is 45°, use

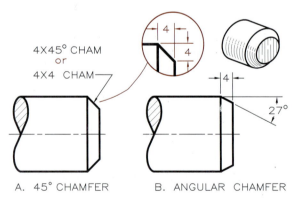

4X45° CHAM
or
4X4 CHAM

A. 45° CHAMFER   B. ANGULAR CHAMFER

19.83 Chamfers

A Dimension 45° chamfers by either of the notes shown.

B Dimension chamfers of all other angles as shown.

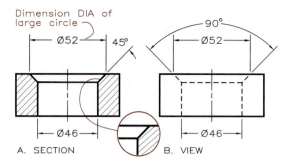

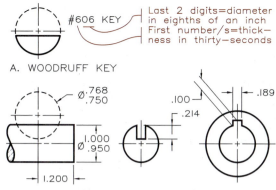

19.84 Dimension chamfers on the insides of cylinders as in this manner.

a note in either of the forms shown in **Fig. 19.83A**. Dimension chamfers of other angles as shown in **Fig. 19.83B**. When inside openings of holes are chamfered, they are dimensioned as shown in **Fig. 19.84**.

19.16 Keyseats

A keyseat is a slot cut into a shaft for aligning and holding a pulley or a collar on a shaft. **Figure 19.85** shows how to dimension keyways and keyseats with dimensions taken from the tables in the Appendix. The double dimensions on the diameter are tolerances (discussed in Chapter 20).

19.17 Knurling

Knurling is the operation of cutting diamond-shaped or parallel patterns on cylindrical surfaces for gripping, decoration, or press fits between mating parts that are permanently assembled. Draw and dimension diamond knurls and straight knurls as shown in **Fig. 19.86**, with notes specifying type, pitch, and diameter.

The abbreviation DP means diametral pitch, or the ratio of the number of grooves on the circumference (N) to the diameter (D) expressed as DP = N/D. The preferred diametral pitches for knurling are 64 DP, 96 DP, 128 DP, and 160 DP.

For diameters of 1 inch, knurling of 64 DP, 96 DP, 128 DP, and 160 DP will have 64, 96, 128, and 160 teeth, respectively, on the circumference.

19.85 These drawings show methods of dimensioning (A) Woodruff keys and (B) keyways used to hold a part on a shaft. Appendix 20 gives their tables of sizes.

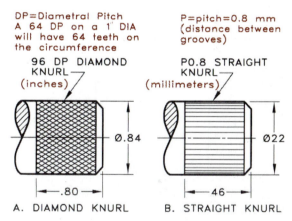

19.86 This diamond knurl (A) has a diametral pitch, DP, of 96 and the straight knurl (B))has a linear pitch, P, of 0.8 mm. Pitch is the distance between the grooves on the circumference.

The note P0.8 means that the knurling grooves are 0.8 mm apart. Make knurling calculations in inches and then convert them to millimeters for metric equivalents. Specify knurls for press fits with the diameter size before knurling and with the minimum diameter size after knurling.

19.18 Necks and Undercuts

A **neck** is a groove cut around the circumference of a cylindrical part. If cut where cylinders of dif-

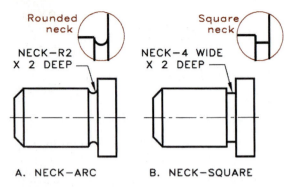

A. NECK–ARC   B. NECK–SQUARE

19.87 Necks are recesses cut into cylinders with rounded or square bottoms, usually at the intersections of concentric cylinders. Dimension necks as shown.

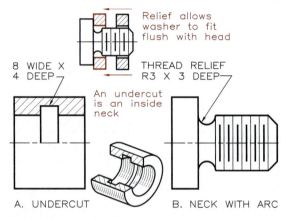

A. UNDERCUT   B. NECK WITH ARC

19.88 Undercuts and necks

A An undercut is a groove cut inside a cylinder.

B A thread relief is a groove cut at the end of a thread to improve the screw's assembly. Dimension both types of necks as shown.

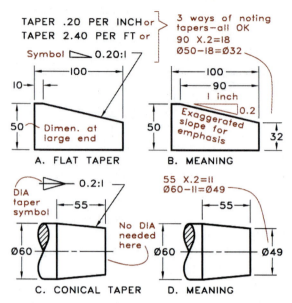

A. FLAT TAPER   B. MEANING

C. CONICAL TAPER   D. MEANING

19.89 Tapers may be specified for either flat or conical surfaces: dimensioning and interpretation for (A and B) a flat taper and (C and D) for a conical taper.

19.19 Tapers

Tapers for both flat planes and conical surfaces may be specified with either notes or symbols. Flat taper is the ratio of the difference in the heights at each end of a surface to its length (**Fig. 19.89A and B**). Tapers on flat surfaces may be expressed as inches per inch (.20 per inch), inches per foot (2.40 per foot), or millimeters per millimeter (0.20:1).

Conical taper is the ratio of the difference in the diameters at each end of a cone to its length (**Fig. 19.89C and D**). Tapers on conical surfaces may be expressed as inches per inch (.25 per inch), inches per foot (3.00 per foot), or millimeters per millimeter (0.25:1).

19.20 Miscellaneous Notes

Notes on detail drawings provide information and specifications that would be difficult to represent by drawings alone (**Figs. 19.90–19.92**). Place notes horizontally on the sheet whenever possible because they are easier to letter and read in that position. Several notes in sequence

ferent diameters join (**Fig. 19.87**), a neck ensures that the assembled parts fit flush at the shoulder of the larger cylinder and allows trash that would cause binding to drop out of the way.

An **undercut** is a recessed neck inside a cylindrical hole (**Fig. 19.88A**). A thread relief is a neck that has been cut at the end of a thread to ensure that the head of the threaded part will fit flush against the part it screws into (**Fig. 19.88B**).

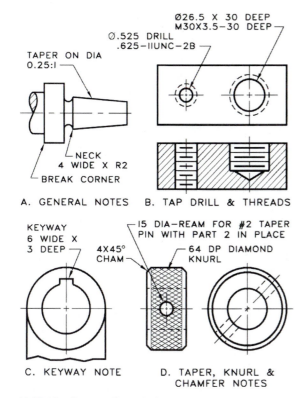

A. GENERAL NOTES   B. TAP DRILL & THREADS

C. KEYWAY NOTE   D. TAPER, KNURL & CHAMFER NOTES

19.90 Miscellaneous dimensioning

A Notes indicate a neck, a taper, and a break corner, which is a slight round to remove corner sharpness.

B Tap drill sizes are sometimes specified in addition to the thread specifications, but selection of the tap drill size usually is left to the shop.

C The keyway is dimensioned by a note.

D The notes for this collar call for chamfering, knurling, and drilling for a #2 taper pin.

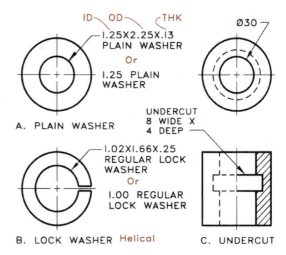

A. PLAIN WASHER   B. LOCK WASHER Helical   C. UNDERCUT

19.91 Washers and undercuts

A and **B** Dimension washers and lock washers by notes by taking sizes from the tables in the Appendix.

C Dimension an undercut with a note.

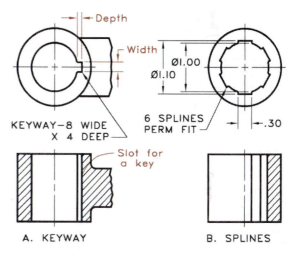

A. KEYWAY   B. SPLINES

19.92 These drawings illustrate how to dimension (A) keyways and (B) splines.

on the same line should be separated with short dashes between them (for example, 15 DIA-30 DIA SPOTFACE). Use standard abbreviations in notes to save space and time.

Problems

1-36. (19.93 and 19.94) Solve these problems on size A paper, one per sheet when drawn full size. Use size B sheets if you draw them double size. The problems are drawn on a 0.20-in. (5 mm) grid. Vary the spacing between views to provide

adequate room for the dimensions. Sketching the views and dimensions to determine the required spacing before laying out the solutions with instruments would be helpful. Supply lines that may be missing in all views.

Supplementary problems:
Problems at the ends of Chapters 13 and 14 can be used as dimensioning exercises.

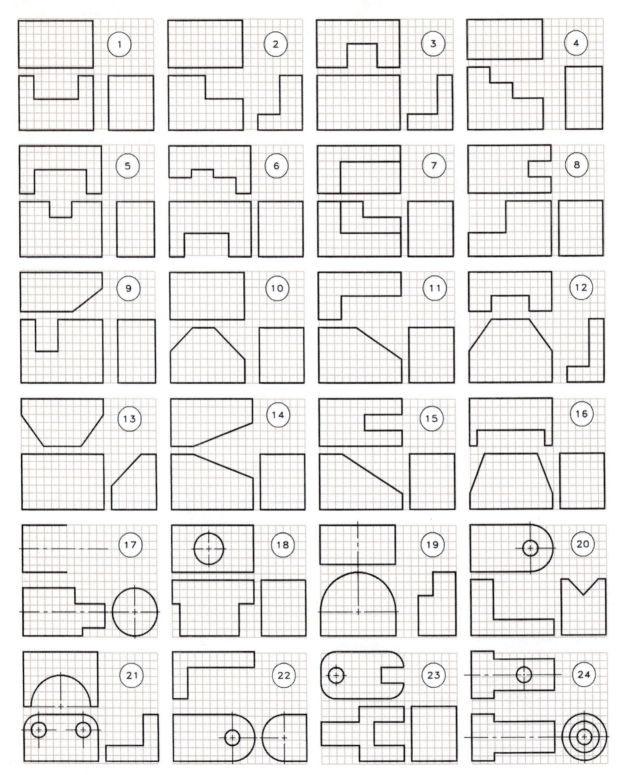

19.93

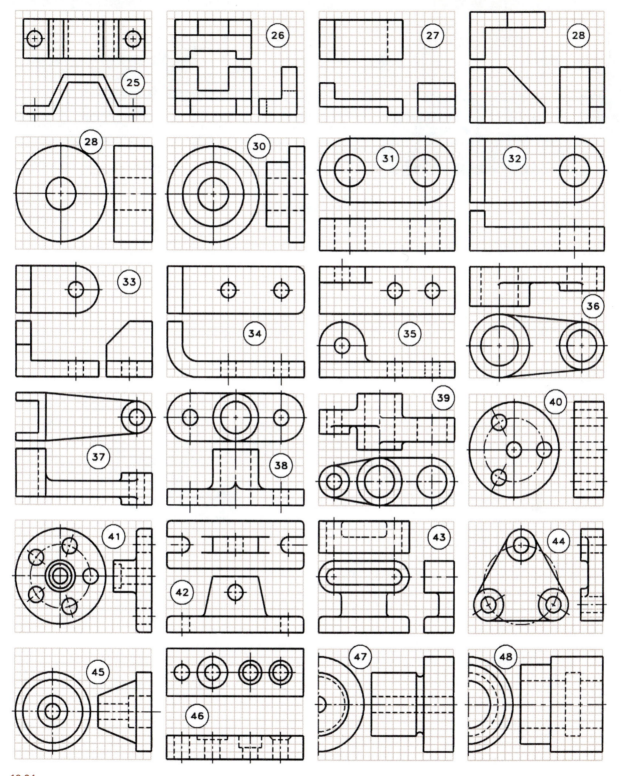

19.94

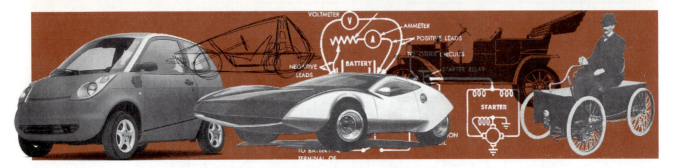

Tolerances

20.1 Introduction

Today's technology requires that parts be specified with increasingly exact dimensions. Many parts, made by different companies at widely separated locations, must be interchangeable, which requires precise size specifications and production.

The technique of dimensioning parts within a required range of variation to ensure interchangeability is called **tolerancing**. Each dimension is allowed a certain degree of variation within a specified zone, or tolerance. For example, a part's dimension might be expressed as 20 ± 0.50, which allows a tolerance (variation in size) of 1.00 mm.

A tolerance should be as **large as possible** without interfering with the function of the part, in order to minimize production costs. Manufacturing costs increase as tolerances become smaller.

The cutting-tool holder in **Fig. 20.1** illustrates a number of parts that must fit within a high degree of precision in order for it to work

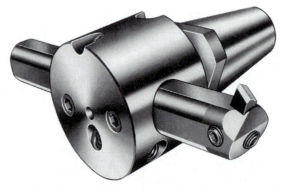

20.1 This cutting-tool holder would not function precisely while being used to make cuts on a lathe unless tolerances were used. All of its parts have been finished within a close tolerance.

properly. It must hold the tool exactly in order to work properly with a lathe.

20.2 Tolerance Dimensions

Three methods of specifying tolerances on dimensions, **Unilateral**, **bilateral**, and **limit** forms, are shown in **Fig. 20.2**. When plus-or-

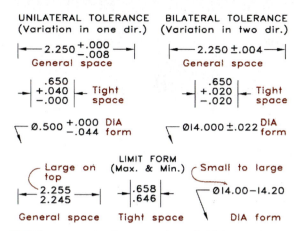

UNILATERAL TOLERANCE
(Variation in one dir.)

2.250 +.000 −.008
General space

.650 +.040 −.000 — Tight space

Ø.500 +.000 −.044 DIA form

BILATERAL TOLERANCE
(Variation in two dir.)

2.250 ±.004
General space

.650 +.020 −.020 — Tight space

Ø14.000 ±.022 DIA form

LIMIT FORM
(Max. & Min.)

Large on top
2.255 2.245
General space

.658 .646
Tight space

Small to large
Ø14.00−14.20
DIA form

20.2 These examples show properly applied tolerances in uni-lateral, bilateral, and limit forms for general and tight spaces.

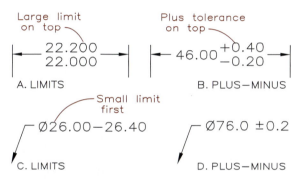

Large limit on top
22.200 22.000
A. LIMITS

Plus tolerance on top
46.00 +0.40 −0.20
B. PLUS−MINUS

Small limit first
Ø026.00−26.40
C. LIMITS

Ø76.0 ±0.2
D. PLUS−MINUS

20.3 Place upper limits either above or to the right of lower limits. In plus-and-minus tolerancing, place the plus limits above the minus limits.

minus tolerancing is used, it is applied to a theoretical dimension called the **basic dimension**. When dimensions can vary in only one direction from the basic dimension (either larger or smaller), tolerancing is **unilateral**. Tolerancing that permits variation in both directions from the basic dimension (larger and smaller) is **bilateral**.

Tolerances may be given in **limit** form, with dimensions representing the largest and smallest sizes for a feature. When tolerances are shown in limit form, the basic dimension will be unknown.

The customary methods of applying tolerance values on dimension lines are shown in

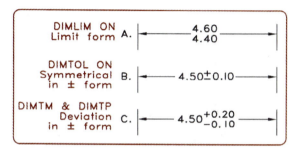

H=1/8   Same no. of decimal places   H/2=1/16   H Max
2.0000 +.0040 −.0020
A. PLUS−MINUS TOLERANCES

H/2=1/16
2.0400 1.9980
B. LIMIT−FORM TOLERANCES

20.4 The spacing and proportions of numerals used to specify tolerances on dimensions are shown here.

DIMLIM ON Limit form   A.   4.60 4.40

DIMTOL ON Symmetrical in ± form   B.   4.50±0.10

DIMTM & DIMTP Deviation in ± form   C.   4.50 +0.20 −0.10

20.5 AutoCAD gives toleranced dimensions in these forms. When *Dimlim* is *On* tolerances will be applied in limit form; when *Dimtol* is *On* tolerances will be in plus-or-minus form.

Fig. 20.3. The spacing and proportions of the tolerance dimensions are shown in **Fig. 20.4**.

Tolerances by Computer

AutoCAD provides an automatic means of showing toleranced dimensions in limit form or plus-and-minus form (**Fig. 20.5**). *Dimlim* must be turned *On* to obtain dimensions in limit form. Assign tolerances to the *Dimtm* and *Dimtp* modes under the *Dim:* command.

In addition to linear dimensions, diametral and radial dimensions are automatically given with either a diameter symbol or an R preceding the dimensions (**Figs. 20.6** and **20.7**). Angular measurements can be toleranced in the plus-and-minus form or the limit form (**Fig. 20.8**). The program measures the angle and automatically computes the upper and lower limits.

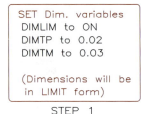

SET Dim. variables
DIMLIM to ON
DIMTP to 0.02
DIMTM to 0.03
(Dimensions will be in LIMIT form)

STEP 1

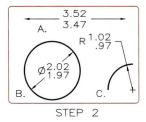

STEP 2

20.6 Limit tolerances by computer

Step 1 Set the dimensioning variables as shown for tolerances to be given in *Limit* form.

Step 2 Linear dimensions will be in limit form, diameters preceded by a diameter sign, and radii preceded by an R.

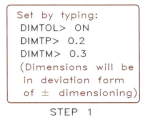

Set by typing:
DIMTOL> ON
DIMTP> 0.2
DIMTM> 0.3
(Dimensions will be in deviation form of ± dimensioning)

STEP 1

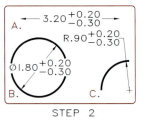

STEP 2

20.7 Plus-or-minus tolerances by computer

Step 1 Set *Dimtol* to On, *Dimtp* (tolerance plus) to 0.2, and *Dimtm* (tolerance minus) to 0.3.

Step 2 Linear dimensions will give a basic diameter followed by plus-and-minus tolerances (deviation form), diameters as linear dimensions preceded by a diameter sign, and radii dimensions preceded by an R.

20.3 Mating Parts

Mating parts must be toleranced to fit within a prescribed degree of accuracy (**Fig. 20.9**). The upper part is dimensioned with limits indicating its maximum and minimum sizes. The slot in the lower part is toleranced to be slightly larger, allowing the parts to assemble with a clearance fit which allows freedom of movement.

Mating parts may be cylindrical forms, such as a pulley, bushing, and shaft (**Fig. 20.10**). The bushing should force fit inside the pulley to provide a good bearing surface for the rotating shaft. At the same time, the shaft and the bush-

Set by typing:
DIMLIM> ON
DIMTP> 0.2
DIMTM> 0.1
DIMDEC> 2
(Dimensions will be in LIMIT form)

STEP 1

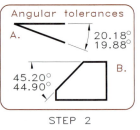

STEP 2

20.8 Angular tolerances by computer

Step 1 Set the dimensioning variables as shown; *Dimdec>* 2 assigns two decimal places.

Step 2 Select the lines forming the angles and the location of the arc, and the toleranced measurements will be given in limit form. Using the *Units* command, you may obtain angular measurements as decimal degrees, minutes and seconds, grads, radians, or surveyor's units.

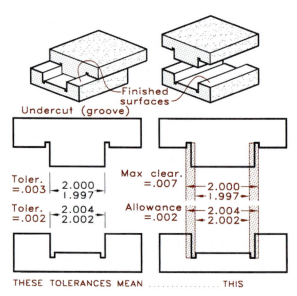

20.9 These mating parts have tolerances (variations in size) of 0.003" and 0.002", respectively. The allowance (tightest fit) between the assembled parts is 0.002".

ing should mate so that the pulley and bushing will rotate on the shaft with a free running fit.

ANSI tables (see Appendices 25–29) prescribe cylindrical-fit tolerances for different applications. Familiarity with the terminology of cylindrical tolerancing is essential to applying the data in these tables.

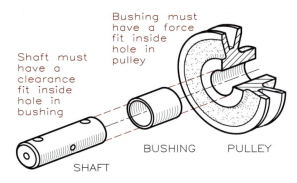

20.10 These parts must be assembled with cylindrical fits that give a clearance and an interference fit.

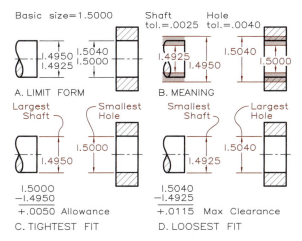

20.11 The allowance (tightest fit) between these assembled parts is +0.005″. The maximum clearance is +0.0115″.

20.4 Tolerancing Terms: English Units

The following terminology and definitions of tolerancing are illustrated in **Fig. 20.11**, which shows two mating cylindrical parts.

Tolerance: The difference between the limits of size prescribed for a single feature, or 0.0025 in. for the shaft and 0.0040 for the hole in **Fig. 20.11A**.

Limits of tolerance: The maximum and minimum sizes of a feature, or 1.4925 and 1.4950 for the shaft and 1.5000 and 1.5040 for the hole in **Fig. 20.11B**.

Allowance: The tightest fit between two mating parts, or +0.0050 in **Fig. 20.11C**. Allowance is negative for an interference fit.

Nominal size: A general size of a shaft or hole, usually expressed with common fractions, 1-1/2 in. or 1.50 in. in **Fig. 20.11**.

Basic size: The size to which plus-and-minus tolerance are applied to obtain the limits of size, 1.5000 in **Fig. 20.11**. The basic diameter cannot be determined from tolerances that are expressed in limit form.

Actual size: The measured size of the finished part.

Fit: The degree of tightness or looseness between two assembled parts, which can be one of the following: **clearance**, **interference**, **transition**, and **line**.

Clearance fit gives a clearance between two assembled mating parts. The shaft and the hole n **Figs. 20.11C** and **D** have a minimum clearance of 0.0050″ and a maximum clearance of 0.0115″.

Interference fit results in a binding fit that requires the parts to be forced together much as if they are welded (**Fig. 20.12A**).

Transition fit may range from an interference to a clearance between the assembled parts. The shaft may be either smaller or larger than the hole and still be within the prescribed tolerances as in **Fig. 20.12B**.

Line fit results in surface contact or clearance when the limits are reached (**Fig. 20.12C**).

Selective assembly: A method of selecting and assembling parts by hand by trial and error that allows parts to be made with larger tolerances at less cost as a compromise between a high manufacturing accuracy and ease of assembly.

Single-limits: Dimensions designated by either minimum (MIN) or maximum (MAX), as shown in **Fig. 20.13**. Depths of holes, lengths, threads, corner radii, and chamfers are sometimes dimensioned in this manner.

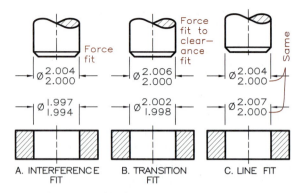

20.12 Three types of fits between mating parts are shown here in addition to the clearance fit shown in Fig. 20.14.

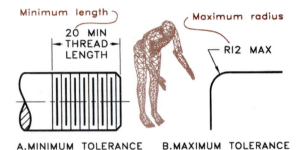

20.13 Single tolerances in maximum (MAX) or minimum (MIN) form can be given in applications of this type.

20.5 Basic Hole System

The **basic hole system** uses the smallest hole size as the **basic diameter** for calculating tolerances and allowances. The basic hole system is best when drills, reamers, and machine tools are used to give precise hole sizes.

The smallest hole size is the basic diameter because a hole can be enlarged by machining but cannot be reduced in size. In **Fig. 20.11** the smallest diameter of the hole is 1.500″. Subtract the allowance, 0.0050″, from it to find the diameter of the largest shaft, 1.4950″. To find the smallest limit for the shaft diameter, subtract the tolerance from 1.4950 in.

20.6 Basic Shaft System

The **basic shaft system** uses the largest diameter as the **basic diameter** to which the tolerances

are applied. This system is applicable when shafts are available in uniform standard sizes.

The largest shaft size is used as the basic diameter because shafts can be machined to smaller size but cannot be enlarged. For example, if the largest permissible shaft size is 1.500″, add the allowance to this dimension to obtain the smallest hole diameter into which the shaft fits. If the parts are to have an allowance of 0.0040″, the smallest hole would have a diameter of 1.5040″.

20.7 Cylindrical Fits

The *ANSI B4.1* standard gives a series of fits between cylindrical features in inches for the basic hole system. The types of fit covered in this standard are:

> **RC:** running or sliding clearance fits
> **LC:** clearance locational fits
> **LT:** transition locational fits
> **LN:** interference locational fits
> **FN:** force and shrink fits

Appendices 25–29 list these five types of fit, each of which has several classes.

Running or sliding clearance fits (RC) provide a similar running performance with suitable lubrication allowance. The clearance for the first two classes (RC 1 and RC 2), which are used chiefly as slide fits, increases more slowly with diameter size than other classes to maintain an accurate location even at the expense of free relative motion.

Locational fits (LC, LT, LN) determine only the location of mating parts; they may provide non-moving rigid locations (interference fits) or permit some freedom of location (clearance fits). The three locational fits are: **clearance fits (LC)**, **transition fits (LT)**, and **interference fits (LN)**.

Force fits (FN) are interference fits characterized by a constant bore pressure throughout the range of sizes. There are five types of force fits: FN1 through FN5, varying from light drive to heavier drives, respectively.

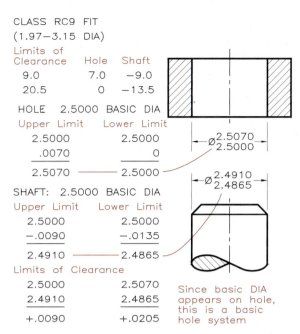

CLASS RC9 FIT
(1.97–3.15 DIA)

Limits of Clearance	Hole	Shaft
9.0	7.0	−9.0
20.5	0	−13.5

HOLE 2.5000 BASIC DIA

Upper Limit	Lower Limit
2.5000	2.5000
.0070	0
2.5070	2.5000

SHAFT: 2.5000 BASIC DIA

Upper Limit	Lower Limit
2.5000	2.5000
−.0090	−.0135
2.4910	2.4865

Limits of Clearance

2.5000	2.5070
2.4910	2.4865
+.0090	+.0205

Since basic DIA appears on hole, this is a basic hole system

20.14 This example shows how to calculate limits and allowances for an RC9 fit between a shaft and hole with a basic diameter of 2.5000″. Values are taken from Appendix 25.

The method of applying tolerance values from the tables in Appendix 25 for an RC9 fit is shown in **Figure 20.14**. The basic diameter of 2.5000″ falls between 1.97″ and 3.15″ in the *Size* column of the table. Limits are in thousandths, which requires that the decimal point be moved three places to the left. For example, +7 is +0.0070″.

Add the limits to the basic diameter when a **plus sign** precedes the values and **subtract** when a **minus sign** is given. Add the limits (+0.0070″ and 0.0000″) to the basic diameter to find the upper and lower limits of the hole (2.5070″ and 2.5000″). Subtract the limits (−.0090″ and −.0135″) from the basic diameter to find the limits of the shaft (2.4910″ and 2.4865″).

The tightest fit (the allowance) between the assembled parts (+0.0090″) is the difference between the largest shaft and the smallest hole.

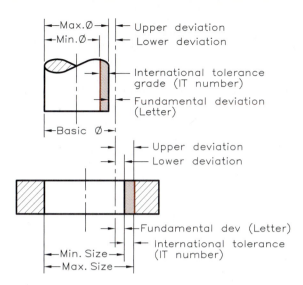

20.15 The terminology and definitions of the metric system of cylindrical fits are given here.

The loosest fit, or maximum clearance, (+0.0205″) is the difference between the smallest shaft and the largest hole. These values appear in the *Limit* column of Appendix 25.

This method of extracting tolerancing dimensions is applied to other types of fits by using their respective tables: force fit, interference fit, transition fit, and locational fit. Subtract negative limits from the basic diameter and add positive limits to it. A **minus sign** preceding limits of clearance in the tables indicates an **interference fit** between the assembled parts, and a **positive limit** of clearance indicates a **clearance fit** between the part.

20.8 Tolerancing: Metric Units

The system recommended by the *International Standards Organization (ISO)* in *ANSI B4.2* for metric measurements are fits that usually apply to cylinders—holes and shafts—but these tables can be used to specify fits between parallel contact surfaces, such as a key in a slot.

Basic size: The size, usually a diameter from which limits or deviations are calculated (**Fig. 20.15**). Select basic sizes from the *First Choice* column in the table in **Fig. 20.16**.

PREFERRED BASIC SIZES (Millimeters)

First Choice	Second Choice	First Choice	Second Choice	First Choice	Second Choice
1	1.1	10	11	100	110
1.2	1.4	12	14	120	140
1.6	1.8	16	18	160	180
2	2.2	20	22	200	220
2.5	2.8	25	28	250	280
3	3.5	30	35	300	350
4	4.5	40	45	400	450
5	5.5	50	55	500	550
6	7	60	70	600	700
8	9	80	90	800	900
				1000	

20.16 Basic sizes for metric fits selected first from the first-choice column are preferred over those in the second-choice column.

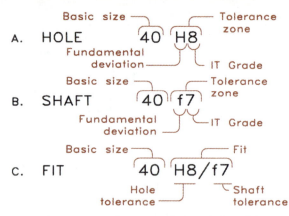

20.17 These metric tolerance symbols and their definitions apply to holes and shafts.

Deviation: The difference between the hole or shaft size and the basic size.

Upper deviation: The difference between the maximum permissible size of a part and its basic size (**Fig. 20.15**).

Lower deviation: The difference between the minimum permissible size of a part and its basic size (**Fig. 20.15**).

Fundamental deviation: The deviation closest to the basic size (**Fig. 20.15**). In the note 40 H8 in **Fig. 20.17**, H represents the fundamental deviation for a hole, and in the note 40 f7, the f represents the fundamental deviation for a shaft.

Tolerance: The difference between the maximum and minimum allowable sizes of a part.

International tolerance (IT) grade: A series of tolerances that vary with basic size to provide a uniform level of accuracy within a given grade (**Fig. 20.15**). In the note 40 H8 in **Fig. 20.17**, the 8 represents the IT grade. There are 16 IT grades: IT01, IT0, IT1, . . . , IT16.

Tolerance zone: A combination of the fundamental deviation and the tolerance grade. The H8 portion of the 40 H8 note in **Fig. 20.17** is the tolerance zone.

Hole basis: A system of fits based on the minimum hole size as the basic diameter. The fundamental deviation letter for a hole-basis system is "H". Appendices 31 and 32 give hole-basis data for tolerances.

Shaft basis: A system of fits based on the maximum shaft size as the basic diameter. The fundamental deviation letter for a shaft-basis system is "h". Appendices 33 and 34 give shaft-basis data for tolerances.

Clearance fit: A fit resulting in a clearance between two assembled parts under all tolerance conditions.

Interference fit: A force fit between two parts, requiring that they be driven together.

Transition fit: A fit that can result in either a clearance or an interference between assembled parts.

Tolerance symbols: Notes giving the specifications of tolerances and fits (**Fig. 20.17**). The basic size is a number, followed by the fundamental deviation letter and the IT number, which give the tolerance zone.

Uppercase letters (H) indicate the fundamental deviations for **holes**, and **lowercase letters** (f) indicate fundamental deviations for **shafts**.

Hole Basis	Shaft Basis	Description	
H11/c11	C11/h11	Loose Running Fit for wide commerical tolerances on external members	
H9/d9	D9/h9	Free Running Fit for large temperature variations, high running speeds, or high journal pressures	
H8/f7	F8/h7	Close Running Fit for accurate location and moderate speeds and journal pressures	
H7/g6	G7/h6	Sliding Fit for accurate fit and location and free moving and turning, not free running	
H7/h6	H7/h6	Locational Clearance for snug fits for parts that can be freely assembled	
H7/k6	K7/h6	Locational Transition Fit for accurate locations	
H7/n6	N7/h6	Locational Transition Fit for more accurate locations and greater interference	
H7/p6	P7/h6	Locational Interference Fit for rigidity and alignment without special bore pressures	
H7/s6	S7/h6	Medium Drive Fit for shrink fits on light sections; tightest fit usable for cast iron	
H7/u6	U7/h6	Force Fit for parts that can be highly stressed and for shrink fits.	

The left portion of the table is grouped vertically as: Clearance Fits (first four rows), Transition Fits (next three rows), and Interference Fits (last three rows).

20.18 This list gives the preferred hole-basis and shaft-basis fits for the metric system.

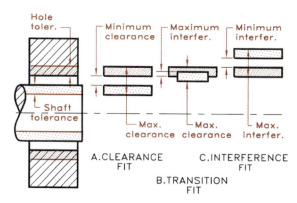

20.19 Types of fits: (A) clearance fit, where there is space between the parts, (B) transition fit, where there can be either interference or clearance, and (C) interference fit, where the parts must be forced together.

Preferred Sizes and Fits

The table in **Fig. 20.16** shows the preferred basic sizes for computing tolerances. Under the *First Choice* heading, each number increases by about 25 percent from the preceding value. Each number in the *Second Choice* column increases by about 12 percent. To minimize cost, select basic diameters from the first column because they correspond to standard stock sizes for round, square, and hexagonal metal products.

Figure **20.18** shows preferred clearance, transition, and interference fits for the hole-basis and shaft-basis systems. Appendices 31–34 contain the complete tables.

Preferred Fits: Hole-Basis System The preferred fits for the hole-basis system, in which the smallest hole is the basic diameter, are shown in **Fig. 20.19**. **Clearance, transition,** and **interfer-** ence fits are options of the hole-basis system. Variations in fit between parts range from a clearance fit of H11/c11 to an interference fit of H7/u6 (**Fig. 20.18**).

Preferred Fits: Shaft-Basis System The preferred fits of the shaft-basis system, in which the largest shaft is the basic diameter. Variations in fit range from a clearance fit of C11/h11 to an interference fit of U7/h6 (**Fig. 20.17**).

Standard Cylindrical Fits

The following examples demonstrate how to calculate and apply tolerances to cylindrical parts. You must use **Fig. 20.16**, **Fig. 20.18**, and data from Appendices 31–34.

Example 1 (Fig. 20.20)

Required: Use the hole-basis system, a close running fit, and a basic diameter of 49 mm.

Solution: Use a preferred basic diameter of 50 mm (**Fig. 20.16**) and fit of H8/f7 (**Fig. 20.18**).

Hole: Find the upper and lower limits of the hole in Appendix 31 under H8 and across from 50 mm. These limits are 50.000 and 50.039 mm.

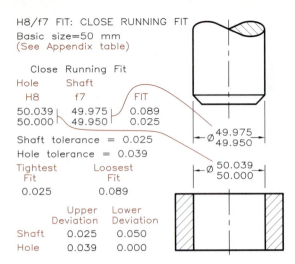

H8/f7 FIT: CLOSE RUNNING FIT
Basic size=50 mm
(See Appendix table)

Close Running Fit

Hole	Shaft	
H8	f7	FIT
50.039	49.975	0.089
50.000	49.950	0.025

Shaft tolerance = 0.025
Hole tolerance = 0.039

Tightest Fit	Loosest Fit
0.025	0.089

	Upper Deviation	Lower Deviation
Shaft	0.025	0.050
Hole	0.039	0.000

Ø 49.975 / 49.950

Ø 50.039 / 50.000

20.20 Example 1—Close running fit: This drawing shows how to calculate and apply metric limits and fits to a shaft and hole (Appendix 31).

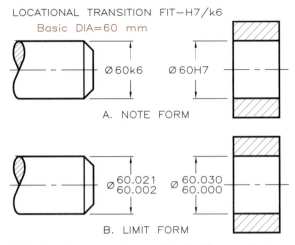

LOCATIONAL TRANSITION FIT—H7/k6
Basic DIA=60 mm

Ø 60k6   Ø 60H7

A. NOTE FORM

Ø 60.021 / 60.002   Ø 60.030 / 60.000

B. LIMIT FORM

20.21 Example 2—Location transition fit: These methods are used to note metric tolerances to a hole and a shaft with a transition fit (Appendix 32).

Shaft: Find the upper and lower limits of the shaft under f7 and across from 50 mm in Appendix 31. These limits are 49.950 and 49.975 mm.

Symbols: **Figure 20.20** shows how to apply toleranced dimensions to the hole and shaft.

Example 2 (Fig. 20.21)

Required: Use the hole-basis system, a location transition fit of medium accuracy, and a basic diameter of 57 mm.

Solution: Use a preferred basic diameter of 60 mm (**Fig. 20.16**) and a fit of H7/k6 (**Fig. 20.18**).

Hole: Find the upper and lower limits of the hole in Appendix 32 under H7 and across from 60 mm. These limits are 60.000 and 60.030 mm.

Shaft: Find the upper and lower limits of the shaft under k6 and across from 60 mm in Appendix 32. These limits are 60.021 and 60.002 mm.

Symbols: **Figure 20.21** shows two methods of applying the tolerance symbols to a drawing, note and limit form.

Example 3 (Fig. 20.22)

Required: Use the hole-basis system, a medium drive fit, and a basic diameter of 96 mm.

Solution: Use a preferred basic diameter of 100 mm (**Fig. 20.16**) and a fit of H7/s6 (**Fig. 20.18**).

Hole: Find the upper and lower limits of the hole in Appendix 32 under H7 and across from 100 mm to obtain limits of 100.035 and 100.000 mm.

Shaft: Find the upper and lower limits of the shaft under s6 and across from 100 mm in Appendix 32. These limits are 100.093 and 100.071 mm. Appendix 32 gives the tightest fit as an interference of −0.093 mm, and the loosest fit as an interference of −0.036 mm. Minus signs in front of these numbers in the fit column indicate interference fits.

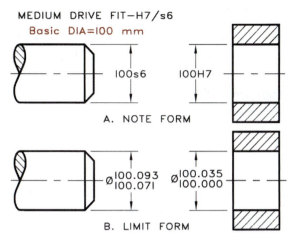

MEDIUM DRIVE FIT—H7/s6
Basic DIA=100 mm

A. NOTE FORM

100s6   100H7

$\varnothing \begin{smallmatrix}100.093\\100.071\end{smallmatrix}$ $\varnothing \begin{smallmatrix}100.035\\100.000\end{smallmatrix}$

B. LIMIT FORM

20.22 Example 3—Interference fit: Either of these formats can be used to apply metric tolerances to a hole and shaft that have an interference fit (Appendix 32).

CALCULATION OF NONSTANDARD LIMITS

FIT: H8/f7   Ø45 BASIC DIA

From Appendix		Hole Limits	45.039
Hole	Shaft		45.000
H8	f7		
0.039	−0.025	Shaft Limits	44.975
0.000	−0.050		44.950

20.23 This calculation is for an H8/f7 non-standard diameter of 45 mm (Appendices 35 and 36).

Symbols: **Figure 20.22** shows how to apply toleranced dimensions to the hole and shaft.

Nonstandard Fits: Nonpreferred Sizes

Limits of tolerances for non-standard sizes can be calculated for any of the preferred fits shown in **Fig. 20.18** for non-standard sizes that do not appear in Appendices 35–36. Limits of tolerances for nonstandard hole sizes are in Appendix 35, and limits of tolerances for nonstandard shaft sizes are in Appendix 36.

Figure 20.22 shows the hole and shaft limits for an H8/f7 fit and a 45-mm DIA. The tolerance limits of 0.000 and 0.039 mm for an H8 hole are taken from Appendix 35, across from the size range of 40-50 mm. The tolerance limits of −0.025 and −0.050 mm for the shaft are from

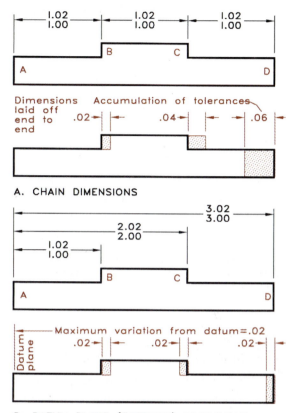

A. CHAIN DIMENSIONS

B. DATUM PLANE (BASELINE) DIMENSIONS

20.24 Chain vs. datum dimensioning

A Dimensions given end to end in a chain fashion may result in an accumulation of tolerances of up to 0.06″ at D instead of the specified 0.02″.

B When dimensioned from a single datum, the variations of B, C, and D cannot deviate more than the specified 0.02″ from the datum.

Appendix 36. Calculate the hole limits by adding the positive tolerances to the 45 mm basic diameter and the shaft limits by subtracting the negative tolerances from the 45 mm basic diameter.

20.9 Chain versus Datum Dimensions

When parts are dimensioned to locate surfaces or geometric features by a chain of dimensions laid end to end (**Fig. 20.24A**), variations may accumulate in excess of the specified tolerance. For example, the tolerance between surfaces A

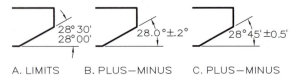

A. LIMITS   B. PLUS—MINUS   C. PLUS—MINUS

20.25 Tolerances on angles can be specified by one of these methods.

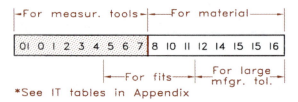

*See IT tables in Appendix

20.26 International tolerance (IT) grades and their applications are shown here. See Appendix 30 to obtain IT tolerance grade values.

and B is 0.02, between A and C it is 0.04, and between A and D it is 0.06.

Tolerance accumulation can be eliminated by measuring from a single plane called a **datum plane** or **baseline**. A datum plane is usually on the object, but it can also be on the machine used to make the part. Because each plane in **Fig. 20.24B** is located with respect to a datum plane, the tolerances between the intermediate planes do not exceed the maximum tolerance of 0.02. Always base the application of tolerances on the function of a part in relationship to its mating parts.

20.10 Tolerance Notes

You should tolerance all dimensions on a drawing either by using the rules previously discussed or by placing a note in or near the title block. For example, the note

TOLERANCE ±1/64

might be given on a drawing for less critical dimensions. Some industries give dimensions in inches with two, three, and four decimal place fractions. A note for dimensions with two and

three decimal places might be given on the drawing as

TOLERANCES XX.XX ±0.10
XX.XXX ±0.005.

Tolerances of four places would be given directly on the dimension lines. The most common method of noting tolerances is to give as large a tolerance as feasible in a note, such as

TOLERANCES ±0.05

and to give tolerances on the dimension lines for dimensions requiring closer tolerances. Give angular tolerances in a general note in or near the title block, such as

ANGULAR TOLERANCES ±0.50° or 30′.

Use one of the formats shown in **Fig. 20.25** to give specific angular tolerances directly on angular dimensions.

20.11 General Tolerances: Metric

All dimensions on a drawing must be specified within certain tolerance ranges when they are not shown on dimension lines. Tolerances not shown on dimension lines should be specified by a general tolerance note on the drawing.

Linear Dimensions: Tolerance linear dimensions by indicating plus and minus (±) one half of an international tolerance (IT) grade as given in Appendix 30. You may select the IT grade from the chart in **Fig. 20.26**, where IT grades for mass-produced items range from IT12 through IT16. IT grades can be selected from **Fig. 20.27** for a particular machining process.

General tolerances using IT grades may be expressed in a note as follows:

UNLESS OTHERWISE SPECIFIED
ALL UNTOLERANCED
DIMENSIONS ARE IT14.

This note means that a tolerance of ±0.700 mm is allowed for a dimension between 315 and 400

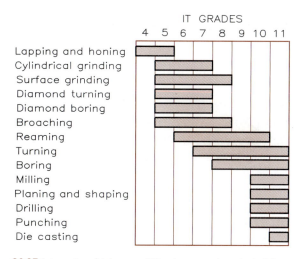

IT GRADES

	4	5	6	7	8	9	10	11
Lapping and honing								
Cylindrical grinding								
Surface grinding								
Diamond turning								
Diamond boring								
Broaching								
Reaming								
Turning								
Boring								
Milling								
Planing and shaping								
Drilling								
Punching								
Die casting								

20.27 International tolerance (IT) values may be selected from this table, which is based on the general capabilities of various machining processes.

GENERAL TOLERANCES:
LINEAR DIMENSIONS (mm)

Basic Dimensions	Fine Series	Medium Series	Coarse Series
0.5 to 3	± 0.05	± 0.1	––
Over 3 to 6	± 0.05	± 0.1	± 0.2
Over 6 to 30	± 0.1	± 0.2	± 0.5
Over 30 to 120	± 0.15	± 0.3	± 0.8
Over 120 to 315	± 0.2	± 0.5	± 1.2
Over 315 to 1000	± 0.3	± 0.8	± 2
Over 1000 to 2000	± 0.5	± 1.2	± 3

20.28 Select general tolerance values from this table for fine, medium, and coarse series. Tolerances vary with dimensions.

Get values from previous table — Specifies a medium series

GENERAL TOLERANCES (mm)							
UNLESS OTHERWISE SPECIFIED, THE FOLLOWING TOLERANCES ARE APPLICABLE							
LINEAR	Over to	0.5 6	6 30	30 120	120 315	315 1000	1000 2000
TOL.	±	0.1	0.2	0.3	0.5	0.8	1.2

20.29 This table for a medium series of values was extracted from Fig. 21.28 for insertion on a working drawing to provide the tolerances for a medium series of sizes.

mm. The value of the tolerance, 1.400 mm, is extracted from Appendix 30.

Figure 20.28 shows recommended tolerances for fine, medium, and coarse series for ranges of size. A medium tolerance, for example, can be specified by the following note:

GENERAL TOLERANCES SPECIFIED
IN ANSI B4.3 MEDIUM SERIES APPLY.

Equivalent tolerances may be given in table form (**Fig. 20.29**) on the drawing, the grade (medium in this example) selected from **Fig. 20.28**. General tolerances may be given in a table for dimensions expressed with one or no decimal places (**Fig. 20.30**). General tolerances may also be notated in the following form:

UNLESS OTHERWISE SPECIFIED
ALL UNTOLERANCED DIMENSIONS
ARE ±0.8 mm.

Use this method only when the dimensions on a drawing are similar in size.

Angular Tolerances: Express angular tolerances as (1) an angle in decimal degrees or in degrees and minutes, (2) a taper expressed in

percentage (mm per 100 mm), or (3) milliradians. (To find milliradian, multiply the degrees of an angle by 17.45.) **Figure 20.31** shows the suggested tolerances for decimal degrees and taper, based on the length of the shorter leg of the angle. General angular tolerances may be notated on the drawing as follows:

UNLESS OTHERWISE SPECIFIED
THE GENERAL TOLERANCES
IN ANSI B4.3 APPLY.

A second method involves showing a portion of the table from **Fig. 20.31** as a table of tolerances on the drawing (**Fig. 20.32**). A third method is a note with a single tolerance, such as:

GENERAL TOLERANCES (mm) UNLESS OTHERWISE SPECIFIED, THE FOLLOWING TOLERANCES ARE APPLICABLE					
LINEAR		OVER TO	120	315	1000
		— 120	315	1000	—
TOL.	ONE DECIMAL ±	0.3	0.5	0.8	1.2
	NO DECIMALS ±	0.8	1.2	2	3

20.30 Placed on a drawing, this table of tolerances would indicate the tolerances for dimensions having one or no decimal places, such as 24.0 and 24, denoting medium and coarse series.

Length of shorter leg (mm)	Up to 10	Over 10 to 50	Over 50 to 120	Over 120 to 400
Degrees	± 1°	± 0° 30'	± 0°20'	± 0°10'
mm per 100	± 1.8	± 0.9	± 0.6	± 0.3

20.31 General tolerances for angular and taper dimensions may be taken from this table of values.

UNLESS OTHERWISE SPECIFIED
ANGULAR TOLERANCES ARE ±0°30'

20.12 Geometric Tolerances

Geometric tolerancing is a system that specifies tolerances that control **location form**, **profile**, **orientation**, **location**, and **runout** on a dimensioned part as covered by the *ANSI Y14.5M Standards* and the *Military Standards* (Mil-Std) of the U.S. Department of Defense. Before discussing those types of tolerancing, however, we need to introduce you to symbols, size limits, rules, three-datum-plane concepts, and applications.

Symbols

The most commonly-used symbols for representing geometric characteristics of dimensioned drawings are shown in **Fig. 20.33**. The proportions of feature control symbols in relation to their feature control frames, based on the letter height, are shown in **Fig. 20.34**. On most

ANGULAR TOLERANCES				
LENGTH OF SHORTER LEG (mm)	UP TO 10	OVER 10 TO 50	OVER 50 TO 120	OVER 120 TO 400
TOLERANCE	±1°	± 0°30'	± 0°20'	±0°10'

Values in degrees and minutes taken from previous table

20.32 This table, extracted from Fig. 21.31, is placed on the drawing to indicate the general tolerances for angles in degrees and minutes.

GEOMETRIC SYMBOLS			
Tolerance		Characteristic	Symbol
INDIVIDUAL FEATURES	Form	Straightness	—
		Flatness	▱
		Circularity	◯
		Cylindricity	⌭
BOTH	Profile	Profile: Line	⌒
		Profile: Surface	⌓
RELATED FEATURES	Orientation	Angularity	∠
		Perpendicularity	⊥
		Parallelism	//
	Location	Position	⊕
		Concentricity	◎
		Symmetry	⟌
	Runout	Runout: Circular	↗
		Runout: Total	↗↗

20.33 These symbols specify the geometric characteristics of a part's features.

drawings, a 1/8-in. or 3-mm letter height is recommended. Examples of feature control frames and their proportions are shown in **Fig. 20.35**.

Size Limits

Three conditions of size are used when geometric tolerances are applied: **maximum material condition**, **least material condition**, and **regardless of feature size**.

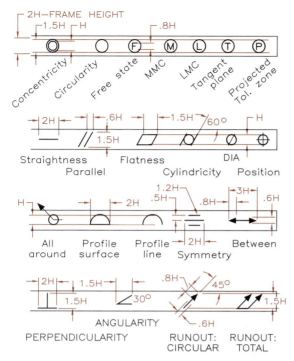

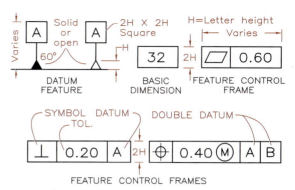

20.35 These are examples of geometric tolerancing frames and feature control symbols used to indicate geometric tolerances. H is the letter height, usually 1/8 inch.

20.34 The proportions of these feature control symbols are based on the letter height, usually 1/8 inch high.

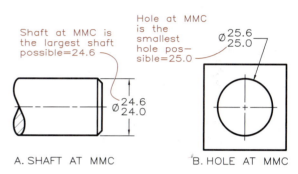

20.36 A shaft is at maximum material condition (MMC) when it is at the largest size permitted by its tolerance. A hole is at MMC when it is at its smallest size.

Maximum material condition (MMC) indicates that a feature contains the maximum amount of material. For example, the shaft shown in **Fig. 20.36** is at MMC when it has the largest permitted diameter of 24.6 mm. The hole is at MMC when it has the most material, or the smallest diameter of 25.0 mm.

Least material condition (LMC) indicates that a feature contains the least amount of material. The shaft in **Fig. 20.36** is at LMC when it has the smallest diameter of 24.0 mm. The hole is at LMC when it has the least material, or the largest diameter of 25.6 mm.

Regardless of feature size (RFS) indicates that tolerances apply to a geometric feature regardless of its size ranging from MMC to LMC.

20.13 Rules for Tolerancing

Two general rules of tolerancing geometric features should be followed.

Rule 1 (**Individual Feature of Size**): When only a tolerance of size is specified on a feature, the limits of size control the variation in its geometric form. The forms of the shaft and hole shown in **Fig. 20.37** are permitted to vary within the tolerance ranges of the dimensions.

Rule 2 (**All Applicable Geometric Tolerances**): Where no modifying symbol is specified, RFS (regardless of features size) applies with respect to the individual tolerance, datum reference, or both. Where required on a drawing, the modifiers MMC or LMC must be specified.

Alternate Practice: For a tolerance of position, RFS may be specified on the drawing with respect to the individual tolerance, datum, reference, or both.

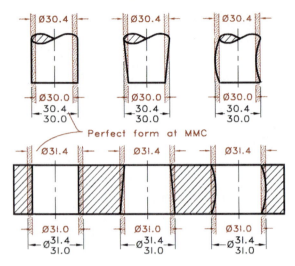

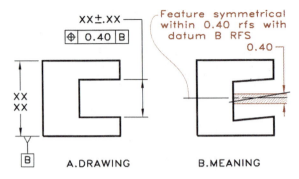

20.38 Tolerances of position should include the note of MMC or LMC to indicate maximum material condition or least material condition, if either is required.

20.37 When only a tolerance of size is specified on a feature, the limits prescribe the form of the features, as shown for these shafts and holes having identical limits.

The specification of symmetry of the part in **Fig. 21.38** is based on a tolerance at RFS from a datum at RFS.

Three-Datum-Plane Concept

A datum plane is used as the origin of a part's features that have been toleranced. Datum planes usually relate to manufacturing equipment, such as machine tables or locating pins.

Three mutually perpendicular datum planes are required to dimension a part accurately. For example, the part shown in **Fig. 20.39** sits on the primary datum plane, with at least three points of its base in contact with the datum. The part is related to the secondary plane by at least two contact points. The third (tertiary) datum is in contact with at least one point on the object.

The priority of datum planes is presented in sequence in feature control frames. For example, in **Fig. 20.40** the primary datum is surface A, the secondary datum is surface B, and the tertiary datum is surface C. **Figure 20.41** lists the order of priority of datum planes A–C sequentially in the feature control frames.

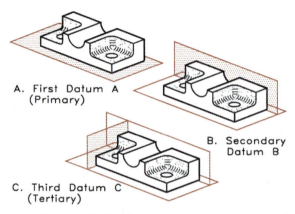

20.39 When an object is referenced to a primary datum plane, it contacts the datum on at least three points. The vertical surface contacts the secondary datum plane on at least two points. The third surface contacts the third datum on at least one point. Datum planes are listed in order of priority in the feature control frame.

20.14 Cylindrical Datum Features

A part with a cylindrical datum feature that is the axis of a cylinder is illustrated in **Fig. 20.42.** Datum K is the primary datum. Datum M is associated with two theoretical planes-the second and third in a three-plane relationship. The two theoretical planes are represented in the circular view by perpendicular centerlines that intersect at the point view of the datum axis. All dimensions originate from the datum axis perpendicular to datum K; the other two intersecting datum planes are used for measurements in the x and y directions.

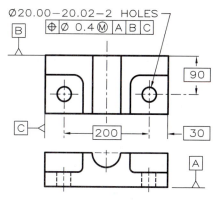

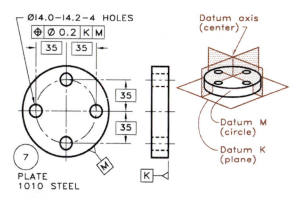

20.40 The three planes of the reference system are noted where they appear as edges. The primary datum plane (A) is given first in the feature control frame; the secondary plane (B), second; and the tertiary plane (C), third. Single numbers in frames are basic dimensions.

20.42 These true-position holes are located with respect to primary datum K and secondary datum M. Because datum M is a circle, the holes are located about two intersecting datum planes at the crossing centerlines in the circular view, satisfying the three-plane concept.

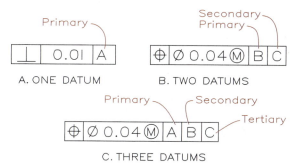

20.41 Use feature control frames to indicate from one to three datum planes in order of priority.

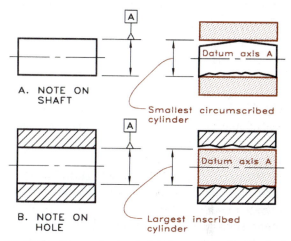

20.43 The datum axis of a shaft is the smallest circumscribed cylinder in contact with the shaft. The datum axis of a hole is the centerline of the largest inscribed cylinder in contact with the hole.

Datum Features at RFS

When size dimensions are applied to a feature at RFS, the processing equipment that comes into contact with surfaces of the part establishes the datum. Variable machine elements, such as chucks or center devices, are adjusted to fit the external or internal features and establish datums.

Primary-Diameter Datums: For an external cylinder (shaft) at RFS, the datum axis is the axis of the smallest circumscribed cylinder that contacts the cylindrical feature (**Fig. 20.43A**). That is, the largest diameter of the part making contact with the smallest cylinder of the machine element holding the part is the datum axis.

For an internal cylinder (hole) at RFS, the datum axis is the axis of the largest inscribed cylinder making contact with the hole. That is, the smallest diameter of the hole making contact with the largest cylinder of the machine element inserted in the hole is the datum axis (**Fig. 20.43B**).

Primary External Parallel Datums: The datum for external features at RFS is the center plane between two parallel planes—at minimum separation—that contact the planes of the

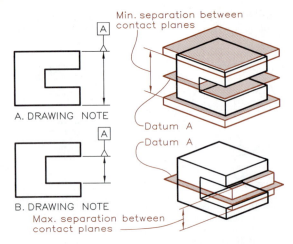

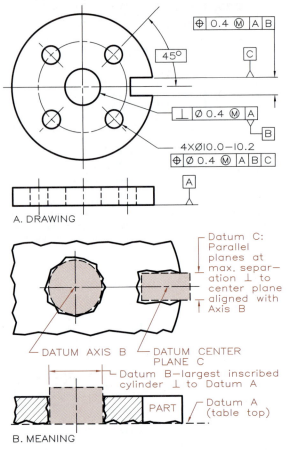

20.44 The datum plane for external parallel surfaces is the center plane between two contact parallel planes at their minimum separation. The datum plane for internal parallel surfaces is the center plane between two contact parallel surfaces at their maximum separation.

20.45 The features of this part have been dimensioned with respect to primary, secondary, and tertiary datum planes.

object (**Fig. 20.44A**). These are planes of a vise-like device at minimum separation that holds the part.

Primary Internal Parallel Datums: The datum for internal features is the center plane between two parallel planes—at their maximum separation—that contact the inside planes of the object (**Fig. 20.44B**).

Secondary Datums: The secondary datum (axis or center plane) for both external and internal diameters (or distances between parallel planes) has the additional requirement that the cylinder in contact with the parallel elements of the hole be perpendicular to the primary datum (**Fig. 20.45**). Datum axis B is the axis of cylinder B.

Tertiary Datums: The third datum (axis or center plane) for both external and internal features has the further requirement that either the cylinder or parallel planes be oriented angularly to the secondary datum. Datum C in **Fig. 20.45** is the tertiary datum plane.

20.15 Location Tolerancing

Tolerances of location specify **position, concentricity,** and **symmetry.**

Position: Location dimensions that are toleranced result in a square (or rectangular) tolerance zone for locating the center of a hole (**Fig. 20.46A**). In contrast, untoleranced location dimensions, called **basic dimensions,** locate the **true position** of a hole's center, about which a circular tolerance zone is specified (**Fig. 20.46B**).

In both methods the size of the hole's diameter is toleranced by identical notes. In the true-position method, a feature control frame specifies the diameter of the circular tolerance zone inside

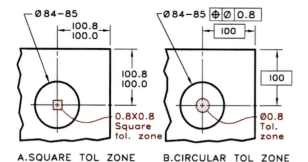

A. SQUARE TOL ZONE **B. CIRCULAR TOL ZONE**

20.46 Toleranced and untoleranced dimensions

A Toleranced location dimensions give a square tolerance zone for the axis of the hole.

B Untoleranced basic dimensions (in frames) locate the true position about which a circular tolerance zone of 0.8 mm is specified.

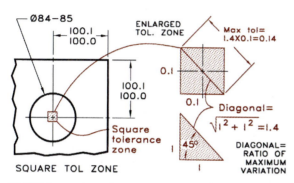

SQUARE TOL ZONE

20.47 Toleranced coordinates give a square tolerance zone with a diagonal that exceeds the specified tolerance by a factor of 1.4.

which the hole's center must lie. A circular position zone gives a more precise tolerance of the hole's true position than does a square.

Figure 20.47 shows an enlargement of the square tolerance zone resulting from the use of toleranced location dimension to locate a hole's center. The diagonal across the square zone is greater than the specified tolerance by a factor of 1.4. Therefore the true-position method, shown enlarged in **Fig. 20.48,** can have a larger circular tolerance zone by a factor of 1.4 and still have the same degree of accuracy specified by the 0.1 square zone. If a variation of 0.14 across the diagonal of the square tolerance zone is

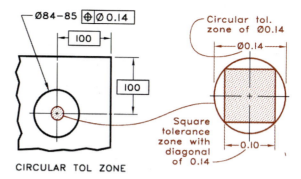

CIRCULAR TOL ZONE

20.48 The true-position method of locating holes results in a circular tolerance zone. The circular zone can be 1.4 times greater than the square tolerance zone and still be as accurate.

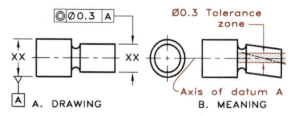

A. DRAWING **B. MEANING**

20.49 Concentricity (related to coaxiality) is a tolerance of location. This feature control frame specifies that the axis of the small cylinder be concentric to datum cylinder A, within a tolerance of a 0.3 mm diameter.

acceptable in the coordinate method, a circular tolerance zone of 0.14, which is greater than the 0.1 tolerance permitted by the square zone, should be acceptable in the true-position tolerance method.

The circular tolerance zone specified in the circular view of a hole extends the full depth of the hole. Therefore, the tolerance zone for the centerline of the hole is a cylindrical zone inside which the axis must lie. Because both the size of the hole and its position are toleranced, these two tolerances establish the diameter of a gauge cylinder for checking conformance of hole sizes and their locations against specifications (**Fig. 20.48**).

Concentricity: Concentricity (closely related to a new term, coaxiality) is a feature of location because it specifies the relationship of two cylinders that share the same axis. In **Fig.**

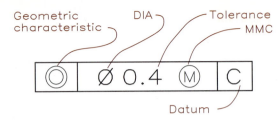

20.50 This typical feature control frame indicates that a surface is concentric to datum C within a cylindrical diameter of 0.4 mm at MMC.

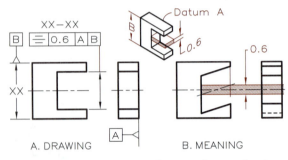

21.51 Symmetry is a tolerance of location that specifies that a part's features be symmetrical about the center plane between parallel surfaces of the part.

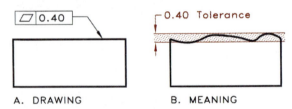

20.52 Flatness is a tolerance of form that specifies a tolerance zone within which a surface must lie.

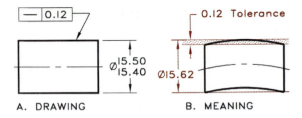

20.53 Straightness is a tolerance of form that indicates that elements of a surface are straight lines. The tolerance frame is applied to the views in which elements appear as straight lines, not points.

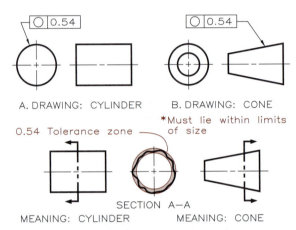

20.54 Circularity (roundness) is a tolerance of form. It indicates that a cross section through a surface of revolution is round and lies within two concentric circles.

20.49, the large cylinder is labeled as datum A to be used as the datum for locating the small cylinder's axis.

Feature control frames of the type shown in **Fig. 20.50** are used to specify concentricity and other geometric characteristics throughout the remainder of this chapter.

Symmetry: Symmetry also is a feature of location in which a feature is symmetrical with the same contour and size on opposite sides of a central plane. **Figure 20.51A** shows how to apply a symmetry feature symbol to the notch that is symmetrical about the part's central datum plane, established by dimension B, for a zone of 0.6 mm (**Fig. 20.51B**).

20.16 Form Tolerancing

Tolerances of form specify flatness, straightness, circularity, and cylindricity.

Flatness: A surface is flat when all its elements are in one plane. A feature control frame specifies flatness within a 0.4 mm tolerance zone in **Fig. 20.52** where no point on the surface may vary more than 0.40 from the highest to the lowest point.

Straightness: A surface is straight if all its elements are straight lines within a specified toler-

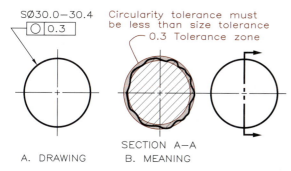

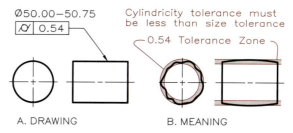

S⌀30.0–30.4 · ○ 0.3

Circularity tolerance must be less than size tolerance
0.3 Tolerance zone

A. DRAWING

SECTION A–A
B. MEANING

20.55 Circularity of a sphere means that any cross section through it is round within the specified tolerance.

⌀50.00–50.75 · ⌀ 0.54

Cylindricity tolerance must be less than size tolerance
0.54 Tolerance Zone

A. DRAWING

B. MEANING

20.56 Cylindricity is a tolerance of form that is a combination of roundness and straightness. It indicates that the surface of a cylinder lies within a tolerance zone formed by two concentric cylinders.

ance zone. The feature control frame shown in **Fig. 20.53** specifies that the elements of a cylinder must be straight within 0.12 mm. On flat surfaces, straightness is measured in a plane passing through control-line elements, and it may be specified in two directions (usually perpendicular) if desired.

Circularity (Roundness): A surface of revolution (a cylinder, cone, or sphere) is circular when all points on the surface intersected by a plane perpendicular to its axis are equidistant from the axis. In **Fig. 20.54** the feature control frame specifies circularity of a cone and cylinder, permitting a tolerance of 0.54 mm on the radius. **Figure 20.55** specifies a 0.30 mm tolerance zone for the roundness of a sphere.

Cylindricity: A surface of revolution is cylindrical when all its elements lie within a cylindrical tolerance zone, which is a combination of tolerances of roundness and straightness (**Fig. 20.66**). Here, a cylindricity tolerance zone of 0.54 mm on the radius of the cylinder is specified.

20.17 Profile Tolerancing

Profile tolerancing involves specifying tolerances for a contoured shape formed by arcs or irregular curves, and it can apply to a surface or a single line. The surface with the unilateral profile tolerance shown in **Fig. 20.57A** is defined by

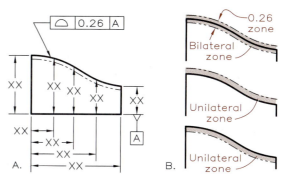

⌒ 0.26 A

A.

0.26 zone
Bilateral zone

Unilateral zone

Unilateral zone

B.

20.57 Profile is a tolerance for irregular curving planes. (A) The curving plane is located by coordinates and is toleranced unidirectionally. (B) The tolerance may be applied by any of these methods.

coordinates. **Figure 20.57B** shows how to specify bilateral and unilateral tolerance zones.

A profile tolerance for a single line is specified as shown in **Fig. 20.58**. The curve is formed by tangent arcs whose radii are given as basic dimensions. The radii are permitted to vary ±0.10 mm from the basic radii.

20.18 Orientation Tolerancing

Tolerances of orientation include **parallelism**, **perpendicularity**, and **angularity**.

Parallelism: A surface or line is parallel when all its points are equidistant from a datum plane or axis. Two types of parallelism tolerance zones are:

1. A planar tolerance zone parallel to a datum plane within which the axis or surface of the

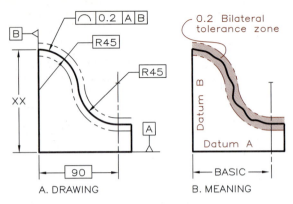

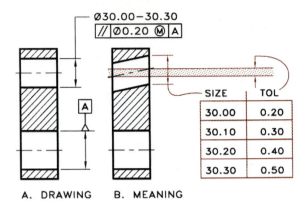

20.58 The profile of a line is a tolerance that specifies the variation allowed from the path of a line. Here, the line is formed by tangent arcs. The tolerance zone may be either bilateral or unilateral, as shown in Fig. 21.57.

20.61 The critical tolerance exists when features are at MMC. (A) The upper hole must be parallel to the hole used as datum A within a 0.20 DIA. (B) As the hole approaches its maximum size of 30.30 mm, the tolerance zone approaches 0.50 mm.

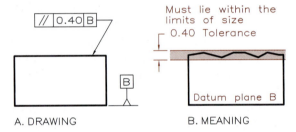

20.59 Parallelism is a tolerance of orientation. It indicates that a plane is parallel to a datum plane within specified limits. Here, plane B is the datum plane.

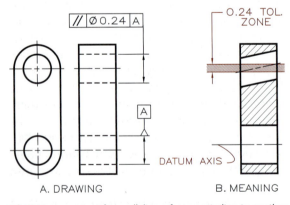

20.60 You may specify parallelism of one centerline to another by using the diameter of one of the holes as the datum.

feature must lie (**Fig. 20.59**). This tolerance also controls flatness.

2. A cylindrical tolerance zone parallel to a datum feature within which the axis of a feature must lie (**Fig. 20.60**).

Figure 20.61 shows the effect of specifying parallelism at MMC, where the modifier M is given in the feature control frame. Tolerances of form apply at RFS when not specified. Specifying parallelism at MMC means that the axis of the cylindrical hole must vary no more than 0.20 mm when the holes are at their smallest permissible size.

As the hole approaches its upper limit of 30.30, the tolerance zone increases to a maximum of 0.50 DIA. Therefore, a greater variation is given at MMC than at RFS.

Perpendicularity: The specifications for the perpendicularity of a plane to a datum are shown in **Fig. 20.62**. The feature control frame shows that the surface perpendicular to datum plane C has a tolerance of 0.32 in. In **Fig. 20.63** a hole is specified as perpendicular to datum plane A.

Angularity: A surface or line is angular when it is at an angle (other than 90°) from a datum or an axis. The angularity of the surface shown in **Fig. 20.64** is dimensioned with a basic angle

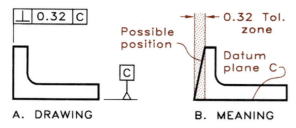

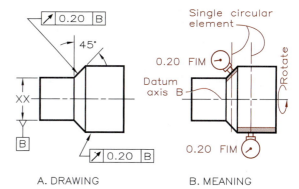

20.62 Perpendicularity is a tolerance of orientation that gives a tolerance zone of .32 for a plane perpendicular to a specified datum plane.

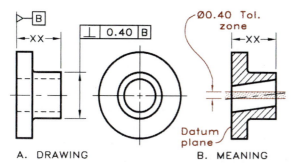

20.63 Perpendicularity can apply to the axis of a feature, such as the centerline of a cylinder.

20.65 Runout tolerance, a composite of several tolerance of form characteristics, is used to specify concentric cylindrical parts. The part is mounted on the datum axis and is gauged as it is rotated.

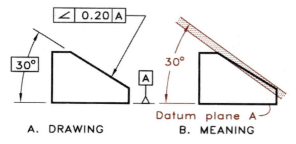

20.64 Angularity is a tolerance of orientation specifying a tolerance zone for an angular surface with respect to a datum plane. Here, the 30° angle is a true, or basic, angle to which a tolerance of 0.20 mm is applied.

(exact angle) of 30° and an angularity tolerance zone of 0.25 mm inside of which the plane must lie.

20.19 Runout Tolerancing

Runout tolerancing is a way of controlling multiple features by relating them to a common datum axis. Features so controlled are surfaces of revolution about an axis and surfaces perpendicular to the axis.

The datum axis, such as diameter B in **Fig. 20.65**, is established by a circular feature that rotates about the axis. When the part is rotated about this axis, the features of rotation must fall within the prescribed tolerance at full indicator movement (FIM).

The two types of runout are **circular runout** and **total runout**. One arrow in the feature control frame indicates circular runout and two arrows indicate total runout.

Circular Runout: Rotating an object about its axis 360° determines whether a circular cross section exceeds the permissible runout tolerance at any point (**Fig. 20.66**). This same technique is used to measure the amount of wobble in surfaces perpendicular to the axis of rotation.

Total Runout: Used to specify cumulative variations of circularity, straightness, concentricity, angularity, taper, and profile of a surface (**Fig. 20.66**), total runout tolerances are measured for all circular and profile positions as the part is rotated 360°. When applied to surfaces perpendicular to the axis, total runout tolerances control variations in perpendicularity and flatness.

The dimensioned part shown in **Fig. 20.67** illustrates several of the techniques of geometric

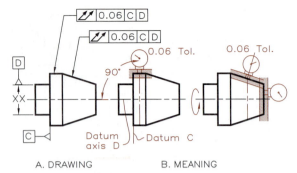

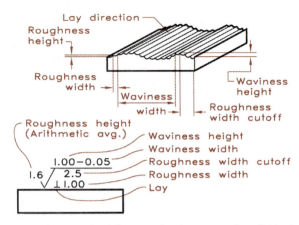

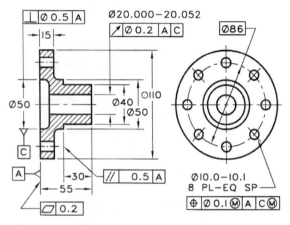

A. DRAWING   B. MEANING

20.66 Here, runout tolerance is measured by mounting the object on the primary datum plane C and the secondary datum cylinder D. The cylinder and conical surface are gauged to check their conformity to a tolerance zone of 0.06 mm. The runout at the end of the cone could have been noted.

20.67 A combination of notes and symbols describe this part's geometric features.

20.68 These are the definitions of surface texture for a finished surface.

tolerancing described in this and previous sections.

20.20 Surface Texture

Because the surface texture of a part affects its function, it must be precisely specified instead of giving an unspecified finished mark, such as a V. **Figure 20.68** illustrates most of the terms that apply to surface texture (surface control).

Surface texture: The variation in a surface, including roughness, waviness, lay, and flaws.

Roughness: The finest of the irregularities in the surface caused by the manufacturing process used to smooth the surface.

Roughness height: The average deviation from the mean plane of the surface measured in microinches (μin.) or micrometers (μm), or millionths of an inch and a meter, respectively.

Roughness width: The width between successive peaks and valleys forming the roughness measured in microinches or micrometers.

Roughness width cutoff: The largest spacing of repetitive irregularities that includes average roughness height (measured in inches or millimeters). When not specified, a value of 0.8 mm (0.030 in.) is assumed.

Waviness: A widely spaced variation that exceeds the roughness width cutoff measured in inches or millimeters. Roughness may be regarded as a surface variation superimposed on a wavy surface.

Waviness height: The peak-to-valley distance between waves measured in inches or millimeters.

Waviness width: The spacing between wave peaks or wave valleys measured in inches or millimeters.

Lay: The direction of the surface pattern caused by the production method used.

Flaws: Irregularities or defects occurring infrequently or at widely varying intervals on a surface, including cracks, blow holes, checks, ridges,

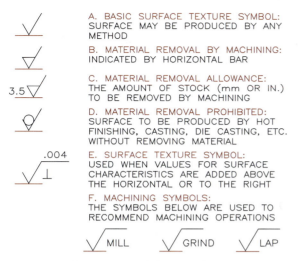

A. BASIC SURFACE TEXTURE SYMBOL: SURFACE MAY BE PRODUCED BY ANY METHOD

B. MATERIAL REMOVAL BY MACHINING: INDICATED BY HORIZONTAL BAR

C. MATERIAL REMOVAL ALLOWANCE: THE AMOUNT OF STOCK (mm OR IN.) TO BE REMOVED BY MACHINING

D. MATERIAL REMOVAL PROHIBITED: SURFACE TO BE PRODUCED BY HOT FINISHING, CASTING, DIE CASTING, ETC. WITHOUT REMOVING MATERIAL

E. SURFACE TEXTURE SYMBOL: USED WHEN VALUES FOR SURFACE CHARACTERISTICS ARE ADDED ABOVE THE HORIZONTAL OR TO THE RIGHT

F. MACHINING SYMBOLS: THE SYMBOLS BELOW ARE USED TO RECOMMEND MACHINING OPERATIONS

MILL   GRIND   LAP

20.69 Use surface texture symbols to specify surface finish on the edge views of finished surfaces.

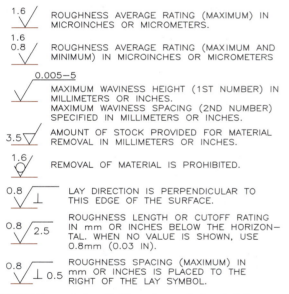

1.6 — ROUGHNESS AVERAGE RATING (MAXIMUM) IN MICROINCHES OR MICROMETERS.

1.6 0.8 — ROUGHNESS AVERAGE RATING (MAXIMUM AND MINIMUM) IN MICROINCHES OR MICROMETERS

0.005–5 — MAXIMUM WAVINESS HEIGHT (1ST NUMBER) IN MILLIMETERS OR INCHES. MAXIMUM WAVINESS SPACING (2ND NUMBER) SPECIFIED IN MILLIMETERS OR INCHES.

3.5 — AMOUNT OF STOCK PROVIDED FOR MATERIAL REMOVAL IN MILLIMETERS OR INCHES.

1.6 — REMOVAL OF MATERIAL IS PROHIBITED.

0.8 — LAY DIRECTION IS PERPENDICULAR TO THIS EDGE OF THE SURFACE.

0.8 2.5 — ROUGHNESS LENGTH OR CUTOFF RATING IN mm OR INCHES BELOW THE HORIZONTAL. WHEN NO VALUE IS SHOWN, USE 0.8mm (0.03 IN).

0.8 0.5 — ROUGHNESS SPACING (MAXIMUM) IN mm OR INCHES IS PLACED TO THE RIGHT OF THE LAY SYMBOL.

20.70 Values may be added to surface control symbols for more precise specifications.

scratches, and the like. The effect of flaws is usually omitted in roughness height measurements.

Contact area: The surface that will make contact with a mating surface.

Symbols for specifying surface texture are shown in **Fig. 20.69**. The point of the V must

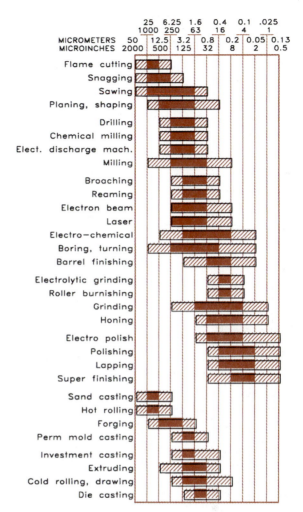

20.71 Various types of production methods result in the surface roughness heights shown in micrometers and microinches (millionths of a meter or an inch).

touch the edge view of the surface, an extension line from it, or a leader pointing to the surface. **Figure 20.70** shows how to specify values as a part of surface texture symbols. Roughness height values are related to the processes used to finish surfaces and may be taken from the table in **Fig. 20.71**. The preferred values of roughness height are listed in **Fig. 20.72**.

The preferred roughness width cutoff values in **Fig. 20.73** are for specifying the sampling width used to measure roughness height. A

Micro− meters μm	Micro− inches μin.	Micro− meters μm	Micro− inches μin.
0.025	1	1.6	63
0.050	2	3.2	125
0.10	4	6.3	250
0.20	8	12.5	500
0.40	16	25	1000
0.80	32	Micrometers=0.001 mm	

20.72 This range of roughness heights is recommended in ANSI Y14.36 standards.

MILLIMETERS	0.08	0.25	0.80	2.5	8.0	25
INCHES	.003	.010	.030	.1	.3	1

20.73 This range of roughness width cutoff values is recommended in the ANSI Y14.36 standards. When unspecified, assume a value of 0.8.

MAXIMUM WAVINESS HEIGHT VALUES

mm	in.	mm	in.
0.0005	.00002	0.025	.001
0.0008	.00003	0.05	.002
0.0012	.00005	0.08	.003
0.0020	.00008	0.12	.005
0.0025	.0001	0.20	.008
0.005	.0002	0.25	.010
0.008	.0003	0.38	.015
0.012	.0005	0.50	.020
0.020	.0008	0.80	.030

20.74 This range of maximum waviness height values is recommended in the ANSI Y14.36 standards.

value of 0.80 mm is assumed if no value is given. When required, maximum waviness height values may be selected from the recommended values shown in **Fig. 20.74**.

Lay symbols indicating the direction of texture (markings made by the machining operation) on a surface (**Fig. 20.75**) may be added to surface texture symbols, as shown in **Fig. 20.76**. The perpendicular sign indicates that lay is perpendicular to the edge view of the surface in this view (where the surface control symbol appears). **Figure 20.77** illustrates how to apply a variety of surface texture symbols to a part.

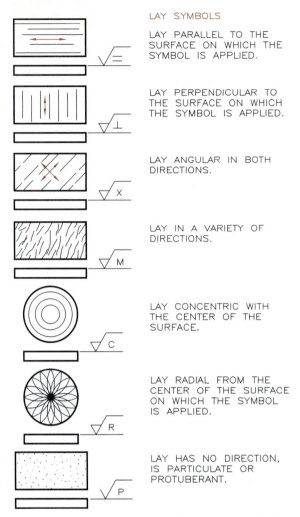

LAY SYMBOLS

LAY PARALLEL TO THE SURFACE ON WHICH THE SYMBOL IS APPLIED.

LAY PERPENDICULAR TO THE SURFACE ON WHICH THE SYMBOL IS APPLIED.

LAY ANGULAR IN BOTH DIRECTIONS.

LAY IN A VARIETY OF DIRECTIONS.

LAY CONCENTRIC WITH THE CENTER OF THE SURFACE.

LAY RADIAL FROM THE CENTER OF THE SURFACE ON WHICH THE SYMBOL IS APPLIED.

LAY HAS NO DIRECTION, IS PARTICULATE OR PROTUBERANT.

20.75 These symbols are used to indicate the direction of lay with respect to the surface where the control symbol is placed.

Problems

Solve the following problems on size A sheets laid out on a grid of 0.20 in. or 5 mm.

Cylindrical Fits
1. (Sheet 1) Draw the shaft and hole shown (it need not be to scale), give the limits for each diameter, and complete the table of values. Use a basic diameter of 1.00 in. (25 mm) and a class RC 1 fit or a metric fit of H8/f7.

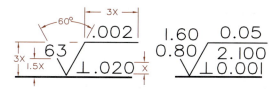

20.76 These are examples and proportions of typical, fully specified surface texture symbols.

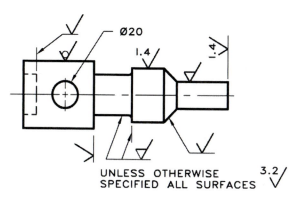

20.77 Various techniques of applying surface texture symbols to a part are illustrated here.

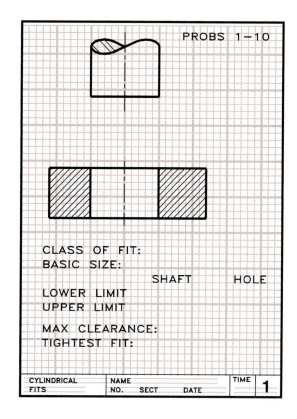

2. Repeat Problem 1, but use a basic diameter of 1.75 in. (45 mm) and a class RC 9 fit or a metric fit of H11/c11.

3. Repeat Problem 1, but use a basic diameter of 2.00 in. (51 mm) and a class RC 5 fit or a metric fit of H9/d9.

4. Repeat Problem 1, but use a basic diameter of 12.00 in. (305 mm) and a class LC 11 fit or a metric fit of H7/h6.

5. Repeat Problem 1, but use a basic diameter of 3.00 in. (76 mm) and a class LC 1 fit or a metric fit of H7/h6.

6. Repeat Problem 1, but use a basic diameter of 8.00 in. (203 mm) and a class LC 1 fit or a metric fit of H7/k6.

7. Repeat Problem 1, but use a basic diameter of 10 in. (254 mm) and a class LN 3 fit or a metric fit of H7/n6.

8. Repeat Problem 1, but use a basic diameter of 11.00 in. (279 mm) and a class LN 2 fit or a metric fit of H7/p6.

9. Repeat Problem 1, but use a basic diameter of 6.00 in. (152 mm) and a class FN 5 fit or a metric fit of H7/s6.

10. Repeat Problem 1, but use a basic diameter of 2.60 in. (66 mm) and a class FN 1 fit or a metric fit of H7/u6.

Tolerances of Location

11. (Sheet 2) Make an instrument drawing of the part shown. Locate the two holes with a size tolerance of 1.00 mm and a position tolerance of 0.50 DIA. Insert the proper symbols and dimensions.

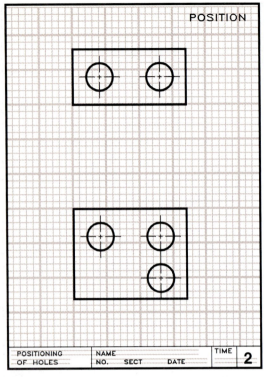

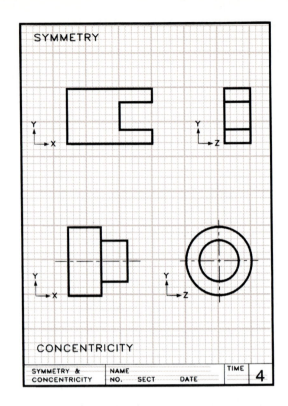

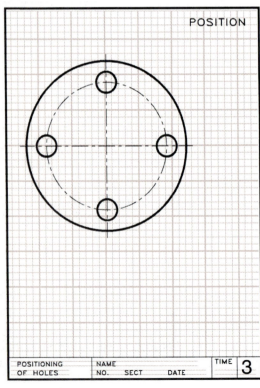

12. **(Sheet 2)** Make an instrument drawing of the part shown. Locate the three holes with a size tolerance of 1.00 mm and a position tolerance of 0.40 DIA. Insert the proper symbols and dimensions.

13. **(Sheet 3)** Using position tolerances, locate the holes and properly note them to provide a size tolerance of 1.50 mm and a locational tolerance of 0.60 DIA.

14. **(Sheet 4)** Using a feature control symbol and the necessary dimensions, indicate that the notch is symmetrical to the height at the left-hand end of the part within 0.60 mm.

15. **(Sheet 4)** Using a feature control symbol and the necessary dimensions, indicate that the small cylinder is concentric with the large one (the datum cylinder) within a tolerance of 0.80 mm.

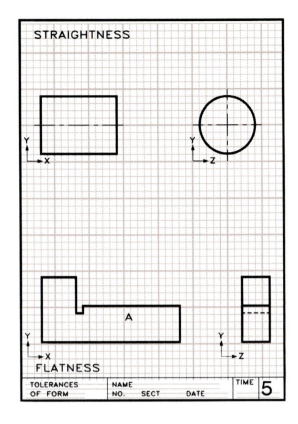

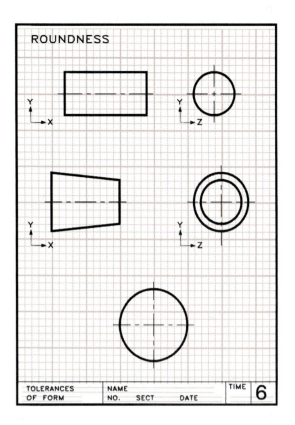

Tolerances of Form

16. (Sheet 5) Using a feature control symbol and the necessary dimensions, indicate that the elements of the cylinder are straight within a tolerance of 0.20 mm.

17. (Sheet 5) Using a feature control symbol and the necessary dimensions, indicate that surface A of the object is flat within a tolerance of 0.08 mm.

18–20. (Sheet 6) Using feature control symbols and the necessary dimensions, indicate that the cross sections of the cylinder, cone, and sphere are round within a tolerance of 0.40 mm.

Tolerances of Profile

21. (Sheet 7) Using a feature control symbol and the necessary dimensions, indicate that the profile of the irregular surface of the object lies within a bilateral or unilateral tolerance zone of 0.40 mm.

22. (Sheet 7) Using a feature control symbol and the necessary dimensions, indicate that the profile of the line formed by tangent arcs lies within a bilateral or unilateral tolerance zone of 0.40 mm.

Tolerances of Orientation

23. (Sheet 8) Using a feature control symbol and the necessary dimensions, indicate that the angularity tolerance of the inclined plane is 0.7 mm from the bottom of the object, the datum plane.

24. (Sheet 8) Using a feature control symbol and the necessary dimensions, indicate that surface A of the object is parallel to datum B within 0.30 mm.

25. (Sheet 9) Using a feature control symbol and the necessary dimensions, indicate that

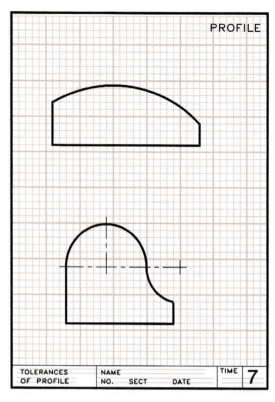

PROFILE

| TOLERANCES OF PROFILE | NAME | TIME | 7 |
| | NO. SECT DATE | | |

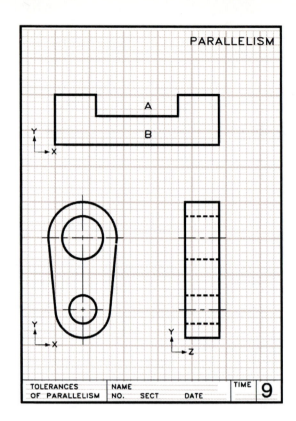

PARALLELISM

| TOLERANCES OF PARALLELISM | NAME | TIME | 9 |
| | NO. SECT DATE | | |

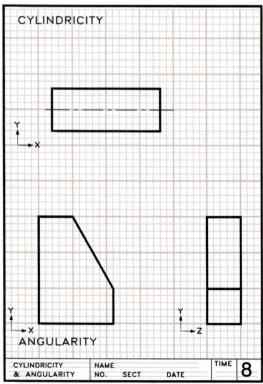

CYLINDRICITY

ANGULARITY

| CYLINDRICITY & ANGULARITY | NAME | TIME | 8 |
| | NO. SECT DATE | | |

surface A is parallel to datum plane B within 0.80 mm.

26. (Sheet 9) Using a feature control symbol and the necessary dimensions, indicate that the small hole is parallel to the large hole, the datum, within a tolerance of 0.80 mm.

27. (Sheet 10) Using a feature control symbol and the necessary dimensions, indicate that the vertical surface B is perpendicular to the bottom of the object, the datum C, within a tolerance of 0.20 mm.

28. (Sheet 10) Using a feature control symbol and the necessary dimensions, indicate that the hole is perpendicular to datum A within a tolerance of 0.08 mm.

Tolerances of Runout

29. (Sheet 11) Using the appropriate geometric tolerancing symbols and cylinder A as the

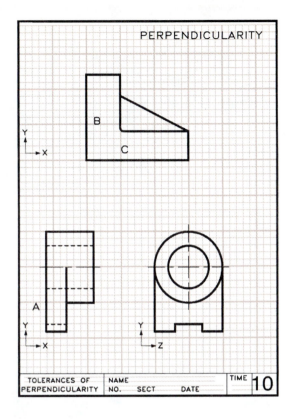

PERPENDICULARITY

TOLERANCES OF PERPENDICULARITY	NAME NO. SECT DATE	TIME	10

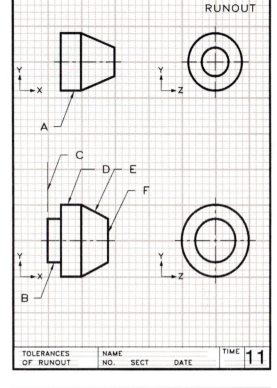

RUNOUT

TOLERANCES OF RUNOUT	NAME NO. SECT DATE	TIME	11

datum, indicate that the conical feature has a runout of 0.80 mm.

30. (Sheet 11) Using a feature control symbol, cylinder B as the primary datum, and surface C as the secondary datum, indicate that surfaces D, E, and F have runouts of 0.60 mm.

31. (Sheet 12) Draw the journal base as it is shown, which is a half-size, two-view drawing. Using metric units and the three-datum planes, locate the two holes (size tolerance of 0.20) to lie within a tolerance zone of 1.6 DIA. Indicate that datum A is flat within 0.8. Indicate that datum B is perpendicular to datum A within 1.2 mm. (Refer to **Fig. 21.40.**)

32. (Sheet 12) Same as problem 22, but in addition to these specifications, give the complete dimensions necessary to fully describe the part. Also indicate that the upper surface in the front view is parallel to the datum A within 1.4 mm.

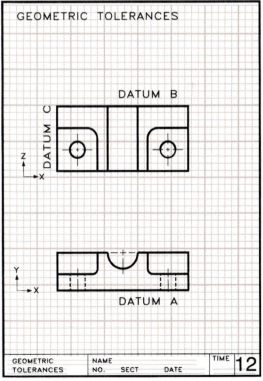

GEOMETRIC TOLERANCES

DATUM C

DATUM B

DATUM A

GEOMETRIC TOLERANCES	NAME NO. SECT DATE	TIME	12

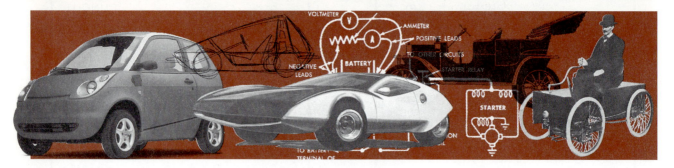

Welding

21.1 Introduction

Welding is the process of permanently joining metal by heating a joint to a suitable temperature with or without applying pressure and with or without using filler material. The welding practices described in this chapter comply with the standards developed by the American Welding Society and the American National Standards Institute (ANSI).

Welding is done in shops, on assembly lines, or in the field, as shown in **Fig. 21.1** where a welder is joining pipes. Welding is a widely used method of fabrication with its own language of notes, specifications, and symbology. You must become familiar with this system of notations in order to make and read drawings containing welding specifications.

Advantages of welding over other methods of fastening include (1) simplified fabrication, (2) economy, (3) increased strength and rigidity, (4) ease of repair, (5) creation of gas- and liquid-tight joints, and (6) reduction in weight and size.

21.1 This welder is joining two pipes in accordance with specifications on a set of drawings. (Courtesy of Texas Eastern; *TE Today*; photo by Bob Thigpen.)

21.2 Welding Processes

Figure 21.2 shows various types of welding processes. The three main types are gas welding, arc welding, and resistance welding.

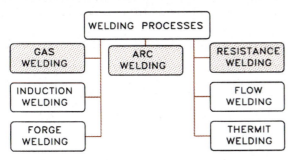

21.2 The three main types of welding processes are gas welding, arc welding, and resistance welding.

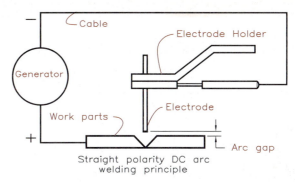

Straight polarity DC arc welding principle

21.4 In arc welding, either AC or DC current is passed through an electrode to heat the joint.

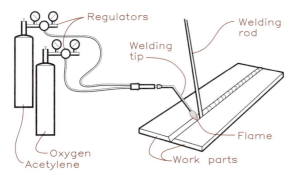

21.3 The gas welding process burns gases such as oxygen and acetylene in a torch to apply heat to a joint. The welding rod supplies the filler material.

Gas welding involves the use of gas flames to melt and fuse metal joints. Gases such as acetylene or hydrogen are mixed in a welding torch and burned with air or oxygen (**Fig. 21.3**). The oxyacetylene method is widely used for repair work and field construction.

Most oxyacetylene welding is done manually with a minimum of equipment. Filler material in the form of welding rods is used to deposit metal at the joint as it is heated. Most metals, except for low- and medium-carbon steels, require fluxes to aid the process of melting and fusing the metals.

Arc welding involves the use of an electric arc to heat and fuse joints, with pressure sometimes required in addition to heat (**Fig. 21.4**).

The filler material is supplied by a consumable or nonconsumable electrode through which the electric arc is transmitted. Metals well-suited to arc welding are wrought iron, low- and medium-carbon steels, stainless steel, copper, brass, bronze, aluminum, and some nickel alloys. In electric-arc welding, **the flux is a material coated on the electrodes that forms a coating on the metal being welded**. This coating protects the metal from oxidation so that the joint will not be weakened by overheating.

Flash welding is a form of arc welding, but it is similar to resistance welding because both pressure and electric current (**Fig. 21.5**) are applied. The pieces to be welded are brought together, and an electric current is passed through them, causing heat to build up between them. As the metal burns, the current is turned off, and the pressure between the pieces is increased to fuse them.

Resistance welding comprises several processes by which metals are fused both by the heat produced from the resistance of the parts to an electric current and by pressure. Fluxes and filler materials normally are not used. All resistance welds are either lap- or butt-type welds.

Resistance spot welding is performed by pressing the parts together, and an electric current fuses them, as illustrated in the lap joint weld in **Fig. 21.6**. A series of small welds spaced

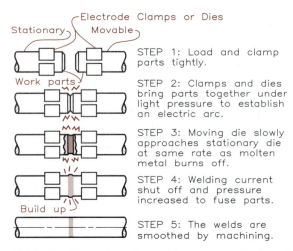

STEP 1: Load and clamp parts tightly.

STEP 2: Clamps and dies bring parts together under light pressure to establish an electric arc.

STEP 3: Moving die slowly approaches stationary die at same rate as molten metal burns off.

STEP 4: Welding current shut off and pressure increased to fuse parts.

STEP 5: The welds are smoothed by machining.

21.5 Flash welding, a type of arc welding, uses a combination of electric current and pressure to fuse two parts.

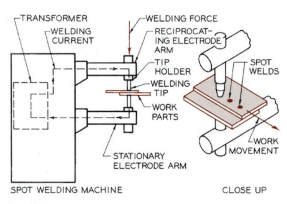

21.6 Resistance spot welding may be used to join lap and butt joints.

Material	Spot Welding	Flash Welding
Low–carbon mild steel		
SAE 1010	Rec.	Rec.
SAE 1020	Rec.	Rec.
Medium–carbon steel		
SAE 1030	Rec.	Rec.
SAE 1050	Rec.	Rec.
Wrought alloy steel		
SAE 4130	Rec.	Rec.
SAE 4340	Rec.	Rec.
High–alloy austenitic stainless steel		
SAE 30301–30302	Rec.	Rec.
SAE 30309–30316	Rec.	Rec.
Ferritic and martensistic stainless steel		
SAE 51410–51430	Satis.	Satis.
Wrought heat–resisting alloys		
19–9–DL	Satis.	Satis.
16–25–6	Satis.	Satis.
Cast iron	NA	Not Rec.
Gray iron	NA	Not Rec.
Aluminum & alum. alloys	Rec.	Satis.
Nickel & nickel alloys	Rec.	Satis.

Rec.—Recommended Satis.—Satisfactory
Not Rec.— Not   NA—Not applicable
    recommended

21.7 Resistance welding processes for various materials are shown here.

at intervals, called **spot welds**, secure the parts. **Figure 21.7** lists the recommended materials and processes to be used for resistance welding.

21.3 Weld Joints and Welds

Figure 21.8 shows the five standard weld joints: **Butt joint**, **corner joint**, **lap joint**, **edge joint**, and **tee joint**. The **butt joint** can be joined with a square groove, V-groove, bevel groove, U-groove, and J-groove weld. The **corner joint** can be

joined with these welds and with the fillet weld. The **lap joint** can be joined with a bevel groove, J-groove, fillet, slot, plug, spot, projection, and seam weld. The **edge joint** uses the same welds as the lap joint, along with square groove, V-groove, U-groove, and seam welds. **The tee joint** can be joined by bevel groove, J-groove, and fillet welds.

Figure 21.9 depicts commonly used welds and their corresponding **ideographs** (symbols). The fillet weld is a built-up weld at the intersection (usually 90°) of two surfaces. The square, bevel, V-groove, J-groove, and U-groove welds all have grooves, and the weld is applied in these grooves. Slot and plug welds have intermittent holes or openings where the parts are welded.

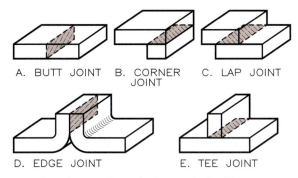

A. BUTT JOINT   B. CORNER   C. LAP JOINT
JOINT

D. EDGE JOINT   E. TEE JOINT

21.8 These diagrams depict the five standard weld joints.

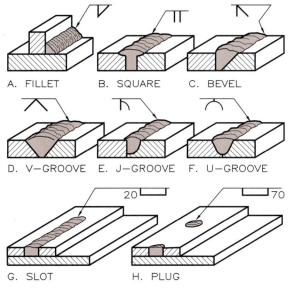

A. FILLET   B. SQUARE   C. BEVEL

D. V—GROOVE   E. J—GROOVE   F. U—GROOVE

G. SLOT   H. PLUG

21.9 These views illustrate standard welds and their corresponding ideographs.

Holes are unnecessary when resistance welding is used.

21.4 Welding Symbols

If a drawing has a general welding note, such as ALL JOINTS ARE WELDED THROUGHOUT, the designer has transferred responsibility to the welder. Welding is too important to be left to chance and should be specified more precisely.

Symbols are used to convey welding specifications on a drawing. The complete welding

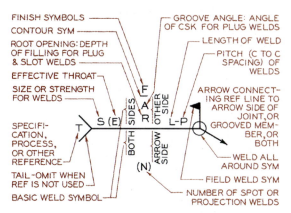

FINISH SYMBOLS
CONTOUR SYM
ROOT OPENING: DEPTH OF FILLING FOR PLUG & SLOT WELDS
EFFECTIVE THROAT
SIZE OR STRENGTH FOR WELDS
SPECIFICATION, PROCESS, OR OTHER REFERENCE
TAIL—OMIT WHEN REF IS NOT USED
BASIC WELD SYMBOL
GROOVE ANGLE: ANGLE OF CSK FOR PLUG WELDS
LENGTH OF WELD
PITCH (C TO C SPACING) OF WELDS
ARROW CONNECTING REF LINE TO ARROW SIDE OF JOINT, OR GROOVED MEMBER, OR BOTH
WELD ALL AROUND SYM
FIELD WELD SYM
NUMBER OF SPOT OR PROJECTION WELDS

21.10 The welding symbol. Usually it is modified to a simpler form for use on drawings.

symbol is shown in **Fig. 21.10**, but it usually appears on a drawing in modified, more general form with less detail. The scale of the welding symbol is based on the letter height used on the drawing, which is the size of the grid on which the symbol is drawn in **Fig. 21.11**. The standard height of lettering on a drawing is usually 1/8 in. or 3 mm.

The **ideograph** is the symbol that denotes the type of weld desired, and it generally depicts the cross-section representation of the weld. **Figure 21.12** shows the ideographs used most often. They are drawn to scale on the 1/8-in. (3-mm) grid (equal to the letter height), which represents their full size when added to the welding symbol.

21.5 Application of Symbols

Fillet Welds

In **Fig. 21.13A,** placement of the fillet weld ideograph below the horizontal line of the symbol indicates that the weld is at the joint on the arrow side—the right side in this case. The vertical leg of the ideograph is always on the left side.

A numeral (either a common fraction or a decimal value) to the right of the ideograph indicates

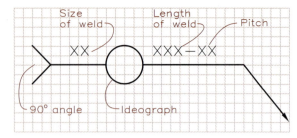

21.11 Welding symbol proportions are based on the letter height used on a drawing, usually 1/8 in. or 3 mm. This grid is equal to the letter height.

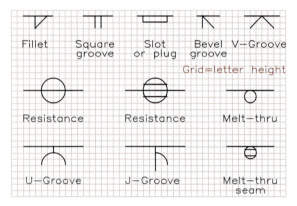

21.12 The sizes of the ideographs shown on the 1/8-in. (3 mm) grid (the letter height) are proportional to the size of the welding symbol (Fig. 21.11).

the size of the weld. You may omit this number from the symbol if you insert a general note elsewhere on the drawing to specify the fillet size, such as:

ALL FILLET WELDS 1/4 IN.
UNLESS OTHERWISE NOTED.

Placing the ideograph above the horizontal line in **Fig. 21.13B** indicates that the weld is to be on the other side; that is, the joint on the other side of the part away from the arrow. When the part is to be welded on both sides, use the ideograph shown in **Fig. 21.13C**. You may omit the tail and other specifications from the symbol when you provide detailed specifications elsewhere.

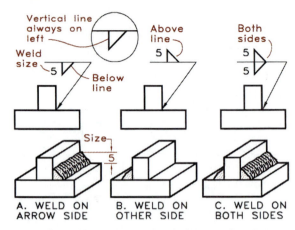

21.13 Fillet welds may be noted with abbreviated symbols. (A) When the ideograph appears below the horizontal line, it specifies a weld on the arrow side. (B) When it is above the line, it specifies a weld on the opposite side. (C) When it is on both sides of the line, it specifies a weld on each side.

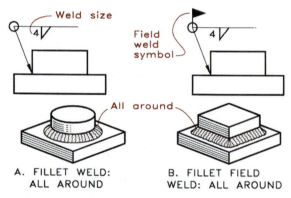

21.14 These symbols indicate fillet welds all around two types of parts.

A single arrow often is used to specify a weld that is to be made all around two joining parts (**Fig. 21.14A**). A circle of 6 mm (twice the letter height) in diameter, drawn at the bend in the leader of the symbol denotes this type of weld. If the welding is to be done in the field rather than in the shop, a solid black triangular "flag" is added also (**Fig. 21.14B**).

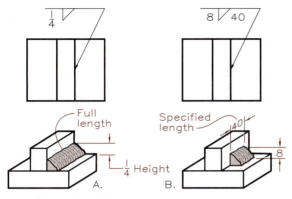

21.15 Fillet weld symbols.

A This symbol indicates full-length fillet welds.

B This symbol indicates fillet welds of specified, but less than, full length.

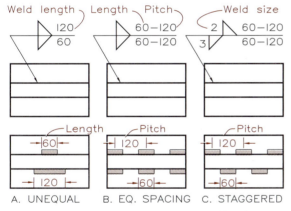

21.16 These symbols specify intermittent welds of varying lengths and alignments.

You may specify a fillet weld that is to run the full length of the two parts, as in **Fig. 21.15A**. The ideograph is on the lower side of the horizontal line, so the weld is on the arrow side. You may specify a fillet weld that is to run shorter than full length, as in **Fig. 21.15B**, where 40 represents the weld's length in millimeters.

You may specify fillet welds to run different lengths and be positioned on both sides of a part, as in **Fig. 21.16A**. The dimension on the lower side of the horizontal gives the length of the weld on the arrow side, and the dimension on the upper side of the horizontal gives the length on the opposite side.

Intermittent welds have a specified length and are spaced uniformly, center to center, at an interval called the pitch. In **Fig. 21.16B**, the welds are equally spaced on both sides, are 60 mm long, and have pitches of 120 mm, as indicated by the symbol shown. The symbol shown in **Fig. 21.16C** specifies intermittent welds that are staggered in alternate positions on opposite sides.

Groove Welds

The standard types of groove welds are **V-groove**, **bevel groove**, **double V-groove**, **U-groove**, and **J-groove** (**Fig. 21.17**). When you do not give the depth of the grooves, angle of the chamfer, and root openings on a symbol, you must specify them elsewhere on the drawing or in supporting documents. In **Fig. 21.17A** and **B**, the angles of the V-joints are labeled 60° and 90° under the ideographs. In **Fig. 21.17B**, the depths of the weld (6) and the root opening (2)—the gap between the two parts—are given.

In a bevel groove weld, only one of the parts is beveled. The symbol's leader is bent and pointed toward the beveled part to call attention to it (**Figs. 21.17C** and **21.18B**). This practice also applies to J-groove welds, where one side is grooved and the other is not (**Fig. 21.18A**).

Notate double V-groove welds by weld size, bevel angle, and root opening (**Figs. 21.17D** and **E**). Omit root opening sizes or show a zero on the symbol when parts fit flush. Give the angle and depth of the groove in the symbol for a U-groove weld (**Fig. 21.17F**).

Seam Welds

A seam weld joins two lapping parts with either a continuous weld or a series of closely spaced spot welds. The seam weld process to be used is

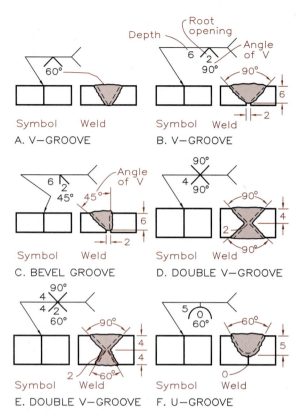

A. V–GROOVE

B. V–GROOVE

C. BEVEL GROOVE

D. DOUBLE V–GROOVE

E. DOUBLE V–GROOVE

F. U–GROOVE

21.17 This drawing shows the various types of groove welds and their general specifications.

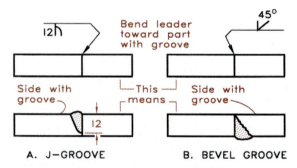

A. J–GROOVE

B. BEVEL GROOVE

21.18 J-groove welds and bevel welds are specified by bent arrows pointing to the side of the joint to be grooved or beveled.

CAW	Carbon—arc w.	IB	Induction brazing
CW	Cold welding	IRB	Infrared brazing
DB	Dip brazing	OAW	Oxyacetylene w.
DFW	Diffusion welding	OHW	Oxyhydrogen w.
EBW	Electric beam w.	PGW	Pressure gas w.
ESW	Electroslag welding	RB	Resist. brazing
EXW	Explosion welding	RPW	Projection weld.
FB	Furnace brazing	RSEW	Resist. seam w.
FOW	Forge welding	RSW	Resist. spot w.
FRW	Friction welding	RW	Resist. welding
FW	Flash welding	TB	Torch brazing
GMAW	Gas metal arc w.	UW	Upset welding
GTAW	Gas tungsten w.	*w.=welding	

21.19 These abbreviations represent the various types of welding processes and are used in welding symbols.

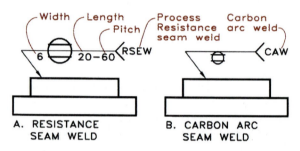

A. RESISTANCE SEAM WELD

B. CARBON ARC SEAM WELD

21.20 The process used for (A) resistance seam welds and (B) arc seam welds is indicated in the tail of the symbol. For the arc weld the symbol must specify the arrow side or the other side of the piece.

the horizontal line of the symbol (**Fig. 21.20A**). The weld's width, length, and pitch are given.

When the seam weld is to be made by arc welding (CAW), the diameter of the ideograph is about 6 mm (twice the letter height) and goes on the upper or lower side of the symbol's horizontal line to indicate whether the seam is to be applied to the arrow side or the opposite side (**Fig. 21.20B**). When the length of the weld is not shown, the seam weld is understood to extend between abrupt changes in the direction of the seam.

Spot welds are similarly specified with ideographs and specifications by diameter, number of welds, and pitch between the welds. The

identified by abbreviations in the tail of the weld symbol (**Fig. 21.19**). The circular ideograph for a resistance weld is about 12 mm (four times the letter height) in diameter and is centered over

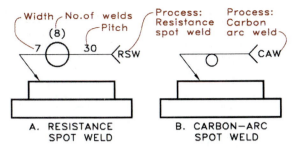

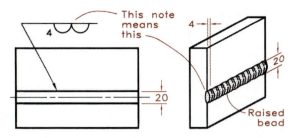

A. RESISTANCE SPOT WELD

B. CARBON-ARC SPOT WELD

21.21 The process to be used for (A) resistance spot welds and (B) arc spot welds is indicated in the tail of the symbol. For the arc weld the symbol must specify the arrow side or the other side of the piece.

21.22 Use this method to apply a symbol to a built-up weld on a surface.

process of resistance spot welding (RSW) is noted in the tail of the symbol (**Fig. 21.21A**). For arc welding, the arrow side or other side must be indicated by a symbol (**Fig. 21.21B**).

Built-Up Welds

When the surface of a part is to be enlarged, or built-up, by welding, indicate this process with a symbol as shown in **Fig. 21.22**. Dimension the width of the built-up weld in the view. Specify the height of the weld above the surface in the symbol to the left of the ideograph. The radius of the circular segment is 6 mm (twice the letter height).

21.6 Surface Contouring

Contour symbols are used to indicate which of the three types of contours, **flush**, **concave**, or **convex**, is desired on the surface of the weld. Flush contours are smooth with the surface or flat across the hypotenuse of a fillet weld. Concave contours bulge inward with a curve, and convex contours bulge outward with a curve (**Fig. 21.23**).

Finishing the weld by an additional process to obtain the desired contour often is necessary. These processes, which may be indicated by their abbreviations, are **chipping** (C), **grinding** (G), **hammering** (H), **machining** (M), **rolling** (R), and **peening** (P), as shown in **Fig. 21.24**.

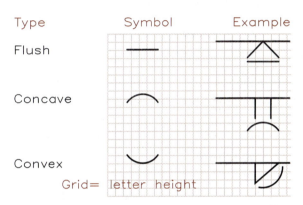

21.23 These contour symbols specify the desired surface finish of a weld.

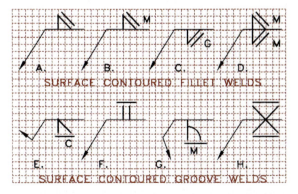

21.24 These examples of contoured weld symbols with letters added indicate the type of finishing to be applied to the weld (M, machining; G, grinding; C, chipping).

21.7 Brazing

Brazing is a method much like welding for joining pieces of metal. Brazing entails heating joints to more than 800°F and distributing by capillary action a nonferrous filler material, with a melting point below that of the base materials, between the closely fitting parts.

Before brazing, the parts must be cleaned and the joints fluxed. The brazing filler is added before or just as the joints are heated beyond the filler's melting point. After the filler material has melted, it is allowed to flow between the parts to form the joint. As **Fig. 21.25** shows, there are two basic brazing joints: lap joints and butt joints.

Brazing is used to join parts, to provide gas- and liquid-tight joints, to ensure electrical conductivity, and to aid in repair and salvage. Brazed joints withstand more stress, higher temperature, and more vibration than soft-soldered joints.

21.8 Soldering

Soldering (pronounced "soddering") is the process of joining two metal parts with a third metal that melts below the temperature of the metals being joined. Solders are alloys of nonferrous metals that melt below 800°F. Widely used in the automotive and electrical industries, soldering is one of the basic techniques of welding and often is done by hand with a soldering iron like the one depicted in **Fig. 21.26**. The iron is placed on the joint to heat it and to melt the solder. Basic soldering is noted on the drawing with a leader simply as SOLDER, and other specifications noted as needed as shown in **Fig. 21.26**.

21.9 Summary

By necessity, the coverage in this chapter is introductory in nature, but it is adequate for a basic understanding of how to specify welding

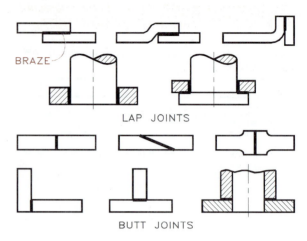

21.25 The two basic types of brazing joints are lap joints and butt joints.

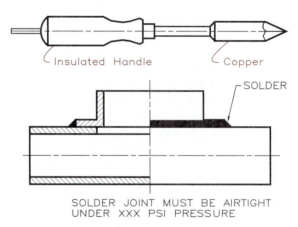

21.26 This typical hand-held soldering iron is used to soft-solder two parts together. The method of notating a drawing for soldering also is shown.

on an engineering drawing. More detailed information on welding is available from the American Welding Society, 2501 N.W. 7th Street, Miami, Florida 33125. This society maintains and publishes guidelines and standards for the technology of welding.

Problems

Solve these problems on size A sheets laid out on a grid of 0.20 inches (5 mm).

1–8. (Fig. 21.27) Give welding notes to include the information specified for each problem. Omit instructional information from the solution.

9. (Fig. 21.28) The shaft socket has a base of 4 in. × 4 in. Draw a top and front view of it; approximate its dimensions; and show the appropriate welding notes for its fabrication.

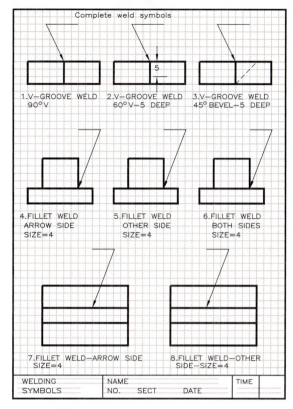

21.27 Problems 1–8.

21.28 Problem 9.

10. (Figure 22.29) The angle fixture has faces of 9 × 12 and 10 × 12. Redesign the fixture to have ribs that are welded instead of cast, as in this example, and show welding symbols. Estimate the unspecified dimensions.

21.29 Problem 10.

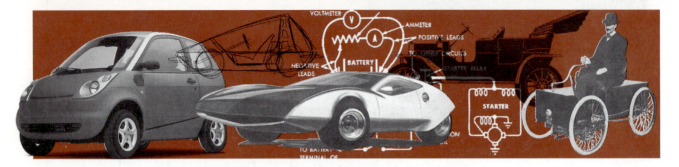

Working Drawings

22.1 Introduction

Working drawings are the drawings from which a design is implemented. All principles of orthographic projection and techniques of graphics can be used to communicate the details of a project in working drawings. A **detail drawing** is a working drawing of a single part (or detail) within the set of working drawings.

Specifications are the written instructions that accompany working drawings. When the design can be represented on a few sheets, the specifications are usually written on the drawings to consolidate the information into a single format.

All parts must interact with other parts to some degree to yield the desired function from a design. Before detail drawings of individual parts are made, the designer must thoroughly analyze the working drawing to ensure that the parts fit properly with mating parts, that the correct tolerances are applied, that the contact surfaces are properly finished, and that the proper motion is possible between the parts.

Much of the work in preparing working drawings is done by the drafter, but the designer, who is usually an engineer, is responsible for their correctness. It is working drawings that bring products and systems into being.

22.2 Working Drawings as Legal Documents

Working drawings are legal contracts that document the design details and specifications as directed by the engineer. Therefore, drawings must be as clear, precise, and thorough as possible. Revisions and modifications of a project at the time of production or construction are much more expensive than when done in the preliminary design stages.

Poorly executed working drawings result in wasted time and resources and increase implementation costs. To be economically competitive, drawings must be as error-free as possible.

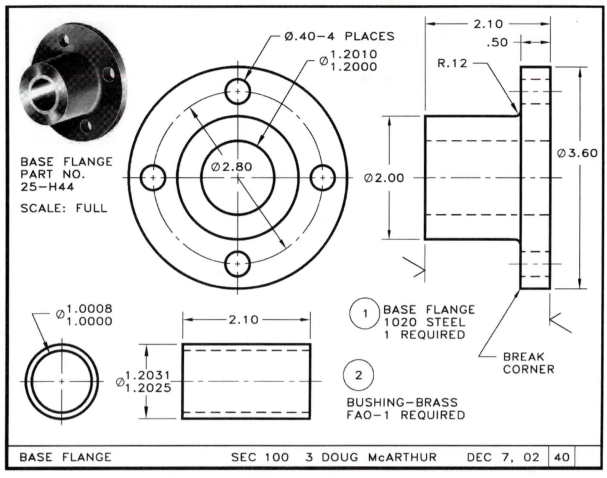

22.1 This revolving clamp assembly holds parts while they are being machined. (*Photo courtesy of Jergens, Incorporated.*)

Working drawings specify all aspects of the design, reflecting the soundness of engineering and function of the finished product and economy of fabrication. The working drawing is the instrument that is most likely to establish the responsibility for any failure to meet specifications during implementation.

22.3 Dimensions and Units

English System

The inch is the basic unit of the English system, and virtually all shop drawings made with English units are dimensioned in inches. This practice is followed even when dimensions are several feet in length.

The base flange shown in **Fig. 22.1** is an example of a relatively simple working drawing of a part. However, there are many drawings of this simplicity that must be designed, developed, and detailed in order for the overall project to come into being.

The base flange is dimensioned with two-place decimal inches, except where four-place decimal inches are used for toleranced dimensions. Inch marks (″) are omitted from dimensions on working drawings because the units are understood to be in inches, and their omission

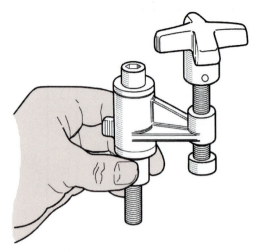

22.2 This revolving clamp assembly holds parts while they are being machined. (*Courtesy of Jergens, Incorporated.*)

22.3 Sheet 1 of 3: This is a computer-drawn working drawing of parts of the clamp assembly shown in Fig. 22.2. (*Figures 22.3–22.5 courtesy of Jergens, Incorporated.*)

saves drafting time. Finish marks are applied to the surfaces that must be machined smooth. Notice that the dimensions are spaced and applied in accordance with the principles covered in Chapters 19 and 20. A photograph showing a three-dimensional view of the flange has been inserted in the corner of the drawing as a raster image by using AutoCAD.

The clamp illustrated in **Fig. 22.2** is detailed in a working drawing of three sheets (**Figs. 22.3–22.5**), which are dimensioned in inches. Decimal fractions are preferable to common fractions, but common fractions are still used (although, mostly by architects). Arithmetic can be done with greater ease using decimal fractions than with common fractions.

Usually, several dimensioned orthographic views of parts are shown on each sheet. However, some companies have policies that views of only one part be drawn on a sheet, even if the part is extremely simple, such as a threaded fastener or the base flange shown in **Fig. 22.1**.

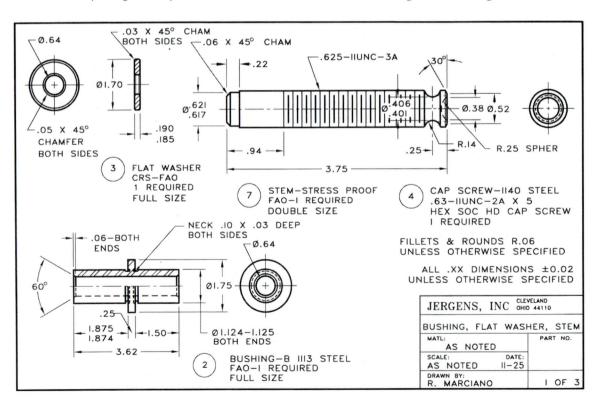

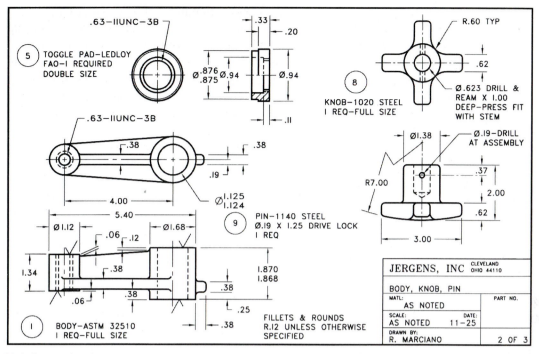

22.4 Sheet 2 of 3 (above): This continuation of Fig. 23.2 shows additional parts of the clamp assembly.

22.5 Sheet 3 of 3 (below): A pad assembly, an overall assembly drawing, and a parts list are shown.

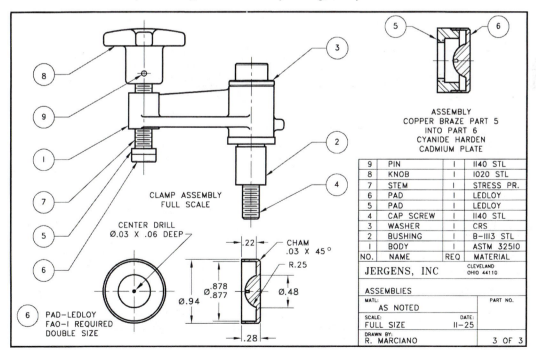

The arrangement of views of parts on the sheet need not attempt to show the relationship of the parts when assembled; the views are simply positioned to best fit the available space on the sheet. The views of each part are labeled with a part number, a name for identification, the material it is made of, the number of the parts required, and any other notes necessary to explain manufacturing procedures.

The purpose of the orthographic assembly drawing shown on Sheet 3 (**Fig. 22.5**) is to illustrate how the parts are to fit together. Each part is numbered and cross-referenced with the part numbers in the parts list, which serves as a bill of materials.

Metric System

The millimeter is the basic unit of the metric system, and dimensions usually are given to the nearest whole millimeter without decimal frac-

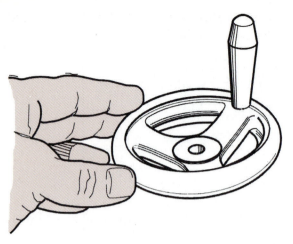

22.6 This drawing of a left-end handcrank is detailed in the working drawing in Figs. 22.7 and 22.8.

22.7 Sheet 1 of 2: This set of working drawings (dimensions in mm) depicts the crank wheel of the left-end handcrank shown in Fig. 22.6.

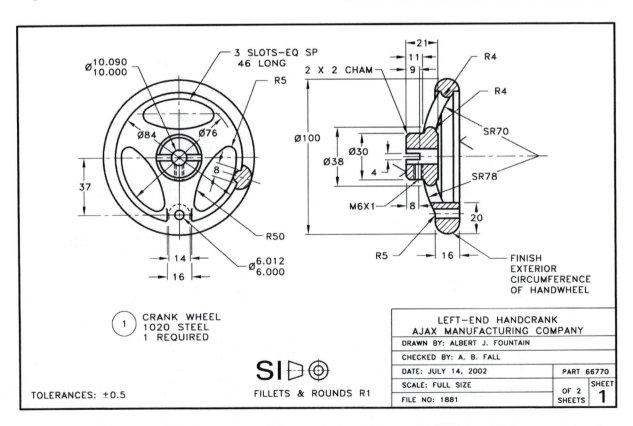

tions (except to specify tolerances which may require three-place decimals). Metric abbreviations (mm) after the numerals are omitted from dimensions because the SI symbol near the title block indicates that all units are metric. If you have trouble relating to the length of a millimeter, recall that the fingernail of your index finger is about 10 mm wide.

The left-end handcrank (**Fig. 22.6**) is depicted and dimensioned in millimeters in the working drawings shown in **Fig. 22.7** and **Fig. 22.8** on size B sheets. Dimensions and notes, along with the descriptive views, give the information needed to construct the four pieces.

The orthographic, sectioned assembly drawing of the left-end handcrank shown in **Fig. 22.8** illustrates how the parts are to be put together. The part numbers in the balloons provide a cross-reference to the parts list that is placed just above the title block.

Dual Dimensions

Some working drawings carry both inch and millimeter dimensions, as shown in **Fig. 22.9**, where the dimensions in parentheses or brackets are millimeters. The units may also appear as millimeters first and then be converted and shown in brackets as inches. Converting from one unit to the other results in fractional round-off errors. An explanation of the primary unit system for each drawing should be noted in the title block.

Metric Working Drawing Example

Figure 22.10 is a photograph of a lifting device used to level heavy equipment such as lathes

22.8 Sheet 2 of 2: This continuation of Fig. 22.7 includes an assembly drawing and parts list.

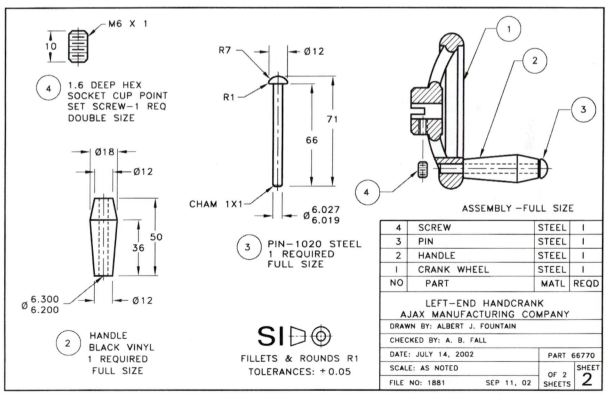

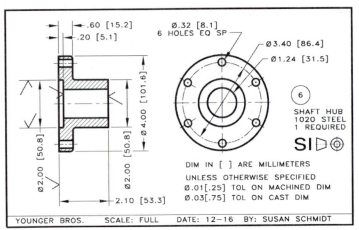

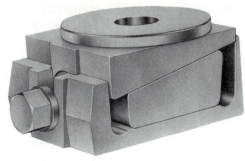

22.10 This Lev-L-Line lifting device is used to level heavy machinery. (*Courtesy of Unisorb Machinery Installation Systems.*)

22.9 In this dual-dimensioned drawing, dimensions are shown in millimeters; their equivalents in inches are given in brackets.

22.11 Sheet 1 of 2: This working drawing (dimensioned in SI units) describes parts of the lifting device shown in Fig. 22.10. (*Courtesy of Unisorb Machinery Installation Systems.*)

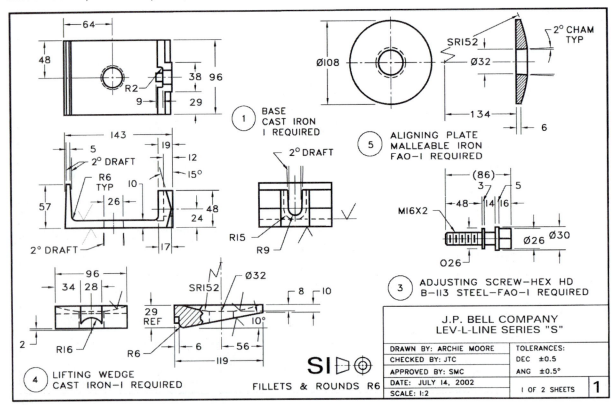

and milling machines. The device raises or lowers the machinery when the screw is rotated, which slides two wedges together. A two-sheet working drawing that gives the details of the parts of the lifting device is shown in **Figs. 22.11** and **22.12**. The SI symbol indicates that the dimensions are in millimeters and the truncated cone indicates that the orthographic views are drawn using third-angle projection. The assembly drawing in **Fig. 22.12** illustrates how the parts are to be assembled together after they have been made.

22.4 Laying out a Detail Drawing

By Computer
You may lay out a simple working drawing of a single part by computer by beginning with the border (**Fig. 22.13**). Although this example is elementary, it is useful in describing the procedures for laying out more complex drawings. Allow a margin of at least 0.25 in. (7 mm) between the edge of the sheet and the borders. Outline space for the title block in the lower right-hand corner of the sheet to ensure that the drawing or notes do not occupy this area.

First, make a freehand sketch to determine the necessary views, the number of dimensions, and their placement so that you can select the proper scale. Then use the computer to produce the views close together to make projection from view to view easier.

Next, *Move* the views apart to make room for notes and dimensions. Finally, add dimensions, notes, the SI symbol, and the title block to complete the drawing.

22.12 Sheet 2 of 2: This continuation of Fig. 22.11 shows the remaining parts in a working drawing and an assembly drawing of the lifting device. (*Courtesy of Unisorb Machinery Installation Systems.*)

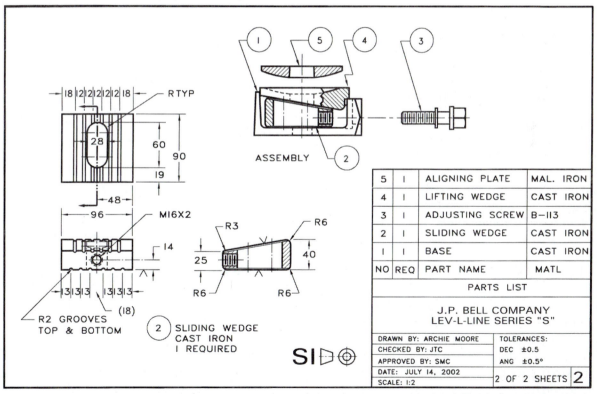

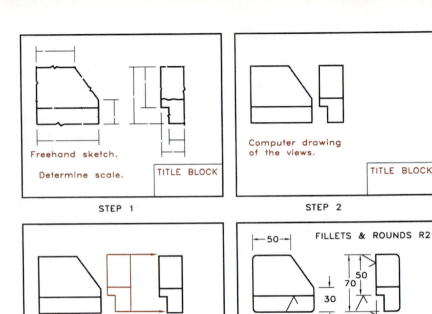

22.13 Laying out a working drawing by computer

Step 1 Make a freehand sketch to determine the views and dimensions needed.

Step 2 Plot the views close together to make projection easier.

Step 3 Use the *Move* command to move the views apart, making room for the dimensions.

Step 4 Insert dimensions and notes and complete the title block.

By Hand

When making a drawing by hand with instruments on paper or film, first lay out the views and dimensions on a different sheet of paper. Then overlay the drawing with vellum or film and trace it to obtain the final drawing. You must use guidelines for lettering for each dimension and note. Lightly draw the guidelines or underlay the drawing with a sheet containing guidelines.

Figure 22.14 shows the standard sheet sizes for working drawings. Paper, film, cloth, and reproduction materials are available in these modular sizes; good practice requires that you make drawings in one of these standard sizes. Modular-sized drawings can be folded to fit standard-sized envelopes, match the sizes of print paper, and fit in standard-size filing cabinets.

22.5 Notes and Other Information

Title Blocks and Parts Lists

Figure 22.15 shows a title block and parts list suitable for most student assignments. Title blocks usually are placed in the lower right-hand corner of the drawing sheet against the borders. The parts list (**Fig. 22.15**) should be placed directly over the title block (see also **Figs. 22.8** and **22.12**).

Title Blocks In practice, title blocks usually contain the title or part name, drafter, date, scale, company, and sheet number. Other information, such as tolerances, checkers, and materials, also may be given. **Figure 22.16** shows another example of a title block, which is typical of those used by various industries. Any modifications or changes added after the first version

ENGLISH SIZES			METRIC SIZES		
A	11 x 8.5		A4	297 X 210
B	17 X 11		A3	420 X 297
C	22 X 17		A2	594 X 420
D	34 X 22		A1	841 X 594
E	44 X 34		A0	1189 X 841

22.14 These are the standard sheet sizes for working drawings dimensioned in inches and millimeters.

2	SHAFT	2	1020 STL	.38
I	BASE	I	CAST IRON	
NO	PART NAME	REQ	MATERIAL	
	PARTS LIST			

—— 5" (Approximately) ——

TITLE		
BY: RED GRANGE	SECT: 500	.38
DATE: MAY 2, 1999	SHEET I	
SCALE: FULL SIZE	OF I SHEETS	

$\frac{1}{8}$" LETTERS

22.15 This typical title block and parts list is suitable for most student assignments.

to improve the design are shown in the revision blocks.

Depending on the complexity of the project, a set of working drawings may contain from one to more than a hundred sheets. Therefore, giving the number of each sheet and the total number of sheets in the set on each sheet is important (for example, sheet 2 of 6, sheet 3 of 6, and so on).

Computer Method A computer shortcut for filling in a title block that will be used on several sheets is shown in **Fig. 22.17**. By computer, you need only draw the title block only once, filling it in with dummy values to establish the positions of the text. By using the *Ddedit* command, the dummy entries can be updated with applicable values after the block is inserted or copied into a drawing.

A similar shortcut in the design of a title block involves the use of *Attributes* (Chapter 26).

REVISIONS	COMPANY NAME COMPANY ADDRESS	
CHG. HEIGHT	TITLE: LEFT—END BEARING	
FAO	DRAWN BY: JOHNNY RINGO	
	CHECKED BY: FRED J. DODGE	
	DATE: JULY 14, 2002	
	SCALE HALF SIZE	SHEET 2 OF 3 SHEETS

22.16 This title block, which includes a revision block, is typical of those used in industry.

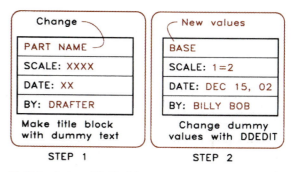

22.17 Producing a title block by computer

Step 1 Draw the title block and add dummy text values, using the desired text style and size. Make a *Block* of the title block.

Step 2 Position the title block against the lower bottom and right borders. *Explode* the *Block* and use the *Ddedit* command to convert the dummy values to actual values.

In that case, the program will prompt you to *Insert* entries into the title block one at a time at the time of insertion.

Parts List The part numbers and part names in the parts list correspond to those given to each part depicted on the working drawings. In addition, the number of identical parts required are given, along with the material used to make each part. Because the exact material (for example, 1020 STEEL) is designated for each part on the drawing, the material in the parts list may be shortened to STEEL, which requires less space.

Patent Rights Note

A note near the title block that names Jack Omohundro as the inventor of the part or process is used to establish ownership of the design (**Fig.**

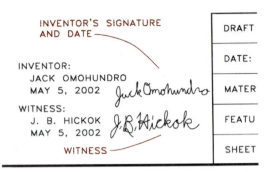

22.18 This note next to the title block names the inventor and is witnessed by an associate to establish ownership of a design for patent purposes.

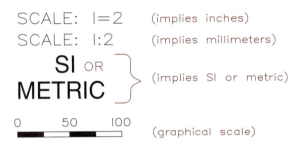

22.19 Specify scales in English and SI units on working drawings with these methods.

22.18). An associate, J. B. Hickok, signs and dates the drawing as a witness to the designer's work. This type of note establishes ownership of the ideas and dates of their development to help the inventor obtain a patent. An even better case for design ownership is made if a second witness signs and dates the drawing. As modifications to the design are made, those drawings should receive the same documentation.

Scale Specification

If all working drawings in a set are the same scale, you need to indicate it only once in the title block on each sheet. If several detail drawings on a working drawing are different scales, indicate them on the drawing under each set of views. In this case, indicate **AS SHOWN** in the title block opposite scale. When a drawing is not to scale, place the abbreviation NTS (not to scale) in the title block.

Figure 22.19 shows several methods of indicating scales. Use of the colon (for example, 1:2) implies the metric system; use of the equal sign (for example, 1=2) implies the English system— but these are not absolute rules. The SI symbol or metric designation on a drawing specifies that millimeters are the units of measurement.

In some cases, you may want to show a graphical scale with calibrations on a drawing to permit the interpretation of linear measurements by transferring them with dividers from the drawing to the scale.

Tolerances

Recall from Chapter 20 that you may use general notes on working drawings to specify the dimension tolerances. **Figure 22.20** shows a table of values with boxes in which you can make a check mark to indicate whether the units are in inches or millimeters. Position plus-and-minus tolerances under each common or decimal fraction. For example, this table specifies that each dimension with two-place decimals will have a tolerance of ±0.10 in. You may also give angular tolerances in general notes ($\pm0.5°$, for example).

Part Labeling

Give each part a name and number, using letters and numbers 1/8-in. (3 mm) high (**Fig. 22.21**). Place part numbers inside circles, called **balloons**, having diameters approximately four times the height of the numerals

Place part numbers near the views to which they apply, so their association will be clear. On assembly drawings, balloons are especially important because the same part numbers are used in the parts list. Show the number of parts required near the part name.

22.6 Drafter's Log

In addition to the individual revision records, drafters should keep a log of all changes made

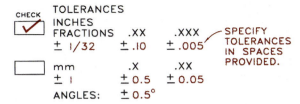

22.20 General tolerance notes on working drawings specify the dimension tolerances permitted.

22.21 Name and number each part on a working drawing for use in the parts list, and indicate the number of parts of this particular part that are needed.

22.22 An assembly drawing explains how the parts of a product, such as this Ford tractor, are to be assembled. (*Courtesy of Ford Motor Company.*)

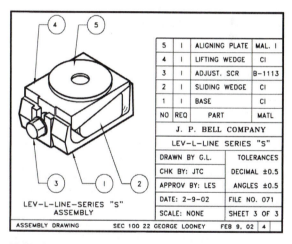

22.23 This isometric assembly drawing depicts the parts of the lifting device shown in Fig. 22.10 fully assembled. Dimensions usually are omitted from assembly drawings and a parts list is given.

during a project. As the project progresses, the drafter should record the changes, dates, and people involved. Such a log allows anyone reviewing the project in the future to understand easily and clearly the process used in arriving at the final design.

Calculations often are made during a drawing's preparation. If they are lost or poorly done, they may have to be redone during a later revision; therefore they should be a permanent part of the log in order to preserve previously expended work.

22.7 Assembly Drawings

After parts have been made according to the specifications of the working drawings, they will be assembled (**Fig. 22.22**) in accordance with the directions of an assembly drawing. Two general types of assembly drawings are **orthographic assemblies** and **pictorial assemblies**. Dimensions usually are omitted from assembly drawings.

The lifting device shown in **Fig. 22.10** is depicted in an isometric assembly in **Fig. 22.23**. Each part is numbered with a balloon and leader

to cross-reference them to the parts list, where more information about each part is given.

Figure 22.24 shows an orthographic exploded assembly drawing. In many applications, the arrangement of parts may be easier to understand when the parts are shown exploded along their centerlines. These views are shown as regular orthographic views, with some lines shown as hidden lines and others omitted.

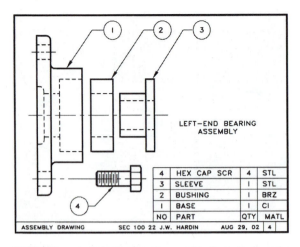

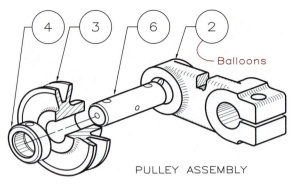

22.24 This exploded orthographic assembly illustrates how the parts shown are to be put together.

22.26 This exploded pictorial assembly drawing is of a shaft bearing assembly. (*Courtesy of Cameron Iron Works, Incorporated.*)

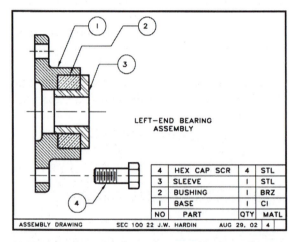

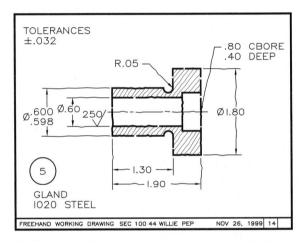

22.25 This sectioned orthographic assembly shows the parts from Fig. 22.24 in their assembled positions, except for the exploded bolt.

22.27 A freehand working drawing with the essential dimensions can be as adequate as an instrument-drawn detail drawing for simple parts.

Assembly of the same part is shown in **Fig. 22.25** in an orthographic assembly drawing, in which the parts are depicted in their assembled positions. The views are sectioned to make them easier to understand.

Figure 22.26 shows a pulley assembly in an exploded pictorial assembly drawing, illustrating how the parts fit together, leaving no doubt as to how the parts relate to each other. Part numbers are given in balloons to complete the drawing.

22.8 Freehand Working Drawings

A freehand sketch can serve the same purpose as an instrument drawing, provided that the part is sufficiently simple and that the essential dimensions are shown (**Fig. 22.27**). Use the same principles of making working drawings with instruments when making working drawings freehand. A sketch can be made quickly, and it can be made in the field, fabrication shop, or other locations where drafting-room instruments are not readily available.

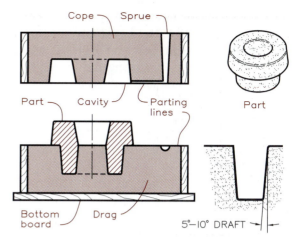

22.28 The left part is a blank that has been forged. It will look like the part on the right after it has been machined.

22.9 Forged Parts and Castings

The two versions of a part shown in **Fig. 22.28** illustrate the difference between a part that has been forged into shape (sometimes called a **blank**) and its final state after the forging has been machined. Recall from Chapter 18 that a forging is a rough form made by hammering (forging) the metal into shape or pressing it between two forms (called dies). The forged part

22.29 A two-part sand mold is used to produce a casting. A draft of from 5° to 10° is needed to permit withdrawal of the pattern from the sand. Some machining is usually required to finish various features of the casting within specified tolerances.

is then machined to its specified finished dimensions and tolerances so it will function as intended.

A casting (**Fig. 22.29**), like a forging, must be machined so that it too will fit and function with

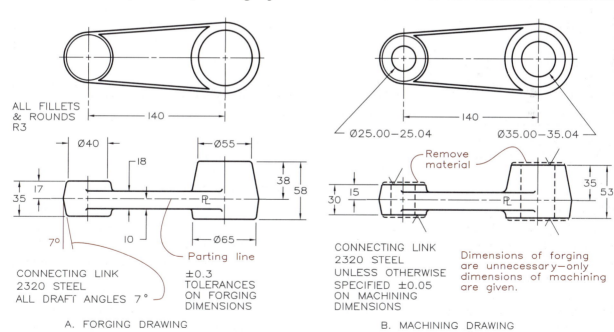

22.30 These separate working drawings, (A) a forging drawing and (B) a machining drawing, give the details of the same part. Often, this information is combined into a single drawing.

other parts when assembled; therefore additional material is added to the areas where metal will be removed by the machining processes. As covered in Chapter 18, castings are formed by pouring molten metal into a mold formed by a pattern that is slightly larger than the finished part to compensate for metal shrinkage. For the pattern to be removable from the sand that forms the mold, its sides have a taper, called a **draft**, of about 5° to 10°.

Some industries require, in addition to preparing drawings of forged and case parts (**Fig. 22.30A**), that supplementary drawings be made to specify the machining operations (**Fig. 22.30B**). More often, however, the parts are detailed on the regular working drawing with the understanding that the features that are to be machined by operations such as grinding or shaping are made oversize by the fabrication shop.

Problems

The following problems will provide exercises in the application of the principles required in making working drawings. You should make rapid, freehand sketches of the views before drawing them with instruments or computer in order to determine the appropriate layout of each sheet. Material covered in all of the previous chapters must be applied in completing these assignments.

Working Drawing Practice

Reproduce the drawings shown in **Figs. 22.31–22.37**, as directed. The purpose of these assignments is to provide experience in laying out a working drawing and improving your draftsmanship on the board or at the computer.

22.31 Duplicate the working drawing of the base plate mount on a size B sheet. (*Courtesy of Omark Industries, Inc.*)

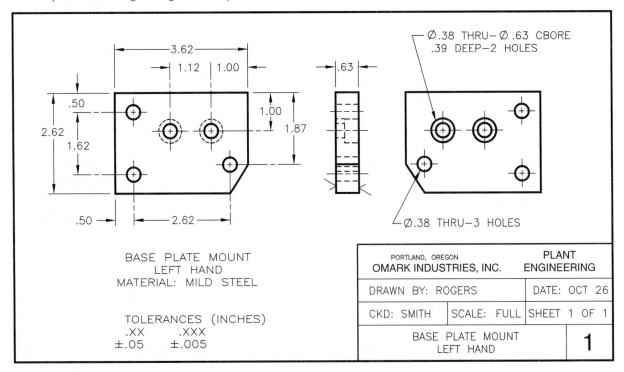

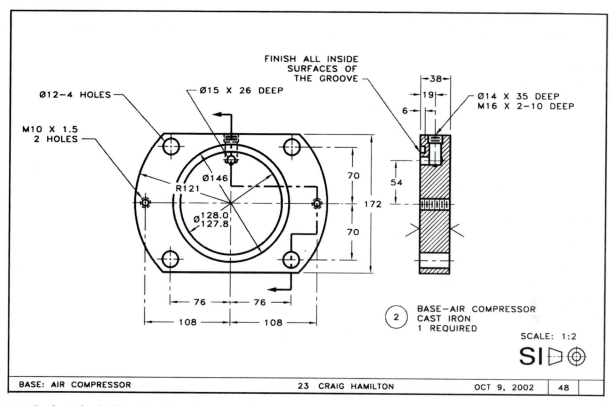

FINISH ALL INSIDE
SURFACES OF
THE GROOVE

Ø15 X 26 DEEP

Ø12–4 HOLES

M10 X 1.5
2 HOLES

Ø14 X 35 DEEP
M16 X 2–10 DEEP

38

19

6

Ø146

R121

Ø128.0
Ø127.8

54

70

70

172

76

76

108

108

2 BASE–AIR COMPRESSOR
CAST IRON
1 REQUIRED

SCALE: 1:2

SI ⮞ ⊚

BASE: AIR COMPRESSOR   23 CRAIG HAMILTON   OCT 9, 2002   48

22.32 Duplicate the detail drawing of the air compressor base on a size B sheet.

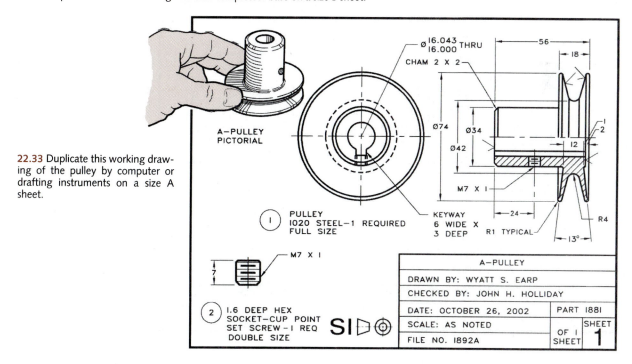

22.33 Duplicate this working drawing of the pulley by computer or drafting instruments on a size A sheet.

A–PULLEY
PICTORIAL

Ø 16.043 / 16.000 THRU
CHAM 2 X 2

56

18

Ø74

Ø34

Ø42

12

M7 X 1

24

R1 TYPICAL

R4

13°

1 PULLEY
1020 STEEL–1 REQUIRED
FULL SIZE

KEYWAY
6 WIDE X
3 DEEP

M7 X 1

7

2 1.6 DEEP HEX
SOCKET–CUP POINT
SET SCREW–1 REQ
DOUBLE SIZE

SI ⮞ ⊚

A–PULLEY	
DRAWN BY: WYATT S. EARP	
CHECKED BY: JOHN H. HOLLIDAY	
DATE: OCTOBER 26, 2002	PART 1881
SCALE: AS NOTED	OF 1 SHEET
FILE NO. 1892A	SHEET 1

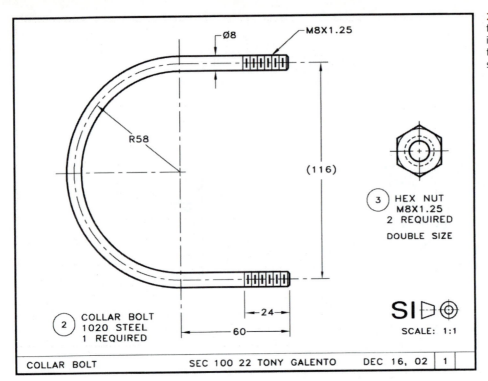

22.34 Sheet 1 of 3: Duplicate these full-size working drawings and assembly (in mm) of the collar bolt on size A sheets.

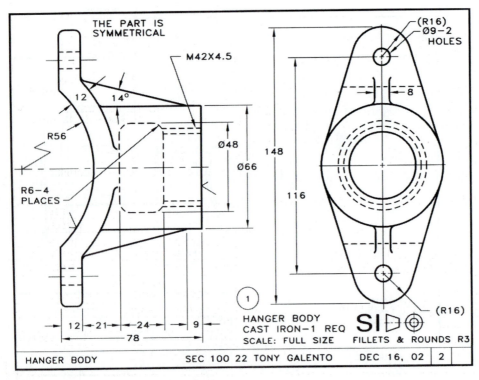

22.35 Sheet 2 of 3: Duplicate this second sheet of the pipe hanger working drawing that shows the hanger body.

22.36 Duplicate this third sheet of the pipe hanger working drawing that gives an assembly which shows how the parts are put together.

22.37 The ball crank has been detailed in the working drawing below. Duplicate the working drawing on a size B sheet. On a second size B sheet, make an assembly drawing of the parts.

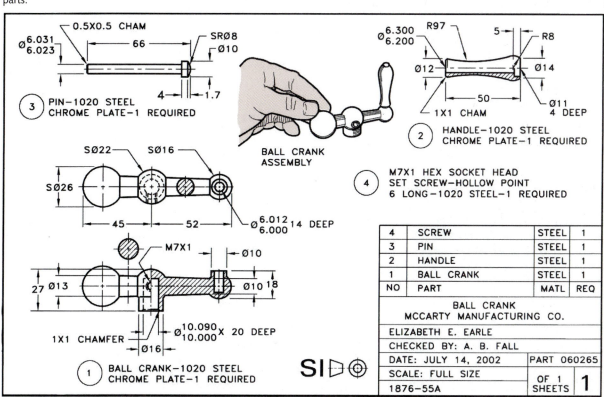

ASSEMBLY—HANGER
SCALE: FULL SIZE

3	HEX NUT	2	CI
2	COLLAR BOLT	1	STEEL
1	BODY	1	CI
NO	NAME	REQ	MATL

HANGER ASSEMBLY   SEC 100 22 TONY GALENTO   DEC 16, 02   3

0.5X0.5 CHAM
Ø 6.031 / 6.023
66
SRØ8
Ø10
4 — 1.7

③ PIN—1020 STEEL
CHROME PLATE—1 REQUIRED

SØ22   SØ16
SØ26
45   52
Ø 6.012 / 6.000 14 DEEP

M7X1
Ø10
27 Ø13
Ø10 18
1X1 CHAMFER
Ø 10.090 / 10.000 X 20 DEEP
Ø16

① BALL CRANK—1020 STEEL
CHROME PLATE—1 REQUIRED

BALL CRANK
ASSEMBLY

Ø 6.300 / 6.200   R97   5 —   R8
Ø12   Ø14
50   Ø11
1X1 CHAM   4 DEEP

② HANDLE—1020 STEEL
CHROME PLATE—1 REQUIRED

④ M7X1 HEX SOCKET HEAD
SET SCREW—HOLLOW POINT
6 LONG—1020 STEEL—1 REQUIRED

4	SCREW	STEEL	1
3	PIN	STEEL	1
2	HANDLE	STEEL	1
1	BALL CRANK	STEEL	1
NO	PART	MATL	REQ

BALL CRANK
MCCARTY MANUFACTURING CO.

ELIZABETH E. EARLE

CHECKED BY: A. B. FALL

DATE: JULY 14, 2002   PART 060265

SCALE: FULL SIZE

1876—55A   OF 1 SHEETS   1

Working drawings: Single parts

Make working drawings of the assigned parts, providing the necessary information, notes, and dimensions. In cases where dimensions may be missing, approximate them using your own judgment.

The determination of the proper scale, selection of sheet sizes, and the choice and positioning of the views on the drawing sheet will be a major portion of all problem assignments. The making of freehand, preliminary sketches will be very helpful in making these decisions and saving layout time.

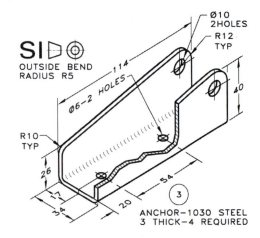

22.38 Size A sheet.

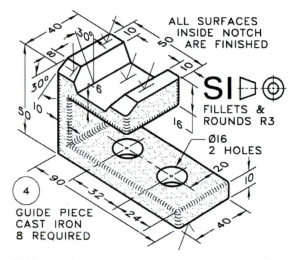

22.39 Size B sheet.

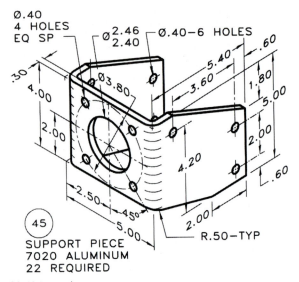

22.40 Size B sheet.

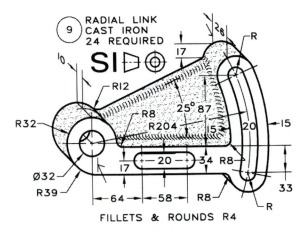

22.41 Size B sheet.

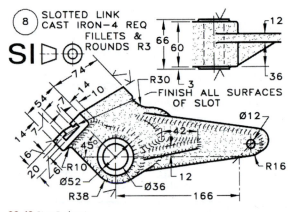

22.42 Size B sheet.

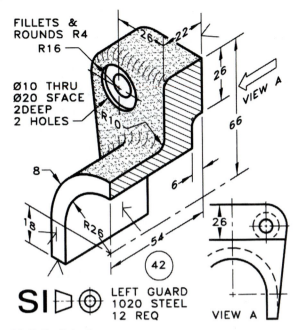

FILLETS & ROUNDS R4
R16
Ø10 THRU
Ø20 SFACE
2DEEP
2 HOLES
R10
8
18
R26
26
22
26
66
6
54
42
VIEW A
26

SI ⊳⊙ LEFT GUARD
1020 STEEL
12 REQ

VIEW A

22.43 Size B sheet.

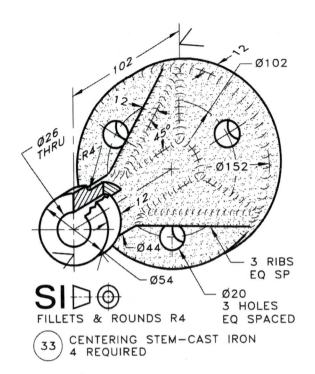

102
12
Ø102
Ø26 THRU
12
R4
45°
Ø152
12
Ø44
Ø54
3 RIBS EQ SP
Ø20 3 HOLES EQ SPACED

SI ⊳⊙
FILLETS & ROUNDS R4

33 CENTERING STEM-CAST IRON
4 REQUIRED

22.45 Size B sheet.

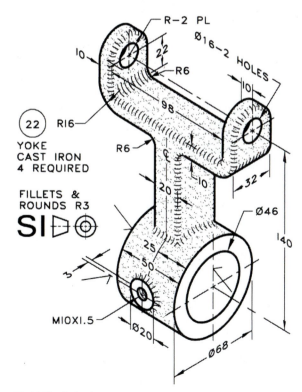

R-2 PL
Ø16-2 HOLES
10
22
R6
10
98
22 R16
R6
32
YOKE
CAST IRON
4 REQUIRED
20
10
140
Ø46
FILLETS & ROUNDS R3
SI ⊳⊙
25
50
3
MIOXI.5
Ø20
Ø68

22.44 Size B sheet.

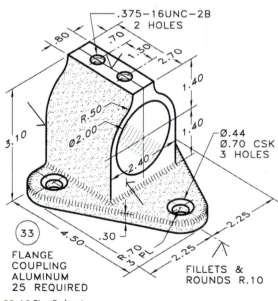

.375-16UNC-2B
2 HOLES
.80
.70
1.30
2.70
1.40
R.50
Ø2.00
2.40
1.40
Ø.44
Ø.70 CSK
3 HOLES
3.10
4.50
.30
R.70
3 PL
2.25
2.25
FILLETS & ROUNDS R.10

33 FLANGE
COUPLING
ALUMINUM
25 REQUIRED

22.46 Size B sheet.

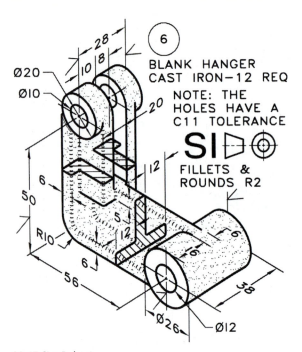

22.47 Size B sheet.

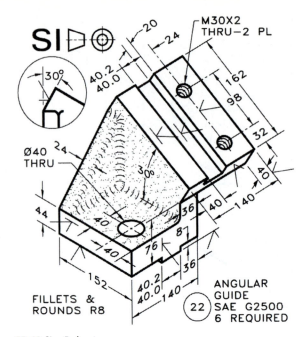

22.49 Size B sheet.

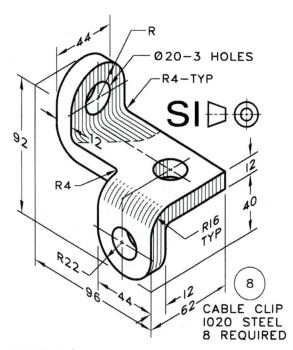

22.48 Size B sheet.

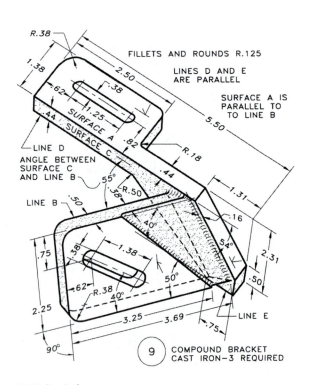

22.50 Size B sheet.

Working Drawings: Multiple Parts

Make working drawings by hand or by computer, as assigned, of the products consisting of multiple parts shown in **Figs. 22.51–22.73** on the suggested sheet sizes. Include a title block, dimensions, and notes necessary for manufacturing the parts. Make an assembly drawing that shows how the parts fit together. More than one sheet may be required.

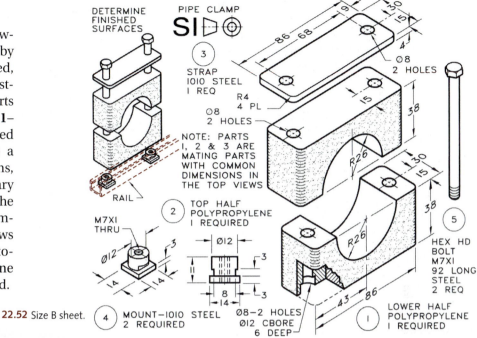

22.52 Size B sheet.

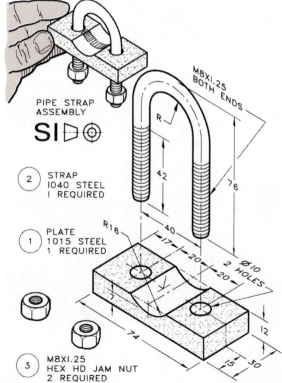

22.51 Size B sheet.

22.53 Size B sheet.

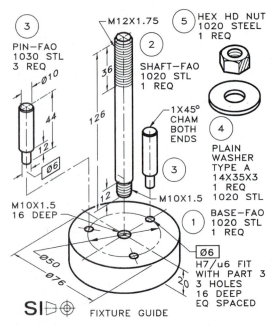

PIN—FAO
1030 STL
3 REQ
∅10
44
12
∅6
M10X1.5
16 DEEP
∅50
∅76
20

M12X1.75

SHAFT—FAO
1020 STL
1 REQ

36
126

1X45°
CHAM
BOTH
ENDS

12

M10X1.5

HEX HD NUT
1020 STEEL
1 REQ

PLAIN
WASHER
TYPE A
14X35X3
1 REQ
1020 STL

BASE—FAO
1020 STL
1 REQ

∅6
H7/u6 FIT
WITH PART 3
3 HOLES
16 DEEP
EQ SPACED

SI

FIXTURE GUIDE

22.54 Make working drawings with an assembly drawing of this adjustable swing stop on size B sheets.

22.57 (Facing page) Make a working drawing with an assembly with a parts list of this adjustable milling stop on size B sheets. The column (part 3) that fits into the base (part 1) must be held in position with a set screw that passes through the end of the base (part 1) and bears against part 3. Select a proper screw for this application and specify it on your working drawing.

22.58 (Facing page) Make a working drawing with an assembly of the rocker tool post on size B sheets. Give a parts list on the assembly sheet using good drawing and dimensioning practices.

22.59 (Facing page) Make a drawing with an assembly of the flange jig on size B sheets. Give a parts list on the assembly sheet using good drawing and dimensioning practices.

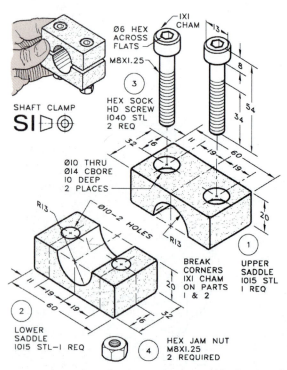

∅6 HEX
ACROSS
FLATS

M8X1.25

IXI
CHAM
13

8
54
34

HEX SOCK
HD SCREW
1040 STL
2 REQ

SHAFT CLAMP
SI

∅10 THRU
∅14 CBORE
10 DEEP
2 PLACES

32
16
11
19
19
60
20

R13
∅10—2 HOLES
R13

11
19
60
19
16
32

BREAK
CORNERS
IXI CHAM
ON PARTS
1 & 2

UPPER
SADDLE
1015 STL
1 REQ

LOWER
SADDLE
1015 STL—1 REQ

HEX JAM NUT
M8X1.25
2 REQUIRED

22.55 Make working drawings with an assembly drawing of this flange jig on size B sheets.

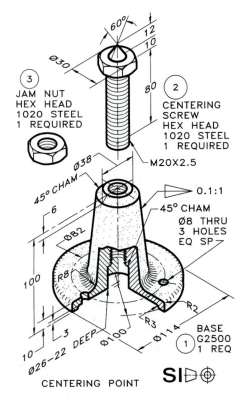

60°
12
10
∅30

80

JAM NUT
HEX HEAD
1020 STEEL
1 REQUIRED

CENTERING
SCREW
HEX HEAD
1020 STEEL
1 REQUIRED

M20X2.5

∅38
45° CHAM
6

0.1:1

45° CHAM
∅8 THRU
3 HOLES
EQ SP

∅82
R8
100

R2
R3

10
∅26—22 DEEP
3
∅100
∅114

BASE
G2500
1 REQ

CENTERING POINT
SI

22.56 Make working drawings with an assembly drawing of this pipe clamp on size B sheets.

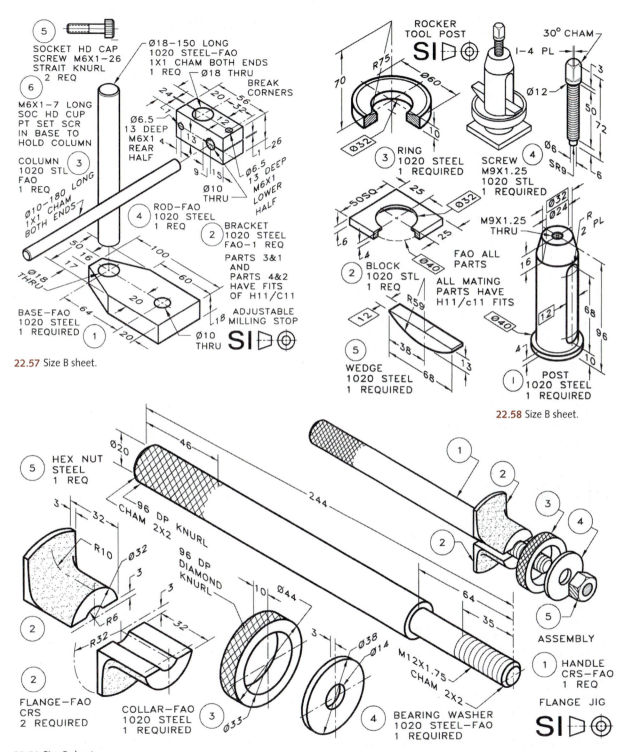

5 SOCKET HD CAP SCREW M6X1–26 STRAIT KNURL 2 REQ

6 M6X1–7 LONG SOC HD CUP PT SET SCR IN BASE TO HOLD COLUMN

COLUMN 1020 STL FAO 1 REQ **3**

Ø10–180 LONG 1X1 CHAM BOTH ENDS

Ø18–150 LONG 1020 STEEL–FAO 1X1 CHAM BOTH ENDS 1 REQ

Ø18 THRU

BREAK CORNERS

24
20
56
32
12
26
13
M6X1
REAR HALF
Ø6.5 13 DEEP
9
15
Ø6.5 13 DEEP M6X1 LOWER HALF
Ø10 THRU

ROD–FAO 1020 STEEL 1 REQ **4**

BRACKET 1020 STEEL FAO–1 REQ **2**

PARTS 3&1 AND PARTS 4&2 HAVE FITS OF H11/C11

50
16
17
100
60
20
64
20
Ø18 THRU
18
Ø10 THRU

BASE–FAO 1020 STEEL 1 REQUIRED **1**

ADJUSTABLE MILLING STOP SI

22.57 Size B sheet.

ROCKER TOOL POST SI

R75
70
Ø60
Ø32
10

RING 1020 STEEL 1 REQUIRED **3**

30° CHAM
I–4 PL
Ø12
3
50
72
Ø6
SR9
6

SCREW M9X1.25 1020 STL 1 REQUIRED **4**

50SQ
25
Ø32
6
Ø40
4

BLOCK 1020 STL 1 REQ **2**

FAO ALL PARTS

ALL MATING PARTS HAVE H11/c11 FITS

M9X1.25 THRU
Ø32
Ø24
R 2 PL
16
Ø40
12
68
96
4
10

R59
12
38
13
68

WEDGE 1020 STEEL 1 REQUIRED **5**

POST 1020 STEEL 1 REQUIRED **1**

22.58 Size B sheet.

5 HEX NUT STEEL 1 REQ

Ø20
46
3
32
R10
Ø32
96 DP KNURL CHAM 2X2
244
96 DP DIAMOND KNURL
R6
R32
3
3
32
10
Ø44
3
Ø38
Ø14
64
35
M12X1.75 CHAM 2X2
Ø33

2 FLANGE–FAO CRS 2 REQUIRED

2

3 COLLAR–FAO 1020 STEEL 1 REQUIRED

4 BEARING WASHER 1020 STEEL–FAO 1 REQUIRED

1
2
3
4
2
5

ASSEMBLY

1 HANDLE CRS–FAO 1 REQ

FLANGE JIG SI

22.59 Size B sheet.

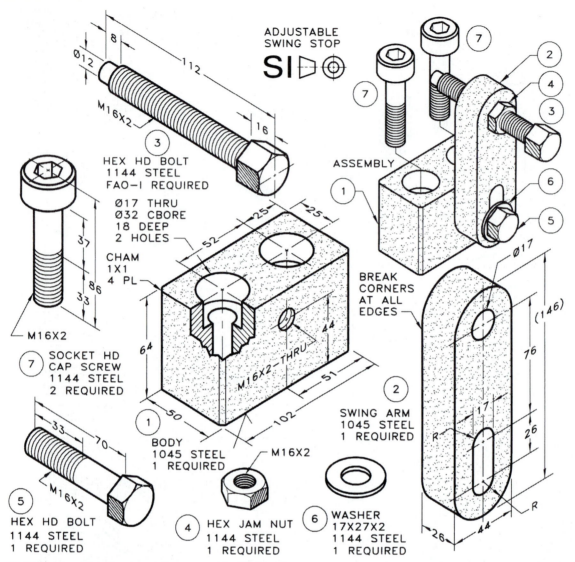

ADJUSTABLE SWING STOP

SI ▷◯

Ø12
8
112
16
M16X2

3 HEX HD BOLT
1144 STEEL
FAO–I REQUIRED

Ø17 THRU
Ø32 CBORE
18 DEEP
2 HOLES

CHAM
1X1
4 PL

37
86
33
M16X2

7 SOCKET HD
CAP SCREW
1144 STEEL
2 REQUIRED

52
25
25
64
44
M16X2–THRU
51
50
102
1 BODY
1045 STEEL
1 REQUIRED

M16X2

33
70
M16X2

5 HEX HD BOLT
1144 STEEL
1 REQUIRED

4 HEX JAM NUT
1144 STEEL
1 REQUIRED

6 WASHER
17X27X2
1144 STEEL
1 REQUIRED

ASSEMBLY

7
2
4
3
1
6
5

BREAK
CORNERS
AT ALL
EDGES

Ø17
(146)
76
17
26
R
R
26
44

2 SWING ARM
1045 STEEL
1 REQUIRED

22.60 Make working drawings with an assembly drawing of this adjustable swing stop on size B sheets.

Thought Questions

1. What is the purpose of the washer (part 6) in this assembly?

2. Why is there a slot in the swing arm (part 2) instead of circular hole?

3. Why did the designer of this assembly use both socket-head cap screws and hex-head cap screws instead of using one type or the other?

4. When assembled, what is the range of adjustment from the upper surface of the body (part 1) and the centerline of the hex-head bolt (part 3)?

5. What is the maximum distance that the 12 DIA end of the hex-head bolt (part 3) can extend beyond the face of swing arm (part 2)?

6. Write a paragraph to verbally give a description of either part 1 or part 2.

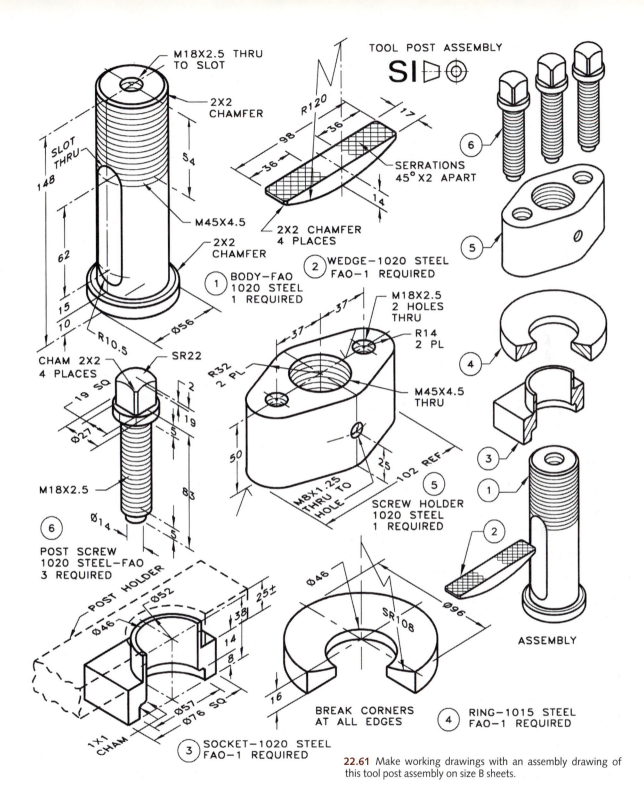

M18X2.5 THRU
TO SLOT

2X2
CHAMFER

TOOL POST ASSEMBLY

SI

R120

98

36

36

54

SLOT
THRU

148

M45X4.5

2X2
CHAMFER

62

2X2 CHAMFER
4 PLACES

2X2
CHAMFER

15

10

R10.5

Ø56

SERRATIONS
45°X2 APART

17

14

6

5

① BODY−FAO
1020 STEEL
1 REQUIRED

② WEDGE−1020 STEEL
FAO−1 REQUIRED

SR22

CHAM 2X2
4 PLACES

19 SQ

2

M18X2.5
2 HOLES
THRU

37

37

Ø27

19

R14
2 PL

R32
2 PL

5

M45X4.5
THRU

4

M18X2.5

83

50

3

5

102 REF

1

Ø14

M8X1.25
THRU TO
HOLE

25

5

5

SCREW HOLDER
1020 STEEL
1 REQUIRED

2

6

POST SCREW
1020 STEEL−FAO
3 REQUIRED

POST HOLDER

Ø52

25±

Ø46

38

Ø46

ASSEMBLY

Ø96

14

8

SR108

Ø57

16

Ø76 SQ

1X1
CHAM

③ SOCKET−1020 STEEL
FAO−1 REQUIRED

BREAK CORNERS
AT ALL EDGES

④ RING−1015 STEEL
FAO−1 REQUIRED

22.61 Make working drawings with an assembly drawing of
this tool post assembly on size B sheets.

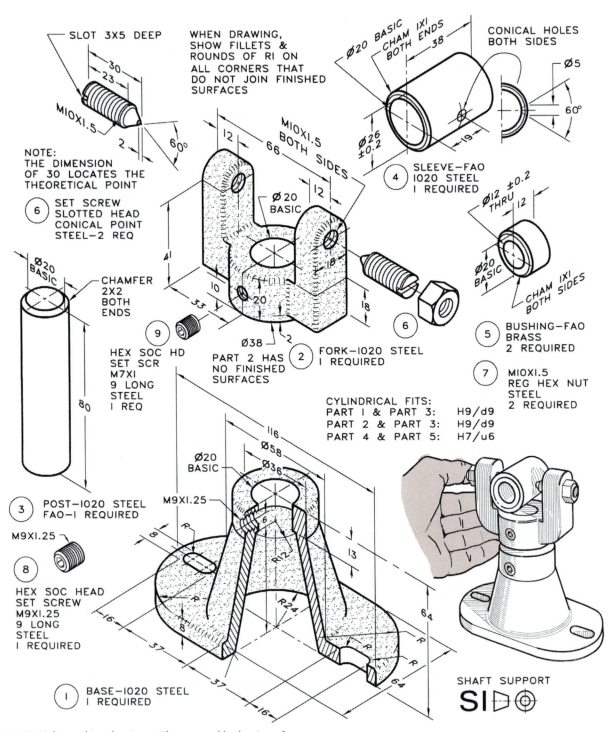

SLOT 3X5 DEEP

30
23

M10X1.5

2

60°

NOTE:
THE DIMENSION
OF 30 LOCATES THE
THEORETICAL POINT

⑥ SET SCREW
SLOTTED HEAD
CONICAL POINT
STEEL-2 REQ

WHEN DRAWING,
SHOW FILLETS &
ROUNDS OF RI ON
ALL CORNERS THAT
DO NOT JOIN FINISHED
SURFACES

M10X1.5
BOTH SIDES

12
66

Ø20
BASIC

12

41

10

20

33

18

Ø38

2

PART 2 HAS
NO FINISHED
SURFACES

② FORK-1020 STEEL
1 REQUIRED

Ø20 BASIC
CHAM IXI
BOTH ENDS

38

CONICAL HOLES
BOTH SIDES

Ø5

60°

Ø26
±0.2

19

④ SLEEVE-FAO
1020 STEEL
1 REQUIRED

Ø12 ±0.2
THRU

12

Ø20
BASIC

CHAM IXI
BOTH SIDES

⑤ BUSHING-FAO
BRASS
2 REQUIRED

⑦ M10X1.5
REG HEX NUT
STEEL
2 REQUIRED

Ø20
BASIC

CHAMFER
2X2
BOTH
ENDS

80

⑨ HEX SOC HD
SET SCR
M7X1
9 LONG
STEEL
1 REQ

⑥

CYLINDRICAL FITS:
PART 1 & PART 3:   H9/d9
PART 2 & PART 3:   H9/d9
PART 4 & PART 5:   H7/u6

③ POST-1020 STEEL
FAO-1 REQUIRED

M9X1.25

⑧ HEX SOC HEAD
SET SCREW
M9X1.25
9 LONG
STEEL
1 REQUIRED

Ø20
BASIC

M9X1.25

116
Ø58
Ø36

R

6

R12

13

R24

R

R

R

64

8

16

37

37

16

8

64

① BASE-1020 STEEL
1 REQUIRED

SHAFT SUPPORT

SI

22.62 Make working drawings with an assembly drawing of
this shaft support on size B sheets.

354 • CHAPTER 22   WORKING DRAWINGS

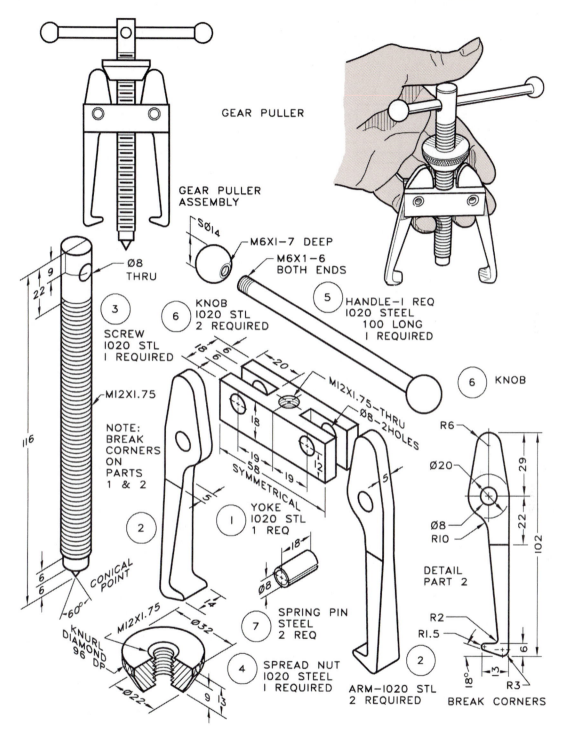

GEAR PULLER

GEAR PULLER
ASSEMBLY

SØ14

M6X1-7 DEEP

M6X1-6
BOTH ENDS

Ø8
THRU

(3)
SCREW
1020 STL
1 REQUIRED

(6) KNOB
1020 STL
2 REQUIRED

(5) HANDLE—1 REQ
1020 STEEL
100 LONG
1 REQUIRED

(6) KNOB

9
22

M12X1.75

116

NOTE:
BREAK
CORNERS
ON
PARTS
1 & 2

18
6
6

20

M12X1.75—THRU
Ø8-2HOLES

18

19

19
58
12
SYMMETRICAL

R6

Ø20

Ø8
R10

DETAIL
PART 2

(2)

(1) YOKE
1020 STL
1 REQ

29

22

102

6
6

CONICAL
POINT

-60°

18
Ø8

(7) SPRING PIN
STEEL
2 REQ

5

R2

R1.5

R3

18°

13

6

KNURL
DIAMOND
96 DP

M12X1.75

Ø32

(4) SPREAD NUT
1020 STEEL
1 REQUIRED

(2)
ARM—1020 STL
2 REQUIRED

BREAK CORNERS

Ø22

9 13

22.63 Make working drawings with an assembly drawing of
this gear puller on size B sheets.

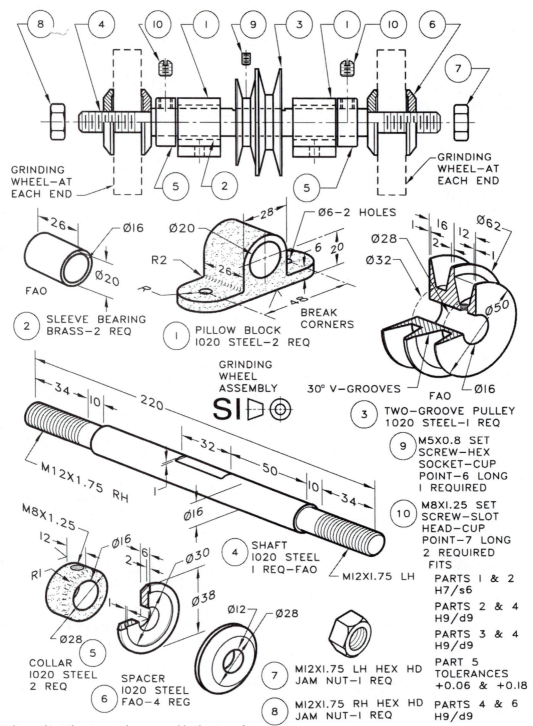

GRINDING
WHEEL—AT
EACH END

GRINDING
WHEEL—AT
EACH END

GRINDING
WHEEL—AT
EACH END

26
Ø16
Ø20
FAO

2 SLEEVE BEARING
BRASS—2 REQ

28
Ø20
R2
26
Ø6—2 HOLES
6 20
48
BREAK
CORNERS

1 PILLOW BLOCK
1020 STEEL—2 REQ

GRINDING
WHEEL
ASSEMBLY

SI

30° V—GROOVES

16
2
12
Ø62
Ø28
Ø32
Ø50
Ø16
FAO

3 TWO—GROOVE PULLEY
1020 STEEL—1 REQ

34 10
220
32
50
10 34
Ø16
M12X1.75 RH
M12X1.75 LH

4 SHAFT
1020 STEEL
1 REQ—FAO

9 M5X0.8 SET
SCREW—HEX
SOCKET—CUP
POINT—6 LONG
1 REQUIRED

10 M8X1.25 SET
SCREW—SLOT
HEAD—CUP
POINT—7 LONG
2 REQUIRED

FITS

PARTS 1 & 2
H7/s6

PARTS 2 & 4
H9/d9

PARTS 3 & 4
H9/d9

PART 5
TOLERANCES
+0.06 & +0.18

PARTS 4 & 6
H9/d9

M8X1.25
12
Ø16
R1
Ø28
Ø16 6
2
Ø30
Ø38

5 COLLAR
1020 STEEL
2 REQ

6 SPACER
1020 STEEL
FAO—4 REQ

Ø12 Ø28

7 M12X1.75 LH HEX HD
JAM NUT—1 REQ

8 M12X1.75 RH HEX HD
JAM NUT—1 REQ

22.64 Make working drawings with an assembly drawing of
this grinding wheel assembly on size B sheets.

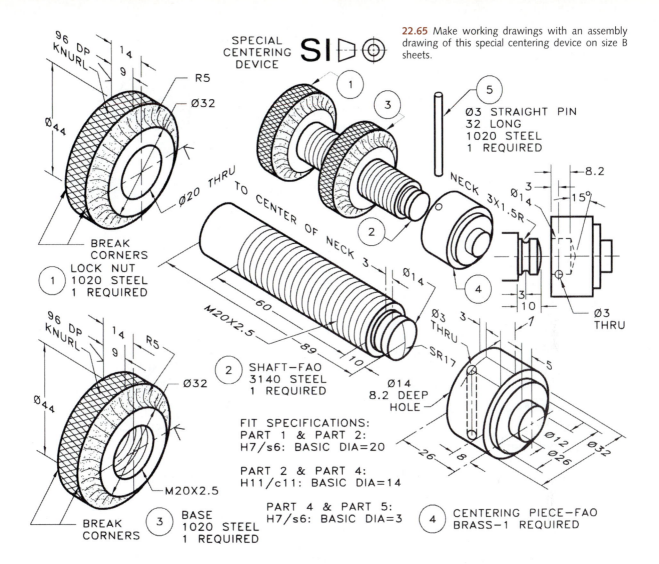

SPECIAL CENTERING DEVICE SI ▷ ◉

22.65 Make working drawings with an assembly drawing of this special centering device on size B sheets.

96 DP KNURL

Ø44

Ø32

R5

Ø20 THRU TO CENTER OF NECK 3

BREAK CORNERS

① LOCK NUT
1020 STEEL
1 REQUIRED

①

③

⑤
Ø3 STRAIGHT PIN
32 LONG
1020 STEEL
1 REQUIRED

NECK 3X1.5R

Ø14

②

Ø14

④

8.2

Ø14

15°

3
10

Ø3
THRU

96 DP KNURL

Ø44

Ø32

R5

M20X2.5

BREAK CORNERS

③ BASE
1020 STEEL
1 REQUIRED

M20X2.5

60

89

10

② SHAFT—FAO
3140 STEEL
1 REQUIRED

Ø14
8.2 DEEP
HOLE

Ø3
THRU

3

SR17

1

5

Ø14
8.2 DEEP HOLE

26

8

Ø12

Ø26

Ø32

FIT SPECIFICATIONS:
PART 1 & PART 2:
H7/s6: BASIC DIA=20

PART 2 & PART 4:
H11/c11: BASIC DIA=14

PART 4 & PART 5:
H7/s6: BASIC DIA=3

④ CENTERING PIECE—FAO
BRASS—1 REQUIRED

Thought Questions

1. What conversion factor would you use to convert the metric dimensions to English units?

2. Why is knurling given on parts 1 and 3? Why was knurling not given on part 4?

3. Why were part 1 and part 2 not designed with threads for attachment to each other?

4. When assembled, will part 4 rotate about the end of part 2? Determine and explain why it attaches as it does.

5. Why was the fit between parts 4 and 5 selected to be H7/s6 instead of H11/c11?

6. What would be the approximate weight of the total assembly if all materials were assumed to weigh 490 lbs per cu. ft.?

7. Can you explain why parts 1 and 3 were designed with bosses (raised surfaces around the holes) as shown?

8. Which of the parts can be specified on a working drawing by a note without a drawing?

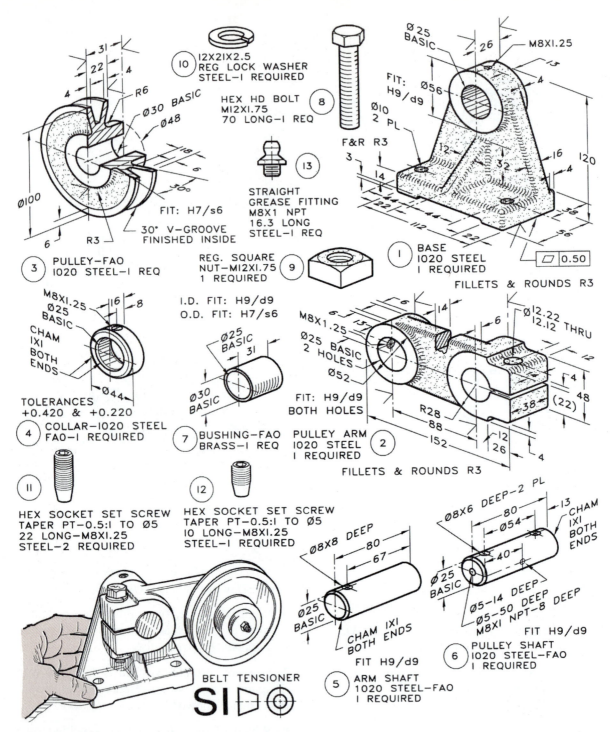

○10 12X21X2.5
REG LOCK WASHER
STEEL—1 REQUIRED

HEX HD BOLT
M12X1.75
70 LONG—1 REQ ○8

STRAIGHT
GREASE FITTING
M8X1 NPT
16.3 LONG
STEEL—1 REQ ○13

○3 PULLEY—FAO
1020 STEEL—1 REQ

30° V—GROOVE
FINISHED INSIDE
FIT: H7/s6
Ø30 BASIC
Ø48
Ø100
R6
R3

REG. SQUARE
NUT—M12X1.75
1 REQUIRED ○9

Ø25
BASIC
FIT:
H9/d9
Ø56
Ø10
2 PL
F&R R3
M8X1.25

○1 BASE
1020 STEEL
1 REQUIRED

FILLETS & ROUNDS R3
□ 0.50

M8X1.25
Ø25
BASIC
CHAM
1X1
BOTH
ENDS
Ø44
16
8

TOLERANCES
+0.420 & +0.220
○4 COLLAR—1020 STEEL
FAO—1 REQUIRED

I.D. FIT: H9/d9
O.D. FIT: H7/s6
Ø25
BASIC
31
Ø30
BASIC
○7 BUSHING—FAO
BRASS—1 REQ

M8X1.25
Ø25 BASIC
2 HOLES
Ø52
FIT: H9/d9
BOTH HOLES
R28
88
152
Ø12.22 THRU
12.12
4
48
38
(22)
12
26
4
PULLEY ARM
1020 STEEL
1 REQUIRED ○2

FILLETS & ROUNDS R3

○11 HEX SOCKET SET SCREW
TAPER PT—0.5:1 TO Ø5
22 LONG—M8X1.25
STEEL—2 REQUIRED

○12 HEX SOCKET SET SCREW
TAPER PT—0.5:1 TO Ø5
10 LONG—M8X1.25
STEEL—1 REQUIRED

Ø8X8 DEEP
80
67
Ø25
BASIC
CHAM 1X1
BOTH ENDS
FIT H9/d9
○5 ARM SHAFT
1020 STEEL—FAO
1 REQUIRED

Ø8X6 DEEP—2 PL
80
Ø54
40
13
CHAM
1X1
BOTH
ENDS
Ø25
BASIC
Ø5—14 DEEP
Ø5—50 DEEP
M8X1 NPT—8 DEEP
FIT H9/d9
○6 PULLEY SHAFT
1020 STEEL—FAO
1 REQUIRED

BELT TENSIONER
SI □▷ ◉

22.66 Make working drawings with an assembly drawing of
this belt tensioner device on size B sheets.

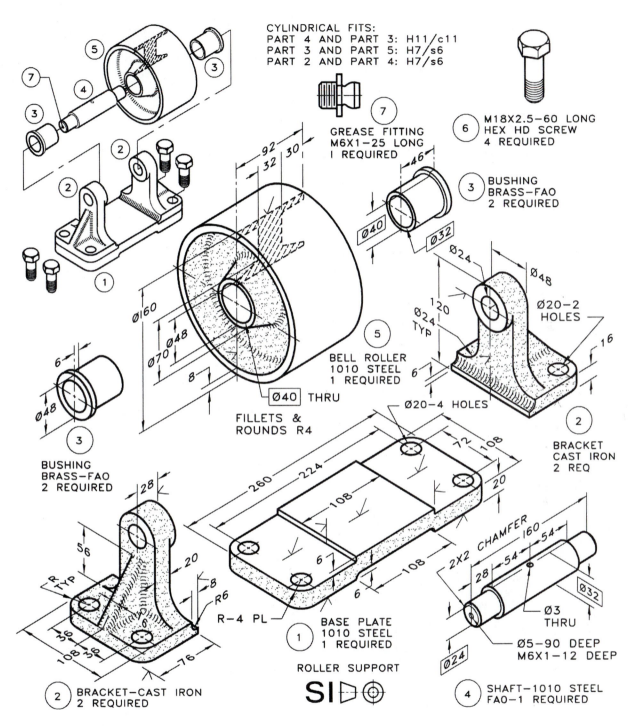

CYLINDRICAL FITS:
PART 4 AND PART 3: H11/c11
PART 3 AND PART 5: H7/s6
PART 2 AND PART 4: H7/s6

⑦ GREASE FITTING
M6X1−25 LONG
1 REQUIRED

⑥ M18X2.5−60 LONG
HEX HD SCREW
4 REQUIRED

③ BUSHING
BRASS−FAO
2 REQUIRED

Ø24
Ø48
Ø20−2
HOLES
120
Ø24
TYP
6
16
② BRACKET
CAST IRON
2 REQ

92
32 30
46
Ø40
Ø32

Ø160
Ø48
Ø70
8
⑤ BELL ROLLER
1010 STEEL
1 REQUIRED
Ø40 THRU
FILLETS &
ROUNDS R4

6
Ø48
③ BUSHING
BRASS−FAO
2 REQUIRED

28
56
R TYP
20
8
R6
36
108 36
6
76
② BRACKET−CAST IRON
2 REQUIRED

Ø20−4 HOLES
72 108
260 224
108
20
6
6
R−4 PL
① BASE PLATE
1010 STEEL
1 REQUIRED
ROLLER SUPPORT
SI▷⊙

2X2 CHAMFER
160
28 54 54
Ø3
THRU
Ø24
Ø5−90 DEEP
M6X1−12 DEEP
Ø32
④ SHAFT−1010 STEEL
FAO−1 REQUIRED

22.67 Make working drawings with an assembly drawing of
this pulley support on size B sheets.

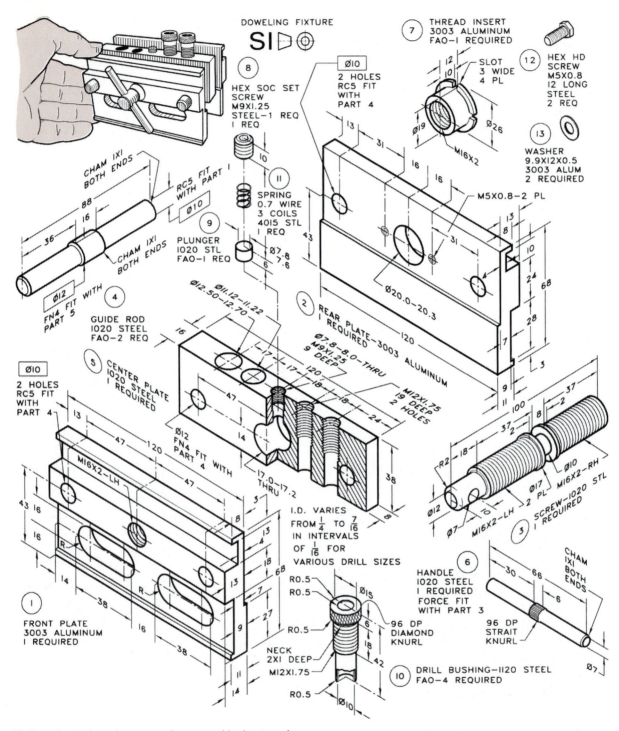

DOWELING FIXTURE

SI ▷◉

8 HEX SOC SET SCREW M9X1.25 STEEL—1 REQ 1 REQ

11 SPRING 0.7 WIRE 3 COILS 4015 STL 1 REQ

9 PLUNGER 1020 STL FAO-1 REQ

Ø10 2 HOLES RC5 FIT WITH PART 4

7 THREAD INSERT 3003 ALUMINUM FAO-1 REQUIRED

SLOT 3 WIDE 4 PL

12 HEX HD SCREW M5X0.8 12 LONG STEEL 2 REQ

13 WASHER 9.9X12X0.5 3003 ALUM 2 REQUIRED

M5X0.8-2 PL

2 REAR PLATE-3003 ALUMINUM 1 REQUIRED

Ø20.0-20.3

CHAM 1X1 BOTH ENDS

RC5 FIT WITH PART 1

Ø10

CHAM 1X1 BOTH ENDS

Ø12 FN4 FIT WITH PART 5

4 GUIDE ROD 1020 STEEL FAO-2 REQ

Ø10 2 HOLES RC5 FIT WITH PART 4

5 CENTER PLATE 1020 STEEL 1 REQUIRED

Ø12 FN4 FIT WITH PART 4

Ø12.50-12.70

Ø11.12—11.22

Ø7.8-8.0-THRU M9X1.25 9 DEEP

M12X1.75 19 DEEP 2 HOLES

17.0-17.2 THRU

3 SCREW-1020 STL 1 REQUIRED

M16X2-RH Ø10 Ø17 2 PL M16X2-LH Ø7 Ø12

MI6X2-LH

M16X2-LH

1 FRONT PLATE 3003 ALUMINUM 1 REQUIRED

I.D. VARIES FROM ¼ TO 7/16 IN INTERVALS OF 1/16 FOR VARIOUS DRILL SIZES

R0.5 R0.5 R0.5 R0.5

Ø15 96 DP DIAMOND KNURL

NECK 2X1 DEEP M12X1.75

Ø10

6 HANDLE 1020 STEEL 1 REQUIRED FORCE FIT WITH PART 3

CHAM 1X1 BOTH ENDS

96 DP STRAIT KNURL

Ø7

10 DRILL BUSHING—1120 STEEL FAO-4 REQUIRED

22.68 Make working drawings with an assembly drawing of this doweling on size B sheets.

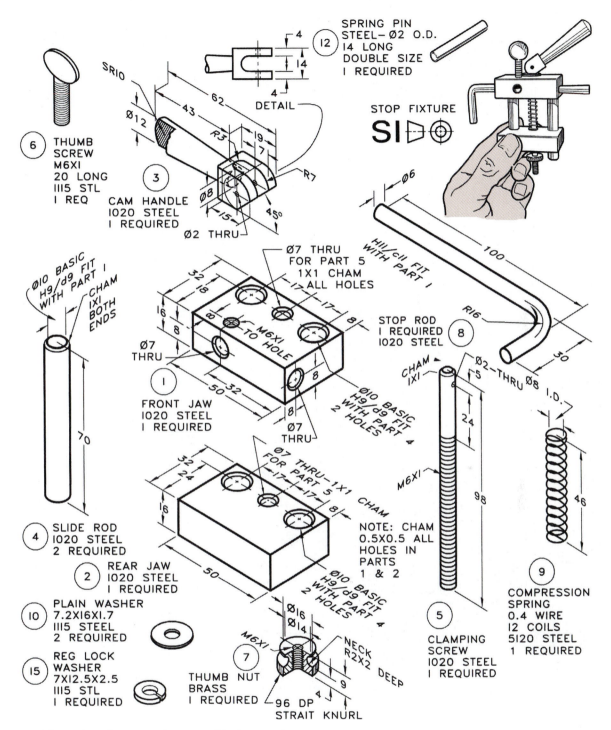

SPRING PIN
STEEL— Ø2 O.D.
14 LONG
DOUBLE SIZE
1 REQUIRED

⑫

4
14
4
62
DETAIL

SRI0
43
Ø12
R3
19
7
R7
Ø8
45°
15
Ø2 THRU

③ CAM HANDLE
1020 STEEL
1 REQUIRED

⑥ THUMB
SCREW
M6X1
20 LONG
1115 STL
1 REQ

STOP FIXTURE

SI ▷⊕

Ø6

H11/c11 FIT
WITH PART 1

100

R16

STOP ROD
1 REQUIRED
1020 STEEL ⑧

Ø7 THRU
FOR PART 5
1X1 CHAM
ALL HOLES

32
8
16
8
8
M6X1
TO HOLE
17
17
8
Ø7
THRU
50
32
8
Ø7
THRU

① FRONT JAW
1020 STEEL
1 REQUIRED

Ø10 BASIC
H9/d9 FIT
WITH PART 1
CHAM
1X1
BOTH
ENDS

70

④ SLIDE ROD
1020 STEEL
2 REQUIRED

Ø10 BASIC
H9/d9 FIT
WITH PART 4
2 HOLES

Ø7 THRU—1X1 CHAM
FOR PART 5
32
24
16
17
17
8

② REAR JAW
1020 STEEL
1 REQUIRED

NOTE: CHAM
0.5X0.5 ALL
HOLES IN
PARTS
1 & 2

Ø10 BASIC
H9/d9 FIT
WITH PART 4
2 HOLES

CHAM
1X1
Ø2 THRU Ø8 I.D.
5
24
M6X1
98

⑤ CLAMPING
SCREW
1020 STEEL
1 REQUIRED

46

⑨ COMPRESSION
SPRING
0.4 WIRE
12 COILS
5120 STEEL
1 REQUIRED

⑩ PLAIN WASHER
7.2X16X1.7
1115 STEEL
2 REQUIRED

⑮ REG LOCK
WASHER
7X12.5X2.5
1115 STL
1 REQUIRED

⑦ THUMB NUT
BRASS
1 REQUIRED

M6X1
Ø16
Ø14
NECK
R2X2 DEEP
9
4
96 DP
STRAIT KNURL

22.69 Make working drawings with an assembly drawing of
this stop fixture on size B sheets.

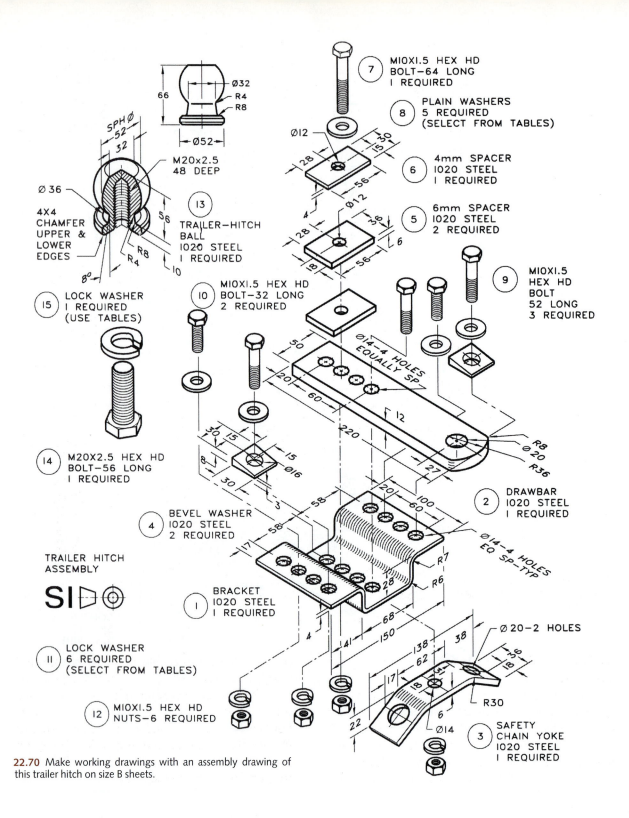

Ø32
R4
R8
66
Ø52

SPHØ
52
32

M20x2.5
48 DEEP

Ø 36

4X4
CHAMFER
UPPER &
LOWER
EDGES

56

R8
R4
10

8°

⑬ TRAILER-HITCH
BALL
1020 STEEL
1 REQUIRED

⑮ LOCK WASHER
1 REQUIRED
(USE TABLES)

⑩ M10X1.5 HEX HD
BOLT-32 LONG
2 REQUIRED

⑭ M20X2.5 HEX HD
BOLT-56 LONG
1 REQUIRED

④ BEVEL WASHER
1020 STEEL
2 REQUIRED

TRAILER HITCH
ASSEMBLY

SI◗◎

⑪ LOCK WASHER
6 REQUIRED
(SELECT FROM TABLES)

⑫ M10X1.5 HEX HD
NUTS-6 REQUIRED

⑦ M10X1.5 HEX HD
BOLT-64 LONG
1 REQUIRED

⑧ PLAIN WASHERS
5 REQUIRED
(SELECT FROM TABLES)

Ø12

30
15
28
56
4

⑥ 4mm SPACER
1020 STEEL
1 REQUIRED

Ø12

30
28
56
18
6

⑤ 6mm SPACER
1020 STEEL
2 REQUIRED

⑨ M10X1.5
HEX HD
BOLT
52 LONG
3 REQUIRED

50
20
60
220
12

Ø14-4 HOLES
EQUALLY SP

R8
Ø 20
R36

27
20
100
50

② DRAWBAR
1020 STEEL
1 REQUIRED

Ø14-4 HOLES
EQ SP-TYP

30
15
15
8
Ø16
30
3

58
58
17

R7
R6
28

① BRACKET
1020 STEEL
1 REQUIRED

4
41
150
68
138
62
17
18
6
22
Ø14

38
Ø 20-2 HOLES
6
18
R30

③ SAFETY
CHAIN YOKE
1020 STEEL
1 REQUIRED

22.70 Make working drawings with an assembly drawing of this trailer hitch on size B sheets.

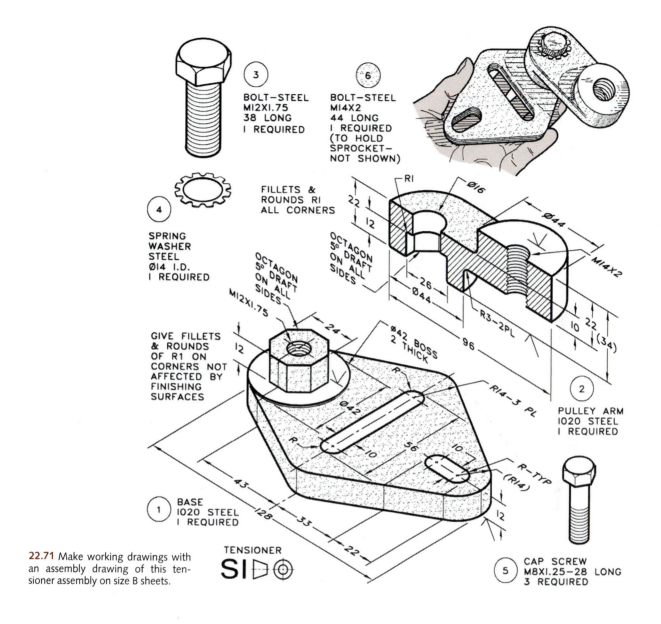

3 BOLT—STEEL M12X1.75 38 LONG 1 REQUIRED

6 BOLT—STEEL M14X2 44 LONG 1 REQUIRED (TO HOLD SPROCKET— NOT SHOWN)

4 SPRING WASHER STEEL Ø14 I.D. 1 REQUIRED

FILLETS & ROUNDS R1 ALL CORNERS

OCTAGON 5° DRAFT ON ALL SIDES

R1

Ø16

Ø44

M14X2

22

12

OCTAGON 5° DRAFT ON ALL SIDES

26

Ø44

R3—2PL

96

10

22

(34)

2 PULLEY ARM 1020 STEEL 1 REQUIRED

M12X1.75

GIVE FILLETS & ROUNDS OF R1 ON CORNERS NOT AFFECTED BY FINISHING SURFACES

24

12

Ø42 BOSS 2 THICK

R14—3 PL

Ø42

R

56

10

R

10

R—TYP (R14)

43

128

33

22

12

1 BASE 1020 STEEL 1 REQUIRED

5 CAP SCREW M8X1.25—28 LONG 3 REQUIRED

TENSIONER
SI ⊳⊙

22.71 Make working drawings with an assembly drawing of this tensioner assembly on size B sheets.

Working Drawings: Multiple Parts With Design Applications

Make dimensioned working drawings of the multiple parts shown in **Figs. 22.71–22.73** on a sheet size of your choice with the necessary dimensions and notes to fabricate the parts. Each part is given in a general format, with partial dimensions, which requires some design effort on your part. You must consider the addition of fillets and rounds, the application of finish marks, and the modification of features of the parts to make them functional and practical. Apply the tolerances to the parts in limit form by using the tables of cylindrical fits in the Appendix. Make an assembly drawing with a parts list to show how the parts are to be put together.

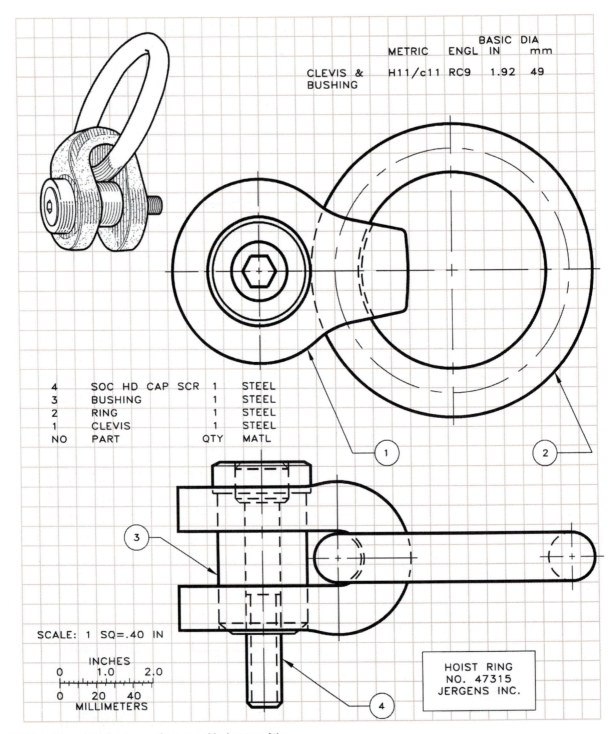

METRIC	ENGL	BASIC DIA IN	BASIC DIA mm
CLEVIS & BUSHING	H11/c11 RC9	1.92	49

NO	PART	QTY	MATL
4	SOC HD CAP SCR	1	STEEL
3	BUSHING	1	STEEL
2	RING	1	STEEL
1	CLEVIS	1	STEEL

SCALE: 1 SQ=.40 IN

INCHES
0   1.0   2.0
0   20   40
MILLIMETERS

HOIST RING
NO. 47315
JERGENS INC.

22.72 Make working drawings with an assembly drawing of the hoist ring on size B sheets.

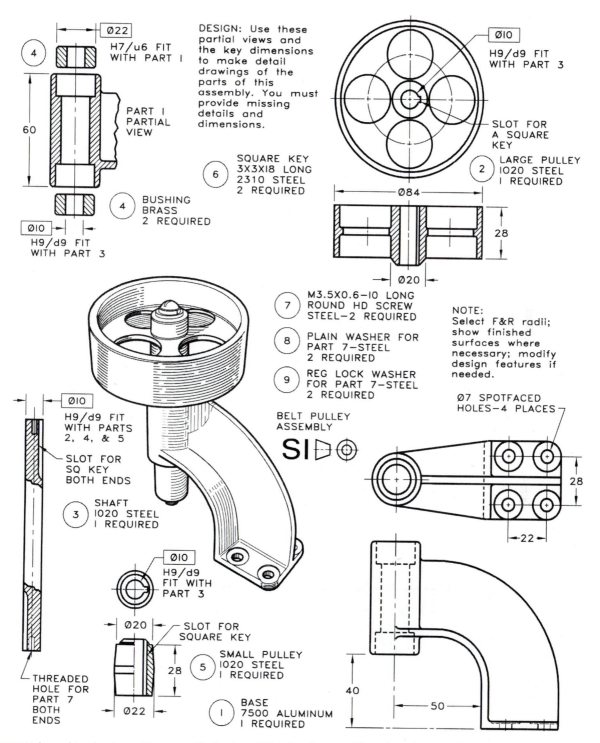

Ø22
H7/u6 FIT
WITH PART 1

4

60

PART 1
PARTIAL
VIEW

4 BUSHING
BRASS
2 REQUIRED

Ø10
H9/d9 FIT
WITH PART 3

DESIGN: Use these
partial views and
the key dimensions
to make detail
drawings of the
parts of this
assembly. You must
provide missing
details and
dimensions.

6 SQUARE KEY
3X3X18 LONG
2310 STEEL
2 REQUIRED

Ø10
H9/d9 FIT
WITH PART 3

SLOT FOR
A SQUARE
KEY

2 LARGE PULLEY
1020 STEEL
1 REQUIRED

Ø84

28

Ø20

7 M3.5X0.6-10 LONG
ROUND HD SCREW
STEEL-2 REQUIRED

8 PLAIN WASHER FOR
PART 7-STEEL
2 REQUIRED

9 REG LOCK WASHER
FOR PART 7-STEEL
2 REQUIRED

BELT PULLEY
ASSEMBLY

SI ▷ ◉

NOTE:
Select F&R radii;
show finished
surfaces where
necessary; modify
design features if
needed.

Ø7 SPOTFACED
HOLES-4 PLACES

28

22

Ø10
H9/d9 FIT
WITH PARTS
2, 4, & 5

SLOT FOR
SQ KEY
BOTH ENDS

3 SHAFT
1020 STEEL
1 REQUIRED

Ø10
H9/d9
FIT WITH
PART 3

SLOT FOR
SQUARE KEY

Ø20

28

THREADED
HOLE FOR
PART 7
BOTH
ENDS

Ø22

5 SMALL PULLEY
1020 STEEL
1 REQUIRED

1 BASE
7500 ALUMINUM
1 REQUIRED

40

50

22.73 Make working drawings with an assembly drawing of this belt pulley assembly on size B sheets. (*Courtesy of Jergens, Incorporated.*)

Working Drawings: Design

The following problems require the application of working drawing principles, creative skills, and judgment. You must determine many of the dimensions, tolerances, and standard features of the parts. Make orthographic, dimensioned working drawings of the parts and assemblies shown in **Fig. 22.74** and **Fig. 22.81** on size A or size B sheets, incorporating the design features where specified. Include a title block, dimensions, and notes necessary for making the part.

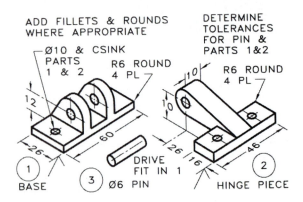

22.74 Size A sheet. Hinge assembly.

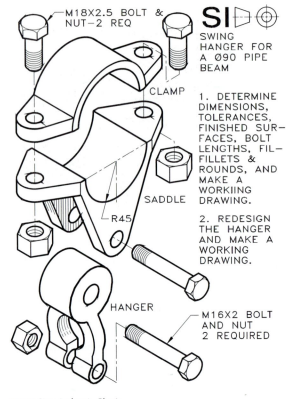

22.76 Size A sheet. Clevis.

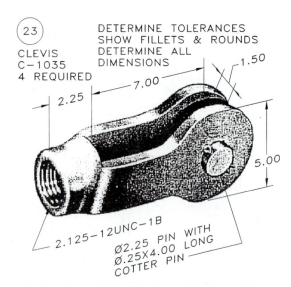

22.75 Size B sheets. Swing hanger.

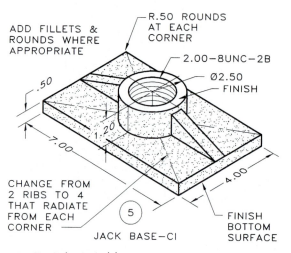

22.77 Size B sheets. Jack base.

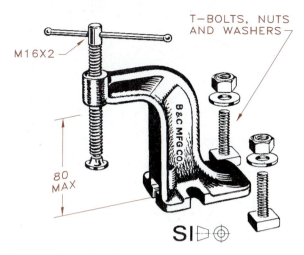

M16X2

T—BOLTS, NUTS
AND WASHERS

80
MAX

B & C MFG CO.

SI

22.78 Make working drawings with an assembly drawing of this hold-down clamp on size B sheets.

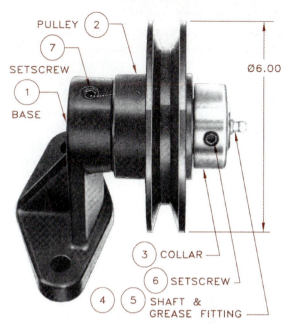

PULLEY ②

⑦

SETSCREW

①

BASE

Ø6.00

③ COLLAR

⑥ SETSCREW

④ ⑤ SHAFT &
GREASE FITTING

PULLEY BRACKET ASSEMBLY

22.80 Make a working drawing with an assembly drawing of this pulley bracket on size B sheets.

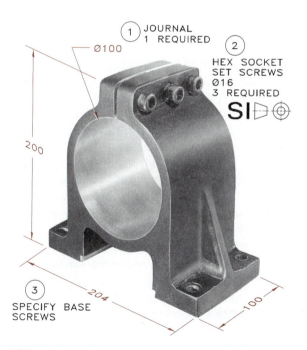

① JOURNAL
1 REQUIRED

② HEX SOCKET
SET SCREWS
Ø16
3 REQUIRED

Ø100

200

204

100

SI

③ SPECIFY BASE
SCREWS

22.79 Make working drawings with an assembly drawing of this journal on size B sheets.

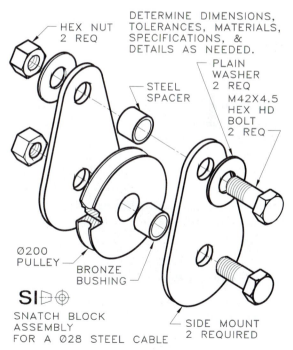

HEX NUT
2 REQ

DETERMINE DIMENSIONS,
TOLERANCES, MATERIALS,
SPECIFICATIONS, &
DETAILS AS NEEDED.

STEEL
SPACER

PLAIN
WASHER
2 REQ

M42X4.5
HEX HD
BOLT
2 REQ

Ø200
PULLEY

BRONZE
BUSHING

SI

SNATCH BLOCK
ASSEMBLY
FOR A Ø28 STEEL CABLE

SIDE MOUNT
2 REQUIRED

22.81 Make working drawings with an assembly drawing of this snatch-block assembly on size B sheets.

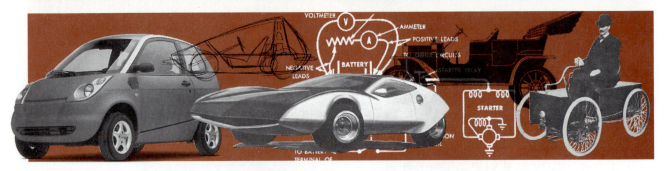

Reproduction of Drawings

23.1 Introduction

So far we have discussed the preparation of drawings and specifications through the working-drawing stage, where detailed drawings are completed on tracing film or paper. Now the drawings must be reproduced, folded, and prepared for transmittal to those who will use them to prepare bids or to fabricate the parts.

Several methods of reproduction are available to engineers and technologists for making copies of their drawings. However, most reproduction methods require strong, well-executed line work on the originals in order to produce good copies.

23.2 Computer Reproduction

Three major types of computer reproduction are (A) **pen plotting**, (B) **ink jet printing**, and (C) **laser printing**.

Pen plotting is done by plotter with a single- or a multiple-ink pen holder with a fiber point that "draws" on the paper or film by moving the pen in x and y directions. Multiple strokes of the pen will give various thicknesses of lines.

Ink jet printing is the process of spraying ink from tiny holes in a flat, disposable printhead onto the drawing surface as it passes through the printer. Prints can be obtained in color and in black and white. Ink jet printers vary in size from 8-1/2 × 11 output (**Fig. 23.1**) to large engineering print sizes (**Fig. 23.2**).

Laser printing is an electrophotographic process that uses a laser beam to draw an image on a photosensitive drum, where it is electrostatically charged to attract the toner. The electrostatically charged paper is rolled against the drum, the image is transferred, and toner is fused to the paper by heat (**Fig. 23.3**). Laser printers make sharp drawings of the highest quality in color or black and white.

Figure 23.4 shows the LaserJet 1200, which is a favorite of offices whose needs do not exceed A-size sheets for both text and graphics. It prints with the highest laser quality of 1200 dots per inch.

23.1 The DesignJet 990c printer provides quiet high-speed operation and high print quality. Its letter- and legal-size format produces excellent color plots of text and graphics. (*Courtesy of Hewlett-Packard Company.*)

23.2 The DesignJet 1050c printer provides quiet high-speed operation and high print quality. This large-format color plotter can print a D-size color line drawing in less than one minute. (*Courtesy of Hewlett-Packard Company.*)

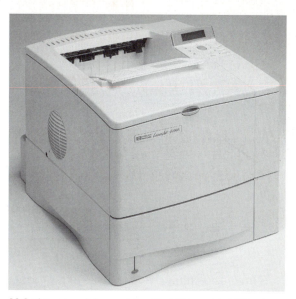

23.3 This network laser printer, the HP LaserJet 4100n, has a speed of 24 pages per minute in order to accommodate more users and higher print volumes. (*Courtesy of Hewlett-Packard Company.*)

23.4 This HP LaserJet 1200 has a speed of 15 pages per minute and a print quality of 1200 dots per inch for black and white prints. (*Courtesy of Hewlett-Packard Company.*)

23.3 Types of Reproduction

Drawings made by a drafter are of little use in their original form. If original drawings were handled by checkers and by workers in the field or shop, they would quickly be soiled and damaged, and no copy would be available as a permanent record of the job. Therefore, the reproduction of drawings is necessary for making inexpensive, expendable copies for use by the people who need to use them.

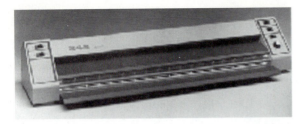

23.5 This typical whiteprinter operates on the diazo process. (*Courtesy of Blu-Ray, Incorporated, Essex, CT.*)

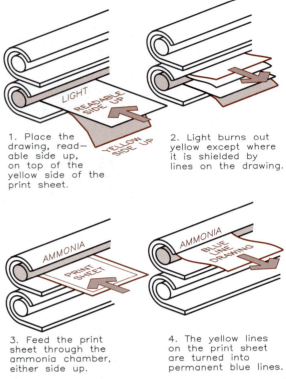

1. Place the drawing, read- able side up, on top of the yellow side of the print sheet.

2. Light burns out yellow except where it is shielded by lines on the drawing.

3. Feed the print sheet through the ammonia chamber, either side up.

4. The yellow lines on the print sheet are turned into permanent blue lines.

23.6 Diazo (blue-line) prints are made by placing the original readable side up and on top of the yellow side of the diazo paper and feeding them under the light, as shown in the steps above.

The most often used processes of reproducing engineering drawings are (1) **diazo printing**, (2) **microfilming**, (3) **xerography**, and (4) **photostating**.

Diazo Printing

The **diazo print** more correctly is called a **whiteprint** or **blue-line print** rather than a **blueprint**, because it has a white background and blue lines. Other colors of lines are available, depending on the type of diazo paper used. (Blueprinting, which creates a print with white lines and a blue background, is a wet process that is almost obsolete at the present.) **Figure 23.5** shows a typical diazo printer.

Diazo printing requires that original drawings be made on semitransparent tracing paper, cloth, or film that light can pass through except where lines have been drawn. The diazo paper on which the blue-line print is copied is chemically treated, giving it a yellow tint on one side. Diazo paper must be stored away from heat and light to prevent spoilage.

The steps of making a diazo print are shown in sequence in **Fig. 23.6**. The drawing is placed face up on the yellow side of the diazo paper and then fed through the diazo-process machine, which exposes the drawing to a built-in light. Light rays pass through the tracing paper and burn away the yellow tint on the diazo paper except where the drawing lines have shielded the paper from the light, similar to how a photographic negative is used. (It is important that your lines be adequately dense to shield the diazo paper enough to make a good print.) The exposed diazo paper becomes a duplicate of the original drawing except that the lines are light yellow and are not permanent.

When the diazo paper is passed through the developing unit of the diazo machine, ammonia fumes develop the yellow lines on it into permanent blue lines. The speed at which the drawing passes under the light determines the darkness of the blue-line copy; the faster the speed, the darker the print is. A slow speed burns out more of the yellow and produces a clear white background, but some of the lighter lines of the drawing may be lost. Most diazo copies are made at a speed fast enough to give a light tint of blue in the background in order to obtain the darkest lines on the copy. Ink drawings, whether made by hand or by computer, give the best reproductions.

Diazo printing has been enhanced by the advent of the computer since computer drawings are made in ink. Thus the print quality is much better than pencil drawings. Also, drawings made by different drafters are more uniform in line weight, lettering, and technique than drawings made by hand.

Microfilming

Microfilming is a photographic process that converts large drawings into film copies—either aperture cards or roll film. Drawings are placed on a copy table and photographed on either 16-mm or 35-mm film.

The roll film or aperture cards are placed in a microfilm enlarger-printer, where the individual drawings can be viewed on a built-in screen. The selected drawings can be printed from the film in standard sizes. Microfilm copies are usually made smaller than the original drawings to save paper and make the drawings easier to use.

Microfilming eliminates the need for large, bulky files of drawings because hundreds of drawings can be stored in permanent archives in miniature on a small amount of film. This is the same process used to preserve newspapers and other large materials by libraries and archives.

Xerography

Xerography is an electrostatic process of duplicating drawings on ordinary, unsensitized paper. Originally developed for business and clerical uses, xerography more recently is currently used for the reproduction of engineering drawings. The xerographic process can also be used to reduce the sizes of the drawings being copied to more convenient and easier-to-use

sizes. The Xerox 2080 can reduce a 24 × 36 inch drawing to 8 × 10 inches.

Photostating

Photostating is a method of enlarging or reducing drawings photographically. The drawing is placed under the glass of the exposure table, which is lit by built-in lamps. The image appears on a glass plate inside the darkroom, where it is exposed on photographically sensitive paper. The exposed negative paper is placed in contact with receiver paper, and the two are fed through the developing solution to obtain a photostatic copy. Photostating also can be used to make reproductions on transparent films and for reproducing halftones (photographs with tones of gray).

23.4 Assembling Drawing Sets

After the original drawings have been copied, they should be stored flat and unfolded in a flat file for future use and updating. Prints made from the originals, however, usually are folded or rolled for ease of transmittal from office to office. The methods of folding size B, C, D, and E sheets so that the image will appear on the outside of the fold are shown in **Fig. 23.7**. Drawings should be folded to show the title block always

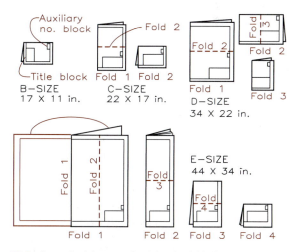

23.7 All standard drawing sheets can be folded to 8-1/2″ × 11″ size for filing and storage.

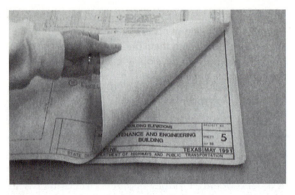

23.8 The title block should appear at the right, usually in the lower right-hand corner of the sheet.

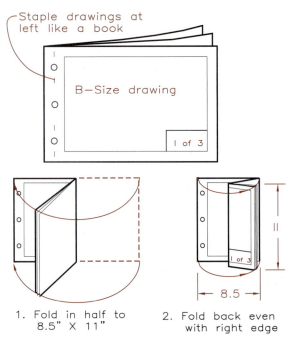

Staple drawings at left like a book

B–Size drawing

1 of 3

1. Fold in half to 8.5" × 11"

2. Fold back even with right edge

8.5

23.9 A set of size B drawings can be assembled by stapling, punching, and folding, as shown here, for safekeeping in a three-ring notebook with the title block visible on top.

on the outside at the right, usually in the lower right-hand corner of the page (**Fig. 23.7**). The final size after folding is 8 1/2 × 11 inches (or 9 × 12 inches).

An alternative method of folding and stapling size B sheets often is used for student assignments so that they can be kept in a three-ring notebook (**Fig. 23.9**). The basic rules of assembling drawings are listed in **Fig. 23.10**.

23.5 Transmittal of Drawings

Prints of drawings are delivered to contractors, manufacturers, fabricators, and others who must use the drawings for implementing the project. Prints usually are placed in standard 9 × 12-inch envelopes for delivery by hand or mail. Sets of large drawings, which may be 30 × 40 inches in size and contain four or more sheets, usually are rolled and sent in a mailing tube when folding becomes impractical. It is not uncommon for a set of drawings to have forty or fifty sheets.

An advanced method of transmitting drawings is by use of large fax machines. Within minutes, large documents can be scanned and transmitted to their destination sites.

Computer drawings can be transmitted on disk by mailing them to their destination, where hard copies can be plotted and reproduced. This procedure offers substantial savings in shipping charges.

Computer drawings can also be transmitted over the Internet in the form of data that is downloaded at its destination. The downloaded data is then printed in the form of a drawing and it is maintained in the database of the computer. In the future, more drawings, documents, and photographs will be sent electronically as data and as scanned images over telephone wires, making them available instantaneously at the desired location.

Only a few years ago, transmission of information and data across the state or nation was time-consuming and carried the risk of loss. Today, any document can be transmitted overnight with certainty of delivery, and most can be transmitted to the receiver within minutes. The OmniShare conferencer (**Fig. 23.11**) lets people in two locations collaborate on the same document at the same time over a single phone line.

WORKING DRAWING CHECKLIST

1. Staple along left edge, like a book. Use several staples, never just one.

2. Fold with drawing on outside.

3. Fold drawings as a set, not one at a time separately.

4. Fold to an 8.5"X 11" modular size.

5. The title block must be visible after folding.

6. Sheets of a set should be uniform in size.

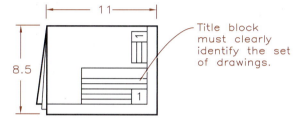

23.10 Follow these basic rules for assembling sets of working drawing prints.

23.11 Hewlett Packard's OmniShare conferencer enables people in two locations to "meet" and collaborate on the same document, at the same time, over a single phone line. (*Courtesy of Hewlett-Packard Company.*)

Hewlett Packard's LaserJet printers have accessories available for fax, copy, file, and read capabilities. Today, the communication of engineering data can be done instantaneously and easily, contributing to an increased productivity (**Fig. 23.12**).

Numerically-controlled manufacturing systems can be actuated directly from engineering data once the designs have been digitized. Such systems can be controlled from remote sites to produce products that previously required a high intensity of work hours by individuals. The future will hold many unique innovations in which business, manufacturing, and construction is done.

23.12 Fast, high-quality output and paper-handling flexibility required of today's business users can be found in the HP LaserJet 4100 printer . In addition, users can add copy, fax, file, and read capabilities by adding the optional LaserJet Companion printer accessory. (*Courtesy of Hewlett-Packard Company.*)

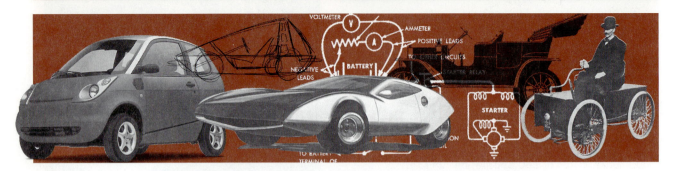

Three-Dimensional Pictorials

24.1 Introduction

A three-dimensional pictorial is a drawing that shows an object's three principal planes, much as they would be captured by a camera. This type of pictorial is an effective means of illustrating a part that is difficult to visualize when only orthographic views are given. Pictorials are especially helpful when a design is complex and when the reader of the drawings is unfamiliar with orthographic drawings.

Sometimes called **technical illustrations**, pictorials are widely used to describe products in catalogs, parts manuals, and maintenance publications (**Fig. 24.1**). The ability to sketch pictorials rapidly to explain a detail to an associate in the field is an important communication skill.

The four commonly used types of pictorials are **(1) obliques, (2) isometrics, (3) axonometrics**, and **(4) perspectives** (**Fig. 24.2**).

Oblique pictorials: Three-dimensional drawings made by projecting from the object with

24.1 Many objects cannot be seen as well in real life as they can in a drawing, as shown in this drawing of a pen set. (*Courtesy of Keuffel & Esser Co.*)

parallel projectors that are oblique to the picture plane (**Fig. 24.2A**).

Isometric and axonometric pictorials: Three-dimensional drawings made by projecting from the object with parallel projectors that

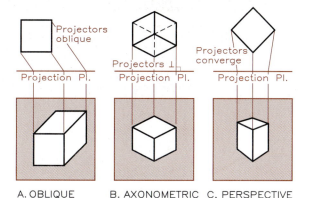

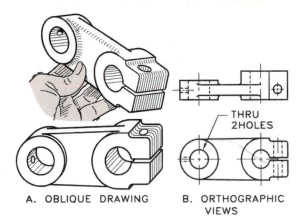

24.2 The three pictorial projection systems are: (A) oblique pictorials, with parallel projectors oblique to the projection plane; (B) axonometric (including isometric) pictorials, with parallel projectors perpendicular to the projection plane; and (C) perspectives, with converging projectors that make varying angles with the projection plane.

24.3 The oblique drawing of this part makes it easier to visualize it than do its orthographic views.

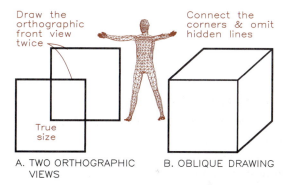

24.4 Draw two true-size surfaces of the box, connect them at the corners, and you have an oblique drawing.

are perpendicular to the picture plane (**Fig. 24.2B**).

Perspective pictorials: Three-dimensional drawings made with projectors that converge at the viewer's eye and make varying angles with the picture plane (**Fig. 24.2C**).

24.2 Oblique Drawings

The pulley arm shown in **Fig. 24.3** is illustrated by orthographic views and an oblique pictorial. Because most parts are drawn before they are made, photographs cannot be taken; therefore the next best option is to draw a three-dimensional pictorial of the part. Details can usually be drawn with more clarity than can be shown in a photograph.

Oblique pictorials are easy to draw. If you can drawn an orthographic view of a part, you are but one step away from drawing an oblique. For example, **Fig. 24.4** shows that drawing a front view of a box twice and connecting its corners yields an oblique drawing.

Thus, an oblique is no more than an orthographic view with a receding axis, drawn at an angle to show the depth of the object. An oblique is a pictorial that does not exist in reality (a camera cannot give an oblique). This type of pictorial is called an oblique because its parallel projectors from the object are oblique to the picture plane.

Types of Obliques

The three basic types of oblique drawings are: **(1) cavalier**, **(2) cabinet**, and **(3) general** (**Fig. 24.5**). For each type, the angle of the receding axis with the horizontal can be at any angle between 0° and 90°. Measurements along the

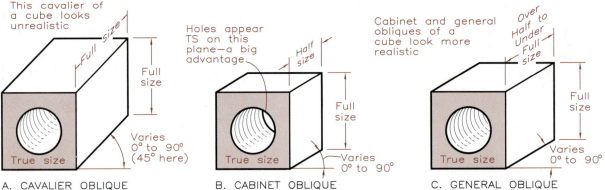

A. CAVALIER OBLIQUE   B. CABINET OBLIQUE   C. GENERAL OBLIQUE

24.5 The three types of obliques

A The cavalier oblique has a receding axis at any angle and true-length measurements on the receding axis.

B The cabinet oblique has a receding axis at any angle and half-size measurements along the receding axis.

C The general oblique has a receding axis at any angle and measurements along the receding axis larger than half size and less than full size.

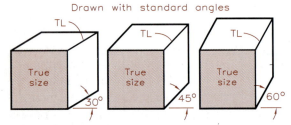

24.6 A cavalier oblique usually has its receding axis at one of the standard angles of drafting triangles. Each gives a different view of a cube.

receding axes of the cavalier oblique are laid off true length, and measurements along the receding axes of the cabinet oblique are laid off half size. The general oblique has measurements along the receding axis that are greater than half size and less than full size.

Figure 24.6 shows three examples of cavalier obliques of a cube. The receding axis for each is drawn at a different angle, but the receding axes are drawn true length. **Figure 24.7** compares cavalier with cabinet obliques.

Constructing Obliques

You can easily begin a cavalier oblique by drawing a box using the overall dimensions of height, width, and depth with light construction lines. As demonstrated in **Fig. 24.8**, first draw the front view as a true-size orthographic view. True measurements must be made parallel to the three axes and transferred from the orthographic views with your dividers. Then remove the notch from the blocked-in construction box to complete the oblique.

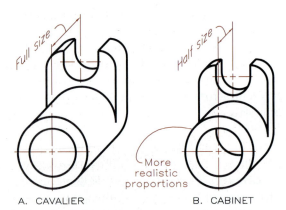

A. CAVALIER   B. CABINET

24.7 Measurements along the receding axis of a cavalier oblique are full size and those in a cabinet oblique are half size.

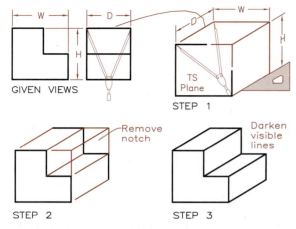

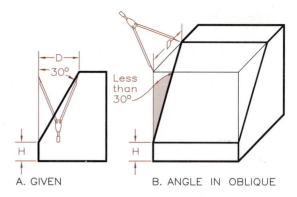

24.10 Angles that do not lie in a true-size plane of an oblique must be located with coordinates.

24.8 Constructing a cavalier oblique

Step 1 Draw the front surface of the object as a true-size plane. Draw the receding axis at a convenient angle and transfer the true distance D from the side view to it with your dividers.

Step 2 Draw the notch on the front plane and project it to the rear plane.

Step 3 Darken the lines to complete the drawing.

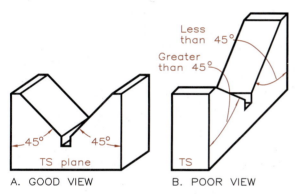

24.9 Objects with angular features should be drawn in oblique so that the angles appear true size. This results in a better pictorial and one that is easier to draw.

Angles

Angular measurements can be made on the true-size plane of an oblique, but not on the other two planes. Note in **Fig. 24.9** that a true angle can be measured on a true-size surface, but in **Fig. 24.10** angles along receding planes are either smaller or larger than their true sizes.

A better, easier-to-draw oblique is obtained when angles are drawn to appear true size.

To construct an angle in an oblique on one of the receding planes, you must use coordinates, as shown in **Fig. 24.10**. To find the surface that slopes 30° from the front surface, locate the vertex of the angle, H distance from the bottom. To find the upper end of the sloping plane, measure the distance D along the receding axis. Transfer H and D to the oblique with your dividers. The angle in the oblique is not equal to the 30° angle in the orthographic view.

Cylinders

The **major advantage** of an oblique is that **circular features can be drawn as true circles** on its frontal plane (**Fig. 24.11**). Draw the centerlines of the circular end at A and construct the receding axis at the desired angle. Locate the end at B by measuring along the axis, draw circles at each end at centers A and B, and draw tangents to both circles.

These same principles apply to the construction of the object having semicircular features shown in **Fig. 24.12**. Position the oblique so that the semicircular features are true size. Locate centers A, B, and C and the two semicircles. Then complete the cavalier oblique.

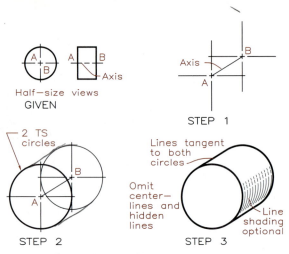

Half–size views
GIVEN

STEP 1

2 TS circles

STEP 2

Lines tangent to both circles

Omit center–lines and hidden lines

Line shading optional

STEP 3

24.11 Drawing a cylinder in oblique

Step 1 Draw axis AB and locate the centers of the circular ends of the cylinder at A and B. Because the axis is true length, this will be a cavalier oblique.

Step 2 Draw a true-size circle with its center at A by using a compass or computer-graphics techniques.

Step 3 Draw the other circular end with its center at B and connect the circles with tangent lines parallel to axis AB.

Circles

Circular features drawn as true circles on a true-size plane of an oblique pictorial appear on the receding planes as **ellipses**.

The four-center ellipse method is a technique of constructing an approximate ellipse with a compass and four centers (**Fig. 24.13**). The ellipse is tangent to the inside of a rhombus drawn with sides equal to the circle's diameter. Drawing the four arcs produces the ellipse.

The four-center ellipse method will not work for the cabinet or general oblique, but coordinates must be used. **Figure 24.14** illustrates the method of locating coordinates on the planes of cavalier and cabinet obliques. For the cabinet oblique, the coordinates along the receding axis are half size, and the coordinates along the horizontal axis (true-size axis) are full size. Draw the

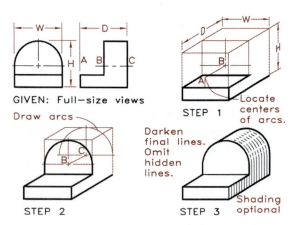

GIVEN: Full–size views

Draw arcs

STEP 2

Locate centers of arcs.

STEP 1

Darken final lines. Omit hidden lines.

Shading optional

STEP 3

24.12 Drawing semicircular features in oblique

Step 1 Block in the overall dimensions of the cavalier oblique with light construction lines, ignoring the semi-circular feature.

Step 2 Locate centers B and C and draw arcs tangent to the sides of the construction boxes with a compass or by computer.

Step 3 Connect the arcs with lines tangent to each arc and parallel to axis BC and darken the lines.

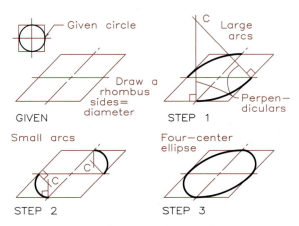

Given circle

Large arcs

STEP 1

Draw a rhombus sides= diameter

Perpendiculars

GIVEN

Small arcs

STEP 2

Four-center ellipse

STEP 3

24.13 Constructing a four-center ellipse in oblique

Given Block in the circle to be drawn in oblique with a square tangent to the circle. This square becomes a rhombus on the oblique plane.

Step 1 Draw construction lines perpendicular to the points of tangency to locate the centers for drawing two segments of the ellipse.

Step 2 Locate the centers for the two remaining arcs with perpendiculars drawn from adjacent tangent points.

Step 3 Draw the four arcs, which yield an approximate ellipse.

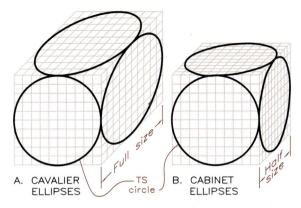

A. CAVALIER ELLIPSES   B. CABINET ELLIPSES

24.14 Circular features on the faces of cavalier and cabinet obliques are compared here. Ellipses on the receding planes of cabinet obliques must be plotted by coordinates. The spacing of the coordinates along the receding axis of cabinet obliques is half size.

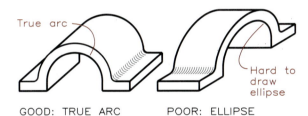

GOOD: TRUE ARC   POOR: ELLIPSE

24.15 An oblique should be positioned so that circular and curving features can be drawn most easily.

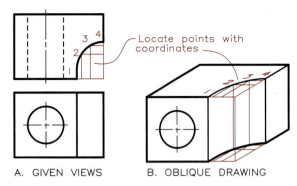

A. GIVEN VIEWS   B. OBLIQUE DRAWING

24.16 Coordinates are used to find points along irregular curves in oblique. Projecting the points downward at a distance equal to the height of the object yields the lower curve.

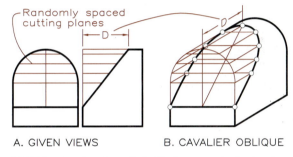

A. GIVEN VIEWS   B. CAVALIER OBLIQUE

24.17 Construction of an elliptical feature on an inclined surface in oblique requires the use of three-dimensional coordinates to locate points on the curve.

ellipse with an irregular curve or an ellipse template that approximates the plotted points.

Whenever possible, oblique drawings of objects with circular features should be positioned so circles can be drawn as true circles instead of ellipses. The view in **Fig. 24.15A** is better than the one in **Fig. 24.15B** because it gives a more descriptive view of the part and is easier to draw.

Curves

Irregular curves in oblique pictorials must be plotted point by point with coordinates (**Fig. 24.16**). Transfer the coordinates from the orthographic to the oblique view and draw the curve

through the plotted points with an irregular curve. If the object has a uniform thickness, plot the points for the lower curve by projecting vertically downward from the upper points a distance equal to the object's height.

To obtain the elliptical feature on the inclined surface shown in **Fig. 24.17**, use a series of coordinates to locate points along its curve. Connect the plotted points by using an irregular curve or ellipse template.

Sketching

Understanding the principles of oblique construction is essential for sketching obliques freehand. The sketch of the part shown in **Fig. 24.18**

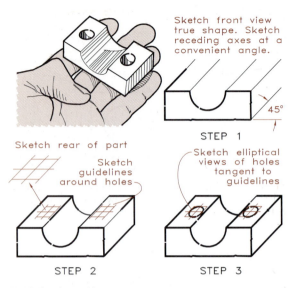

24.18 Sketching obliques

Step 1 Sketch the front of the object as a true-size surface and draw a receding axis from each corner.

Step 2 Lay off the depth, D, along the receding axes to locate the rear of the part. Lightly sketch pictorial boxes as guidelines for drawing the holes.

Step 3 Sketch the holes inside the boxes and darken all lines.

is based on the principles discussed, but its proportions were determined by eye instead of with scales and dividers.

Lightly drawn guidelines need not be erased when you darken the final lines. When sketching on tracing vellum, you can place a printed grid under the sheet to provide guidelines. Refer to Chapter 13 to review sketching techniques if needed.

Dimensioned Obliques

Dimensioned sectional views of obliques provide excellent, easily understood depictions of objects (**Fig. 24.19**). Apply numerals and lettering in oblique pictorials by using either the **aligned** method (with numerals aligned with the dimension lines) or the **unidirectional** method (with numerals positioned horizontally regardless of the direction of the dimension lines), as

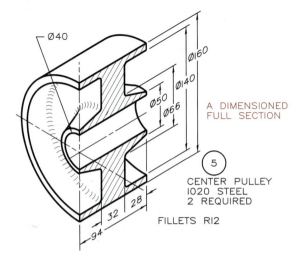

24.19 Oblique pictorials can be drawn as sections and dimensioned to serve as working drawings.

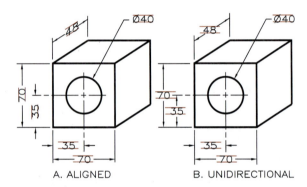

24.20 Either of these methods of lettering, aligned or unidirectional, is acceptable for dimensioning obliques.

shown in **Fig. 24.20**. Notes connected with leaders are positioned horizontally in both methods.

24.3 Isometric Pictorials

In **Fig. 24.21**, the pulley arm is drawn in orthographic views and as a three-dimensional pictorial drawing. The pictorial is an **isometric drawing** in which the three planes of the object are equally foreshortened, representing the object more realistically than an oblique drawing can.

With more realism comes more difficulty of construction. In particular, circles and curves do

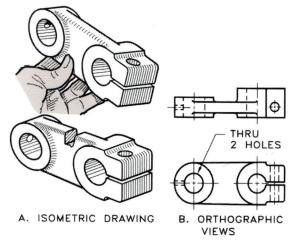

A. ISOMETRIC DRAWING   B. ORTHOGRAPHIC VIEWS

THRU 2 HOLES

24.21 An isometric drawing gives a more realistic view of a part than an oblique drawing does.

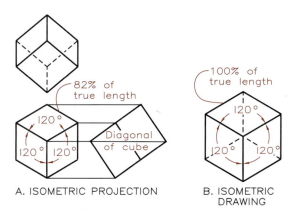

82% of true length

Diagonal of cube

120° 120° 120°

A. ISOMETRIC PROJECTION

100% of true length

120° 120° 120°

B. ISOMETRIC DRAWING

24.22 Projection vs. drawing

A A true isometric projection is found by constructing a view in which the diagonal of a cube appears as a point and the axes are foreshortened.

B An isometric drawing is not a true projection because the dimensions are true size rather than foreshortened.

not appear true shape on any of the three isometric planes.

Isometric Projection versus Drawing

In isometric projection, parallel projectors are perpendicular to the imaginary projection (picture) plane in which the diagonal of a cube appears as a point (**Fig. 24.22**). An isometric pictorial constructed by projection is called an iso-

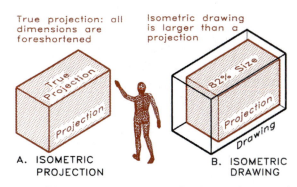

True projection: all dimensions are foreshortened

Isometric drawing is larger than a projection

A. ISOMETRIC PROJECTION

B. ISOMETRIC DRAWING

24.23 The true isometric projection is foreshortened to 82% of full size. The isometric drawing is drawn full size for convenience.

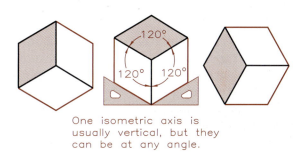

120° 120° 120°

One isometric axis is usually vertical, but they can be at any angle.

24.24 Isometric axes are spaced 120° apart, but they can be revolved into any position. Usually, one axis is vertical, but it can be at any angle with axis spacing remaining the same.

metric projection, with the three axes foreshortened to 82% of their true lengths and 120° apart. The name isometric, which means equal measurement, aptly describes this type of projection because the planes are equally foreshortened.

An **isometric drawing** is a convenient approximate isometric pictorial in which the measurements are shown full size along the three axes, rather than at 82% as in **isometric projection** (**Fig. 24.23**). Thus the isometric drawing method allows you to measure true dimensions with standard scales and lay them off with dividers along the three axes. The only difference between the two is the larger size of the drawing. Consequently, isometric drawings are used much more often than isometric projections.

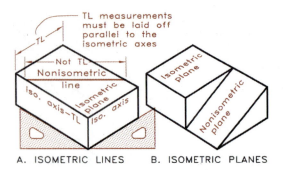

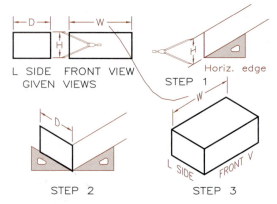

24.25 Isometric lines and planes

A Isometric lines (parallel to the three axes) give true measurements, but nonisometric lines do not.

B Here, the three isometric planes are equally foreshortened, and the nonisometric plane is inclined at an angle to one of the isometric planes.

The axes of isometric drawings are separated by 120° (**Fig. 24.24**), but more often than not, one of the axes selected is vertical, since most objects have vertical lines. However, isometrics without a vertical axis are still isometrics.

24.4 Isometric Drawings

An isometric drawing is begun by drawing three axes 120° apart. Lines parallel to these axes are called **isometric lines** (**Fig. 24.25A**). You can make true measurements along isometric lines but not along nonisometric lines. The three surfaces of a cube in an isometric drawing are called **isometric planes** (**Fig. 24.25B**). Planes parallel to those planes also are isometric planes.

To draw an isometric pictorial, you need a scale, dividers, and a 30°–60° triangle (**Fig. 24.26**). Begin by selecting the three axes and then constructing a plane of the isometric from the dimensions of height, H, and depth, D. Add the third dimension of width, W, and complete the isometric drawing.

Use light construction lines to block in all isometric drawings (**Fig. 24.27**) and the overall dimensions W, D, and H. Take other dimensions from the given views with dividers and measure along their isometric lines to locate notches in the blocked-in drawing.

24.26 Drawing an isometric of a box

Step 1 Use a 30°-60° triangle and a horizontal straight edge to construct a vertical line equal to the height, H, and draw two isometric lines through each end.

Step 2 Draw two 30° lines and locate the depth, D, by transferring depth from the given views with dividers.

Step 3 Locate the width, W, of the object, complete the surfaces of the isometric box, and darken the lines.

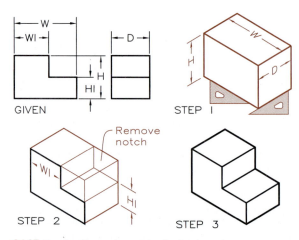

24.27 Constructing an isometric of a simple part

Step 1 Construct an isometric drawing of a box with the overall dimensions W, D, and H from the given views.

Step 2 Locate the notch by transferring dimensions W1 and H1 from the given views with your dividers.

Step 3 Darken the lines to complete the drawing.

Figure 24.28 shows an isometric drawing of a slightly more complex object, with two notches.

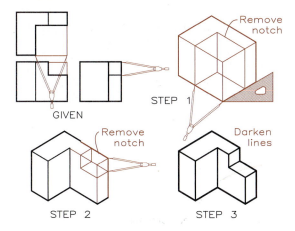

24.28 Laying out an isometric drawing

Step 1 Use the overall dimensions given to block in the object with light lines and remove the large notch.

Step 2 Remove the small notch.

Step 3 Darken the lines to complete the drawing.

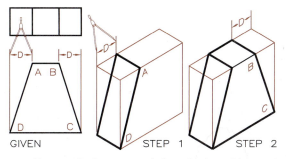

24.29 Use coordinates measured along the isometric axes to obtain inclined surfaces. Angular lines are not true length in isometric.

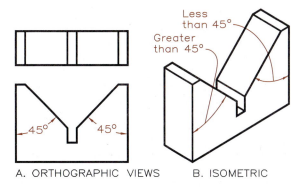

24.30 Angles in isometric may appear larger or smaller than they actually are.

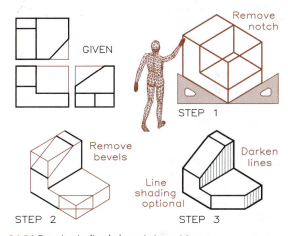

24.31 Drawing inclined planes in isometric

Step 1 Block in the object with light lines, using the overall dimensions, and remove the notch.

Step 2 Locate the ends of the inclined planes by using measurements parallel to the isometric axes.

Step 3 Darken the lines to complete the drawing.

The object was blocked in by using the H, W, and D dimensions. Remove the notches in the block to complete the drawing.

Angles

You cannot measure an angle's true size in an isometric drawing because the surfaces of an isometric are not true size. Instead, you must locate angles with isometric coordinates measured parallel to the axes (**Fig. 24.29**). Lines AD and BC are equal in length in the orthographic view, but they are shorter and longer than true length in the isometric drawing. **Figure 24.30** shows a similar situation, where two angles drawn in isometric are less than and greater than their true dimensions in the orthographic view.

Figure 24.31 shows how to construct an isometric drawing of an object with inclined surfaces. Blocking in the object with its overall dimensions with light construction lines is followed by removal of the inclined portions.

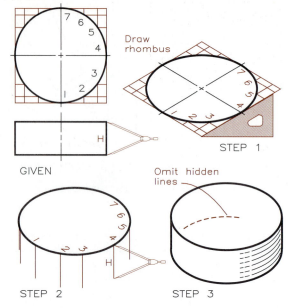

GIVEN

Draw rhombus

STEP 1

Omit hidden lines

STEP 2

STEP 3

24.32 Plotting circles in isometric

Step 1 Block in the circle by using its overall dimensions. Transfer the coordinates that locate points on the circle to the isometric plane and connect them with a smooth curve.

Step 2 Project each point a distance equal to the height of the cylinder to obtain the lower ellipse.

Step 3 Connect the two ellipses with tangent lines and darken all lines.

Circles

Three methods of constructing circles in isometric drawings are **(1) point plotting**, **(2) four-center ellipse construction**, and **(3) ellipse template usage**.

Point plotting is a method of using a series of x and y coordinates to locate points on a circle in the given orthographic views (**Fig. 24.32**). The coordinates are then transferred with dividers to the isometric drawing to locate the points on the ellipse one at a time.

Block in the cylinder with light construction lines and show the centerlines. Draw coordinates on the upper plane and use the height dimension to locate the points on the lower plane. Draw the ellipses with an irregular curve or an ellipse template.

A plotted ellipse is a true ellipse and is equivalent to a 35° ellipse drawn on an isometric

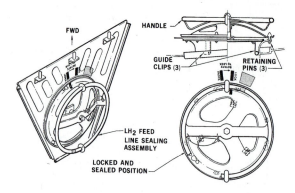

24.33 This handwheel assembly proposed for use in an orbital workshop is an example of parts with circular features drawn as ellipses in isometric. (*Courtesy of NASA.*)

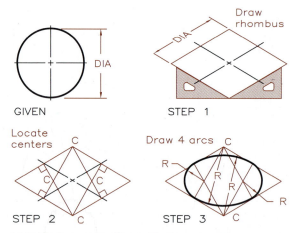

GIVEN

Draw rhombus

STEP 1

Locate centers

STEP 2

Draw 4 arcs

STEP 3

24.34 The four-center ellipse method

Step 1 Use the diameter of the given circle to draw an isometric rhombus and the centerlines.

Step 2 Draw light construction lines perpendicularly from the midpoints of each side to locate four centers.

Step 3 Draw four arcs from the centers to represent an ellipse tangent to the rhombus.

plane. An example of a design composed of circular features drawn in isometric is the handwheel shown in **Fig. 24.33**.

Four-center ellipse construction is the method of producing an approximate ellipse (**Fig. 24.34**) by using four arcs drawn with a compass. Draw an isometric rhombus with its sides equal to the diameter of the circle to be repre-

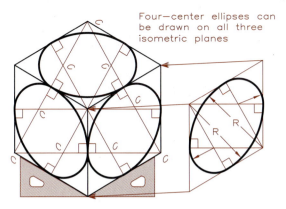

Four—center ellipses can be drawn on all three isometric planes

24.35 Four-center ellipses may be drawn on all three surfaces of an isometric drawing.

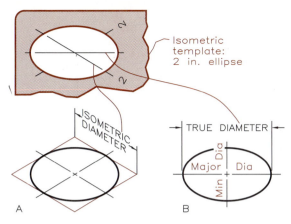

Isometric template: 2 in. ellipse

24.37 Ellipse terminology

A Measure the diameter of a circle along the isometric axes. The major diameter of an isometric ellipse thus is larger than the measured diameter.

B The minor diameter is perpendicular to the major diameter.

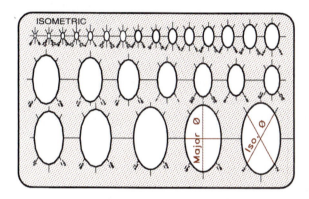

ISOMETRIC

24.36 The isometric template (a 35° ellipse angle) is designed for drawing elliptical features in isometric. The isometric diameters of the ellipses are not major diameters of the ellipses, but are diameters that are parallel to the isometric axes.

sented. Find the four centers by constructing perpendiculars to the sides of the rhombus at the midpoints of each side, and draw the four arcs to complete the ellipse. You may draw four-center ellipses on all three isometric planes, because each plane is equally foreshortened (**Fig. 24.35**). Although it is only an approximate ellipse, the four-center ellipse technique is acceptable for drawing large ellipses and as a way to draw ellipses when an ellipse template is unavailable.

Isometric ellipse templates are specially designed for drawing ellipses in isometric (**Fig. 24.36**). The numerals on the templates represent

the isometric diameters of the ellipses because diameters are measured parallel to the isometric axes of an isometric drawing (**Fig. 24.37**). Recall that the maximum diameter across the ellipse is its major diameter, which is a true diameter. Thus the size of the diameter marked on the template is less than the ellipse's major diameter. You may use the isometric ellipse template to draw an ellipse by constructing centerlines of the ellipse in isometric and aligning the ellipse template with those isometric lines (**Fig. 24.37**).

Cylinders

A cylinder may be drawn in isometric by using the four-center ellipse method (**Fig. 24.38**). Use the isometric axes and centerline axis to construct a rhombus at each end of the cylinder. Then draw the ellipses at each end, connect them with tangent lines, and darken the lines to complete the drawing.

An easier way to draw a cylinder is to use an isometric ellipse template (**Fig. 24.39**). Draw the axis of the cylinder and construct perpendiculars at each end. Because the axis of a right cylinder is

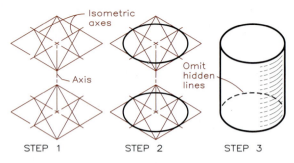

24.38 A cylinder drawn with the four-center method

Step 1 Draw an isometric rhombus at each end of the cylinder's axis.

Step 2 Draw a four-center ellipse within each rhombus.

Step 3 Draw lines tangent to each rhombus to complete the drawing.

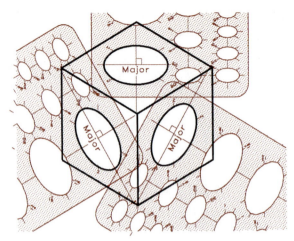

24.40 Position the isometric ellipse template as shown for drawing ellipses of various sizes on the three isometric planes.

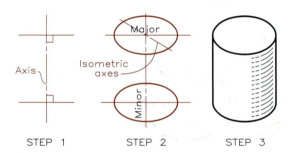

24.39 A cylinder using the ellipse template method

Step 1 Establish the length of the axis of the cylinder and draw perpendiculars at each end.

Step 2 Draw the elliptical ends by aligning the major diameter of the ellipse template with the perpendiculars at the ends of the axis. The isometric diameters of the isometric ellipse template will align with two isometric axes.

Step 3 Connect the ellipses with tangent lines to complete the drawing and omit hidden lines.

perpendicular to the major diameter of its elliptical ends, position the ellipse template with its major diameter perpendicular to the axis. Draw the ellipses at each end, connect them with tangent lines, and darken the visible lines to complete the drawing.

The isometric ellipse template (**Fig. 24.40**) can be used to draw ellipses on all three planes

of an isometric drawing, as shown in **Fig. 24.42**. On each plane, the major diameter is perpendicular to the isometric axis of the adjacent perpendicular plane. The isometric diameters marked on the template align with the isometric axes. Rounded corners (fillets or rounds) can be drawn with an ellipse template by using only a quarter of the ellipse.

Inclined Planes

Inclined planes in isometric may be located by coordinates, but they cannot be measured with a protractor because they do not appear true size. **Figure 24.41** illustrates the coordinate method. Use horizontal and vertical coordinates (in the x and y directions) to locate key points on the orthographic views. Transfer these coordinates to the isometric drawing with dividers to show the features of the inclined surface.

Curves

Irregular curves in isometric must be plotted point by point, with coordinates locating each point. Locate points A through F in the orthographic view with coordinates of width and depth (**Fig. 24.42**). Then transfer them to the isometric

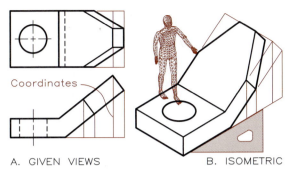

A. GIVEN VIEWS   B. ISOMETRIC

24.41 Inclined surfaces in isometric must be located with three-dimensional coordinates parallel to the isometric axes. True angles cannot be measured in isometric drawings.

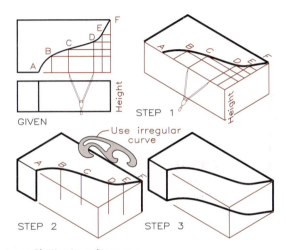

GIVEN   STEP 1

Use irregular curve

STEP 2   STEP 3

24.42 Plotting irregular curves

Step 1 Block in the shape by using the overall dimensions. Locate points on the irregular curve with coordinates transferred from the orthographic views.

Step 2 Project these points downward the distance H from the upper points to obtain the lower curve.

Step 3 Connect the points and darken the lines.

view of the blocked-in part and connect them with an irregular curve.

Project points on the upper curve downward a distance of H, the height of the part, to locate points on the lower ellipse. Connect these points with an irregular curve and darken the lines to complete the isometric.

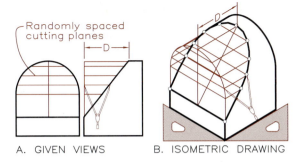

Randomly spaced cutting planes

A. GIVEN VIEWS   B. ISOMETRIC DRAWING

24.43 To construct ellipses on inclined planes, draw coordinates to locate points in the orthographic views. Then transfer the three-dimensional coordinates to the isometric drawing and connect them with a smooth curve.

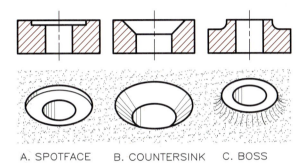

A. SPOTFACE   B. COUNTERSINK   C. BOSS

24.44 These examples of circular features in isometric may be drawn by using ellipse templates.

Ellipses on Nonisometric Planes

Ellipses on nonisometric planes in an isometric drawing, such as the one shown in **Fig. 24.43**, must be found by locating a series of points on the curve. Locate three-dimensional coordinates in the orthographic views and then transfer them to the isometric with your dividers. Connect the plotted points with an irregular curve or an ellipse template selected to approximate the plotted points. The more points you select, the more accurate will be the final ellipse. It will not be an isometric ellipse template, but one that fits the plotted points.

24.5 Technical Illustration

Orthographic and isometric views of a spotface, a countersink, and a boss are shown in **Fig. 25.44**.

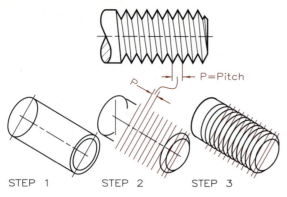

24.45 Threads in isometric

Step 1 Using an ellipse template, draw the cylinder to be threaded.

Step 2 Lay off perpendiculars, spacing them apart at a distance equal to the pitch of the thread, P (usually drawn larger than actual size).

Step 3 Draw a series of ellipses to represent the threads. Draw the chamfered end by using an ellipse whose major diameter is equal to the root diameter of the threads.

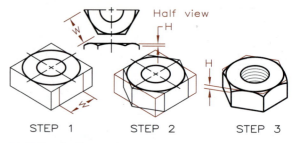

24.46 Constructing a nut

Step 1 Use the overall dimensions of the nut to block in the nut.

Step 2 Construct the hexagonal sides at the top and bottom.

Step 3 Draw the chamfer with an irregular curve. Draw the threads to complete the drawing.

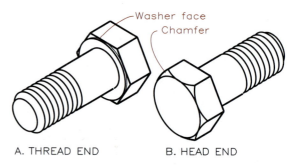

24.47 Isometric drawings of the lower and upper sides of a hexagon-head bolt.

These features may be drawn in isometric by point-by-point plotting of the circular features, the four-center method, or the ellipse template method (the easiest method of the three).

A threaded shaft may be drawn in isometric as shown in **Fig. 24.45**. First draw the cylinder in isometric. Draw the major diameters of the crest lines equally separated by distance P, the pitch of the thread. Then draw ellipses by aligning the major diameter of the ellipse template with the perpendiculars to the cylinder's axis. Use a smaller ellipse at the end for the 45° chamfered end.

Figure 24.46 shows how to draw a hexagon-head nut with an ellipse template. Block in the nut and draw an ellipse tangent to the rhombus. Construct the hexagon by locating distance W across a flat parallel to the isometric axes. To find the other sides of the hexagon, draw lines tangent to the ellipse. Lay off distance H at each corner to establish the chamfers.

Figure 24.47 depicts a hexagon-head bolt in two positions. The washer face is on the lower side of the head, and the chamfer is on the upper side.

A portion of a sphere is drawn to represent a round-head screw in **Fig. 24.48**. Construct a hemisphere and locate the centerline of the slot along one of the isometric planes. Measure the head's thickness, E, from the highest point on the sphere.

Sections

A full section drawn in isometric can clarify internal details that might otherwise be overlooked (**Fig. 24.49**). Half sections also may be used advantageously.

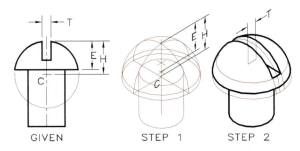

GIVEN   STEP 1   STEP 2

24.48 Drawing spherical features

Step 1 Use an isometric ellipse template to draw the elliptical features of a round-head screw.

Step 2 Draw the slot in the head and darken the lines to complete the drawing.

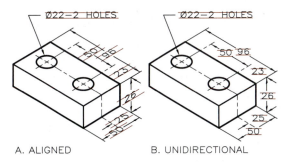

A. ALIGNED   B. UNIDIRECTIONAL

24.50 Either of the techniques shown—aligned or unidirectional—is acceptable for placing dimensions on isometric drawings. Guidelines should always be used for lettering.

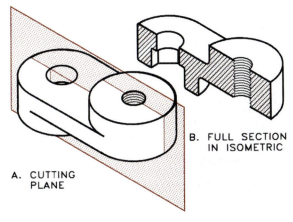

B. FULL SECTION IN ISOMETRIC

A. CUTTING PLANE

24.49 Isometric sections can be used to clarify the internal features of a part.

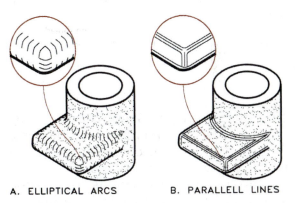

A. ELLIPTICAL ARCS   B. PARALLELL LINES

24.51 Either of these two methods can be used to represent fillets and rounds on the pictorial view of a part.

Dimensioned Isometrics

When you dimension isometric drawings, place numerals on the dimension lines, using either **aligned** or **unidirectional** numerals (**Fig. 24.50**). In both cases, notes connected with leaders usually are positioned horizontally, but drawing them to lie in an isometric plane is permissible. Always use guidelines for your lettering and numerals.

Fillets and Rounds

Fillets and rounds in isometric may be represented by either of the techniques shown in **Fig.**

24.51 for added realism. The enlarged detail in the balloon shows how to draw intersecting guidelines equal in length to the radii of the fillets and rounds with arcs drawn tangent to them. These arcs may be drawn either freehand or with an ellipse template. The stipple shading can be applied by using an adhesive overlay film or a computer pattern.

When fillets and rounds of a dimensioned part are shown, it is much easier to understand its features than it is when the part is represented by orthographic views (**Fig. 24.52**).

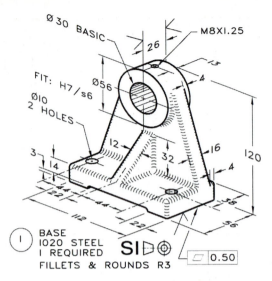

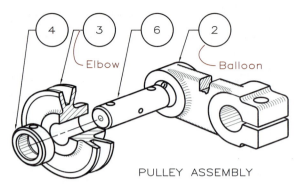

24.54 This exploded isometric assembly shows how parts are to be put together.

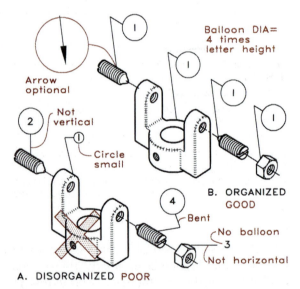

24.52 This three-dimensional drawing has been drawn to show fillet and rounds, dimensions, and notes in order for it to be used as a working drawing.

24.53 This drawing shows (A) common mistakes in applying leaders and part numbers in balloons of an assembly, and (B) acceptable techniques of applying leaders and part numbers to an assembly.

Assemblies

Assembly drawings illustrate how to put parts together. **Figure 24.53A** shows common mistakes in applying leaders and balloons to an assembly, and **Fig. 24.53B** shows the correct

method of applying them. The numbers in the balloons correspond to the part numbers in the parts list. **Figure 24.54** shows an exploded assembly that illustrates the relationship of four mating parts. Illustrations of this type are excellent for inclusion in parts catalogs and maintenance manuals.

24.6 Isometrics by Computer

AutoCAD provides an *Isometric* grid for drawing isometrics. The *Style* option of the *Snap* command allows changing the rectangular *Grid*, called *Standard* (S), to *Isometric* (I) with dots shown vertically and at 30° to the horizontal (**Fig. 24.55**). In this mode, you can make the cursor's cross hairs *Snap* to the grid points and align with the axes of isometric drawings.

Isometric drawings made with this system (**Fig. 24.56**) are not a true three-dimensional drawings system. Instead, they are two-dimensional isometrics that cannot be rotated to show other views.

Circles that will appear as ellipses in isometric can be drawn when *Snap* has been set to *Isometric*. From the *Draw* menu, choose *Ellipse*, and *I* (isometric circle). Specify the center point and the radius or diameter, and the isometric ellipse is drawn. When using this command, the cursor is aligned with each of the three isometric planes by pressing (Ctrl-E) on the keyboard

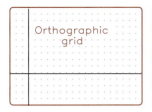
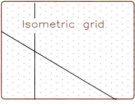

A. ORTHOGRAPHIC GRID   B. ISOMETRIC GRID

24.55 The *Snap* command permits you to use the orthographic grid *(Standard)* or the isometric grid option (isometric) for drawing isometric pictorials.

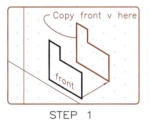
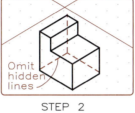

STEP 1   STEP 2

24.56 Isometrics by computer

Step 1 Set the isometric grid on the screen (*Snap* and *I*), and set *Snap* to the grid. Draw the front view as an isometric and copy it to the backside with the *Copy* command.

Step 2 Connect the visible corner points and *Erase* hidden lines to complete the drawing.

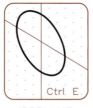
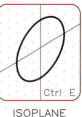
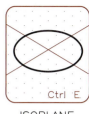

ISOPLANE   ISOPLANE   ISOPLANE
LEFT   RIGHT   TOP

24.57 Use the *Ellipse* command and the *Isocircle* option to draw circles in isometric. By pressing (Ctrl-E), you may alternatively rotate the isometric ellipses 120° to fit the three isometric planes.

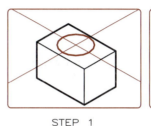
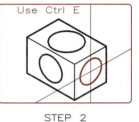

STEP 1   STEP 2

24.58 Isometric ellipses by computer

Step 1 Use *Snap's* isometric-grid mode to draw isometric ellipses.

Command: ELLIPSE (Enter)

Specify axis endpoint of ellipse or [Arc/ Center/ Isocircle]: I (Enter).

Specify center of isocircle: (Select with cursor.)

Specify radius of isocircle or [Diameter]: (Select radius with cursor.)

Step 2 Change the orientation of the cursor for drawing isometric ellipses on the other two planes by pressing (Ctrl-E). Repeat the process in Step 1.

(**Fig. 24.57**). When the cursor is aligned with the proper axes of an isometric plane, you may select the center of the isometric ellipse or its diameter's endpoints (**Fig. 24.58**).

The *Isoplane* command changes the position of the cursor in the same way (Ctrl-E) does. *Isoplane* will prompt you to select from *Left/Top/Right/[Toggle]:* options. To use the Toggle option, press (Enter) to successively move the cursor position from plane to plane.

24.7 Axonometric Projection

An axonometric projection is a type of orthographic projection in which the pictorial view is projected perpendicularly onto the picture plane with parallel projectors. The object is positioned at an angle to the picture plane so that its pictorial projection will be a three-dimensional view. The three types of axonometric projections are: (**1**) **isometric**, (**2**) **dimetric**, or (**3**) **trimetric** (**Fig. 24.59**).

Recall that the isometric projection is the type of pictorial in which the diagonal of a cube is seen as a point, the three axes and planes of the cube are equally foreshortened, and the axes are equally spaced 120° apart. Measurements along the three axes will be equal but less than true length because the isometric projection is true projection.

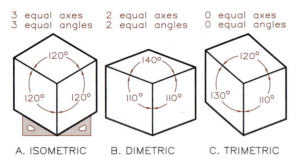

3 equal axes
3 equal angles

2 equal axes
2 equal angles

0 equal axes
0 equal angles

A. ISOMETRIC | B. DIMETRIC | C. TRIMETRIC

24.59 This drawing illustrates the three types of axonometric projection.

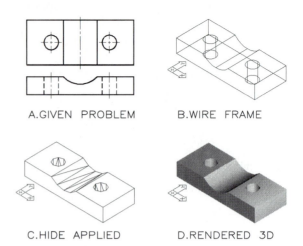

A. GIVEN PROBLEM | B. WIRE FRAME

C. HIDE APPLIED | D. RENDERED 3D

24.60 Modeling a simple part

A Two orthographic views of the part are given.

B A wire frame drawing of the part is made.

C The hidden lines are suppressed to give a three-dimensional model.

D The model is rendered to give it a realistic look.

A **dimetric projection** is a pictorial in which two planes are equally foreshortened and two of the axes are separated by equal angles. Measurements along two axes of the cube are equal.

A **trimetric projection** is a pictorial in which all three planes are unequally foreshortened. The lengths of the axes are unequal, and the angles between them are different.

24.8 Three-dimensional Modeling

Objects drawn with AutoCAD as true three-dimensional solids can be rotated and viewed from any angle as if they were held in your hand. The object in **Fig. 24.60** is an example of a simple object represented by two orthographic views, a wire-frame drawing, a hidden-line wire frame drawing, and a rendered solid. The capability to depict objects as rendered solids is a powerful design and communications tool.

Another example of a three-dimensional part that would be difficult to draw by hand is the pulley shown in **Fig. 24.61**. A typical section through the pulley and its axis are drawn, the section is revolved about the axis, and the wire frame diagram is rendered. In addition to being able to select various views of the pulley, different lighting combinations and materials can be applied to it in infinite combinations of effects.

An example of an industrial application is given in **Fig. 24.62**, which shows an apparatus of

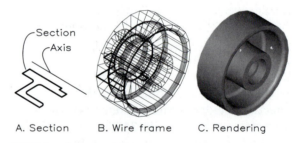

A. Section | B. Wire frame | C. Rendering

24.61 A model by revolution

A A typical section of the pulley and its axis is drawn.

B The section is rotated about the axis to obtain a wire- frame drawing.

C The wire frame is rendered to obtain a realistic view of the pulley.

a higher degree of complexity that would be a rigorous assignment if drawn by hand. Although is no easy chore to draw it as a series of solids by computer, the computer drawing enables you to obtain many different views of the parts, and to

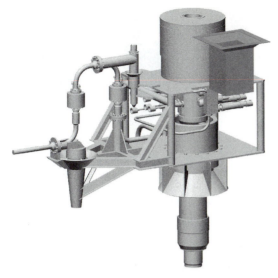

24.62 This apparatus is an example of a rendered three-dimensional model of a moderately complex application. (*Courtesy of Cameron.*)

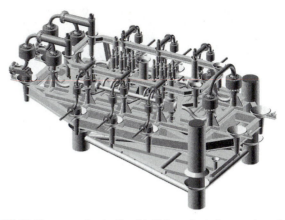

24.63 The apparatus in Fig. 24.62 is replicated a number of times in this equipment assembly used in subsea production. (*Courtesy of Cameron.*)

replicate drawings in combination. For example, the apparatus in **Fig. 24.62** is applied repetitively in the subsea production-equipment assembly in **Fig. 24.63**. The savings in time and effort becomes highly significant, and the final rendering greatly improves the understanding of the unit as a whole.

An introduction to three-dimensional modeling by several methods is given in Chapter 27. You will find that solid modeling begins with and understanding of the underlying fundamentals covered in this chapter. The ability to sketch three-dimensional drawings is an invaluable skill that you will use to develop and communicate design applications.

24.9 The Human Figure

An ultimate aspiration of the illustrator has always been the ability to represent the human form in a realistic manner. In addition to determining the interactions between parts, assemblies, and equipment, it is equally important to

24.64 The computer-drawn scene illustrates the interaction between people and equipment. (*Courtesy McDonnell Douglas Space & Defense System—Kennedy Space Center.*)

study the relationship of personnel to their working environment. An example of this type of application in **Fig. 24.64** shows workers performing maintenance on a spacecraft. The figures can

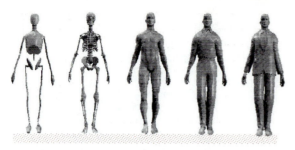

A.Stick   B.Skeleton   C.Nude   D.Casual   E.Formal

24.65 These are several of the rendering options that are available as part of *Poser 2*.

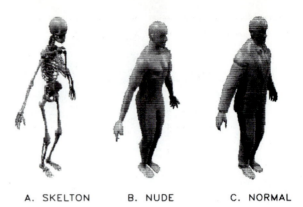

A. SKELTON   B. NUDE   C. NORMAL

24.66 With *Poser 2*, the human figure can be viewed as orthographic, axonometric, and perspective views.

be moved about the work area and placed in an infinite variety of poses.

Several software packages have been developed that can be used with AutoCAD and other programs that adapt well with computer graphics. The software, *Poser*® by *Fractal Design,* offers many options for representing the human body, from stick figures to formally-dressed figures (**Fig. 24.65**). Choices of body styles can be made from many categories, a few of which are age, sex, weight, and pose. Bodies can be positioned and controlled to fit almost any application. Figures can be rotated to obtain orthographic, axonometric, or perspective views of them (**Fig. 24.66**). Clothing options range from casual to a formal business suit or dress, in the case of a female. Since all designs and projects are undertaken to fulfill the needs of people, it is important that the human body interacts with design concepts at all stages of their development.

The Future

The future of 3D graphics is truly exciting. What is available today for the microcomputer was not possible even on much larger and more expensive computers just a few years ago. The capabilities of 3D programs will continue to become more powerful and easier to use. Graphics in the future will include more solid modeling, animation, and sound effects. Get ready for an exciting trip!

Problems

Draw your solutions to the following problems (**Fig. 24.67**) on size A or B sheets, as assigned. Select an appropriate scale to take advantage of the space available on each sheet. By letting each square represent 0.20 in. (5 mm), you can draw two solutions on each size A sheet. By setting each square to 0.40 inch (10 mm), you can draw one solution on each size B sheet.

Oblique Pictorials
1–24. Construct cavalier, cabinet, or general obliques of the parts assigned.

Isometric Pictorials
1–24. Construct isometrics of the parts assigned.

24.67 Problems 1–24.

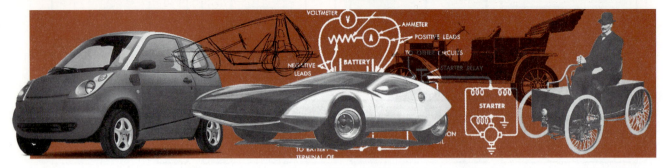

Graphs

25.1 Introduction

Data and information expressed as numbers and words are usually difficult to analyze or evaluate unless transcribed into graphical form, or as a **graph.** The term **chart** is an acceptable substitute for graph, but it is more appropriate when applied to maps, a specialized form of graphs.

Graphs are especially useful in presenting data at briefings where the data must be interpreted and communicated quickly to those in attendance. Graphs are a convenient way to condense and present data visually, allowing the data to be grasped much more easily than when presented as tables of numbers or verbally.

Several different types of graphs are widely used. Their application depends on the data and the nature of the presentation required. The most common types of graphs are:

1. Pie graphs

2. Bar graphs

3. Linear coordinate graphs

4. Logarithmic coordinate graphs

5. Semilogarithmic coordinate graphs

Proportions

Graphs are used on large display boards, in technical reports, as slides for a projector, and as transparencies for an overhead projector. Consequently, the proportion of the graph must be determined before it is constructed in order to match the page, slide, or transparency.

A graph that is to be photographed with a 35-mm camera must be drawn to the proportions of the film, or approximately $3'' \times 2''$ (**Fig. 25.1**). This area may be enlarged or reduced proportionally by using the diagonal-line method.

The proportions of an overhead projector transparency are approximately $10'' \times 8''$. The image size should not exceed 9.5 inches $\times$ 7.5 inches to allow adequate margin for mounting the transparency on a frame (usually made of cardboard).

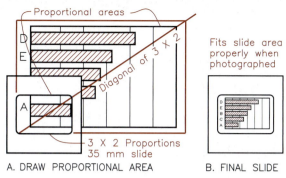

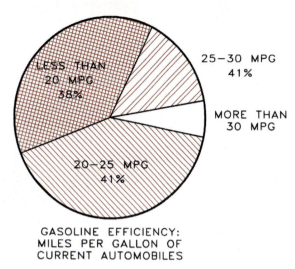

GASOLINE EFFICIENCY:
MILES PER GALLON OF
CURRENT AUTOMOBILES

25.1 This diagonal-line method may be used to lay out drawings that are proportional to the area of a 35-mm slide.

25.2 A pie graph shows the relationship of parts to a whole. It is most effective when there are only a few parts.

25.2 Pie Graphs

Pie graphs compare the relationships of parts to a whole. For example, **Fig. 25.2** shows a pie graph that compares the energy efficiency in miles per gallon of the current models of automobiles on the market.

Figure 25.3 illustrates the steps involved in drawing a pie graph. The data in this example, as simple as it is, are not as easily compared in numerical form as when drawn as a pie graph. Position thin sectors of a pie graph as nearly hor-

izontal as possible to provide more space for labeling. When space is not available within the sectors, place labels outside the pie graph and, if necessary, use leaders (**Fig. 25.2**). Showing the percentage represented by each sector is important and giving the actual numbers or values as part of the label is also desirable.

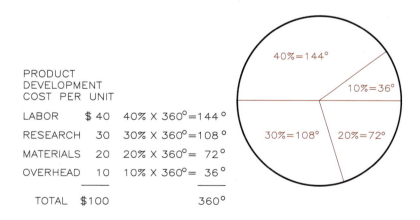

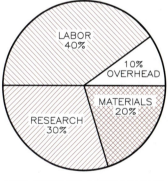

NEW PRODUCT DEVELOPMENT
COST PER UNIT

PRODUCT DEVELOPMENT COST PER UNIT		
LABOR	$ 40	40% X 360°=144°
RESEARCH	30	30% X 360°=108°
MATERIALS	20	20% X 360°= 72°
OVERHEAD	10	10% X 360°= 36°
TOTAL	$100	360°

25.3 Drawing pie graphs

Step 1 Find the sum of the parts and the percentage of the total that each part comprises. Multiply each percentage by 360° to obtain the angle of each sector.

Step 2 Draw the circle and construct each sector using the degrees of each from Step 1. Place small sectors as nearly horizontal as possible.

Step 3 Label sectors with their proper names and percentages. Exact numbers also may be included in each sector to add more clarity.

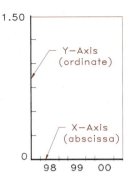

DIVIDENDS PAID
BY THE
APEX COMPANY

YEAR	DIVIDEND
1998	$0.40
1999	0.60
2000	0.90

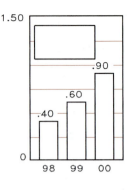

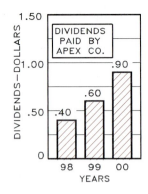

25.4 Drawing a bar graph

Given These numerical data are to be plotted as a bar graph for better presentation in a report.

Step 1 Scale the vertical and horizontal axes so that the data will fit on the grid. Begin the bars at zero.

Step 2 The width of the bars should be greater than the space between them. Lines should not cross the bars.

Step 3 Strengthen lines, place a title in the graph, label the axes, and cross-hatch the bars.

25.3 Bar Graphs

Bar graphs are widely used for comparing values because the general public understands them. **Figure 25.4** shows how to convert data into a bar graph that can be used in a report or briefing. The axes of the graph carry labels, and its title appears inside the graph where space is available.

The bars of a bar graph should be sorted in ascending or descending order unless there is an overriding reason not to, such as a chronological sequence. An arbitrary arrangement of the bars, such as in alphabetical or numerical order, makes a graph difficult to evaluate (**Fig. 25.5A**). However, ranking the categories by bar length allows easier comparisons from smallest to largest (**Fig. 25.5B**). If the data are sequential and involve time, such as sales per month, a better arrangement of the bars is chronologically to show the effect of time.

Bars in a bar graph may be horizontal (**Fig. 25.6**) or vertical. Data cannot be compared accurately unless each bar is full length and originates at zero. Also, bars should not extend beyond the limits of the graph (giving the impression that the data were "too hot" to hold).

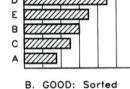

A. POOR: Not sorted   B. GOOD: Sorted

25.5 Arranging bars by length

A When bars are arbitrarily arranged, such as alphabetically, the bar graph is difficult to interpret.

B When the bars are sorted by length, the graph is much easier to interpret.

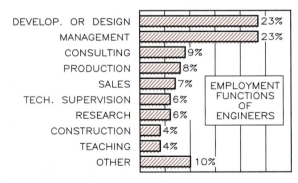

25.6 The horizontal bars of this graph are arranged in descending order to show the employment functions of engineers.

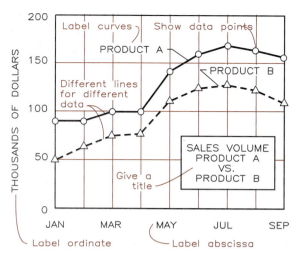

25.7 This basic linear coordinate graph illustrates the important features on a graph.

25.4 Linear Coordinate Graphs

Figure 25.7 shows a typical linear coordinate graph, with notes explaining its important features. Divided into equal divisions, the axes are referred to as linear scales. Data points are plotted on the grid by using measurements, called coordinates, along each axis from zero. The plotted points are marked with symbols such as circles or squares that may be easily drawn with a template. The horizontal scale of the graph is called the **abscissa** or x axis. The vertical scale is called the **ordinate** or y axis.

When the points have been plotted, a curve is drawn through them to represent the data. The line drawn to represent data points is called a **curve** regardless of whether it is a straight line, smooth curve, or broken line. The curve should not extend through the plotted points; rather, the points should be left as open circles or other symbols.

The curve is the most important part of the graph, so it should be drawn as the most prominent (thickest) line. If there are two curves in a graph, they should be drawn as different line types and labeled. The title of the graph is placed in a box inside the graph and units are given along the x and y axes with labels identifying the scales of the graph.

Broken-Line Graphs

The steps required to draw a linear coordinate graph are shown in **Fig. 25.8**. Because the data points represent sales, which have no predictable pattern, the data do not give a smooth

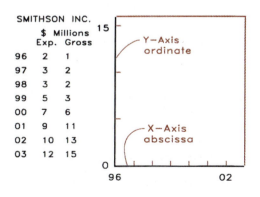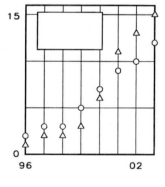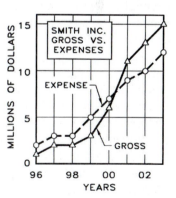

25.8 A broken-line graph

Given A record of the Smith Company's gross income and expenses.

Step 1 Lay off the vertical (ordinate) and horizontal (abscissa) axes to provide space for the largest values.

Step 2 Draw division lines and plot the data, using different symbols for each set of data.

Step 3 Connect points with straight lines, label the axes, title the graph, darken the lines, and label the curves.

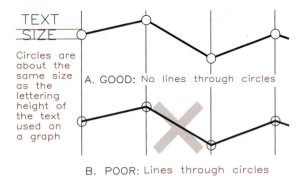

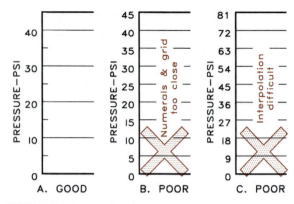

25.9 The curve of a graph drawn from point to point should not extend through the symbols used to represent data points.

25.11 Calibrating graph scales.

A The scale is properly labeled and calibrated. It has about the right number of grid lines and divisions, and the numbers are well-spaced and easy to interpolate.

B The numbers are too close together, and there are too many grid lines.

C The increments selected make interpolation difficult.

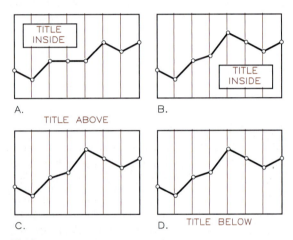

25.10 Placement of titles on a graph.

A and **B** The title of a graph may be placed inside a box within the graph. Box perimeter lines should not coincide with grid lines.

C The title may be placed over the graph.

D The title may be placed under the graph.

Titles The title of a graph may be located in any of the positions shown in **Fig. 25.10**. A graph's title should never be as meaningless as "graph" or "coordinate graph." Instead, it should identify concisely what the graph shows.

Calibration and Labeling The calibration and labeling of the axes affects the appearance and readability of a graph. **Figure 25.11A** shows a properly calibrated and labeled axis. **Figures 25.11B** and **25.11C** illustrate common mistakes: placing the grid lines too close together and labeling too many divisions along the axis. In **Fig. 25.11C**, the choice of the interval between the labeled values (9 units) makes interpolation between them difficult. For example, locating the value 22 by eye is more difficult on this scale than on the one shown in **Fig. 25.11A**.

Smooth-Line Graphs

The strength of concrete related to its curing time is plotted in **Fig. 25.12**. The strength of concrete changes gradually and continuously in relation to curing time. Therefore, the data

progression from point to point. Therefore, the points are connected with a **broken-line curve** drawn as an angular line from point to point.

Again, leave the symbols used to mark the data points open rather than extending grid lines or the data curve through them (**Fig. 25.9**). Each circle or symbol used to plot points should be about 1/8 in. (3 mm) in diameter.

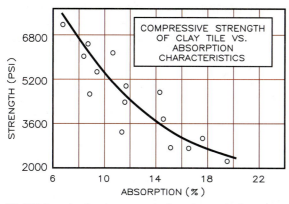

25.12 When the data being graphed involve gradual, continuous changes in relationships, the curve is drawn as a smooth line, which estimates the true trend of the data.

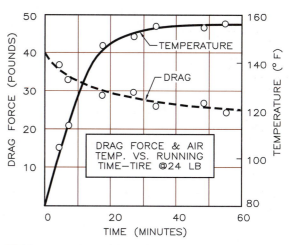

25.14 A two-scale graph has different scales along each y axis, and labels identify which scale applies to which curve.

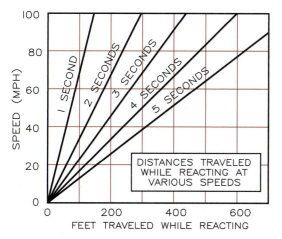

25.13 This graph may be used to determine a third value from the other two variables. For example, select a speed of 70 mph and a time of 5 seconds to find a distance traveled of 550 ft.

points are connected with a smooth-line curve rather than a broken-line curve. These relationships are represented by the **best-fit curve**, a smooth curve that is an average representation of the points.

A smooth-line curve on a graph implies that interpolations between data points can be made to estimate other values. Data points connected by a broken-line curve imply that interpolations between the plotted points cannot be made.

Straight-Line Graphs

Some graphs have neither broken-line curves nor smooth-line curves, but straight-line curves (**Fig. 25.13**). On this graph, a third value can be determined from the two given values. For example, if you are driving 70 miles per hour and you take 5 seconds to react and apply your brakes, you will have traveled 550 feet in that time.

Two-Scale Coordinate Graphs

Graphs may contain different scales in combination, as shown in **Fig. 25.14**, where the vertical scale at the left is in units of pounds and the one at the right is in degrees of temperature. Both curves are drawn with respect to their y axes and each curve is labeled. Two-scale graphs of this type may be confusing unless they are clearly labeled. Two-scale graphs are effective for comparing related variables, as shown here.

Optimization Graphs

Optimization graphs are effective in comparing two related variables, such as an automobile's

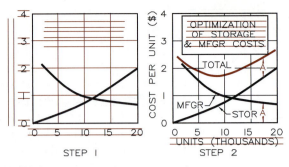

25.15 Constructing an optimization graph

Step 1 Lay out the graph and plot the curves from the data given.

Step 2 Graphically add the two curves to find a third curve. For example, transfer distance A to locate a point on the third curve. The lowest point of the "total" curve is the optimum point, or 8000 units.

depreciation in comparison to increasing maintenance costs to determine the optimum time for replacing the car. The point of optimization is at the time when the cost of maintenance is equal to the value of the car.

The steps involved in drawing an optimization graph are illustrated in **Fig. 25.15**. Here, the manufacturing cost per unit reduces as more units are made, causing warehousing costs to increase. Adding the two curves to get a third (total) curve indicates that the optimum num-

ber to manufacture at a time is about 8000 units (the low point on the total curve). When more or fewer units are manufactured, the total cost per unit is greater.

Break-Even Graphs

Break-even graphs help in evaluating marketing and manufacturing costs to determine the selling price of a product. As **Fig. 25.16** shows, if the desired break-even point for a product is 10,000 units, it must sell for $3.50 per unit to cover the costs of manufacturing and development.

25.5 Semilogarithmic Coordinate Graphs

Semilogarithmic graphs are called **ratio graphs** because they graphically represent ratios. One scale, usually the vertical scale, is logarithmic, and the other is linear (divided into equal divisions).

The same data plotted on a linear grid and on a semilogarithmic grid are compared in **Fig. 25.17**. The semilogarithmic graph reveals that the percentage change from 0 to 5 is greater for curve B than for curve A because here curve B is steeper. The plot on the linear grid appears to show the opposite result.

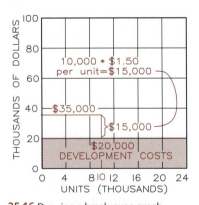

25.16 Drawing a break-even graph

Step 1 Plot the development cost ($20,000). At $1.50 per unit to make, the total cost would be $35,000 for 10,000 units, the break-even point.

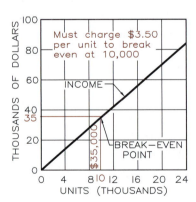

Step 2 To break even at 10,000, the manufacturer must sell each unit for $3.50. Draw a line from zero through the break-even point of $35,000 to represent income.

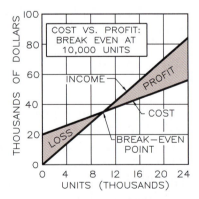

Step 3 There is a loss of $20,000 at zero units, but progressively less until the break-even point is reached. Profit is the difference between curves at the right of the break-even point.

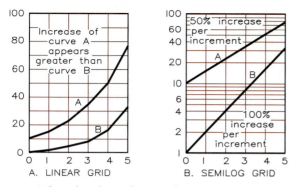

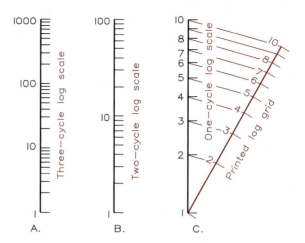

25.17 When plotted on a linear grid, curve A appears to be increasing at a greater rate than curve B. However, plotting the data on a semilogarithmic grid reveals the true rate of change.

25.19 Logarithmic scales may have several cycles: (A) three-cycle scales; (B) two-cycle scales, and (C) one-cycle scales. Calibrations may be projected to a scale of any length from a printed scale, as shown here.

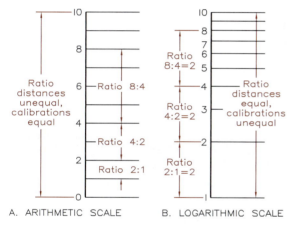

25.18 The divisions on an arithmetic scale are equal and represent unequal ratios between points. The divisions on logarithmic scales are unequal and represent equal ratios.

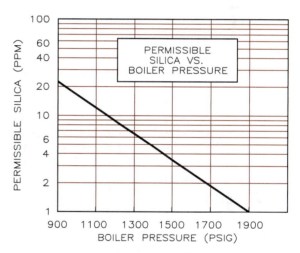

25.20 This semilogarithmic graph relates permissible silica (parts per million) to boiler pressure.

Figure 25.18 shows the relationship between the linear scale and the logarithmic scale. Equal divisions along the linear scale have unequal ratios, but unequal divisions along the log scale have equal ratios.

Log scales may have one or many cycles. Each cycle increases by a factor of 10. For example, the scale shown in **Fig. 25.19A** is a three-cycle scale, and the one shown in **Fig. 25.19B** is a two-cycle scale. When scales must be drawn to a certain length, commercially printed log scales may be used to graphically transfer the calibrations to the scale being used (**Fig. 25.19C**).

An application of a semilogarithmic graph for presenting industrial data is illustrated in **Fig. 25.20**. People who do not realize that semilog graphs are different from linear coordinate graphs may misunderstand them. Also, zero values cannot be shown on log scales.

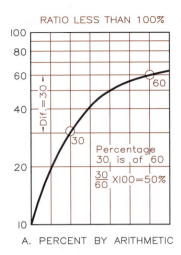

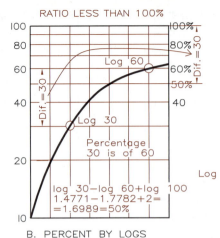

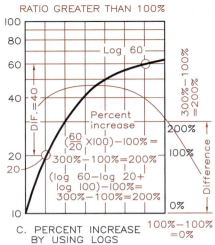

| A. PERCENT BY ARITHMETIC | B. PERCENT BY LOGS | C. PERCENT INCREASE BY USING LOGS |

25.21 Percentage graphs

A To find the percentage that one data point is of another point (the percentage that 30 is of 60, for example), you may calculate it mathematically: (30/60)(100) = 50%.

B Find the percentage that 30 is of 60 mathematically by using the logarithms of the numbers. Or find it graphically by transferring the distance between 30 and 60 to the scale at the right, which shows that 30 is 50%.

C To find a percentage increase greater than 100%, divide the smaller number into the larger number. Find the difference between the logs of 60 and 20 with dividers and measure upward from 100% to find the increase of 200%.

Percentage Graphs

The percentage that one number is of another, or the percentage increase of one number to a greater number can be determined on a semi-logarithmic graph (**Fig. 25.21**). Data plotted in **Fig. 25.21A** are used to find the percentage that 30 is of 60 (two points on the curve) by arithmetic. The vertical distance between them is the difference between their logarithms, so the percentage can be found graphically in **Fig 25.21B**. The distance from 30 to 60 is transferred to the log scale at the right of the graph and subtracted from the log of 100 to find the value of 50% as a direct reading of percentage.

In **Fig. 25.21C**, the percentage increase between two points is transferred from the grid to the lower end of the log scale and measured upward because the increase is greater than zero. These methods may be used to find percentage increases or decreases for any set of points on the grid.

Problems

Draw your solutions to these problems on size A sheets. Apply the techniques and principles covered in this chapter.

Pie Graphs

1. Draw a pie graph that shows the comparative sources of retirees' income: investments, 34%; employment, 24%; social security, 21%; pensions, 19%; other, 2%.

2. Draw a pie graph that shows the number of members of the technological team: engineers, 985,000; technicians, 932,000; scientists, 410,000.

3. Construct a pie graph of the employment status of graduates of two-year technician programs a year after graduation: employed, 63%; continuing full-time study, 23%; considering job offers, 6%; military, 6%; other, 2%.

4. Draw a pie graph showing the types of degrees held by aerospace engineers: bachelor's, 65%; master's, 29%; Ph.D.'s, 6%.

Bar Graphs

5. Draw a bar graph that shows expected job growth by city: Austin, 1.3%; San Antonio, 0.8%; Houston, 1.6%; Fort Worth, 0%; Dallas, 0.4%; all of Texas, 0.8%.

6. Draw a single-bar bar graph that represents 100% of a die casting alloy. The proportional parts of the alloy are: tin, 16%; lead, 24%; zinc, 38.8%; aluminum, 16.4%; copper, 4.8%.

7. Draw a bar graph that compares the number of skilled workers employed in various occupations. Use the following data and arrange the graph for ease of comparing occupations: carpenters, 82,000; all-round machinists, 310,000; plumbers, 350,000; bricklayers, 200,000; appliance servicers, 185,000; automotive mechanics, 760,000; electricians, 380,000; and painters, 400,000.

8. Draw a bar graph that shows the characteristics of a typical U.S. family's spending: housing, 29.6%; food, 15.1%; transportation, 16.7%; clothing, 5.9%; retirement, 8.6%; entertainment, 4.9%; insurance, 5.2%; health care, 3.0%; charity, 3.1%; other, 7.9%.

9. Draw a bar graph that compares the corrosion resistance of the materials listed in the following table.

	Loss in Weight (%)	
	In Atmosphere	*In Sea Water*
Common steel	100	100
10% nickel steel	70	80
25% nickel steel	20	55

10. Draw a bar graph of the data from Problem 1.

11. Draw a bar graph of the data from Problem 2.

12. Draw a bar graph of the data from Problem 3.

13. Construct a bar graph comparing sales and earnings of Apple Computer from 1980 through 1989. Data are by year for sales and earnings (profit) in billions of dollars: 1980, 0 and 0; 1981, 0.33 and 0.05; 1982, 0.60 and 0.07; 1983, 1.00 and 0.09; 1984, 1.51 and 0.08; 1985, 1.90 and 0.07; 1986, 1.85 and 0.12; 1987, 2.70 and 0.25; 1988, 4.15 and 0.40; 1989, 5.50 and 0.45.

Linear Coordinate Graphs

14. Draw a linear coordinate graph to show the estimated population growth in the U.S. from 1992 through 2050 in millions of people: 1992, 255; 2000, 270; 2010, 295; 2020, 325; 2030, 348; 2040, 360; 2050, 383.

15. Construct a linear coordinate graph that shows the relationship of energy costs (mills per kilowatt-hour) on the y axis to the percent capacity of a nuclear power plant and a gas-or oil-fired power plant on the x axis. Gas- or oil-fired plant data: 17 mills, 10%; 12 mills, 20%; 8 mills, 40%; 7 mills, 60%; 6 mills, 80%; 5.8 mills, 100%. Nuclear plant data: 24 mills, 10%; 14 mills, 20%; 7 mills, 40%; 5 mills, 60%; 4.2 mills, 80%; 3.7 mills, 100%.

16. Plot the data from Problem 13 as a linear coordinate graph.

17. Construct a linear coordinate graph to show the relationship between the transverse resilience in inch-pounds (ip) on the y axis and the single-blow impact in foot-pounds (fp) on the x axis of gray iron. Data: 21 fp, 375 ip; 22 fp, 350 ip; 23 fp, 380 ip; 30 fp, 400 ip; 32 fp, 420 ip; 33 fp, 410 ip; 38 fp, 510 ip; 45 fp, 615 ip; 50 fp, 585 ip; 60 fp, 785 ip; 70 fp, 900 ip; 75 fp, 920 ip.

18. Draw a linear coordinate graph to illustrate the trends in the export of U.S. services and products from 1980 through 1993: 1980, +8.5%; 1981, +2.5%; 1982, −7.5%; 1983, −4.5%; 1984, +7%; 1985, −2%; 1986, +7%; 1987, +12.5%; 1988, +17.5%; 1989, +10%; 1990, +6%; 1991, +3%; 1992, +5%; 1993, +7%.

19. Draw a linear coordinate graph for the centrifugal pump test data for water HP and electric HP in the following table. The units along the x axis are to be gallons per minute. Use two curves to represent the variables given.

Gallons per Minute	Discharge Pressure	Water HP	Electric HP	Efficiency (%)
0	19.0	0.00	1.36	0.0
75	17.5	0.72	2.25	32.0
115	15.0	1.00	2.54	39.4
154	10.0	1.00	2.74	36.5
185	5.0	0.74	2.80	26.5
200	3.0	0.63	2.83	22.2

20. Draw a linear coordinate graph that compares two of the values shown in **Table 25.1**—ultimate strength and elastic limit—with degrees of temperature (x axis).

Table 25.1

F°	Ultimate Strength	Elastic Limit
400	257,500	208,000
500	247,000	224,500
600	232,500	214,000
700	207,500	193,500
800	180,500	169,000
900	159,500	146,500
1000	142,500	128,500
1100	126,500	114,000
1200	114,500	96,500
1300	108,000	85,500

Break-Even Graphs

21. Draw a break-even graph that shows the earnings for a new product that has a development cost of $12,000. The break-even point is at 8000 units and each costs $0.50 to manufacture. What would be the profit at volumes of 20,000 and 25,000?

22. Repeat Problem 21 except that the development costs are $80,000, the manufacturing cost of the first 10,000 units is $2.30 each, and the desired break-even point is 10,000 units. What is the profit at volumes of 20,000 and 30,000?

Logarithmic Graphs

23. Use the data given in **Table 25.2** to construct a logarithmic graph. Plot the vibration amplitude (A) as the ordinate and the vibration frequency (F) as the abscissa. The data for curve 1 represent the maximum limits of machinery in good condition with no danger from vibration. The data for curve 2 are the lower limits of machinery that is being vibrated excessively to the danger point. The vertical scale is three cycles, and the horizontal scale is two cycles.

24. Plot this data on a two-cycle log graph to show the current in amperes (y axis) versus the voltage in volts (x axis) of precision temperature-sensing resistors. Data: 1 volt, 1.9 amps; 2 volts, 4 amps; 4 volts, 8 amps; 8 volts, 17 amps; 10 volts, 20 amps; 20 volts, 30 amps; 40 volts, 36 amps; 80 volts, 31 amps; 100 volts, 30 amps.

25. Plot the data in Problem 9 as a logarithmic graph.

26. Plot the data in Problem 20 as a logarithmic graph.

Semilogarithmic Graphs

27. Construct a semilogarithmic graph with the y axis a two-cycle log scale from 1 to 100 and the x axis a linear scale from 1 to 7. The object of the graph is to show the survivability of a shelter at varying distances from the atmospheric detonation of a one-megaton thermonuclear bomb. Plot overpressure in psi along the y axis, and distance from ground zero in miles along the x axis. The data points represent an 80% chance of survival of the shelter. Data: 1 mile, 55 psi; 2 miles, 11 psi; 3 miles, 4.5 psi; 4 miles, 2.5 psi; 5 miles, 2.0 psi; 6 miles, 1.3 psi.

Table 25.2

F	100	200	500	1000	2000	5000	10,000
A(1)	0.0028	0.002	0.0015	0.001	0.0006	0.0003	0.00013
A(2)	0.06	0.05	0.04	0.03	0.018	0.005	0.001

28. The growth of Division A and Division B of a company is shown by the following data. Plot the data on a semilog graph with a one-cycle log scale on the y axis for sales in thousands of dollars and a linear scale on the x axis for years. Data: first year, A = $11,700 and B = $44,000; second year, A = $19,500 and B = $50,000; third year, A = $25,000 and B = $55,000; fourth year, A = $32,000 and B = $64,000; fifth year, A = $42,000 and B = $66,000; sixth year, A = $48,000 and B = $75,000. Which division has the better growth rate?

29. Draw a semilog chart showing probable engineering progress based on the following indices: 40,000 B.C., 21; 30,000 B.C., 21.5; 20,000 B.C., 22; 16,000 B.C., 23; 10,000 B.C., 27; 6000 B.C., 34; 4000 B.C., 39; 2000 B.C., 49; 500 B.C., = 60; A.D. 1900, 1000. Use a horizontal scale of 1 in. = 10,000 years, a height of about 5 in., and two-cycle printed paper, if available.

30. Plot the data in Problem 19 as a semilogarithmic graph.

31. Plot the data in Problem 20 as a semilogarithmic graph.

Percentage Graphs

32. Using the graph plotted in Problem 30, determine the percentage of increase of Division A and Division B growth from year 1 to year 4. What percentage of sales of Division A are the sales of Division B at the end of year 2? At the end of year 6?

33. Plot the values for water horsepower and electric horsepower from Problem 22 on semilog paper against gallons per minute along the x axis. What percentage of electric horsepower is water horsepower when 75 gallons per minute are being pumped?

34. Plot the data below as a semilog graph to determine percentages and ratios for the data. What is the percentage increase in the demand for water from 1980 to 1920? What percentage of demand is the supply for 1900, 1930, and 1970?

	Supply*	Demand*
1890	80	35
1900	90	35
1910	110	60
1920	135	80
1930	155	110
1940	240	125
1950	270	200
1960	315	320
1970	380	410
1980	450	550

*Billions of gallons per day.

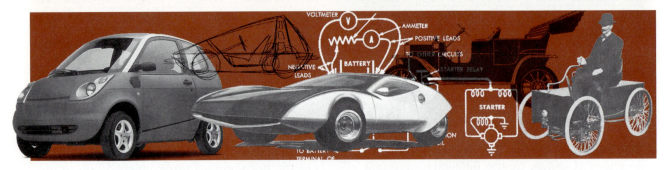

CHAPTER TWENTY SIX

AutoCAD 2002 2D Computer Graphics

26.1 Introduction

This chapter provides an introduction to computer graphics using AutoCAD® 2002, which runs on an Intel 486 or Pentium processor with 32 MB (64 MB preferred) of RAM, at least 200 Mb of hard disk space, a mouse (or tablet), and an A-B plotter and/or printer. Windows 98, Windows 2000, or Windows NT are recommended as the operating systems. AutoCAD was selected as the software for presenting computer graphics because it is the most widely used computer graphics program.

The coverage of AutoCAD in this book is brief and many operations could not be included because of space limitations. AutoCAD's concisely written *User's Guide* has 856 pages and other manuals on the market have as many as 1500 pages. However, AutoCAD is covered here sufficiently well to guide you through the applications necessary for a typical engineering design graphics course.

You will find that learning computer graphics and its next upgrades will be a career-long experience. You should begin this self-teaching by experimenting with the peripheral commands and options that are not covered in this book. Also, reference to *Help* should be made routinely as a means of learning new commands and refreshing your memory when necessary.

26.2 Computer Graphics Overview

The major areas of computer graphics are **CAD** (computer-aided design), **CADD** (computer-aided design and drafting), **CAD/CAM** (computer-aided manufacturing), and **CIM** (computer-integrated manufacturing).

CAD (computer-aided design) is used to solve design problems, analyze design data, and store design information for easy retrieval. Many CAD systems perform these functions in an integrated manner, greatly increasing the designer's productivity.

CADD (computer-aided design and drafting) is the computer process of making engi-

26.1 This automatic Chrysler assembly line uses computer-controlled robots for welding body parts together. (*Courtesy of Chrysler Corporation.*)

2. **Increased drawing speed.** Engineering drawings and documents can be prepared more quickly, especially when standard details from existing libraries are incorporated in new drawings.

3. **Easy to revise.** Drawings can be more easily modified, changed, and revised than is possible by hand techniques.

4. **Better design analysis.** Alternative designs can be analyzed quickly and easily. Software is available to simulate a product's operation and test it under a variety of conditions, which lessens the need for models and prototypes.

5. **Better presentation.** Drawings can be presented in 2D or 3D, and rendered as technical illustrations in order to better communicate designs.

6. **Libraries of drawing aids.** Databases of details, symbols, and figures that are used over and over can be archived for immediate use in making drawings.

7. **Improved filing.** Drawings can be conveniently filed, retrieved, and transmitted on disks and tapes.

neering drawings and technical documents more closely related to drafting.

CAD/CAM (computer-aided design/computer-aided manufacturing) is a system that can be used to design a part or product, devise the production steps, and electronically communicate this data to control the operation of manufacturing equipment and robots.

CIM (computer-integrated manufacturing) is a more advanced system than CAD/CAM that coordinates and operates all stages of manufacturing from design to finished product (**Fig. 26.1**).

Advantages of CAD and CADD

Computer-graphics systems offer the designer and drafter some or all of the following advantages.

1. **Increased accuracy.** CAD systems are capable of producing drawings that are essentially 100% accurate.

26.3 Computer Hardware

The hardware of a computer graphics system includes the **computer**, **monitor**, **input devices** (keyboard, digitizers, and light pens), and **output devices** (plotters and printers).

Computer

The computer, with an installed **program**, receives input from the user from the keyboard, executes the instructions, and produces output. The part of the computer that follows the program's instructions is the **CPU** (central processing unit). The computer graphics computer should have at least 32 MB of RAM, and its hard disk storage should be large, preferably 8 gigabytes or larger (**Fig. 26.2**).

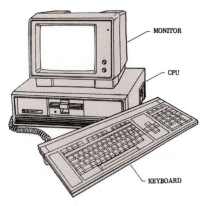

26.2 The basic components of a desktop computer system are the CPU (central processing unit), keyboard, and monitor.

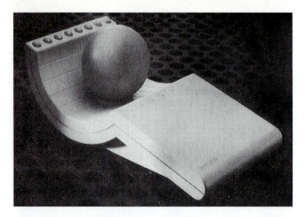

26.4 The Spaceball® digitizer is manipulated to move an object in 3D space on the screen by pushing, pulling, and twisting it. (*Courtesy of CalCom Corporation.*)

26.3 Current technology enables computers to send 3D graphics over networks for instantaneous communication. (*Courtesy of Hewlett-Packard Company.*)

26.5 The DeskJet 990c series of printers produces photo-quality color images that are as close to traditional photographs as desktop printers have ever come. (*Courtesy of Hewlett-Packard Company.*)

The monitor is a **CRT (cathode-ray tube)** with an electron gun that emits a beam that sweeps rows of raster lines on the screen. Each line consists of dots called **pixels**. Raster-scanned CRTs refresh the picture display many times per second. A measure of monitor quality is **resolution**, which is the number of pixels per inch that can be produced on the screen. The greater the number of pixels, the greater will be the clarity of the image on the screen (**Fig. 26.3**)

Input Devices

Besides the standard keyboard, the **digitizer** (stylus) is used to enter graphic data to the computer. The **mouse**, a hand-held device that is moved about the table top to transmit information to the computer, is the most commonly used input device. Variations of the mouse are **thumbwheels** operated by fingertips, **joysticks** that let the user "steer" about the screen by tilting a lever, and **spherical balls** that can be rotated to input 3D data to the screen (**Fig. 26.4**).

A **tablet** and digitizer used in combination are an alternative to the mouse. The digitizer can be used to select commands from the menu attached to the tablet. Also, drawings can be attached to tablets and "traced" with the stylus to convert it to x and y coordinates. The **light pen** enables the user to "draw" on the screen with it to select point and lines.

Output Devices

The **plotter** makes a drawing on paper or film with a pen in the same manner a drawing is made by hand. Plotter types are **flatbed plotters**, **drum plotters**, and **sheet-fed plotters**. With flatbed plotters, the drawing paper is held stationary while pens are moved about its surface. Drum plotters roll the paper up and down over a cylinder while the pen moves left and right to make the drawing. Sheet-fed plotters hold the paper with grit wheels in a flat position as the sheet is moved forward and backward and the pen moves left and right to make the drawing.

Printers are of the impact type (much like typewriters) or the nonimpact type, where images are formed by sprays, laser beams, photography, or heat (**Fig. 26.5**). The laser printer gives excellent resolution of dense, accurately drawn lines in color as well as in black and white. Ink-jet technology has enabled images to be sprayed onto the drawing surface in color or black ink that approaches the quality of the laser. Larger nonimpact printers ($24'' \times 36''$ and larger) are most often ink-jet printers since large lasers are much more expensive.

26.4 Your First AutoCAD Session

If this is your first session, you are anxious to turn the computer on, make a drawing on the

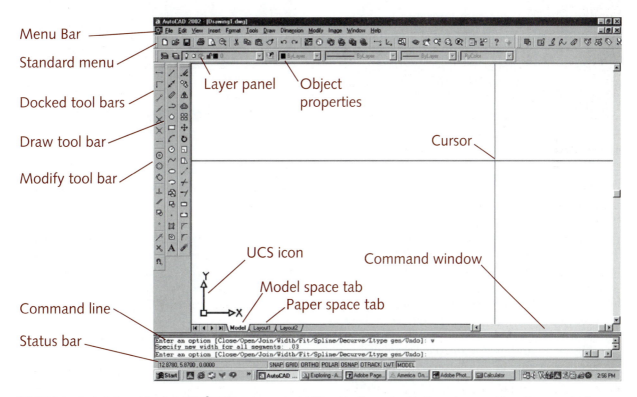

26.6 This is a typical view of the AutoCAD® 2002 main screen. Additional toolbars can added to and removed from the screen by the user.

screen, and plot it without reading the instructions. This section is what you're looking for.

Format of Presentation

In this chapter, the progression from one step of a command to the next level will be separated by an angle pointing to the right (>) in order to simplify presentation and reduce explanatory text. Since there are about three different ways of actuating most commands, these methods will be used alternatively in the following examples. The commands and prompts that appear on the screen will be given in *italics* to distinguish them from supplementary notes of explanation. (Enter) refers to the keyboard key with this name. Once a command is selected, additional prompts will be given at the *Command* line at the bottom of the screen or in dialogue boxes that must be followed.

Booting Turn on the computer and boot the system by typing ACAD2002 (or the command used by your system) to activate the program (**Fig. 26.6**). Experiment by moving the cursor around the screen with your mouse, selecting items, and trying the pull-down menu.

Mouse Most interactions with the computer will be accomplished with a mouse (**Fig. 26.7**), but many commands can be entered at the keyboard, and perhaps more quickly after you learn them. Press the left mouse button to click on, select, or pick a command or object; a double click is needed in some cases. The right button has the same effect as pressing (Enter) on the keyboard.

Creating a File To create a new file on a disk, place your formatted disk in its slot, pick *Files* from the *Main menu* and *New* from the dialogue box (**Fig. 26.8**), and the *Create New Drawing* dialogue box will appear on the screen (**Fig. 26.9**). Select the *Use a Wizard* icon button, *Quick setup,* and *OK,* and the *Quick Setup* box will appear where *Size Units* can be specified (**Fig. 26.10**);

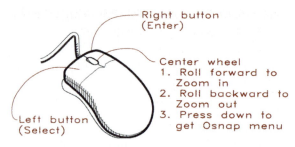

26.7 The left mouse button is used for picking points when drawing and selecting operational buttons. The right mouse button has the same effect as pressing the (Enter) button on the keyboard. The center wheel can be rolled forward to *Zoom* in, rolled backward to *Zoom* out, and pressed down on to obtain an Osnap menu.

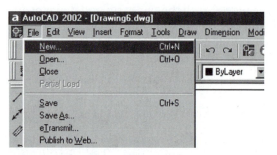

26.8 Open a new drawing *(Main menu> File> New)* to obtain the *Create New Drawing box.*

26.9 In the *Create New Drawing* box, select the *Use a Wizard* icon button> *Quick Setup>* and *OK.*

select *Decimal* units and then select the *Next* button. When the *Area* box appears on the screen, insert the *Width* and *Length* (11 × 8.5)

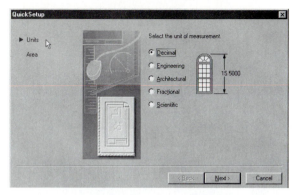

26.10 In the *Quick Setup* box, specify the type of *Units* you wish to have, *Decimal* units in this example, and select *Next*.

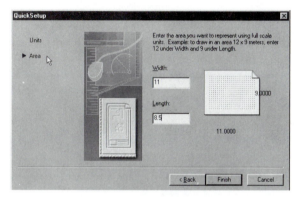

26.11 In the *Quick Setup* box, type the dimensions for *Width* and *Length* (11 and 8.5 for an A-size sheet) and select *Finish* to obtain a drawing screen.

and select the *Finish* button (**Fig. 26.11**). The program returns the screen and its command menus ready for your drawing.

Making a Drawing Since you don't have the menus and toolbars figured out, type L (for *Line*), press (Enter), and draw some lines on the screen with the mouse for the fun of it by selecting endpoints with the left button, as shown in **Fig. 26.12**. A line on the screen "rubberbands" from point to point. To disengage the rubberband, press the right mouse button, which is the same as pressing (Enter). Press the right button again to return to the *Line* command.

Instead of typing L to enter the *Line* command, pick the *Main menu> Draw,* and select

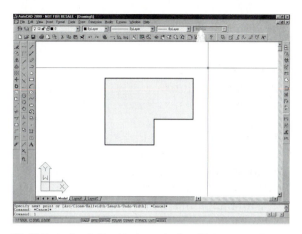

26.12 By typing L (for *Line*) or selecting *Main menu> Draw> Line,* endpoints of lines can be selected on the screen with the cursor to draw a figure.

the *Line* option to get the prompt line *Specify first:* in the *Command* line at the bottom of the screen. Now, use your mouse to draw on the screen. The *Line* command can also be selected from the *Draw* toolbar that you will learn about soon. Try drawing circles and other objects on the screen by selecting icons from the *Draw* pull-down menu.

Repeat Commands By pressing (Enter) on the keyboard (or the right mouse button) twice after the previous command, the command can be repeated. For example, *Line* will appear in the *Command* line at the bottom of the screen after pressing (Enter) twice, if *Line* was the previous command.

Saving Your File Click on *File* on the *Main menu* and pick *Save As* from the pull-down menu to get the menu box shown in **Fig. 26.13**. Type A:DRW-5 (if your disk is in Drive A) and select the *Save* button; the light over drive A will blink briefly and the drawing, DRW-5, is saved to the disk in the A drive.

Plotting Your Drawing Select *File* (**Fig. 26.14**) and the *Plot* option from its pull-down to get the *Plot* dialogue box. Select the *Plot Device* tab,

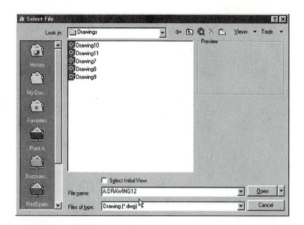

26.13 Select *Main menu> File> Save As* to obtain the *Save Drawing As* box, type the drawing drive (A:) and file name *(DRW-5)* in *File name* box, and select *Save*. *A:DRW-5.DWG* is saved as a file.

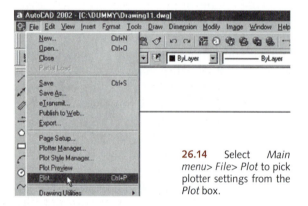

26.14 Select *Main menu> File> Plot* to pick plotter settings from the *Plot* box.

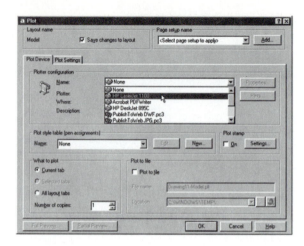

26.15 In the *Plot box*, select the *Plot Device* tab and the name of the plotter or printer that you will use, and then select the *Plot Settings* tab.

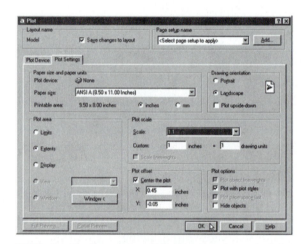

26.16 Specify *Paper size* (8.5x11), *Drawing orientation* (Landscape), *Plot area* (*Limits* button), *Plot scale* (1:1), Check *Center the plot*, and click on *Full Preview* to obtain a view of what will be plotted. If it looks correct, press the right mouse button, select *Plot*, and the drawing is printed.

click on the pull-down window of the *Plotter configuration* area, and pick the plotter that you intend to use (**Fig. 26.15**). Select the *Plot Settings tab* of the *Plot box* (**Fig. 26.16**), select *Limits*, set *Scale* to 1:1, and select *Center* under *Plot Offset*. Load the A-size paper sheet in the printer or plotter; pick *Full Preview* to see how the drawing will appear when plotted. If it appears correct, press the right mouse button and select *Plot* on the pop-up menu, and the drawing is plotted.

Quitting AutoCAD To be sure that your latest changes have been saved to disk, select *File* from the *Main menu* and pick *Save* from the pull-

down menu to update *A:DRW-5*. To quit AutoCAD, close the active file *(Main menu> File> Close)* and the file will close and leave the screen if it has been *Saved* in its current form (**Fig. 26.17**). If changes have been made to it since its last *Save*, the pop-up box in **Fig. 26.18** lets you decide whether to *Save* it or not (*Yes* or *No*), or *Cancel*. To quit your session, select *Main*

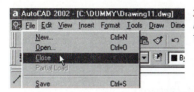

26.17 *Main menu> File> Close* to close the current file.

26.18 If the file has not been *Saved*, this dialogue prompts you to decide whether or not you want to save (*Yes*, *No*, or *Cancel*).

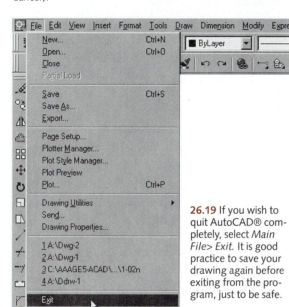

26.19 If you wish to quit AutoCAD® completely, select *Main File> Exit.* It is good practice to save your drawing again before exiting from the program, just to be safe.

26.20 The icons in the upper right of the screen can be used minimize a drawing (pick dash), reduce it to partial size (pick boxes), or close the file (pick X).

26.21 Minimized files are displayed as an icon box above the *Command* line.

26.22 A partial screen can be enlarged to full-screen size by selecting the box button.

26.23 Select the lower right corner, hold down the left mouse button, and "drag" the border to size the screen as you desire.

menu> *File> Exit,* and AutoCAD closes (**Fig. 26.19**). If you intend to continue your session, do not *Exit* now, but close the current file and continue with other drawings. When working from a floppy disk, do not remove it from its drive until it has been saved with either the *Save* or the *Save As* option.

That's a quick review of how it works. Now, let's get into the details.

26.5 Introduction to Windows

The recommended operating system for AutoCAD 2002® for a single user is Windows 98 or higher, which allows several programs to be open and running at the same time. For exam-

ple, a word-processing program can be running in addition to AutoCAD 2002.

A drawing file can be manipulated with the three buttons in the upper-right corner of the window (**Fig. 26.20**). The "overlapping boxes" button is selected to display the file in a format that covers only a portion of the screen in order to allow other files or programs to share the screen. The "X" button closes the current file. The "dash" button minimizes a file to an icon box (that retains the three buttons of the original) located above the *Command* line (**Fig. 26.21**). Maximize the minimized file to fill the screen by selecting the "box" button (**Fig. 26.22**), and it will return to the screen and cover the other displays on the screen.

Windows can be resized by selecting a border, or the corner of the border, while holding down the left mouse button and "dragging" to size the window (**Fig. 26.23**).

When several overlapping program windows appear on the screen, select any point on a window to move it to the front and make it the current program.

26.6 Format of Presentation

AutoCAD has several ways of using a command in almost all cases. For example, a circle can be drawn by typing C at the *Command* line; selecting the *circle icon* from the *Draw* toolbar; or using the *Main menu* bar> *Draw*> *Circle* on the drop-down menu. In each of these examples, you must select from options–*Center, radius; Center, diameter,* and others–before drawing the circle.

In this chapter, the progression from one step of a command to the next level will be separated by an angle pointing to the right (>) in order to simplify presentation and reduce explanatory text. The commands and prompts that appear on the screen will be given in *italics* type to distinguish them from supplementary notes of explanation. (Enter) refers to the keyboard key with this name. Once a command is selected, additional prompts given at the *Command* line at the bottom of the screen and/or in dialogue boxes must be responded to.

Command line   When a circle is drawn by typing at the *Command* line, it will be presented as follows: *Command:*> Circle *(or C)*> *Center point*> P1> *Radius*> type 4 (Enter). Entries that are typed in response to prompts are underlined. The underlined P1 is a point on the screen and the underlined 4 is the radius that is typed at the command line in response to the prompt, *Radius.*

Main menu   When the *Main menu* is used to draw a circle, the sequence of steps is presented as: *Main menu*> *Draw*> *Circle*> *Center, radius*> *Center point*> P1> *Radius*> drag to a radius of 4.

Draw Toolbar   When the *Draw toolbar* is used to draw a circle, the steps are presented as: *Main menu*> *View*> *Draw toolbar*> *Circle icon*> *Center, radius*> *Center point*> P1> *Radius*> type 4.

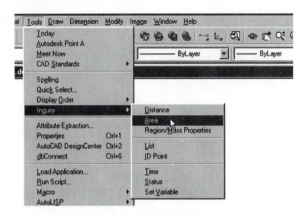

26.24 The *Main menu* has pull-down menus. Commands in the pull-down menu followed by black arrows have sub-dialogue boxes. The sequence in this example is *Main menu*> *Tools*> *Inquiry*> *Area.*

26.7 Using Dialogue Boxes

AutoCAD 2002 has many dialogue boxes with names beginning with *DD (DDlmodes,* for example) to interact with the user. The command *Filedia* can be used to turn off (0 = off and 1 = on) the dialogue boxes if you prefer to type the commands without dialogue boxes. When a command on a menu that is followed by three dots (...) or an arrow (>) is selected, supplemental dialogue boxes will be displayed (**Fig. 26.24**) and some of these boxes will have subdialogue boxes.

Definition boxes are provided to identify the functions of each box on the screen. By placing the cursor on a box, a *flyout* will appear to define its function, as shown in **Fig. 26.25**.

Double clicking the mouse (quickly pressing the left button twice) in some applications enables you to skip a step. In contrast, when a **Single click** is used to select a file to *Open* from a list, you must select a second *Open* box to con-

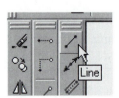

26.25 *Definition* boxes are flyout boxes that explain the functions of the various icons when the cursor is rested on them briefly.

26.26 *Main menu> File> Open* gives the *Select File* box that helps you find the file that you wish to open. A thumbnail view of the selected file is previewed in the window before it is opened.

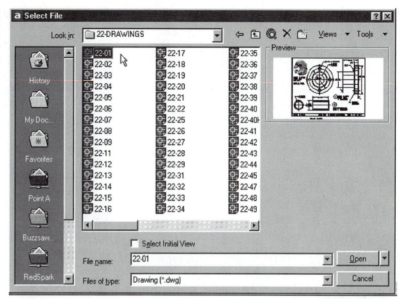

26.27 *Main menu> File> Open> Select File box> Tools> Find> Browse> Browse for Folder box>* type in drive or folder names (use wild cards if you like) *Find Now> Find:* box (Double click on the file of your choice and a list appears from which you can make selections and get thumbnail views).

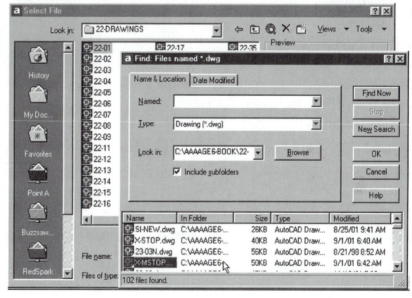

firm your intent. With experimentation you will soon learn where double clicking can be best applied.

Right clicking when the cursor (right mouse key) is placed over an icon will display a set of commands that are related to that particular command.

The *Select File* box in **Fig. 26.26** has dialogue boxes, lists, blanks, and buttons that can be selected by the cursor. When a file is selected, it is darkened by a gray bar and a thumbnail illustration of it is shown in the window. To *Find* thumbnail images of drawing files, select *Tools> Find>* type the file name or folder to look in and press the *Find Now* button, and a directory of the files will appear (**Fig. 26.27**). Select a file from the directory and its thumbnail will appear ready for your selection for display on the screen.

26.28 These function keys on the keyboard control the options indicated by the notes.

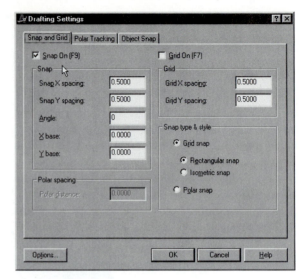

26.29 The *Drafting Settings* dialogue box (or type *DDrmodes*) has three tabs from which to make settings: *Snap and Grid, Polar Tracking,* and *Object Snap.*

In many cases, speed is increased if you type commands at the *Command* line instead of using dialogue boxes. What could be easier than typing L and pressing (Enter) for drawing a *Line?*

26.8 Drawing Aids

Function Keys

Convenient drawing aids are available from the function keys on the keyboard, which can be pressed to turn settings on and off (**Fig. 26.28**).

F2 (Flip screen) alternates between the graphics and text modes. *F6* (Coordinates) sets coordinates of the cursor to "on" to show the numerical coordinates in the *Status* bar at the bottom of the screen as the cursor is moved. *F7* (Grid) turns the grid on or off and refreshes the screen in the process, removing any blips or erasures. *F8* (Ortho) forces all lines to be drawn either horizontally or vertically. *F9 (Snap),* when on, makes all object points lie on points within an invisible grid. *F10* (Tablet) activates a digitizing tablet, if one is attached to your computer.

To set the drawing area of the screen that will be filled with the *Grid* dots when *F7* is pressed, type *Limits,* or *(Main menu> Format> Drawing Limits).* A drawing that fills an A-size sheet (11 × 8.5 inches) has a plotting area of about 10.4 × 7.8 inches, or 254 × 198 mm. The drawing area is specified with the *Limits* command as follows:

Command line: Limits (Enter)

Specify lower left corner[ON/OFF] <0.00, 0,00>: (Enter) Accepts default of 0,0.

Specify upper right corner <12.00,9.00>: 11,8.5 (Enter)

Press *F7* and the dot pattern fills the *Limits.*

Type *Zoom* (Enter)> type *All* (Enter) The grid dots fill the screen.

Limits can be reset at any time during the drawing session by repeating these steps.

Drafting Settings

The *Drafting Settings* box is found by *Main menu> Tools> Drafting Settings,* right clicking on the *Osnap* icon above the *Command* line, and selecting *Settings,* or by typing *DDrmodes* (**Fig. 26.29**). The *Snap and Grid* tab gives buttons for selection and blanks for filling in to activate these settings. *Snap* forces the cursor to stop only at points on an imaginary grid of a specified spacing. The *Snap X* and *Snap Y* values can be set by typing values in the blanks. *Snap* can also

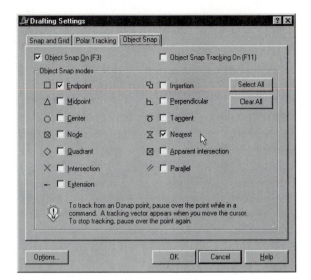

26.30 *Osnap* settings can be made from the *Object Snap* tab of the *Drafting Settings* dialogue box *(or type DDrmodes).*

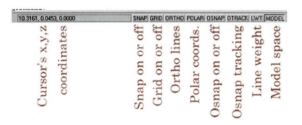

26.31 *Drawing Aides* boxes in the *Status bar* beneath the *Command* line at the bottom of the screen display current settings. Click on them to turn them on or off.

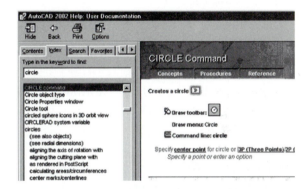

26.32 Pick *Main menu> Help> AutoCAD Help> Index tab>* type Circle, pick *Display* button, and a help window tells you how to draw a circle. With experimentation, you will learn how to have a "manual" on the screen.

be set by typing *Snap* at the *Command* line and specifying the interval desired. When *On,* the *Snap* icon in the *Status* line at the bottom of the screen is highlighted. *Snap* can be toggled on and off by double clicking on this icon or by pressing *F9.*

Grid of the *Drafting Settings* box fills the *Limits* area with dots spaced apart by typing values in the *Grid X spacing* and *Grid Y spacing* boxes. With the following selections, *Snap type & style> Grid snap> Rectangular snap,* the cursor will snap to the grid if the *Snap* and *Grid* spacings are equal.

The *Object Snap* tab (**Fig. 26.30**) gives options for making lines and other geometry of a drawing *Snap* to previously drawn objects at specified points. *Osnap* is covered in **Section 26.42**.

The *Status Window* at the bottom of the screen displays several of the settings discussed above if set to *On* (**Fig. 26.31**). Double clicking on these buttons toggles them off or on.

Blips (Command:> Blips) are temporary marks made on the screen when selections are made with the mouse. They are removed by refreshing the screen by pressing *F7.*

26.9 General Assistance Commands

Several examples of helpful commands that can be typed at the *Command line* are discussed below.

Help *(Main menu> Help> AutoCAD Help)* gives menus *Contents, Index, Search, Favorites,* and *Querry* to help you with all aspects of AutoCAD. Under *Search,* you will be able to insert key words for commands and steps that you need assistance with, as shown in **Fig. 26.32**. When a topic, *Circle* for example, is selected and *Display* is picked, a screen of instructions will appear to help you with using the *Circle* command (**Fig. 26.33**). Additional options are provided under *Help* that are self-explanatory as you experiment with them.

Purge *(Main menu> File> Drawing Utilities> Purge> All)* can be used at any time to remove

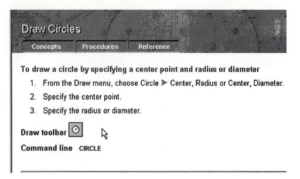

26.33 By selecting *Circle (Draw menu)* from the *Index tab*, a window of instructions is given for drawing a circle. Type CIRCLE in all caps as the keyword, pick *Display*, and instructions for drawing a circle from the *Command line* are given.

unused layers, blocks, and other attributes from files. *Purge* the activated by:

Command: PURGE (Enter)
Enter type of unused object to purge [Blocks/ Dimstyles/LAyers/LTypes/Plotstyles/Text/ Mlinestyles/All]: ALL (Enter)

The *All* option is used to eliminate all unused references one at a time, as prompted. The other options purge specific features of a drawing.

List *(Main menu> Tools> Inquiry> List)* asks you to select any object drawn on the screen and gives information about it. For example, it will give the radius, circumference, and area of a selected circle plus the coordinates of its center point.

Copy *Object (Modify toolbar> Copy Object icon)* is used to select objects on the screen (single objects or groups of objects) with the cursor, pick a new position, and make a duplicate of the selection. The *Multiple (M)* option can be selected for making more than a single copy. *Unlock* is used to select *Locked* files; pick OK and the files are unlocked.

26.10 Drawing Layers

An almost infinite number of layers can be created, each assigned a *Name, Color, Linetype,* *Lineweight,* and *Plot Style* on which to draw. For example, a yellow layer named *Hidden* for drawing dashed lines may be created.

Architects use separate copies of the same floor plan for different applications: dimensions, floor finishes, electrical details, and so forth. The same basic plan is used for all these applications by turning on the needed layers and turning the others off.

Working with Layers   Layers and their settings are created and manipulated in the *Layer Properties Manager* box, which is displayed by selecting the paper-stack icon next to the *Layer Control* panel (**Fig. 26.34**). For most working drawings, the layers shown in the *Layer Properties Manager* box in **Fig. 26.35** are sufficient. Layers are assigned linetypes, lineweights, and different colors so they can be easily distinguished from each other. The 0 (zero) layer is the default layer, which can be turned off or frozen, but not deleted.

Layers can be created by selecting the *New* box to obtain *Layer1,* the default name, which can be replaced by a new name (**Fig. 26.35**). The new layer will appear in the listing of layers with a default color of white and a continuous linetype, all of which can be changed to your specifications.

Color is assigned to the new layer by picking the default color (white) to obtain the *Select Color* menu, choosing a color for that layer, and picking the *OK* button (**Fig. 26.36**).

Linetypes are found by clicking on the default linetype of the new layer in the *Layer Properties Manager* box so that the *Select Linetype* box appears; select *Load* and the *Load or Reload Linetypes* box appears with a list of linetypes from which to select (**Fig. 26.37**). To assign a hidden *Linetype* to a layer named *Hidden,* select the linetype of the layer, select *Hidden* from the *Select Linetype* box, pick *OK,* and the line is assigned to the layer. All lines drawn on the hidden layer will be dashed lines.

26.34 Select the paper stack next to *Layer Control* panel to obtain the *Layer Properties Manager* box for setting all layer properties.

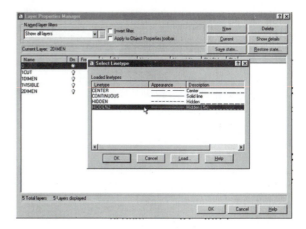

26.37 *Main menu> Format> Layer> Select Linetype* (or type *DDltype*) and *Load* to get this box, from which linetypes can be selected and assigned to layers.

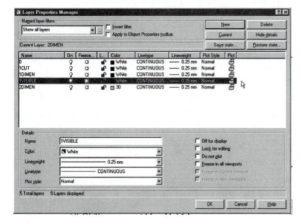

26.35 *Layer Properties Manager* box (*Main menu> Format> Layer,* or type DDlmodes), which lists layers and their properties. From this box, layers can be created and deleted, linetypes and colors assigned, and other settings made.

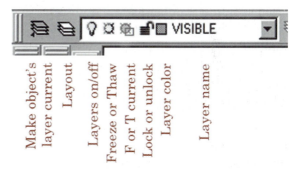

26.38 The *Layer Control* bar offers access to layers and their properties by selecting one of the icons shown here.

Ltscale, when typed at the *Command* line, modifies the lengths of line segments of non-continuous lines, such as hidden lines.

Layer Control Panel

A layer must be selected as the current layer in order to draw on it using the assigned color and linetype. The *Layer Control* bar offers the quickest method of selecting a layer as the current layer (**Fig. 26.38**). By picking a point anywhere within the *Layer Control Panel*, a drop-down list of the defined layers and their properties is displayed, from which a layer can be selected as the current layer (**Fig. 26.39**). Now you can draw on the current layer.

This drop-down list of the *Layer Control* Panel can also be used to make other layer assignments: *On* and *Off, Freeze* and *Thaw, Lock*

26.36 *Main menu> Format> Color> Select Color box* (or type *DDcolor*) to get this box, from which colors can be selected and assigned to layers.

Lineweights are found by clicking on the default lineweight of a layer in the *Layer Properties Manager* box so that the *Lineweight* box appears with a list of linetypes from which to select. Choose the desired lineweight and pick *OK to assign* the lineweight to that layer. All lines on this layer will be drawn with this assigned line thickness.

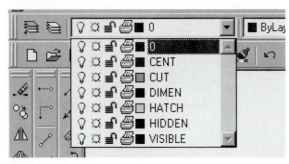

26.39 Select any point on the *Layer Control panel* or select the down-arrow button, and this drop-down list of the layers appears.

and *Unlock,* and others. By selecting the *Layers* icon (**Fig. 26.38**), the *Layers Properties Manager* box will be displayed, from which the previously covered setting can be made (**Fig. 26.35**). This box can also be obtained by *Command:* LA (Enter).

Renaming a layer can be done from the *Layers Properties Manager* box by dragging the cursor across the existing name and typing a new one in its place.

On/Off is applied to a layer in the *Layer Control Panel* by selecting the lightbulb icon (**Fig. 26.39**). Layers can be turned on or off with buttons from the *Layers Properties Manager* box (**Fig. 26.37**), or by typing LA and *Off* at the *Command* line. An *Off* layer that is selected as the current layer can be drawn on, but this is seldom done.

The *Freeze* and *Thaw* options (sun icon) under the *Layer Control Panel* are used like the *On* and *Off* options (**Fig. 26.39**). *Freeze* a layer and it will (unlike an *Off* layer) be ignored by the computer until it has been *Thawed,* which makes regeneration faster than when *Off* is used.

26.11 Toolbars

Main menu> View> Toolbars gives a list of toolbars that can be selected to suit the current application (**Fig. 26.40**). A portion of the *Standard* toolbar (**Fig. 26.41**) gives a sequence of icons for commands from *New* to *Tracking Point.* The

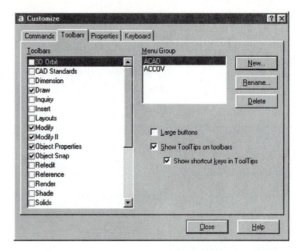

26.40 Select *Main menu> View> Toolbars* to obtain this listing of toolbars that can be activated or deactivated by checking a box.

26.41 This half of the *Standard toolbar* provides many routine operations that can be accessed with the cursor.

26.42 The second half of the *Standard toolbar* has more helpful commands that you will need for most drawings.

remainder of the *Standard* toolbar commands, from *UCS* to *Help,* are given in **Fig. 26.42**.

Toolbars can be moved about the screen by selecting a point on one of their edges, holding

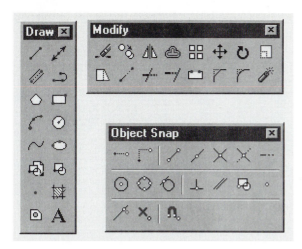

26.43 *Toolbars* can be arranged on the screen by dragging their corners to make single, double, or triple strips that are horizontal or vertical. They can be "docked" at the borders or left "floating" on the screen.

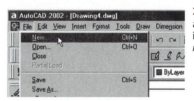

26.44 Begin the creation of a new drawing as follows: *Main menu> File> New.*

down the select button of the mouse, and moving the cursor to a new position. *Toolbars* can be "docked" by moving them into contact with a border of the screen. They can be changed from single strips to double and triple blocks by moving the corners of the toolbars, or they can be changed into vertical or horizontal strips, depending on which border of the screen they are moved to (**Fig. 26.43**). When located in the open area of the screen, toolbars will appear as "floating" menus. When a small icon needs explanation, place the pointer on an icon and a "flyout" box will appear with its definition.

26.12 A New Drawing

Title Block

To create a new drawing, select *Main menu> File> New>* (**Fig. 26.44**) and the *Create New*

26.45 From the *Create New Drawing* box, select the *Use a Wizard* icon and you will be offered two options: *Advanced Setup* and *Quick Setup*. Select *Advanced Setup*.

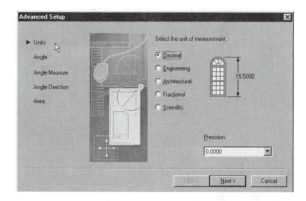

26.46 Set *Units* to *Decimal* and *Precision* to *0.00* (2 decimal places or X.00, for example).

Drawing box appears, giving two options: *Advanced Setup* or *Quick Setup* (**Fig. 26.45**). Pick *Advanced Setup,* set the *Units* to *Decimal* with a *Precision* (decimal places) of *0.00*, and select *Next* (**Fig. 26.46**). In the following screen (**Fig. 26.47**), set the *Angle* to *Decimal Degrees* with a *Precision* of *0.00* and pick *Next.*

In the *Angle Measure* box (**Fig. 26.48**), set the angle measurement to *East* and pick *Next.* In the *Angle Direction* box (**Fig. 26.49**), set the angle direction to *Counter Clockwise* and pick *Next.* In the *Area* box (**Fig. 26.50**), set the values for *Width* (11) and *Length* (8.5) and pick *Finish.*

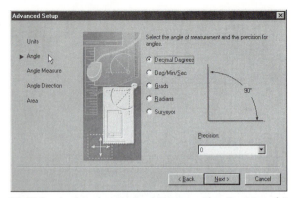

26.47 For *Angle*, select *Decimal Degrees* with a *Precision* of 0 and pick *Next*.

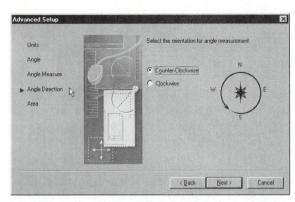

26.49 For *Angle Direction*, select *Counter-Clockwise* and *Next*. Angles will be measured counter-clockwise from the x axis.

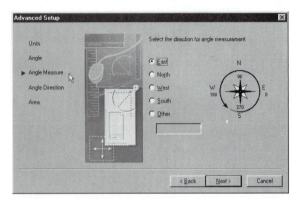

26.48 For *Angle Measure*, select *East* and the *Next* button. The angles will be measured from the +X axis.

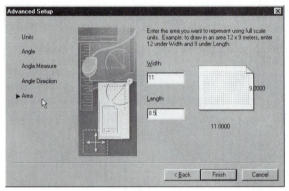

26.50 For *Area*, type values for *Width* (11) and *Length* (8.5) for a standard 11 × 8.5 sheet size and pick *Next*.

Prototype Drawing

The drawing screen appears ready for drawing. If the grid dots do not show, press *F7* to show them; the upper right dot having coordinates of about 11, 8.5, the assigned sheet size. Draw a border and title strip using *Line*> 0,0> 10.4, 0> 10.4, 7.8> 0, 7.8> 0,0 to get a 10.4 × 7.8 border (**Fig. 26.51**). Save this A-size border for use as a prototype file for making drawings with these same settings (*Main menu*> *File*> *SaveAs*> A:ABORD-HORIZ (Enter)). Close this file (*Main menu*> *File*> *Close*) and the drawing leaves the screen.

Using the Prototype Drawing

So far, you have been working entirely in *Model Space*, which is adequate for the two-dimensional

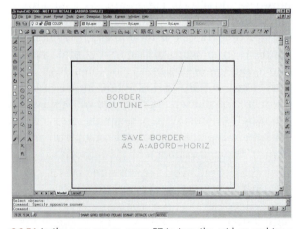

26.51 In the new screen, press *F7* to turn the grid on and type *Zoom*> *All* to make the grid fill the drawing area. Draw a border (10.4 × 7.8) and *SaveAs* > A:ABORD-HORIZ. *Close* the file.

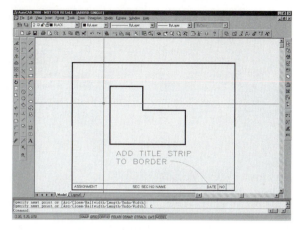

26.52 *Open* A:ABORD-HORIZ, save the file (*Main menu> SaveAs> DRW-5* (Enter)), and DWG-5 becomes the current drawing located on drive A. Make your drawing, complete the title strip, and save the file (*Main menu> File> Save*).

26.53 When using *Save As,* this box asks if you want to update the file. Select *Yes* and the named file is replaced by the current file.

26.54 Select *Main menu> Insert> Block* to insert a file into another file.

drawing covered in this chapter. The application of *Model Space* and *Paper Space* in combination will be covered in Chapter 27.

To make a drawing using the settings and border made in the previous sequence, open the prototype file (*Main menu> File> Open> A:ABORD-HORIZ*), and the border and grid appear on the screen as they did at the end of the last drawing (**Fig. 26.52**). Save the file with a new name (*Main menu> File> SaveAs> DRW-5>* (Enter)), and DWG5 becomes the current file and replaces the prototype file. (This same procedure can be used to create a new file by saving the prototype file to a new name, while preserving the prototype file in its original form.)

Update the title strip in the border for your name, date, and other information required by your instructor. You may consider making this information part of your prototype file so it will be displayed every time it is used: *File> SaveAs> A:ABORD-HORIZ*. Since you are saving to an existing file, the *Save Drawing As* box in **Fig. 26.53** will ask you if you want to replace it; select *Yes*.

Prototype file A:ABORD-HORIZ is updated so the title strip will be included when it is used next.

Make your drawing within the border, save it (*Main menu> File> Save As> DRW-5*), and your drawing is ready to be plotted.

Section 26.66 covers the techniques of customizing your title block for classroom drawings, but first you must learn more about the operation of AutoCAD. If this section seems a little advanced for you, leave it, and come back when you have learned a few more drawing principles.

26.13 Drawing Scale

It is best (and easiest) to work with a drawing at a full-size scale, in which 1 inch is equal to 1 inch for instance. The previous examples of files and title blocks were developed as full-size layouts, which permits text size and measurements to be easily handled.

Half-size drawings can be made by creating a new drawing, DRW-6, by using the *Advanced Setup* steps covered in the last section. Now, insert (**Fig. 26.54**) the prototype drawing, A:ABORD-HORIZ, with the following steps: (*Main menu> Insert> Block> File> A:ABORD-HORIZ>* Set parameters: check *Uniform Scale,* type 2 in *X-Scale window> Ok>* type 0,0 at the *Command* line as the insertion point (**Fig. 26.55**). These commands insert the border and

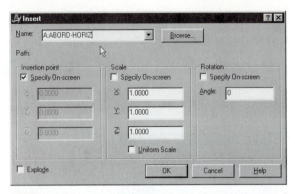

26.55 Type the name of the file to insert, A:ABORD-HORIZ, and set parameters: select *Uniform Scale,* and give a scale factor of 2. Select *OK* and insert the file at 0,0 at the *Command* Line.

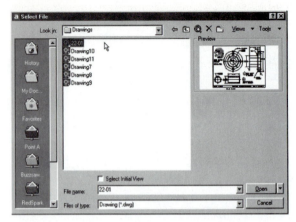

26.56 Name the file, select the drive to save it to, and save it by using this dialogue box *(Main menu> File> Save As).*

title strip at double size (scale = 2). For a double-size metric drawing, the scale would be 25.4 × 2 = 50.8 for millimeters. A full-size drawing is made within the double-size border.

At plot time, the double-size border must be reduced to half size (0.5) so it will fit on its sheet, and the full-size drawing within it is reduced to half size.

Double-size drawings can be made with the same steps as half-size drawings, except the A:ABORD-HORIZ file is inserted at a *Scale* of 0.5 (half size). (The factor would be 25.4 × 0.5 = 12.7 for millimeters.)

At plot time, the half-size border must be enlarged by a factor of 2 so it will fill the sheet, and the full-size drawing within it will be doubled.

Using this logic, other combinations of scale factors can be determined for drawings of any scale. The most important point to remember is that it is best to work with full-size drawings and scale them at plot time.

26.14 Saving and Exiting

The pull-down file *(Main menu> File)* gives options for saving a drawing *(Save, SaveAs,* and *Exit)* that can be selected from the pull-down menu, the toolbar, or by typing at the *Command* line.

Saving

Type Save to "quick save" to the current file's name if the file has been previously named and saved. If the file is unnamed, the *Save* command prompts for a name by displaying the *Save Drawing As* dialogue box in **Fig. 26.56**. Select the directory and name the file (A:NEW7) to save it on the disk in drive A. Drawing A:NEW7 becomes the current file on the screen.

Ending the Session

To exit the drawing session and close AutoCAD, choose *Main menu> File> Exit.* If you have not saved immediately before selecting *Exit,* the dialogue box shown in **Fig. 26.53** asks if you want to save the updated drawing. Select *Yes* and the *Save Drawing As* menu box appears for assigning the drive, directory, file name, and file type. To exit without saving, respond *to Save Changes?* with *No* and the latest changes made since the last *Save* will be discarded.

Type *Close* at the *Command* line and you will be prompted to *Save* the drawing if it has been changed since the last *Save.* If the drawing has not been previously named, the *Save Drawing As* dialogue box will prompt you for a file name. The previous version of the drawing is automati-

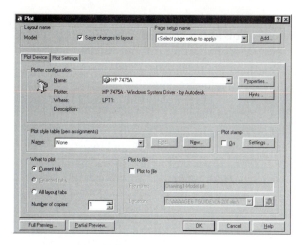

26.57 Begin from the *Plot Device tab* and select the printer to be used. The printing options for a laser printer (without physical pens) are specified in this box *(Main menu> Plot> Plot Device* tab).

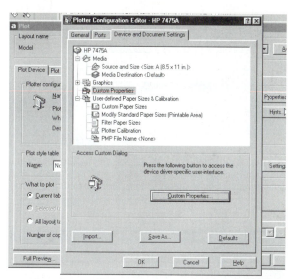

26.58 Pen assignments for a plotter with separate physical pens are set in the the lower portion of this figure, which is found by *Main menu> File> Plot> Plot Device* tab> *Properties> Custom Properties* box> *Device Options* tab> and set pen specifications.

cally saved as a backup file with a *.Bak* extension and the current drawing is saved with a *.dwg* extension. Several drawing files can be open at the same time during a session.

26.15 Plotting Parameters

To plot a drawing before ending a drawing session, select *File> Plot* to obtain the *Plot* box (**Fig. 26.57**). Select the *Plot Device* tab to obtain the subdialogue box for selecting *HP 7475 plotter* to make a pen drawing. (A *plotter* has physical pens that plot a drawing, whereas a *printer* has no pins, but sprays the ink onto the drawing at specified line widths.)

Plotter Settings (Model Space)

Main menu> Plot> Plot Device tab> *HP7475A > Properties* box> *Device and Document settings tab > Custom Properties* box> *Device Options* tab to obtain a table of pen specifications that can be modified to fit your needs (**Fig. 26.58**). Since plotters use physical pens, the pens to be used by each color on the screen must be specified. The colors of the lines on the paper plot depend

upon the colors of the physical pens, which may be all one color, and lineweights will be determined by the lineweights of the physical pens (P.3 and P.7).

A *Color* of Red, a pen *Speed* of 9 inches per sec (228 mm per sec), and a *Width* of .03 in. (.7) is assigned to pen 1 (the slot occupied by the pen in the pen holder). All lines drawn in red on the screen will plot with pen 1 at this speed. Select *Save As> Pen Plotter HP7475A* and the settings are saved with a *.PC3* extension for this setup.

Printer Settings (Model Space)

Main menu> Plot> Plot Device tab and select the configured printer that you intend to use for plotting your drawing. Select the *Plot Settings* tab, select *Drawing orientation (Portrait* or *Landscape),* specify *Plot Area (Limits, Extents,* or *Display),* assign a *Scale,* set *Plot offset* to *Center the plot.* Save this *Page setup* by selecting the *Add* button (**Fig. 26.59**) and naming it in the

26.59 Settings made in the *Plot* menu can be saved with the *Add...* button for use in future drawings. The *Previous Plot* option enables you to specify settings identical to the last plot.

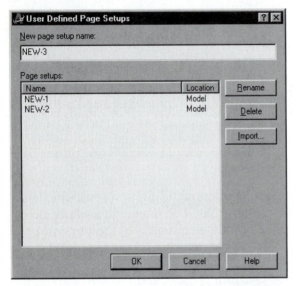

26.60 From the *Add...* button, the *User Defined Page Setups* box appears, in which you can name a new page setup and select *OK* to save it for future drawings.

setup in the box that appears on the screen (**Fig. 26.60**), and pick *OK*. These settings will be saved with the drawing when the file is saved.

General

These approaches to making settings for plotters and printers while working from *Model Space* is the simplest approach to plotting drawings, yet they are sufficient for essentially all two-dimen-

sional drawings required in a beginning graphics course. The application of *Plot Styles* is not covered in this chapter for this reason. Plot Styles will be touched on in Chapter 27 where three-dimensional principles are covered.

Plot Settings Tab

Plot settings (**Fig. 26.61**) applicable to both plotters and printers are covered below.

Extents plots a drawing to its extents if the scale selected permits. It is good practice to apply *Zoom> Extents* to ready a drawing for plotting.

Limits is used to plot the portion of the drawing bounded by the grid pattern defined by its *Limits*.

Display plots the portion of the drawing shown on the screen.

View lists saved *Views* that can be selected and plotted. This box is gray if no views are saved.

Window specifies the portion of a drawing to be plotted when *Pick* is chosen and the window is sized with the cursor, or coordinates are typed from the keyboard.

Hide Lines removes hidden lines from 3D drawings that are plotted. *Adjust Area Fill* pulls in the boundaries of the filled area by one-half pen width for a more precisely drawn fill area.

Paper Size... lists standard and user-specified plot sizes (**Fig. 26.62**).

Drawing Orientation offers *Portrait* and *Landscape* options.

Scale is typed in the edit boxes, *Custom = Drawing Units* (**Fig. 26.63**). 1 = 1 is full size, 1 = 2 is half size, and 2 = 1 is double size.

Scaled to Fit calculates the scale that makes the drawing's extents fill the plotting area and be as large as possible (**Fig. 26.64**).

Plot Offset can be set with x and y coordinates or centered (**Fig. 26.64**).

Partial Preview shows rectangles representing paper size and the drawing area (**Fig. 26.65**). The part of the drawing area that exceeds the paper size cannot be plotted unless the scale, origin, or both are adjusted.

26.61 The *Plot area* section of the *Plot* box is used to specify the portion of the drawing that will be plotted: *Limits, Extents,* or *Display.*

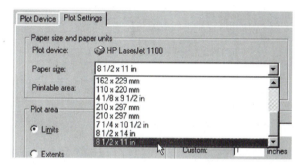

26.62 The *Paper Size* box gives a listing of the plot sizes that are available for selection.

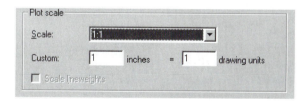

26.63 Type the desired plotting scale (1=1, or full size in this case). If *Scaled to Fit* is selected, the drawing will be enlarged or reduced to fill the sheet if the placement of the origin permits.

Full Preview shows the entire drawing on the screen and its relationship to the paper limits when plotted (**Fig. 26.66**). Press (Enter) to *Pan* and *Zoom* about the preview drawing. Press (Enter) to return to the *Plot* dialogue box.

To update the *Page setup* settings, *Plot box> Add...>* Select the named file> *OK>* type <u>Yes</u> when asked if you want to replace the existing file.

26.64 Check *Center the Plot* in this box for specifying that the drawing will be centered on the sheet.

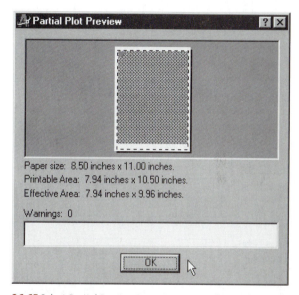

26.65 Select *Partial Preview* to get two rectangles on the screen that represent the paper size and drawing size.

26.16 Plotting or Printing

Plotter

Load paper in the plotter, as shown in **Fig. 26.67**, with the thick pen (P.7) in slot 1 and the thin pen (P.3) in slot 2, as specified by *Pen Assignments* in **Fig. 26.57**. Press (Enter) and the plot will begin. Plotting can be cancelled by pressing (Esc), but it may take almost a minute for it to take effect. When completed, select *File> Exit* to close Auto-CAD and end the session.

Printer

Load the printer with the necessary sheets of paper, be sure the printer is on, pick the OK button, and the drawing file is sent to the printer,

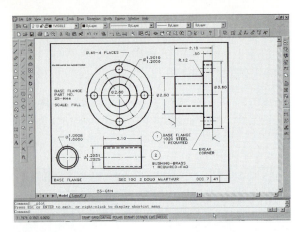

26.66 Select *Full Preview* to get this box for specifying rotation of the plot and its x- and y-offsets.

```
1. Load paper, lower lever
2. Pens: P.7 (Slot 1); P.3 (Slot 2)
3. Set for A–Size
4. Press P1 and P2
```

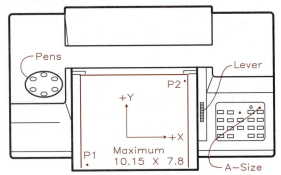

26.67 The Hewlett-Packard 7475A plotter is often the plotter of choice for size A and size B plots with pens.

where the drawing is plotted. A laser printer has no physical pens; the ink is sprayed on the paper (**Fig. 26.68**).

Now that we know how to set a few drawing aids, save files, and plot, it is time to learn how to make drawings.

26.17 2D Lines (Draw Toolbar)

Open your prototype drawing, *Main menu> File> Open> A:ABORD-HORIZ*, and use *Save As* to name the drawing as A:NO1, which becomes the current drawing with the same settings of

26.68 The Hewlett-Packard LaserJet 1200 printer has no physical pens; the ink is sprayed onto the paper. (*Courtesy of Hewlett-Packard Company.*)

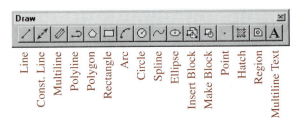

26.69 The *Draw* toolbar makes it easy for you to select commands with the cursor. *Main menu> View> Toolbars> Draw.*

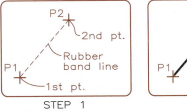

26.70 Line

Step 1 *Main menu> Draw> Line> Specify first point:* P1
Specify next point or [Undo]: P2

Step 3 *Specify next point or [Close/Undo]:* P3. (Enter)
(Enter) to disconnect rubber band from last point.

A:ABORD-HORIZ. Load the *Draw* toolbar *(View> Toolbars> Draw)* to obtain the commands shown in **Fig. 26.69**.

A *Line* (called an object) can be drawn by using the keyboard, the *Draw toolbar,* or the *Main menu (Main menu> Draw> Line).* At the *Command* line, type *Line* or *L* and respond to the prompts as shown in **Fig. 26.70** to draw lines by picking endpoints with the left mouse button. The current line will rubberband from the last point and lines are drawn in succession until (Enter) or the right mouse button is pressed.

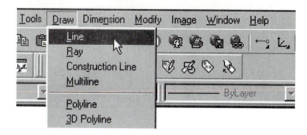

These types of lines can be selected from the *Draw* drop-down menu or from the *Main menu* toolbar.

The *Draw toolbar* can be used to select four types of lines: *Line, Ray, Construction,* and *Multilines.* These types of lines can also be selected from *Main menu> Draw* (**Fig. 26.71**). A *Construction line* is drawn across the whole length of the screen and a *Ray* is drawn from the selected point to the edge of the screen.

A comparison of absolute and polar coordinates is shown in **Fig. 26.72**. *Delta coordinates* can be typed as @2,4 to specify the end of a line 2 units in the x-direction and 4 units in the y-direction from the current end.

Polar coordinates are *2D* coordinates and are typed as @3.6<56 to draw a 3.6-long line from the current (and active) end of a line at an angle of 56° with the x-axis. *Last coordinates* are found by typing @ while in the *Line* command. This causes the cursor to move to the last point.

World coordinates locate points in the *World Coordinate System* regardless of the *User Coordinate System* being used by preceding the coordinates with an asterisk (*). Examples are *4,3; *90<44; and @*1,3.

The *Status line* at the bottom of the screen shows the length of the line and its angle from the last point as it is rubberbanded from point to point. The *Close* command will close a continuous series of lines from the last to the first point selected.

26.18 Circles (Draw Toolbar)

The *Circle* command *(Main menu> Draw> Circle)* draws circles when you select a center

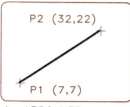
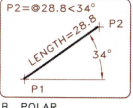

A. ABSOLUTE COORDINATES

B. POLAR COORDINATES

26.72 Lines: By coordinates

A Absolute coordinates can be typed (7,7 and 32,22) at the *Command* line to establish the ends of a line.

B Polar coordinates are relative to the current point and are specified with a length and the angle measured clockwise from the horizontal (@28.8<34).

and radius, a center and diameter, or three points (**Fig. 26.73**). Typing C at the *Command* line may be the fastest means of activating the *Circle* command, but the circle icon on the *Draw Toolbar* (**Fig. 26.69**) can also be selected. **Figure 26.74** illustrates how a circle is drawn.

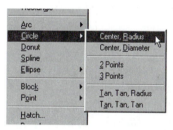

26.73 The *Circle* command *(Main menu> Draw> Circle>* has a flyout menu with these options for drawing circles.

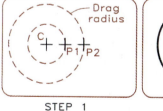
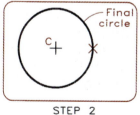

STEP 1

STEP 2

26.74 Circle

Step 1 *Main menu> Draw> Circle> Center, Radius> Specify center point for circle or [3P/2P/Ttr (tan tan radius)]:* C (Enter)
Specify radius of circle or [Diameter] <0.0000>: (Drag radius to P1 and P2 to enlarge the circle.)

Step 2 Select the final end of the radius (P2) with the left mouse button and the final circle is drawn.

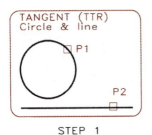
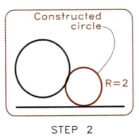
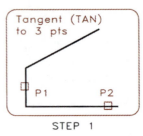
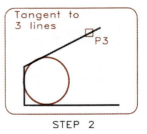

| STEP 1 | STEP 2 | STEP 1 | STEP 2 |

26.75 Circle: Tangent to 2 objects (TTR)

Step 1 *Main menu> Draw> Circle> (Tan, Tan, Radius)*

Specify center point for circle or [3P/ 2P/ Ttr (tan, tan, radius)]: Ttr (Enter)

Specify point on object for first tangent of circle: P1

Step 2 *Specify point on object for second tangent of circle:* P2, *Specify radius of circle <0.0000>:* 2 (Enter)

26.76 Circle: Tangent to 3 lines (TTT)

Step 1 *Main menu> Draw> Circle> (Tan, Tan, Tan)*

Specify point on object for first tangent of circle: P1

Specify point on object for second tangent of circle: P2

Step 2 *Specify point on object for third tangent of circle:* P3

The *Ttr (tangent, tangent, radius)* option of *Circle* draws a circle tangent to a circle and a line, three lines, three circles, or two lines and a circle. A circle is drawn tangent to a line and a circle by selecting the circle, the line, and giving the radius (**Fig. 26.75**). The *TTT option* (Main menu > circle > Tan, Tan, Tan) calculates the radius length and draws a circle tangent to three lines, as shown in **Fig. 26.76**.

26.19 Arc (Draw Toolbar)

The *Arc* command *(Main menu> Draw> Arc>* options) (**Fig. 26.77**) or the *Arc* icon in the *Draw toolbar* (**Fig. 26.69**) has eleven combinations of variables that use abbreviations for starting point, center, angle, ending point, length of chord, and radius. The *S, C, E* version requires that you locate the starting point *S*, the center *C*, and the ending point *E* (**Fig. 26.78**). The arc begins at point S and is drawn counterclockwise to a point near *E*.

A line can be continued with an arc drawn from the last point of a line and tangent to it, as shown in **Fig. 26.79**, for drawing runouts of fillets and rounds. It can be used to draw a tangent line from an arc by applying the commands in reverse and dragging the line to its final length.

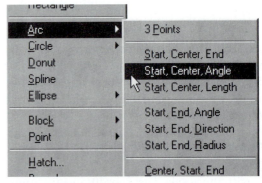

26.77 Select *Main menu> Draw> Arc>* to obtain these options. When using the *Start, Center, Angle* option, these elements must be specified in this sequence on the screen. The *Draw toolbar* also can be used.

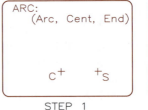
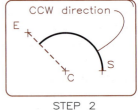

| STEP 1 | STEP 2 |

26.78 Arc: Start, Center, End option (SCE)

Step 1 *Main menu> Draw> Arc> Start, Center, End> Specify start point of arc or [CEnter]:* S (Enter)

Specify center point of arc: C

Step 2 *Specify end point of arc or [Angle/chord Length]:* Drag the arc to the end of the radial line CE, click the left mouse button, and the arc is drawn.

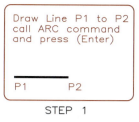
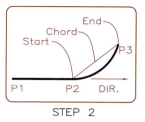

STEP 1 STEP 2

26.79 Arc: Tangent to the end of a line

Step 1 *Main menu> Draw> Line> Specify first point:* P1
Specify next point or [Undo]: P2 (Enter) or right mouse button.

Step 2 *Draw toolbar> Arc> Continue:* (Arc automatically begins at P2.) *Specify end point of arc:* Drag tangent arc to P3.

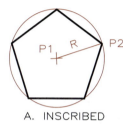
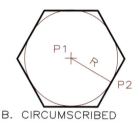

A. INSCRIBED   B. CIRCUMSCRIBED

26.80 Polygons: inscribed and circumscribed

A *Main menu> Draw> Polygon> Enter number of sides <4>:* 5 (Enter), *Specify center of polygon or [Edge]:* P1

Enter and option [Inscribed in circle/Circumscribed about circle] <I>: I (Enter) *Specify radius of circle:* Drag to radius P2.

B Same as above, but enter C for *Circumscribed:* Drag radius to P2 to size the circumscribed polygon.

26.20 Polygon (Draw Toolbar)

An equal-sided polygon can be drawn as shown in **Fig. 26.80** with *Main menu> Draw> Polygon,* or the *Polygon* icon can be selected from the *Draw toolbar* (**Fig. 26.81**) and the prompts responded to in the same manner. A polygon is drawn in a counterclockwise direction about the center point. Polygons can have a maximum of 1024 sides.

26.21 Ellipse (Draw Toolbar)

The *Ellipse* command in the *Draw Toolbar* gives icons for 3 types of ellipses (**Fig. 26.82**). An ellipse is drawn by selecting the endpoints of the major axis and a third point, P3, to give the length of the minor radius (**Fig. 26.83**).

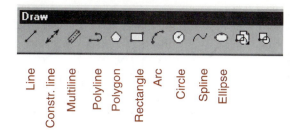

Line Constr. line Multiline Polyline Polygon Rectangle Arc Circle Spline Ellipse

26.81 Select the *Polygon* icon from the *Draw toolbar* and respond to the prompts as described in Fig. 26.76.

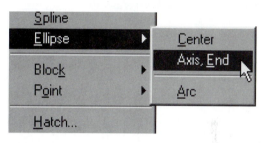

26.82 *Main menu> Draw> Ellipse> Axis, End* can be used for drawing ellipses.

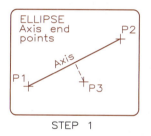
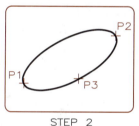

STEP 1 STEP 2

26.83 Ellipse: Endpoint option

Step 1 *Main menu> Draw> Ellipse> Axis, End>*
Specify axis endpoint or [Arc/Center]: P1
Specify other endpoint of axis: P2

Step 2 *Specify distance to other axis or [Rotation]:* P3, Ellipse is drawn through P1, P2, and a point on the perpendicular from the midpoint of the axis established by P3.

In **Fig. 26.84**, points are picked at the center of the ellipse at P1, one axis endpoint at P2, and the second axis length from P1 to P3. The ellipse is drawn through point P2 and the endpoint of the minor diameter specified by P3. The endpoints of the axis can be located and the rotation angle specified. An angle of 0° gives a full circle, and an angle of 90° gives an edge.

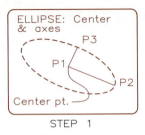

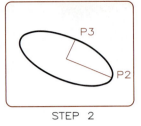

26.84 Ellipse: Center option

Step 1 *Main menu> Draw> Ellipse> Center*

Specify axis endpoint of ellipse or [Arc/Center]: C *Specify center of ellipse:* P1, *Specify endpoint of axis:* P2

Step 2 *Specify distance to other axis or [Rotation]:* P3, *The ellipse is drawn*

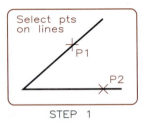

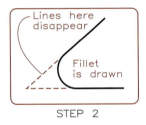

26.85 Fillets: Between lines

Step 1 *Main menu> Modify> Fillet*

Current settings: Mode=TRIM, Radius=0.5000

Select first object or [Polyline/Radius/Trim]: R (Enter), *Specify fillet radius <0.5000>:* 1 (Enter) (Enter).

Step 2 *Command:* Fillet, *Current settings: Mode =Trim, Radius =1.00, Select first object or [Polyline/Radius/Trim]:* P1, *Select second object:* P2, *The tangent arc is drawn.*

26.22 Fillet (Modify Menu)

The corners of two lines can be rounded with the *Fillet* command *(Main menu> Modify> Fillet)* whether or not they intersect. When the fillet is drawn, the lines are either trimmed or extended as shown in **Fig. 26.85**. The assigned radius is remembered until it is changed. By setting the radius to 0, lines will be extended to a perfect intersection. Fillets of a specified radius can be drawn tangent to circles or arcs as shown in **Figs. 26.86** and **26.87**.

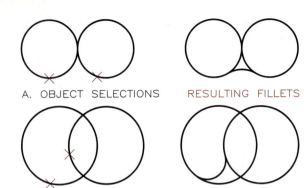

A. OBJECT SELECTIONS   RESULTING FILLETS

B. OBJECT SELECTIONS   RESULTING FILLETS

26.86 Fillets: Tangent arcs

A Tangent arcs (drawn with the fillet command) are drawn at the lower arcs of the circles when selected at P1 and P2.

B Tangent arcs (drawn with the fillet command) are drawn as shown when selected at points P1 and P2.

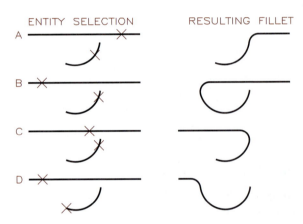

26.87 The applications of fillets between lines and arcs are determined by the positions of the selection points.

26.23 Chamfer (Modify Menu)

The *Chamfer* command *(Main menu> Modify> Chamfer)* draws angular bevels at intersections of lines or polylines. After assigning chamfer distances *(D)*, select two lines and they are trimmed or extended, and the *Chamfer* is drawn **(Fig. 26.88)**. Press (Enter) to repeat this command using the previous settings. Chamfer distances can be equal or unequal in length.

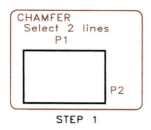
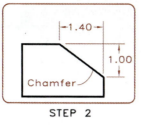

26.88 Chamfer

Step 1 *Main menu> Modify> Chamfer> (Trim mode) Current chamfer Dist1=0.5000, Dist2=0.5000*

Select first line or [Polyline/Distance/Angle/Trim/Method]: <u>D</u>

Specify first chamfer distance <0.5000>: <u>1.40</u> (Enter)

Specify second chamfer distance <1.4000>: <u>1.00</u> (Enter)

Step 2 (Enter) *Chamfer*

(Trim mode) Current chamfer Dist1=1.4000, Dist2=1.0000

Select first line or [Polyline/Distance/Angle/Trim/Method]: <u>P1</u>> *Select second line:* <u>P2</u>, The chamfer is drawn.

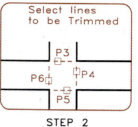
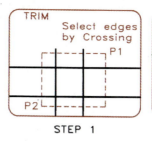

26.90 Trim: Crossing window

Step 1 *Main menu> Modify> Trim> Current settings: Projection=UCS Edge=Extend Select cutting edges...*

Select objects: <u>P1</u>, *Specify opposite corner:* <u>P2</u>

4 found, Select objects: (Enter)

Step 2 *Select object to trim or [Project/Edge/Undo]:* <u>P3</u>

Select object to trim or [Project/Edge/Undo]: <u>P4</u>

Select object to trim or [Project/Edge/Undo]: <u>P5</u>

Select object to trim or [Project/Edge/Undo]: <u>P6</u>

The four lines are trimmed.

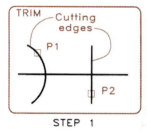
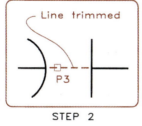

26.89 Trim: Cutting edges

Step 1 *Main menu> Modify> Trim> Current settings: Projection=UCS Edge=Extend Select cutting edges...*

Select objects: <u>P1</u>, *1 found*

Select objects: <u>P2</u> ,*1 found> Select objects:* (Enter)

Step 2 *Select object to trim or [Project/Edge/Undo]:* <u>P3</u>, The line between the cutting edges is removed.

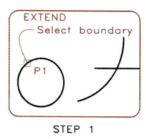
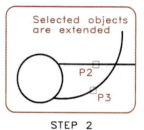

26.91 Extend

Step 1 *Main menu> Modify> Extend*

Current settings: Projection=UCS Edge=Extend

Select boundary edges... Select objects: <u>P1</u>, *1 found*

Step 2 *Select objects: Select object to extend or [Project/Edge/Undo]:* <u>P2</u>

Select object to extend or [Project/Edge/Undo]: <u>P3</u>

26.24 Trim (Modify Menu)

The *Trim* command *(Main menu> Modify> Trim)* selects cutting edges that trim selected lines, arcs, or circles that cross them up to their points of intersection, as illustrated in **Fig. 26.89**. The *Crossing* option of *Trim* is used to select four cutting edges at once and all four of the lines are trimmed as shown in **Fig. 26.90**.

26.25 Extend (Modify Menu)

The *Extend* command lengthens lines, plines, and arcs to intersect a selected boundary (**Fig. 26.91**). You are prompted to select the boundary object and the object to be extended, which will extend the object to the boundary. More than one object can be extended. *Extend* will not work on "closed" polylines such as a polygon.

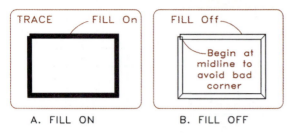

A. FILL ON   B. FILL OFF

26.92 Trace

A *Command:* Fill, *Enter mode [On/Off]: <On>* (Enter) *Command:* Trace (Enter), *Specify trace width <0.0500>:* .02, *Specify start point:* P1, *Select next point:* P2, *Select next point:* Continue point selection; (Enter) to end.

B To obtain a *Trace* with unfilled lines: *Command:* Fill, Set mode to *Off,* (Enter) *Command:* Regen (Enter) Draw the Trace following the steps as in A above.

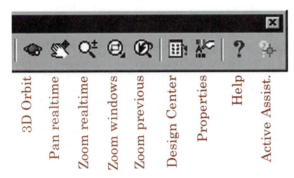

3D Orbit — Pan realtime — Zoom realtime — Zoom windows — Zoom previous — Design Center — Properties — Help — Active Assist.

26.93 This part of the *Standard toolbar* contains many options for *Panning* and *Zooming* on the screen.

26.26 Trace (Command line)

Wide lines made with multiple strokes by the plotter can be drawn with the *Trace* command. At the *Command* line, type *Fill* and set *On* and the *Trace* will be drawn as shown in **Fig. 26.92A**. When *Fill* is *Off,* the lines will be drawn as parallel lines with "mitered" angles (**Fig. 26.92B**).

26.27 Zoom and Pan (Standard Toolbar)

Parts of a drawing can be enlarged or reduced by the *Zoom* command *(View> Standard toolbar> Zoom> options for Zooming),* as shown in **Fig. 26.93**. Other zooms can be selected from the *Zoom* toolbar > *View> Zoom* toolbar*)* shown in

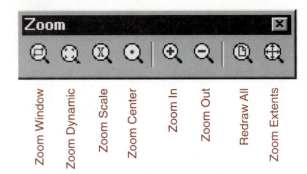

Zoom Window — Zoom Dynamic — Zoom Scale — Zoom Center — Zoom In — Zoom Out — Redraw All — Zoom Extents

26.94 The *Zoom toolbar* contains these options for *Zooming* on the screen.

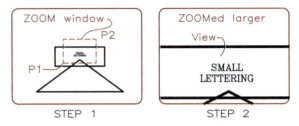

STEP 1   STEP 2

26.95 Zoom

Step 1 *Standard toolbar> Zoom realtime* icon>

Right-click to activate pop-up menu

Specify corner of window, enter a scale factor (nX or nXP), or [All/Center/Dynamic/Extents/ previous/Scale/Window] <real time>: Hold down select button and window the *Zoom* area (P1 and P2)

Step 2 The area in the window box is expanded to fill as much of the screen as possible.

Fig. 26.94. An example of using a *Zoom* window to enlarge part of a drawing is shown in **Fig. 26.95**.

Zoom (Z, when typing) has the following options: *All, Center, Dynamic, Extents, Previous, Scale, Window,* and *Realtime.*

All expands the drawing's *Limits* (dot pattern) to fill the screen.

Center is picked to specify the center of the *Zoomed* image and specify its magnification or reduction.

Dynamic lets you *Zoom* and *Pan* by selecting points with the cursor.

Extents enlarges the drawing to its maximum size on the screen.

Previous displays the last *Zoomed* view.

Scale X/XP magnifies a drawing relative to paper space. By typing 1/4XP, or .25XP, the

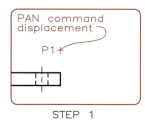
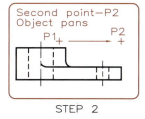

STEP 1 STEP 2

26.96 Pan

Step 1 *Standard toolbar> Pan icon*

Step 2 Pick <u>P1</u>, hold down select button, and drag to <u>P2</u> to change your view of the screen.

drawing will be scaled so that 0.25 inch equals 1 inch.

Window lets you pick the diagonal corners of a window to fill the screen.

Realtime (the default) lets you drag to the left to make a crossing window, or to the right for a window to specify the area to be enlarged.

The *Pan (P)* command (**Fig. 26.96**) is used to pan the view across the screen by selecting two points. The drawing is not relocated as in the *Move* command; only your viewpoint of it is changed.

26.28 Selecting Objects

A recurring prompt, *Select objects:*, asks you to select an object or objects that are to be *Erased, Changed,* or modified in some way. Type *Select* when in a current command that requires a select *(Move,* for example) and the options will be displayed: *Window, Last, Crossing, BOX, ALL, Fence, WPolygon, CPolygon, Group, Add, Remove, Multiple, Previous, Undo, AUto,* and *SIngle.* **Figure 26.97** shows ways of selecting objects for applicable commands, such as *Copy.* The application of the options of *SIngle* and *Multiple, Window, Crossing,* and *BOX* are shown in parts A, B, C, and D, respectively.

Window selects objects that lie completely within the solid-line window.

Last is used to pick the most recently drawn object.

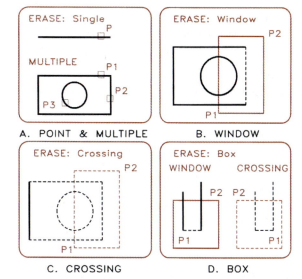

A. POINT & MULTIPLE   B. WINDOW

C. CROSSING   D. BOX

26.97 Select options

A When prompted *Select objects:*, select the objects one at a time.

B *Window (W)* is used to select objects lying completely within the window, defined by solid lines.

C *Crossing Window (C)* is used to select objects within or crossed by the window, defined by dotted lines.

D The *Box* option is used to make a *Window* or a *Crossing Window,* determined by the direction the box is dragged.

Crossing (C) selects objects that are crossed by or lie completely within the dotted-line window.

BOX lets you make a window by selecting a point and dragging to the right. A crossing window can be made by dragging to the left.

Other techniques for selecting objects are shown in **Fig. 26.98**.

WPolygon (WP) forms a solid-line polygon that has the same effect as a window.

CPolygon (CP) forms a dotted-line polygon that has the same effect as a crossing window.

Fence (F) selects corner points of a polyline that will select any object it crosses the same as a crossing window.

ALL selects everything on the screen.

Add and *Remove* are used while selecting objects to add an object by typing <u>A</u> (Add) or to

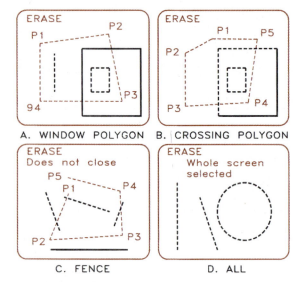

26.98 Selection of objects

A *Window Polygon (WP)* selects objects inside it.

B *Crossing Polygon (CP)* selects objects inside it and crossed by it.

C *Fence (F)*, a nonclosing polyline, selects objects that it crosses.

D *All* selects all objects on the screen.

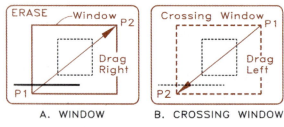

26.99 Selection windows

A *Window* is formed by holding down the select button while dragging a diagonal corner to the right.

B *Crossing Window* is formed in the same manner, but is dragged to the **left**.

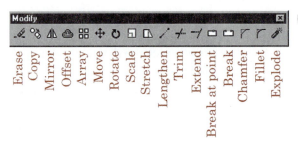

26.100 The *Modify toolbar,* a portion of which is shown here, has options for making changes in a drawing.

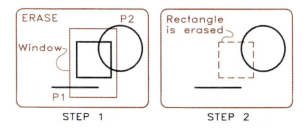

26.101 Erase: Window option

Step 1 *Modify toolbar> Erase* icon

Select objects: P1, *Other corner:* P2.

Step 2 *Select objects:* (Enter) The box lying completely within the erasing window is removed.

remove one by typing R. When finished, press (Enter) to end the *Select/remove* prompt.

Multiple (M) selects multiple points without highlighting in order to speed up the selection process.

Previous (P) recalls the previously selected set of objects. For example, enter *Move* and type P, and the last selected objects are recalled.

Undo (U) removes objects in reverse order one at a time by typing U (undo) repetitively.

AUto (AU) selects an object by pointing to it, and pointing to a blank area selects the first corner of a box defined by the *BOX* option.

Single (SI) causes the program to act on the object or sets of objects without pausing for a response.

A *Window* or a *Crossing Window* can be obtained automatically by pressing the pick button (left button), holding it down, and selecting the diagonal of a window. By dragging it to the right a window is obtained; by dragging it to the left a crossing window is obtained (**Fig. 26.99**).

26.29 Erase and Break (Modify Toolbar)

The *Erase* command *(Modify toolbar> Erase icon)* (**Fig. 26.100**) deletes specified parts of a drawing. The selection techniques described previously can be used to select objects to be

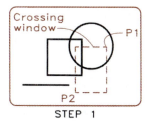
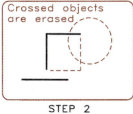

26.102 Erase: Crossing option

Step 1 *Modify toolbar> Erase icon*

Select objects: P1, *Other corner:* P2 (Right to left for a crossing window).

Step 2 *Select objects:* (Enter) The lines crossed by the crossing window are removed.

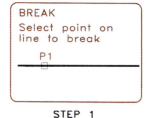
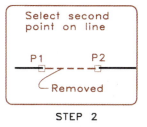

26.103 Break

Step 1 *Modify toolbar> Break icon*

Select object: P1,

Step 2 *Specify second break point or [First point]:* P2 Line between P1 and P2 is removed.

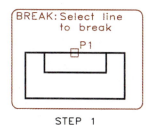
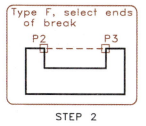

26.104 Break: F option

Step 1 *Modify toolbar> Break icon> Select object:* P1,

Step 2 *Specify second break point or [First point]:* F (Enter)
Specify first break point: P2,
Specify second break point: P3, Line P2–P3 is removed.

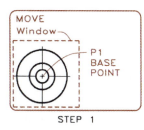
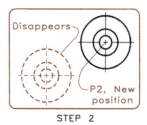

26.105 Move

Step 1 *Modify toolbar> Move icon*
Select objects: W , Crossing window around part
Specify base point or displacement: P1

Step 2 *Specify second point of displacement or <use first point as displacement>:* P2, Drag to new position.

erased as shown in **Figs. 26.101** and **26.102**. The default of the *Erase* command, *Select Objects*, allows you to pick one or more objects and delete them by pressing (Enter). Type *Oops* to restore the last erasure—but only the last one.

The *Break* command (*Modify toolbar> Break* icon) removes part of a line, pline, arc, or circle (**Fig. 26.103**). To specify a break at an intersection with another line as shown in **Fig. 26.104**, select the line to be broken and select the *F* option. Now the endpoints can be selected without fear of selecting the wrong lines.

26.30 Move and Copy (Modify Toolbar)

The *Move* command (*Modify toolbar> Move* icon) repositions a drawing (**Fig. 26.105**) and the *Copy* command duplicates it, leaving the original in its same position. Both the *Move* and the *Copy* commands are applied in the same manner. The *Copy* command has a *Multiple* option for locating a series of copies of drawings in different positions.

26.31 Undo (Standard Toolbar)

Standard toolbar> Undo icon (or *Command:* Undo or U) can reverse the previous commands one at a time back to the beginning of a session. The *Redo* command reverses the last *Undo; Oops* will not work. The *Undo* command has options of: *Auto, Control, BEgin, End, Mark, Back,* and *Number.*

Command: Undo (Enter)
Auto/Control/BEgin/End/Mark/Back/
<Number>: 4 (Enter)

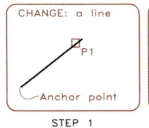
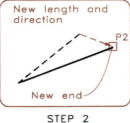

STEP 1   STEP 2

26.106 Change: Line

Step 1 *Command:> Change>* (Enter)
Select objects: P1, 1 found> Select objects: (Enter)
Step 2 *Specify change point or [Properties]: P2*
The end of the line moves to P2.

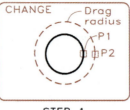
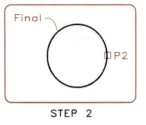

STEP 1   STEP 2

26.107 Change: Circle

Step 1 *Command:> Change>* (Enter)
Select objects: P1, 1 found
Select objects: (Enter)
Step 2 *Specify change point or [Properties]: P2*
The circle's size is changed.

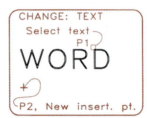
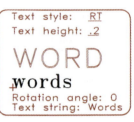

STEP 1   STEP 2

26.108 Change: Text

Step 1 *Command: Change>* (Enter)
Select objects: P1, 1 found, Select objects: (Enter)
Specify change point of [Properties]: (Enter)
Specify new text insertion point <no change>: P2
Step 2 *Enter new text style <Outline>:* Romans (Enter)
Specify new height <0.5000>: .20 (Enter)
Specify new rotation angle <0>: (Enter)
Enter new text <WORD>: words (Enter)

Entering 4 has the same effect as using the *U* command four separate times.

Mark identifies a point in the drawing process to which subsequent additions can be undone by the *Back* option. Only the part of the drawing added after placing the *Mark* will be undone at the prompt:

This will undo everything.
OK? <Y>: Y (Enter)

By responding Y, the *Mark* will be removed, making it possible for the next *Undo (U)* to proceed backward past the mark.

The *BEgin* and *End* options group a sequence of operations until *End* terminates the group. *Undo* treats the group as a single operation. The *Control* subcommand has three options: *All, None,* and *One. All* turns on the full features of the *Undo* command, *None* turns them off, and *One* uses *Undo* commands for single operations and requires the least disk space.

26.32 Change (Modify Toolbar)

Type *Change* to modify features: *Lines, Circles, Text, Attribute Definitions, Blocks, Color, Layers, Linetypes,* and *Thickness.* The position of an endpoint of a *Line* is changed by selecting one end and locating a new endpoint (**Fig. 26.106**).

Change varies the size of a circle by picking a point on its arc and dragging to a new size (**Fig. 26.107**).

Text can be modified with the *Change* command by pressing (Enter) until the prompts *Insertion point, Style, Height, Rotation Angle,* and *New Text* appear in sequence (**Fig. 26.108**). *Attribute Definitions,* including *Tag, Prompt String,* and *Default Value,* can be revised with the *Change* command. *Blocks* can be moved or rotated with the *Change* command as shown in **Fig. 26.109**.

Property changes of the *Change* command, *LAyer, Color, LType,* and *Thickness,* are made by selecting objects and typing *P (Properties),* as

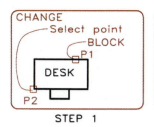
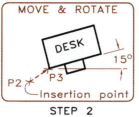

26.109 Change: Block

Step 1 *Command:> Change> Select objects:* <u>P1</u>,
1 found> Select objects: (Enter)

Step 2 *Specify change point or [Properties]:* <u>P2</u>
Specify new block rotation angle <0>: <u>15</u> (Enter).

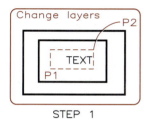
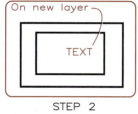

26.110 Change: Layers

Step 1 *Command:> Change* (Enter)
Select objects: <u>W</u>, *Window with* <u>P1</u> *and* <u>P2</u> *1 found*
Select objects: (Enter)
Specify change point of [Properties]: <u>P</u> (Enter)

Step 2 *Enter property to change*
[Color/Elev/LAyer/LType/ltScale/. . . /PLotstyle]: <u>LA</u> (Enter)
Enter new layer name <0>: <u>Visible</u> (Enter)

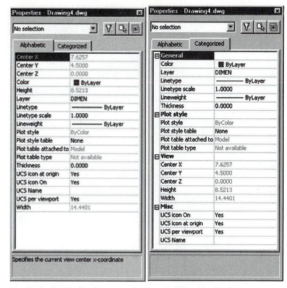

A. Alphabetical tab   **B. Categorized tab**

26.111 *Main menu> Modify> Properties (or Command:* <u>Properties</u> *(Enter)) to modify objects in the same manner as the Change command is used.*

shown in **Fig. 26.110**. Type *LA (Layer)* and the name of the layer onto which the text is to be changed.

Multiple *Colors* and *LTypes* can be assigned to objects on the same layer by the *Change* command, but it is better for each layer to have only one layer and linetype. The *Thickness* property is the height of an extrusion in the z-direction of a three-dimensional object drawn with the *Elev* and *Thickness* options (as covered in Chapter 27). *Changing* the *Thickness* of a 2D surface 0 to a nonzero value converts it to an extruded 3D drawing.

At the command line, type <u>DDmodify</u>, *(Main menu> Modify> Properties)* and select an object when prompted to obtain a *Modify* box for changing colors, layers, linetypes, thickness, linetype scale, and ends of lines and properties of other objects (**Fig. 26.111**). The *Modify* box can also be found by double clicking on an object.

26.33 Grips (Tools Menu)

Grips are small squares that appear on selected objects at midpoints and ends of lines, at centers and quadrant points of circles, and at insertion points of text. *Grips* are used to *Stretch, Move, Rotate, Scale,* and *Mirror.*

The *Grips* dialogue box *(DDgrips)* is found under *Main menu> Tools> Options...> Selection* tab for making settings (**Fig. 26.112**). The *Enable Grips* check box turns on grips for all objects. *Enable Grips Within Blocks* turns on grips for objects within a *Block;* when *Off,* a single grip is given at the insertion point of the *Block.*

Grip Colors turns on the *Color* dialogue box for assigning colors to selected and unselected grips; unselected grips are not filled in. *Grip Size* sets the size of grip boxes with a slider box.

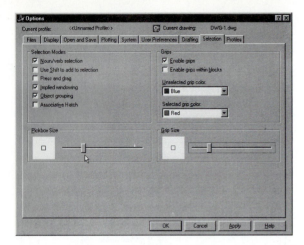

26.112 *Main menu> Tools> Options>Selection* tab to obtain this box for *Enabling Grips,* setting *Grip size,* and setting *Grip color.*

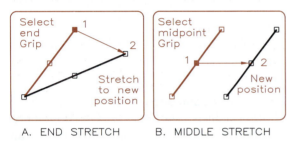

A. END STRETCH   B. MIDDLE STRETCH

26.113 Grips: Stretch

A Click on the line and grips appear; click on end grip 1 and select a position at 2, and the end of the line is moved.

B Select the midpoint grip 1, pick second point 2, and the line is moved.

Using Grips: By clicking on an object with the cursor, grips will appear on it as open boxes. A grip that is picked is made the "hot" point and is filled with color. By holding down the *Shift* key, more than one grip can be picked as a "hot" point, but the last grip of a series must be selected without pressing *Shift.* Press the *Escape* key to remove grips. By turning grips on and successively pressing (Enter), the options *Stretch, Move, Rotate, Scale,* and *Move* will be sequentially activated, each with subcommands. These option can be obtained by pressing the right mouse button after clicking on an object.

Stretch lets the endpoint grip of a line be selected as the "hot" point, and a second point

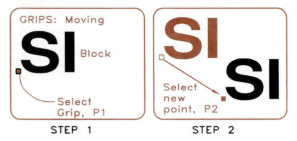

STEP 1   STEP 2

26.114 Grips: Move

Step 1 Click on the block and a grip appears at the insertion point. Pick this grip, P1

Step 2 Move the cursor to a new position, P2, click, and the block is moved.

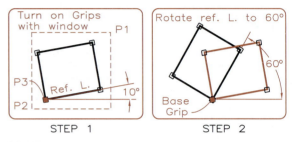

STEP 1   STEP 2

26.115 Grips: Rotation

Step 1 Turn on grips by windowing the object (P1 and P2); Select P3 as the pivot point, press (Enter or right button), repeatedly until **ROTATE** appears.

Step 2 *Specify rotation angle or [Base point/Copy/Undo/ Reference/eXit]:* 50 (Enter) (Esc) The object is rotated.

as the new end of the line (**Fig. 26.113**). Select the midpoint grip to *Move* the line to a new position.

To *Move* the *Block* in **Fig. 26.114**, select the insertion point as the hot point. Options of *Base Point, Copy, Undo,* and *eXit* can be used for these applications.

Rotate revolves an object about a selected *Grip.* The *Reference* option rotates an object about a selected grip by dragging or typing a number. The object in **Fig. 26.115** is rotated 50° from the reference line by typing 50.

Scale uses the grip selected as a base point to size the object (**Fig. 26.116**). The scale factor is assigned by typing, by dragging, or by selecting a reference dimension and giving it a new dimension.

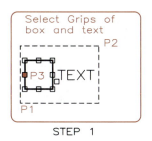
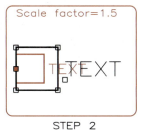

26.116 Grips: Scale

Step 1 Turn on grips by windowing object (P1 and P2); select P3 as the base, continue to press (Enter) until ****SCALE**** appears.

Step 2 *Specify scale factor or [Base point/Copy/Undo/Reference/eXit]:* 1.5 (Enter) (Esc)

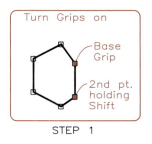
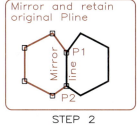

26.117 Grips: Mirroring

Step 1 Turn on grips by windowing object; select P1 as the base grip, press (Enter) until ****MIRROR**** appears.

Step 2 *Specify second point or [Base point/Copy/Undo/eXit]:* Hold down (shift) and pick P2 The object is mirrored. (Enter) (Esc)

Mirror makes a mirror image of an object. The original object is removed when two grips are selected to specify a mirror line. Hold down the *Shift* key while selecting the second grip point on the mirror line and the initial drawing will be retained (**Fig. 26.117**).

26.34 Polyline (Draw Toolbar)

The *Polyline (PL)* command from the *Draw* toolbar (**Fig. 26.118**) is used for drawing 2D polylines, which are lines of continuously connected segments instead of the separate segments drawn by the *Line* command. The thickness of a *Pline* can be varied as well, which requires multiple pen strokes when plotting with a pen plotter (**Fig. 26.119**).

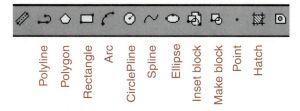

26.118 The *Pline* icon on the *Draw* toolbar is selected for drawing *Polylines*.

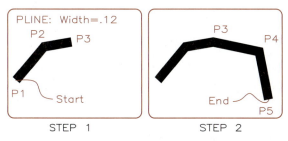

26.119 Pline: Width option

Step 1 *Draw toolbar> Select Pline icon> Specify start point:* P1

Current line-width is 0.000> Specify next point or [Arc/Close/Halfwidth/Length/Undo/Width]: W (Enter) *Specify starting width <0.0000>:* .12 (Enter)

Specify ending width <0.12000>: (Enter)

Specify next point, or [Arc/Close/Halfwidth/Length/Undo/Width]: P2

Specify next point, or [Arc/Close. . ./Width]: P3

Step 2 *Specify next point, or [Arc/Close . . . /Width]:* P4 *Specify next point, or [Arc/Close . . . /Width]:* P5 (Enter) (Enter)

The *Pline* options are *Arc, Close, Halfwidth, Length, Undo,* and *Width. Close* automatically connects the last end of the polyline with its beginning point and ends the command. *Length* continues a *Pline* in the same direction by typing the length of the segment. If the first line was an arc, a line is drawn tangent to and from the arc. *Undo* erases the last segment of the polyline, and it can be repeated to continue erasing segments. *Halfwidth* specifies the width of the line measured on both sides of its center line.

The *Arc* option of *Pline* is selected to obtain the prompts shown in **Fig. 26.120**. The default draws the arc tangent from the endpoint of the last line and through the next selected point. *Angle* gives the prompt, *Included angle:*, to

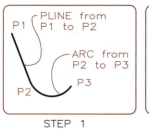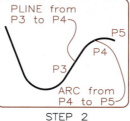

STEP 1   STEP 2

26.120 Pline: Lines and arcs

Step 1 *Draw* toolbar> Select *Pline* icon> *Specify start point:*> P1 (Enter)
Current line-width is 0.1200> Specify next point or [Arc/Close/Halfwidth/Length/Undo/Width]: P2
Specify next point or [Arc/Close . . . /Width]: Arc
Specify endpoint of arc or [Arc/Close . . . /Width]: P3

Step 2 *Specify endpoint of arc or [Arc/Close . . ./Width]:* Line
Specify next point or [Arc/ Close . . . /Width]: Length
Specify length of line: P4
Specify endpoint of arc or [Arc/Close . . . /Width]: Arc
Specify endpoint of arc or [Arc/Close . . . /Width]: P5
Specify endpoint of arc or [Arc/ . . . /Width]: (Enter)

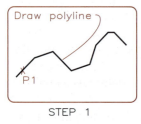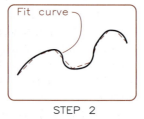

STEP 1   STEP 2

26.121 Pedit: Fit curve

Step 1 *Modify II* toolbar> Select *Pedit* icon> *Select polyline:* P1 (Enter)

Step 2 *[Close/ Join/ Width/ Edit vertex/ Fit/ . . .Undo/ eXit <X>]:* Fit (Enter) The curve is changed to a series of arcs that pass through all vertex points.

which a positive or negative value is given. The next prompt asks for *Center/Radius/<End point>:* to draw an arc tangent to the previous line segment. Select *Center* and you will be prompted for the center of the next arc segment.

The next prompt is *Angle/Length/<Endpoint>:*, where *Angle* is the included angle, and *Length* is the chordal length of the arc. *Close* causes the *Plines'* arc segment to close to its beginning point.

Direction lets you override the default, which draws the next arc tangent to the last *Pline* segment. When prompted with *Direction from starting point:*, pick the beginning point and respond to the next prompt, *Endpoint*, by picking a second point to give the direction of the arc.

Line switches the *Pline* command back to the straight-line mode. *Radius* gives the prompt, *Radius:*, for specifying the size of the next arc. The next prompt, *Angle/Length/<Endpoint>:*, lets you specify the included angle or the arc's chordal length. *Second Pt* gives two prompts, *Second point:* and *Endpoint:*, for selecting points on an arc.

26.35 Pedit (Modify II Toolbar)

The *Pedit* command from the *Modify II* toolbar modifies *Plines* with the following options: *Close, Join, Width, Edit vertex, Fit, Spline, Decurve, Ltype gen, Undo,* and *eXit.* If the *Pline* is already closed, the *Close* command will be replaced by the *Open* option.

Join (J) gives the prompt, *Select objects,* for selecting segments to join into a polyline. Segments of polylines must have exact meeting points to be joined.

Width (W) gives the prompt, *Specify new width for all segments:*, for assigning a new width to a *Pline.*

Fit (F) converts a polyline into a line composed of circular arcs that pass through each vertex (**Fig. 26.121**).

Spline (S) modifies the polyline as did *Fit*, but it draws cubic curves passing through the first and last points, and not necessarily through the other points (**Fig. 26.122**).

Decurve (D) converts *Fit* or *Spline* curves to their original straight-line forms.

Ltype gen (L) applies dashed lines (such as hidden lines) in a continuous pattern on curved polylines. Without applying this option, dashed lines may omit gaps in curved lines (**Fig. 26.123**). *Command:* Plinegen> 0 and dashed lines will

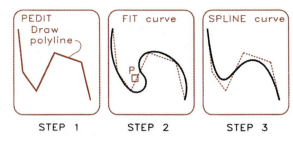

STEP 1   STEP 2   STEP 3

26.122 Pedit: Fit and Spline

Step 1 Draw a polyline (Pline).

Step 2 *Modify II toolbar> Pedit icon> Select polyline:* P

Close/ Join/ Width/ Edit vertex/ Fit/ . . .Undo/ eXit <X>: Fit
(Enter).

The curve of arcs passes through all points.

Step 3 *Pedit* in the same way, but use the *Spline* option to obtain a "best curve" that may not pass through all the selected points.

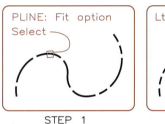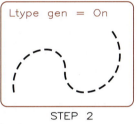

STEP 1   STEP 2

26.123 Pedit: Ltype generate

Step 1 *Modify II* toolbar> *Select Pedit icon> Select polyline:* P1
(Enter)

Step 2 *Enter an option [Close/ Join/ Width/ Edit vertex/ Fit/ . . . Ltype gen/ Undo/ eXit <X>]:* Ltype (Enter)

Enter polyline linetype generation option [ON/OFF] <Off>: ON, (Enter) Dashes are uniform around curves.

begin and end with a dash at each vertex. Set *Plinegen* to 1 and the dashed lines will be continuous around the vertexes.

Undo (U) reverses the most recent *Pedit* editing step.

Edit Vertex (E) selects vertexes of the *Pline* for editing by placing an X on the first vertex when the polyline is picked. The following options appear: *Next/ Previous/ Break/ Insert/ Move/ Regen/ Straighten/ Tangent/ Width/ eXit/ <N>:* Next (Enter).

Next (N) and *Previous* (P) options move the X marker to next or previous vertexes by pressing

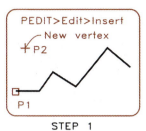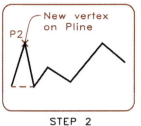

STEP 1   STEP 2

26.124 Pedit: Edit vertex—Insert

Step 1 *Modify II toolbar> Select Pedit icon> Select polyline:* P1
(Enter)

Enter an option [Close/Join/Width/Edit vertex . . . Undo]: Edit
(Enter)

Enter a vertex editing option [Next/ . . . /Insert/ . . ./eXit] <N>: Insert (Enter) Vertex to be inserted after P1.

Specify location for new vertex: P2

Step 2 *Enter a vertex editing option [Next/ . . . / Insert/ . . ./ eXit] <N>:* X (Enter)

(Enter). *Break* (B) prompts you to select a vertex with the X marker. Then use *Next* or *Previous* to move to a second point and pick *Go* to remove the line between the vertexes. Select *eXit* to leave the *Break* command and return to *Edit Vertex*.

Insert adds a new vertex to the polyline between a selected vertex and the next vertex (**Fig. 26.124**). *Move (M)* relocates a selected vertex (**Fig. 26.125**).

Straighten (S) converts the polyline into a straight line between two selected points as shown in **Fig. 26.126**. An X marker appears at the current vertex and the prompt, *Next/Previous/ Go/eXit/<N>*, appears. Move the X marker to a new vertex with *Next* or *Previous,* select *Go,* and the line is straightened between the vertices. Enter X to *eXit* and return to the *Edit Vertex* prompt.

Tangent (T) lets a tangent direction be selected at the vertex marked by the X for curve fitting by responding to the prompt *Direction of tangent.* Enter the angle from the keyboard or by cursor.

Width (W) sets the beginning and ending widths of an existing line segment from the X-marked vertex. Use *Next* and *Previous* to confirm in which direction the line will be drawn from

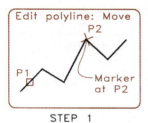
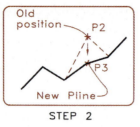

26.125 Pedit: Edit vertex—Move

Step 1 *Modify II toolbar> Pedit icon> Select polyline:* <u>P1</u>

Enter an option [Close/Join/Width/Edit vertex . . . Undo]: <u>Edit</u>
(Enter) (Enter) (Enter) Move marker to P2.

Step 2 *Select a vertex editing option [Next/ . . . /*
Move/ . . ./eXit] <N>: <u>Move</u> (Enter)

Specify a new location for marked vertex: <u>P3</u>

Enter a vertex editing option [Next/ . . . /Move/ . . ./eXit]
<N>:<u>X</u> (Enter) to exit the command.

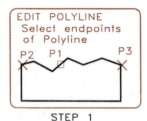
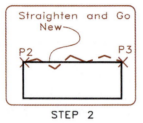

26.126 Pedit: Edit vertex—Straighten

Step 1 *Modify II toolbar> Select Pedit icon> Select polyline or*
[Multiple]: <u>P1</u> (Enter)

Enter an option [Close/. . . /Edit vertex/. . . /Undo]: <u>E</u> (Enter)
Marker is at P2.

Enter a vertex editing option [Next/ . . . /Straighten/ . . ./eXit]
<N>: <u>Straighten</u> (Enter)

Enter an option [Next/Previous/Go/eXit] <N>: Press (Enter)
until the marker is on <u>P3</u>.

Step 2 *Next/ Previous/ Go/ eXit <N>:* <u>Go</u> (Enter) The line is
straightened between P2 and P3.

the X marker. The polyline will be changed to its
new thickness when the screen is regenerated
with *Regen* (R). Use *eXit* to escape from the *Pedit*
command.

26.36 Spline (Draw Toolbar)

The *Spline* command *(Draw* toolbar> *Spline*
icon) draws a smooth curve with a sequence of
points within a specified tolerance as shown in

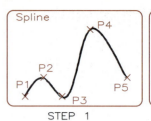
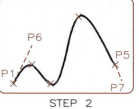

26.127 Spline

Step 1 *Draw toolbar> Spline icon> Specify first point or*
[Object]: <u>P1</u> *Specify next point:* <u>P2</u>

Specify next point or [Close/Fit tolerance] <start tangent>: <u>P3</u>
Continue specifying points until <u>P5</u> (Enter)

Step 2 *Specify start tangent:* Rubberband to <u>P6</u>

Specify end tangent: Rubberband to <u>P7</u>

26.128 *Draw* toolbar> *Select Hatch icon* to begin hatching a
sectioned area.

Fig. 26.127. By setting *Fit Tolerance* to <u>0</u>, the
curve will pass through the points; when set to a
value greater than 0, it will pass within a tolerance of each point. The *Close* option makes the
spline a closed figure. The *Endpoint Tangents*
determine the angle of the spline at each end.

26.37 Hatch (Draw Toolbar)

Hatching is a pattern of lines that fills sectioned
areas, bars on graphs, and similar applications.
From the *Draw* toolbar (**Fig. 26.128**), the *Bhatch*
(boundary hatch) dialogue box is displayed (**Fig.
26.129**). By selecting the down arrow at the
Pattern box, a listing of pattern names is given
from which to select. When one is selected, a
view of the pattern will appear in the *Swatch*
window. Examples of some predefined ANSI
patterns are shown in **Fig. 26.130**.

The *Boundary Hatch* box (**Fig. 26.129**) lets
you specify *Predefined, User-defined,* or *Custom*
patterns. *Predefined* patterns are those provided
by AutoCAD®.

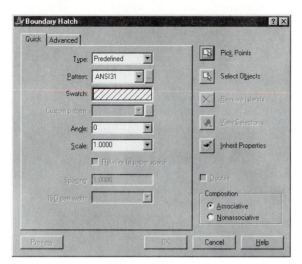

26.129 When the *Hatch icon* is selected, this *Boundary Hatch box* appears on the screen.

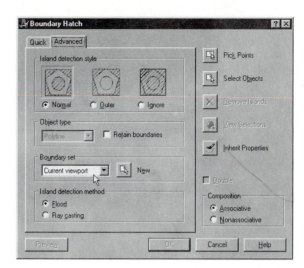

26.131 Select *Advanced tab* in the *Boundary Hatch box* (Fig. 26.129) to display this dialogue box.

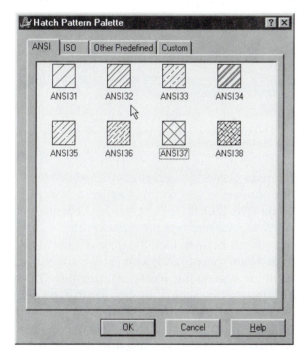

26.130 When the *Pattern button* in the *Boundary Hatch box* is selected, the ANSI hatch patterns and their names are displayed in this *Hatch Pattern Palette*.

Scale sets the spacing between the lines of a pattern and *Angle* assigns their direction. The *Advanced* button displays the *Advanced Options* dialogue box (**Fig. 26.131**), from which options

of *Normal, Outer,* or *Ignore* can be selected. A square with a pentagon and a circle inside it illustrates the effect of each choice. *Normal* hatches every other nested area, beginning with the outside. *Outer* hatches the outside area, and *Ignore* hatches the entire area from the outer boundary. When text within the hatching area is selected, it will appear in an opening and hatch lines will not pass through it.

Select Pick Points and *Select Objects* (**Fig. 26.129**) are used to select areas inside of boundaries and then boundaries themselves (**Fig. 26.132**). When points are selected outside the boundary or if the boundary is not closed, error messages will appear. Composition can be specified as *Associative* or *Nonassociative. Associative* hatching is automatically updated when the size of the hatching area is changed. Select the *Inherit Properties icon,* pick the symbols within a hatched area, select the area to be hatched, and it is filled with the same hatching symbols.

26.38 Text and Numerals

Command: <u>Dtext></u> *Justify* and you will be prompted for the placement of the insertion

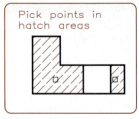

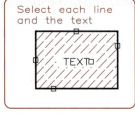

A. PICK POINTS | B. SELECT OBJECTS

26.132 Hatching areas

A The *Pick Points* option (Fig. 26.131) of *Boundary Hatch* prompts for points inside the boundaries for hatching.

B The *Select Objects* option requires that boundary lines be selected.

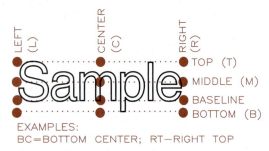

EXAMPLES:
BC=BOTTOM CENTER; RT—RIGHT TOP

26.133 Text can be added to a drawing by using any of the insertion points above. For example, *BC* means the bottom center of a word or sentence that will be located at the cursor point.

point for text (**Fig. 26.133**). *BC* means bottom center, *RT* means right top, and so forth.

Figure 26.134 illustrates how multiple lines of *Dtext* are automatically spaced by pressing (Enter) at the end of each line. The special characters shown in **Fig. 37.135** can be inserted by typing a double percent sign (%%) in front of them.

Type Qtext and select *On* to reduce screen regeneration time by converting text to boxes (**Fig. 26.136**). When *Qtext* is *Off,* the full text will be restored after regeneration (*Command: Regen*).

26.39 Text Style (Format Menu)

Many of AutoCAD's text fonts and their names are shown in **Fig. 26.137**. The default style, *Standard,* uses the *Txt* font. Select *Main menu>*

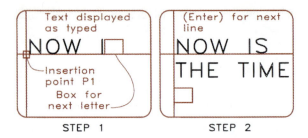

STEP 1 | STEP 2

26.134 Dtext

Step 1 *Command:> Dtext>* (Enter)
Current text style: "Standard" Text height 0.5000
Specify start point of text or [Justify/Style]: P
Specify height <0.5000>: .125 (Enter)
Specify rotation angle of text <0>: (Enter)
Enter text: NOW IS

Step 2 (Enter) *Enter text:* THE TIME (Enter) (Enter)

%%O	Start or stop Overline of text
%%U	Start or stop Underline of text
%%D	Degree symbol: 45%%D =45°
%%P	Plus—minus: %%P0.05=±0.05
%%C	Diameter: %%C20=⌀20
%%%	Percent sign: 80%%% =80%
%%nnn	Special character number nnn

26.135 The special characters that begin with %% are used with *Dtext* to obtain these symbols.

Format> Text Style, and the *Text Style* dialogue box appears where you can assign a *New Style* name (**Fig. 26.138**). Select the *New* button, get the *New Style* box, type the name (Romand), and the style is named. Pick the down arrow at the *Font Name* panel, and pick the font that you want to assign to the new style (*Romand*). Other options can be assigned: *Height* (0 is recommended), *Width factor,* and *Oblique Angle.* Your preferences are shown in the *Preview* window.

The *Style names* are listed in a drop-down menu in the window beneath the heading, *Style Name* of the *Text Style* dialog box. An example of the text font is displayed when a *Style* is selected (**Fig. 26.138**). A defined *Style* will retain its settings until they are changed.

If you later change a named *Style* with new settings or fonts, and select *Apply* in the *Text*

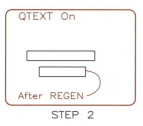

QTEXT Off	QTEXT On
Ø24 CBORE 16 DEEP	After REGEN
STEP 1	STEP 2

26.136 Qtext

Step 1 *Command:* <u>Qtext</u> (Enter), *On/ Off:* <u>On</u> (Enter)

Step 2 *Command:* <u>Regen</u> (Enter) Text is shown as boxes.

TXT	PRELIMINARY PLOTS
MONOTXT	FOR SPEED ONLY
	Simplex fonts
ROMANS	FOR WORKING DRAWINGS
SCRIPTS	*Handwritten Style, 1234*
GREEKS	ΓΡΕΕΚ ΣΙΜΠΛΕΞ, 12345
	Duplex fonts
ROMAND	**THICK ROMAN TEXT**
	Complex fonts
ROMANC	ROMAN WITH SERIFS
ITALICC	*ROMAN ITALICS TEXT*
SCRIPTC	*Thick-Stroke Script Text*
GREEKC	ΓΡΕΕΚ ΩΙΤΗ ΣΕΡΙΦΣ
	Triplex fonts
ROMANT	**TRIPLE-STROKE ROMAN**
ITALICT	*Triple-Stroke Italics*
	Gothic fonts
GOTHICE	**English Gothic Text**
GOTHICG	**German Gothic Text, 12**
GOTHICI	**Italian Gothic Text, 12**

26.137 Examples of some of AutoCAD's available fonts are shown here.

Style box, all text previously entered under this style name will be updated with the new properties. This technique is used to change the *Txt* and *Monotxt* fonts to more attractive fonts at plot time. Beforehand, time is saved by using *Txt* and *Monotxt* fonts because they regenerate quickly.

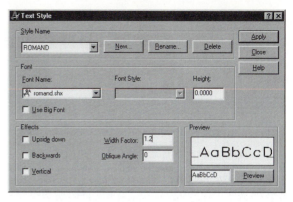

26.138 *Main menu> Format> Text Style* (or type *Style* at the *Command* line) to display this *Text Style* box. From here, a *New style* can be named, *Fonts* can be assigned, *Width Factors* can be specified, and other assignments can be made.

26.139 *Modify II toobar>* Select *Edit Text* icon (or type <u>DDedit</u> at the *Command* line), select a line of text on the screen, and it will appear in this *Edit Text* box for editing.

The *DDedit or (View> Toolbars> Modify II> Text Edit* icon) is used to select a line of text to be displayed in a dialogue box for editing (**Fig. 26.139**). Correct the text, select the *OK* button, and it is revised on the screen.

26.40 Multiline (Draw Toolbar)

From the *View> Toolbars> Draw toolbar,* select the *A icon (Text),* pick an insertion point, and specify the size of the text boundary by the diagonal window option by specifying the width with *W,* or by specifying two points with *2P.* The *Multiline Text Editor* dialogue box will appear and the paragraph of text can be typed in its window (**Fig. 26.140**). Select *OK* to place the paragraph on the drawing.

Four tabs, each having a variety of settings, are: *Character, Properties, Line Spacing,* and *Find/Replace.* Most of the options provided by the tabs box are obvious after a degree of experimentation and applying the *Help* command

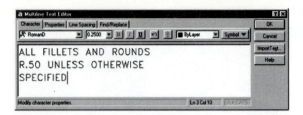

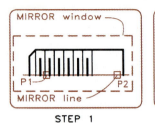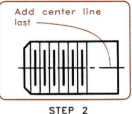

STEP 1   STEP 2

26.140 *Draw* toobar> *Multiline text*> Select a window on the screen with two diagonal corners to specify the area for the lines of text and this *Multiline Text Editor* appears. Type lines of text in the box, pick *OK,* and the lines are drawn on the screen in the specified box. Four tabs—*Character, Properties, Line Spacing* and *Find/ Replace*—of this box provide additional options.

26.142 Mirror.

Step 1 Draw the half to be mirrored. *Modify toolbar> Mirror icon> Select objects:* <u>W</u> (Enter)
Select objects: <u>Window the drawing</u>.
Specify first point of mirror line: <u>P1</u>,
Specify second point of mirror line: <u>P2</u>

Step 2 *Delete old objects? <N>:* <u>No</u> (Enter) The drawing is mirrored.

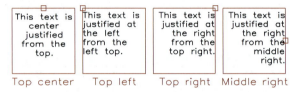

This text is center justified from the top.	This text is justified at the left from the left top.	This text is justified at the right from the top right.	This text is justified at the right from the middle right.
Top center	Top left	Top right	Middle right

26.141 Under the *Properties tab,* types of *Justification* can be selected. Several examples are shown here.

when needed. Fonts specifications, line spacing, layers, and similar settings can be made. Examples of text applied by the *Attach* option are shown in **Fig. 26.141**.

26.41 Mirror (Modify Toolbar)

Select the *Mirror (Modify toolbar> Mirror icon* (or *Command:* <u>Mirror</u>) to *Mirror* partial figures about an axis (**Fig. 26.142**). A line that coincides with the *Mirror line* (P1-P2, for example) will be drawn twice when mirrored; therefore, parting lines should be drawn after the drawing has been mirrored.

A system variable, *Mirrtext (Command:* <u>Setvar</u>> <u>Mirrtext</u>*)*, is used for mirroring text. By setting *Mirrtext* to 0, *Mirrtext* is set to *Off* and text will not be mirrored. If the *Mirrtext* variable is set to 1 *(On),* the text will be mirrored along with the drawing.

26.42 Osnap (Object Snap Toolbar)

By using *Osnap (Object Snap),* you can snap to objects of a drawing rather than to the *Snap* grid. *Osnap* icons from the *Object snap* toolbar (**Fig.**

26.143 The *Object Snap* toolbar has these options for drawing to and from object features on the screen.

26.143) give the following options: *Endpoint, Midpoint, Intersection, Apparent Extension, Center, Quadrant, Tangent, Perpendicular, Parallel, Insertion point, Node, Nearest, None,* and *Settings. Osnap* is used as an accessory to other commands: *Line, Move, Break,* and so forth.

Figure 26.144 shows how a line is drawn from an intersection to the endpoint of a line. In **Fig. 26.145**, a line is drawn from <u>P1</u> tangent to the circle by using the *Tangent option* of *Osnap.* The *Tangent option* can be used to draw a line tangent to two arcs.

Of the various options, *Node* snaps to a *Point, Quadrant* snaps to one of the four compass points on a circle, *Insert* snaps to the insertion point of a *Block,* and *None* turns off *Osnap* for the next selection.

Osnap settings can be temporarily retained as "running" *Osnaps* for repetitive use. One way

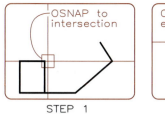 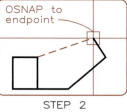

26.144 Osnap: Intersection and end

Step 1 *Draw* toolbar> *Line* icon> *Line from point:* Pick *Intersection* icon, *Int of:* P1

Step 2 *To point:* Pick *Endpoint* icon on *Osnap* toolbar.

To point: P2, The line is drawn to the endpoint.

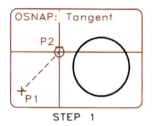

26.145 Osnap: Tangent

Step 1 *Draw* toolbar> *Line* icon> *Line from point:* P1

To point: Select *Tangent* icon.

Step 2 *Tan to:* P2 The line is drawn from P1 to true tangent point near P2.

to set running *Osnaps* is to right click on the *Osnap* tab in the *Status line* at the bottom of the screen to obtain options of *On, Off,* and *Settings.* The *Settings* option displays the *Drafting Settings* box that lists the *Osnap* options by selecting the *Object Snap tab.* The settings can be retained, but turned on and off by selecting this button.

When *Osnap* is on, the cursor has an aperture target at its intersection for picking endpoints and centers of arcs. Remove running *Osnap* settings by right clicking on the OSNAP button in the *Status line,* picking *Settings,* picking *Object Snap,* and deselecting the different settings by removing the checks from the various option boxes. Select the *Option* button of the *Drafting Settings* box and the *Options* box

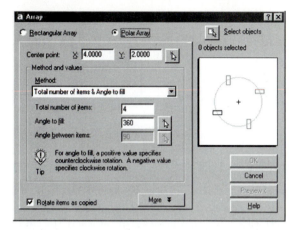

26.146 *Draw* toolbar> *Array* icon to obtain the *Array box* from which to make selections for *rectangular* and *polar* arrays.

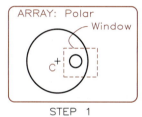 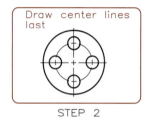

26.147 Array: Polar

Step 1 *Modify* toolbar> *Array* icon> *Select objects:* W (Enter) (Window the hole.) *Select objects: Enter the type of array [Rectangular/Polar] <R>:* P (Enter) *Specify center point of array:* C

Step 2 *Enter the number of items in the array:* 4 (Enter) *Specify the angle to fill(+=ccw, -=cw) <360>:* 360 (Enter) *Rotate arrayed objects? [Yes/No] <Y>:* (Enter)

will appear, from which you can set aperture sizes from 1 to 50 pixels for snapping to objects.

26.43 Array (Draw Toolbar)

Draw toolbar> *Array* is used to draw rectangular patterns (rows and columns) or polar layouts of selected drawings using the *Array* dialogue box (**Fig. 26.146**). A series of holes can be drawn on a bolt circle by drawing the first hole and *Arraying* it as a *polar* array (**Fig. 26.147**).

A *rectangular* array is begun by making the drawing in the lower left corner and following the steps in **Fig. 26.148**. Rectangular arrays may

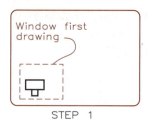
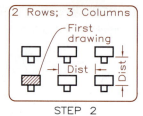

STEP 1   STEP 2

26.148 Array: Rectangle

Step 1 *Draw* toolbar> *Array icon> Select objects:* <u>W</u> (Enter) (Window the desk.) *Select objects: Enter the type of array [Rectangular/Polar] <R>:* <u>Rectangular</u> (Enter)

Step 2 *Enter the number of rows (—) <1>:* <u>2</u> (Enter)

Enter the number of columns (| | |) <1>: <u>3</u> (Enter),

Enter the distance between rows or specify unit cell (–) <1>: <u>4</u> (Enter)

Specify the distance between columns (111) <1>: <u>3.5</u> (Enter)

be drawn at angles by using the *Snap* mode to *Rotate* the grid. The first object is drawn in the lower left corner of the array and the number of rows, columns, and the cell distances are specified when prompted.

26.44 Scale (Modify Toolbar)

The *Scale* command reduces or enlarges previously drawn objects. The desk in **Fig. 26.149** is enlarged by windowing it, selecting a base point, and typing a scale factor of 1.6. The drawing and its text are enlarged in the x- and y-directions.

A second option of *Scale* lets you select a length of a given object, specify its present length, and assign a length as a ratio of the first dimension (**Fig. 26.150**). The lengths can be given by the cursor or typed at the keyboard in numeric values.

26.45 Stretch (Modify Toolbar)

The *Stretch* command *(Modify* toolbar> *Stretch* icon) lengthens or shortens a portion of a drawing while one end is left stationary. The window symbol in the floor plan (**Fig. 26.151**) is *Stretched* to a new position, leaving the lines of the wall

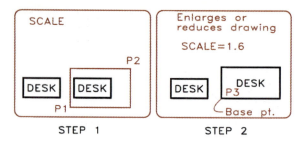

STEP 1   STEP 2

26.149 Scale: Numeric

Step 1 *Modify toolbar> Scale icon> Select objects:* <u>W</u> (Enter) Window the desk with <u>P1</u> and <u>P2</u>.

Step 2 *Specify base point:* <u>P3</u> *Specify scale factor or [Reference]:* <u>1.6</u> (Enter) The desk is drawn 60% larger.

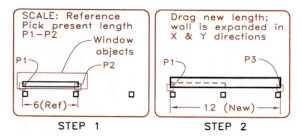

STEP 1   STEP 2

26.150 Scale: Reference.

Step 1 *Modify* toolbar> *Scale* icon

Select objects: <u>Select 4 objects,</u>

Base point: Select <Scale factor>/ Reference: <u>R</u> (Enter)

Reference length <1>: <u>P1</u> and <u>P2</u>.

Step 2 *New length:* Drag to <u>P3</u>. The drawing is enlarged in all directions.

unchanged. A *Crossing Window* must be used to select lines that will be stretched, a regular window will not work.

26.46 Rotate (Modify Toolbar)

A drawing can be rotated about a selected base point by using *Command:* <u>Rotate</u> or *(Modify* toolbar> *Rotate* icon) as shown in **Fig. 26.152**. *Window* the drawing to be rotated, select it's base point, and type the rotation angle, or select the angle by dragging the cursor on the screen, and the drawing is rotated. Drawings made on multiple layers can be rotated also.

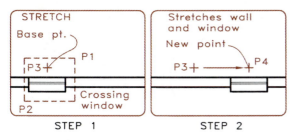

26.151 Stretch

Step 1 *Modify toolbar> Stretch icon> Select objects:* Use P1 and P2 to form a crossing window.

Specify base point or displacement: P3

Step 2 *Specify second point of displacement:* P4 The windowed portion of the drawing is repositioned.

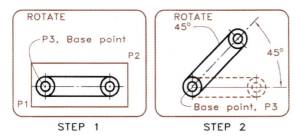

26.152 Rotate

Step 1 *Modify* toolbar> *Rotate* icon> *Select objects:* P1 and P2 to window link.

Specify base point: P3

Step 2 *Specify rotation angle or [Reference]:* 45 (Enter) Object is rotated 45° counterclockwise.

26.47 Setvar (Command Line)

Many system variables (several hundred) can be inspected by *Command:* Setvar> ? (Enter) and changed if they are not read-only commands. To change one or more variables (*Textsize,* for example), respond as follows:

Command: Setvar (Enter)
Variable name or ?: Textsize (Enter)
Enter new value for Textsize <0.18>: 0.125 (Enter)

By entering the *Setvar* command with an apostrophe in front of it *('Setvar),* it can be used transparently without the necessity of exiting from the command in progress.

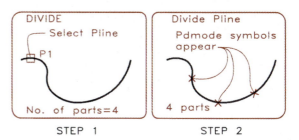

26.153 Divide

Step 1 *Command:* Divide (Enter)
Select object to divide: P1

Step 2 *Enter the number of segments or [Block]:* 4 (Enter)

Pdmode symbols are placed along the line dividing it.

26.48 Divide (Draw Menu)

Command: Divide (or *Main menu> Draw> Point> Divide)* is used to place markers on a line to show a specified number of equal divisions. The line in **Fig. 26.153** is selected by the cursor, the number of divisions is specified, and markers are equally spaced along it. The markers will be of the type and size set by the *Pdmode* and *Pdsize* variables under the *Setvar* command. Set *Pdmode* to 3 to get an X when the *Point* command is used.

The *Block* option of *Divide* allows saved blocks of any number of objects (rectangles in this example) to be used as markers on the line (**Fig. 26.154**). *Blocks* can be either *Aligned* or *Not Aligned,* as shown.

26.49 Measure (Draw Menu)

Command: Measure (or *Main menu> Draw> Point> Measure)* repeatedly measures off a specified distance along an arc, circle, polyline, or line and places markers at these distances along the selected object (**Fig. 26.155**). Respond to the *Select object to measure* prompt by picking a point near the end where you want the measuring to begin. When prompted, give the segment length, and markers are displayed along the line at equal intervals. The last segment is usually a shorter length.

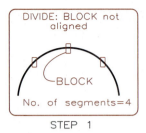

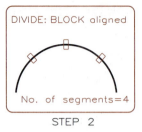

| STEP 1 | STEP 2 |

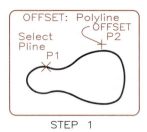

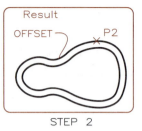

| STEP 1 | STEP 2 |

26.154 Divide: Arc

A *Command:* Divide (Enter)
Select object to divide: Select arc.
Enter the number of segments or [Block]: Block (Enter)
Enter the name of block to insert: S (Enter)
Align block with object? [Yes/No]:<Y>: No (Enter)
Enter the number of segments: 4 (Enter)
Blocks are drawn to radiate from the arc's center.

B Same as A above but do not align Blocks, and they will be inserted each in the same direction.

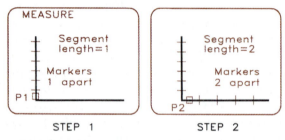

| STEP 1 | STEP 2 |

26.155 Measure

Step 1 *Command:* Measure (Enter)
Select object to measure: P1 (on the vertical line.)
Specify length of segment or [Block]: 1 (Enter)
Markers are placed 1 apart starting at end nearest P1.

Step 2 *Command:* Measure (Enter)
Select object to measure: P2 (on the horizontal line.)
Specify length of segment or [Block]: 2 (Enter) Markers are placed 2 units apart starting at the end nearest P2.

26.50 Offset (Modify Toolbar)

A line, arc, or polyline can be drawn parallel to and offset from other objects of the same type by *Command:* Offset (or *Modify* toolbar> *Offset* icon) (**Fig. 26.156**). *Offset* prompts for the distance or the point through which the offset line must pass, and then prompts for the side of the offset. The offset distance can be typed as numerals or defined by two points located by the cursor. The *Offset* command is helpful when drawing parallel lines to represent walls of a floor plan.

26.156 Offset

Step 1 *Command:* Offset (Enter)
Specify offset distance or [Through] <1>: T (Enter)
Select object to offset or <exit>: P1

Step 2 *Specify through point:* P2. An enlarged *Pline* is drawn that passes through P2.

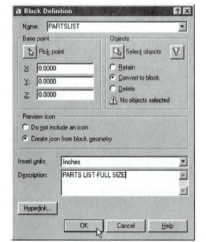

26.157 *Draw* toolbar> *Make block* icon will open this *Block Definition* box on the screen for making a *Block*.

26.51 Blocks (Draw Toolbar)

One of the most productive features of computer graphics is the capability of creating drawings called *Blocks* for repetitive use. *Draw* toolbar> *Block> Make> Block definition* box is used to make a block (**Fig. 26.157**). The SI symbol in **Fig. 26.158** is a typical drawing that is made into a *Block* and inserted into drawings using icons from the *Draw* toolbar shown in **Fig. 26.159**. The *Insert* heading on the *Main menu> Insert> Block)* gives the *Insert* dialogue box (**Fig. 26.160**) for inserting both *Blocks*. You can select a block from the window or *Browse* for other files to insert as *Blocks* (**Fig. 26.161**).

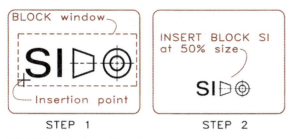

26.158 Block: Make and Insert

Step 1 *Command:* <u>Block</u> (Enter) Get *Block Definition* box (see above). *Name:* <u>SI-M</u>> *Pick point button*> <u>P2</u>) *Select objects button* (Window drawing) (Enter)

OK button, and the Block is made.

Step 2 *Command:*> *Insert* (Enter)> *Insert* box> Give name of Block> <u>SI-M</u>> *Scale:* <u>0.5</u>, Check *Uniform Scale* box> *OK*> *Specify insertion point:* <u>P2</u>

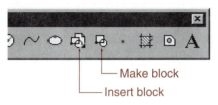

26.159 The *Make block* and *Insert block icons* can be selected from the *Draw* toolbar.

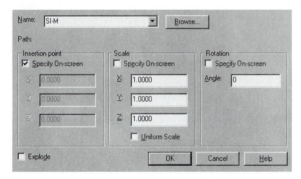

26.160 *Main menu> Insert>* to get *Insert* box to specify *Blocks* or *Files (Wblocks)* to be inserted in a drawing.

When a *Block* is selected on the screen (to be *Moved,* for example), it is selected as a total unit. However, *Blocks* that were *Inserted* by selecting the *Explode* box first, or by typing a star in front of the *Block* name (*SI,* for example), can be selected one object part at a time. An inserted *Block* can be separated into individual entities by typing *Explode* and picking the *Block.*

26.161 To insert a Block, *Command:* <u>Insert</u> (Enter)> *Browse*> Select a defined block from the list> *Open*> Select an insertion point on the screen.

Blocks are parts of files that can be used only in the current drawing file unless they are converted to *Wblocks (Write Blocks),* which become independent files, not parts of files. This conversion is performed by typing *Wblock* at the *Command* line to get the *Write Block* dialogue box. Select the *Block* button and type the name of the *Block* that is to be converted to a file. Give the location of the block in the *Destination File Name,* and press *OK.*

Blocks can be redefined by selecting a previously used *Block* name to receive the prompt, *Redefine it? <N>:.* Type <u>Y</u> (Yes), and select the new drawing to be blocked. After doing so, the redefined *Block* automatically replaces the one in the current drawing with the same name. *Command line> Insert> Block> Browse* can be used to display thumbnail illustrations of *Wblocks* (Files), as illustrated in **Fig. 26.161**.

26.52 Transparent Commands

Transparent commands are commands that can be used while another command is in progress by typing an apostrophe in front of the command name at the *Command* line. If you are dimensioning a part and wish to use *Pan,* type <u>'Pan,</u> (Enter), do the pan, and then complete the dimensioning command. Commands that can

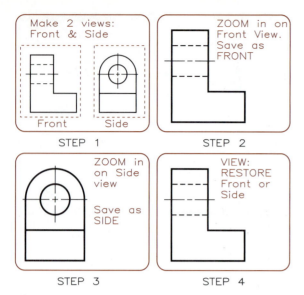

26.162 View

Step 1 Make a two-view drawing for saving as separate views.

Step 2 *Zoom* the front view to fill the screen.
Command: <u>View</u> (Enter)
?/ Delete/ Restore/ Save/ Window: <u>Save</u> (Enter)
View name to save: <u>FRONT</u> (Enter)

Step 3 *Zoom* the side view to fill the screen.
Command: <u>View</u> (Enter)
View name to save: <u>SIDE</u> (Enter)

Step 4 To display a view, *Command:* <u>View</u> (Enter)
?/ Delete/ Restore/ Save/ Window: <u>Restore</u> (Enter)
View name to restore: <u>SIDE</u> (Enter) The view is displayed.

be used transparently are *'Graphscr, 'Help, 'Pan, 'Redraw, 'Resume, 'Setvar, 'Textscr, 'View,* and *'Zoom.*

26.53 View (Command Line)

Portions of drawings can be saved as separate views by *Command:* <u>View</u>, as shown in **Fig. 26.162**, and the *View* box appears. The entire screen can be made into a *View* by picking the *New option* and naming it when prompted. The *Window* option makes a *View* of the windowed portion of the drawing. To display a view, type <u>View</u>, select the name view from the list of named views (FRONT, for example), and pick *Set Current* and *OK.*

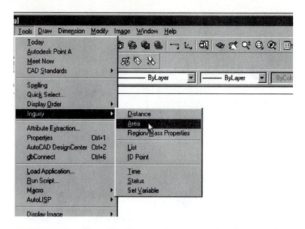

26.163 *Main menu> Tools> Inquiry* menu offers these options to assist you in learning about the details of a particular drawing.

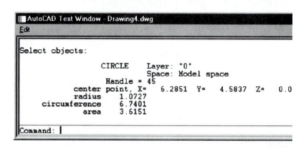

26.164 *Main menu> Tools* menu> *Inquiry> List* icon> select a circle on the screen. This box appears and gives circle's center, radius, circumference, and area.

26.54 Inquiry Commands (Tools)

From *Main menu> Tools> Inquiry* (or *Command:* <u>Inquiry</u>) to obtain information about objects and files with *Dist, Area, Mass Properties, List, ID Point, Time, Status,* and *Set Variables* (**Fig. 26.163**). *List* is selected (or typed) and the circle (or any object) is selected when prompted to obtain information about it (**Fig. 26.164**).

Dist measures the distance, its angle, and its delta-x and delta-y distances between selected points without drawing a line. *ID* gives the x-, y-, and z-coordinates of a point that is picked on the screen. *Area* gives the perimeter and area space on the screen. Prompts request *First point:, Next point:, Next point:,* and so on to pick

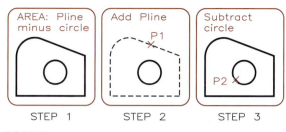

26.165 Area

Step 1 Draw the object with a *Pline* outline and a circular hole in it.

Step 2 *Main menu> Tools> Inquiry> Area> <First point>/*
Specify first corner point or [Object/Add/Subtract]: <u>Add</u> (Enter)
Specify first corner point or [Object/Subtract]: <u>O</u> (Enter)
(ADD mode) Select objects: <u>P1</u>
Area= 4.0300 Perimeter =24.8560
Total area = 4.0300

Step 3 *Specify first corner point or [Object/Subtract]:* <u>S</u>
Specify first corner point or [Object/Add]: <u>Object</u>
(SUBTRACT mode) Select objects: <u>P2</u>
Area= 0.4910, Perimeter= 7.8540
Total area= 3.5400

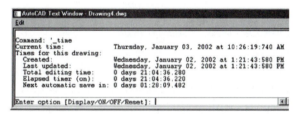

26.166 *Main menu> Tools> Inquiry> Time* is used for inspecting the time spent on a drawing and for setting the time for an assignment.

all points; then press (Enter). *Area*s can be added and removed when they are being selected, as shown in **Fig. 26.165**.

The *Status* option gives information about the settings, layers, coordinates, and disk space. *Time* displays information about the time spent on a drawing (**Fig. 26.166**). The timer can be *Reset* and turned *On* to record the time of a drawing session, but the cumulative time cannot be erased without deleting the drawing file. After *Resetting, Display* shows the time of the current session opposite the heading *Elapsed time:*.

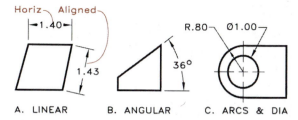

26.167 The basic types of dimensions that may appear on a drawing.

26.168 *Command:* <u>Dim</u> > <u>Status</u>, and (Enter) to obtain a listing of the dimension system variables.

26.55 Dimensioning Introduction

Figure 26.167 shows common types of dimensions that are applied to drawings. **Drawings should be drawn full size on the screen** since they are measured by the dimensioning commands; scaling should be done at plotting time.

Dimensions can be applied as *associative* or as *nonassociative (Exploded)* dimensions. *Associative* dimensions (when *Dimaso* is *On*) are inserted as if the dimension line, extension lines, text, and arrows were parts of a single *Block*. Exploded dimensions are applied as individual objects that can be modified independently by setting *Dimaso* to *Off*. Except where noted, the examples that follow will be associative dimensions.

Many variables must be set before dimensioning is usable: Arrowheads and numerals must be sized, extension line offsets specified, text fonts assigned, and units adopted, to name a few.

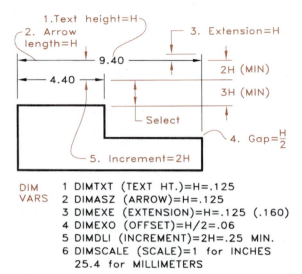

1. Text height=H
2. Arrow length=H
3. Extension=H
9.40
4.40
2H (MIN)
3H (MIN)
Select
4. Gap=$\frac{H}{2}$
5. Increment=2H

DIM VARS		
1	DIMTXT (TEXT HT.)=H=.125	
2	DIMASZ (ARROW)=H=.125	
3	DIMEXE (EXTENSION)=H=.125 (.160)	
4	DIMEXO (OFFSET)=H/2=.06	
5	DIMDLI (INCREMENT)=2H=.25 MIN.	
6	DIMSCALE (SCALE)=1 for INCHES	
	25.4 for MILLIMETERS	

26.169 Dimensioning variables are based on the height of the lettering (text), usually about 1/8-inch high. It is recommended that the arrow length (DIMASZ) be a little longer than 0.125 but less than 1.60.

26.56 Dimension Style Variables

To get a list of the current dimensioning variables as shown in **Fig. 26.168**, *Command:* <u>Dim</u>> <u>Status</u>> (Enter). Sizes of dimensioning variables are based on the letter height, which is most often 0.125″ (**Fig. 26.169**).

To set and save a few variables needed for basic applications, *Open (*or *Create)* the file *A:PROTO1.* Each variable is set by typing *Setvar* and the name of the dimensioning variable (*Dimtxt,* text height, for example) and assigning a numerical value. A list of most of the dimensioning variables is given in **Figs. 26.170** and **26.171**. Assign the basic variable values of *Dimtxt, Dimasz, Dimexe, Dimexo, Dimtad, Dimdli, Dimaso,* and *Dimscale* (**Fig. 26.169**) to *B:PROTO1,* since they apply to most applications. Type <u>Units</u> and set decimal fractions to two decimal places for inches.

Save these settings to *A:PROTO1* with no drawings on it and use it as the prototype when creating a new file. Load *A: PROTO1* and *Save As A:DWG-3,* for example, which becomes the current file with the same settings as *A:PROTO1.*

Dim Vars	Default	Description
DIMADEC	−1	Decimal places for ang. dims.
DIMALT	OFF	Alternate units selected
DIMALTD	2	Alternate unit decimal places
DIMALTF	25.4	Alternate unit scale factor
DIMALTTD	2	Alternate tolerance dec. places
DIMALTTZ	0	Alternate tolerance zero suppress.
DIMALTU	2	Alternate units
DIMALTZ	0	Alternate unit zero suppression
DIMAPOST	—	Default suffix for alternate text
DIMASO	ON	Create associative dimensions
DIMASZ	.125	Arrow length
DIMAUNIT	0	Angular unit format
DIMBLK	—	Arrow block name
DIMBLK1	—	First arrow block name
DIMBLK2	—	Second arrow block name
DIMCEN	.09	Center mark size
DIMCLRD	BYLAYER	Dimension line color
DIMCLRE	BYLAYER	Extension line & leader color
DIMCLRT	BYLAYER	Dimension & extension color
DIMDEC	4	Decimal places for dimensions
DIMDLE	0	Dimension line extension
DIMDLI	.38	Dim. increment for continuation
DIMEXE	.125	Extension beyond dimension line
DIMEXO	.06	Extension line offset
DIMFIT	3	Fit text
DIMGAP	.06	Justification of text on dim. line
DIMJUST	0	Gap from dimension line to text
DIMLFAC	1	Length factor
DIMLIM	OFF	Gives tolerances in limit form
DIMPOST	—	Character suffix after dimensions

26.170 Type *Dimstyle* at the *Command* line > *Status* to obtain a listing of the dimension variables, their settings, and definitions.

Dim Vars	Default	Description
DIMRND	0	Rounding value for distances
DIMSAH	OFF	Separate arrowheads at each end
DIMSCALE	1	Scale factor for all dim. vars.
DIMSD1	OFF	Suppress first dimension line
DIMSD2	OFF	Suppress second dimension line
DIMSE1	OFF	Suppress first extension line
DIMSE2	OFF	Suppress second extension line
DIMSHO	ON	Changes dimens. while dragging
DIMSOXD	OFF	Suppress outside dimension lines
DIMSTYLE	STANDARD	Current dimensioning stype
DIMTAD	0	Text placed above dimension line
DIMTDEC	4	Tolerance decimal places
DIMTFAC	1	Tolerance text scale factor
DIMTIH	ON	Text inside extension lines horiz.
DIMTIX	OFF	Text forced inside extension lines
DIMTM	0	Minus tolerance value
DIMTOFL	OFF	Forces dim. line inside, text out
DIMTOH	ON	Text outside ext. lines is horiz
DIMTOL	OFF	Applies tolerances to dimensions
DIMTOLJ	1	Tolerance vertical justification
DIMTP	0	Plus tolerance value
DIMTSZ	0	Tick size
DIMTVP	0	Text over or under dimen. line
DIMTXSTY	STANDARD	Text style
DIMTXT	.125	Text height
DIMTZIN	0	Tolerance zero suppression
DIMUNIT	2	Unit format
DIMUPT	OFF	User positioned text
DIMZIN	0	Zero suppression

26.171 Additional dimension variables are shown here as a continuation of the previous figure by pressing (Enter).

Dimensioning variables can be set from dialogue boxes also, instead of being typed; these techniques are covered later. You will be more proficient by becoming familiar with both meth-

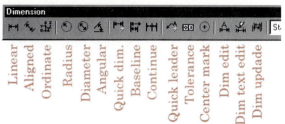

26.172 The *Dimension* toolbar has these options from which to select.

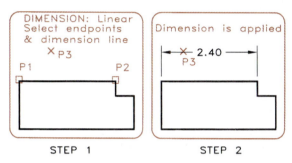

STEP 1   STEP 2

26.173 Dimensioning: Line

Step 1 *Main menu> View> Toolbars> Dimension* toolbar> *Linear* icon> *First extension line origin or <Select object>:* P1

Specify second extension line origin: P2

Dimension line location (Text/ Angle/ Horizontal/ Vertical/ Rotated): P3

Step 2 *Dimension text <2.40>:* (Enter) The dimension line is drawn.

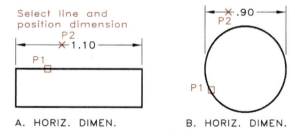

A. HORIZ. DIMEN.   B. HORIZ. DIMEN.

26.174 Dimensioning: Semiautomatic-Linear

A *Dimension* toolbar> *Aligned> Specify first extension line origin or <select object>:* (Enter)

Select object to dimension: P1

Select dimension line location or [Mtext/Text/Angle]: P2

Dimension text <1.10>: (Enter)

B Use these same steps and select a point on the circle (P1) to dimension its diameter.

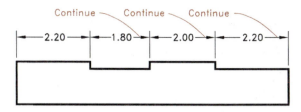

26.175 When dimensions are placed end to end, the *Continue* option is used to specify the second extension line origin after the first dimension line has been drawn.

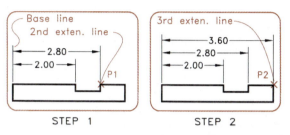

STEP 1   STEP 2

26.176 Dimensioning: Baseline option

Step 1 Place a *Linear* dimension (2.00); the first extension line becomes the baseline. From the *Dimension* toolbar, select *Baseline* icon.

Specify a second extension line origin or [Undo/Select] <Select>: P1 > *Dimension text=2.80* (Enter) The 2.80 dimension is drawn.

Step 2 *Specify a second extension line origin or [Undo/Select] <Select>:* P2 >*Dimension text=3.60* (Enter)

The 3.60 dimension is drawn. (Enter) to exit.

ods of assigning variables. For now, use the *A:DWG-3* file to explore the fundamentals of dimensioning.

26.57 Linear Dimensions (Dimension Toolbar)

The *Dimension* toolbar (**Fig. 26.172**) is a convenient means of selecting dimensioning commands. Select the *Linear Dimension* icon, the points as prompted, and the horizontal option, as shown in **Fig. 26.173**.

A dimension is applied semiautomatically in **Fig. 26.174** by pressing (Enter) when prompted for *Endpoints,* selecting the line or circle to be dimensioned, and locating its dimension line.

Main menu> Dimension> Continue (or *Command:* Dimcontinue line) to continue a

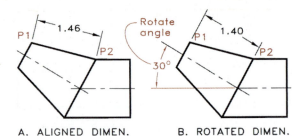

A. ALIGNED DIMEN. **B. ROTATED DIMEN.**

26.177 Dimensioning: Oblique lines

A Linear dimensions can be aligned by selecting the *Aligned Dimension icon*, selecting endpoints P1 and P2.

B Linear dimensions can be rotated by selecting the *Linear icon*, the *Rotate* option (assign an angle), and endpoints P1 and P2.

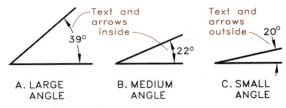

A. LARGE ANGLE **B. MEDIUM ANGLE** **C. SMALL ANGLE**

26.178 Angles will be dimensioned in any of these three formats.

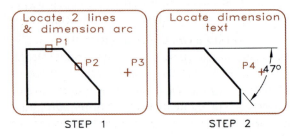

STEP 1 STEP 2

26.179 Dimensioning: Angles

Step 1 Select *Angular* icon> *Select arc, circle, line, or <specify vertex>:* P1 > *Select second line:* P2

Specify dimension arc line location or [Mtext/Text/Angle]: P3

Step 2 *Dimension text <47>:* (Enter)

Enter text location (or press Enter): P4

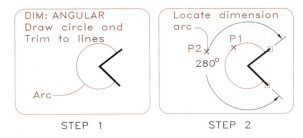

STEP 1 STEP 2

26.180 Dimensioning: Arcs

Step 1 Draw an arc with its center at the vertex and *Trim* it to end at the lines.

Step 2 *Select Angular icon> Select arc, circle, line, or <specify vertex>:* P1 > *Specify dimension arc line location or [Mtext/Text/Angle]:* P2> Dimension text = 280 (Enter)> Enter text location (or press Enter):* P3

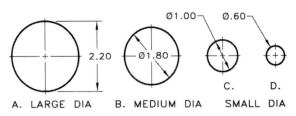

A. LARGE DIA **B. MEDIUM DIA** **C.** **D. SMALL DIA**

26.181 Examples of methods of dimensioning circles.

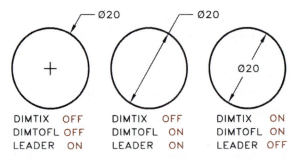

DIMTIX OFF	DIMTIX OFF	DIMTIX ON
DIMTOFL OFF	DIMTOFL ON	DIMTOFL ON
LEADER ON	LEADER ON	LEADER OFF

26.182 Examples of circle dimensions and their associated dimensioning variables.

chain of linear, angular, or ordinate dimensions from the last extension line (**Fig. 26.175**). *Baseline* applies dimensions from a single endpoint and each dimension is incrementally offset by the dimension line increment variable, *Dimdli* (**Fig. 26.176**).

Select the *Aligned* command from the *Dimension* toolbar and you will be prompted to select the first and second extensions lines and the position of the dimension line (**Fig. 26.177A**). The dimension line will be inserted in a position aligned with line P1–P2. Extension lines can be automatically drawn by pressing (Enter) at the first prompt, selecting the line to be dimensioned, and selecting its location. A rotated dimension can be applied with the

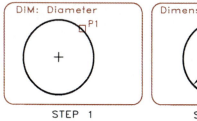 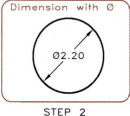 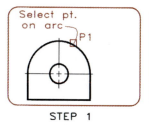 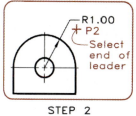

STEP 1   STEP 2   STEP 1   STEP 2

26.183 Dimensioning: Circle

Step 1 *Command:* <u>Dim</u>, (Enter) *Dim:* <u>Dia</u> (Enter) *Select arc or circle:* <u>P1</u>

Step 2 *Enter dimension text <2.20>: (Enter)*

Specify dimension line location or [Mtext/Text/Angle]: (Enter)

26.185 Dimensioning: Leader

Step 1 *Command:* <u>Dim</u> (Enter)
Dim: <u>Radius</u> (Enter) *Select arc or circle:* <u>P1</u>

Step 2 *Dimension text=1.00*
Specify dimension line location or [Mtext/Text/Angle]: <u>P2</u> (Enter)

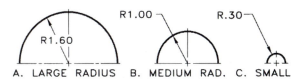

26.184 Arcs are dimensioned by one of the formats given here, depending on the size of the radius.

Rotate option and an assigned angle of rotation (**Fig. 26.177B**).

26.58 Angular Dimensions (Dimension Toolbar)

Figure 26.178 shows variations of formats for dimensioning angles, depending on the space available. Select the *Angular* icon, select lines of the angle, and locate the dimension line arc as shown in Step 1 of **Fig. 26.179**. If space permits, the dimension text will be centered in the arc between the arrows as shown in Step 2.

An angular dimension can be applied by selecting its vertex and the endpoints of each line as shown in Step 1 of **Fig. 26.180**. For angles over 180°, draw an arc using the vertex as its center; and with *Dim > Ang*, select the arc and place the dimensions as shown in Step 2.

26.59 Diameter (Dimension Toolbar)

Diameters of circles can be placed as shown in **Fig. 26.181**, depending on the available space. By changing system variables *Dimtix* and *Dimtofl*, circles can be dimensioned as shown in **Figs. 26.182** and **26.183**. By setting the *Dimtix* system variable *On*, the text is forced inside the extension lines regardless of the available space. The *Dimtofl (On)* dimension variable forces a dimension line to be drawn between the arrows when the text is located outside. By specifying whether or not a dimension has a *Leader* use *Main menu> Format> Dimension style> Fit.*

26.60 Radius (Dimension Toolbar)

Select *Radius* from the *Dimension* toolbar to dimension areas with an *R* placed in front of the text (R1.00, for example), as shown in **Fig. 26.184**. An example of dimensioning an arc with a radius and leader is shown in **Fig. 26.185**.

The *Leader* command is used to add a dimension or a note to a drawing, but it cannot measure the circle; it inserts the value of the last measurement made. The circle's diameter must be known and typed to override this measurement (**Fig. 26.186**).

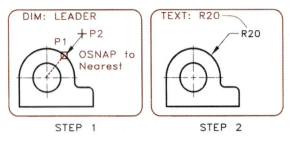

STEP 1   STEP 2

26.186 Dimensioning: Leader

Step 1 *Dimension* toolbar> *Leader* icon> *Leader start:* P1> *To point:* P2,> *To point:* (Enter)

Step 2 *Dimension text <0.0000>:* R20 (Enter)

The leader is completed and the text is drawn.

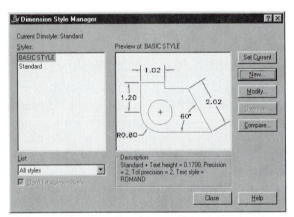

26.187 *Dimension* toolbar> *Dimstyle* icon to get this *Dimension Style Manager* box for setting dimensioning variables.

26.61 Dimension Style Manager (Dimension Toolbar)

Select the *Dimension Style* icon (or type *DDim*) from the *Dimension* toolbar to display the *Dimension Style Manager* dialogue box shown in **Fig. 26.187**, from which a number of variables can be assigned to different tabs. Each group of settings can be made and saved by style name (*NEW-4*, for example) for future use.

Lines and Arrows Tab
Click on the *New box* to get the *Lines and Arrows* menu shown in **Fig. 26.188**. From here, settings

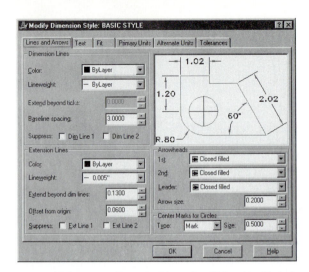

26.188 *Main menu> Format> Dimension Style> Modify button> Modify Dimen Style> Lines and Arrows tab* to obtain options for various settings.

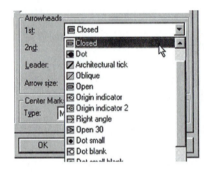

26.189 From the *Arrowheads* area on the menu, a drop-down listing of the types of *Arrowheads* is given from which to select.

can be made for *Dimension lines, Extension lines, Arrowheads,* and *Center marks.* When *Oblique-Stroke* arrows are used, the value placed in the *Arrow-size* box specifies the distance the dimension line extends beyond the extension line. The *Baseline Spacing* box is used to set *Dimdli,* which controls the spacing between baseline dimensions. The *Color* button displays the color menu from which to select a color for the dimension line *(Dimclrd).*

The options of the *Extension-Line* group (**Fig. 26.188**) control the following variables: *Lineweight, Extend beyond dim lines, Color,* and *Offset from origin.* The *Suppress 1st* and *2nd* boxes turn *On* the *Dimse1* and *Dimse2* variables

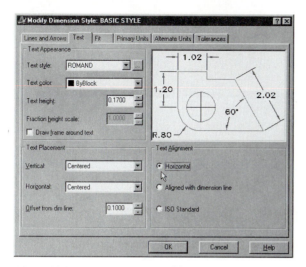

26.190 *Main menu> Format> Modify Dimension Style> Text tab opens this menu box for making a variety of text settings.*

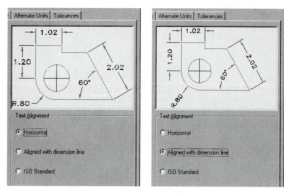

26.191 These examples show the results of having the *Unidirectional (Horizontal)* and *Aligned* text in dimension lines.

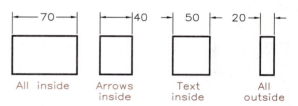

26.192 Examples of dimensions applied using the *Best Fit* option.

to suppress the first and second extension lines. The value typed in the *Extension* box specifies the distance the extension line extends beyond the dimensioning arrowhead *(Dimexe)*. The *Origin Offset* option is used to specify the size of the gap between the object and the extension line *(Dimexo)*. The *Color* button lets you select the color of the extension lines *(Dimclre)*.

The options of the *Arrowheads* group (**Fig. 26.189**) control the following variables: *Dimasz, Dimtsz, Dimblk1,* and *Dimblk2*. The value typed in the *Arrow Size* box gives the size of the arrowhead, the *Dimasz* variable. By selecting scroll arrows next to the *1st* or *2nd* boxes, the types of arrowheads for each end of the dimension are listed (**Fig. 26.189**). If only the *1st* arrow type is selected, it is automatically applied to the second end unless a *2nd* arrow type is specified. *Tick marks* are given when *Oblique* is selected, the *Dimtsz* variable. When *User Arrow* is selected, custom-made arrows can be inserted (*Dimblk1* and *Dimblk2*).

Under *Center Marks for Circles,* select *Mark, Line,* or *None* (equivalent to the *Dimcenter* command) to draw center marks, center lines, or

nothing on arcs and circles when diameter or radius dimensions are placed outside by the *Dimdiameter* and *Dimradius* commands. The value placed in the *Size* box gives the size of the center mark (a plus mark). A minus value gives center lines and a zero gives none.

Text Tab

Click on the *Text tab* (**Fig. 26.188**) to get the menu shown in **Fig. 26.190**, which controls the dimensioning text. *Text Appearance* includes settings for *Text color, Text style,* and *Text height*. *Text Placement* allows you to specify *horizontal* and *vertical* text placement and assign its *distance* from the dimension line. *Text Alignment* is used to set text as unidirectional or aligned (**Fig. 26.191**). *Text Styles* can be selected from the pull-down window or created by pressing the button next to the style window. *Text Placement*

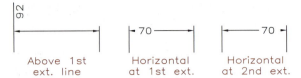

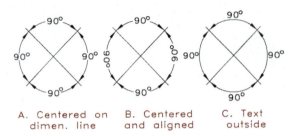

26.193 Examples of *Text Placement* settings.

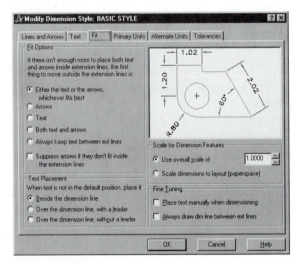

A. Centered on dimen. line   **B. Centered and aligned**   **C. Text outside**

26.194 Examples of *Text Placement* settings on arcs.

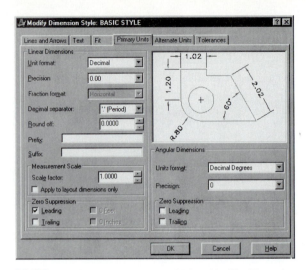

26.196 *Main menu> Dimension Style> Modify Dimension Style> Primary Units tab* lets you make changes to the dimension text settings.

0 Ft 0 In	1/4"	4"	1'	1'−01/4"
No options	0'−01/4"	0'−6"	2'−0"	1'−01/4"
0 In	0'−01/4"	0'−4"	1'	1'−01/4"
0 Ft	1/4"	4"	1'−0"	1'−01/4"

26.197 The *Zero Suppression (Dimzin)* options control the leading and trailing zeros in dimensioning, especially when applied to architectural dimensions.

26.195 *Main menu> Format> Dimension Style> Modify Dimen Style> Fit tab* gives this menu for placing text on dimensions.

options let dimensioning text be positioned as shown in **Fig. 26.192** through **Fig. 26.194**.

Fit Tab

Under *Fit tab, Fit options, Text Placement, Scale for Dimension Features,* and *Fine Tuning* adjustments can be made (**Fig. 26.195**). The *Use overall scale of* box controls the scale of all the dimensioning variables on the screen—arrow size, text

height, extension-line offsets, center size, and others. It is very useful in changing the scales of dimensioning settings from English to metric units by entering a scale factor of 25.4.

Primary Units Tab

Select the *Primary Units tab* to obtain options for *Linear Units, Measurement Scale, Zero Suppression,* and *Angular Dimensions* (**Fig. 26.196**). Use the scroll arrow under *Precision* and select the number of decimals places (or fractions) desired. From the *Angle* area, the *Units Format* of degrees and their *Precision* can be specified in the same manner as above.

Entries in the *Zero Suppression (Dimzin)* boxes suppress zeros that are leading or trailing

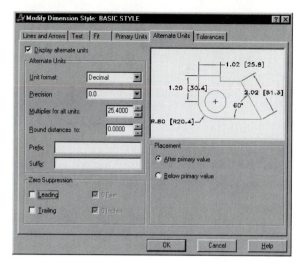

26.198 *Main menu> Dimension Style> Modify Dimension Style> Alternate Units* tab gives this window for assigning alternate and dual dimensions.

A. Inches and mm   B. mm and inches

26.199 Examples of alternate units (dual dimensions) made in inches and millimeters.

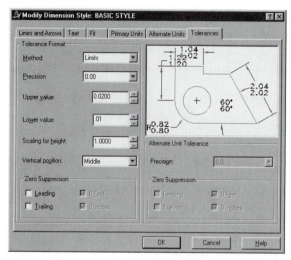

26.200 *Main menu> Format> Dimension Style> Modify Dimension Style> Tolerance tab* gives a menu for formatting dimensions with tolerances.

2.0000 ±.0020   2.0000 $^{+.0030}_{-.0020}$ 2.0030
1.9980

DIMTP & DIMTM   DIMTP & DIMTM   DIMLIM
SAME   DIFFERENT

26.201 Examples of various formats for tolerancing.

decimal points. Select *Leading* to make 0.20 become .20. **Figure 26.197** shows the results of applying the four options to architectural units. From under *Measurement Scale Factor (Dimlfac)*, units for measurements can be specified.

Alternate Units Tab

Select the *Display Alternate Units* button and two dimensions appear on each dimension in the example drawing in **Fig. 26.198**. *Unit Format* and *Precision* are used to define units and decimal points. If *Multiplier for all units* is set to 25.4, the millimeter equivalents for inches are given as the alternate dimension. Examples of dimensions with alternate units are shown in **Fig. 26.199**.

Values can be placed in the *Prefix* and *Suffix* panels (**Fig. 26.198**) so dimensions can have text such as inches before or after the dimensions; 26 mm or 42 inches, for example. *Placement* options allow alternate dimensions to be placed below or after the primary units.

Tolerances Tab

Tolerance Format in **Fig. 26.200** can be selected from options of *None, Symmetrical, Deviation,*

Limits, and *Basic.* Examples of applications of these options are shown in **Fig. 26.201**. The number of decimal points is set with *Precision,* and *Upper* and *Lower* values are selected from their respective pull-down menus. *Height* is specified as a ratio of the primary text height, the basic dimension, and is recommended to be about 80%.

26.62 Saving Dimension Styles

When the settings of this new *Dimension Style* are complete, press the *OK* button on the current tab and the first menu of the *Dimension*

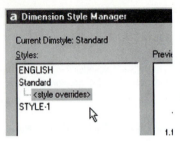

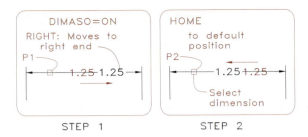

26.202 The new style, NEW-4, is displayed in the list of styles. If a style is *Overridden* (values changed), a style override subheading is displayed beneath the primary style.

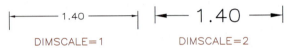

26.203 When *Dimscale* is changed from 1 to 2 and *Override* used, the selected dimension is updated.

26.205 Dimensioning: Associative— Left, right, home

Step 1 *Dimension* toolbar> *Dimension text edit* icon> *Select dimension* P1, *Enter text location (Left/ Right/ Home/ Angle):* Right (Enter) *Numeral moves to right.*

Step 2 *Command:* (Enter) *Select dimension:* P2

Enter text location (Left/ Right/ Home/ Angle): Home (Enter) *Dimension moves to center of dimension line.*

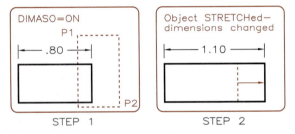

26.204 Dimensioning: Associative—Dimaso

Step 1 *Command:* Dimaso (Enter) *Enter new value for Dimaso <On>:* On *Apply dimensions to the part. Use the Stretch command and a Crossing window at the end of the part.*

Step 2 *Drag to a new endpoint for the part and it will be lengthened and a new dimension will be calculated and shown.*

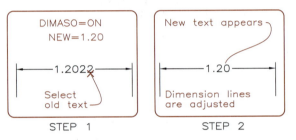

26.206 Dimensioning: Associative—New text

Step 1 *Dimension* toolbar> *Dimension Edit* icon> *Select dimension:* Pick text

Step 2 *Enter type of dimension editing [Home/New/Rotate/Oblique] <Home>:* New (Enter) *Place new dimension* 1.20 *in dialogue box.> Select objects:* Pick a point on the dimension line and the numeral is changed.

Style Manager will appear on the screen, showing the new style, NEW-4 (**Fig. 26.202**). Options of *Modify* (change any settings), *Override* (make temporary changes in a style), and *Compare* (list the settings side-by-side of any two selected styles) are available. An often-used override is the change of the *overall scale factor (Dimscale)* by changing a single multiplier (**Fig. 26.203**). This text style can be used in the future with the assigned values.

26.63 Editing Dimensions

When the dimensioning variable *Dimaso* is set to *on*, the dimensioning entities (arrows, text, extension lines, etc.) become a single unit (associative) once a dimension has been inserted into a drawing.

A related dimensioning variable, *Dimsho*, can be set on to show the dimensioning numerals being dynamically changed on the screen as the dimension line is *Stretched*. When *Dimaso* is on and *Dimsho* is off, the numerals will be changed after the *Stretch* (**Fig. 26.204**), but not dynamically during the *Stretch*.

When in the associative dimensioning mode, the *Dimension edit* can be selected from *Dimension toolbar* to obtain the options of

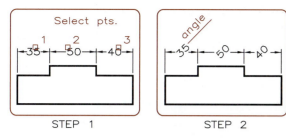

26.207 Dimensioning: Associative—Rotated text

Step 1 *Dimension* toolbar> *Dimension Edit icon> Enter type of dimension editing [Home/New/Rotate/Oblique] <Home>:* Rotate (Enter)

Step 2 *Specify angle for dimension text:* 45 (Enter)
Select objects: 1 *1 found> Select objects:* 2, *1 found, 2 total>*
Select objects: 3 , *1 found, 3 total* (Enter)

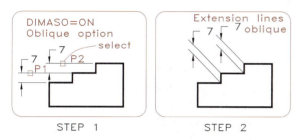

26.208 Dimensioning: Associative—Oblique extension lines

Step 1 Dimension as usual with vertical, associative dimensions. *Dimension* toolbar> *Dimension edit icon> Enter type of dimension editing [Home/New/Rotate/Oblique] <Home>:* Oblique (Enter)
Select objects: P1, *Select objects:* P2,

Step 2 *Select objects:* (Enter)
Enter obliquing angle (ENTER for none): 135 (Enter)

2.0000 ±.0020	2.0000 $^{+.0030}_{-.0020}$	2.0030 1.9980
DIMTP & DIMTM SAME	DIMTP & DIMTM DIFFERENT	DIMLIM

26.209 Dimensions can be toleranced in any of these three formats.

Home, New, Rotate, and *Oblique* for changing existing dimensions. *Home* repositions text to its standard position at the center of the dimension line after being changed by the *Stretch* commands (**Fig. 26.205**). *New* changes text within a dimension line (**Fig. 26.206**) by pressing (Enter) when prompted and inserting the new text.

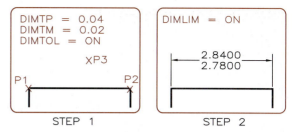

26.210 Dimensioning: Tolerances—Limit form

Step 1 Set the *Dimension variables* above to the values shown here. Apply the dimension line by selecting the endpoints P1 and P2.

Step 2 Locate the dimension lines with P3.

The dimension will be shown with its upper and lower limits, based on the limits given by *Dimtp* and *Dimtm*.

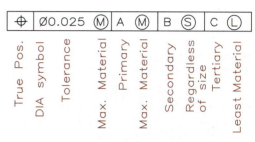

26.211 The parts of the feature control frame that give geometric tolerance specifications are defined here.

Rotate positions dimension text at any specified angle (**Fig. 26.207**). *Oblique* converts extension lines to angular lines (**Fig. 26.208**).

26.64 Toleranced Dimensions

Dimensions can be toleranced automatically using *Main menu> Format> Dimension Styles box> Modify box> Tolerances* tab defined previously, in which the settings shown in **Fig. 26.209** were made: *Dimtol* (tolerance on), *Dimtp* (plus tolerance), and *Dimtm* (minus tolerance). When *Dimlim* is *On,* the upper and lower limits of the size are given (**Fig. 26.210**).

Dimtfac is a scale factor that controls the text height of the tolerance values, which is about 80% of the basic dimension.

Second tolerance value ─────────────

Material condition symbol ─────────

First tolerance value ─────────

First tolerance value
DIA symbol ─────

Geometric symbol ─────

2nd line of tolerances ─────

Primary datum

2nd datum

3rd datum

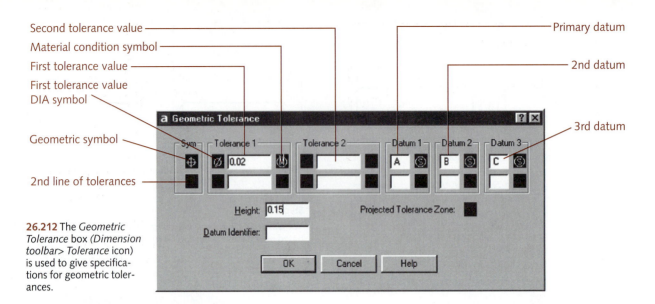

26.212 The *Geometric Tolerance* box *(Dimension toolbar> Tolerance* icon) is used to give specifications for geometric tolerances.

26.213 The *Symbol box* gives the various types of geometric tolerance symbols that can be chosen.

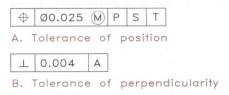

A. Tolerance of position

B. Tolerance of perpendicularity

26.214 Typical applications of *Geometric Tolerances* in the feature control frames are shown here.

26.65 Geometric Tolerances (Dimension Toolbar)

Geometric tolerances specify the permissible variations in form, profile, orientation, location, and runout. A typical geometric tolerance feature control frame is given in **Fig. 26.211**.

From the *Dimensioning* toolbar, select the *Tolerance* icon to obtain the *Geometry Tolerance* box (**Fig. 26.212**); pick the *Symbol* icon to display the *Symbol* menu (**Fig. 26.213**); select the desired symbol, and pick *OK*. Continue the process of responding to the prompts and icons to complete the geometric tolerance frame necessary for it to comply with the guidelines covered in Chapter 20. Examples of completed feature control frames as they would appear on a drawing are shown in **Fig. 26.214**.

26.66 Custom Title Block and Border

Having covered most of the basics of 2D drawing, you may wish to make your own customized title blocks with their own unique parameters that can be used to start up new drawings, as introduced in **Section 26.12**. The format shown in **Fig. 26.215** is used for laying out problems given at the ends of the chapters in this book.

To make a border identical to the one used in this example, draw the border 7.6 in. wide × 10.3 in. high, with its lower left corner at 0,0 with a polyline that is .06 thick. Draw a title strip across the bottom that has two rows of 1/8-inch text with margins of 1/8 inch above and below each

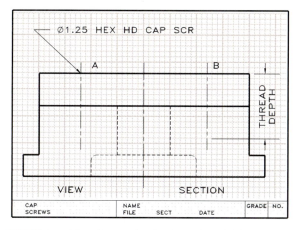

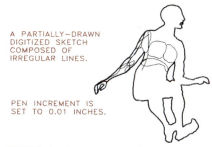

A PARTIALLY—DRAWN
DIGITIZED SKETCH
COMPOSED OF
IRREGULAR LINES.

PEN INCREMENT IS
SET TO 0.01 INCHES.

26.215 A problem sheet with a border and a title block of this type can be drawn and saved as a template file.

26.216 This drawing was made with *Sketch* command and a tablet instead of a mouse. The drawing was taped to the tablet and traced with a stylus at increments of .01 inches.

line. Fill out the title strip using the *Romand* font (double-stroke Gothic) and fill in all blanks (name, date, etc.); they will be changed later. Set *Snap* and *Grid* to 0.2 inches, set any other variables to be based on a letter height of 1/8 in. Save the drawing *(Main menu> Save As> File Name>:* <u>PROB-1.DWG</u>), or by selecting the *Save as* box and typing the file name.

When you create a new drawing *(Main menu> File> Open> PROB-1),* the border and title block appear on the screen. *Main menu> File> Save As> <u>NEW-1</u>* (Enter) and a new file named NEW-1 is ready for drawing. Use *DDedit (Modify II* toolbar*> Text edit* icon) to select the title strip text that needs to be edited and update each entry. Save this setup to a file *(Main menu> File> Save>* (Enter)) and the drawing is saved again as NEW-1.

26.67 Digitizing with the Tablet

Drawings on paper can be taped to a digitizing tablet and digitized point-by-point. A drawing is calibrated in the following manner:

Command: <u>Tablet</u> (Enter)
Option (ON/OFF/CAL/CFG): <u>CAL</u> (Enter)
(Calibrate tablet for use.)

Digitize first known point: (Digitize point.)
Enter coordinates for first point: <u>1,1</u> (Enter)
Digitize second known point: (Digitize point.)
Enter coordinates for second point: <u>10,1</u>
(Enter)

Digitize points from left to right, or from bottom to top of the drawing. Use *On* or *Off* to turn the tablet mode on or off. Function key *F10* also turns the tablet off so the cursor can select from the screen menus. To draw lines, select the *Line command* from one of the menus (or type <u>L</u>), and pick points on the tablet with the stylus.

26.68 Sketch (Miscellaneous Toolbar)

The *Sketch* command can be used with the tablet for tracing drawings composed of irregular lines (**Fig. 26.216**). Tape the drawing to the tablet and calibrate it as discussed previously, following these steps:

Command: <u>Sketch</u> (Enter)
Record increment <0.1>: <u>0.01</u> (Enter)
Sketch. Pen eXit Quit Record Erase Connect.

The record increment specifies the distances between the endpoints of the connecting lines that are sketched. Other options are:

Pen	raises or lowers pen.
eXit	records lines and exits.
Quit	discards temporary lines and exits.
Record	records temporary lines.
Erase	deletes selected lines.

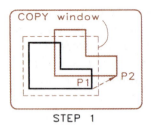
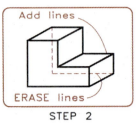

STEP 1   STEP 2

26.217 Pictorial: Oblique

Step 1 Draw the front surface of the oblique and *Copy* the view from P1 to P2.

Step 2 Connect the corner points and erase the invisible lines to complete the oblique.

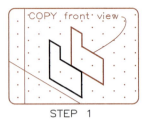
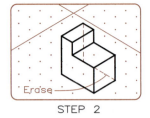

STEP 1   STEP 2

26.219 Pictorial: Isometric

Step 1 Set the grid to *Isometric*. Draw the front plane of the iso-metric and *Copy* it at its proper depth.

Step 2 Connect the corner points and erase the invisible lines. The cursor lines can be moved into three positions using *Ctrl E* for *Isoplane*.

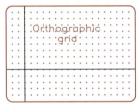
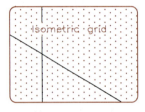

A. ORTHOGRAPHIC GRID   B. ISOMETRIC GRID

26.218 Types of screen grids

A The orthographic grid is called the *Standard style.* (*Command* line> *Snap*> *Style*> (*Standard/Isometric*)) S (Enter)

B The *isometric (I)* style of the *Snap* mode.

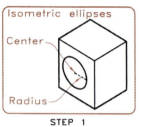

STEP 1   STEP 2

26.220 Pictorial: Isometric Ellipse

Step 1 When in *Isometric Style* of the *Snap* mode:
Command line: Ellipse (Enter)
<Axis endpoint 1> /Center/ Isocircle: Iso (Enter)
Center of circle: Select center.
<Circle radius>/ Diameter: Drag or type radius.

Step 2 The isometric ellipse is drawn in this manner on each *Isoplane.*

Connect   joins current line to last end point.

. (period)   draws a line from the current point to the last endpoint.

Begin sketching by moving your pointer to the first point, lower the pen *(P)*, move the stylus over the line, and the line is sketched on the screen. To erase, raise the pen *(P)*, enter *Erase (E)*, move the stylus backward from the current point, and select the point where the erasure is to stop. All lines are temporary until you select *Record (R)* or *eXit (X)* to save them. Begin new lines by repeating these steps.

The *Skpoly variable* can be set as follows: *Command> Setvar> Skpoly> 1 (On).* When using the *Sketch* command with *Skpoly* activated, all lines will be drawn connected as a single contin-uous polyline. When *Skpoly* is *Off (0)*, the lines drawn end-to-end will remain as individual line segments.

26.69 Oblique Pictorials

An oblique pictorial can be constructed as shown in **Fig. 26.217**. The front orthographic view is drawn and *Copied* behind the first view at the angle selected for the receding axis. The visible endpoints are connected with *Osnap On*, and invisible lines are erased. Circles are drawn as true circles on the true-size front surface, but cir-cular features should be avoided on the receding planes since their construction is complex.

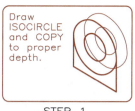

STEP 1   STEP 2

26.221 Pictorial: Isometric

Step 1 Draw an *Isocircle* (ellipse) as shown in Step 1 of Figure 26.220. *Copy* the *Isocircle* to establish the part's depth.

Step 2 Use the *Trim* command to remove the unneeded portions of the isocircles. Add missing lines.

26.70 Isometric Pictorials

The *Style* option of the *Snap* command is used to change the rectangular *Grid* from *Standard (S)* to *Isometric (I)* to show the grid dots in an isometric pattern (vertically and at 30° with the horizontal) (**Fig. 26.218**). The cursor will align with two of the isometric axes and can be *Snapped* to the grid. The axes of the cursor are rotated 120° by pressing *Ctrl E* or by typing *Isoplane* at the *Command* line. When *Ortho* is *On,* lines are forced parallel to the isometric axes. **Figure 26.219** shows the steps for constructing an isometric drawing.

When the *Grid* is set to the isometric mode, the *Ellipse* command will give the following options: *<Axis endpoint 1>/Center/Isocircle:* I (Enter). Select the *Isocircle option* and ellipses are positioned in one of the isometric orientations shown in **Fig. 26.220** by using *Ctrl E*. An example of an isometric with partial ellipses is shown in **Fig. 26.221**.

The oblique and isometric drawings covered here are 2D drawings that appear to be 3D views, but they cannot be rotated on the screen to obtain different viewpoints of them as can real 3D drawings.

Problems

1. Reconstruct the example problems given in the figures of this chapter and follow the step-by-step instructions given with each example to obtain the final drawing. Experiment with the related commands and options that may not have been covered in the examples.

2. Select suitable practice problems from the ends of the chapters throughout the textbook and solve them by computer instead of by pencil. You may wish to sketch the solutions first, and then use the sketches as a guide in completing the computer drawings.

CHAPTER TWENTY SEVEN

AutoCAD 2002 3D MODELING

27.1 Introduction

This chapter provides an introduction to the principles of making true 3D pictorial drawings that can be rotated on the screen and viewed from any angle as if they were held in your hand. The three major divisions of this chapter are **fundamentals of 3D drawing**, **solid modeling**, and **rendering**.

AutoCAD provides several methods of executing most commands: From the *Command* line, *Main menu,* and *Toolbars.* Each of these techniques is used in the coverage that follows in this chapter. You are encouraged to use the online *Help* for each command and to experiment with various options.

27.2 Paper Space and Model Space

The two distinctly different ways of obtaining views of objects are from *Model space* or *Paper space.* When in *Model space,* the screen can be divided into viewports (*Vports*) that, abut each other in standard arrangements, as do flooring

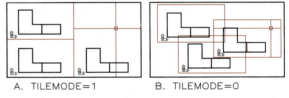

A. TILEMODE=1   B. TILEMODE=0

27.1 Model tab vs. Layout tab

A When *Model tab* is current (*Tilemode*=1), the viewports are arranged to abut each other like flooring "tiles."

B When *Layout1* (Paper space) is current, 3D viewports can be made with *Vports* that can abut or overlap.

tiles (**Fig. 27.1A**). When in *Paper space*, the viewports are created with *Vports* in standard abutting or nonstandard positions (floating viewports) as shown in **Fig. 27.1B**. By typing *Tilemode* at the *Command* line, abutting *Vports* can be turned on when set to 1 or turned off when set to 0 (zero).

Model Space

Type *Vports* (viewports) at the *Command* line, and from the *New Viewports* tab, specify the number of

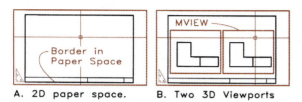

A. MODEL TAB current
Plots active viewport.

B. Plot of the active
viewport only.

27.2 When the *Model tab* is current only the active viewport can be plotted to paper.

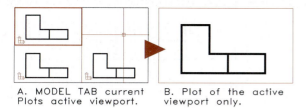

A. 2D paper space.

B. Two 3D Viewports

27.3 Layout1 tab: Paper Space (PS)

A When the *Layout1* tab is picked, the screen is set to *Paper Space* where a 2D border can be inserted or drawn.

B Type *Vports* (or *Mview*) and define the diagonal corners of two windows into 3D model space.

abutting viewports to display on the screen, three are shown in this example (**Fig. 27.2**). Drawings made before applying the *Vports* command will be duplicated in each viewport as if multiple monitors were wired to your computer. Only the active viewport, shown with a heavy outline, can be plotted from *Model Space*.

Model Space

Up until now, all examples have been given in *Model Space* where drawings can be made in two dimensions (2D) and three dimensions (3D). Select the *Layout1 tab* at the bottom of the screen (you are in 2D *Paper Space*) and the *Page Setup* menu appears on the screen for choosing a plotter and specifying a page layout. The word *Paper* appears in the command bar at the bottom of the screen, and a triangle icon appears at the lower left of the drawing area. You can move to and from *Paper Space* and *Model Space* by clicking on the *Paper* button below the *Status line* or by typing *PS*. While in *Paper Space (PS)*, where drawings are in 2D, insert or draw a 2D border to define the drawing area (**Fig. 27.3A**).

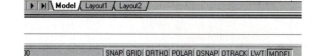

27.4 Select the *Layout1* tab and you are in *Paper Space* where a plotter and a page layout can be specified. By alternately picking the *Paper/Model* buttons in the *Status line,* you can move from *Paper Space (PS)* to *Model Space (MS)* for drawing in either 2D or 3D.

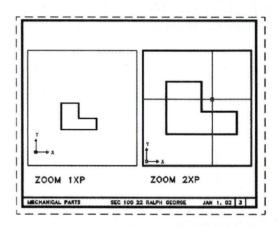

27.5 Set the *Model/Paper* button to *Model* to enter model space and type *Zoom> 1XP* to show the drawing full-size in that viewport. Select the other viewport, type *Zoom,* and *2XP* to obtain a double-size view in that viewport.

From *Paper Space,* type Vports> *New Viewports* tab> *Single* and open two model-space windows by selecting their diagonal corners (**Fig. 27.3B**). (You will get a single viewport by default that should be erased before inserting multiple ports.) Type *MS* or double click on the *Paper/Model* button at the bottom of the screen in the *Status bar* to set it to *Model (Model space).* The cursor will appear in the active viewport (**Fig. 27.4**). Move to a new viewport and select it with the cursor. The drawing in the model-space port is scaled by typing *Zoom* and *1XP* for a full-size drawing, *2XP* for a double-size drawing, and *0.5XP* for a half-size drawing (**Fig. 27.5**).

To make a plot, return to paper space with the *Model/Paper* button; the triangular paper space icon reappears, and *Paper* replaces *Model* at the bottom of the screen in the *Status bar.* Plot

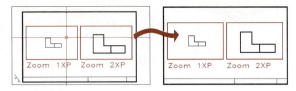

27.6 Plotting from *Paper Space*

A Select *PS* to enter *Paper Space* for plotting a drawing.

B Both *Paper Space* and *Model Space* drawings will be plotted.

from paper space and both the 2D and 3D drawings will plot as they appear on the screen (**Fig. 27.6**).

27.3 Paper Space Versus Model Space

The following points summarize what you can do from *Paper Space (PS):*

1. *Vports* makes *Model Space (MS)* viewports.
2. *Stretch, Move,* and *Scale* MS viewports.
3. *Erase* MS viewports.
4. *Freeze* MS outlines.
5. *Insert* 2D drawings.
6. *Hideplot* removes invisible lines from selected viewports.
7. *Text* can be added across MS viewports.

The following points summarize what you can do from *Model Space (MS):*

1. *Modify* a 3D drawing.
2. *Rotate* the *User Coordinate System (UCS).*
3. *Pan, Zoom, Scale,* etc., MS drawings.
4. *Attach* dimensions to the MS drawing.
5. *Erase* the contents of an MS viewport.

27.4 Fundamentals of 3D Drawing

Experiment with 3D drawing; set the *Model/ Paper* button to *Model,* type *UCSicon,* set it to *On,* and the *2D UCS icon* may appear as shown in **Fig. 27.7**. Type *Ucsicon>* Select *Properties* to get a dialogue box that will let you change the UCS icon to appear as shown in **Fig. 27.8**. Type *Ucsicon>* Select the *ORigin* option to make the UCS icon appear at the origin of the UCS with a plus sign in its corner. (You may need to *Pan* the 0,0 origin up and to the right of the screen's cor-

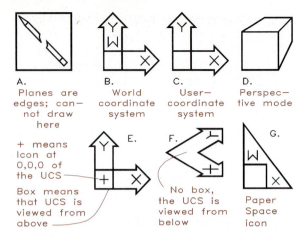

27.7 Various *2D UCS icons* that appear on the screen to show the X- and Y-axes when using the *Vport* and *UCS* commands are shown here.

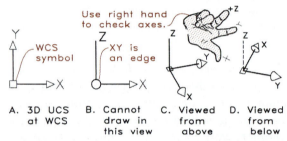

27.8 *3D UCS icons* can be used as alternatives to the *2D UCS icons* in Fig. 27.7. Point the thumb of your right hand in the +x direction, your index finger in the +y direction, and your middle finger points in the +z direction.

ner so that the *UCS icon* has room to sit on the origin.) When a *W* appears on the 2D icon it is in the *World Coordinate System* (WCS). Without the *W,* you are in the *User Coordinate System* (UCS). The broken-pencil icon warns that the XY plane appears as an edge, making it impractical to draw in that viewpoint. The oblique-box icon indicates that the current drawing is a perspective. The triangular icon tells you that the screen is in 2D paper space. The *2D UCS icon* never shows the *Z-axis;* it is found by the right-hand rule shown in **Fig. 27.8**. The 3D icons at B-D show the x, y, and z directions.

The standard *Vports* are shown in the *Vports* menu in **Fig. 27.9**. *Vports* must be named, in

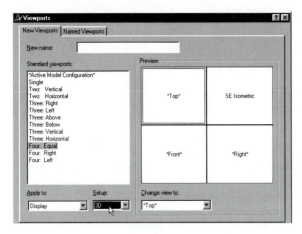

order for them to be *Saved,* by typing a name in the panel of the *Vports* menu.

27.5 Elementary Extrusions

Using elementary extrusions, 3D objects can be drawn with the *Elev, Thickness, Plan,* and *Hide* commands. *Elev* (elevation) sets the level of the base plane of the drawing. *Thickness* is the distance of the extrusion in a direction parallel to the z-axis. *Plan* changes the *UCS* to give a true-size view of the *XY icon* and the surfaces parallel to it. *Hide* removes invisible lines of the extruded surfaces.

Type *UCSicon>* On to obtain the *XY icon,* type *Elev>* 0 (zero), type *Thickness>* 4, and draw the plan view of the object with the *Line* command (**Fig. 27.10A**). The X- and Y-axes are true size in the *Plan* view (top view) and the *Z-axis* is perpendicular to them and pointing toward you.

Type *Vpoint* (Viewpoint) and specify a line of sight with settings of 1,-1,1 to obtain an isometric view of the extruded block in **Fig. 27.10B**. Type *Plan* and the x-y axes of the *UCS icon* are shown true size and planes of the object that are parallel to it appear true size as well. You may use most of the regular *Draw* commands such as *Line, Circle,* and *Arc* to draw features, all of

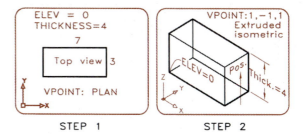

27.10 Elevation and Thickness: Drawing a box
Step 1 *Command:* Elev (Enter)
Specify new default elevation <0>: 0 (Enter)
Specify new default thickness <0>: 4 (Enter)
Command: Line (Enter)
Specify first point (Draw a 7 × 3 rectangle as a top view.)
Step 2 *Command:* Vpoint (Enter)
Specify a view point or Rotate/ <display compass and tripod>: 1,-1,1 An isometric view of the extruded box appears.

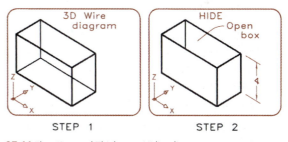

27.11 Elevation and Thickness: Hiding lines
Step 1 After the box is drawn, it appears as a wire frame on the screen.
Step 2 *Command:* Hide (Enter) The vertical surfaces become opaque (solid) planes and the top is open.

which will be extruded 4 units in the z-direction. The extrusion value of 4 units will remain in effect until reset.

Type *Hide* and (Enter) to remove hidden lines from an extruded object and give an "empty-box" look (**Fig. 27.11**). Type *3Dface* and *Osnap* (object snap) to the corner points on the upper surface to make the top of the box opaque when the *Hide* command is applied (**Fig. 27.12**).

The *Solid* command can be used to make the top surface opaque by assigning it an *Elev* equal to the *Thickness* (4), setting its *Thickness* to zero,

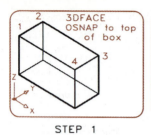 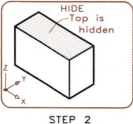 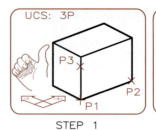 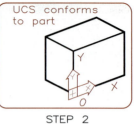

| STEP 1 | STEP 2 | STEP 1 | STEP 2 |

27.12 3DFace

Step 1 *Command:* Osnap (Enter)

Object snap modes: End (Enter)

Command: 3Dface (Enter)

Specify first point or [Invisible]: 1 > *Specify second point or [Invisible]:* 2 > *Specify third point or [Invisible]:* 3 > *Specify fourth point or [Invisible] <created three-sided face>:* 4 > *Specify first point or [Invisible]:* (Enter)

Step 2 *Command:* Hide (Enter)

The top surface appears as an opaque surface.

27.13 UCS: 3 Point option

Step 1 *Main menu> Tools> New UCS>* 3 Point (to rotate the UCS 90° about the x-axis).

Specify new origin point <0,0,0>: P1

Specify point on positive portion of the x-axis: P2

Step 2 *Specify point on the positive Y portion of the UCS XY plane:* P3

The *UCS icon* is transferred to the origin. The plus sign at its corner box indicates that it is at the origin.

and applying a solid area to the top by selecting the four corners. Type *Hide* and the top appears opaque.

27.6 Coordinate Systems

Almost all drawing is done in the plane of the active coordinate system indicated by the *XY icon*. The two coordinate systems are the *World Coordinate System (WCS)* and the *User Coordinate System (UCS)*.

 World Coordinate System (WCS) has an origin where X, Y, and Z are 0 and, usually, the x- and y-axes are true length in the top (the plan view). The *UCSicon* has a *W* and a plus sign on it when it is at the *WCS* origin.

 A *User Coordinate System (UCS)* can be located within the *WCS* with its origin at any selected point and its x- and y-axes in any direction. Type *UCSicon> ON> ORigin* to set the icon at the origin of a *User Coordinate System* that is established in the following manner:

Command: UCS (Enter)
Enter and option [New/ Move/ orthoGraphic/ Prev/ Restore/ Save/ Del/ Apply/ ?/ World] <World>: Move (Enter)

Specify new origin point or [Zdepth] <0,0,0>: Select with cursor (Enter)

 The options of the *UCS command* are:

New: Defines a new coordinate system by one of six methods: *Origin, Z axis, 3 point, Object, Face, View,* and *X,Y,Z.* An application of the *3 Point* option is given in **Fig. 27.13**.

Move: Redefines the origin without changing the orientation of the X-, Y-, and Z-axes by picking a point.

orthoGraphic: Specifies one of six UCSs, mostly for 3D editing.

Previous: Steps back through the previous list of UCSs, one at a time.

Restore: Restores a named UCS and makes it current, however the *Viewpoint* is not restored.

Save: Saves the current UCS to a specified name.

Delete: Removes a saved UCS from a list of saved UCSs.

Apply: Assigns the current UCS to a specified *Viewport* or *Viewports.*

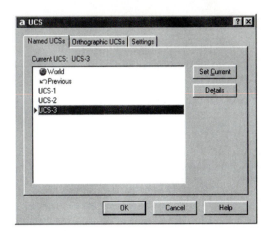

27.14 *Main menu> Tools> UCS* box> *Named UCSs* tab> a list of saved *UCSs* is displayed.

? (List UCSs): Lists names of UCS and their origins and X-, Y-, and Z-axes for each.

World: Set the UCS to the *World Coordinate System.*

Save a *UCS* as follows: *Command:* UCS (Enter)> Save> type name when prompted. Select *Main Menu> Tools> UCS* box> *Named UCS* tab (**Fig. 27.14**) to obtain a list of the saved coordinate systems. The *World* coordinate system is listed first. The current *UCS* is indicated by the pointer but a new one can be selected with the cursor (*UCS-2*, for example), and picking the *Set Current* button. Delete a *UCS* by right clicking on it and selecting *Delete*, or *Rename* it by right-clicking on it and typing a new name. *OK* confirms any action made and *Cancel* closes the dialogue box. Three tabs are given in the *UCS* box: *Named UCSs, Orthographic UCSs,* and *Settings.*

The *UCS icon* is turned on in the following manner:

Command: UCSicon (Enter) *Enter an option [ON/ OFF/ All/ Noorigin/ ORigin] <ON>:* ON (Enter)

The functions of these *UCSicon* options are:

ON/OFF turns the icon on and off.

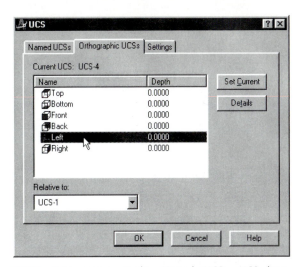

27.15 *Main menu> Tools> Named UCS> UCS* box> *Othographic UCSs* tab> to get a list of UCSs from which to select.

All displays the icon in all viewports.

Noorigin displays the icon at the lower left corner regardless of the location of the UCS origin.

Origin places the icon at the origin of the current coordinate system if space permits, or at the lower left, if space is unavailable.

Properties gives options for choosing the type of icon: 2D or 3D plus additional features.

27.7 Setting Viewpoints (Vpoints)

The *Vpoint* command sets the viewpoint of a *UCS* with the *UCS box,* the *tripod axes,* or by *typing coordinates. Main menu> Tools> UCS* box> *Orthographic UCSs* tab> to get the UCS orientations for principal orthographic views (**Fig. 27.15**). For example, select the *top view* icon, specify the *origin* when prompted, pick *Set Current,* and type *Plan* to obtain a top view of the *UCSicon* where the plane of the X- and Y-axes is true size.

When the *UCS icon* symbol is selected, the *axis tripod* (a set of x-, y-, and z-axes) appears on

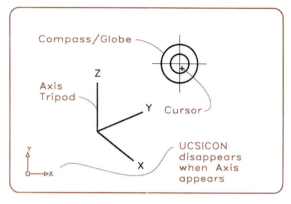

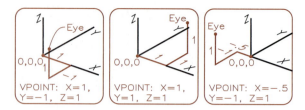

27.19 Graphical examples of three *Vpoints* found by typing x-, y-, and z-coordinates at the keyboard.

27.16 *Command:* Vpoint (Enter) (Enter) and a globe and axes appear on the screen for selecting a viewpoint.

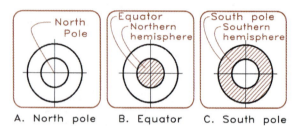

A. North pole   B. Equator   C. South pole

27.17 The compass globe

A The north pole is at the intersections of the crosshairs.

B The small circle locates viewpoints on the equator.

C The large circle locates the viewpoint at the south pole.

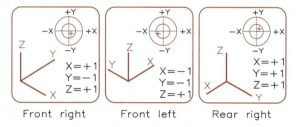

Front right   Front left   Rear right

27.18 The relationship between the points on the *Vpoint* globe and the *Vpoint* values selected from the keyboard.

the screen (**Fig. 27.16**). A viewpoint of the object is found by selecting a point on the compass globe, as described in **Fig. 27.17**. Repeat this command by pressing (Enter) and selecting other views until the desired view is found.

Figure 27.18 compares the viewpoints found on the compass globe with those specified with

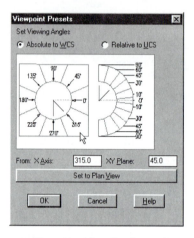

27.20 *Main menu> View> 3D Views> View Presets box* from which to select a view. The point of view in the XY-plane and from the XY-plane is selected with the cursor or by typing.

numbers at the keyboard. A *Vpoint* of 1,-1,1 means that the origin (0,0,0) is viewed from a point that is 1 unit in the positive X-direction, 1 unit in the negative Y-direction, and 1 unit in the positive Z-direction from 0,0,0 (**Fig. 27.19**).

A pop-up box, found by picking *View> 3D Views> View presets,* can be used to select a viewpoint (**Fig. 27.20**). The six principal orthographic views can be picked from *3D Viewport Presets* under *View,* or by typing *Vpoint* at the *Command* line as follows:

Presets	By Typing
Top view	0,0,1
Front view	0,-1,0
Right-side view	1,0,0
Left-side view	-1,0,0
Rear view	0,1,0
Bottom view	0,0,-1

27.8 Application of Extrusions

An extruded box similar to the one in **Fig. 27.10**, is shown in isometric by typing *Vpoint,* (Enter),

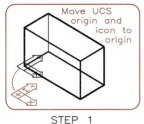
STEP 1

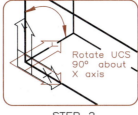
STEP 2

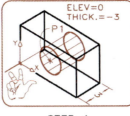
STEP 1

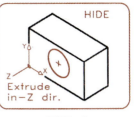
STEP 2

27.21 Setting the UCS

Step 1 *Command:* UCSicon (Enter)

Enter an option [On/Off/All/. . . /ORigin] <ON>: ORigin (Enter)

Specify new origin point <0,0,0>: Select object's corner.

Step 2 *Command:* UCS (Enter)

Enter and option [New/Move . . ./?/World]<World>: New (Enter)

Specify origin of new UCS or [ZAxis/ . . . /X/Y/Z]: X (Enter)

Specify rotation angle about X axis: 90*. The UCS icon rotates parallel to the frontal plane of the object.*

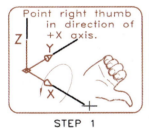
STEP 1

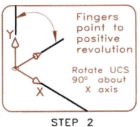
STEP 2

27.22 Rotating the UCS

Step 1 *Command:* UCS (Enter)

Enter and option [New/Move . . ./?/World] <World>: New (Enter)

Specify origin of new UCS or [ZAxis/. . . /X/Y/Z]: X (Enter)

Step 2 *Specify rotation angle about X axis:* 90,

The UCS icon rotates 90°.

and giving coordinates of 1,-1,1 in **Fig. 27.21**. The *UCSicon* is moved to the object's lower left corner by the *UCS* command and rotated 90° about the X-axis to lie in the frontal plane of the box. The right-hand rule is used to determine the direction of rotation by pointing your right thumb in the positive direction of the axis of rotation (**Fig. 27.22**). Type *Plan* and the *UCSicon* and the front view will appear true size.

27.23 Extruding a hole

Step 1 *Command:* Elev (Enter)

Specify new default elevation <0>: 0 (Enter)

Specify new current thickness <4>: -3 (Enter)

Command: Circle (Enter) *Circle specify center point for circle or [3P/2P/Ttr (tan tan radius)]:* P1

Specify radius of circle or [Diameter]: .5*, A 1 inch diameter cylinder is extruded 3 inches deep into the box.*

Step 2 *Command:* Hide (Enter) The outline of the hole is shown, but it cannot be seen through.

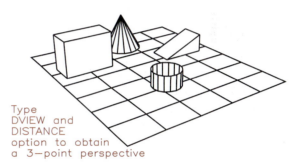

Type DVIEW and DISTANCE option to obtain a 3-point perspective

27.24 *Command:* Dview (Enter)> *Select objects> Window objects> [CAmera/ TArget/ Distance . . . Undo]:* Distance (Enter) *A perspective view of the objects is obtained.*

The circle is drawn as an extrusion by setting the *Elev* to 0 and *Thickness* to -3 (the depth of the box) to draw a cylindrical hole (**Fig. 27.23**). Apply *3Dfaces* to the upper and lower planes of the box and type *Hide* to remove invisible lines.

27.9 Dynamic View (Dview)

The *Dview* command is similar to the *Vpoint* command, but *Dview* changes the viewpoints of an object dynamically as they are changed by the cursor. As **Fig. 27.24** shows, axonometric views (parallel projections) and three-point perspectives can be obtained for the most realistic

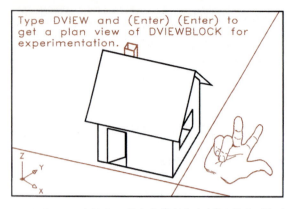

Type DVIEW and (Enter) (Enter) to get a plan view of DVIEWBLOCK for experimentation.

27.25 *Command:* <u>Dview</u> (Enter) (Enter) and the *DviewBlock* house is displayed for experimenting with the various options.

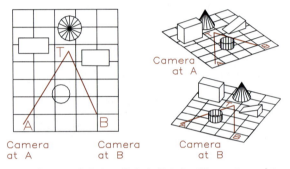

Camera at A Camera at B Camera at B

27.26 *Command:* <u>Dview</u> (Enter) (Enter)> *CAmera* is used to obtain different views of a stationary target point by moving the position of the camera about it.

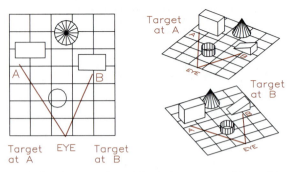

Target at A EYE Target at B

27.27 The *TArget* option of the *Dview* command is used to obtain views of a scene by moving the target to different locations about a stationary camera (the eye).

pictorials. The *Dview* command has the following options:

Command: <u>Dview</u> (Enter)
[CAmera/TArget/Distance/POints/PAn/Zoom/TWist/CLip/Hide/Off/Undo]:

By typing *Dview* and (Enter) (Enter), the top view of the *DviewBlock* house appears, which can be used for experimentation with the following options (**Fig. 27.25**):

CAmera rotates your viewpoint as if you were using a camera and moving about the target (**Fig. 27.26**). As the cursor (the camera) is moved, the view is dynamically changed until a viewpoint is selected.

TArget is identical to the *CAmera* option, except the camera remains stationary and the target (and the drawing containing it) is rotated about the camera (**Fig. 27.27**).

Distance uses the current camera position and turns the view into a perspective. The xy-icon is replaced with the perspective-box icon. When prompted, give a distance to the target by typing the value, or by using the slider bar, with a range from 0X to 16X; 1X is the current distance to the target.

POints specifies the target point and the camera position for viewing a drawing. This command is necessary to specify viewpoints for perspectives.

PAn moves the view of a drawing without changing its magnification or true position.

Zoom changes the magnification of a drawing in the same manner as the *Zoom/Center* command when perspective is *Off.* When the perspective mode is *On (Dist=On), Zoom* dynamically changes the magnification.

TWist rotates the drawing about an axis that is perpendicular to the screen.

CLip places cutting planes perpendicular to the line of sight to remove portions of a drawing either in front or in back of the plane by selecting *Back/Front/<Off>* (**Fig. 27.28**).

Off exits from *CLip.* When *Distance* is *On* (perspective mode), the frontal clipping plane remains *On* at the camera position.

Hide suppresses invisible lines.

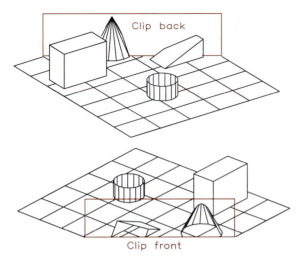

— 3D Orbit

27.28 *Command:* Dview (Enter) (Enter)> *Clip* is used to remove the *Back* or *Front* portions of a drawing. The clipping plane is parallel to the drawing screen.

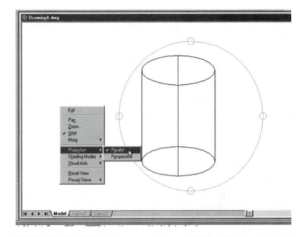

27.30 The *3D Obit* places a circle (an arcball) on the screen that can be used to rotate objects on the screen. By right-clicking anywhere outside the ball, a pop-up window appears from which options appear including perspective views.

OFF turns off the perspective mode enabled by *Distance=On.*

Undo reverses the previous *Dview* operations, one at a time.

27.10 3D Orbit

3D objects can be positioned in space using *3D Orbit* that is activated by selecting its icon on the *Standard Toolbar* (**Fig. 27.29**). A circle appears on the screen with four handles located at its compass points and an xyz icon (**Fig. 27.30**). The circle can be thought of as a view of a sphere that encloses a 3D object (the object can exceed the size of the circle). *3D Orbit* can manipulate the view of the part in four basic ways (each has it own symbol at the cursor):

Horizontal rotation: Select one of the handles at 3 and 9 o'clock and drag to rotate the object about a vertical axis.

Vertical rotation: Select one of the handles at 12 and 6 o'clock and drag to rotate the object about a horizontal axis.

Roll: Select a point outside the arcball and drag to rotate the object about an axis that is perpendicular to the screen.

Free rotation: Select a point inside the arcball and drag in any direction to rotate the object about any or all of the axes.

By right clicking outside the arcball, a pop-up menu appears with a list of options, many of which have sub-options for affecting the object. The entire screen of objects need not be selected, but only those that you want to observe during the process, which enhances the computer's performance.

27.11 Basic 3D Shapes (Surfaces)

From the *Surfaces toolbar* (**Fig. 27.31**), or by typing *3D* at the *Command* line (or *Main menu>*

27.31 *Main menu > View> Toolbars> Surfaces gives this menu for drawing 3D surfaces (meshes).*

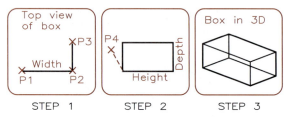

STEP 1 STEP 2 STEP 3

27.32 Surfaces: Box

Step 1 *Surface* toolbar> *Box icon> Specify corner of box:* P1

Specify length of box: P2> *Specify width of box or [Cube]:* P3 *Specify height of box:* P4

Step 2 *Specify rotation angle about Z axis or [Reference]:* 0 (Enter). *Command:* Vpoint> set to 1,-1,1 to get an isometric view.

View> Toolbars> Surfaces to obtain the *Surfaces* toolbar), you can select a basic 3D shape or surface from the following: *Box, Cone, DIsh, DOme, Mesh, Pyramid, Sphere, Torus,* and *Wedge.* These shapes are wire frames until *Hide* is used to make them appear as solids. Think of them as hollow shapes with meshes (or faces) applied to their surfaces. Remember that these shapes are drawn with respect to the xy plane; consequently, the *xy icon* must be observed at all times:

Box draws a cube or a box when you select a corner, specify length, width, and height and give the angle of rotation about the *z-axis* (**Fig. 27.32**).

Cone draws a cone to its apex (**Fig. 27.33**) or it can be a truncated cone without an apex.

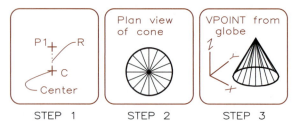

STEP 1 STEP 2 STEP 3

27.33 Surfaces: Cone

Step 1 *Surface toolbar> Cone icon> Specify center point for base of cone:* C

Specify radius for base of cone or [Diameter]: P1

Step 2 Specify radius for top of cone or [Diameter] <0>: (Enter)

Step 2 *Specify height of cone:* 3 (Enter) *Enter number of segments for surface of cone <16>:* (Enter)

Step 3 *Command:* Vpoint (Enter) and set coordinates to 1,-1,1 to obtain an isometric of the cone.

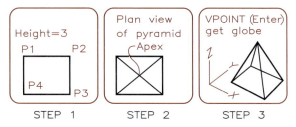

STEP 1 STEP 2 STEP 3

27.34 Surfaces: Pyramid

Step 1 *Surface toolbar> Pyramid icon>*

Specify first corner point for base of pyramid: P1

Specify second corner for base of pyramid: P2

Specify third corner point for base of pyramid: P3

Specify fourth corner. . . . of pyramid or [Tetrahedron]: P4

Step 2 *Specify apex point of pyramid or [Ridge/Top]:* .XY (Enter) *of (Need Z):* 2 (Enter)

Step 3 *Command:* Vpoint > set to 1,-1,1 to get an isometric view.

DIsh draws the lower hemisphere of a sphere by selecting its center and radius.

DOme draws the upper hemisphere of a sphere by selecting its center and radius in the same manner as *Dish.*

Mesh is used to apply web to a flat or curving surface to give it a "skin."

Pyramid draws a pyramid extending to its apex (**Fig. 27.34**), or it can be a truncated pyramid without an apex.

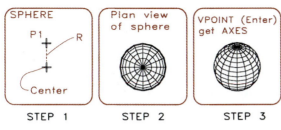

STEP 1   STEP 2   STEP 3

27.35 Surfaces: Sphere

Step 1 *Surface* toolbar> *Sphere* icon>

Specify center point of sphere: C (center)

Specify radius of sphere or [Diameter]: P1

Step 2 *Enter number of longitudinal segments for surface of sphere <16>: (Enter) >Enter number of latitudinal segments for surface of sphere <16>: (Enter)*

Step 3 *Command:* Vpoint *> set to* 1,-1,1 *to get an isometric view. Command:* Hide *(Enter)*

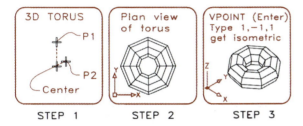

STEP 1   STEP 2   STEP 3

27.36 Surfaces: Torus

Step 1 *Surface* toolbar> *Torus* icon>

Specify center of torus: C

Specify radius of torus or [Diameter]: P1

Specify radius of tube or [Diameter]: P2

Enter number of segments around tube circumference <16>: 8 (Enter)> *Enter number of segments around torus circumference <16>:* 8 (Enter)

Step 2 *The plan view of the torus is drawn.*

Step 3 *Command:* Vpoint *> set to* 1,-1,1 *to get an isometric.* Command: Hide (Enter)

Sphere draws a ball by selecting its center and radius (**Fig. 27.35**). Its center lies on the xy plane of the *UCS*.

Torus draws a donut shape called a torus or toroid as shown in **Fig. 27.36**.

Wedge draws a wedge with the same steps used to draw the box (**Fig. 27.37**).

Other operations available from the *Surfaces toolbar* are covered in **Section 27.12**.

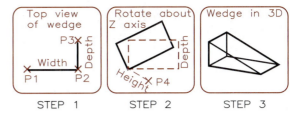

STEP 1   STEP 2   STEP 3

27.37 Surfaces: Wedge

Step 1 *Surface* toolbar> *Wedge* icon>

Specify corner of wedge: P1 *Specify length of wedge:* P2 *Specify width of wedge:* P3

Step 2 *Specify height of wedge:* P4

Step 3 *Specify rotation angle of wedge about the Z axis:* -15 (Enter) *Command:* Vpoint *> set to* 1,-1,1 *to get an isometric.*

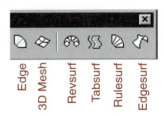

Edge   3D Mesh   Revsurf   Tabsurf   Rulesurf   Edgesurf

27.38 Facing options from the *Surfaces Toolbar* for putting "skins" on wire frames.

27.12 Surface Modeling

Faces (or *meshes*) can be applied to cover wire frames with "skins" to make them look solid. Commands from the *Surfaces* toolbar for applying these meshes are *Rulesurf, Tabsurf, Revsurf, Edgesurf,* and *3Dmesh* (**Fig. 27.38**).

The application of these commands is illustrated by applying them to a wire frame beginning with **Fig. 27.39**. Set *Vpoint* to 1,-1,1 to obtain an isometric view of the 3D frame. Type *Setvar,* (Enter), *Surftab1,* and set it to 20, the number of faces to be applied.

Rulesurf (ruled surface) applies a surface (20 faces, as specified by *Surftab1*) between the circular ends (**Fig. 27.39**). The applied surface is *Moved* to 0,5,0 from the wire frame. *Rulesurf* can be used to place surfaces between two objects (curves, arcs, polylines, lines, or points) as shown in **Fig. 27.40**.

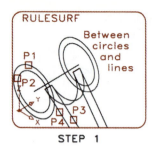

STEP 1   STEP 2

27.39 Part 1: Rulesurf

Step 1 *Command:* <u>Rulesurf</u> (Enter)

Select first defining curve: <u>P1</u>

Select second defining curve: <u>P2</u> Circles are faced.

Select first defining curve: <u>P3</u>

Select second defining curve: <u>P4</u> Ends are faced.

Step 2 *Command:* <u>Move</u> (Enter)

Select objects? Select faces. (Enter)

Base point or displacement: <u>0,5,0</u> (Enter) Faces are moved.

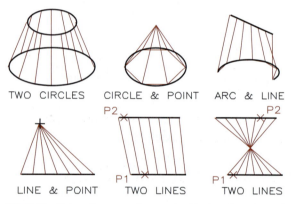

TWO CIRCLES   CIRCLE & POINT   ARC & LINE

LINE & POINT   TWO LINES   TWO LINES

27.40 The *Rulesurf* command connects objects with a series of *3D Faces* as shown in these examples.

Tabsurf (tabulated surface) applies a surface from a curve that is parallel and equal in length to a directional vector (**Fig. 27.41**). Select *Path Curve* (the circle) and *Select Direction Vector* and the cylinder is drawn. The *Surftab1* system variable (set to 20) applies 20 faces.

Revsurf (revolved surface) revolves lines or shapes about an axis (**Fig. 27.42**) and is *Moved* to 0,5,0 to add it to the hollow shell. Lines, polylines, arcs, or circles can be revolved to form a surface of revolution controlled by *Surftab1*. If a circle or a closed polyline is to be revolved (to

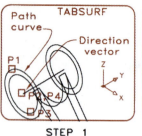

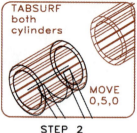

STEP 1   STEP 2

27.41 Part 2: Tabsurf

Step 1 *Command:* <u>Tabsurf</u> (Enter) *Select object for path curve:* <u>P1</u> >*Select object for direction vector:* <u>P2</u> The spacing between tabulated vectors is determined by the *Surftab1* variable.

Step 2 *Command:* <u>Move</u> (Enter)

Select objects?: <u>Select faces</u>.

Base point or displacement: <u>0,5,0</u> (Enter) The faces are moved to a new position.

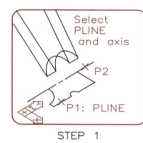

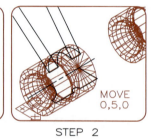

STEP 1   STEP 2

27.42 Part 3: Revsurf

Step 1 *Command:* <u>Revsurf</u> (Enter) *Current wire frame density:* *SURFTAB1=16 SURFTAB2=4 Select object to revolve:* <u>P1</u>

Select axis that defines the axis of revolution: <u>P2</u>

Specify start angle <0>: (Enter)

Specify included angle (+=ccw, -=cw) <360>: <u>360</u> (Enter)

Step 2 *Command:* <u>Move</u> (Enter) *Select objects?:* Pick faces.

Base point or displacement: <u>0,5,0</u> (Enter) Faces are moved.

make a torus, for example), system variable *Surftab2* controls the mesh density of the line, circle, arc, or polyline that is being revolved, and *Surftab1* controls the density of the path of revolution.

Edgesurf (edge surface) applies a mesh to four edges (joined boundary lines) as shown in **Fig. 27.43**. System variables *Surftab1* and *Surftab2* control the density of the first and second objects selected, respectively. The surfaces

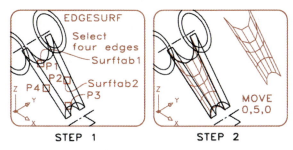

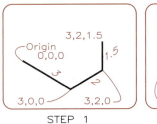

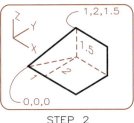

STEP 1	STEP 2

27.43 Part 4: Edgesurf

Step 1 *Command:* <u>Edgesurf</u> (Enter)

Current wire frame density: SURFTAB1=5 SURFTAB2=4

Select object 1 for surface edge: <u>P1</u>

Select object 2 for surface edge: <u>P2</u>

Select object 3 for surface edge: <u>P3</u>

Select object 4 for surface edge: <u>P4</u>

Mesh is drawn in boundaries. *Surftab1* and *Surftab2* variables determine the density of the mesh.

Step 2 *Command:* <u>Move</u> (Enter) *Select objects?:* Pick faces.

Base point or displacement: <u>0,5,0</u> (Enter) Faces are moved.

27.45 3Dpoly: Absolute coordinates

Step 1 *Command:* <u>3Dpoly</u> or <u>Line</u> (Enter)

Specify start point of polyline: <u>0,0,0</u> (Enter)

Specify endpoint of line or [Undo]: <u>3,0,0</u> (Enter)

Specify endpoint of line or [Undo]: <u>3,2,0</u> (Enter)

Specify endpoint of line or [Close/Undo]: <u>3,2,1.5</u> (Enter)

Step 2 *Specify endpoint of line or [Close/Undo]:* <u>1,2,1.5</u> (Enter)> *Specify endpoint of line or [Close/Undo]:* <u>Close</u> (Enter)

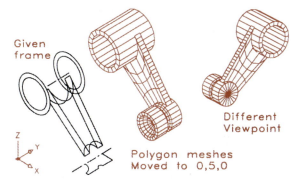

Given frame

Different Viewpoint

Polygon meshes Moved to 0,5,0

27.44 The given frame of the connector and the resulting 3D hollow shells from two viewpoints are shown here after using the *Hide* command to remove hidden lines.

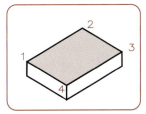

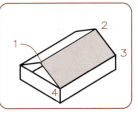

A. HORIZONTAL SURFACE	B. SLOPING SURFACE

27.46 3Dface: On wire frames

3Dface is used to opaque planes of wire frames by snapping to endpoints and drawing opaque faces. *3Dface* is applied to a horizontal surface at **A** and to a sloping surface at **B**.

are moved to 0,-5,0 to complete the hollow shell of the connector.

The beginning frame and two final views of the meshed connector are shown in **Fig. 27.44** after the *Hide* command has been applied.

27.13 Line, Pline, and 3Dpoly

The *Line* command draws 2D lines when x- and y-values are specified, and 3D lines when x-, y-, and z-coordinates are given. *Pline* draws a 2D polyline and *3Dpoly* draws 3D polylines with x-, y-, and z-coordinates.

3Dpoly or *Line* commands draw lines with absolute coordinates from 0,0,0 located in 3D space in **Fig. 27.45**. Relative coordinates can be typed in the form of @X,Y,Z or @3,0,0 to locate their endpoints with respect to the last point.

All *Osnap* modes apply to *Lines, Plines,* and *3DFaces*. 3D objects can be *Stretched* in the plane of the *UCSicon* (in the x- and y-directions), but not in the z-direction. Height dimensions are modified by rotating the *UCS* so height lies in the x- or y-directions where *Stretch* can be used.

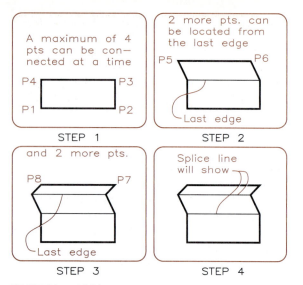

27.47 3Dface: Visible seam

Step 1 *Command:* 3Dface *(Enter) Specify first point or [Invisible]:* P1 > *Specify second point or [Invisible]:* P2 *Specify third point or [Invisible]:* P3

Specify fourth point or [Invisible]: P4

Step 2 *Specify third point or [Invisible]:* P5

Specify fourth point or [Invisible]: P6

Step 3 *Specify third point or [Invisible]:* P7

Specify fourth point or [Invisible]: P8

Step 4 *Specify third point :* (Enter) Splice lines show.

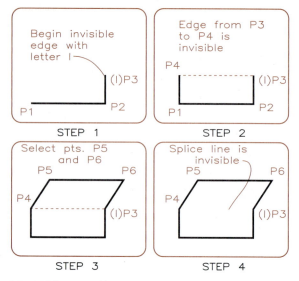

27.48 3Dface: Invisible seam

Step 1 *Command:* 3Dface *(Enter) Specify first point or [Invisible]:* P1 *Specify second point or [Invisible]:* P2 *Specify third point or [Invisible]:* Invisible *(Enter)*

Specify third point or [Invisible]: P3

Step 2 *Specify fourth point or [Invisible]:* P4

Step 3 *Specify third point or [Invisible]:* P5

Step 4 *Specify fourth point or [Invisible]:* P6> *Specify third point or [Invisible]:* (Enter) P3-P4 is invisible.

27.14 3Dface Command

3Dface is used to apply faces that can be made opaque by the *Hide* command (**Fig. 27.46**). *3Dface* is applied to wire frames by *Snapping* to their endpoints with *Osnap*.

  Figure 27.47 illustrates how corners of a *3Dface* are used to form an opaque plane. After selecting four points with the *3Dface* command, you will be prompted for points 3 and 4, using the previous two points as points 1 and 2. Successively added four-sided areas are connected with splice lines yielding a "patchwork" area of faces. By typing *I* (for invisible) and (Enter) prior to selecting the beginning point of a splice line, the splice will be invisible (**Fig. 27.48**).

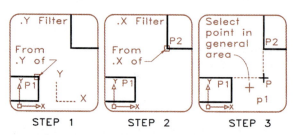

27.49 X and Y filters

Step 1 *Command:* Line *(Enter)*

Specify first point: .Y *(Enter)*

of P1 *(need XZ):* .X *(Enter)*

Step 2 *of* P2 *(need Z):*

Step 3 Select a point in the area of the desired position; a point appears at the intersection of the y-coordinate from the side view and the x-coordinate from the top view.

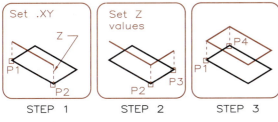

STEP 1   STEP 2   STEP 3

27.50 3D Filters

Step 1 *Command:* 3Dpoly (or Line) (Enter)
Specify start point of polyline: .XY of P1
(need Z): 2 (Enter)
Specify start endpoint of polyline: .XY of P2
(need Z): 2 (Enter)

Step 2 *Specify start . . . polyline:* .XY of P3
(need Z): 2 (Enter)

Step 3 *Specify start. . . polyline:* .XY of P4
(need Z): 2 (Enter)

27.51 *Main menu> View> Toolbars> Solids to get this Solids*
toolbar on your screen.

27.15 XYZ Filters

Filters are used for picking points that adopt the coordinates of 3D points (**Fig. 27.49**). When a command prompts for a point (as in the *Line* command), type a period (.) followed by one- or two-letter coordinates (.*X* or .*XY* for example) and select the point with the cursor. Respond to the prompt for the missing coordinate or coordinates with a number or numbers.

To locate the front view of a point projected from the left side and top views, select the .*Y* of the left point (Step 1) and the .*X* of the top point (Step 2), and the front view of the point sharing these coordinates is found (Step 3).

A 3D drawing is made in **Fig. 27.50** using filters where the .XY coordinates of a given point are selected and *Z* is specified as 2. *Osnap* was set to *End* for selecting endpoints. When the

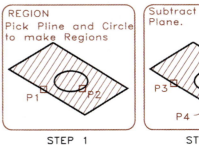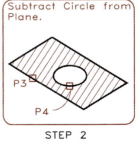

STEP 1   STEP 2

27.52 2D Regions

Step 1 *Command:* Region (Enter) *Select objects:* P1
1 found> Select objects: P2 (Enter) *2 Regions created.*

Step 2 *Command:* Subtract (Enter) *Select solids and regions to subtract from . . >* *Select objects:* P3 *1 found> Select objects:* (Enter)
Select solids and regions to subtract . . .
Select objects: P4 *> 1 found > Select objects:* (Enter)

points are filtered in the XZ plane, a prompt will ask for the Y-coordinate to locate the point in 3D space.

27.16 Solid Modeling: Introduction

AutoCAD 2000 provides solid modeling capabilities of *Regions* (2D solids) and *Solids* (3D solids). The various commands for solid modeling found in the *Solids* toolbar (**Fig. 27.51**) are used to create solid primitives—*boxes, cylinders, spheres,* and others—that can be added or subtracted from each other to form a composite object.

Regions

Region modeling is a 2D version of solid modeling in which a closed surface can be converted into a solid plane (an object) (**Fig. 27.52**). The upper plane of a wire frame enclosed by a *Pline* is made into a 2D solid by typing *Region* and selecting the polyline. The circle is made into a region and is removed from the rectangular *Region* by the *Subtract* command.

Extrude

The *Extrude* command (from the *Solids* toolbar) is used with closed polylines, polygons, circles,

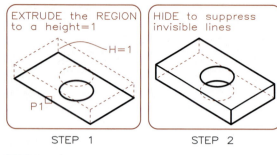

EXTRUDE the REGION to a height=1	HIDE to suppress invisible lines
STEP 1	STEP 2

27.53 Extruding a Region

Step 1 *View> Toolbars> Solids> Extrude* icon> *Select objects: P1 1 found > Select objects:* (Enter)

Step 2 *Specify height of extrusion or [Path]: 1 (Enter)*

Specify angle of taper for extrusion <0>: (Enter)

Region is extruded.

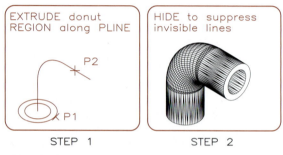

EXTRUDE donut REGION along PLINE	HIDE to suppress invisible lines
STEP 1	STEP 2

27.54 Extruding a Region

Step 1 *Command:* Extrude (Enter) *Select objects:* P1 > 1 found> *Select objects:* (Enter) *Specify height of extrusion or [Path]:* Path (Enter)

Step 2 *Select extrusion path:* P2 > Hide. Region is extruded and its hidden lines removed.

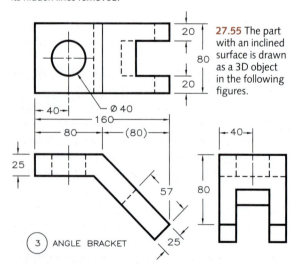

27.55 The part with an inclined surface is drawn as a 3D object in the following figures.

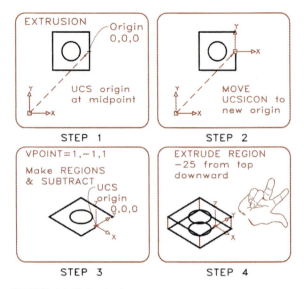

EXTRUSION — Origin 0,0,0	
UCS origin at midpoint	MOVE UCSICON to new origin
STEP 1	STEP 2
VPOINT=1,−1,1 Make REGIONS & SUBTRACT UCS origin 0,0,0	EXTRUDE REGION −25 from top downward
STEP 3	STEP 4

27.56 Part 1: First extrusion

Step 1 Draw the top view of the bracket and set the *UCS* origin at the midpoint of the line as shown.

Step 2 Use *UCS icon* and ORigin to place the icon at the origin.

Step 3 Set a *Vpoint* of 1,-1,1 to obtain an isometric view of the plane. Make the plane into a *Region* with a hole in it.

Step 4 *Extrude* the *Region* to a height of −25.

ellipses, and 3D entities to extrude them to a specified height, with tapered sides if desired. **Figure 27.53** shows the extrusion of the 2D *Region,* developed in **Fig. 27.52**, to an assigned height of 1. Polylines with crossing or intersecting segments cannot be extruded.

Regions can be extruded paths (usually a polyline) to form a 3D shape, as illustrated in **Fig. 27.54**. Extruded shapes can be hidden and rendered.

27.17 An Extrusion Example

While in *Model Space,* assign limits of about 200 × 180 in which to draw the first portion of the angle bracket shown in **Fig. 27.55**. Begin drawing the bracket as follows:

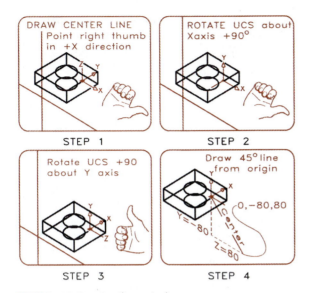

| STEP 1 | STEP 2 |
| DRAW CENTER LINE Point right thumb in +X direction | ROTATE UCS about Xaxis +90° |

| STEP 3 | STEP 4 |
| Rotate UCS +90 about Y axis | Draw 45° line from origin |

27.57 Part 2: Drawing the center line

Step 1 *Command:* <u>UCS</u> (Enter) *Enter an option [New/ Move/. . ./World]:* <u>New</u> (Enter) *Specify origin of new UCS:* <u>X</u> (Enter)

Step 2 *Specify rotation angle about X axis:* <u>90</u> (Enter)

Step 3 *Command:* <u>UCS</u> (Enter) *Enter an option [New/ Move/. . ./World]:* <u>New</u> (Enter)

Specify origin of new UCS: <u>Y</u> (Enter)

Specify rotation angle about Y axis: <u>90</u> (Enter)

Step 4 *Command:* <u>Line</u> (Enter)

Specify first point: <u>0,0,0</u> (Enter)

Specify next point: <u>0,-80,80</u> (Enter) *Center line is drawn.*

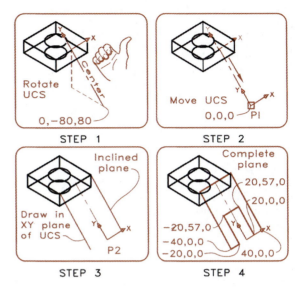

| STEP 1 | STEP 2 |
| Rotate UCS 0,-80,80 | Move UCS 0,0,0 P1 |

| STEP 3 | STEP 4 |
| Inclined plane Draw in XY plane of UCS P2 | Complete plane 20,57,0 20,0,0 -20,57,0 -40,0,0 -20,0,0 40,0,0 |

27.58 Part 3: Drawing the inclined plane

Step 1 *Command:* <u>UCS</u> (Enter) *Enter an option [New/ Move/. . ./World]:* <u>New</u> (Enter) *Specify origin of new UCS:* <u>X</u> (Enter)

Specify rotation angle about X axis: <u>−45</u> (Enter)

Step 2 *Command:* <u>UCS</u> (Enter) *Enter an option [New/ Move/. . ./World]:*<u>Move</u> (Enter)

Specify origin of new UCS: <u>P1</u>(Enter) *End of center line.*

Step 3 *Command:* <u>Pline</u> (Enter) *Draw the two outside lines that lie in the plane of the UCS.*

Step 4 *Command:* <u>Pline</u> (Enter) *Continue drawing the notch in the inclined plane by using the coordinates of each point. Pedit> Join to make the lines on the inclined plane one continuous polyline.*

Part 1—First Extrusion: (Fig. 27.56) Draw the top view of the bracket as a polyline with a circle in it, and set the *UCS origin* at the midpoint of the line shown. *Move* the *UCS icon* to the *UCS ORigin,* convert the plane into a *Region,* and *Subtract* the circle from the rectangular plane. Obtain an isometric view (*Vpoint*=1,-1,1), and *Extrude* the *Region* to -25 mm below the upper surface.

Part 2—Draw the inclined center line: (Fig. 27.57) Rotate the UCS 90° about the X axis and 90° about the Y axis. Draw a line from 0,0,0 (the UCS origin) to 0,-80,80 to find the centerline of the inclined surface.

Part 3—Draw the inclined surface: (Fig. 27.58) Rotate the UCS −45° about the X axis so

that it lies in the plane of the inclined surface. Draw a closed *Pline* using the coordinates of the inclined plane to locate its corners.

Part 4—Extruding the inclined surface: (Fig. 27.59) Convert the inclined plane into a *Region.* Type *Extrude* from the *Command* line and enter a height of −25 when prompted. Use the *Union* command, select the two extrusions, and join them together into a single solid.

Part 5—Four equal views: (Fig. 27.60) Pick the *Layout1 tab* at the bottom of the screen and you will get a dialogue box that will let you open a single viewport. When it is opened, erase this viewport, which leaves no viewport. Select *Four Equal* (3D) ports from the *Viewports* box (**Fig.**

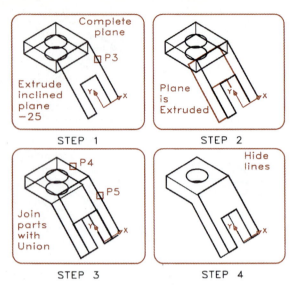

STEP 1   **STEP 2**

STEP 3   **STEP 4**

27.59 Part 4: The inclined surface

Step 1 *Command:* <u>Region</u> (Enter)

Select object: <u>P3</u> (Enter)

Command: <u>Extrude</u> (Enter)

Step 2 *Specify height of extrusion or [path]:* <u>-25</u> (Enter)

Step 3 *Command:* <u>Union</u> (Enter) *Select object:* <u>P4</u>

Select object: <u>P5</u> (Enter) The parts are joined.

Step 4 *Command:* <u>Hide</u> (Enter) Invisible lines are hidden.

27.60); when prompted, select the diagonal corner of the area of the four ports. The four viewports will appear as shown in **Fig. 27.61** with top, front, side, and isometric views. It is usually necessary to size the views to a uniform scale by using *Zoom> nXP (.3XP* for example). *Hide* can be used in each port to remove invisible lines. When printing from *Paper Space,* invisible lines can be suppressed by selecting the viewports with hidden lines, right-clicking inside the port, and selecting *Hide plot.*

27.18 Solids: Primitives

Solid primitives—*box, sphere, wedge, cone, cylinder,* and *torus*—can be selected from the *Solids* toolbar shown in **Fig. 27.51**. Hidden lines in solid primitives are suppressed by typing *Hide.*

    Box creates a box as shown in **Fig. 27.62** where its base is drawn in the plane of the current *UCS.*

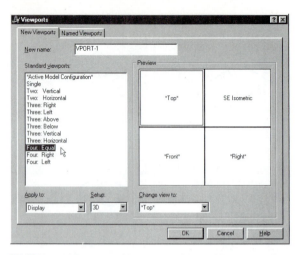

27.60 To set Viewports: *Main menu> View> Viewports> New Viewports* to obtain this dialogue box. Select *Four Equal* windows and *3D* in *Setup* as your viewports option.

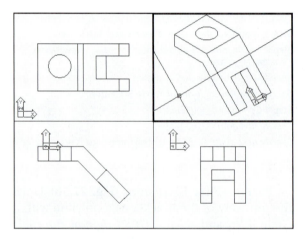

27.61 Part 5: Four equal views

Select the *Layout1tab* (Enter) and a single *MS* viewport appears in paper space. *Erase* the window. *Main menu> View> Viewports> New Viewports> Four: Equal[grat] 3D in*

The dimensions of the box can be created with separate widths and depths, diagonal corners of the base, or as a cube by typing values at the keyboard, or selecting them with the cursor.

    Sphere creates a ball by responding to the prompts with the center and radius, or center

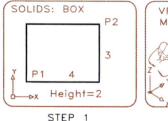

27.62 Solids: *Box*

Step 1 *Command:* Box (Enter)

Specify corner of box or [Center] <0,0,0>: P1 (Enter)

Specify corner or [Cube/Length]: P2 (Enter)

Specify height: 2 (Enter)

Step 2 *Command:* Vpoint (Enter)

Specify a view point or [Rotate] <display compass and tripod>: 1,-1,1 (Enter) The box is shown as a wire frame. Type Hide to suppress hidden lines.

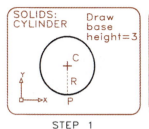
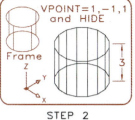

27.64 Solids: *Cylinder*

Step 1 *Command:* Cylinder (Enter)

Specify center point for base of cylinder or [Elliptical]<0,0,0>: Center (Enter)

Specify radius for base of cylinder or [Diameter]: 2.5 (Enter)

Specify height of cylinder or [Center of]: 3 (Enter)

Step 2 *Command:* Vpoint (Enter)

Specify a view point or [Rotate] <display compass and tripod>: 1,-1,1 (Enter) 3D view of the cylinder is obtained. Type Hide to suppress invisible lines.

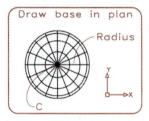

27.63 Solids: *Sphere*

Step 1 *Command:* Sphere (Enter)

Specify center of sphere <0,0,0>: Center (Enter)

Specify radius of sphere or [Diameter]: 2 (Enter)

Step 2 *Command:* Vpoint (Enter)

Specify a view point or [Rotate] <display compass and tripod>: 1,-1,1 (Enter) 3D view of the sphere is obtained. Type Hide to suppress invisible lines.

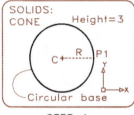
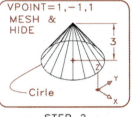

27.65 Solids: *Cone*

Step 1 *Command:* Cone (Enter)

Specify center point for base of cone or [Elliptical]: <0,0,0>: Center (Enter)

Specify radius for base of cone or [Diameter]: P1 (Enter)

Specify height of cone or [Apex]: 3 (Enter)

Step 2 *Command:* Vpoint (Enter)

Specify a view point or [Rotate] <display compass and tripod>: 1,-1,1 (Enter) 3D view of the cone is obtained. Type Hide to suppress invisible lines.

and diameter of the ball as shown in **Fig. 27.63**. The axis of the sphere connecting its north and south poles is parallel to the Z-axis of the current *UCS,* and its center is on the plane of the *UCS.*

Cylinder draws a cylinder in a similar manner to drawing a cone. **Figure 27.64** illustrates the steps of drawing a cylinder with a circular base, but cylinders with elliptical bases also may be drawn.

Cone draws cones with circular or elliptical bases. The example in **Fig. 27.65** illustrates a cone drawn with a circular base and its center, axis endpoints, and height specified when prompted.

Wedge draws the base that lies in the plane of the current *UCS* with the upper plane sloping

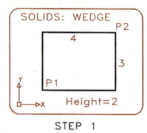 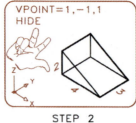

STEP 1   STEP 2

27.66 Solids: *Wedge*

Step 1 *Command:* Wedge (Enter)

Specify first corner of wedge or [CEnter]<0,0,0>: P1 (Enter)

Specify corner or [Cube/Length]: P2 (Enter)

Specify height: 2 (Enter)

Step 2 *Command:* Vpoint (Enter)

Specify a view point or [Rotate] <display compass and tripod>: 1,-1,1 (Enter) 3D view of the wedge is obtained. Type Hide (Enter) to suppress invisible lines.

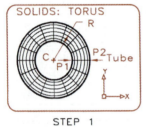 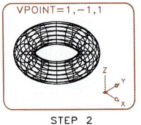

STEP 1   STEP 2

27.67 Solids: *Torus*

Step 1 *Command:* Torus (Enter)

Specify center of torus <0,0,0>: C (Enter)

Specify radius of torus or [Diameter]: 6 (Enter)

Specify radius of tube or [Diameter]: 2 (Enter)

Step 2 *Command:* Vpoint (Enter)

Specify a view point or [Rotate] <display compass and tripod>: 1,-1,1 (Enter) 3D view of the torus is obtained. Type Hide to suppress invisible lines.

toward the second point selected (**Fig. 27.66**). Prompts ask for the length, width, and height of the wedge.

Torus draws a donut solid by giving its center, diameter or radius of the tube, and diameter or radius of torus (**Fig. 27.67**). The diameter of the torus will lie in the plane of the current *UCS*.

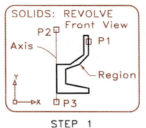 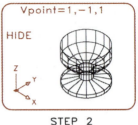

STEP 1   STEP 2

27.68 Solids: *Revolve*

Step 1 *Command:* Revolve (Enter) *Select objects:* P1

Axis of revolution-object/X/Y/<Start point of axis>: P2

<End point of axis>: P3

Angle of revolution <full circle>: (Enter)

Surface is revolved.

Step 2 *Command:* Vpoint (Enter)

Rotate/<Viewpoint><0,0,0>: 1,-1,1 (Enter)

3D view of revolution is drawn.

Type Hide (Enter) to suppress invisible lines.

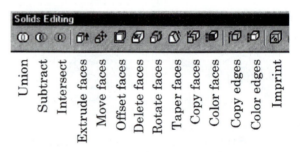

27.69 This *Solids Editing* toolbar is used to make changes in solid models.

Revolve is used to sweep polylines, polygons, circles, ellipses, and 3D poly objects about an axis if they have at least 3, but less than 300, vertices. In **Fig. 27.68**, a polyline is revolved a full 360° about an axis. The path of revolution can start and end at any point between 0 and 360°. Polylines that have been *Fit* or *Splined* will require extensive calculations.

27.19 Modifying Solids

Once drawn, *Solids* can be modified and edited by a number of commands including *Union, Subtract, Explode, Chamfer, Fillet, Extend,* and *Trim.* Some of these tools and others can be

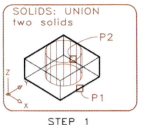

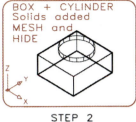

27.70 Solids: *Union*
Step 1 *Command:* <u>Union</u> (Enter)
Select objects: <u>P1</u> (Enter)
Select objects: <u>P2</u> (Enter)
Step 2 *Select objects:* (Enter)
The solids are unified (added) into a single part.
Type <u>Hide</u> (Enter) to remove the invisible lines.

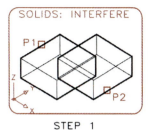

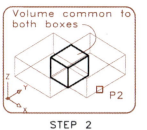

27.72 Solids: *Interfere*
Step 1 *Command:* <u>Interfere</u> (Enter)
Select first set of solids: Select objects: <u>P1</u> (Enter)
Select second set of solids:
Step 2 *Select objects:* <u>P2</u> (Enter)
Create interference solids? <N>: <u>Yes</u> (Enter) Interference solid is created and nonoverlapping portions are discarded. Type <u>Hide</u> (Enter) to suppress invisible lines.

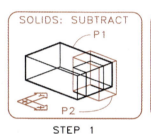

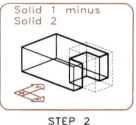

27.71 Solids: *Subtract*
Step 1 *Main menu > Modify> Solids editing> Subtract> Select solids and regions to subtract from . . .*
Select objects: <u>P1</u> (Enter)
Select solids and regions to subtract: <u>P2</u> (Enter)
Step 2 The notch is cut into the part. Type <u>Hide</u> to remove the hidden lines.

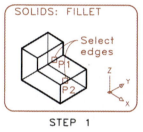

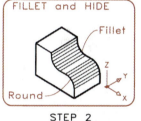

27.73 Solids: *Fillet*
Step 1 *Command:* <u>Fillet</u> (Enter)> *Select first object or [Polyline/Radius/Trim]:* <u>P1</u>
Enter fillet radius: <u>3</u> (Enter)> *Select an edge or [Chain/Radius]:* <u>P2</u> (Enter) *2 edges selected for fillet*
Step 2 The *Fillets* are drawn. Type <u>Hide</u> (Enter) to remove the hidden lines.

accessed from the *Solids Editing* toolbar (**Fig. 27.69**).

Union is used to join intersecting solids to form a single composite solid model. **Figure 27.70** shows how a box and cylinder are unified into a single solid.

Subtract is used to remove one intersecting solid from another, as illustrated in **Fig. 27.71**.

Intersect is used to obtain a solid that is common to two intersecting solids. An interference solid is found in **Fig. 27.72** with this command.

Explode is used to separate solids or regions that were combined by the *Subtract* and *Union* commands to permit editing or correcting before redoing *Subtract* and *Union* commands.

Fillet is used to apply rounded intersections between planes by selecting the common edges between solids and giving the diameter or radius of the fillet as shown in **Fig. 27.73**. The *Fillet* command can also be used to fillet the edges of a cylindrical or curved features.

Chamfer applies beveled edges by selecting the base surface, the adjoining surface, and the edges to be chamfered, giving the first and second

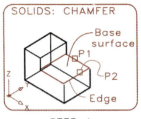

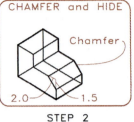

STEP 1   STEP 2

27.74 Solids: *Chamfer*

Step 1 *Command:* <u>Chamfer</u> (Enter) *Select first line or [Polyline/Distance/Angle/ Trim/Method]:* <u>D</u> (Enter)

Base surface selection... Enter surface selection option [Next/OK (current)] <OK>: (Enter)

Specify base surface chamfer distance <1.000>: <u>2</u> (Enter) *Specify other surface chamfer distance <1.000>:* <u>1.5</u> (Enter)

Select an edge or [Loop]: <u>P2</u>

Step 2 The *Chamfer* is drawn. Type <u>Hide</u> (Enter) to remove the hidden lines.

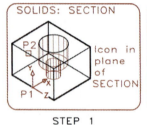

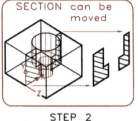

STEP 1   STEP 2

27.75 Solids: *Section*

Step 1 Position the UCS in the plane of the section.

Command: <u>Section</u> (Enter) *Select objects:* <u>P1</u> (Enter)

Specify the first point on Section plane by [Object/. . . /XY/YZ/ZX]: <u>XY</u> (Enter)> *Specify a point on the XY plane <0,0,0>:* <u>P2</u> This section establishes a *Region* in the plane of the UCS icon.

Step 2 *Command:* <u>Move</u> (Enter) *Move the Region* outside the part; apply section lines to it if you like.

chamfer distances (**Fig. 27.74**). When these prompts have been satisfied, the chamfers are automatically drawn.

27.20 Section

Section is used to pass a sectioning plane through a 3D solid to show a *Region* that defines its internal features (**Fig. 27.75**). *Bhatch* (hatch pattern) can be used to assign the hatching pattern to the *Region* if it lies in the plane of the

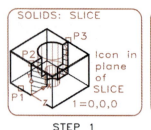

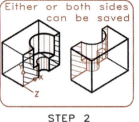

STEP 1   STEP 2

27.76 Solids: *Slice*

Step 1 Move the *UCS* to the plane of the *Slice*.

Command: <u>Slice</u> (Enter) *Select objects:* Pick the box.

Specify first point on slicing plane by Object/...XY / YZ...: <u>P1</u> (Enter) > *Specify first point on plane:* <u>2</u>

Specify second point on plane: <u>3</u>

Step 2 *Specify a point on desired side of the plane or [keep Both sides]:* <u>Both</u> (Enter) Move views apart.

UCS. The hatch pattern is set to ANSI31 for cast iron hatching symbols.

The *UCSicon* is placed on the object to establish the plane of the section, *Section* is typed, and the plane passing through the object appears. The section plane can be moved as shown in this example. Other sections through the object are found in this same manner by positioning the icon in the cutting plane or by selecting from one of the following options: *3point, Object, Zaxis, View, XY, YZ,* or *ZX.*

27.21 Slice

With the *Slice* command an object can be cut through and made into separate parts, either or both of which can be retained as shown in **Fig. 27.76**. The *Slice* command has the following options:

3points defines three points on the slice plane.

Object aligns the cutting plane with a circle, ellipse, 2D spline, or 2D polyline element.

Zaxis defines a plane by picking an origin point on the Z axis that is perpendicular to the selected points.

View makes the cutting plane parallel with the viewport's viewing plane when a single point is selected.

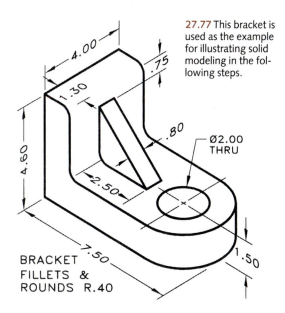

27.77 This bracket is used as the example for illustrating solid modeling in the following steps.

BRACKET
FILLETS &
ROUNDS R.40

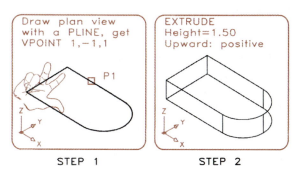

STEP 1   STEP 2

27.78 Part 1: *Extrude* base

Step 1 Draw the base with a closed *Pline*.

Command: Vpoint (Enter)

Specify a view point or [Rotate]<display compass and tripod>: 1,-1,1 (Enter) *Get an isometric view of base.*

Command: Extrude (Enter) *Select objects:* P1 (Enter)

Step 2 *Specify height of extrusion or [Path]:* 1.50 (Enter)

Specify angle of taper for extrusion <0>: (Enter) *Base is extruded 1.50 inches high.*

XY, YZ, or *ZX* aligns the cutting plane with the planes of the *UCS* by selecting only one point.

27.22 A Solid Model Example

The bracket shown in **Fig. 27.77** is to be drawn as a solid model by using the commands from the *Solids* toolbar. Create the outline of the base

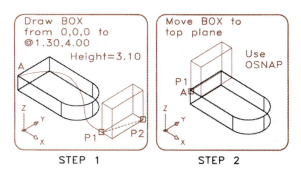

STEP 1   STEP 2

27.79 Part 2: Draw the *box*

Step 1 *Command:* Box (Enter)

Specify corner of box or [CEenter]: P1 (Enter)

Specify corner or [Cube/Length]: [at]1,30,4 (Enter)

Specify height: 3.1 (Enter) *Box is drawn.*

Step 2 Set *Osnap* to *End.* *Command:* Move (Enter)

Select objects: Pick box.

Specify base point or displacement: P1 (Enter)

Second point of displacement: A (Enter) *Box is moved.*

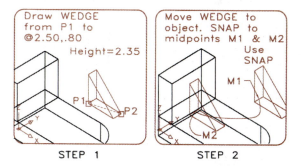

STEP 1   STEP 2

27.80 Part 3: Draw the *wedge*

Step 1 *Command:* Wedge (Enter)

Specify first corner of wedge of [CEnter]: P1 (Enter)

Specify corner or [Cube/Length]: [at]2.5,0.8 (Enter)

Specify height: 2.35 *The Wedge is drawn.*

Step 2 Set *Osnap* to *Midpoint.* *Command:* Move (Enter)

Select objects: Pick wedge. Set *Osnap* to *Midpoint.*

Specify base point or displacement: M1 (Enter)

Specify second point or displacement or <use first point as displacement>: M2 (Enter) *Wedge is moved to base.*

with a *Pline* and obtain an isometric view of it by a *Vpoint* of 1,-1,1 (**Fig. 27.78**). Then, *Extrude* the base to a height of 1.50 units.

A *Box* of 1.30 × 4.00 × 3.10 is drawn (**Fig. 27.79**) and moved to the base by *Snapping End* P1 of the box *End A.* Use *Wedge* to draw the bracket's rib as shown in **Fig. 27.80**. Move the rib

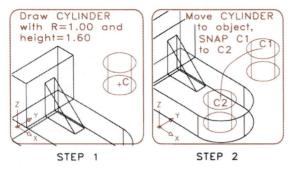

| Draw CYLINDER with R=1.00 and height=1.60 | Move CYLINDER to object, SNAP C1 to C2 |

STEP 1   **STEP 2**

27.81 Part 4: Draw the cylinder

Step 1: *Command:* <u>Cylinder</u> (Enter)
Specify center point for base of cylinder or [Elliptical] <0,0,0>: <u>Center</u> (Enter)
Specify radius for base of cylinder or [Diameter]: <u>1.00</u> (Enter)
Specify height for base of cylinder or [Center of other end]: <u>1.60</u> (Enter) Cylinder is drawn.

Step 2 Set *Osnap* to *Center. Command:* <u>Move</u> (Enter)
Select objects: <u>Pick cylinder.</u>
Specify base point or displacement: <u>C1</u>
Specify second point of displacement: <u>C2</u> Hole is placed.

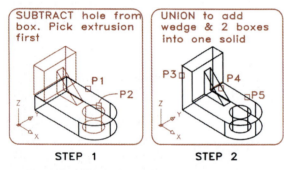

| SUBTRACT hole from box. Pick extrusion first | UNION to add wedge & 2 boxes into one solid |

STEP 1   **STEP 2**

27.82 Part 5: *Subtract* and *Union*

Step 1 *Command:* <u>Subtract</u> (Enter) *Select solids and regions to subtract from . . . Select objects:* <u>P1</u> (Enter)
Select objects: <u>P2</u> (Enter) Hole is subtracted from base.

Step 2 *Command:* <u>Union</u> (Enter)

Select objects: <u>P3, P4, P5</u> (Enter) *Select objects:* (Enter)
The bracket is unified into one solid.

to join the base and the upright box by using the *Midpoint* option of *Snap.*

In **Fig. 27.81**, use *Cylinder* to represent the hole and *Move* it to the center of the semicircular end of the base using the *Center* option of *Snap.* Use *Subtract* to create the hole in the base (**Fig. 27.82**). Use the *Union* command to join the base, upright box, and wedge together into a composite solid.

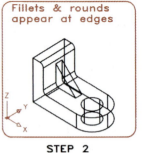

| Use FILLET to add fillets of R.40 | Fillets & rounds appear at edges |

STEP 1   **STEP 2**

27.83 Part 6: *Fillets*

Step 1 *Command:* <u>Fillet</u> (Enter) (Trim mode)
Select first object or [Polyline/Radius/ Trim]<Select first object>: <u>P1</u>
Enter fillet radius: <u>.40</u> (Enter)
Command: <u>Fillet</u> (Enter)
Select and edge or [Chain/Radius]: <u>P2</u>
Select and edge or [Chain/Radius]: <u>P3</u>

Step 2 *Select and edge or [Chain/Radius]:* (Enter)

Fillets and rounds are applied.

| WIRE–FRAME diagram | HIDE to remove hidden lines. |

STEP 1   **STEP 2**

27.84 Part 7: *Hide* invisible lines

Step 1 *Command:* <u>Hide</u> (Enter)

Step 2 The object is shown as solid with hidden lines suppressed.

Fillet is used in **Fig. 27.83** to select the edges to be rounded with a radius of 0.40 and *Hide* suppresses the invisible lines (**Fig. 27.84**). An infinite number of views of the bracket can be obtained with *Vpoint* or *Dview*.

27.23 Three-View Drawing

A drawing composed of three orthographic views (top, front, and side) with an isometric

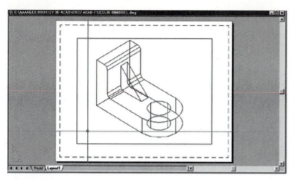

27.85 A single viewport in the *Paper Space (Layout1 tab)* shows the isometric of the bracket that was drawn in *Model Space*. Erase this viewport.

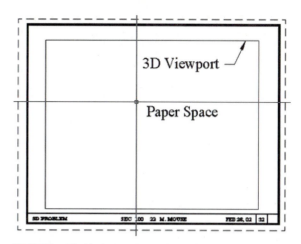

27.87 The title block is in *Paper Space (Layout1 tab)* and no viewports into *Model Space* are defined at this point.

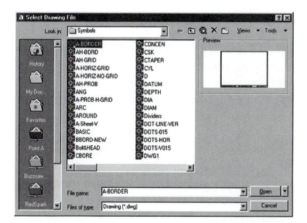

27.86 *Main menu> Insert> Block> Browse>* select ABORD-HOR and insert it into *Paper Space*. This previously saved title block establishes the drawing area.

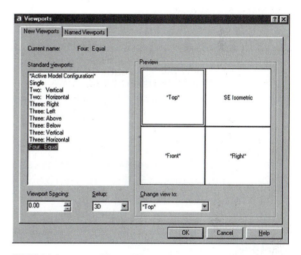

27.88 *Main menu> View> Viewports> New Viewports> 3D* (in the *Setup* window)> *Four: Equal*. When prompted, specify the diagonal of the window into which the four viewports are to fit within the border.

view is a classic arrangement for an engineering drawing suitable for depicting most parts. This layout can be obtained by drawing an object in *Model Space* as the bracket in **Fig. 27.77** was drawn (see the previous examples).

Select the *Layout1 tab* at the bottom of the screen to obtain a dialogue box and obtain a single viewport in *Paper Space* that shows the bracket (**Fig. 27.85**). Use the steps outlined in

Fig. 27.86 to insert a title block into *Paper Space* as shown in **Fig. 27.87**. Erase the *Model Space* window and the 3D image disappears.

Specify four 3D viewports following the steps given in **Fig. 27.88**. The four viewports will appear within *Model Space,* as illustrated in **Fig. 27.89**, but the views of the bracket may not be scaled uniformly. Double-click on a viewport to enter the *Model Space* (*UCS icons* will appear) of that

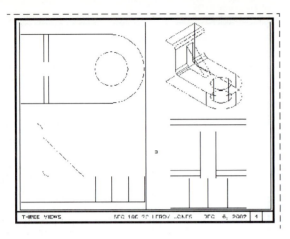

27.89 The four viewports that open into *Model Space* appear in the window specified by diagonal corners.

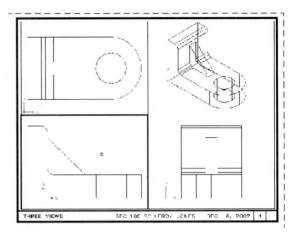

27.90 Size each view with the same factor. For example, use *Zoom* nXP (.5XP perhaps) in order for the orthographic views to be equal in size.

viewport where you can use a *Zoom* factor to size that view of the bracket; *Zoom* .5XP, for example. Select the other viewports by double-clicking on them, and assign the same *Zoom* factor to them in order to size them uniformly (**Fig. 27.90**).

If the views need to be aligned vertically and/or horizontally, type <u>*Mvsetup*</u> at the *Command line> Enter an option [Align/ Create... /Undo]:* <u>Align</u> (Enter). Select the horizontal option, pick a base point in a given view and the corresponding point in an adjacent view, and the views will be horizontally aligned. Refer to **Fig. 14.34**.

Double-click on a *Paper Space* area (the title block) to return to *Paper Space* and the triangular icon reappears. A plot can be made from *Paper Space* that will show the four viewports, but the outlines of the viewports will plot and hidden lines will plot as solid lines.

To remove the viewport outlines, create a new layer, select the outlines from *PS*, and *Change* them to the new layer. *Freeze* the new layer at plot time and the outlines will not be plotted.

The hidden lines can be suppressed if you select a viewport border (from *PS*), right-click inside the viewport, and pick *Hide plot* from the pop-up menu. These options are available from *Main menu> Tools> Properties* as well. Each viewport must be manipulated in this manner to suppress its hidden lines.

However, you would probably prefer to show invisible lines as dashed lines rather than omit them altogether. *Main Menu> Draw> Solids> Setup> Profile* and click on the front view of the bracket in *Model Space* (Enter) to get the following prompts:

Display hidden profile lines on separate layer? <Y>: (Enter)
Project profile lines onto a plane? <Y>: (Enter)
Delete tangential edges? <Y>: (Enter)

When each viewport with hidden lines has been manipulated in this manner, single planes (profiles) representing each view of the 3D solid have been created and placed in front of the solid. Therefore, it is necessary to *Freeze* the layer on which the 3D solid is drawn in each view leaving only the profiles that were created with dashed lines to represent invisible lines. Double-click on a paper space area to return to *Paper Space;* turn *Off* the *Layer* on which the

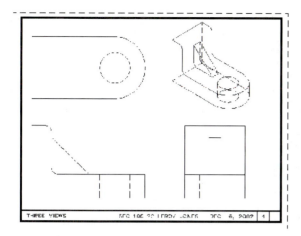

27.91 The *Vport* outlines can be removed and hidden lines generated by the *Profile* command to make the layout of views appear in the standard format.

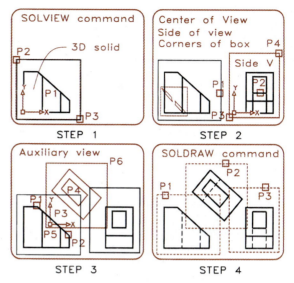

27.92 *Solview* and *Soldraw*

Step 1 *Command:* <u>Solview</u> (Enter)
Ucs/ Ortho/ Auxiliary/ Section/ <eXit>: <u>UCS</u> (Enter)
Named/ World/ ?/ <Current>: (Enter)
Enter view scale <1.00>: (Enter) *View Center:* <u>P1</u> (Enter)
Specify first corner of viewport: <u>P2</u>
Specify opposite corner of viewport: <u>P3</u>
Enter view name: <u>Front</u> (Enter)

Step 2 *Enter an option [Ucs/ Ortho/ Auxiliary/ Section]:* <u>Ortho</u>
(Enter)
Specify side of viewport to project: <u>P1</u>
Specify view center: <u>P2</u> (Enter)
Specify first corner of viewport: <u>P3</u>
Specify opposite corner of viewport: <u>P4</u>
Enter view name: <u>Rside</u> (Enter)

Step 3 *Enter an option [Ucs/ Ortho/ Auxiliary/ Section]:*
<u>Auxiliary</u> (Enter)
Specify first point of inclined plane: <u>P1</u>
Specify second point of inclined plane: <u>P2</u>
Specify side to view from: <u>P3</u>
Specify view center: <u>P4</u> (Enter)
Specify first corner of viewport: <u>P5</u>
Specify opposite corner of viewport: <u>P6</u>
Enter view name: <u>Aux1</u> (Enter)

Step 4 *Command:* <u>Soldraw</u> (Enter)
Select viewport to draw: <u>P1, P2, P3,</u> (Enter) Solid lines that are
invisible are converted to hidden (dashed lines). *Freeze the
Vports* layer to remove the windows.

solid model was drawn in order to leave only the profile planes to represent the views of the bracket. *Main Menu> Format> Layer> Layer Properties Manager* and pick the layer whose name begins with "PH" (not "PV") and change the line type to *Hidden* and pick <u>Ok</u>. Now the invisible lines appear as dashed lines (**Fig. 27.91**).

27.24 Views of a Solid

Two commands, *Solview* and *Soldraw,* are used together to convert a 3D solid into orthographic views, auxiliary views, or sections. Once a 3D solid has been drawn, select the *Setup View* icon from the *Solids* toolbar (or type *Solview*), the screen will enter *Paper Space* and you will be given the options of *UCS, Ortho, Auxiliary,* and *Section.* Select *UCS/* and follow the prompts as shown in **Fig. 27.92**.

You will be asked to select the *view center* and two *viewport corners* (the diagonals of a *MS* view port). When asked to name the *view* select *<Current>* (Enter) to use the *xy plane* of the current *UCS* to create an orthographic view.

The next prompt will ask for the type of view you want. Choose *Ortho* for a side view and select the right edge of the window so it will be

projected to the right of the front view. Select the *view center* point when prompted to position the side view; several selections can be made to obtain the best location. Select the *corner* points to establish the *MS* window.

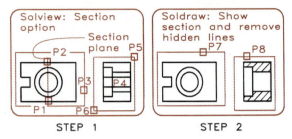

STEP 1   STEP 2

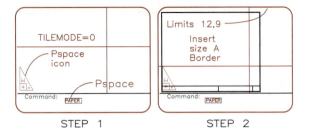

STEP 1   STEP 2

27.93 *Solview:* Section option

Step 1 Draw the front view of the solid to be sectioned using the steps illustrated in previous examples. To find the section view:

Type Solview> *Enter an option [UCS/ Ortho/ Auxiliary/ Section]:* Section

Specify first point of cutting plane: P1

Specify second point of cutting plane: P2

Specify side to view from: P3

Enter view scale <1.000>: .40 (Enter)

Specify view center: P4

Specify first corner of viewport: P5

Specify opposite corner of viewport: P6

Enter view name: SECT (Enter)

Step 2 *Command:* Soldraw (Enter) Select viewports to draw: P7, P8. Solid lines that are invisible are omitted and the cut surface of the section is hatched.

Since the object has an inclined plane (Step 3), specify the next view as an *Auxiliary* and select two points on the inclined plane in the front view. Pick a point on the side where the auxiliary is to be drawn; pick the *view center,* pick the diagonal corners of the viewport window; and the auxiliary view is drawn. *Solview* automatically creates four layers for each named view. The name of the layer is followed by a dash and the abbreviations, -VIS, -HID, -DIM, and -Hat for visible, hidden, dimension, and hatch respectively on which these features can be drawn.

In Step 4, *Solid toolbar> Setup Drawing* icon (or type Soldraw at the *Command line*) and you will be prompted for *Viewports to draw.* Select points on the *MS* windows and invisible lines will be converted to hidden (dashed) lines. It is necessary that linetype *Hidden* be loaded before using this command. From the *Layer* toolbar, *Freeze* the layer *Vports* to remove the outline of the *MS* windows.

27.94 PS option: *Layout 1*

Step 1 From *Model Space,* select the *Layout1* (or *Model* in the *Status* bar) to get the *Page Setup* box from which to make plotting assignments. Make printer and paper assignment and pick OK. You are in paper space where a viewport into 3D is shown. Erase this box to close it.

Step 2 *Command:* Insert (Enter)

Block name (or ?): Border-A (Enter)

Specify Insertion point or [Scale/X/Y/Z.Rotate/PScale/PX/ PY/PZ/PRotate]: 0,0 (Enter)

The title block is inserted into paper space at the scale to which it was drawn, full size in this case.

A sectional view is illustrated in **Fig. 27.93** where the same steps are followed but instead of *Ortho* or *Aux, Section* is selected when prompted. The hatching is automatically applied to the section view and hidden lines are omitted when *Soldraw* is used to select the *MS* windows from paper space. Crosshatching can be varied by *HPname, HPscale,* and *HPangle* to set the name of the hatch pattern, its scale, and angle, respectively.

Dimensions can be applied to the *Solid Views* by using the layers labeled with -Dim following the view's name (Front-Dim, for example). These dimensions are applied in much the same manner as discussed in section 27.24.

27.25 Mass Properties (Massprop)

Various properties of regions and solids can be obtained with the *Massprop* command. An explanation of the options available from this command are given below:

Area computes the area of a region or solid.

Perimeter calculates the perimeter of a region. It is not available for solids.

Bounding Box gives coordinates of the diagonal corners of a region's enclosing rectangle. For

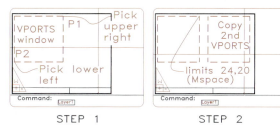

STEP 1   STEP 2

27.95 PS option: *Vports*

Step 1 While in Paper Space, *Main Menu> View> Viewports> New Viewports* to obtain the *Viewports* dialogue box. Select *Single* and pick P1 and P2 to form a floating viewport into 3D space.

Step 2 Copy this viewport to make a second one. Return to *Model Space* by selecting the *Model* tab in the *Status Line* and set the view ports *Limits* to 24,20. A 3D viewport can be made current by double-clicking inside it, and *Paper space* entered by double-clicking outside viewport.

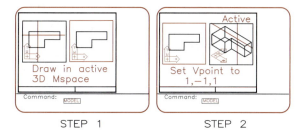

STEP 1   STEP 2

27.96 MS option: Drawing in *Model Space*

Step 1 Double-click inside one of the viewports to make it current and draw and extruded 3D part. It will show in both views.

Step 2 Pick the right viewport to make it active.

Command: Vpoint (Enter) *Specify viewpoint:* 1,-1,1 (Enter) An isometric drawing of the part is obtained.

---

a solid, coordinates of the diagonal and opposite corners of a 3D box are given.

Volume gives the space enclosed in a solid.

Mass gives the weight of a solid.

Centroid gives the coordinates of the center of a region or the 3D center of a solid.

Moments of Inertia is given for regions and solids.

Products of Inertia is given for regions and solids.

Radii of Gyration is given for regions and solids.

Matlib (materials library) assigns material types that can be assigned to solids that will have an effect on the mass properties listed above. The *Materials Library* box is found under the *Render* toolbar.

27.26 Paper Space and Model Space

By selecting the *Layout1* tab we can plot all *Vports* just as they appear on the screen, not just the active *viewport*. (An overview of *Paper Space* and *Model Space* was covered in Section 27.2.)

Type UCSicon and On so the icon will appear. Double-click in an area of *Paper Space*

and the screen returns to *Paper Space* with a *Pspace* icon (a triangle) in its lower left corner, and *Paper* appears in the *Command* line (**Fig. 27.94**). Then set the paper space *Limits* large enough to contain the border, about $12'' \times 9''$, and insert a size-A border. (You may design your own border and save it as a *Wblock*.)

Type Mview, select diagonal corners of a model-space viewport with the cursor, *Copy* it, and double-click in one of the ports to enter *Model Space* in that particular port (**Fig. 27.95**). Set the *Limits* in this 3D viewport to 24×20, large enough to contain the drawing. Move between *MS* and *PS* by double clicking on the button below the *Command line* that will be either *Model* or *Paper*.

By typing *-Vports* in the *Command line* you will obtain the following prompts:

On/Off: Selects and turns off viewports to save regeneration time; leave at least one on.

Hideplot: When turned on, it removes the hidden lines from the selected viewports.

Fit: Makes a viewport fill the screen.

2/3/4: Lets you create an area and specify the number of viewports within it.

Restore: Recalls a viewport configuration *Saved* by *Vports*.

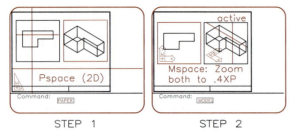

STEP 1   STEP 2

27.97 PS option: *Zoom to Scale*

Step 1 Double click in the paper space area (or select *Model* in the *Status* bar) to enter paper space and the cursor spans the screen. Since *PS* had limits of 12,9 and *MS* had limits of 24,20, the *MS* ports must be *Zoomed* to about 0.20 size for both to fit in the border.

Step 2 Double-click on one of the 3D ports to make it active. *Command*: Zoom (Enter)
All/Center/ . . . /<Scale (X/XP)>: .2XP (Enter)
The active port is scaled to 0.2 size to fit in the 2D border. Select and Zoom the other port to .2XP also.

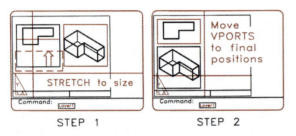

STEP 1   STEP 2

27.98 PS option: *Stretch*

Step 1 Double click in *Paper* to switch to paper space. Use *Stretch* to reduce the size of the viewport.

Step 2 *Move* the viewports to their final positions within the 2D border in paper space.

Figure 27.96 shows a 3D object drawn by the *Extrude* command in one of the 3D viewports and shows it simultaneously in a second port. Select an isometric *Vpoint* and double-click on a paper-space area to enter paper space. The cursor spans the screen in paper space. Now the drawing must be scaled.

The paper-space *Limits* are 12,9 inside of which are two model-space viewports each with *Limits* of 24,20. These *MS* ports must be sized to fit, which requires calculations. The combined width of the two 24-in.-wide model spaces is 48. When scaled to half size, their width is 24, too

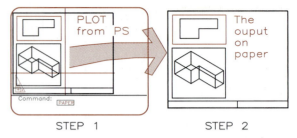

STEP 1   STEP 2

27.99 PS option: *Plot*

Step 1 *Main menu> File> Plot* and give specifications for plotters and plotting from paper space.

Step 2 The size-A layout is plotted to show both 2D (paper space) and 3D (model space) drawings in the same plot.

wide to fit. If scaled to 0.20 (two-tenths), their width is 9.6, small enough to fit inside the A-size border.

From model space, type Zoom and use the *X/XP* (2/10XP or 0.2XP) option to size the contents of each viewport (**Fig. 27.97**). This factor changes the width limit of each viewport from 24 to 4.8, with both drawings having the same scale on the screen. In other words, you may scale viewports with width limits of 24 inches to a full-size width of 4.8 in paper space.

Double-click on a paper-space area to enter paper space and use *Stretch* to reduce the size of the *Vports* outlines (**Fig. 27.98**). Reposition the model-space views for plotting with *Move*.

Plotting must be performed from *Paper Space* for both the 2D and 3D drawings to be plotted at the same time, including the outlines of the model-space ports (**Fig. 27.99**). To remove the window outlines, *Change* them to a separate *Layer* (*Window,* for example), *Freeze* it, and *Plot* in the usual manner.

Remove hidden lines when plotting by selecting a *Vport* from *PS*, right-clicking in the port, and selecting *Hide Plot* from the pop-up menu. Repeat this for each port in which the lines are to be hidden when plotted. Use *Vplayer* to select *3D viewports* from paper space in which layers can be turned *Off* or *Frozen* while remaining *On* or *Thawed* in other viewports.

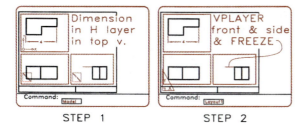

STEP 1   STEP 2

27.100 Dimensioning: Width and Depth

Step 1 Create layer *H* and set it *On*. Set the *Dimscale* variable to *0* and the dimensioning variables in model space will match those in paper space. Move the *UCS icon* to the plane of the dimension (top view) and apply the width and depth by snapping to the endpoints of the part.

Step 2 When a dimension is applied in one viewport it is shown in all 3D viewports, and the dimensioning variables are the same size in *MS* as in *PS*. Dimensions appear as edges in the front and side views.

27.27 Dimensioning in 3D

Dimensions can be applied to objects in model space to match the dimensioning variables set for paper space by setting *Dimscale=0* (**Fig. 27.100**). Create two new layers, *H* and *F*, on which horizontal and frontal dimensions will be placed. Set associative dimensions on *(Dimaso= On)*, set the layer *H* on, set the *UCS* to *Plan* in the top view (see xy icon), and *Snap* to the endpoints of the object to attach width and depth dimensions to the top view. These dimensions appear as edges in the front and side views.

Select the front viewport and rotate the *xy* icon parallel to the frontal plane *(UCS/X/ 90°)* as shown in **Fig. 27.101**. Attach a vertical height dimension to the object by *Snapping* to the endpoints of the front view and the dimension appears as an edge in the top and side views.

Since the horizontal dimensions cannot be seen in the front and side views, select these ports, type <u>Vplayer</u>, and <u>Freeze</u> the *H* layer (**Fig. 27.102**). Since the vertical dimensions cannot be seen in the top and side views, select these ports, type <u>Vplayer</u>, and <u>Freeze</u> the *F* layer. Other dimensions can be added and edited in this manner. Options under *Vplayer* that operate

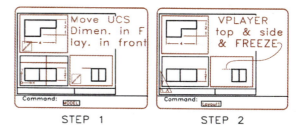

STEP 1   STEP 2

27.101 Dimensioning: Height

Step 1 Create layer *F* and set it *On*. Move the *UCS icon* to the plane of the frontal dimension. Apply the dimension of height in the front view.

Step 2 The height dimension appears as an edge in the top and side views.

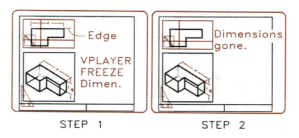

STEP 1   STEP 2

27.102 Dimensioning: *Vplayer* option

Step 1 Since the dimensions of depth and width in the top view are not readable in the side view, set *Vplayer* to *On*, select the border of the side view viewport (while in *PS*) and *Freeze* layer *H*.

Step 2 The dimensions are removed in the side view. *Freeze* the *F* layer in the top and side views also in this same manner.

from paper space are *Freeze, Thaw, Reset, Newfrz*, and *Vpvisdflt*.

Freeze/Thaw: Allows specified layers in selected *Vports* to be frozen or thawed. *Thaw* does not work on globally frozen layers.

Reset: Changes visibility of one or more layers in selected *Vports* to their current default setting.

Newfrz: Creates a new layer that is visible in the current viewport and frozen in the rest.

Vpvisdflt: Used to set default visibility by viewport for any layer. The default setting makes layers frozen or thawed in new viewports.

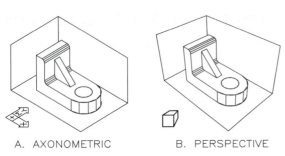

A. AXONOMETRIC   B. PERSPECTIVE

27.103 This part is used to illustrate rendering techniques in the following examples.

27.104 *Main menu > View> Toolbars> Render* to obtain this toolbar for rendering 3D models.

27.28 Render

Rendering is the process that gives 3D objects a realistic appearance by adding color, lighting, and materials to them. The following examples illustrate how 3D drawings are rendered.

The bracket from **Fig. 27.77** is displayed in two viewports as an axonometric and a perspective (**Fig. 27.103**). From the *Render* toolbar in (**Fig. 27.104**), select *Render Preferences* to obtain the dialogue box shown in **Fig. 27.105**. Rendering options are *Smooth Shading, Apply Materials, Shadows,* and *Render Cache.* The *More Options* box gives *Gouraud* and *Phong* options to specify rendering quality (**Fig. 27.106**). The *Phong* option gives the smoother, more realistic rendering.

While a view of the bracket is on the screen, select *Render* from the *Render* toolbar, or type <u>Render</u>, and the *Render dialogue* box appears (**Fig. 27.105**). Make selections and the bracket is rendered as shown in **Fig. 27.107**.

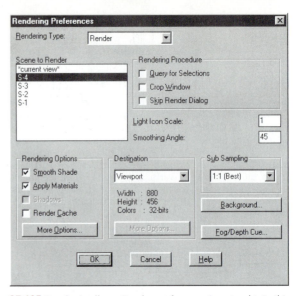

27.105 *Render toolbar> Render preferences* icon to obtain this dialogue box.

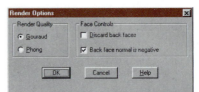

27.106 The *More options* button in the *Render Preferences* menu gives this dialogue box of options.

27.107 A sample rendering of the angle bracket.

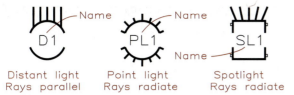

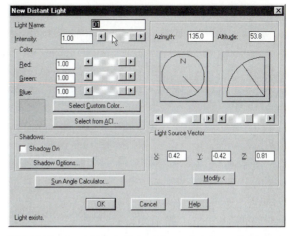

27.108 *Distant light, point light*, and *spotlight* symbols are placed on drawings to indicate the positions for lighting.

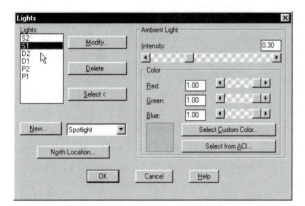

27.109 The *Lights dialogue* box is used to set and modify lights for rendering.

27.29 Lights

A rendering is enhanced by *point lights, distant lights, spotlights,* and *ambient lighting* that are under your control.

Point light emits rays in all directions from a point source.

Distant light emits parallel beams like those of sunlight.

Spotlight emits a cone of light to a target surface.

Ambient light comes from no particular source and provides a constant illumination to all surfaces of an object.

New Lights

Light sources can be added to a drawing and indicated with the symbols shown in **Fig. 27.108**. From the *Render* toolbar, select *Lights* to get the *Lights* dialogue box shown in **Fig. 27.109** where several lights are listed. *Select Distant*

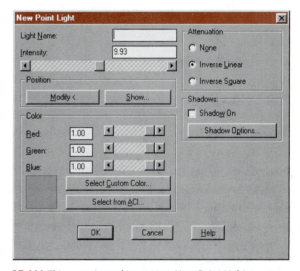

27.110 The *New Distant Light* dialogue box is used to create and name a new light source.

27.111 This menu is used to create a *New Point Light.*

Light next to the *New* button, pick *New* to get the *New Distant Light* dialogue box (**Fig. 27.110**). From this menu, you can name the distant light, set its directions, and pick its colors. Select the *Distant Light* button and pick *Ok* (**Fig. 27.110**). *Light Intensity* (0=off, 1=bright) is set with the slider bar or by typing. Leave intensity set to 1, select *Ok* to return to *Lights* where D2 is listed, and pick *Ok* to exit. Select *Render* from the pull-down menu to obtain a new image of the bracket using distant light D2.

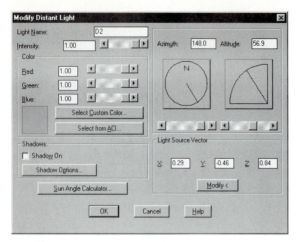

27.112 The *Modify Distant Light* dialogue box is used to make changes in an existing *Distant Lights*.

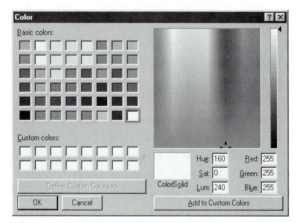

27.113 *Render toolbar> Lights icon> Select Custom Color> Color* menu is displayed for selecting colors.

If you had selected *Point Light* and *New,* the *New Point Light dialogue* box would have appeared on the screen (**Fig. 27.111**). This dialogue box is different from the *New Distant Light* box since point lights have different characteristics.

Modifying Lights

Select *Lights* from the *Render* toolbar menu, select *Distant Light* to obtain the dialogue box shown in **Fig. 27.109** and double click on *D1*

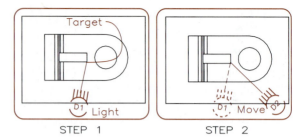

27.114 Moving a light

Step 1 Select *Modify* from the *Modify Distant Light* dialogue box (Fig. 27.112) and you are transferred to the drawing. *Enter light target <current>:* (Enter)

Select current target.

Step 2 *Enter light location <current>:* .XY (Enter)

(Need Z): 6 (Enter) The *Modify Distant Light* box reappears. Click on *Ok* to exit. *Render* the bracket.

(distant light) to obtain the *Modify Distant Light* box (**Fig. 27.112**). The *Select Custom Color* button can be picked to obtain the *Color* dialogue box (**Fig. 27.113**). Experiment with *Intensity* at other settings (for example, 0.2 and 0.6) and render an object to observe variations in the brightness of the image.

Moving Lights

To move distant light *D2,* type Plan to get a top view of the bracket, where the light sources are shown as symbols. Each light can be moved with the *Move* command (**Fig. 27.114**). You can also select *Modify* from the *Light* menu, pick distant light *D1*, and pick *Modify* to obtain the *Modify Distant Light* menu (**Fig. 27.112**). Select *Modify* under the heading, *Light Source Vector,* and the screen returns to the drawing where you are prompted for the direction of the light rays. The direction can also be changed by the *Azimuth* and *Altitude* adjustments (**Fig. 27.112**).

In Step 1 (**Fig. 27.114**), the prompt *"Enter light direction To <current>:"* appears with a rubber-band line attached to the target. Press (Enter) to retain the current target and obtain a rubber-band line attached to it and the prompt *"Enter light direction FROM <current>."* In Step 2, type .XY, pick the light location with the cursor

A. Distant Light: Pos. 1   B. distant Light: Pos. 2

27.115 A comparison of the rendered views of the bracket with *Distant Light D1* and *D2* in positions 1 and 2.

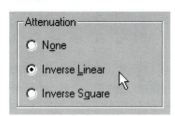

27.116 The type of point light fall-off can be specified as either *Inverse Linear* or *Inverse Square*.

and respond to the prompt, *"of (Need Z)"* with <u>6</u> to locate the light source and establish the direction of the parallel light rays.

Type <u>Vpoint</u> and settings of <u>1,-1,1</u> to obtain an isometric view of the bracket. Select *Render* from the *Render* toolbar to observe the original and new light positions (**Fig. 27.115**).

Light Fall-off

The characteristic whereby light becomes dimmer as it travels farther from its source is called *fall-off*. *Point Lights* and *Spotlights* are affected by fall-off; *Distant* and *Ambient Lights* have uniform intensity at all distances and are not affected. From the *Lights menu*, select *P1 (Point Light)*, select *Modify* to get the *Modify Point Light* box, which has an *Attenuation* area. The options available here are *None, Inverse Linear*, and *Inverse Square* (**Fig. 27.116**):

None is a light with no fall-off, giving all objects the same brightness.

Inverse Linear makes a surface that is 4 units from the light one-fourth as bright, and one-eighth as bright when it is 8 units away.

A. Inverse Linear   B. Inverse Square

27.117 *Light Fall-off* options are *None, Inverse Linear,* and *Inverse Square.* By using *Inverse Linear,* an object 4 units away is one-fourth as bright as one that is 1 unit away from the light. By using *Inverse Square,* an object 4 units away is one-sixteenth as bright as one that is 1 unit away. The options are not available for *Distant Lights.*

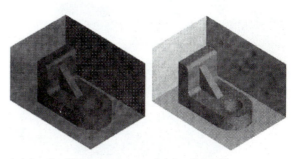

A. Intensity=0.30   B. Intensity=0.60

27.118 A comparison of *Ambient light* set at two intensities is shown here.

Inverse Square makes an object 4 units from the light one-sixteenth as bright, and one-sixty-fourth as bright when 8 units away.

A comparison of the effects of lighting set to *Inverse Linear* and *Inverse Square* is shown in **Fig. 27.117**.

Ambient Light

So far, ambient light has been set to 0.3. From the *Render* toolbar obtain the *Lights dialogue* box and set ambient intensity to 0.85 by typing or using the slider bar. The variation in lighting the bracket is shown in **Fig. 27.118**.

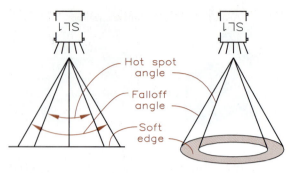

27.119 The definitions of the characteristics of a spotlight are shown here.

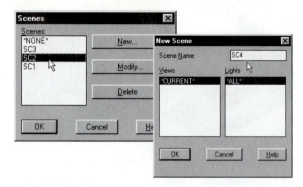

27.121 *Render toolbar> Scenes* icon gives the *Scenes* dialogue box where the *New* button can be picked to obtain the *New Scene* box for naming a new scene.

27.120 An example of a *Spotlight* applied to the rendered bracket.

Spotlights

Spotlights emit cones of light, as defined in **Fig. 27.119**, to highlight features. The creation of a *Spotlight* begins from the *Lights* dialogue box (**Fig. 27.109**) where *Spotlight* and *New* are selected to display the *Create New Spotlight* box. You can see the effects of a spotlight in **Fig. 27.120**.

27.30 Working with Scenes

Views and light settings can be saved in combinations as *Scenes*, which can have several lights (or no lights), but only one *View*. A viewpoint of a drawing can be saved as a *View* by typing *View*

and giving it a name. Other viewpoints can be saved in this manner. To recall a *View*, type *View* and *Restore*, and give its name when prompted.

Restored Views of the bracket used in the previous examples are selected from *Scenes* of the *Render* toolbar menu to obtain the *Scenes* dialogue box (**Fig. 27.121**). Select *New* and the *New Scene* box appears in which all model-space *Views* and lights are listed. Type the name of the *Scene* in the box (*S2*, for example). The name is truncated to eight characters if it is longer than eight. Select *V2* as the *View* in *S2*, select point-light *P1* and distant-light *D1*, select *OK*, and the *Scenes* dialogue box reappears. Other scenes can be created by using these steps.

If **None** were selected as the scene to render, all lights would be on in the current view. If no lights existed, an over-the-shoulder distant-light would be given. Select *S2* from the dialogue box, pick *OK*, and choose *Render* to obtain a rendered *S2*. A comparison of *S1* and *S2* is given in **Fig. 27.122** after they have been rendered.

A *Scene* can be modified by selecting it from the *Scenes* dialogue box (**Fig. 27.121**) and picking *Modify* to obtain the *Modify Scene* dialogue box, which is similar to the *New Scene* box. Different lights can be selected or deselected.

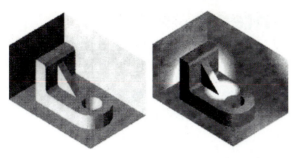

A. Scene 1: 2 Lights

B. Scene 2: 2 Lights and a Spotlight

27.122 Examples of *Scenes* are shown here with different combinations of lights.

Select *Ok* to keep your modifications and return to the *Scenes* dialogue box, select *Ok* to exit and *Render* the modified *Scene.*

27.31 Materials

Select the *Materials Library* icon from the *Render toolbar* to get the *Materials Library dialogue* box (**Fig. 27.123**). The material of an object determines the reflective quality of its surfaces from dull to shiny. Materials can be selected one at a time from the listing and previewed by selecting the *Preview* button. To add a material to the *Materials List* for future use, pick *Import*. Click on *Save* to add the material to the *Materials List* file. Type *Ok* to exit the *Materials Library* dialogue box and return to the drawing.

From the *Render toolbar,* select *Materials* to get the dialogue box shown in **Fig. 27.123**. To *Attach* a material to a part, select it from the list, select *Attach,* and the drawing reappears. You are prompted, *"Select objects to attach 'MATL' to:"* Select the part and the *Materials dialogue* box returns; click on *Ok* to exit. *Render* the object to see the results.

By selecting *Modify* from the *Materials dialogue* box (**Fig. 27.123**), the *Modify Standard Materials* box (**Fig. 27.124**) lets you modify the selected material. These settings are *Color, Ambient light, Reflection,* and *Roughness.*

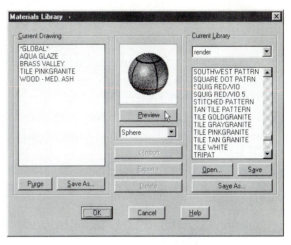

27.123 Select the *Materials Library* icon from the *Render* toolbar to get this dialogue box that gives the materials that can be assigned to 3D models. A preview of their application is shown on the sphere.

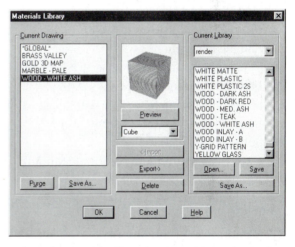

27.124 The Materials *Library* box is used to preview various materials as they are assigned to a part.

Experiment with different settings and observe the results of these changes by picking *Preview.*

Problems

The problems at the ends of the previous chapters can be drawn and plotted using the computer graphics techniques covered in this chapter and in previous chapters.

Appendix Contents

LENGTH

1 millimeter (mm) = 0.03937 inch
1 centimeter (cm) = 0.39370 inch
1 meter (m) = 39.37008 inches
1 meter = 3.2808 feet
1 meter = 1.0936 yards
1 kilometer (km) = 0.6214 miles
1 inch = 25.4 millimeters
1 inch = 2.54 centimeters
1 foot = 304.8 millimeters
1 foot = 0.3048 meters
1 yard = 0.9144 meters
1 mile = 1.609 kilometers

AREA

1 square millimeter = 0.00155 square inch
1 square centimeter = 0.155 square inch
1 square meter = 10.764 square feet
1 square meter = 1.196 square yards
1 square kilometer = 0.3861 square mile
1 square inch = 645.2 square millimeters
1 square inch = 6.452 square centimeters
1 square foot = 929 square centimeters
1 square foot = 0.0929 square meter
1 square yard = 0.836 square meter
1 square mile = 2.5899 square kilometers

DRY CAPACITY

1 cubic centimeter (cm3) = 0.061 cubic inches
1 liter = 0.0353 cubic foot
1 liter = 61.023 cubic inches
1 cubic meter (m3) = 35.315 cubic feet
1 cubic meter = 1.308 cubic yards
1 cubic inch = 16.38706 cubic centimeters
1 cubic foot = 0.02832 cubic meter
1 cubic foot = 28.317 liters
1 cubic yard = 0.7646 cubic meter

LIQUID CAPACITY

1 liter = 1.0567 U.S. quarts
1 liter = 0.2642 U.S. gallons
1 liter = 0.2200 Imperial gallons
1 cubic meter = 264.2 U.S. gallons
1 cubic meter = 219.969 Imperial gallons
1 U.S. quart = 0.946 liters
1 Imperial quart = 1.136 liters
1 U.S. gallon = 3.785 liters
1 Imperial gallon = 4.546 liters

WEIGHT

1 gram (g) = 15.432 grains
1 gram = 0.03215 ounce troy
1 gram = 0.03527 ounce avoirdupois
1 kilogram (kg) = 35.274 ounces avoirdupois
1 kilogram = 2.2046 pounds
1000 kilograms = 1 metric ton (t)
1000 kilograms = 1.1023 tons of 2000 pounds
1000 kilograms = 0.9842 tons of 2240 pounds
1 ounce avoirdupois = 28.35 grams
1 ounce troy = 31.103 grams
1 pound = 453.6 grams
1 pound = 0.4536 kilogram
1 ton of 2240 pounds = 1016 kilograms
1 ton of 2240 pounds = 1.016 metric tons
1 grain = 0.0648 gram
1 metric ton = 0.9842 tons of 2240 pounds
1 metric ton = 2204.6 pounds

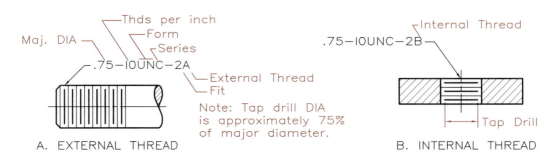

A. EXTERNAL THREAD

B. INTERNAL THREAD

Note: Tap drill DIA is approximately 75% of major diameter.

Nominal Diameter	Basic Diameter	Coarse NC & UNC		Fine NF & UNF		Extra Fine NEF/UNEF	
		Thds per in.	Tap Drill DIA	Thds per in.	Tap Drill DIA	Thds per in.	Tap Drill DIA
0	.060			80	.0469		
1	.073	64	No. 53	72	No. 53		
2	.086	56	No. 50	64	No. 50		
3	.099	48	No. 47	56	No. 45		
4	.112	40	No. 43	48	No. 42		
5	.125	40	No. 38	44	No. 37		
6	.138	32	No. 36	40	No. 33		
8	.164	32	No. 29	36	No. 29		
10	.190	24	No. 25	32	No. 21		
12	.216	24	No. 16	28	No. 14	32	No. 13
1/4	.250	20	No. 7	28	No. 3	32	.2189
5/16	.3125	18	F	24	I	32	.2813
3/8	.375	16	.3125	24	Q	32	.3438
7/16	.4375	14	U	20	.3906	28	.4062
1/2	.500	13	.4219	20	.4531	28	.4688
9/16	.5625	12	.4844	18	.5156	24	.5156
5/8	.625	11	.5313	18	.5781	24	.5781
11/16	.6875	...	...	...	...	24	.6406
3/4	.750	10	.6563	16	.6875	20	.7031
13/16	.8125	...	...	...	...	20	.7656
7/8	.875	9	.7656	14	.8125	20	.8281
15/16	.9375	...	...	...	...	20	.8906

Nominal Diameter	Basic Diameter	Coarse NC & UNC		Fine NF & UNF		Extra Fine NEF/UNEF	
		Thds per in.	Tap Drill DIA	Thds per in.	Tap Drill DIA	Thds per in.	Tap Drill DIA
1	1.000	8	.875	12	.922	20	.953
1-1/16	1.063	...	...	...	...	18	1.000
1-1/8	1.125	7	.904	12	1.046	18	1.070
1-3/16	1.188	...	...	...	...	18	1.141
1-1/4	1.250	7	1.109	12	1.172	18	1.188
1-5/16	1.313	...	...	...	...	18	1.266
1-3/8	1.375	6	1.219	12	1.297	18	1.313
1-7/16	1.438	...	...	...	...	18	1.375
1-1/2	1.500	6	1.344	12	1.422	18	1.438
1-9/16	1.563	...	...	...	...	18	1.500
1-5/8	1.625	...	...	...	...	18	1.563
1-11/16	1.688	...	...	...	...	18	1.625
1-3/4	1.750	5	1.563	...	...	...	...
2	2.000	4.5	1.781	...	...	...	...
2-1/4	2.250	4.5	2.031	...	...	...	...
2-1/2	2.500	4	2.250	...	...	...	...
2-3/4	2.750	4	2.500	...	...	...	...
3	3.000	4	2.750	...	...	...	...
3-1/4	3.250	4	...	...	...	...	...
3-1/2	3.500	4	...	...	...	...	...
3-3/4	3.750	4	...	...	...	...	...
4	4.000	4	...	...	...	...	...

Source: ANSI/ASME B1.1—1989

Appendix 3 • Screw Threads: American National and Unified (inches)
Constant-Pitch Threads

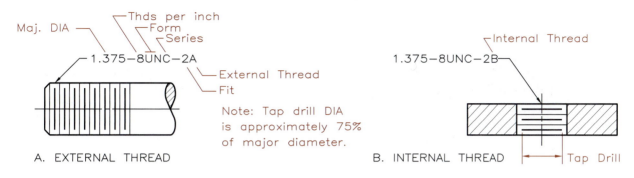

A. EXTERNAL THREAD

B. INTERNAL THREAD

Note: Tap drill DIA is approximately 75% of major diameter.

Nominal Diameter	8 Pitch 8N & 8UN		12 Pitch 12N & 12UN		16 Pitch 16N & 16UN		Nominal Diameter	8 Pitch 8N & 8UN		12 Pitch 12N & 12UN		16 Pitch 16N & 16UN	
	Thds per in.	Tap Drill DIA	Thds per in.	Tap Drill DIA	Thds per in.	Tap Drill DIA		Thds per in.	Tap Drill DIA	Thds per in.	Tap Drill DIA	Thds per in.	Tap Drill DIA
.500	...	...	12	.422	...	...	2.063	...	...	...	...	16	2.000
.563	...	...	12	.484	...	...	2.125	...	...	12	2.047	16	2.063
.625	...	...	12	.547	...	...	2.188	...	...	...	...	16	2.125
.688	...	...	12	.609	...	...	2.250	8	2.125	12	2.172	16	2.188
.750	...	...	12	.672	16	.688	2.313	...	...	...	...	16	2.250
.813	...	...	12	.734	16	.750	2.375	...	...	12	2.297	16	2.313
.875	...	...	12	.797	16	.813	2.438	...	...	...	...	16	2.375
.934	...	...	12	.859	16	.875	2.500	8	2.375	12	2.422	16	2.438
1.000	8	.875	12	.922	16	.938	2.625	...	...	12	2.547	16	2.563
1.063	...	...	12	.984	16	1.000	2.750	8	2.625	12	2.717	16	2.688
1.125	8	1.000	12	1.047	16	1.063	2.875	...	...	12	...	16	...
1.188	...	...	12	1.109	16	1.125	3.000	8	2.875	12	...	16	...
1.250	8	1.125	12	1.172	16	1.188	3.125	...	...	12	...	16	...
1.313	...	...	12	1.234	16	1.250	3.250	8	...	12	...	16	...
1.375	8	1.250	12	1.297	16	1.313	3.375	...	...	12	...	16	...
1.434	...	...	12	1.359	16	1.375	3.500	8	...	12	...	16	...
1.500	8	1.375	12	1.422	16	1.438	3.625	...	...	12	...	16	...
1.563	...	...	...	...	16	1.500	3.750	8	...	12	...	16	...
1.625	8	1.500	12	1.547	16	1.563	3.875	...	...	12	...	16	...
1.688	...	...	...	...	16	1.625	4.000	8	...	12	...	16	...
1.750	8	1.625	12	1.672	16	1.688	4.250	8	...	12	...	16	...
1.813	...	...	...	...	16	1.750	4.500	8	...	12	...	16	...
1.875	8	1.750	12	1.797	16	1.813	4.750	8	...	12	...	16	...
1.934	...	...	...	...	16	1.875	5.000	8	...	12	...	16	...
2.000	8	1.875	12	1.922	16	1.938	5.250	8	...	12	...	16	...

Source: ANSI/ASME B1.1—1989.

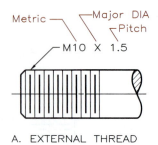

Metric — Major DIA — Pitch

M10 X 1.5

A. EXTERNAL THREAD

Note: Tap drill DIA is approximately 75% of major diameter.

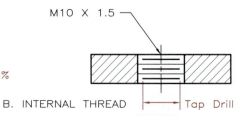

M10 X 1.5

B. INTERNAL THREAD — Tap Drill

COARSE		FINE		COARSE		FINE	
MAJ. DIA & THD PITCH	TAP DRILL	MAJ. DIA & THD PITCH	TAP DRILL	MAJ. DIA & THD PITCH	TAP DRILL	MAJ. DIA & THD PITCH	TAP DRILL
M1.6 × 0.35	1.25			M20 × 2.5	17.5	M20 × 1.5	18.5
M1.8 × 0.35	1.45			M22 × 2.5	19.5	M22 × 1.5	20.5
M2 × 0.4	1.6			M24 × 3	21.0	M24 × 2	22.0
M2.2 × 0.45	1.75			M27 × 3	24.0	M27 × 2	25.0
M2.5 × 0.45	2.05			M30 × 3.5	26.5	M30 × 2	28.0
M3 × 0.5	2.5			M33 × 3.5	29.5	M33 × 2	31.0
M3.5 × 0.6	2.9			M36 × 4	32.0	M36 × 3	33.0
M4 × 0.7	3.3			M39 × 4	35.0	M39 × 3	36.0
M4.5 × 0.75	3.75			M42 × 4.5	37.5	M42 × 3	39.0
M5 × 0.8	4.2			M45 × 4.5	40.5	M45 × 3	42.0
M6 × 1	5.0			M48 × 5	43.0	M48 × 3	45.0
M7 × 1	6.0			M52 × 5	47.0	M52 × 3	49.0
M8 × 1.25	6.8	M8 × 1	7.0	M56 × 5.5	50.5	M56 × 4	52.0
M9 × 1.25	7.75			M60 × 5.5	54.5	M60 × 4	56.0
M10 × 1.5	8.5	M10 × 1.25	8.75	M64 × 6	58.0	M64 × 4	60.0
M11 × 1.5	9.5			M68 × 6	62.0	M68 × 4	64.0
M12 × 1.75	10.3	M12 × 1.25	10.5	M72 × 6	66.0	M72 × 4	68.0
M14 × 2	12.0	M14 × 1.5	12.5	M80 × 6	74.0	M80 × 4	76.0
M16 × 2	14.0	M16 × 1.5	14.5	M90 × 6	84.0	M90 × 4	86.0
M18 × 2.5	15.5	M18 × 1.5	16.5	M100 × 6	94.0	M100 × 4	96.0

Source: ANSI/ASME B1.13

APPENDIX 5 • Square and Acme Threads

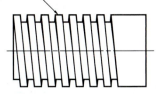

2.00−2.5 SQUARE

Typical thread note

Dimensions are in inches		Thds per inch			Thds per inch			Thds per inch
Size	Size		Size	Size		Size	Size	
3/8	.375	12	1-1/8	1.125	4	3	3.000	1-1/2
7/16	.438	10	1-1/4	1.250	4	3-1/4	3.125	1-1/2
1/2	.500	10	1-1/2	1.500	3	3-1/2	3.500	1-1/3
9/16	.563	8	1-3/4	1.750	2-1/2	3-3/4	3.750	1-1/3
5/8	.625	8	2	2.000	2-1/2	4	4.000	1-1/3
3/4	.75	6	2-1/4	2.250	2	4-1/4	4.250	1-1/3
7/8	.875	5	2-1/2	2.500	2	4-1/2	4.500	1
1	1.000	5	2-3/4	2.750	2	Larger		1

APPENDIX 6 • American Standard Taper Pipe Threads (NPT)

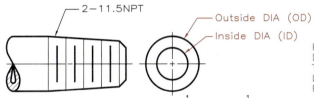

— 2−11.5NPT

— Outside DIA (OD)

— Inside DIA (ID)

PIPES THRU 12 INCHES IN DIA ARE SPECIFIED BY THEIR INSIDE DIAMETERS. LARGER PIPES ARE SPECIFIED BY THEIR OD.

$\frac{1}{16}$ DIA to $1\frac{1}{4}$ DIA   Dimensions in inches

Nominal ID	$\frac{1}{16}$	$\frac{1}{8}$	$\frac{1}{4}$	$\frac{3}{8}$	$\frac{1}{2}$	$\frac{3}{4}$	1	1-1/4
Outside DIA	0.313	0.405	0.540	0.675	0.840	1.050	1.315	1.660
Thds/Inch	27	27	18	18	14	14	$11\frac{1}{2}$	$11\frac{1}{2}$

$1\frac{1}{2}$ DIA to 6 DIA

Nominal ID	$1\frac{1}{2}$	2	$2\frac{1}{2}$	3	$3\frac{1}{2}$	4	5	6
Outside DIA	1.900	2.375	2.875	3.500	4.000	4.500	5.563	6.625
Thds/Inch	$11\frac{1}{2}$	$11\frac{1}{2}$	8	8	8	8	8	8

8 DIA to 24 DIA

Nominal ID	8	10	12	14 OD	16 OD	18 OD	20 OD	24 OD
Outside DIA	8.625	10.750	12.750	14.000	16.000	18.000	20.000	24.000
Thds/Inch	8	8	8	8	8	8	8	8

Source: ANSI B2.1.

Appendix 7 • Square Bolts (inches)

DIA	E Max.	F Max.	G Avg.	H Max.	R Max.
1/4	.250	.375	.530	.188	.031
5/16	.313	.500	.707	.220	.031
3/8	.375	.563	.795	.268	.031
7/16	.438	.625	.884	.316	.031
1/2	.500	.750	1.061	.348	.031
5/8	.625	.938	1.326	.444	.062
3/4	.750	1.125	1.591	.524	.062
7/8	.875	1.313	1.856	.620	.062
1	1.000	1.500	2.121	.684	.093
1-1/8	1.125	1.688	2.386	.780	.093
1-1/4	1.250	1.875	2.652	.876	.093
1-3/8	1.375	2.625	2.917	.940	.093
1-1/2	1.500	2.250	3.182	1.036	.093

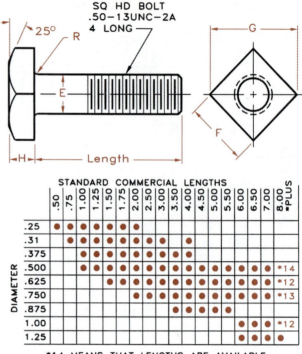

*14 MEANS THAT LENGTHS ARE AVAILABLE AT 1 INCH INCREMENTS UP 14 INCHES.

Appendix 8 • Square Nuts

Dimensions are in inches.

DIA	DIA	F Max.	G Avg.	H Max.
1/4	.250	.438	.619	.235
5/16	.313	.563	.795	.283
3/8	.375	.625	.884	.346
7/16	.438	.750	1.061	.394
1/2	.500	.813	1.149	.458
5/8	.625	1.000	1.414	.569
3/4	.750	1.125	1.591	.680
7/8	.875	1.313	1.856	.792
1	1.000	1.500	2.121	.903
1-1/8	1.125	1.688	2.386	1.030
1-1/4	1.250	1.875	2.652	1.126
1-3/8	1.375	1.063	2.917	1.237
1-1/2	1.500	2.250	3.182	1.348

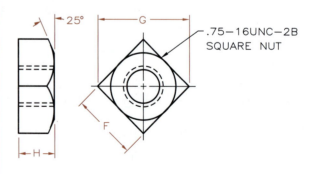

Dimensions are in inches.

DIA	E Max.	F Max.	G Avg.	H Max.	R Max.
1/4	.250	.438	.505	.163	.025
5/16	.313	.500	.577	.211	.025
3/8	.375	.563	.650	.243	.025
7/16	.438	.625	.722	.291	.025
1/2	.500	.750	.866	.323	.025
9/16	.563	.812	.938	.371	.045
5/8	.625	.938	1.083	.403	.045
3/4	.750	1.125	1.299	.483	.045
7/8	.875	1.313	1.516	.563	.065
1	1.000	1.500	1.732	.627	.095
1-1/8	1.125	1.688	1.949	.718	.095
1-1/4	1.250	1.875	2.165	.813	.095
1-3/8	1.375	2.063	2.382	.878	.095
1-1/2	1.500	2.250	2.598	.974	.095
1-3/4	1.750	2.625	3.031	1.134	.095
2	2.000	3.000	3.464	1.263	.095
2-1/4	2.250	3.375	3.897	1.423	.095
2-1/2	2.500	3.750	4.330	1.583	.095
2-3/4	2.750	4.125	4.763	1.744	.095
3	3.000	4.500	5.196	1.935	.095

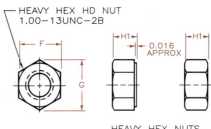

*10 MEANS THAT LENGTHS ARE AVAILABLE AT 1 INCH INCREMENTS UP TO 10 INCHES.

Appendix 10 • Hex Nuts and Hex Jam Nuts

MAJOR DIA		F Max.	G Avg.	H1 Max.	H2 Max.
1/4	.250	.438	.505	.226	.163
5/16	.313	.500	.577	.273	.195
3/8	.375	.563	.650	.337	.227
7/16	.438	.688	.794	.385	.260
1/2	.500	.750	.866	.448	.323
9/16	.563	.875	1.010	.496	.324
5/8	.625	.938	1.083	.559	.387
3/4	.750	1.125	1.299	.665	.446
7/8	.875	1.313	1.516	.776	.510
1	1.000	1.500	1.732	.887	.575
1-1/8	1.125	1.688	1.949	.899	.639
1-1/4	1.250	1.875	2.165	1.094	.751
1-3/8	1.375	2.063	2.382	1.206	.815
1-1/2	1.500	2.250	2.589	1.317	.880

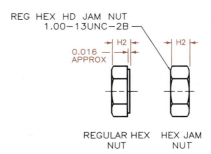

HEAVY HEX NUTS AND HEX JAM NUTS

REGULAR HEX NUT   HEX JAM NUT

APPENDIX 11 • Round Head Cap Screws

Dimensions are in inches.

DIA	D Max.	A Max.	H Avg.	J Max.	T Max.
1/4	.250	.437	.191	.075	.117
5/16	.313	.562	.245	.084	.151
3/8	.375	.625	.273	.094	.168
7/16	.438	.750	.328	.094	.202
1/2	.500	.812	.354	.106	.218
9/16	.563	.937	.409	.118	.252
5/8	.625	1.000	.437	.133	.270
3/4	.750	1.250	.546	.149	.338

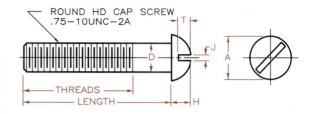

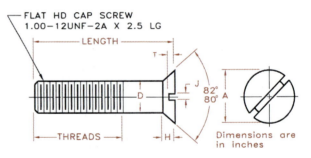

OTHER LENGTHS AND DIAMETERS ARE AVAILABLE, BUT THESE ARE THE MORE STANDARD ONES.

APPENDIX 12 • Flat Head Cap Screws

Dimensions are in inches.

DIA	D Max.	A Max.	H Avg.	J Max.	T Max.
1/4	.250	.500	.140	.075	.068
5/16	.313	.625	.177	.084	.086
3/8	.375	.750	.210	.094	.103
7/16	.438	.813	.210	.094	.103
1/2	.500	.875	.210	.106	.103
9/16	.563	1.000	.244	.118	.120
5/8	.625	1.125	.281	.133	.137
3/4	.750	1.375	.352	.149	.171
7/8	.875	1.625	.423	.167	.206
1	1.000	1.875	.494	.188	.240
1-1/8	1.125	2.062	.529	.196	.257
1-1/4	1.250	2.312	.600	.211	.291
1-3/8	1.375	2.562	.665	.226	.326
1-1/2	1.500	2.812	.742	.258	.360

OTHER LENGTHS AND DIAMETERS ARE AVAILABLE, BUT THESE ARE THE MORE STANDARD ONES.

APPENDIX 13 • Fillister Head Cap Screws

Dimensions are in inches.

DIA	D Max.	A Max.	H Avg.	J Max.	T Max.
1/4	.250	.375	.172	.075	.097
5/16	.313	.437	.203	.084	.115
3/8	.375	.562	.250	.094	.142
7/16	.438	.625	.297	.094	.168
1/2	.500	.750	.328	.106	.193
9/16	.563	.812	.375	.118	.213
5/8	.625	.875	.422	.133	.239
3/4	.750	1.000	.500	.149	.283
7/8	.875	1.125	.594	.167	.334
1	1.000	1.312	.656	.188	.371

Source: ANSI B18.6.2.

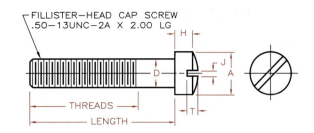

FILLISTER—HEAD CAP SCREW
.50—13UNC—2A X 2.00 LG

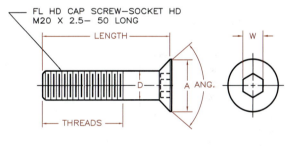

Appendix 14 • Flat Socket Head Cap Screws

Diameter mm	inches	Pitch	A	Ang.	W
M3	.118	.5	6	90	2
M4	.157	.7	8	90	2.5
M5	.197	.8	10	90	3
M6	.236	1	12	90	4
M8	.315	1.25	16	90	5
M10	.394	1.5	20	90	6
M12	.472	1.75	24	90	8
M14	.551	2	27	90	10
M16	.630	2	30	90	10
M20	.787	2.5	36	90	12

FL HD CAP SCREW—SOCKET HD
M20 X 2.5— 50 LONG

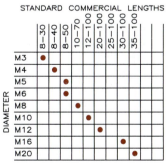

DIA 8—16: LENGTHS AT INTERVALS OF 2 MM
DIA 20—100: LENGTHS AT INTERVALS OF 5 MM

APPENDIX 15 • Socket Head Cap Screws

Diameter mm	inches	Pitch	A	H	W
M3	.118	.5	6	3	2
M4	.157	.7	8	4	3
M5	.187	.8	10	5	4
M6	.236	1	12	6	6
M8	.315	1.25	16	8	6
M10	.394	1.5	20	10	8
M12	.472	1.75	24	12	10
M14	.551	2	27	14	12
M16	.630	2	30	16	14
M20	.787	2.5	36	20	17

APPENDIX 16 • Round Head Machine Screws

Dimensions are in inches.

DIA	D Max.	A Max.	H Avg.	J Max.	T Max.
0	.060	.113	.053	.023	.039
1	.073	.138	.061	.026	.044
2	.086	.162	.069	.031	.048
3	.099	.187	.078	.035	.053
4	.112	.211	.086	.039	.058
5	.125	.236	.095	.043	.063
6	.138	.260	.103	.048	.068
8	.164	.309	.120	.054	.077
10	.190	.359	.137	.060	.087
12	.216	.408	.153	.067	.096
1/4	.250	.472	.175	.075	.109
5/16	.313	.590	.216	.084	.132
3/8	.375	.708	.256	.094	.155
7/16	.438	.750	.328	.094	.196
1/2	.500	.813	.355	.106	.211
9/16	.563	.938	.410	.118	.242
5/8	.625	1.000	.438	.133	.258
3/4	.750	1.250	.547	.149	.320

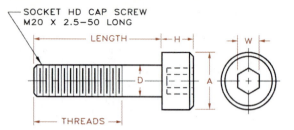

SOCKET HD CAP SCREW
M20 X 2.5–50 LONG

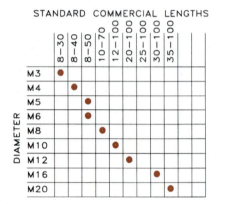

STANDARD COMMERCIAL LENGTHS

DIA 8–16: LENGTHS AT INTERVALS OF 2 MM
DIA 20–100: LENGTHS AT INTERVALS OF 5 MM

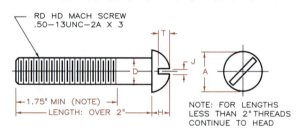

RD HD MACH SCREW
.50–13UNC–2A X 3

1.75" MIN (NOTE)
LENGTH: OVER 2"

NOTE: FOR LENGTHS
LESS THAN 2" THREADS
CONTINUE TO HEAD

STANDARD LENGTHS

OTHER LENGTHS AND DIAMETERS
ARE AVAILABLE; THESE ARE THE
MORE STANDARD ONES.

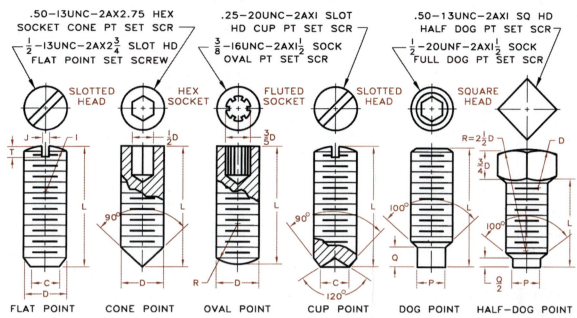

D	I	J	T	R	C		P		Q	q
	Radius of Headless Crown	Width of Slot	Depth of Slot	Oval Point Radius	Diamter of Cup and Flat Points		Diameter of Dog Point		Length of Dog Point	
Nominal Size					Max	Min	Max	Min	Full	Half
5 0.125	0.125	0.023	0.031	0.094	0.067	0.057	0.083	0.078	0.060	0.030
6 0.138	0.138	0.025	0.035	0.109	0.047	0.064	0.092	0.087	0.070	0.035
8 0.164	0.164	0.029	0.041	0.125	0.087	0.076	0.109	0.103	0.080	0.040
10 0.190	0.190	0.032	0.048	0.141	0.102	0.088	0.127	0.120	0.090	0.045
12 0.216	0.216	0.036	0.054	0.156	0.115	0.101	0.144	0.137	0.110	0.055
$\frac{1}{4}$ 0.250	0.250	0.045	0.063	0.188	0.132	0.118	0.156	0.149	0.125	0.063
$\frac{5}{16}$ 0.3125	0.313	0.051	0.076	0.234	0.172	0.156	0.203	0.195	0.156	0.078
$\frac{3}{8}$ 0.375	0.375	0.064	0.094	0.281	0.212	0.194	0.250	0.241	0.188	0.094
$\frac{7}{16}$ 0.4375	0.438	0.072	0.190	0.328	0.252	0.232	0.297	0.287	0.219	0.109
$\frac{1}{2}$ 0.500	0.500	0.081	0.125	0.375	0.291	0.270	0.344	0.344	0.250	0.125
$\frac{9}{16}$ 0.5625	0.563	0.091	0.141	0.422	0.332	0.309	0.391	0.379	0.281	0.140
$\frac{5}{8}$ 0.625	0.625	0.102	0.156	0.469	0.371	0.347	0.469	0.456	0.313	0.156
$\frac{3}{4}$ 0.750	0.750	0.129	0.188	0.563	0.450	0.425	0.563	0.549	0.375	0.188

Dimensions for the set screws shown in ANSI Fig. 18.44 (dimensions in inches)

Source: Courtesy of ANSI; B18.6.2.

Appendix 18 • Cotter Pins: American National Standard

Nominal Diameter	Maximum DIA A	Minimum DIA B	Hole Size
0.031	0.032	0.063	0.047
0.047	0.048	0.094	0.063
0.062	0.060	0.125	0.078
0.078	0.076	0.156	0.094
0.094	0.090	0.188	0.109
0.109	0.104	0.219	0.125
0.125	0.120	0.250	0.141
0.141	0.176	0.281	0.156
0.156	0.207	0.313	0.172
0.188	0.176	0.375	0.203
0.219	0.207	0.438	0.234
0.250	0.225	0.500	0.266
0.312	0.280	0.625	0.313
0.375	0.335	0.750	0.375
0.438	0.406	0.875	0.438
0.500	0.473	1.000	0.500
0.625	0.598	1.250	0.625
0.750	0.723	1.500	0.750

Source: Courtesy of ANSI: B18.8.1—1983.

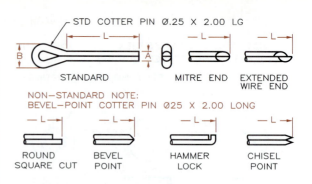

Appendix 19 • Straight Pins

Nominal DIA	Diameter A		Chamfer B
	Max	Min	
0.062	0.0625	0.0605	0.015
0.094	0.0937	0.0917	0.015
0.109	0.1094	0.1074	0.015
0.125	0.1250	0.1230	0.015
0.156	0.1562	0.1542	0.015
0.188	0.1875	0.1855	0.015
0.219	0.2187	0.2167	0.015
0.250	0.2500	0.2480	0.015
0.312	0.3125	0.3095	0.015
0.375	0.3750	0.3720	0.030
0.438	0.4345	0.4345	0.030
0.500	0.4970	0.4970	0.030

Source: Courtesy of ANSI: B5.20.

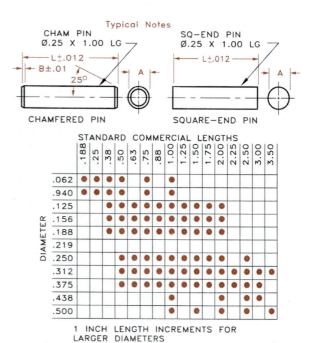

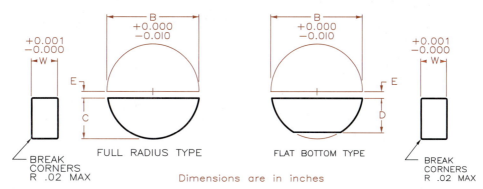

FULL RADIUS TYPE   FLAT BOTTOM TYPE

BREAK CORNERS R .02 MAX

Dimensions are in inches

Key No.	W × B	C Max.	D Max.	E
204	1/16 × 1/2	.203	.194	.047
304	3/32 × 1/2	.203	.194	.047
404	1/8 × 1/2	.203	.194	.047
305	3/32 × 5/8	.250	.240	.063
405	1/8 × 5/8	.250	.240	.063
505	5/32 × 5/8	.250	.240	.063
406	1/8 × 3/4	.313	.303	.063

Key No.	W × B	C Max.	D Max.	E
506	5/32 × 3/4	.313	.303	.063
606	3/16 × 3/4	.313	.303	.063
507	5/32 × 7/8	.375	.365	.063
607	3/16 × 7/8	.375	.365	.063
807	1/4 × 7/8	.375	.365	.063
608	3/16 × 1	.438	.428	.063
609	3/16 × 1-1/8	.484	.475	.078

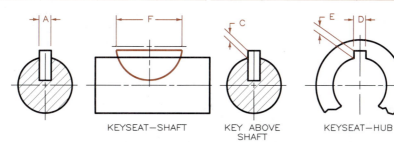

KEYSEAT—SHAFT   KEY ABOVE SHAFT   KEYSEAT—HUB

Key No.	A Min.	C +.005 −.000	F	D +.005 −.000	E +.005 −.000
204	.0615	.0312	.500	.0635	.0372
304	.0928	.0469	.500	.0948	.0529
404	.1240	.0625	.500	.1260	.0685
305	.0928	.0625	.625	.0948	.0529
405	.1240	.0469	.625	.1260	.0685
505	.1553	.0625	.625	.1573	.0841
406	.1240	.0781	.750	.1260	.0685

Key No.	A Min.	C +.005 −.000	F	D +.005 −.000	E +.005 −.000
506	.1553	.0781	.750	.1573	.0841
606	.1863	.0937	.750	.1885	.0997
507	.1553	.0781	.875	.1573	.0841
607	.1863	.0937	.875	.1885	.0997
807	.2487	.1250	.875	.2510	.1310
608	.1863	.3393	1.000	.1885	.0997
609	.1863	.3853	1.125	.1885	.0997

KEY SIZES VS. SHAFT SIZES

Shaft DIA	to .375	to .500	to .750	to 1.313	to 1.188	to 1.448	to 1.750	to 2.125	to 2.500
Key Nos.	204	304 305	404 405 406	505 506 507	606 607 608 609	807 808 809	810 811 812	1011 1012	1211 1212

Appendix 21 • Standard Keys and Keyways

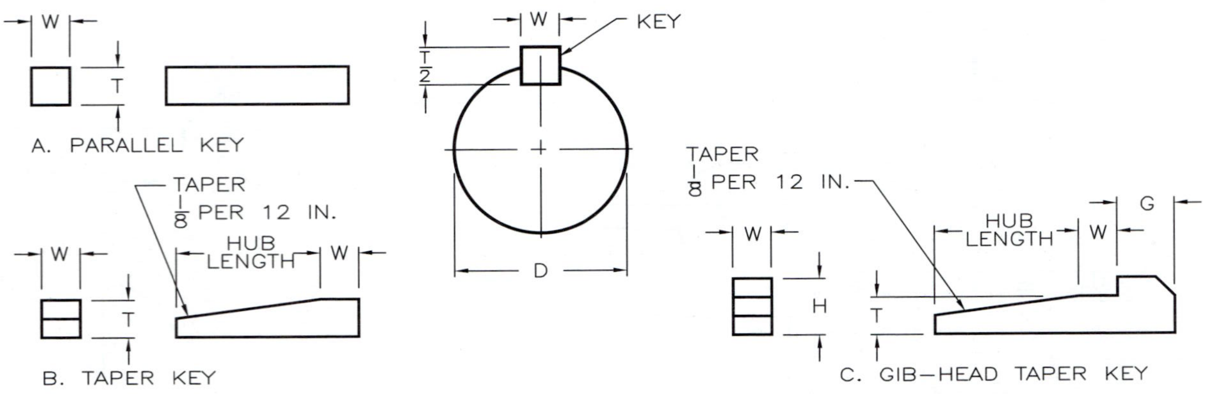

W
T
A. PARALLEL KEY
KEY
T/2
D
TAPER
1/8 PER 12 IN.
HUB LENGTH
W
T
B. TAPER KEY
TAPER
1/8 PER 12 IN.
HUB LENGTH
W
G
H
T
C. GIB–HEAD TAPER KEY

Sprocket Bore (= Shaft Diam.)	Keyway Dimensions — Inches		Key Dimensions—Inches			Gib Head Dimensions—Inches				Key Tolerances Taper and Gib Head	
	For Square Key	For Flat Key	Square	Flat	Tolerance on W and T	Square Key		Flat Key			
Inches D	Width W × Depth T/2	Width W × Depth T/2	Width W × Height T	Width W × Height T	(–)	H	G	H	G	W (–)	T (–)
1/2—9/16	1/8 × 1/16	1/8 × 3/64	1/8 × 1/8	1/8 × 3/32	0.002	1/4	7/32	3/16	1/8	0.002	0.002
5/8—7/8	3/16 × 3/32	3/16 × 1/16	3/16 × 3/16	3/16 × 1/8	0.002	5/16	9/32	1/4	3/16	0.002	0.002
13/16—1 1/4	1/4 × 1/8	1/4 × 3/32	1/4 × 1/4	1/4 × 3/16	0.002	7/16	11/32	5/16	1/4	0.002	0.002
1 5/16—1 3/8	5/16 × 5/32	5/16 × 1/8	5/16 × 5/16	5/16 × 1/4	0.002	9/16	13/32	3/8	5/16	0.002	0.002
1 7/16—1 3/4	3/8 × 3/16	3/8 × 1/8	3/8 × 3/8	3/8 × 1/4	0.002	11/16	15/32	7/16	3/8	0.002	0.002
1 13/16—2 1/4	1/2 × 1/4	1/2 × 3/16	1/2 × 1/2	1/2 × 3/8	0.0025	7/8	19/32	5/8	1/2	0.0025	0.0025
2 5/16—2 3/4	5/8 × 5/16	5/8 × 7/32	5/8 × 5/8	5/8 × 7/16	0.0025	1 1/16	23/32	3/4	5/8	0.0025	0.0025
2 7/8—3 1/4	3/4 × 3/8	3/4 × 1/4	3/4 × 3/4	3/4 × 1/2	0.0025	1 1/4	7/8	7/8	3/4	0.0025	0.0025
3 3/8—3 3/4	7/8 × 7/16	7/8 × 5/16	7/8 × 7/8	7/8 × 5/8	0.003	1 1/2	1	1 1/16	7/8	0.003	0.003
3 7/8—4 1/2	1 × 1/2	1 × 3/8	1 × 1	1 × 3/4	0.003	1 3/4	1 3/16	1 1/4	1	0.003	0.003
4 3/4—5 1/2	1 1/4 × 5/8	1 1/4 × 7/16	1 1/4 × 1 1/4	1 1/4 × 7/8	0.003	2	1 7/16	1 1/2	1 1/4	0.003	0.003
5 3/4—7 3/8	1 1/2 × 3/4	1 1/2 × 1/2	1 1/2 × 1 1/2	1 1/2 × 1	0.003	2 1/2	1 3/4	1 3/4	1 1/2	0.003	0.003
7 1/2—9 7/8	1 3/4 × 7/8	.. ..	1 3/4 × 1 3/4	.. ..	0.004	3	2	..	..	0.004	0.004
10—12 1/2	2 × 1	.. ..	2 × 2	.. ..	0.004	3 1/2	2 3/8	..	..	0.004	0.004

Standard Keyway Tolerances: Straight Keyway—Width (W) +.005 −.000 Depth (T/2) +.010 −.000

Taper Keyway—Width (W) +.005 −.000 Depth (T/2) +.000 −.010

APPENDIX 22 • Plain Washers (inches)

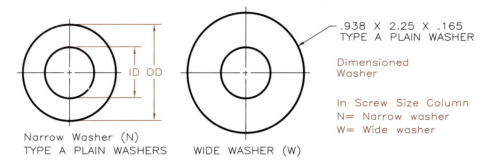

.938 X 2.25 X .165
TYPE A PLAIN WASHER

Dimensioned
Washer

In Screw Size Column
N= Narrow washer
W= Wide washer

Narrow Washer (N)
TYPE A PLAIN WASHERS

WIDE WASHER (W)

SCREW SIZE	ID SIZE	OD SIZE	THICK-NESS	SCREW SIZE	ID SIZE	OD SIZE	THICK-NESS
0.138	0.156	0.375	0.049	0.875 N	0.938	1.750	0.134
0.164	0.188	0.438	0.049	0.875 W	0.938	2.250	0.165
0.190	0.219	0.500	0.049	1.000 N	1.062	2.000	0.134
0.188	0.250	0.562	0.049	1.000 W	1.062	2.500	0.165
0.216	0.250	0.562	0.065	1.125 N	1.250	2.250	0.134
0.250 N	0.281	0.625	0.065	1.125 W	1.250	2.750	0.165
0.250 W	0.312	0.734	0.065	1.250 N	1.375	2.500	0.165
0.312 N	0.344	0.688	0.065	1.250 W	1.375	3.000	0.165
0.312 W	0.375	0.875	0.083	1.375 N	1.500	2.750	0.165
0.375 N	0.406	0.812	0.065	1.375 W	1.500	3.250	0.180
0.375 W	0.438	1.000	0.083	1.500 N	1.625	3.000	0.165
0.438 N	0.469	0.922	0.065	1.500 W	1.625	3.500	0.180
0.438 W	0.500	1.250	0.083	1.625	1.750	3.750	0.180
0.500 N	0.531	1.062	0.095	1.750	1.875	4.000	0.180
0.500 W	0.562	1.375	0.109	1.875	2.000	4.250	0.180
0.562 N	0.594	1.156	0.095	2.000	2.125	4.500	0.180
0.562 W	0.594	1.469	0.190	2.250	2.375	4.750	0.220
0.625 N	0.625	1.312	0.095	2.500	2.625	5.000	0.238
0.625 N	0.625	1.750	0.134	2.750	2.875	5.250	0.259
0.750 W	0.812	1.469	0.134	3.000	3.125	5.500	0.284
0.750 W	0.812	2.000	0.148				

SCREW SIZE	ID SIZE	OD SIZE	THICK-NESS
3	3.2	9	0.8
4	4.3	12	1
5	5.3	15	1.5
6	6.4	18	1.5
8	8.4	25	2
10	10.5	30	2.5
12	13	40	3
14	15	45	3
16	17	50	3
18	19	56	4
20	21	60	4
2.6	2.8	5.5	0.5
3	3.2	6	0.5
4	4.3	8	0.5
5	5.3	10	1.0
6	6.4	11	1.5
8	8.4	15	1.5
10	10.5	18	1.5
12	13	20	2.0
14	15	25	2.0
16	17	27	2.0
18	19	30	2.5
20	21	33	2.5

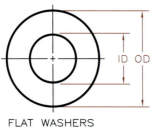

FLAT WASHERS
DIN 9021

17 X 27 X 2
WROUGHT WASHER

Dimensioned
Washer

DIN= German Industrial
Standard (ISO)

WROUGHT WASHERS
DIN 433

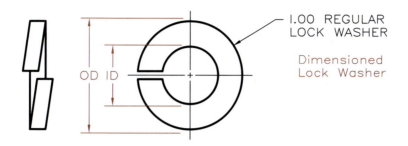

Dimensioned Lock Washer

LOCK WASHERS—inches

SCREW SIZE	ID SIZE	OD SIZE	THICK-NESS
0.164	0.168	0.175	0.040
0.190	0.194	0.202	0.047
0.216	0.221	0.229	0.056
0.250	0.255	0.263	0.062
0.312	0.318	0.328	0.078
0.375	0.382	0.393	0.094
0.438	0.446	0.459	0.109
0.500	0.509	0.523	0.125
0.562	0.572	0.587	0.141
0.625	0.636	0.653	0.156
0.688	0.700	0.718	0.172
0.750	0.763	0.783	0.188
0.812	0.826	1.367	0.203
0.875	0.890	1.464	0.219
0.938	0.954	1.560	0.234
1.000	1.017	1.661	0.250
1.062	1.080	1.756	0.266
1.125	1.144	1.853	0.281
1.188	1.208	1.950	0.297
1.250	1.271	2.045	0.312
1.312	1.334	2.141	0.328
1.375	1.398	2.239	0.344
1.438	1.462	2.334	0.359
1.500	1.525	2.430	0.375

METRIC LOCK WASHERS—DIN 127 (Millimeters)

SCREW SIZE	ID SIZE	OD SIZE	THICK-NESS
4	4.1	7.1	0.9
5	5.1	8.7	1.2
6	6.1	11.1	1.6
8	8.2	12.1	1.6
10	10.2	14.2	2
12	12.1	17.2	2.2
14	14.2	20.2	2.5
16	16.2	23.2	3
18	18.2	26.2	3.5
20	20.2	28.2	3.5
22	22.5	34.5	4
24	24.5	38.5	5
27	27.5	41.5	5
30	30.5	46.5	6
33	33.5	53.5	6
36	36.5	56.5	6
39	39.5	59.5	6
42	42.5	66.5	7
45	45.5	69.5	7
48	49	73	7

Limits are in thousandths of an inch.
Limits for hole and shaft are applied algebraically to the basic size to obtain the limits of size for the parts.
Data in bold face are in accordance with ABC agreements.
Symbols H5, g5, etc., are Hole and Shaft designations used in ABC System.

Nominal Size Range Inches		Class RC1			Class RC2			Class RC3			Class RC4		
		Limits of Clearance	Standard Limits		Limits of Clearance	Standard Limits		Limits of Clearance	Standard Limits		Limits of Clearance	Standard Limits	
Over	To		Hole H5	Shaft g4		Hole H6	Shaft g5		Hole H7	Shaft f6		Hole H8	Shaft f7
0	−0.12	0.1	+0.2	−0.1	0.1	+0.25	−0.1	0.3	+0.4	−0.3	0.3	+0.6	−0.3
		0.45	0	−0.25	0.55	0	−0.3	0.95	0	−0.55	1.3	0	−0.7
0.12	−0.24	0.15	+0.2	−0.15	0.15	+0.3	−0.15	0.4	+0.5	−0.4	0.4	+0.7	−0.4
		0.5	0	−0.3	0.65	0	−0.35	1.12	0	−0.7	1.6	0	−0.9
0.24	−0.40	0.2	0.25	−0.2	0.2	+0.4	−0.2	0.5	+0.6	−0.5	0.5	+0.9	−0.5
		0.6	0	−0.35	0.85	0	−0.45	1.5	0	−0.9	2.0	0	−1.1
0.40	−0.71	0.25	+0.3	−0.25	0.25	+0.4	−0.25	0.6	+0.7	−0.6	0.6	+1.0	−0.6
		0.75	0	−0.45	0.95	0	−0.55	1.7	0	−1.0	2.3	0	−1.3
0.71	−1.19	0.3	+0.4	−0.3	0.3	+0.5	−0.3	0.8	+0.8	−0.8	0.8	+1.2	−0.8
		0.95	0	−0.55	1.2	0	−0.7	2.1	0	−1.3	2.8	0	−1.6
1.19	−1.97	0.4	+0.4	−0.4	0.4	+0.6	−0.4	1.0	+1.0	−1.0	1.0	+1.6	−1.0
		1.1	0	−0.7	1.4	0	−0.8	2.6	0	−1.6	3.6	0	−2.0
1.97	−3.15	0.4	+0.5	−0.4	0.4	+0.7	−0.4	1.2	+1.2	−1.2	1.2	+1.8	−1.2
		1.2	0	−0.7	1.6	0	−0.9	3.1	0	−1.9	4.2	0	−2.4
3.15	−4.73	0.5	+0.6	−0.5	0.5	+0.9	−0.5	1.4	+1.4	−1.4	1.4	+2.2	−1.4
		1.5	0	−0.9	2.0	0	−1.1	3.7	0	−2.3	5.0	0	−2.8
4.73	−7.09	0.6	+0.7	−0.6	0.6	+1.0	−0.6	1.6	+1.6	−1.6	1.6	+2.5	−1.6
		1.8	0	−1.1	2.3	0	−1.3	4.2	0	−2.6	5.7	0	−3.2
7.09	−9.85	0.6	+0.8	−0.6	0.6	+1.2	−0.6	2.0	+1.8	−2.0	2.0	+2.8	−2.0
		2.0	0	−1.2	2.6	0	−1.4	5.0	0	−3.2	6.6	0	−3.8
9.85	−12.41	0.8	+0.9	−0.8	0.8	+1.2	−0.8	2.5	+2.0	−2.5	2.5	+3.0	−2.5
		2.3	0	−1.4	2.9	0	−1.7	5.7	0	−3.7	7.5	0	−4.5
12.41	−15.75	1.0	+1.0	−1.0	1.0	+1.4	−1.0	3.0	+	−3.0	3.0	+3.5	−3.0
		2.7	0	−1.7	3.4	0	−2.0	6.6	0	−4.4	8.7	0	−5.2
15.75	−19.69	1.2	+1.0	−1.2	1.2	+1.6	−1.2	4.0	+1.6	−4.0	4.0	+4.0	−4.0
		3.0	0	−2.0	3.8	0	−2.2	8.1	0	−5.6	10.5	0	−6.5
19.69	−30.09	1.6	+1.2	−1.6	1.6	+2.0	−1.6	5.0	+3.0	−5.0	5.0	+5.0	−5.0
		3.7	0	−2.5	4.8	0	−2.8	10.0	0	−7.0	13.0	0	−8.0
30.09	−41.49	2.0	+1.6	−2.0	2.0	+2.5	−2.0	6.0	+4.0	−6.0	6.0	+6.0	−6.0
		4.6	0	−3.0	6.1	0	−3.6	12.5	0	−8.5	16.0	0	−10.0
41.49	−56.19	2.5	+2.0	−2.5	2.5	+3.0	−2.5	8.0	+5.0	−8.0	8.0	+8.0	−8.0
		5.7	0	−3.7	7.5	0	−4.5	16.0	0	−11.0	21.0	0	−13.0
56.19	−76.39	3.0	+2.5	−3.0	3.0	+4.0	−3.0	10.0	+6.0	−10.0	10.0	+10.0	−10.0
		7.1	0	−4.6	9.5	0	−5.5	20.0	0	−14.0	26.0	0	−16.0
76.39	−100.9	4.0	+3.0	−4.0	4.0	+5.0	−4.0	12.0	+8.0	−12.0	12.0	+12.0	−12.0
		9.0	0	−6.0	12.0	0	−7.0	25.0	0	−17.0	32.0	0	−20.0
100.9	−131.9	5.0	+4.0	−5.0	5.0	+6.0	−5.0	16.0	+10.0	−16.0	16.0	+16.0	−16.0
		11.5	0	−7.5	15.0	0	−9.0	32.0	0	−22.0	36.0	0	−26.0
131.9	−171.9	6.0	+5.0	−6.0	6.0	+8.0	−6.0	18.0	+8.0	−18.0	18.0	+20.0	−18.0
		14.0	0	−9.0	19.0	0	−11.0	38.0	0	−26.0	50.0	0	−30.0
171.9	−200	8.0	+6.0	−8.0	8.0	+10.0	−8.0	22.0	+16.0	−22.0	22.0	+25.0	−22.0
		18.0	0	−12.0	22.0	0	−12.0	48.0	0	−32.0	63.0	0	−38.0

Source: Courtesy of USASI; B4.1—1955.

| Class RC 5 | | | Class RC 6 | | | Class RC 7 | | | Class RC 8 | | | Class RC 9 | | | Nominal Size Range Inches | |
Limits of Clearance	Hole H8	Shaft e7	Limits of Clearance	Hole H9	Shaft e8	Limits of Clearance	Hole H9	Shaft d8	Limits of Clearance	Hole H10	Shaft c9	Limits of Clearance	Hole H11	Shaft	Over	To
0.6	+0.6	−0.6	0.6	+1.0	−0.6	1.0	+1.0	−1.0	2.5	+1.6	−2.5	4.0	+2.5	−4.0	0	− 0.12
1.6	−0	−1.0	2.2	−0	−1.2	2.6	0	−1.6	5.1	0	−3.5	8.1	0	−5.6		
0.8	+0.7	−0.8	0.8	+1.2	−0.8	1.2	+1.2	−1.2	2.8	+1.8	−2.8	4.5	+3.0	−4.5	0.12	− 0.24
2.0	−0	−1.3	2.7	−0	−1.5	3.1	0	−1.9	5.8	0	−4.0	9.0	0	−6.0		
1.0	+0.9	−1.0	1.0	+1.4	−1.0	1.6	+1.4	−1.6	3.0	+2.2	−3.0	5.0	+3.5	−5.0	0.24	− 0.40
2.5	−0	−1.16	3.3	−0	−1.9	3.9	0	−2.5	6.6	0	−4.4	10.7	0	−7.2		
1.2	+1.0	−1.2	1.2	+1.6	−1.2	2.0	+1.6	−2.0	3.5	+2.8	−3.5	6.0	+4.0	−6.0	0.40	− 0.71
2.9	−0	−1.9	3.8	−0	−2.2	4.6	0	−3.0	7.9	0	−5.1	12.8	−0	−8.8		
1.6	+1.2	−1.6	1.6	+2.0	−1.6	2.5	+2.0	−2.5	4.5	+3.5	−4.5	7.0	+5.0	−7.0	0.71	− 1.19
3.6	−0	−2.4	4.8	−0	−2.8	5.7	0	−3.7	10.0	0	−6.5	15.5	0	−10.5		
2.0	+1.6	−2.0	2.0	+2.5	−2.0	3.0	+2.5	−3.0	5.0	+4.0	−5.0	8.0	+6.0	−8.0	1.19	− 1.97
4.6	−0	−3.0	6.1	−0	−3.6	7.1	0	−4.6	11.5	0	−7.5	18.0	0	−12.0		
2.5	+1.8	−2.5	2.5	+3.0	−2.5	4.0	+3.0	−4.0	6.0	+4.5	−6.0	9.0	+7.0	−9.0	1.97	− 3.15
5.5	−0	−3.7	7.3	−0	−4.3	8.8	0	−5.8	13.5	0	−9.0	20.5	0	−13.5		
3.0	+2.2	−3.0	3.0	+3.5	−3.0	5.0	+3.5	−5.0	7.0	+5.0	−7.0	10.0	+9.0	−10.0	3.15	− 4.73
6.6	−0	−4.4	8.7	−0	−5.2	10.7	0	−7.2	15.5	0	−10.5	24.0	0	−15.0		
3.5	+2.5	−3.5	3.5	+4.0	−3.5	6.0	+4.0	−6.0	8.0	+6.0	−8.0	12.0	+10.0	−12.0	4.73	− 7.09
7.6	−0	−5.1	10.0	−0	−6.0	12.5	0	−8.5	18.0	0	−12.0	28.0	0	−18.0		
4.0	+2.8	−4.0	4.0	+4.5	−4.0	7.0	+4.5	−7.0	10.0	+7.0	−10.0	15.0	+12.0	−15.0	7.09	− 9.85
8.6	−0	−5.8	11.3	−0	−6.8	14.3	0	−9.8	21.5	0	−14.5	34.0	0	−22.0		
5.0	+3.0	−5.0	5.0	+5.0	−5.0	8.0	+5.0	−8.0	12.0	+8.0	−12.0	18.0	+12.0	−18.0	9.85	− 12.41
10.0	0	−7.0	13.0	0	−8.0	16.0	0	−11.0	25.0	0	−17.0	38.0	0	−26.0		
6.0	+3.5	−6.0	6.0	+6.0	−6.0	10.0	+6.0	−10.0	14.0	+9.0	−14.0	22.0	+14.0	−22.0	12.41	− 15.75
11.7	0	−8.2	15.5	0	−9.5	19.5	0	13.5	29.0	0	−20.0	45.0	0	−31.0		
8.0	+4.0	−8.0	8.0	+6.0	−8.0	12.0	+6.0	−12.0	16.0	+10.0	−16.0	25.0	+16.0	−25.0	15.75	− 19.69
14.5	0	−10.5	18.0	0	−12.0	22.0	0	−16.0	32.0	0	−22.0	51.0	0	−35.0		
10.0	+5.0	−10.0	10.0	+8.0	−10.0	16.0	+8.0	−16.0	20.0	+12.0	−20.0	30.0	+20.0	−30.0	19.69	− 30.09
18.0	0	−13.0	23.0	0	−15.0	29.0	0	−21.0	40.0	0	−28.0	62.0	0	−42.0		
12.0	+6.0	−12.0	12.0	+10.0	−12.0	20.0	+10.0	−20.0	25.0	+16.0	−25.0	40.0	+25.0	−40.0	30.09	− 41.49
22.0	0	−16.0	28.0	0	−18.0	36.0	0	−26.0	51.0	0	−35.0	81.0	0	−56.0		
16.0	+8.0	−16.0	16.0	+12.0	−16.0	25.0	+12.0	−25.0	30.0	+20.0	−30.0	50.0	+30.0	−50.0	41.49	− 56.19
29.0	0	−21.0	36.0	0	−24.0	45.0	0	−33.0	62.0	0	−42.0	100	0	−70.0		
20.0	+10.0	−20.0	20.0	+16.0	−20.0	30.0	+16.0	−30.0	40.0	+25.0	−40.0	60.0	+40.0	−60.0	56.19	− 76.39
36.0	0	−26.0	46.0	0	−30.0	56.0	0	−40.0	81.0	0	−56.0	125	0	−85.0		
25.0	+12.0	−25.0	25.0	+20.0	−25.0	40.0	+20.0	−40.0	50.0	+30.0	−50.0	80.0	+50.0	−80.0	76.39	− 100.9
45.0	0	−33.0	57.0	0	−37.0	72.0	0	−52.0	100	0	−70.0	160	0	−110		
30.0	+16.0	−30.0	30.0	+35.0	−30.0	50.0	+25.0	−50.0	60.0	+40.0	−60.0	100	+60.0	−100	100.9	− 131.9
56.0	0	−40.0	71.0	0	−46.0	91.0	0	−66.0	125	0	−85.0	200	0	−140		
35.0	+20.0	−35.0	35.0	+30.0	−35.0	60.0	+30.0	−60.0	80.0	+50.0	−80.0	130	+80.0	−130	131.9	− 171.9
57.0	0	−47.0	85.0	0	−55.0	110.0	0	−80.0	160	0	−110	260	0	−180		
45.0	+25.0	−45.0	45.0	+40.0	−45.0	80.0	+40.0	−80.0	100	+60.0	−100	150	+100	−150	171.9	− 200
86.0	0	−61.0	110.0	0	−70.0	145.0	0	−105.0	200	0	−140	310	0	−210		

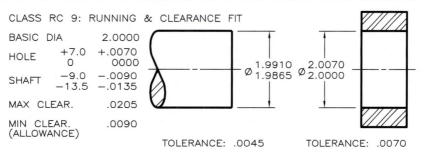

CLASS RC 9: RUNNING & CLEARANCE FIT

BASIC DIA		2.0000
HOLE	+7.0	+.0070
	0	.0000
SHAFT	−9.0	−.0090
	−13.5	−.0135
MAX CLEAR.		.0205
MIN CLEAR. (ALLOWANCE)		.0090

Ø 1.9910 / 1.9865   Ø 2.0070 / 2.0000

TOLERANCE: .0045   TOLERANCE: .0070

Limits are in thousandths of an inch.
Limits for hole and shaft are applied algebraically to the basic size to obtain the limits of size for the parts.
Data in bold face are in accordance with ABC agreements.
Symbols H9, f8, etc., are Hole and Shaft designations used in ABC System.

Nominal Size Range Inches		Class LC 1			Class LC2			Class LC 3			Class LC 4			Class LC 5		
		Limits of Clearance	Standard Limits		Limits of Clearance	Standard Limits		Limits of Clearance	Standard Limits		Limits of Clearance	Standard Limits		Limits of Clearance	Standard Limits	
Over	To		Hole H6	Shaft h5		Hole H7	Shaft h6		Hole H8	Shaft h7		Hole H10	Shaft h9		Hole H7	Shaft g6
0	−0.12	0	+0.25	+0	0	+0.4	+0	0	+0.6	+0	0	+1.6	+0	0.1	+0.4	−0.1
		0.45	−0	−0.2	0.65	−0	−0.25	1	−0	−0.4	2.6	−0	−1.0	0.75	−0	−0.35
0.12	−0.24	0	+0.3	+0	0	+0.5	+0	0	+0.7	+0	0	+1.8	+0	0.15	+0.5	−0.15
		0.5	−0	−0.2	0.8	−0	−0.3	1.2	−0	−0.5	3.0	−0	−1.2	0.95	−0	−0.45
0.24	−0.40	0	+0.4	+0	0	+0.6	+0	0	+0.9	+0	0	+2.2	+0	0.2	+0.6	−0.2
		0.65	−0	−0.25	1.0	−0	−0.4	1.5	−0	−0.6	3.6	−0	−1.4	1.2	−0	−0.6
0.40	−0.71	0	+0.4	+0	0	+0.7	+0	0	+1.0	+0	0	+2.8	+0	0.25	+0.7	−0.25
		0.7	−0	−0.3	1.1	−0	−0.4	1.7	−0	−0.7	4.4	−0	−1.6	1.35	−0	−0.65
0.71	−1.19	0	+0.5	+0	0	+0.8	+0	0	+1.2	+0	0	+3.5	+0	0.3	+0.8	−0.3
		0.9	−0	−0.4	1.3	−0	−0.5	2	−0	−0.8	5.5	−0	−2.0	1.6	−0	−0.8
1.19	−1.97	0	+0.6	+0	0	+1.0	+0	0	+1.6	+0	0	+4.0	+0	0.4	+1.0	−0.4
		1.0	−0	−0.4	1.6	−0	−0.6	2.6	−0	−1	6.5	−0	−2.5	2.0	−0	−1.0
1.97	−3.15	0	+0.7	+0	0	+1.2	+0	0	+1.8	+0	0	+4.5	+0	0.4	+1.2	−0.4
		1.2	−0	−0.5	1.9	−0	−0.7	3	−0	−1.2	7.5	−0	−3	2.3	−0	−1.1
3.15	−4.73	0	+0.9	+0	0	+1.4	+0	0	+2.2	+0	0	+5.0	+0	0.5	+1.4	−0.5
		1.5	−0	−0.6	2.3	−0	−0.9	3.6	−0	−1.4	8.5	−0	−3.5	2.8	−0	−1.4
4.73	−7.09	0	+1.0	+0	0	+1.6	+0	0	+2.5	+0	0	+6.0	+0	0.6	+1.6	−0.6
		1.7	−0	−0.7	2.6	−0	−1.0	4.1	−0	−1.6	10	−0	−4	3.2	−0	1.6
7.09	−9.85	0	+1.2	+0	0	+1.8	+0	0	+2.8	+0	0	+7.0	+0	0.6	+1.8	−0.6
		2.0	−0	−0.8	3.0	−0	−1.2	4.6	−0	−1.8	11.5	−0	−4.5	3.6	−0	−1.8
9.85	−12.41	0	+1.2	+0	0	+2.0	+0	0	+3.0	+0	0	8.0	+0	0.7	+2.0	−0.7
		2.1	−0	−0.9	3.2	−0	−1.2	5	−0	−2.0	13	−0	−5	3.9	−0	−1.9
12.41	−15.75	0	+1.4	+0	0	+2.2	+0	0	+3.5	+0	0	+9.0	+0	0.7	+2.2	−0.7
		2.4	−0	−1.0	3.6	−0	−1.4	5.7	−0	−2.2	15	−0	−6	4.3	−0	−2.1
15.75	−19.69	0	+1.6	+0	0	+2.5	+0	0	+4	+0	0	+10.0	+0	0.8	+2.5	−0.8
		2.6	−0	−1.0	4.1	−0	−1.6	6.5	−0	−2.5	16	−0	−6	4.9	−0	−2.4
19.69	−30.09	0	+2.0	+0	0	+3	+0	0	+5	+0	0	+12.0	+0	0.9	+3.0	−0.9
		3.2	−0	−1.2	5.0	−0	−2	8	−0	−3	20	−0	−8	5.9	−0	−2.9
30.09	−41.49	0	+2.5	+0	0	+4	+0	0	+6	+0	0	+16.0	+0	1.0	+4.0	−1.0
		4.1	−0	−1.6	6.5	−0	−2.5	10	−0	−4	26	−0	−10	7.5	−0	−3.5
41.49	−56.19	0	+3.0	+0	0	+5	+0	0	+8	+0	0	+20.0	+0	1.2	+5.0	−1.2
		5.0	−0	−2.0	8.0	−0	−3	13	−0	−5	32	−0	−12	9.2	−0	−4.2
56.19	−76.39	0	+4.0	+0	0	+6	+0	0	+10	+0	0	+25.0	+0	1.2	+6.0	−1.2
		6.5	−0	−2.5	10	−0	−4	16	−0	−6	41	−0	−16	11.2	−0	−5.2
76.39	−100.9	0	+5.0	+0	0	+8	+0	0	+12	+0	0	+30.0	+0	1.4	+8.0	−1.4
		8.0	−0	−3.0	13	−0	−5	20	−0	−8	50	−0	−20	14.4	−0	−6.4
100.9	−131.9	0	+6.0	+0	0	+10	+0	0	+16	+0	0	+40.0	+0	1.6	+10.0	−1.6
		10.0	−0	−4.0	16	−0	−6	26	−0	−10	65	−0	−25	17.6	−0	−7.6
131.9	−171.9	0	+8.0	+0	0	+12	+0	0	+20	+0	0	+50.0	+0	1.8	+12.0	−1.8
		13.0	−0	−5.0	20	−0	−8	32	−0	−12	8	−0	−30	21.8	−0	−9.8
171.9	−200	0	+10.0	+0	0	+16	+0	0	+25	+0	0	+60.0	+0	1.8	+16.0	−1.8
		16.0	−0	−6.0	26	−0	−10	41	−0	−16	100	−0	−40	27.8	−0	−11.8

Source: Courtesy of USASI; B4.1—1955.

LC 6 Limits of Clearance	LC 6 Hole H9	LC 6 Shaft f8	LC 7 Limits of Clearance	LC 7 Hole H10	LC 7 Shaft e9	LC 8 Limits of Clearance	LC 8 Hole H10	LC 8 Shaft d9	LC 9 Limits of Clearance	LC 9 Hole H11	LC 9 Shaft c10	LC 10 Limits of Clearance	LC 10 Hole H12	LC 10 Shaft	LC 11 Limits of Clearance	LC 11 Hole H13	LC 11 Shaft	Nominal Size Over	Nominal Size To
0.3	+1.0	−0.3	0.6	+1.6	−0.6	1.0	+0.6	−1.0	2.5	+2.5	−2.5	4	+4	−4	5	+6	−5	0	0.12
1.9	0	−0.9	3.2	0	−1.6	3.6	−0	−2.0	6.6	−0	−4.1	12	−0	−8	17	−0	−11		
0.4	+1.2	−0.4	0.8	+1.8	−0.8	1.2	+1.8	−1.2	2.8	+3.0	−2.8	4.5	+5	−4.5	6	+7	−6	0.12	0.24
2.3	0	−1.1	3.8	0	−2.0	4.2	−0	−2.4	7.6	−0	−4.6	14.5	−0	−9.5	20	−0	−13		
0.5	+1.4	−0.5	1.0	+2.2	−1.0	1.6	+2.2	−1.6	3.0	+3.5	−3.0	5	+6	−5	7	+9	−7	0.24	0.40
2.8	0	−1.4	4.6	0	−2.4	5.2	−0	−3.0	8.7	−0	−5.2	17	−0	−11	25	−0	−16		
0.6	+1.6	−0.6	1.2	+2.8	−1.2	2.0	+2.8	−2.0	3.5	+4.0	−3.5	6	+7	−6	8	+10	−8	0.40	0.71
3.2	0	−1.6	5.6	0	−2.8	6.4	−0	−3.6	10.3	−0	−6.3	20	−0	−13	28	−0	−18		
0.8	+2.0	−0.8	1.6	+3.5	−1.6	2.5	+3.5	−2.5	4.5	+5.0	−4.5	7	+8	−7	10	+12	−10	0.71	1.19
4.0	0	−2.0	7.1	0	−3.6	8.0	−0	−4.5	13.0	−0	−8.0	23	−0	−15	34	−0	−22		
1.0	+2.5	−1.0	2.0	+4.0	−2.0	3.0	+4.0	−3.0	5	+6	−5	8	+10	−8	12	+16	−12	1.19	1.97
5.1	0	−2.6	8.5	0	−4.5	9.5	−0	−5.5	15	−0	−9	28	−0	−18	44	−0	−28		
1.2	+3.0	−1.2	2.5	+4.5	−2.5	4.0	+4.5	−4.0	6	+7	−6	10	+12	−10	14	+18	−14	1.97	3.15
6.0	0	−3.0	10.0	0	−5.5	11.5	−0	−7.0	17.5	−0	−10.5	34	−0	−22	50	−0	−32		
1.4	+3.5	−1.4	3.0	+5.0	−3.0	5.0	+5.0	−5.0	7	+9	−7	11	+14	−11	16	+22	−16	3.15	4.73
7.1	0	−3.6	11.5	0	−6.5	13.5	−0	−8.5	21	−0	−12	39	−0	−25	60	−0	−38		
1.6	+4.0	−1.6	3.5	+6.0	−3.5	6	+6	−6	8	+10	−8	12	+16	−12	18	+25	−18	4.73	7.09
8.1	0	−4.1	13.5	0	−7.5	16	−0	−10	24	−0	−14	44	−0	−28	68	−0	−43		
2.0	+4.5	−2.0	4.0	+7.0	−4.0	7	+7	−7	10	+12	−10	16	+18	−16	22	+28	−22	7.09	9.85
9.3	0	−4.8	15.5	0	−8.5	18.5	−0	−11.5	29	−0	−17	52	−0	−34	78	−0	−50		
2.2	+5.0	−2.2	4.5	+8.0	−4.5	7	+8	−7	12	+12	−12	20	+20	−20	28	+30	−28	9.85	12.41
10.2	0	−5.2	17.5	0	−9.5	20	−0	−12	32	−0	−20	60	−0	−40	88	−0	−58		
2.5	+6.0	−2.5	5.0	+9.0	−5	8	+9	−8	14	+14	−14	22	+22	−22	30	+35	−30	12.41	15.75
12.0	0	−6.0	20.0	0	−11	23	−0	−14	37	−0	−23	66	−0	−44	100	−0	−65		
2.8	+6.0	−2.8	5.0	+10.0	−5	9	+10	−9	16	+16	−16	25	+25	−25	35	+40	−35	15.75	19.69
12.8	0	−6.8	21.0	0	−11	25	−0	−15	42	−0	−26	75	−0	−50	115	−0	−75		
3.0	+8.0	−3.0	6.0	+12.0	−6	10	+12	−10	18	+20	−18	28	+30	−28	40	+50	−40	19.69	30.09
16.0	0	−8.0	26.0	−0	−14	30	−0	−18	50	−0	−30	88	−0	−58	140	−0	−90		
3.5	+10.0	−3.5	7.0	+16.0	−7	12	+16	−12	20	+25	−20	30	+40	−30	45	+60	−45	30.09	41.49
19.5	0	−9.5	33.0	−0	−17	38	−0	−22	61	−0	−36	110	−0	−70	165	−0	−105		
4.0	+12.0	−4.0	8.0	+20.0	−8	14	+20	−14	25	+30	−25	40	+50	−40	60	+80	−60	41.49	56.19
24.0	0	−12.0	40.0	−0	−20	46	−0	−26	75	−0	−45	140	−0	−90	220	−0	−140		
4.5	+16.0	−4.5	9.0	+25.0	−9	16	+25	−16	30	+40	−30	50	+60	−50	70	+100	−70	56.19	76.39
30.5	0	−14.5	50.0	−0	−25	57	−0	−32	95	−0	−55	170	−0	110	270	−0	−170		
5.0	+20.0	−5	10.0	+30.0	−10	18	+30	−18	35	+50	−35	50	+80	−50	80	+125	−80	76.39	100.9
37.0	0	−17	60.0	−0	−30	68	−0	−38	115	−0	−65	210	−0	−130	330	−0	−205		
6.0	+25.0	−6	12.0	+40.0	−12	20	+40	−20	40	+60	−40	60	+100	−60	90	+160	−90	100.9	131.9
47.0	0	−22	67.0	−0	−27	85	−0	−45	140	−0	−80	260	−0	−160	410	−0	−250		
7.0	+30.0	−7	14.0	+50.0	−14	25	+50	−25	50	+80	−50	80	+125	−80	100	+200	−100	131.9	171.9
57.0	0	−27	94.0	−0	−44	105	−0	−55	180	−0	−100	330	−0	−205	500	−0	−300		
7.0	+40.0	−7	14.0	+60.0	−14	25	+60	−25	50	+100	−50	90	+160	−90	125	+250	−125	171.9	200
72.0	0	−32	114.0	−0	−54	125	−0	−65	210	−0	−110	410	−0	−250	625	−0	−375		

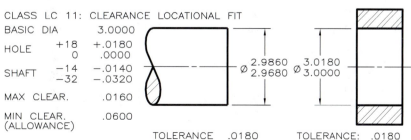

CLASS LC 11: CLEARANCE LOCATIONAL FIT

BASIC DIA		3.0000
HOLE	+18 / 0	+.0180 / .0000
SHAFT	−14 / −32	−.0140 / −.0320
MAX CLEAR.		.0160
MIN CLEAR. (ALLOWANCE)		.0600

Ø 2.9860 / 2.9680   Ø 3.0180 / 3.0000

TOLERANCE .0180   TOLERANCE: .0180

APPENDIX 27 • American Standard Transition Locational Fits (hole basis)

Limits are in thousandths of an inch.
Limits for hole and shaft are applied algebraically to the basic size to obtain the limits of size for the mating parts.
Data in bold face are in accordance with ABC agreements.
"Fit" represents the maximum interference (minus values), and the maximum clearance (plus values).
Symbols H7, js6, etc., are Hole and Shaft designations used in ABC System.

Nominal Size Range Inches Over	To	Class LT 1 Fit	Standard Limits Hole H7	Standard Limits Shaft js6	Class LT 2 Fit	Standard Limits Hole H8	Standard Limits Shaft js7	Class LT 3 Fit	Standard Limits Hole H7	Standard Limits Shaft k6	Class LT 4 Fit	Standard Limits Hole H8	Standard Limits Shaft k7	Class LT 5 Fit	Standard Limits Hole H7	Standard Limits Shaft n6	Class LT 6 Fit	Standard Limits Hole H7	Standard Limits Shaft n7
0	0.12	−0.10 / +0.50	+0.4 / −0	+0.10 / −0.10	−0.2 / +0.8	+0.6 / −0	+0.2 / −0.2							−0.5 / +0.15	+0.4 / −0	+0.5 / +0.25	−0.65 / +0.15	+0.4 / −0	+0.65 / +0.25
0.12	0.24	−0.15 / +0.65	+0.5 / −0	+0.15 / −0.15	−0.25 / +0.95	+0.7 / −0	+0.25 / −0.25							−0.6 / +0.2	+0.5 / −0	+0.6 / +0.3	−0.8 / +0.2	+0.5 / −0	+0.8 / +0.3
0.24	0.40	−0.2 / +0.8	+0.6 / −0	+0.2 / −0.2	−0.3 / +1.2	+0.9 / −0	+0.3 / −0.3	−0.5 / +0.5	+0.6 / −0	+0.5 / +0.1	−0.7 / +0.8	+0.9 / −0	+0.7 / +0.1	−0.8 / +0.2	+0.6 / −0	+0.8 / +0.4	−1.0 / +0.2	+0.6 / −0	+1.0 / +0.4
0.40	0.71	−0.2 / +0.9	+0.7 / −0	+0.2 / −0.2	−0.35 / +1.35	+1.0 / −0	+0.35 / −0.35	−0.5 / +0.6	+0.7 / −0	+0.5 / +0.1	−0.8 / +0.9	+1.0 / −0	+0.8 / +0.1	−0.9 / +0.2	+0.7 / −0	+0.9 / +0.5	−1.2 / +0.2	+0.7 / −0	+1.2 / +0.5
0.71	1.19	−0.25 / +1.05	+0.8 / −0	+0.25 / −0.25	−0.4 / +1.6	+1.2 / −0	+0.4 / −0.4	−0.6 / +0.7	+0.8 / −0	+0.6 / +0.1	−0.9 / +1.1	+1.2 / −0	+0.9 / +0.1	−1.1 / +0.2	+0.8 / −0	+1.1 / +0.6	−1.4 / +0.2	+0.8 / −0	+1.4 / +0.6
1.19	1.97	−0.3 / +1.3	+1.0 / −0	+0.3 / −0.3	−0.5 / +2.1	+1.6 / −0	+0.5 / −0.5	−0.7 / +0.9	+1.0 / −0	+0.7 / +0.1	−1.1 / +1.5	+1.6 / −0	+1.1 / +0.1	−1.3 / +0.3	+1.0 / −0	+1.3 / +0.7	−1.7 / +0.3	+1.0 / −0	+1.7 / +0.7
1.97	3.15	−0.3 / +1.5	+1.2 / −0	+0.3 / −0.3	−0.6 / +2.4	+1.8 / −0	+0.6 / −0.6	−0.8 / +1.1	+1.2 / −0	+0.8 / +0.1	−1.3 / +1.7	+1.8 / −0	+1.3 / +0.1	−1.5 / +0.4	+1.2 / −0	+1.5 / +0.8	−2.0 / +0.4	+1.2 / −0	+2.0 / +0.8
3.15	4.73	−0.4 / +1.8	+1.4 / −0	+0.4 / −0.4	−0.7 / +2.9	+2.2 / −0	+0.7 / −0.7	−1.0 / +1.3	+1.4 / −0	+1.0 / +0.1	−1.5 / +2.1	+2.2 / −0	+1.5 / +0.1	−1.9 / +0.4	+1.4 / −0	+1.9 / +1.0	−2.4 / +0.4	+1.4 / −0	+2.4 / +1.0
4.73	7.09	−0.5 / +2.1	+1.6 / −0	+0.5 / −0.5	−0.8 / +3.3	+2.5 / −0	+0.8 / −0.8	−1.1 / +1.5	+1.6 / −0	+1.1 / +0.1	−1.7 / +2.4	+2.5 / −0	+1.7 / +0.1	−2.2 / +0.4	+1.6 / −0	+2.2 / +1.2	−2.8 / +0.4	+1.6 / −0	+2.8 / +1.2
7.09	9.85	−0.6 / +2.4	+1.8 / −0	+0.6 / −0.6	−0.9 / +3.7	+2.8 / −0	+0.9 / −0.9	−1.4 / +1.6	+1.8 / −0	+1.4 / +0.2	−2.0 / +2.6	+2.8 / −0	+2.0 / +0.2	−2.6 / +0.4	+1.8 / −0	+2.6 / +1.4	−3.2 / +0.4	+1.8 / −0	+3.2 / +1.4
9.85	12.41	−0.6 / +2.6	+2.0 / −0	+0.6 / −0.6	−1.0 / +4.0	+3.0 / −0	+1.0 / −1.0	−1.4 / +1.8	+2.0 / −0	+1.4 / +0.2	−2.2 / +2.8	+3.0 / −0	+2.2 / +0.2	−2.6 / +0.6	+2.0 / −0	+2.6 / +1.4	−3.4 / +0.6	+2.0 / −0	+3.4 / +1.4
12.41	15.75	−0.7 / +2.6	+2.2 / −0	+0.7 / −0.7	−1.0 / +4.5	+3.5 / −0	+1.0 / −1.0	−1.6 / +2.0	+2.2 / −0	+1.6 / +0.2	−2.4 / +3.3	+3.5 / −0	+2.4 / +0.2	−3.0 / +0.6	+2.2 / −0	+3.0 / +1.6	−3.8 / +0.6	+2.2 / −0	+3.8 / +1.6
15.75	19.69	−0.8 / +2.9	+2.5 / −0	+0.8 / −0.8	−1.2 / +5.2	+4.0 / −0	+1.2 / −1.2	−1.8 / +2.3	+2.5 / −0	+1.8 / +0.2	−2.7 / +3.8	+4.0 / −0	+2.7 / +0.2	−3.4 / +0.7	+2.5 / −0	+3.4 / +1.8	−4.3 / +0.7	+2.5 / −0	+4.3 / +1.8

Source: Courtesy of ANSI; B4.1–1955.

Limits are in thousandths of an inch.
Limits for hole and shaft are applied algebraically to the basic size to obtain the limits of size for the parts.
Data in bold face are in accordance with ABC agreements.
Symbols H7, p6, etc., are Hole and Shaft designations used in ABC System.

Nominal Size Range Inches		Class LN 1			Class LN 2			Class LN 3		
Over	To	Limits of Interference	Standard Limits Hole H6	Standard Limits Shaft n5	Limits of Interference	Standard Limits Hole H7	Standard Limits Shaft p6	Limits of Interference	Standard Limits Hole H7	Standard Limits Shaft r6
0	− 0.12	**0**	**+0.25**	**+0.45**	**0**	**+0.4**	**+0.65**	0.1	+0.4	+0.75
		0.45	**−0**	**+0.25**	**0.65**	**−0**	**+0.4**	0.75	−0	+0.5
0.12	− 0.24	**0**	**+0.3**	**+0.5**	**0**	**+0.5**	**+0.8**	0.1	+0.5	+0.9
		0.5	**−0**	**+0.3**	**0.8**	**−0**	**+0.5**	0.9	0	+0.6
0.24	− 0.40	**0**	**+0.4**	**+0.65**	**0**	**+0.6**	**+1.0**	0.2	+0.6	+1.2
		0.65	**−0**	**+0.4**	**1.0**	**−0**	**+0.6**	1.2	−0	+0.8
0.40	− 0.71	**0**	**+0.4**	**+0.8**	**0**	**+0.7**	**+1.1**	0.3	+0.7	+1.4
		0.8	**−0**	**+0.4**	**1.1**	**−0**	**+0.7**	1.4	−0	+1.0
0.71	− 1.19	**0**	**+0.5**	**+1.0**	**0**	**+0.8**	**+1.3**	0.4	+0.8	+1.7
		1.0	**−0**	**+0.5**	**1.3**	**−0**	**+0.8**	1.7	−0	+1.2
1.19	− 1.97	**0**	**+0.6**	**+1.1**	**0**	**+1.0**	**+1.6**	0.4	+1.0	+2.0
		1.1	**−0**	**+0.6**	**1.6**	**−0**	**+1.0**	2.0	−0	+1.4
1.97	− 3.15	**0.1**	**+0.7**	**+1.3**	**0.2**	**+1.2**	**+2.1**	0.4	+1.2	+2.3
		1.3	**−0**	**+0.7**	**2.1**	**−0**	**+1.4**	2.3	−0	+1.6
3.15	− 4.73	**0.1**	**+0.9**	**+1.6**	**0.2**	**+1.4**	**+2.5**	0.6	+1.4	+2.9
		1.6	**−0**	**+1.0**	**2.5**	**−0**	**+1.6**	2.9	−0	+2.0
4.73	− 7.09	**0.2**	**+1.0**	**+1.9**	**0.2**	**+1.6**	**+2.8**	0.9	+1.6	+3.5
		1.9	**−0**	**+1.2**	**2.8**	**−0**	**+1.8**	3.5	−0	+2.5
7.09	− 9.85	**0.2**	**+1.2**	**+2.2**	**0.2**	**+1.8**	**+3.2**	1.2	+1.8	+4.2
		2.2	**−0**	**+1.4**	**3.2**	**−0**	**+2.0**	4.2	−0	+3.0
9.85	−12.41	**0.2**	**+1.2**	**+2.3**	**0.2**	**+2.0**	**+3.4**	1.5	+2.0	+4.7
		2.3	**−0**	**+1.4**	**3.4**	**−0**	**+2.2**	4.7	−0	+3.5
12.41	−15.75	**0.2**	**+1.4**	**+2.6**	**0.3**	**+2.2**	**+3.9**	2.3	+2.2	+5.9
		2.6	**−0**	**+1.6**	**3.9**	**−0**	**+2.5**	5.9	−0	+4.5
15.75	−19.69	**0.2**	**+1.6**	**+2.8**	**0.3**	**+2.5**	**+4.4**	2.5	+2.5	+6.6
		2.8	**−0**	**+1.8**	**4.4**	**−0**	**+2.8**	6.6	−0	+5.0
19.69	−30.09		+2.0		0.5	+3	+5.5	4	+3	+9
			−0		5.5	−0	+3.5	9	−0	+7
30.09	−41.49		+2.5		0.5	+4	+7.0	5	+4	+11.5
			−0		7.0	−0	+4.5	11.5	−0	+9
41.49	−56.19		+3.0		1	+5	+9	7	+5	+15
			−0		9	−0	+6	15	−0	+12
56.19	−76.39		+4.0		1	+6	+11	10	+6	+20
			−0		11	−0	+7	20	−0	+16
76.39	−100.9		+5.0		1	+8	+14	12	+8	+25
			−0		14	−0	+9	25	−0	+20
100.9	−131.9		+6.0		2	+10	+18	15	+10	+31
			−0		18	−0	+12	31	−0	+25
131.9	−171.9		+8.0		4	+12	+24	18	+12	+38
			−0		24	−0	+16	38	−0	+30
171.9	− 200		+10.0		4	+16	+30	24	+16	+50
			−0		30	−0	+20	50	−0	+40

Source: Courtesy of ANSI; B4.1–1955.

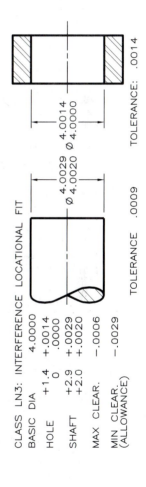

Limits are in thousandths of an inch.
Limits for hole and shaft are applied algebraically to the basic size to obtain the limits of size for the parts.
Data in bold face are in accordance with ABC agreements.
Symbols H7, s6, etc., are Hole and Shaft designations used in ABC System.

Nominal Size Range Inches Over	To	Class FN 1 Limits of Interference	Standard Limits Hole H6	Shaft	Class FN 2 Limits of Interference	Standard Limits Hole H7	Shaft s6	Class FN 3 Limits of Interference	Standard Limits Hole H7	Shaft t6	Class FN 4 Limits of Interference	Standard Limits Hole H7	Shaft u6	Class FN 5 Limits of Interference	Standard Limits Hole H8	Shaft x7
0	− 0.12	0.05	+0.25	+0.5	0.2	+0.4	+0.85				0.3	+0.4	+0.95	0.3	+0.6	+1.3
		0.5	−0	+0.3	0.85	−0	+0.6				0.95	−0	+0.7	1.3	−0	+0.9
0.12	− 0.24	0.1	+0.3	+0.6	0.2	+0.5	+1.0				0.4	+0.5	+1.2	0.5	+0.7	+1.7
		0.6	−0	+0.4	1.0	−0	+0.7				1.2	−0	+0.9	1.7	−0	+1.2
0.24	− 0.40	0.1	+0.4	+0.75	0.4	+0.6	+1.4				0.6	+0.6	+1.6	0.5	+0.9	+2.0
		0.75	−0	+0.5	1.4	−0	+1.0				1.6	−0	+1.2	2.0	−0	+1.4
0.40	− 0.56	0.1	−0.4	+0.8	0.5	+0.7	+1.6				0.7	+0.7	+1.8	0.6	+1.0	+2.3
		0.8	−0	+0.5	1.6	−0	+1.2				1.8	−0	+1.4	2.3	−0	+1.6
0.56	− 0.71	0.2	+0.4	+0.9	0.5	+0.7	+1.6				0.7	+0.7	+1.8	0.8	+1.0	+2.5
		0.9	−0	+0.6	1.6	−0	+1.2				1.8	−0	+1.4	2.5	−0	+1.8
0.71	− 0.95	0.2	+0.5	+1.1	0.6	+0.8	+1.9				0.8	+0.8	+2.1	1.0	+1.2	+3.0
		1.1	−0	+0.7	1.9	−0	+1.4				2.1	−0	+1.6	3.0	−0	+2.2
0.95	− 1.19	0.3	+0.5	+1.2	0.6	+0.8	+1.9	0.8	+0.8	+2.1	1.0	+0.8	+2.3	1.3	+1.2	+3.3
		1.2	−0	+0.8	1.9	−0	+1.4	2.1	−0	+1.6	2.3	−0	+1.8	3.3	−0	+2.5
1.19	− 1.58	0.3	+0.6	+1.3	0.8	+1.0	+2.4	1.0	+1.0	+2.6	1.5	+1.0	+3.1	1.4	+1.6	+4.0
		1.3	−0	+0.9	2.4	−0	+1.8	2.6	−0	+2.0	3.1	−0	+2.5	4.0	−0	+3.0
1.58	− 1.97	0.4	+0.6	+1.4	0.8	+1.0	+2.4	1.2	+1.0	+2.8	1.8	+1.0	+3.4	2.4	+1.6	+5.0
		1.4	−0	+1.0	2.4	−0	+1.8	2.8	−0	+2.2	3.4	−0	+2.8	5.0	−0	+4.0
1.97	− 2.56	0.6	+0.7	+1.8	0.8	+1.2	+2.7	1.3	+1.2	+3.2	2.3	+1.2	+4.2	3.2	+1.8	+6.2
		1.8	−0	+1.3	2.7	−0	+2.0	3.2	−0	+2.5	4.2	−0	+3.5	6.2	−0	+5.0
2.56	− 3.15	0.7	+0.7	+1.9	1.0	+1.2	+2.9	1.8	+1.2	+3.7	2.8	+1.2	+4.7	4.2	+1.8	+7.2
		1.9	−0	+1.4	2.9	−0	+2.2	3.7	−0	+3.0	4.7	−0	+4.0	7.2	−0	+6.0
3.15	− 3.94	0.9	+0.9	+2.4	1.4	+1.4	+3.7	2.1	+1.4	+4.4	3.6	+1.4	+5.9	4.8	+2.2	+8.4
		2.4	−0	+1.8	3.7	−0	+2.8	4.4	−0	+3.5	5.9	−0	+5.0	8.4	−0	+7.0
3.94	− 4.73	1.1	+0.9	+2.6	1.6	+1.4	+3.9	2.6	+1.4	+4.9	4.6	+1.4	+6.9	5.8	+2.2	+9.4
		2.6	−0	+2.0	3.9	−0	+3.0	4.9	−0	+4.0	6.9	−0	+6.0	9.4	−0	+8.0
4.73	− 5.52	1.2	+1.0	+2.9	1.9	+1.6	+4.5	3.4	+1.6	+6.0	5.4	+1.6	+8.0	7.5	+2.5	+11.6
		2.9	−0	+2.2	4.5	−0	+3.5	6.0	−0	+5.0	8.0	−0	+7.0	11.6	−0	+10.0
5.52	− 6.30	1.5	+1.0	+3.2	2.4	+1.6	+5.0	3.4	+1.6	+6.0	5.4	+1.6	+8.0	9.5	+2.5	+13.6
		3.2	−0	+2.5	5.0	−0	+4.0	6.0	−0	+5.0	8.0	−0	+7.0	13.6	−0	+12.0
6.30	− 7.09	1.8	+1.0	+3.5	2.9	+1.6	+5.5	4.4	+1.6	+7.0	6.4	+1.6	+9.0	9.5	+2.5	+13.6
		3.5	−0	+2.8	5.5	−0	+4.5	7.0	−0	+6.0	9.0	−0	+8.0	13.6	−0	+12.0
7.09	− 7.88	1.8	+1.2	+3.8	3.2	+1.8	+6.2	5.2	+1.8	+8.2	7.2	+1.8	+10.2	11.2	+2.8	+15.8
		3.8	−0	+3.0	6.2	−0	+5.0	8.2	−0	+7.0	10.2	−0	+9.0	15.8	−0	+14.0
7.88	− 8.86	2.3	+1.2	+4.3	3.2	+1.8	+6.2	5.2	+1.8	+8.2	8.2	+1.8	+11.2	13.2	+2.8	+17.8
		4.3	−0	+3.5	6.2	−0	+5.0	8.2	−0	+7.0	11.2	−0	+10.0	17.8	−0	+16.0
8.86	− 9.85	2.3	+1.2	+4.3	4.2	+1.8	+7.2	6.2	+1.8	+9.2	10.2	+1.8	+13.2	13.2	+2.8	+17.8
		4.3	−0	+3.5	7.2	−0	+6.0	9.2	−0	+8.0	13.2	−0	+12.0	17.8	−0	+16.0
9.85	− 11.03	2.8	+1.2	+4.9	4.0	+2.0	+7.2	7.0	+2.0	+10.2	10.0	+2.0	+13.2	15.0	+3.0	+20.0
		4.9	−0	+4.0	7.2	−0	+6.0	10.2	−0	+9.0	13.2	−0	+12.0	20.0	−0	+18.0
11.03	− 12.41	2.8	+1.2	+4.9	5.0	+2.0	+8.2	7.0	+2.0	+10.2	12.0	+2.0	+15.2	17.0	+3.0	+22.0
		4.9	−0	+4.0	8.2	−0	+7.0	10.2	−0	+9.0	15.2	−0	+14.0	22.0	−0	+20.0
12.41	− 13.98	3.1	+1.4	+5.5	5.8	+2.2	+9.4	7.8	+2.2	+11.4	13.8	+2.2	+17.4	18.5	+3.5	+24.2
		5.5	−0	+4.5	9.4	−0	+8.0	11.4	−0	+10.0	17.4	−0	+16.0	24.2	+0	+22.0
13.98	− 15.75	3.6	+1.4	+6.1	5.8	+2.2	+9.4	9.8	+2.2	+13.4	15.8	+2.2	+19.4	21.5	+3.5	+27.2
		6.1	−0	+5.0	9.4	−0	+8.0	13.4	−0	+12.0	19.4	−0	+18.0	27.2	−0	+25.0
15.75	− 17.72	4.4	+1.6	+7.0	6.5	+2.5	+10.6	9.5	+2.5	+13.6	17.5	+2.5	+21.6	24.0	+4.0	+30.5
		7.0	−0	+6.0	10.6	−0	+9.0	13.6	−0	+12.0	21.6	−0	+20.0	30.5	−0	+28.0
17.72	− 19.69	4.4	+1.6	+7.0	7.5	+2.5	+11.6	11.5	+2.5	+15.6	19.5	+2.5	+23.6	26.0	+4.0	+32.5
		7.0	−0	+6.0	11.6	−0	+10.0	15.6	−0	+14.0	23.6	−0	+22.0	32.5	−0	+30.0

Courtesy of ANSI; B4.1

Dimensions are in mm.

Basic sizes		Tolerance grades[3]																		
Over	Up to and including	IT01	IT0	IT1	IT2	IT3	IT4	IT5	IT6	IT7	IT8	IT9	IT10	IT11	IT12	IT13	IT14	IT15	IT16
0	3	0.0003	0.0005	0.0008	0.0012	0.002	0.003	0.004	0.006	0.010	0.014	0.025	0.040	0.060	0.100	0.140	0.250	0.400	0.600
3	6	0.0004	0.0006	0.001	0.0015	0.0025	0.004	0.005	0.008	0.012	0.018	0.030	0.048	0.075	0.120	0.180	0.300	0.480	0.750
6	10	0.0004	0.0006	0.001	0.0015	0.0025	0.004	0.006	0.009	0.015	0.022	0.036	0.058	0.090	0.150	0.220	0.360	0.580	0.900
10	18	0.0005	0.0008	0.0012	0.002	0.003	0.005	0.008	0.011	0.018	0.027	0.043	0.070	0.110	0.180	0.270	0.430	0.700	1.100
18	30	0.0006	0.001	0.0015	0.0025	0.004	0.006	0.009	0.013	0.021	0.033	0.052	0.084	0.130	0.210	0.330	0.520	0.840	1.300
30	50	0.0006	0.001	0.0015	0.0025	0.004	0.007	0.011	0.016	0.025	0.039	0.062	0.100	0.160	0.250	0.390	0.620	1.000	1.600
50	80	0.0008	0.0012	0.002	0.003	0.005	0.008	0.013	0.019	0.030	0.046	0.074	0.120	0.190	0.300	0.460	0.740	1.200	1.900
80	120	0.001	0.0015	0.0025	0.004	0.006	0.010	0.015	0.022	0.035	0.054	0.087	0.140	0.220	0.350	0.540	0.870	1.400	2.200
120	180	0.0012	0.002	0.0036	0.005	0.008	0.012	0.018	0.025	0.040	0.063	0.100	0.160	0.250	0.400	0.630	1.000	1.600	2.500
180	250	0.002	0.003	0.0045	0.007	0.010	0.014	0.020	0.029	0.046	0.072	0.115	0.185	0.290	0.460	0.720	1.150	1.850	2.900
250	315	0.0025	0.004	0.006	0.008	0.012	0.016	0.023	0.032	0.052	0.081	0.130	0.210	0.320	0.520	0.810	1.300	2.100	3.200
315	400	0.003	0.005	0.007	0.009	0.013	0.018	0.025	0.036	0.057	0.089	0.140	0.230	0.360	0.570	0.890	1.400	2.300	3.600
400	500	0.004	0.006	0.008	0.010	0.015	0.020	0.027	0.040	0.063	0.097	0.156	0.250	0.400	0.630	0.970	1.550	2.500	4.000
500	630	0.0045	0.006	0.009	0.011	0.016	0.022	0.030	0.044	0.070	0.110	0.175	0.280	0.440	0.700	1.100	1.750	2.800	4.400
630	800	0.005	0.007	0.010	0.013	0.018	0.025	0.035	0.050	0.080	0.125	0.200	0.320	0.500	0.800	1.250	2.000	3.200	5.000
800	1000	0.0055	0.008	0.011	0.015	0.021	0.029	0.040	0.056	0.090	0.140	0.230	0.360	0.560	0.900	1.400	2.300	3.600	5.600
1000	1250	0.0065	0.009	0.013	0.018	0.024	0.034	0.046	0.066	0.105	0.165	0.260	0.420	0.660	1.050	1.650	2.600	4.200	6.600
1250	1600	0.008	0.011	0.015	0.021	0.029	0.040	0.054	0.078	0.125	0.195	0.310	0.500	0.780	1.250	1.950	3.100	5.000	7.800
1600	2000	0.009	0.013	0.018	0.025	0.035	0.048	0.065	0.092	0.150	0.230	0.370	0.600	0.920	1.500	2.300	3.700	6.000	9.200
2000	2500	0.011	0.015	0.022	0.030	0.041	0.057	0.077	0.110	0.175	0.280	0.440	0.700	1.100	1.750	2.800	4.400	7.000	11.000
2500	3150	0.013	0.018	0.026	0.036	0.050	0.069	0.093	0.135	0.210	0.330	0.540	0.860	1.350	2.100	3.300	5.400	8.600	13.500

[3]IT Values for tolerance grades larger than IT16 can be calculated by using the following formulas:
IT17 = IT12 × 10; IT18 = IT13 × 10; etc.

APPENDIX 31 • Preferred Hole Basis Clearance Fits—Cylindrical Fits (ANSI B4.2)

AMERICAN NATIONAL STANDARD PREFERRED METRIC LIMITS AND FITS ANSI B4.2—1978
Dimensions are in mm.

BASIC SIZE		LOOSE RUNNING Hole H11	LOOSE RUNNING Shaft c11	LOOSE RUNNING Fit	FREE RUNNING Hole H9	FREE RUNNING Shaft d9	FREE RUNNING Fit	CLOSE RUNNING Hole H8	CLOSE RUNNING Shaft f7	CLOSE RUNNING Fit	SLIDING Hole H7	SLIDING Shaft g6	SLIDING Fit	LOCATIONAL CLEARANCE Hole H7	LOCATIONAL CLEARANCE Shaft h6	LOCATIONAL CLEARANCE Fit
1	MAX	1.060	0.940	0.180	1.025	0.980	0.070	1.014	0.994	0.030	1.010	0.998	0.018	1.010	1.000	0.016
	MIN	1.000	0.880	0.060	1.000	0.955	0.020	1.000	0.984	0.006	1.000	0.992	0.002	1.000	0.994	0.000
1.2	MAX	1.260	1.140	0.180	1.225	1.180	0.070	1.214	1.194	0.030	1.210	1.198	0.018	1.210	1.200	0.016
	MIN	1.200	1.080	0.060	1.200	1.155	0.020	1.200	1.184	0.006	1.200	1.192	0.002	1.200	1.194	0.000
1.6	MAX	1.660	1.540	0.180	1.625	1.580	0.070	1.614	1.594	0.030	1.610	1.598	0.018	1.610	1.600	0.016
	MIN	1.600	1.480	0.060	1.600	1.555	0.020	1.600	1.584	0.006	1.600	1.592	0.002	1.600	1.594	0.000
2	MAX	2.060	1.940	0.180	2.025	1.980	0.070	2.014	1.994	0.030	2.010	1.998	0.018	2.010	2.000	0.016
	MIN	2.000	1.880	0.060	2.000	1.955	0.020	2.000	1.984	0.006	2.000	1.992	0.002	2.000	1.994	0.000
2.5	MAX	2.560	2.440	0.180	2.525	2.480	0.070	2.514	2.494	0.030	2.510	2.498	0.018	2.510	2.500	0.016
	MIN	2.500	2.380	0.060	2.500	2.455	0.020	2.500	2.484	0.006	2.500	2.492	0.002	2.500	2.494	0.000
3	MAX	3.060	2.940	0.180	3.025	2.980	0.070	3.014	2.994	0.030	3.010	2.998	0.018	3.010	3.000	0.016
	MIN	3.000	2.880	0.060	3.000	2.955	0.020	3.000	2.984	0.006	3.000	2.992	0.002	3.000	2.994	0.000
4	MAX	4.075	3.930	0.220	4.030	3.970	0.090	4.018	3.990	0.040	4.012	3.996	0.024	4.012	4.000	0.020
	MIN	4.000	3.855	0.070	4.000	3.940	0.030	4.000	3.978	0.010	4.000	3.988	0.004	4.000	3.992	0.000
5	MAX	5.075	4.930	0.220	5.030	4.970	0.090	5.018	4.990	0.040	5.012	4.996	0.024	5.012	5.000	0.020
	MIN	5.000	4.855	0.070	5.000	4.940	0.030	5.000	4.978	0.010	5.000	4.988	0.004	5.000	4.992	0.000
6	MAX	6.075	5.930	0.220	6.030	5.970	0.090	6.018	5.990	0.040	6.012	5.996	0.024	6.012	6.000	0.020
	MIN	6.000	5.855	0.070	6.000	5.940	0.030	6.000	5.978	0.010	6.000	5.988	0.004	6.000	5.992	0.000
8	MAX	8.090	7.920	0.260	8.036	7.960	0.112	8.022	7.987	0.050	8.015	7.995	0.029	8.015	8.000	0.024
	MIN	8.000	7.830	0.080	8.000	7.924	0.040	8.000	7.972	0.013	8.000	7.986	0.005	8.000	7.991	0.000
10	MAX	10.090	9.920	0.260	10.036	9.960	0.112	10.022	9.987	0.050	10.015	9.995	0.029	10.015	10.000	0.024
	MIN	10.000	9.830	0.080	10.000	9.924	0.040	10.000	9.972	0.013	10.000	9.986	0.005	10.000	9.991	0.000
12	MAX	12.110	11.905	0.315	12.043	11.950	0.136	12.027	11.984	0.061	12.018	11.994	0.035	12.018	12.000	0.029
	MIN	12.000	11.795	0.095	12.000	11.907	0.050	12.000	11.966	0.016	12.000	11.983	0.006	12.000	11.989	0.000
16	MAX	16.110	15.905	0.315	16.043	15.950	0.136	16.027	15.984	0.061	16.018	15.994	0.035	16.018	16.000	0.029
	MIN	16.000	15.795	0.095	16.000	15.907	0.050	16.000	15.966	0.016	16.000	15.983	0.006	16.000	15.989	0.000
20	MAX	20.130	19.890	0.370	20.052	19.935	0.169	20.033	19.980	0.074	20.021	19.993	0.041	20.021	20.000	0.034
	MIN	20.000	19.760	0.110	20.000	19.883	0.065	20.000	19.959	0.020	20.000	19.980	0.007	20.000	19.987	0.000
25	MAX	25.130	24.890	0.370	25.052	24.935	0.169	25.033	24.980	0.074	25.021	24.993	0.041	25.021	25.000	0.034
	MIN	25.000	24.760	0.110	25.000	24.883	0.065	25.000	24.959	0.020	25.000	24.980	0.007	25.000	24.987	0.000
30	MAX	30.130	29.890	0.370	30.052	29.935	0.169	30.033	29.980	0.074	30.021	29.993	0.041	30.021	30.000	0.034
	MIN	30.000	29.760	0.110	30.000	29.883	0.065	30.000	29.959	0.020	30.000	29.980	0.007	30.000	29.987	0.000

Source: American National Standard Preferred Metric Limits and Figs, ANSI B4.2—1978.

APPENDIX 31 • (continued)

BASIC SIZE		LOOSE RUNNING Hole H11	Shaft c11	Fit	FREE RUNNING Hole H9	Shaft d9	Fit	CLOSE RUNNING Hole H8	Shaft f7	Fit	SLIDING Hole H7	Shaft g6	Fit	LOCATIONAL CLEARANCE Hole H7	Shaft h6	Fit
40	MAX	40.160	39.880	0.440	40.062	39.920	0.204	40.039	39.975	0.089	40.025	39.991	0.050	40.025	40.000	0.041
	MIN	40.000	39.720	0.120	40.000	39.858	0.080	40.000	39.950	0.025	40.000	39.975	0.009	40.000	39.984	0.000
50	MAX	50.160	49.870	0.450	50.062	49.920	0.204	50.039	49.975	0.089	50.025	49.991	0.050	50.025	50.000	0.041
	MIN	50.000	49.710	0.130	50.000	49.858	0.080	50.000	49.950	0.025	50.000	49.975	0.009	50.000	49.984	0.000
60	MAX	60.190	59.860	0.520	60.074	59.900	0.248	60.046	59.970	0.106	60.030	59.990	0.059	60.030	60.000	0.049
	MIN	60.000	59.670	0.140	60.000	59.826	0.100	60.000	59.940	0.030	60.000	59.971	0.010	60.000	59.981	0.000
80	MAX	80.190	79.850	0.530	80.074	79.900	0.248	80.046	79.970	0.106	80.030	79.990	0.059	80.030	80.000	0.049
	MIN	80.000	79.660	0.150	80.000	79.826	0.100	80.000	79.940	0.030	80.000	79.971	0.010	80.000	79.981	0.000
100	MAX	100.220	99.830	0.610	100.087	99.880	0.294	100.054	99.964	0.125	100.035	99.988	0.069	100.035	100.000	0.057
	MIN	100.000	99.610	0.170	100.000	99.793	0.120	100.000	99.929	0.036	100.000	99.966	0.012	100.000	99.978	0.000
120	MAX	120.220	119.820	0.620	120.087	119.880	0.294	120.054	119.964	0.125	120.035	119.988	0.069	120.035	120.000	0.057
	MIN	120.000	119.600	0.180	120.000	119.793	0.120	120.000	119.929	0.036	120.000	119.966	0.012	120.000	119.978	0.000
160	MAX	160.250	159.790	0.710	160.100	159.855	0.345	160.063	159.957	0.146	160.040	159.986	0.079	160.040	160.000	0.065
	MIN	160.000	159.540	0.210	160.000	159.755	0.145	160.000	159.917	0.043	160.000	159.961	0.014	160.000	159.975	0.000
200	MAX	200.290	199.760	0.820	200.115	199.830	0.400	200.072	199.950	0.168	200.046	199.985	0.090	200.046	200.000	0.075
	MIN	200.000	199.470	0.240	200.000	199.715	0.170	200.000	199.904	0.050	200.000	199.956	0.015	200.000	199.971	0.000
250	MAX	250.290	249.720	0.860	250.115	249.830	0.400	250.072	249.950	0.168	250.046	249.985	0.090	250.046	250.000	0.075
	MIN	250.000	249.430	0.280	250.000	249.715	0.170	250.000	249.904	0.050	250.000	249.956	0.015	250.000	249.971	0.000
300	MAX	300.320	299.670	0.970	300.130	299.810	0.450	300.081	299.944	0.189	300.052	299.983	0.101	300.052	300.000	0.084
	MIN	300.000	299.350	0.330	300.000	299.680	0.190	300.000	299.892	0.056	300.000	299.951	0.017	300.000	299.968	0.000
400	MAX	400.360	399.600	1.120	400.140	399.790	0.490	400.089	399.938	0.208	400.057	399.982	0.111	400.057	400.000	0.093
	MIN	400.000	399.240	0.400	400.000	399.650	0.210	400.000	399.881	0.062	400.000	399.946	0.018	400.000	399.964	0.000
500	MAX	500.400	499.520	1.280	500.155	499.770	0.540	500.097	499.932	0.228	500.063	499.980	0.123	500.063	500.000	0.103
	MIN	500.000	499.120	0.480	500.000	499.615	0.230	500.000	499.869	0.068	500.000	499.940	0.020	500.000	499.960	0.000

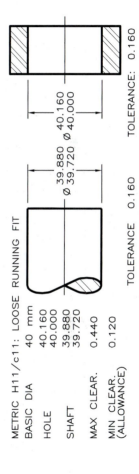

METRIC H11/c11: LOOSE RUNNING FIT

BASIC DIA   40 mm

HOLE   40.160 / 40.000

SHAFT   39.880 / 39.720

MAX CLEAR.   0.440

MIN CLEAR. (ALLOWANCE)   0.120

Ø 39.880   Ø 40.160 / Ø 39.720   Ø 40.000

TOLERANCE   0.160   TOLERANCE: 0.160

APPENDIX 32 • Preferred Hole Basis Transition and Interference Fits—Cylindrical Fits (ANSI B4.2)

Dimensions are in mm.

BASIC SIZE		LOCATIONAL TRANSN. Hole H7	Shaft k6	Fit	LOCATIONAL TRANSN. Hole H7	Shaft n6	Fit	LOCATIONAL INTERF. Hole H7	Shaft p6	Fit	MEDIUM DRIVE Hole H7	Shaft s6	Fit	FORCE Hole H7	Shaft u6	Fit
1	MAX	1.010	1.006	0.010	1.010	1.010	0.006	1.010	1.012	0.004	1.010	1.020	-0.004	1.010	1.024	-0.008
	MIN	1.000	1.000	-0.006	1.000	1.004	-0.010	1.000	1.006	-0.012	1.000	1.014	-0.020	1.000	1.018	-0.024
1.2	MAX	1.210	1.206	0.010	1.210	1.210	0.006	1.210	1.212	0.004	1.210	1.220	-0.004	1.210	1.224	-0.008
	MIN	1.200	1.200	-0.006	1.200	1.204	-0.010	1.200	1.206	-0.012	1.200	1.214	-0.020	1.200	1.218	-0.024
1.6	MAX	1.610	1.606	0.010	1.610	1.610	0.006	1.610	1.612	0.004	1.610	1.620	-0.004	1.610	1.624	-0.008
	MIN	1.600	1.600	-0.006	1.600	1.604	-0.010	1.600	1.606	-0.012	1.600	1.614	-0.020	1.600	1.618	-0.024
2	MAX	2.010	2.006	0.010	2.010	2.010	0.006	2.010	2.010	0.004	2.010	2.020	-0.004	2.010	2.024	-0.008
	MIN	2.000	2.000	-0.006	2.000	2.004	-0.010	2.000	2.006	-0.012	2.000	2.014	-0.020	2.000	2.018	-0.024
2.5	MAX	2.510	2.506	0.010	2.510	2.510	0.006	2.510	2.512	0.004	2.510	2.520	-0.004	2.510	2.524	-0.008
	MIN	2.500	2.500	-0.006	2.500	2.504	-0.010	2.500	2.506	-0.012	2.500	2.514	-0.020	2.500	2.518	-0.024
3	MAX	3.010	3.006	0.010	3.010	3.010	0.006	3.010	3.012	0.004	3.010	3.020	-0.004	3.010	3.024	-0.008
	MIN	3.000	3.000	-0.006	3.000	3.004	-0.010	3.000	3.006	-0.012	3.000	3.014	-0.020	3.000	3.018	-0.024
4	MAX	4.012	4.009	0.011	4.012	4.016	0.004	4.012	4.020	0.000	4.012	4.027	-0.007	4.012	4.031	-0.011
	MIN	4.000	4.001	-0.009	4.000	4.008	-0.016	4.000	4.012	-0.020	4.000	4.019	-0.027	4.000	4.023	-0.031
5	MAX	5.012	5.009	0.011	5.012	5.016	0.004	5.012	5.020	0.000	5.012	5.027	-0.007	5.012	5.031	-0.011
	MIN	5.000	5.001	-0.009	5.000	5.008	-0.016	5.000	5.012	-0.020	5.000	5.019	-0.027	5.000	5.023	-0.031
6	MAX	6.012	6.009	0.011	6.012	6.016	0.004	6.012	6.020	0.000	6.012	6.027	-0.007	6.012	6.031	-0.011
	MIN	6.000	6.001	-0.009	6.000	6.008	-0.016	6.000	6.012	-0.020	6.000	6.019	-0.027	6.000	6.023	-0.031
8	MAX	8.015	8.010	0.014	8.015	8.019	0.005	8.015	8.024	0.000	8.015	8.032	-0.008	8.015	8.037	-0.013
	MIN	8.000	8.001	-0.010	8.000	8.010	-0.019	8.000	8.015	-0.024	8.000	8.023	-0.032	8.000	8.028	-0.037
10	MAX	10.015	10.010	0.014	10.015	10.019	0.005	10.015	10.024	0.000	10.015	10.032	-0.008	10.015	10.037	-0.013
	MIN	10.000	10.001	-0.010	10.000	10.010	-0.019	10.000	10.015	-0.024	10.000	10.023	-0.032	10.000	10.028	-0.037
12	MAX	12.018	12.012	0.017	12.018	12.023	0.006	12.018	12.029	0.000	12.018	12.039	-0.010	12.018	12.044	-0.015
	MIN	12.000	12.001	-0.012	12.000	12.012	-0.023	12.000	12.018	-0.029	12.000	12.028	-0.039	12.000	12.033	-0.044
16	MAX	16.018	16.012	0.017	16.018	16.023	0.006	16.018	16.029	0.000	16.018	16.039	-0.010	16.018	16.044	-0.015
	MIN	16.000	16.001	-0.012	16.000	16.012	-0.023	16.000	16.018	-0.029	16.000	16.028	-0.039	16.000	16.033	-0.044
20	MAX	20.021	20.015	0.019	20.021	20.028	0.006	20.021	20.035	-0.001	20.021	20.048	-0.014	20.021	20.054	-0.020
	MIN	20.000	20.002	-0.015	20.000	20.015	-0.028	20.000	20.022	-0.035	20.000	20.035	-0.048	20.000	20.041	-0.054
25	MAX	25.021	25.015	0.019	25.021	25.028	0.006	25.021	25.035	-0.001	25.021	25.048	-0.014	25.021	25.061	-0.027
	MIN	25.000	25.002	-0.015	25.000	25.015	-0.028	25.000	25.022	-0.035	25.000	25.035	-0.048	25.000	25.048	-0.061
30	MAX	30.021	30.015	0.019	30.021	30.028	0.006	30.021	30.035	-0.001	30.021	30.048	-0.014	30.021	30.061	-0.027
	MIN	30.000	30.002	-0.015	30.000	30.015	-0.028	30.000	30.022	-0.035	30.000	30.035	-0.048	30.000	30.048	-0.061

Source: American National Standard Preferred Metric Limit and Fits, ANSI B4.2—1978.

APPENDIX 32 • (continued)

BASIC SIZE		LOCATIONAL TRANSN. Hole H7	LOCATIONAL TRANSN. Shaft k6	LOCATIONAL TRANSN. Fit	LOCATIONAL TRANSN. Hole H7	LOCATIONAL TRANSN. Shaft n6	LOCATIONAL TRANSN. Fit	LOCATIONAL INTERF. Hole H7	LOCATIONAL INTERF. Shaft p6	LOCATIONAL INTERF. Fit	MEDIUM DRIVE Hole H7	MEDIUM DRIVE Shaft s6	MEDIUM DRIVE Fit	FORCE Hole H7	FORCE Shaft u6	FORCE Fit
40	MAX	40.025	40.018	0.023	40.025	40.033	0.008	40.025	40.042	−0.001	40.025	40.059	−0.018	40.025	40.076	−0.035
	MIN	40.000	40.002	−0.018	40.000	40.017	−0.033	40.000	40.026	−0.042	40.000	40.043	−0.059	40.000	40.060	−0.076
50	MAX	50.025	50.018	0.023	50.025	50.033	0.008	50.025	50.042	−0.001	50.025	50.059	−0.018	50.025	50.086	−0.045
	MIN	50.000	50.002	−0.018	50.000	50.017	−0.033	50.000	50.026	−0.042	50.000	50.043	−0.059	50.000	50.070	−0.086
60	MAX	60.030	60.021	0.028	60.030	60.039	0.010	60.030	60.051	−0.002	60.030	60.072	−0.023	60.030	60.106	−0.057
	MIN	60.000	60.002	−0.021	60.000	60.020	−0.039	60.000	60.032	−0.051	60.000	60.053	−0.072	60.000	60.087	−0.106
80	MAX	80.030	80.021	0.028	80.030	80.039	0.010	80.030	80.051	−0.002	80.030	80.078	−0.029	80.030	80.121	−0.072
	MIN	80.000	80.002	−0.021	80.000	80.020	−0.039	80.000	80.032	−0.051	80.000	80.059	−0.078	80.000	80.102	−0.121
100	MAX	100.035	100.025	0.032	100.035	100.045	0.012	100.035	100.059	−0.002	100.035	100.093	−0.036	100.035	100.146	−0.089
	MIN	100.000	100.003	−0.025	100.000	100.023	−0.045	100.000	100.037	−0.059	100.000	100.071	−0.093	100.000	100.124	−0.146
120	MAX	120.035	120.025	0.032	120.035	120.045	0.012	120.035	120.059	−0.002	120.035	120.101	−0.044	120.035	120.166	−0.109
	MIN	120.000	120.003	−0.025	120.000	120.023	−0.045	120.000	120.037	−0.059	120.000	120.079	−0.101	120.000	120.144	−0.166
160	MAX	160.040	160.028	0.037	160.040	160.052	0.013	160.040	160.068	−0.003	160.040	160.125	−0.060	160.040	160.215	−0.150
	MIN	160.000	160.003	−0.028	160.000	160.027	−0.052	160.000	160.043	−0.068	160.000	160.100	−0.125	160.000	160.190	−0.215
200	MAX	200.046	200.033	0.042	200.046	200.060	0.015	200.046	200.079	−0.004	200.046	200.151	−0.076	200.046	200.265	−0.190
	MIN	200.000	200.004	−0.033	200.000	200.031	−0.060	200.000	200.050	−0.079	200.000	200.122	−0.151	200.000	200.236	−0.265
250	MAX	250.046	250.033	0.042	250.046	250.060	0.015	250.046	250.079	−0.004	250.046	250.169	−0.094	250.046	250.313	−0.238
	MIN	250.000	250.004	−0.033	250.000	250.031	−0.060	250.000	250.050	−0.079	250.000	250.140	−0.169	250.000	250.284	−0.313
300	MAX	300.052	300.036	0.048	300.052	300.066	0.018	300.052	300.088	−0.004	300.052	300.202	−0.118	300.052	300.382	−0.298
	MIN	300.000	300.004	−0.036	300.000	300.034	−0.066	300.000	300.056	−0.088	300.000	300.170	−0.202	300.000	300.350	−0.382
400	MAX	400.057	400.040	0.053	400.057	400.073	0.020	400.057	400.098	−0.005	400.057	400.244	−0.151	400.057	400.471	−0.378
	MIN	400.000	400.004	−0.040	400.000	400.037	−0.073	400.000	400.062	−0.098	400.000	400.208	−0.244	400.000	400.435	−0.471
500	MAX	500.063	500.045	0.058	500.063	500.080	0.023	500.063	500.108	−0.005	500.063	500.292	−0.189	500.063	500.580	−0.477
	MIN	500.000	500.005	−0.045	500.000	500.040	−0.080	500.000	500.068	−0.108	500.000	500.252	−0.292	500.000	500.540	−0.580

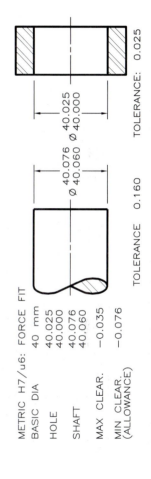

```
METRIC  H7/u6:  FORCE  FIT
BASIC DIA        40 mm
HOLE             40.025
                 40.000
SHAFT            40.076
                 40.060
MAX CLEAR.      −0.035
MIN CLEAR.      −0.076
(ALLOWANCE)
```

Ø 40.076 Ø 40.025
Ø 40.060 Ø 40.000

TOLERANCE 0.160   TOLERANCE: 0.025

APPENDIX 33 • Preferred Shaft Basis Clearance Fits—Cylindrical Fits (ANSI B4.2)

Dimensions are in mm.

BASIC SIZE		LOOSE RUNNING			FREE RUNNING			CLOSE RUNNING			SLIDING			LOCATIONAL CLEARANCE		
		Hole C11	Shaft h11	Fit	Hole D9	Shaft h9	Fit	Hole F8	Shaft h7	Fit	Hole G7	Shaft h6	Fit	Hole H7	Shaft h6	Fit
1	MAX	1.120	1.000	0.180	1.045	1.000	0.070	1.020	1.000	0.030	1.012	1.000	0.018	1.010	1.000	0.016
	MIN	1.060	0.940	0.060	1.020	0.975	0.020	1.006	0.990	0.006	1.002	0.994	0.002	1.000	0.994	0.000
1.2	MAX	1.320	1.200	0.180	1.245	1.200	0.070	1.220	1.200	0.030	1.212	1.200	0.018	1.210	1.200	0.016
	MIN	1.260	1.140	0.060	1.220	1.175	0.020	1.206	1.190	0.006	1.202	1.194	0.002	1.200	1.194	0.000
1.6	MAX	1.720	1.600	0.180	1.656	1.600	0.070	1.620	1.600	0.030	1.612	1.600	0.018	1.610	1.600	0.016
	MIN	1.660	1.540	0.060	1.620	1.575	0.020	1.606	1.590	0.006	1.602	1.595	0.002	1.600	1.594	0.000
2	MAX	2.120	2.000	0.180	2.045	2.000	0.070	2.020	2.000	0.030	2.012	2.000	0.018	2.010	2.000	0.016
	MIN	2.060	1.940	0.060	2.020	1.975	0.020	2.006	1.990	0.006	2.002	1.994	0.002	2.000	1.994	0.000
2.5	MAX	2.620	2.500	0.180	2.545	2.500	0.070	2.520	2.500	0.030	2.512	2.500	0.018	2.510	2.500	0.016
	MIN	2.560	2.440	0.060	2.520	2.475	0.020	2.506	2.490	0.006	2.502	2.494	0.002	2.500	2.494	0.000
3	MAX	3.120	3.000	0.180	3.045	3.000	0.070	3.020	3.000	0.030	3.012	3.000	0.018	3.010	3.000	0.016
	MIN	3.060	2.940	0.060	3.020	2.975	0.020	3.006	2.990	0.006	3.002	2.994	0.002	3.000	2.994	0.000
4	MAX	4.145	4.000	0.220	4.060	4.000	0.090	4.028	4.000	0.040	4.016	4.000	0.024	4.012	4.000	0.020
	MIN	4.070	3.925	0.070	4.030	3.970	0.030	4.010	3.988	0.010	4.004	3.992	0.004	4.000	3.992	0.000
5	MAX	5.145	5.000	0.220	5.060	5.000	0.090	5.028	5.000	0.040	5.016	5.000	0.024	5.012	5.000	0.020
	MIN	5.070	4.925	0.070	5.030	4.970	0.030	5.010	4.988	0.010	5.004	4.992	0.004	5.000	4.992	0.000
6	MAX	6.145	6.000	0.220	6.060	6.000	0.090	6.028	6.000	0.040	6.016	6.000	0.024	6.012	6.000	0.020
	MIN	6.070	5.925	0.070	6.030	5.970	0.030	6.010	5.988	0.010	6.004	5.992	0.004	6.000	5.992	0.000
8	MAX	8.170	8.000	0.260	8.076	8.000	0.112	8.035	8.000	0.050	8.020	8.000	0.029	8.015	8.000	0.024
	MIN	8.080	7.910	0.080	8.040	7.964	0.040	8.013	7.985	0.013	8.005	7.991	0.005	8.000	7.991	0.000
10	MAX	10.170	10.000	0.260	10.076	10.000	0.112	10.035	10.000	0.050	10.020	10.000	0.029	10.015	10.000	0.024
	MIN	10.080	9.910	0.080	10.040	9.964	0.040	10.013	9.985	0.013	10.005	9.991	0.005	10.000	9.991	0.000
12	MAX	12.205	12.000	0.315	12.093	12.000	0.136	12.043	12.000	0.061	12.024	12.000	0.035	12.018	12.000	0.029
	MIN	12.095	11.890	0.095	12.050	11.957	0.050	12.016	11.982	0.016	12.006	11.989	0.006	12.000	11.989	0.000
16	MAX	16.205	16.000	0.315	16.093	16.000	0.136	16.043	16.000	0.061	16.024	16.000	0.035	16.018	16.000	0.029
	MIN	16.095	15.890	0.095	16.050	15.957	0.050	16.016	15.982	0.016	16.006	15.989	0.006	16.000	15.989	0.000
20	MAX	20.240	20.000	0.370	20.117	20.000	0.169	20.053	20.000	0.074	20.028	20.000	0.041	20.021	20.000	0.034
	MIN	20.110	19.870	0.110	20.065	19.948	0.065	20.020	19.979	0.020	20.007	19.987	0.007	20.000	19.987	0.000
25	MAX	25.240	25.000	0.370	25.117	25.000	0.169	25.053	25.000	0.074	25.028	25.000	0.041	25.021	25.000	0.034
	MIN	25.110	24.870	0.110	25.065	24.948	0.065	25.020	24.979	0.020	25.007	24.987	0.007	25.000	24.987	0.000
30	MAX	30.240	30.000	0.370	30.117	30.000	0.169	30.053	30.000	0.074	30.028	30.000	0.041	30.021	30.000	0.034
	MIN	30.110	29.870	0.110	30.065	29.948	0.065	30.020	29.979	0.020	30.007	29.987	0.007	30.000	29.987	0.000

Source: American National Standard Preferred Metric Limits and Fits, ANSI B4.2—1978.

BASIC SIZE		LOOSE RUNNING Hole C11	Shaft h11	Fit	FREE RUNNING Hole D9	Shaft h9	Fit	CLOSE RUNNING Hole F8	Shaft h7	Fit	SLIDING Hole G7	Shaft h6	Fit	LOCATIONAL CLEARANCE Hole H7	Shaft h6	Fit
40	MAX	40.280	40.000	0.440	40.142	40.000	0.204	40.064	40.000	0.089	40.034	40.000	0.050	40.025	40.000	0.041
	MIN	40.120	39.840	0.120	40.080	39.938	0.080	40.025	39.975	0.025	40.009	39.984	0.009	40.000	39.984	0.000
50	MAX	50.290	50.000	0.450	50.142	50.000	0.204	50.064	50.000	0.089	50.034	50.000	0.050	50.025	50.000	0.041
	MIN	50.130	49.840	0.130	50.080	49.938	0.080	50.025	49.975	0.025	50.009	49.984	0.009	50.000	49.984	0.000
60	MAX	60.330	60.000	0.520	60.174	60.000	0.248	60.076	60.000	0.106	60.040	60.000	0.059	60.030	60.000	0.049
	MIN	60.140	59.810	0.140	60.100	59.926	0.100	60.030	59.970	0.030	60.010	59.981	0.010	60.000	59.981	0.000
80	MAX	80.340	80.000	0.530	80.174	80.000	0.248	80.076	80.000	0.106	80.040	80.000	0.059	80.030	80.000	0.049
	MIN	80.150	79.810	0.150	80.100	79.926	0.100	80.030	79.970	0.030	80.010	79.981	0.010	80.000	79.981	0.000
100	MAX	100.390	100.000	0.610	100.207	100.000	0.294	100.090	100.000	0.125	100.047	100.000	0.069	100.035	100.000	0.057
	MIN	100.170	99.780	0.170	100.120	99.913	0.120	100.036	99.965	0.036	100.012	99.979	0.012	100.000	99.979	0.000
120	MAX	120.400	120.000	0.620	120.207	120.000	0.294	120.090	120.000	0.125	120.047	120.000	0.069	120.035	120.000	0.057
	MIN	120.180	119.780	0.180	120.120	119.913	0.120	120.036	119.965	0.036	120.012	119.978	0.012	120.000	119.978	0.000
160	MAX	160.460	160.000	0.710	160.245	160.000	0.345	160.106	160.000	0.146	160.054	160.000	0.079	160.040	160.000	0.065
	MIN	160.210	159.750	0.210	160.145	159.900	0.145	160.043	159.960	0.043	160.014	159.975	0.014	160.000	159.975	0.000
200	MAX	200.530	200.000	0.820	200.285	200.000	0.400	200.122	200.000	0.168	200.061	200.000	0.090	200.046	200.000	0.075
	MIN	200.240	199.710	0.240	200.170	199.885	0.170	200.050	199.954	0.050	200.015	199.971	0.015	200.000	199.971	0.000
250	MAX	250.570	250.000	0.860	250.285	250.000	0.400	250.122	250.000	0.168	250.061	250.000	0.090	250.046	250.000	0.075
	MIN	250.280	249.710	0.280	250.170	249.885	0.170	250.050	249.954	0.050	250.015	249.971	0.015	250.000	249.971	0.000
300	MAX	300.650	300.000	0.970	300.320	300.000	0.450	300.137	300.000	0.189	300.069	300.000	0.101	300.052	300.000	0.084
	MIN	300.330	299.680	0.330	300.190	299.870	0.190	300.056	299.948	0.056	300.017	299.968	0.017	300.000	299.968	0.000
400	MAX	400.760	400.000	1.120	400.350	400.000	0.490	400.151	400.000	0.208	400.075	400.000	0.111	400.057	400.000	0.983
	MIN	400.400	399.640	0.400	400.210	399.860	0.210	400.062	399.943	0.062	400.018	399.964	0.018	400.000	399.964	0.000
500	MAX	500.880	500.000	1.280	500.385	500.000	0.540	500.165	500.000	0.228	500.083	500.000	0.123	500.063	500.000	0.103
	MIN	500.480	499.600	0.480	500.230	499.845	0.230	500.068	499.937	0.068	500.020	499.960	0.020	500.000	499.960	0.000

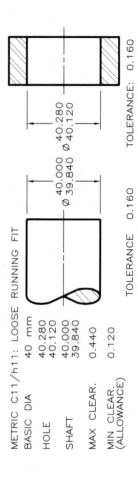

```
                        40.280   40.280
                        40.120   40.120
                                            TOLERANCE:  0.160

            Ø 40.000  Ø 40.280
            Ø 39.840  Ø 40.120

                        TOLERANCE  0.160

METRIC  C11/h11:  LOOSE  RUNNING  FIT
  BASIC  DIA        40  mm
  HOLE             40.280
                   40.120
  SHAFT            40.000
                   39.840
  MAX  CLEAR.      0.440
  MIN  CLEAR.      0.120
  (ALLOWANCE)
```

APPENDIX 34 • Preferred Shaft Basis Transition and Interference Fits—Cylindrical Fits (ANSI B4.2)

Dimensions are in mm.

BASIC SIZE		LOCATIONAL TRANSN. Hole K7	Shaft h6	Fit	LOCATIONAL TRANSN. Hole N7	Shaft h6	Fit	LOCATIONAL INTERF Hole P7	Shaft h6	Fit	MEDIUM DRIVE Hole S7	Shaft h6	Fit	FORCE Hole U7	Shaft h6	Fit
1	MAX	1.000	1.000	0.006	0.996	1.000	0.002	0.994	1.000	0.000	0.986	1.000	−0.008	0.982	1.000	−0.012
	MIN	0.990	0.994	−0.010	0.986	0.994	−0.014	0.984	0.994	−0.016	0.976	0.994	−0.024	0.972	0.994	−0.028
1.2	MAX	1.200	1.200	0.006	1.196	1.200	0.002	1.194	1.200	0.000	1.186	1.200	−0.008	1.182	1.200	−0.012
	MIN	1.190	1.194	−0.010	1.186	1.194	−0.014	1.184	1.194	−0.016	1.176	1.194	−0.024	1.172	1.194	−0.028
1.6	MAX	1.600	1.600	0.006	1.596	1.600	0.002	1.594	1.600	0.000	1.586	1.600	−0.008	1.582	1.600	−0.012
	MIN	1.590	1.594	−0.010	1.586	1.594	−0.014	1.584	1.594	−0.016	1.576	1.594	−0.024	1.572	1.594	−0.028
2	MAX	2.000	2.000	0.006	1.996	2.000	0.002	1.994	2.000	0.008	1.986	2.000	−0.008	1.982	2.000	−0.012
	MIN	1.990	1.994	−0.010	1.986	1.994	−0.014	1.984	1.994	−0.016	1.976	1.994	−0.024	1.972	1.994	−0.028
2.5	MAX	2.500	2.500	0.006	2.496	2.500	0.002	2.494	2.500	0.000	2.486	2.500	−0.008	2.482	2.500	−0.012
	MIN	2.490	2.494	−0.010	2.486	2.494	−0.014	2.484	2.494	−0.016	2.476	2.494	−0.024	2.472	2.494	−0.028
3	MAX	3.000	3.000	0.006	2.996	3.000	0.002	2.994	3.000	0.000	2.986	3.000	−0.008	2.982	3.000	−0.012
	MIN	2.990	2.994	−.010	2.986	2.994	−0.014	2.984	2.994	−0.016	2.976	2.994	−0.024	2.972	2.994	−0.028
4	MAX	4.003	4.000	0.011	3.996	4.000	0.004	3.992	4.000	0.000	3.985	4.000	−0.007	3.981	4.000	−0.011
	MIN	3.991	3.992	−0.009	3.984	3.992	−0.016	3.980	3.992	−0.020	3.973	3.992	−0.027	3.969	3.992	−0.031
5	MAX	5.003	5.000	0.011	4.996	5.000	0.004	4.992	5.000	0.000	4.985	5.000	−0.007	4.981	5.000	−0.011
	MIN	4.991	4.992	−0.009	4.984	4.992	−0.016	4.980	4.992	−0.020	4.973	4.992	−0.027	4.969	4.992	−0.031
6	MAX	6.003	6.000	0.011	5.996	6.000	0.004	5.992	6.000	0.000	5.985	6.000	−0.007	5.981	6.000	−0.011
	MIN	5.991	5.992	−0.009	5.984	5.992	−0.016	5.980	5.992	−0.020	5.973	5.992	−0.027	5.969	5.992	−0.031
8	MAX	8.005	8.000	0.014	7.986	8.000	0.005	7.991	8.000	0.000	7.983	8.000	−0.008	7.978	8.000	−0.013
	MIN	7.990	7.991	−0.010	7.981	7.991	−0.019	7.976	7.991	−0.024	7.968	7.991	−0.032	7.963	7.991	−0.037
10	MAX	10.005	10.000	0.014	9.996	10.000	0.005	9.991	10.000	0.0000	9.983	10.000	−0.008	9.978	10.000	−0.013
	MIN	9.990	9.991	−0.010	9.981	9.991	−0.019	9.976	9.991	−0.024	9.968	9.991	−0.032	9.963	9.991	−0.037
12	MAX	12.006	12.000	0.017	11.995	12.000	0.006	11.989	12.000	0.000	11.979	12.000	−0.010	11.974	12.000	−0.015
	MIN	11.988	11.989	−0.012	11.977	11.989	−0.023	11.971	11.989	−0.029	11.961	11.989	−0.039	11.956	11.989	−0.044
16	MAX	16.006	16.000	0.017	15.995	16.000	0.006	15.989	16.000	0.000	15.979	16.000	−0.010	15.974	16.000	−0.015
	MIN	15.988	15.989	−0.012	15.977	15.989	−0.023	15.971	15.989	−0.029	15.961	15.989	−0.039	15.956	15.989	−0.044
20	MAX	20.006	20.000	0.019	19.993	20.000	0.006	19.986	20.000	−0.001	19.973	20.000	−0.014	19.967	20.000	−0.020
	MIN	19.985	19.987	−0.015	19.972	19.987	−0.028	19.965	19.987	−0.035	19.952	19.987	−0.048	19.946	19.987	−0.054
25	MAX	25.006	25.000	0.019	24.993	25.000	0.006	24.986	25.000	−0.001	24.973	25.000	−0.014	24.960	25.000	−0.027
	MIN	24.985	24.987	−0.015	24.972	24.987	−0.028	24.965	24.987	−0.035	24.952	24.987	−0.048	24.939	24.987	−0.061
30	MAX	30.006	30.000	0.019	29.993	30.000	0.006	29.986	30.000	−0.001	29.973	30.000	−0.014	29.960	30.000	−0.027
	MIN	29.985	29.987	−0.015	29.972	29.987	−0.028	29.965	29.987	−0.035	29.952	29.987	−0.048	29.939	29.987	−0.061

Source: American National Standard Preferred Metric Limits and Fits, ANSI B4.2—1978.

Dimensions are in mm.

BASIC SIZE		LOCATIONAL TRANSN. Hole K7	Shaft h6	Fit	LOCATIONAL TRANSN. Hole N7	Shaft h6	Fit	LOCATIONAL INTERF. Hole P7	Shaft h6	Fit	MEDIUM DRIVE Hole S7	Shaft h6	Fit	FORCE Hole U7	Shaft h6	Fit
40	MAX	40.007	40.000	0.023	39.992	40.000	0.008	39.983	40.000	-0.001	39.966	40.000	-0.018	39.949	40.000	-0.035
	MIN	39.982	39.984	-0.018	39.967	39.984	-0.033	39.958	39.984	-0.042	39.941	39.984	-0.059	39.924	39.984	-0.076
50	MAX	50.007	50.000	0.023	49.992	50.000	0.008	49.983	50.000	-0.001	49.966	50.000	-0.018	49.939	50.000	-0.045
	MIN	49.982	49.984	-0.018	49.967	49.984	-0.033	49.958	49.984	-0.042	49.941	49.984	-0.059	49.914	49.984	-0.086
60	MAX	60.009	60.000	0.028	59.991	60.000	0.010	59.979	60.000	-0.002	59.958	60.000	-0.023	59.924	60.000	-0.057
	MIN	59.979	59.981	-0.021	59.961	59.981	-0.039	59.949	59.981	-0.051	59.928	59.981	-0.072	59.894	59.981	-0.106
80	MAX	80.009	80.000	0.028	79.991	80.000	0.010	79.979	80.000	-0.002	79.952	80.000	-0.029	79.909	80.000	-0.072
	MIN	79.979	79.981	-0.021	79.961	79.981	-0.039	79.949	79.981	-0.051	79.922	79.981	-0.078	79.879	79.981	-0.121
100	MAX	100.010	100.000	0.032	99.990	100.000	0.012	99.976	100.000	-0.002	99.942	100.000	-0.036	99.889	100.000	-0.089
	MIN	99.975	99.978	-0.025	99.955	99.978	-0.045	99.941	99.978	-0.059	99.907	99.978	-0.093	99.854	99.978	-0.146
120	MAX	120.010	120.000	0.032	119.990	120.000	0.012	119.976	120.000	-0.002	119.934	120.000	-0.044	119.869	120.000	-0.109
	MIN	119.975	119.978	-0.025	119.955	119.978	-0.045	119.941	119.978	-0.059	119.899	119.978	-0.101	119.834	119.978	-0.166
160	MAX	160.012	160.000	0.037	159.988	160.000	0.013	159.972	160.000	-0.003	159.915	160.000	-0.060	159.825	160.000	-0.150
	MIN	159.972	159.975	-0.028	159.948	159.975	-0.052	159.932	159.975	-0.068	159.875	159.975	-0.125	159.785	159.975	-0.215
200	MAX	200.013	200.000	0.042	199.986	200.000	0.015	199.967	200.000	-0.004	199.895	200.000	-0.076	199.781	200.000	-0.190
	MIN	199.967	199.971	-0.033	199.940	199.971	-0.060	199.921	199.971	-0.079	199.849	199.971	-0.151	199.735	199.971	-0.265
250	MAX	250.013	250.000	0.042	249.986	250.000	0.015	249.967	250.000	-0.004	249.877	250.000	-0.094	249.733	250.000	-0.238
	MIN	249.967	249.971	-0.033	249.940	249.971	-0.060	249.921	249.971	-0.079	249.831	249.971	-0.169	249.687	249.971	-0.313
300	MAX	300.016	300.000	0.048	299.986	300.000	0.018	299.964	300.000	-0.004	299.850	300.000	-0.188	299.670	300.000	-0.298
	MIN	299.964	299.968	-0.036	299.934	299.968	-0.066	299.912	299.968	-0.088	299.798	299.968	-0.202	299.618	299.968	-0.382
400	MAX	400.017	400.000	0.053	399.984	400.000	0.020	399.959	400.000	-0.005	399.813	400.000	-0.151	399.586	400.000	-0.378
	MIN	399.960	399.964	-0.040	399.927	399.964	-0.073	399.902	399.964	-0.08	399.756	399.964	-0.244	399.529	399.964	-0.471
500	MAX	500.018	500.000	0.058	499.983	500.000	0.023	499.955	500.000	-0.005	499.771	500.000	-0.189	499.483	500.000	-0.477
	MIN	499.955	499.960	-0.045	499.920	499.960	-0.080	499.892	499.960	-0.1808	499.708	499.960	-0.292	499.420	499.960	-0.580

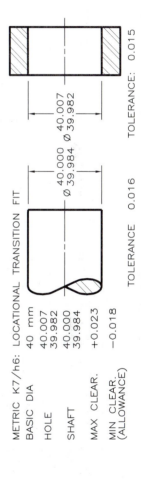

METRIC K7/h6: LOCATIONAL TRANSITION FIT

BASIC DIA	40 mm
HOLE	40.007 / 39.982
SHAFT	40.000 / 39.984
MAX CLEAR.	+0.023
MIN CLEAR. (ALLOWANCE)	-0.018

Ø 40.000 Ø 39.984   TOLERANCE 0.016

Ø 40.007 Ø 39.982   TOLERANCE: 0.015

APPENDIX 35 • Hole Sizes for Nonpreferred Diameters (millimeters)

Basic Size		C11	D9	F8	G7	H7	H8	H9	H11	K7	N7	P7	S7	U7
OVER	0	+0.120	+0.045	+0.020	+0.012	+0.010	+0.014	+0.025	+0.060	0.000	−0.004	−0.006	−0.014	−0.018
TO	3	+0.060	+0.020	+0.006	+0.002	0.000	0.000	0.000	0.000	−0.010	−0.014	−0.016	−0.024	−0.028
OVER	3	+0.145	+0.060	+0.028	+0.016	+0.012	+0.018	+0.030	+0.075	+0.003	−0.004	−0.008	−0.015	−0.019
TO	6	+0.070	+0.030	+0.010	+0.004	0.000	0.000	0.000	0.000	−0.009	−0.016	−0.020	−0.027	−0.031
OVER	6	+0.170	+0.076	+0.035	+0.020	+0.015	+0.022	+0.036	+0.090	+0.005	−0.004	−0.009	−0.017	−0.022
TO	10	+0.080	+0.040	+0.013	+0.005	0.000	0.000	0.000	0.000	−0.010	−0.019	−0.024	−0.032	−0.037
OVER	10	+0.205	+0.093	+0.043	+0.024	+0.018	+0.027	+0.043	+0.110	+0.006	−0.005	−0.011	−0.021	−0.026
TO	14	+0.095	+0.050	+0.016	+0.006	0.000	0.000	0.000	0.000	−0.012	−0.023	−0.029	−0.039	−0.044
OVER	14	+0.205	+0.093	+0.043	+0.024	+0.018	+0.027	+0.043	+0.110	+0.006	−0.005	−0.011	−0.021	−0.026
TO	18	+0.095	+0.050	+0.016	+0.006	0.000	0.000	0.000	0.000	−0.012	−0.023	−0.029	−0.039	−0.044
OVER	18	+0.240	+0.117	+0.053	+0.028	+0.021	+0.033	+0.052	+0.130	+0.006	−0.007	−0.014	−0.027	−0.033
TO	24	+0.110	+0.065	+0.020	+0.007	0.000	0.000	0.000	0.000	−0.015	−0.028	−0.035	−0.048	−0.054
OVER	24	+0.240	+0.117	+0.053	+0.028	+0.021	+0.033	+0.052	+0.130	+0.006	−0.007	−0.014	−0.027	−0.040
TO	30	+0.110	+0.065	+0.020	+0.007	0.000	0.000	0.000	0.000	−0.015	−0.028	−0.035	−0.048	−0.061
OVER	30	+0.280	+0.142	+0.064	+0.034	+0.025	+0.039	+0.062	+0.160	+0.007	−0.008	−0.017	−0.034	−0.051
TO	40	+0.120	+0.080	+0.025	+0.009	0.000	0.000	0.000	0.000	−0.018	−0.033	−0.042	−0.059	−0.076
OVER	40	+0.290	+0.142	+0.064	+0.034	+0.025	+0.039	+0.062	+0.160	+0.007	−0.008	−0.017	−0.034	−0.061
TO	50	+0.130	+0.080	+0.025	+0.009	0.000	0.000	0.000	0.000	−0.018	−0.033	−0.042	−0.059	−0.086
OVER	50	+0.330	+0.174	+0.076	+0.040	+0.030	+0.046	+0.074	+0.190	+0.009	−0.009	−0.021	−0.042	−0.076
TO	65	+0.140	+0.100	+0.030	+0.010	0.000	0.000	0.000	0.000	−0.021	−0.039	−0.051	−0.072	−0.106
OVER	65	+0.340	+0.174	+0.076	+0.040	+0.030	+0.046	+0.074	+0.190	+0.009	−0.009	−0.021	−0.048	−0.091
TO	80	+0.150	+0.100	+0.030	+0.010	0.000	0.000	0.000	0.000	−0.021	−0.039	−0.051	−0.078	−0.121
OVER	80	+0.390	+0.207	+0.090	+0.047	+0.035	+0.054	+0.087	+0.220	+0.010	−0.010	−0.024	−0.058	−0.111
TO	100	+0.170	+0.120	+0.036	+0.012	0.000	0.000	0.000	0.000	−0.025	−0.045	−0.059	−0.093	−0.146

Basic Size	C11	D9	F8	G7	H7	H8	H9	H11	K7	N7	P7	S7	U7
OVER 100	+0.400	+0.207	+0.090	+0.047	+0.035	+0.054	+0.087	+0.220	+0.010	-0.010	-0.024	-0.066	-0.131
TO 120	+0.180	+0.120	+0.036	+0.012	0.000	0.000	0.000	0.000	-0.025	-0.045	-0.059	-0.101	-0.166
OVER 120	+0.450	+0.245	+0.106	+0.054	+0.040	+0.063	+0.100	+0.250	+0.012	-0.012	-0.028	-0.077	-0.155
TO 140	+0.200	+0.145	+0.043	+0.014	0.000	0.000	0.000	0.000	-0.028	-0.052	-0.068	-0.117	-0.195
OVER 140	+0.460	+0.245	+0.106	+0.054	+0.040	+0.063	+0.100	+0.250	+0.012	-0.012	-0.028	-0.085	-0.175
TO 160	+0.210	+0.145	+0.043	+0.014	0.000	0.000	0.000	0.000	-0.028	-0.052	-0.068	-0.125	-0.215
OVER 160	+0.480	+0.245	+0.106	+0.054	+0.040	+0.063	+0.100	+0.250	+0.012	-0.012	-0.028	-0.093	-0.195
TO 180	+0.230	+0.145	+0.043	+0.014	0.000	0.000	0.000	0.000	-0.028	-0.052	-0.068	-0.133	-0.235
OVER 180	+0.530	+0.285	+0.122	+0.061	+0.046	+0.072	+0.115	+0.290	-0.013	-0.014	-0.033	-0.105	-0.219
TO 200	+0.240	+0.170	+0.050	+0.015	0.000	0.000	0.000	0.000	-0.033	-0.060	-0.079	-0.151	-0.265
OVER 200	+0.550	+0.285	+0.122	+0.061	+0.046	+0.072	+0.115	+0.290	+0.013	-0.014	-0.033	-0.113	-0.241
TO 225	+0.260	+0.170	+0.050	+0.015	0.000	0.000	0.000	0.000	-0.033	-0.060	-0.079	-0.159	-0.287
OVER 225	+0.570	+0.285	+0.122	+0.061	+0.046	+0.072	+0.115	+0.290	+0.013	-0.014	-0.033	-0.123	-0.267
TO 250	+0.280	+0.170	+0.050	+0.015	0.000	0.000	0.000	0.000	-0.033	-0.060	-0.079	-0.169	-0.313
OVER 250	+0.620	+0.320	+0.137	+0.069	+0.052	+0.081	+0.130	+0.320	+0.016	-0.014	-0.036	-0.138	-0.295
TO 280	+0.300	+0.190	+0.056	+0.017	0.000	0.000	0.000	0.000	-0.036	-0.066	-0.088	-0.190	-0.347
OVER 280	+0.650	+0.320	+0.137	+0.069	+0.052	+0.081	+0.130	+0.320	+0.016	-0.014	-0.036	-0.150	-0.330
TO 315	+0.330	+0.190	+0.056	0.017	0.000	0.000	0.000	0.000	-0.036	-0.066	-0.088	-0.202	-0.382
OVER 315	+0.720	+0.350	+0.151	+0.075	+0.057	+0.089	+0.140	+0.360	+0.017	-0.016	-0.041	-0.169	-0.369
TO 355	+0.360	+0.210	+0.062	+0.018	0.000	0.000	0.000	0.000	-0.040	-0.073	-0.058	-0.226	-0.426
OVER 355	+0.760	+0.350	+0.151	+0.075	+0.057	+0.089	+0.140	+0.360	+0.017	-0.016	-0.041	-0.187	-0.414
TO 400	+0.400	+0.210	+0.062	+0.018	0.000	0.000	0.000	0.000	-0.040	-0.073	-0.058	-0.244	-0.471
OVER 400	+0.840	+0.385	+0.165	+0.083	+0.063	+0.097	+0.155	+0.400	+0.018	-0.017	-0.045	-0.209	-0.467
TO 450	+0.440	+0.230	+0.068	+0.020	0.000	0.000	0.000	0.000	-0.045	-0.080	-0.108	-0.272	-0.530
OVER 450	+0.880	+0.385	+0.165	+0.083	+0.063	+0.097	+0.155	+0.400	+0.018	-0.017	-0.045	-0.229	-0.517
TO 500	+0.480	+0.230	+0.068	+0.020	0.000	0.000	0.000	0.000	-0.045	-0.080	-0.108	-0.292	-0.580

Appendix 36 • Shaft Sizes for Nonpreferred Diameters (millimeters)

Basic Size		c11	d9	f7	g6	h6	h7	h9	h11	k6	n6	p6	s6	u6
OVER	0	−0.060	−0.020	−0.006	−0.002	0.000	0.000	0.000	0.000	+0.006	+0.010	+0.012	+0.020	+0.024
TO	3	−0.120	−0.045	−0.016	−0.008	−0.006	−0.010	−0.025	−0.060	0.000	+0.004	+0.006	+0.014	+0.018
OVER	3	−0.070	−0.030	−0.010	−0.004	0.000	0.000	0.000	0.000	+0.009	+0.016	+0.020	+0.027	+0.031
TO	6	−0.145	−0.060	−0.022	−0.012	−0.008	−0.012	−0.030	−0.075	+0.001	+0.008	+0.012	+0.019	+0.023
OVER	6	−0.080	−0.040	−0.013	−0.005	0.000	0.000	0.000	0.000	+0.010	+0.019	+0.024	+0.032	+0.037
TO	10	−0.170	−0.076	−0.028	−0.014	−0.009	−0.015	−0.036	−0.090	+0.001	+0.010	+0.024	+0.023	+0.028
OVER	10	−0.095	−0.050	−0.016	−0.006	0.000	0.000	0.000	0.000	+0.012	+0.023	+0.029	+0.039	+0.044
TO	14	−0.205	−0.093	−0.034	−0.017	−0.011	−0.018	−0.043	−0.110	+0.001	+0.012	+0.018	+0.028	+0.033
OVER	14	−0.095	−0.050	−0.016	−0.006	0.000	0.000	0.000	0.000	+0.012	+0.023	+0.029	+0.039	+0.044
TO	18	−0.205	−0.093	−0.034	−0.017	−0.011	−0.018	−0.043	−0.110	+0.001	+0.012	+0.018	+0.028	+0.033
OVER	18	−0.110	−0.065	−0.020	−0.007	0.000	0.000	0.000	0.000	+0.015	+0.028	+0.035	+0.048	+0.054
TO	24	−0.240	−0.117	−0.041	−0.020	−0.013	−0.021	−0.052	−0.130	+0.002	+0.015	+0.022	+0.035	+0.041
OVER	24	−0.110	−0.065	−0.020	−0.007	0.000	0.000	0.000	0.000	+0.015	+0.028	+0.035	+0.048	+0.061
TO	30	−0.240	−0.117	−0.041	−0.020	−0.013	−0.021	−0.052	−0.130	+0.002	+0.015	+0.022	+0.035	+0.048
OVER	30	−0.120	−0.080	−0.025	−0.009	0.000	0.000	0.000	0.000	+0.018	+0.033	+0.042	+0.059	+0.076
TO	40	−0.280	−0.142	−0.050	−0.025	−0.016	−0.025	−0.062	−0.160	+0.002	+0.017	+0.026	+0.043	+0.060
OVER	40	−0.130	−0.080	−0.025	−0.009	0.000	0.000	0.000	0.000	+0.018	+0.033	+0.042	+0.059	+0.086
TO	50	−0.290	−0.142	−0.050	−0.025	−0.016	−0.025	−0.062	−0.160	+0.002	+0.017	+0.026	+0.043	+0.070
OVER	50	−0.140	−0.100	−0.030	−0.010	0.000	0.000	0.000	0.000	+0.021	+0.039	+0.051	+0.072	+0.106
TO	65	−0.330	−0.174	−0.060	−0.029	−0.019	−0.030	−0.074	−0.190	+0.002	+0.020	−0.032	+0.053	+0.087
OVER	65	−0.150	−0.100	−0.030	−0.010	0.000	0.000	0.000	0.000	+0.021	+0.039	+0.051	+0.078	+0.121
TO	80	−0.340	−0.174	−0.060	−0.029	−0.019	−0.030	−0.074	−0.190	+0.002	+0.020	+0.032	+0.059	+0.102
OVER	80	−0.170	−0.120	−0.036	−0.012	0.000	0.000	0.000	0.000	+0.025	+0.045	+0.059	+0.093	+0.146
TO	100	−0.390	−0.207	−0.071	−0.034	−0.022	−0.035	−0.087	−0.220	+0.003	+0.023	+0.037	+0.071	+0.124

Basic Size		c11	d9	f7	g6	h6	h7	h9	h11	k6	n6	p6	s6	u6
OVER	100	−0.180	−0.120	−0.036	−0.012	0.000	0.000	0.000	0.000	+0.025	+0.045	+0.059	+0.101	+0.166
TO	120	−0.400	−0.207	−0.071	−0.034	−0.022	−0.035	−0.087	−0.220	+0.003	+0.023	+0.037	+0.079	+0.144
OVER	120	−0.200	−0.145	−0.043	−0.014	0.000	0.000	0.000	0.000	+0.028	+0.052	+0.068	+0.117	+0.195
TO	140	−0.450	−0.245	−0.083	−0.039	−0.025	−0.040	−0.100	−0.250	+0.003	+0.027	+0.043	+0.092	+0.170
OVER	140	−0.210	−0.145	−0.043	−0.014	0.000	0.000	0.000	0.000	+0.028	+0.052	+0.068	+0.125	+0.215
TO	160	−0.460	−0.245	−0.083	−0.039	−0.025	−0.040	−0.100	−0.250	+0.003	+0.027	+0.043	+0.100	+0.190
OVER	160	−0.230	−0.145	−0.043	−0.014	0.000	0.000	0.000	0.000	+0.028	+0.052	+0.068	+0.133	+0.235
TO	180	−0.480	−0.245	−0.083	−0.039	−0.025	−0.040	−0.100	−0.250	+0.003	+0.027	+0.043	+0.108	+0.210
OVER	180	−0.240	−0.170	−0.050	−0.015	0.000	0.000	0.000	0.000	+0.033	+0.060	+0.079	+0.151	+0.265
TO	200	−0.530	−0.285	−0.096	−0.044	−0.029	−0.046	−0.115	−0.290	+0.004	+0.031	+0.050	+0.122	+0.236
OVER	200	−0.260	−0.170	−0.050	−0.015	0.000	0.000	0.000	0.000	+0.033	+0.060	+0.079	+0.159	+0.287
TO	225	−0.550	−0.285	−0.096	−0.044	−0.029	−0.046	−0.115	−0.290	+0.004	+0.031	+0.050	+0.130	+0.258
OVER	225	−0.280	−0.170	−0.050	−0.015	0.000	0.000	0.000	0.000	+0.033	+0.060	+0.079	+0.169	+0.313
TO	250	−0.570	−0.285	−0.096	−0.044	−0.029	−0.046	−0.115	−0.290	+0.004	+0.031	+0.050	+0.140	+0.284
OVER	250	−0.300	−0.190	−0.056	−0.017	0.000	0.000	0.000	0.000	+0.036	+0.066	+0.088	+0.190	+0.347
TO	280	−0.620	−0.320	−0.108	−0.049	−0.032	−0.052	−0.130	−0.320	+0.004	+0.034	+0.056	+0.158	+0.315
OVER	280	−0.330	−0.190	−0.056	−0.017	0.000	0.000	0.000	0.000	+0.036	+0.066	+0.088	+0.202	+0.382
TO	315	−0.650	−0.320	−0.108	−0.049	−0.032	−0.052	−0.130	−0.320	+0.004	+0.034	+0.056	+0.170	+0.350
OVER	315	−0.360	−0.210	−0.062	−0.018	0.000	0.000	0.000	0.000	+0.040	+0.073	+0.098	+0.226	+0.426
TO	355	−0.720	−0.350	−0.119	−0.054	−0.036	−0.057	−0.140	−0.360	+0.004	+0.037	+0.062	+0.190	+0.390
OVER	355	−0.400	−0.210	−0.062	−0.018	0.000	0.000	0.000	0.000	+0.040	+0.073	+0.098	+0.244	+0.471
TO	400	−0.760	−0.350	−0.119	−0.054	−0.036	−0.057	−0.140	−0.360	+0.004	+0.037	+0.062	+0.208	+0.435
OVER	400	−0.440	−0.230	−0.068	−0.020	0.000	0.000	0.000	0.000	+0.045	+0.080	+0.108	+0.272	+0.530
TO	450	−0.840	−0.385	−0.131	−0.060	0.040	0.063	−0.155	0.400	+0.005	+0.040	+0.068	+0.232	+0.490
OVER	450	−0.480	−0.230	−0.068	−0.020	0.000	0.000	0.000	0.000	+0.045	+0.080	+0.108	+0.292	+0.580
TO	500	−0.880	−0.385	−0.131	−0.060	−0.040	−0.063	−0.155	−0.400	+0.005	+0.040	+0.068	+0.252	+0.540

The following LISP programs were written by Professor Leendert Kersten of the University of Nebraska and are given here with his permission. These programs were introduced in Chapter 15, in which the principles of orthographic projection are covered. These very valuable programs can be duplicated and added as supplements to your AutoCAD software.

```
)
(defun C:PARALLEL ()
  (setvar "aperture" 5)
    (setq sp (getpoint "\nSelect START point of
      parallel line:"))
    (setq ep (getpoint "\nSelect END point of
      parallel line:"))
    (setvar "osmode" 1)
    (setq sl (getpoint "\nSelect 1st point on line
      for parallelism:"))
    (setq el (getpoint "\nSelect 2nd point on line
      for parallelism:"))
    (setvar "osmode" 0)
    (setq pa (angle sl el ))
    (setq la (angle sp ep))
    (setq ll (distance sp ep))
    (setq m -1)
    (setq d 0)
    (if (> pa d) (setq m 1))
    (if (> la d) (setq d 1))
    (if (/= m d) (setq pa (+ pa 3.141593)))
    (setq ep (polar sp pa ll))
    (setvar "cmdecho" 0)
    (command line sp ep "" )
    (restore)
)
(defun C:PERPLINE ()
    (setvar "aperture" 5) (setvar "cmdecho" 0)
    (setq sp (getpoint "\nSelect START point of
      perpendicular line:"))
    (setvar "osmode" 128)
    (setq cc (getpoint sp "\nSelect ANY point on
      line to which perp'lr:"))
    (setq beta (angle sp cc)) (setvar "osmode" 0)
(setq ep
(getpoint "\nSelect END point of desired
 perpendicular (for length only): "))
    (setq length (distance sp ep))
    (setq ep (polar sp beta length))
    (command "line sp ep "")
    (restore)
)
(defun C:TRANSFER ()
    (setvar "aperture" 5) (setvar "cmdecho" 0)
    (setvar "osmode" 1)
    (setq aa (getpoint "\nSelect start of transfer
      distance:"))
    (setvar "osmode" 128)
    (setq bb (getpoint aa "\nSelect the reference
      plane:"))
    (setq length (distance aa bb))
    (setvar "osmode" 1)
    (setq cc (getpoint "\nSelect point to be
      projected:"))
    (setvar "osmode" 128)
    (setq dd (getpoint oc "\nSelect other reference
      plane:"))
(setvar "osmode" 0)
    (setq alpha (angle cc dd))
    (setq ep (polar dd alpha length))
    (COMMAND "CIRCLE" EP 0.05)
    (restore)
)
```

```
(defun RESTORE ()
    (setvar "aperture" 10)
    (setvar "cmdecho" 1)
    (setvar "osmode" 0)
)
(DEFUN *ERROR* (MSG)
(SETVAR "OSMODE" 0)
(setvar "aperture" 10)
( setvar "cmdecho" 1)
(PRINC "error: ")
(princ msg)
(terpri)
)
(defun C:COPYDIST ()
      (setvar "aperture"5)
      (setvar "cmdecho" 0)
    (setvar "osmode" 1)
      (setq p1 (getpoint "\nSelect start point of
        line distance to be copied: "))
      (setq p2 (getpoint "\nEnd point?: "))
    (setvar "osmode" 0)
      (setq dist (distance p1 p2))
      (setq p1 (getpoint "\nStart point of new
        distance location:"))
      (setq ang (getangle p1 "\nWhich
        direction?: "))
      (setq p2 (polar p1 ang diet))
    (setvar "osmode" 0)
      (command "circle" p2 0.05)
      (restore)
)
(defun C:BISECT ()
    (setvar "aperture" 5)
    (setvar "osmode" 32)
    (setq sp (getpoint "\nSelect Corner of angle:"))
    (setvar "osmode" 2)
    (setq aa (getpoint "\nSelect first side
        (remember CCW):"))
    (setq alpha (angle sp aa))
    (setq bb (getpoint "\nSelect other side:"))
    (setvar "osmode" 0)
    (setq beta (angle sp bb))
    (setq m (/ (+ alpha beta) 2))
    (if (> alpha beta) (setq ang (+ pi m))
        (setq ang m))
(setq ep
    (getpoint "\nSelect endpoint of bisecting line
        (for length only): "))
    (setq length (distance sp ep))
    (setq ep (polar sp ang length))
    (setvar "cmdecho" 0)
    (command "line sp ep "")
    (restore)
}
```

This graph can be used to determine the individual grades of members of a team and to compute grade averages for those who do extra assignments.

The percent participation of each team member should be determined by the team as a whole (see Section 7.7).

Example: written or oral report grades

Overall team grade: 82

Team members N=5	Contribution C=%	F=CN	Grade (graph)
J. Doe	20%	100	82.0
H. Brown	16%	80	75.8
L. Smith	24%	120	86.0
R. Black	20%	100	82.0
T. Jones	20%	100	82.0
	100%		

Example: quiz or problem sheet grades

Number assigned: 30
Number extra: 6
Total 36

Average grade for total (36): 82

$$F = \frac{\text{No. completed} \times 100}{\text{No. assigned}} = \frac{36 \times 100}{30} = 120$$

Final grade (from graph): 86.0

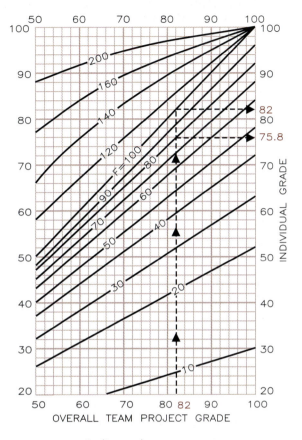

Figure A38-1 Grading graph.

SUBSTANCE	WEIGHT LB. PER CU. FT.	SPECIFIC GRAVITY	SUBSTANCE	WEIGHT LB. PER CU. FT.	SPECIFIC GRAVITY
METALS, ALLOYS, ORES			**TIMBER, U.S. SEASONED**		
Aluminum, cast,			Moisture Content by		
hammered	165	2.55–2.75	Weight		
Brass, cast, rolled	534	8.4–8.7	Seasoned timber 15 t0 20%		
Bronze, 7.9 to 14% Sn	509	7.4–8.9	Green timber up to 50%		
Bronze, aluminum	481	7.7	Ash, white, red	40	0.62–0.65
Copper, cast, rolled	556	8.8–9.0	Cedar, white, red	22	0.32–0.38
Copper ore, pyrites	262	4.1–4.3	Chestnut	41	0.66
Gold, cast, hammered	1205	19.25–19.3	Cypress	30	0.48
Iron, cast, pig	450	7.2	Fir, Douglas spruce	32	0.51
Iron, wrought	485	7.6–7.9	Fir, eastern	25	0.40
Iron, spiegel-eisen	466	7.5	Elm, white	45	0.72
Iron, ferro-silicon	437	6.7–7.3	Hemlock	29	0.42–0.52
Iron ore, hematite	325	5.2	Hickory	49	0.74–0.84
Iron ore, hematite in bank	160–180	—	Locust	46	0.73
Iron ore, hematite loose	130–160	—	Maple, hard	43	0.68
Iron ore, limonite	237	3.6–4.0	Maple, white	33	0.53
Iron ore, magnetite	315	4.9–5.2	Oak, chestnut	54	0.86
Iron slag	172	2.5–3.0	Oak, live	59	0.95
Lead	710	11.37	Oak, red, black	41	0.65
Lead ore, galena	465	7.3–7.6	Oak, white	46	0.74
Magnesium, alloys	112	1.74–1.83	Pine, Oregon	32	0.61
Manganese	475	7.2–8.0	Pine, red	30	0.48
Manganese ore, pyrolusite	259	3.7–4.6	Pine, white	26	0.41
Mercury	849	13.6	Pine, yellow, long-leaf	44	0.70
Monel Metal	556	8.8–9.0	Pine, yellow, short-leaf	38	0.61
Nickel	565	8.9–9.2	Poplar	30	0.48
Platinum, cast, hammered	1330	21.1–21.5	Redwood, California	26	0.42
Silver, cast, hammered	656	10.4–10.6	Spruce, white, black	27	0.40–0.46
Steel, rolled	490	7.85	Walnut, black	38	0.61
Tin, cast, hammered	459	7.2–7.5			
Tin ore, cassiterite	418	6.4–7.0			
Zinc, cast, rolled	440	6.9–7.2			
Zinc ore, blends	253	3.9–4.2	**VARIOUS LIQUIDS**		
			Alcohol, 100%	49	0.79
			Acids, muriatic 40%	75	1.20
VARIOUS SOLIDS			Acids, nitric 91%	94	1.50
			Acids, sulphuric 87%	112	1.80
Cereals, oats ....bulk	32	—	Lye, soda	106	1.70
Cereals, barley ....bulk	39	—	Oils, vegetable	58	0.91–0.94
Cereals, corn, rye ....bulk	48	—	Oils, mineral, lubricants	57	0.90–0.93
Cereals, wheat ....bulk	48	—	Water, 4°C. max, density	62.428	1.0
Hay and Straw ....bales	20	—	Water, 100°C	59.830	0.9584
Cotton, Flax, Hemp	93	1.47–1.50	Water, ice	56	0.88–0.92
Fats	58	0.90–0.97	Water, snow, fresh fallen	8	.125
Flour, loose	28	0.40–0.50	Water, sea water	64	1.02–1.03
Flour, pressed	47	0.70–0.80			
Glass, common	156	2.40–2.60			
Glass, plate or crown	161	2.45–2.72	**GASES**		
Glass, crystal	184	2.90–3.00			
Leather	59	0.86–1.02	Air, 0°C. 760 mm.	.08071	1.0
Paper	58	0.70–1.15	Ammonia	.0478	0.5920
Potatoes, piled	42	—	Carbon dioxide	.1234	1.5291
Rubber, caostchouc	59	0.92–0.96	Carbon monoxide	.0781	0.9673
Rubber goods	94	1.0–2.0	Gas, illuminating	.028–.036	0.35–0.45
Salt, granulated, piled	48	—	Gas, natural	.038–.039	0.47–0.48
Saltpeter	67	—	Hydrogen	.00559	0.0693
Starch	96	1.53	Nitrogen	.0784	0.9714
Sulphur	125	1.93–2.07	Oxygen	.0892	1.1056
Wool	82	1.32			

The specific gravities of solids and liquids refer to water at 4°C., those of gases to air at 0°C. and 760 mm. pressure. The weights per cubic foot are derived from average specific gravities, except where stated that weights are for bulk, heaped or loose materials, etc.

(Courtesy of the American Institute of Steel Construction.)

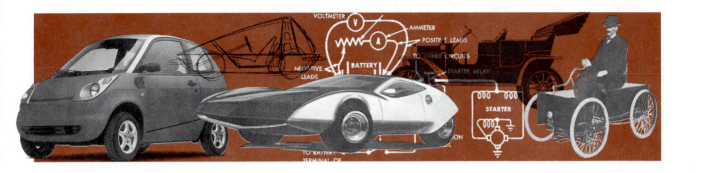

Index

Horizontal orthographic
   planes, 183
Horizontal planes,
   of orthographic projection,
      156
Horizontal reference plane
   (HRP), 185–186
Hose spool
   short design problem, 90
Hot water supply
   systems design problem, 91
HRP. *See* Horizontal reference
   plane
Human factors
   and design analysis, 50,
      51–52
Human figure, 394
Hunting blind
   product design problem, 91
Hunting seat
   comparative pricing of, 58
Hyperbolas, 127

I

Ideographs, 321
   for fillet welds, 322
   for resistance welds, 324
Ignore hatches, 447
IMEXO, 462
Implementation, 9, 72
   and assembly drawings, 73
   of design process, 12
   for exercise bench, 75–76
   with hanger bracket prob-
      lem, 17–18
   miscellaneous considera-
      tions, 73–75
   of patent drawings, 78–80

and patents, 77–79
   and patent searches, 80
   specifications, 73–74
   and working drawings,
      72–73
Inch(es)
   dimensions in millimeters
      converted to, 262
   working drawings dimen-
      sioned in, 329
Inclined planes
   in isometric drawings,
      385–386
India ink
   for patent drawings, 79
   for presentation lettering,
      68
Individual approach
   with design process, 29
Informal presentations, 66
Information accumulation
   and creativity, 28
Information center
   systems design problem, 91
Ingots, 247
Ink
   for patent drawings, 79
Ink drawings, 370
Ink jet printers, 368, 412
Ink jet printing
   for reproduction of draw-
      ings, 368
Input devices, 409, 410
Inquiry commands (Tools),
   456–457
INSERT command, 231, 337
Insert option, 445
Instant coffee spoon, 28

Instrument drawings, 45
   for design problems, 85
   triangles for, 161, 162
Instruments
   orthographic drawing with,
      154–173
Instrument set
   for drawing, 98
Insurance
   warehousing, 59
INTERFERE command, 492
Interference
   and patent applications, 82
Interference fit (LN), 293, 295
   English units, 291
   metric units, 294
Interlocking dies, 251
Intermittent welds, 323
Internal micrometer, 270
   calipers, 255
Internal threads, 219, 222, 223,
      236
International Standards
   Organization (ISO), 104
   threads, 218
   thread table, 223
   tolerancing system of, 293
International tolerance (IT)
   grade, 298
   metric units, 294
Intersecting lines, 160
Inventors
   joint, 82
   patents applied for by,
      77–79
   sole, 82
Inverse linear option, 507
Inverse square option, 507